D1072723

THE GLOBAL POLITICAL ECONOMY OF ISRAEL

Praise for the Hebrew and English editions

'*The Global Political Economy of Israel* is hard to review without superlatives.... I read it as a desert traveller who has finally reached an oasis. It is full of details, flatters the reader, but demands an intellectual effort. In return, it explains not only the "how" but also the "why". Nitzan and Bichler have put aside the justifications, the misleading terminology, the dis-information, the speculation in blood. They came to the party with their cameras, only that instead of conventional film, they used x-rays.'

– *Haim Baram*, Kol Ha'eer

'The reader will find in this book a whole world, Kafkanesque in nature and scope.... Naturally, it deserves attention from economists ... but it could also be read as a first-class cultural document. Above all, it is a grand, perpetual deconstruction of Israel's material reality, a penetrating, sarcastic and well-written study of 'where we live'. Rarely does a single book transform the entire worldview of a reader. This book does it. Eye opening. Depressing.'

– *Dror Burstein*, Kol Ha'eer

'You could agree or disagree with *The Global Political Economy of Israel*, but it is undoubtedly the most riveting and outstanding political economy book you would have read this year.'

– Globes

'An arresting and creative book. Moving beyond standard explanations, the authors reveal the underpinnings of Israel's history and politics, and in doing so provide a new framework to examine other such societies in global politics'.

– *Jeffrey Harrod, Professor of International Political Economy, University of Amsterdam*

'I devoured it in few days. It is a great, impressive and illuminating book, as well as a fascinating read. The enemies of Nitzan and Bichler, but also their admirers, will now be a thousand-fold.'

– *Aryeh Kofsky, Professor of Comparative Religion, Haifa University*

'I read the hundreds of pages of this book like a thriller.... There is a great deal of anger in this book and a great deal of humor. Reading economic literature is usually very boring. This book is fascinating. Marxists and socialists of all kinds, if they don't want to give answers from the day before yesterday to yesterday's questions, should definitely read it'.

– Itzhak Laor, Professor of Literature, Tel Aviv University

'Nitzan and Bichler are without doubt two of the more innovative political economists in the world right now. Relying primarily on data gathered by themselves, with brutal precision and unwavering logic they dispense with the thick layer of ideologies and mystification to lay bare the innermost structures of power of Israeli society. This accessible but deeply disturbing book is not only the most authoritative study of the Israeli State to date, but also a significant contribution to state theory and globalisation. I would place it on par with Poulantzas' work in the seventies. It is a masterpiece.'

– Ronen Palan, Professor of International Political Economy,
University of Sussex

'This innovative and thoroughly researched examination of Israel in the global political economy is a brilliant addition to the growing "new political economy" literature. The volume is distinguished by its engaging style. Theories are laid out clearly and evaluated empirically with reference to a rich descriptive and quantitative data base that includes economic and political variables. Indeed, among the greatest strengths of this work is the way that economics and politics are fully integrated throughout; another is how well the authors site Israel's domestic political economy in a larger web of external strategic and economic relationships. I recommend it highly and look forward to sharing it with my students.'

– Mary Ann Tétreault, Distinguished Professor of International Affairs,
Trinity University

'Professional academics will, of course, hate it. They will say it is not "science" and they will say it is not scholarship, it will be called "journalism" and all that. But you guys knew of course what you were doing. And I am glad you did it this way, because I would have never even opened the book if it were classical scholarship. Life is too short. I found it a good read, a very good read, illuminating, very funny at times, and even when I did not agree (because my views on life, social justice, political organization, are very different than yours), I found it challenging and engaging. I also loved, just loved, all the gossipy snippets. A "Must" read for anyone interested in the debate about globalization and its discontents, this book pricks and deflates all hot air balloons in sight.'

– Joseph H.H. Weiler, Jean Monnet Professor of Law, NYU School of Law

The Global Political Economy of Israel

Jonathan Nitzan and
Shimshon Bichler

Pluto  Press

LONDON • STERLING, VIRGINIA

First published 2002 by Pluto Press
345 Archway Road, London N6 5AA
and 22883 Quicksilver Drive, Sterling, VA 20166–2012, USA

www.plutobooks.com

British Library Cataloguing in Publication Data
A catalogue record for this book is available from the British Library

ISBN 0 7453 1676 X hardback
ISBN 0 7453 1675 1 paperback

Library of Congress Cataloguing in Publication Data
A catalogue record for this book is available

10   9   8   7   6   5   4   3   2   1

Designed and produced for Pluto Press by
Chase Publishing Services, Fortescue, Sidmouth EX10 9QG
Typeset from disk by Stanford DTP Services, Towcester
Printed in the European Union by Antony Rowe Ltd, Chippenham, England

To Geneviève and Elvire, with love, from Jonathan

To Dassi, with love, from Shimshon

Contents

List of Figures

List of Tables

Acknowledgements

Radical research in the social sciences is difficult to publish in mainstream journals. Writers who wish to challenge the status quo learn this the hard way. Their papers usually get rejected. Often, they are not even considered. They just don't 'fit'. But not all journals are like that. Some of the research leading to this book has been previously published in *Capital & Class, Review of International Political Economy, Review of Radical Political Economics*, and *Science & Society*. We wish to express our gratitude to the editors and reviewers of these journals. Your rigour, honesty and openness make your publications, along with a few others, stand out in a sea of complacency.

We also like to thank George Archer, Hagai Forshner, Stephen Gill, Jeffrey Harrod, Gibin Hong, Daniel Moure, Kinhide Mushakoji, Tom Naylor, Dan O'Meara, Akiva Orr, Ronen Palan, Jeffrey Rudolph, Terisa Turner, and Mary Ann Tétreault. Your intellectual engagement and moral encouragement helped us think with greater clarity and purpose.

Finally, we would like to thank the Social Sciences and Humanities Research Council of Canada, whose financial support helped us bring this book to completion.

1

Introduction

The natives, by and large, had to be driven to work with clubs, they preserved that much dignity, whereas the whites, perfected by public education, worked of their own free will.

— Louis-Ferdinand Céline, *Journey to the End of the Night*

Looking into the twenty-first century, the future of Israel seems uncertain as ever. While the country's economy grows increasingly integrated into the global market, its politics remain internally divided and regionally isolated. Which of these processes is likely to prevail? Will neoliberalism win over xenophobic nationalism, driving Israel toward further openness and, eventually, toward regional integration? Or will the spectre of conflict continue to haunt it, leading to renewed isolationism, authoritarianism, and perhaps disintegration? Or maybe there is really no contradiction here? Perhaps economic liberalisation could coexist comfortably with internal political conflict in a quasi-war economy? What are the crucial forces at work here? Is it the 'policy makers' who run the show, or are these officials merely pawns in a predetermined historical trajectory? Who stand to gain? And who shall bear the cost?

The future of course remains unknown. But, then, simply *asking* these questions is already a significant step forward. Indeed, until only a decade ago, most Israelis and many in the West took it for granted that Israel really had no option. The country, went the argument, was surrounded by hostile and backward Arab regimes, and therefore had to maintain a 'garrison state'; and given its allegiance to freedom, it had both the right and obligation to line up with the United States and Europe against 'Soviet expansionism' in the region. The main domestic conflict, to the extent that such conflict was at all acknowledged, was usually blamed on ethnicity rather than class. Economic under-performance was said to be rooted in the dead weight of a socialist past. Economists preached the blessing of free competition, accusing power-hungry politicians and fossilised labour leaders for Israel's failure to achieve it. Israeli democracy was hardly in doubt, and military occupation of Arab land was justified by historic right, or as enlightened colonialism. According to the prevailing 'consensus', propagated by academics and public opinion makers,

1

Israel was in fact unique. Whereas the history of other societies shared common patterns, or 'laws of motion', that of Israel paved its own special course.

This intellectual cocoon has finally been pierced. Over the past decade, more and more people have begun questioning the 'no-choice' ideology. And with the future no longer seen as predetermined, neither is the past. Sacred cows are being slaughtered daily, and the word 'consensus' is no longer a useful weapon in the hands of domestic elites. Yet for all the apparent openness, not everything is really subject to debate. In fact, the critical discourse is confined largely to the so-called 'political' domain. The 'economic' discourse, by contrast, is far less critical. While there is growing recognition that globalisation is altering the nature of the Israeli economy, there is little discussion of whether this is good or bad. In fact, according to the conventional wisdom, such discussion is largely unnecessary. The 'Washington Consensus' of liberalisation, deregulation, privatisation, sound finance and the unwinding of the welfare state, is seen not as one of several possible paths of development, but as the natural course of things. It is almost as if the collapse of the old political consensus of Zionism has given way to a new economic consensus of free markets: 'Laissez-faire – good; state intervention – bad.'

This asymmetry between critical politics and uncritical economics is highly suspect. It raises suspicion because in the real world of production and ideology, power and cooperation, sweat and blood, well-being and control, the realms of 'politics' and 'economics' are in fact indistinguishable. Indeed, until the early part of this century, they were studied not separately, but rather as a unified discipline of 'political economy'. The chief interest of political economy was always the relationship between power and well-being. Its moral task was to find that social organisation which best suited the 'good life'. For the dominant group in society, political economy was a means of justification; for the critics, a method of attack.

Seen from this broader perspective, the current discourse in Israel is largely conservative, serving to bolster rather than undermine the existing power structure. This is achieved largely by presenting issues such as war, peace, ethnicity, religion, and formal political institutions, as if they were separate problems in need of separate solutions. These issues, though, are neither separate, nor are they 'problems' – at least not for everyone. Instead, they are part of a much larger process on which there is practically no debate at all: *the progressive emergence of Israel as a capitalist society*. The new debates about international relations, identity, and domestic politics appear critical in tone only because the broader context in which they are embedded remains uncontested. If we were instead to shift our focus, making capitalism and accumulation the centre of analysis, the current 'political' discourse would look anything but radical.

For Israel's ruling class, or at least the bulk of it, the shift from Zionist nationalism to openness and regional integration is far from a challenge; indeed, given the changing nature of capitalism, globally and locally, the reorientation is rather necessary. Until the late 1980s, Israeli capitalism operated in the broader context of superpower confrontation, and under local conditions of war economy and stagflation (combined stagnation and inflation). These circumstances mandated a strong nationalist ideology, an emphasis on ethnicity, and colonial occupation. In time, though, that mode of accumulation ran into insurmountable barriers. The end of the Cold War, the progressive globalisation of trade and investment, the gradual loss of control over the stagflationary process at home, and, finally, the Palestinian uprising, have together driven Israel toward an alternative regime. The hallmark of this regime is transnational accumulation, with local capital increasingly integrated into the global circuits of ownership. This latter process is inconsistent with a war economy; hence, the attacks on the nationalist consensus and its associated features, the demise of collectivism in favour of individualism, the decline of the welfare state in lieu of sound finance, and the disintegration of organised labour in the face of rising business power.

The purpose of this book is to situate this latest transition as part of Israel's century-long evolution as a capitalist society. We seek to tell what has happened, as well as why, trying to interweave the processes of accumulation, class and globalisation into one single story. In writing this story, we attempted, as much as possible, to avoid unnecessary jargon and explain the terms we use. However, the issues we deal with are often not simple, and therefore warrant more than a short introduction. The present chapter aims to give a systematic presentation of the main questions and themes of the book, concentrating specifically on why we think these questions and themes are important, and on the broader framework which ties them into a coherent whole.

The Conventional Wisdom

Until recently, most of those writing on Israeli society seemed to share the following three assumptions: (1) that their subject matter was best analysed within a 'statist' frame of reference; (2) that the historical development of Israel was predetermined by 'unique' circumstances; and (3) that as a consequence of these unique circumstances, Israel has evolved into a 'special case' of classless society, a society in which the process of accumulation and the role of elites could be safely ignored. Over the past decade, the rise of neoliberalism made many writers uneasy with this model, although few if any have been able to transcend it. Let us look more closely at these conventional beliefs and what they mean.

Statism

The 'statist', or 'realist' approach has grown increasingly fashionable since the 1970s.[1] The basic unit of analysis here is the nation state, whose actions are dominated by an amorphous group of 'central-decision makers', 'state officials', or 'rulemakers'. This group is supposedly driven by the 'national interest', seeking to achieve broad macroeconomic goals, such as growth and a favourable balance of payments, or macropolitical aims, like military prowess and social stability (see for instance Arian 1989). These broad ends are perceived as independent of the particular interests of various societal groups, and are often emphasised precisely for their universal nature.

The aims of the state are formulated in aggregate terms – a habit of thinking which emerged and consolidated with the postwar Keynesian paradigm (Tsuru 1968). Within this aggregate framework, practitioners habitually subdivide society into two systems of 'economics' and 'politics'. In the Israeli context, it is customarily to assume that the economic system would guarantee universal welfare – that is, if only the system were allowed to function 'efficiently'. The political system undermines that efficiency when it seeks to achieve additional goals, such as 'national security' – but then fails to find the optimal rate of substitution between security and economic growth along the nation's production-possibilities frontier.[2] With its foundations deeply embedded in the neoclassical paradigm of economics, this focus on 'aggregate welfare' enables the writer to remain within the boundaries of the national consensus (Robinson 1962: 117–18), and has driven many Israeli academics to accept the supremacy of the political echelon.

Thus, Eitan Berglas, an economics professor who later became chairman of Bank Hapoalim, asserts that 'the central problem of the economic policy in Israel is choosing the right point on the curve [production-possibilities frontier]', yet he immediately adds that this choice must be determined by 'security considerations' which are 'beyond the domain of this article' (1970: 194). That

---

1 Cf. Tilly and Ardant (1975); Krasner (1978a); and Skocpol (1985). 'Statism' remains particularly popular in the study of International Relations, not only because of its universal character, but also since its analytical units and research categories correspond closely to official bureaucratic structures. For an extreme application of this approach to Israeli, see Migdal (1989) and Barnett (1992).
2 The production-possibilities frontier is a hypothetical curve describing the trade-off between different types of goods and services – in this case, 'security' and 'investment' – which can be produced when the economy operates at full employment and maximum efficiency. Since all productive resources are assumed to be fully and efficiently utilised, an increase in one type of output (for instance, security) necessitates a decrease in the other (investment), and vice versa, and it is up to society to decide which combination of the two is 'optimal'. The 'misallocation' arises when the politicians' choice differs from the 'optimal' one. The only problem is that, so far, nobody has been able to either draw this frontier for any actual economy, or to explain how an 'optimal' choice can ever be made in a conflict-ridden society, where the loss of one is the gain of another.

particular paper was written at a sensitive period, right at the end of the Israel–Egyptian war of attrition – although time has done little to change the author's basic presumption. Thirteen years later, after the 1982 Israeli entanglement in Lebanon, we can still find Berglas claiming that 'the purpose of military expenditures [in Israel] is both to deter potential enemies from starting a war and to achieve superiority once a war has started', and that 'it is thus difficult even in retrospect to assess the success or failure of a military expenditure program' (Berglas 1983: 16). Likewise, Hasid and Lesser, while working as senior economists at the Ministry of Defence, asserted that although 'Israeli society is democratic, free, peace-seeking and striving for a standard and quality of life much like the progressive Western states, Israel is coerced into a permanent state of war'. In this context, they explained, 'the allocation of resources for security involves national risks which are very difficult to assess in any objective way' (Hasid and Lesser 1981: 243). These assertions may be all true of course, but then there arises the simple question: if the size of the military budget, decisions about the occupied territories, the fate of the settlements, and the dependency on the United States are all determined by autonomous state officials, uncompromising Arab regimes and built-in ideological inclinations, why the scientific pretensions of rational economism?

The total subjugation of the economy to the state is manifest in Ezra Sadan (1985: 119), an economics professor and General Director of the Finance Ministry at the time: 'In Israel', he asserts, 'economic goals arise naturally from the general goal of the survival of the state.' Indeed, 'planning for survival includes economic growth, and even when this is not an objective in and of itself, it is a means for making possible the establishment of the defence system required for future wars'. (Sadan, previously a member of the far-right HaTehia, or Revival Party, has since converted to advocating peaceful regional integration.) The Hobbesian view of 'survivalism' has been so thoroughly accepted in Israeli political literature, that some researchers have decided to skip the analysis altogether and turn directly to policy implications. Kleiman (1992), for example, although writing after George Bush's declaration of a 'New World Order', still has little doubt about the militaristic course of Israeli society. For him, the main issue remains the benefit for the 'state', and the principal question is 'how can Israel best respond to mounting challenges in the global weapon market and how should it preserve its position and competitive advantage?' (p. 326). The answer is succinctly summarised in Kleiman's own words: 'In order for the Israeli arms industry not to perish, it should continue with its tradition of domestic dexterity and external cunning.' In his opinion, the key is a proper reading of the world armament market, leading to a most revealing conclusion, namely, that 'those who foresee the future and respond adequately will get the juiciest market share' (p. 336).

The substitution of advice for serious research is typical of an academic community locked into a rigid consensus. Perhaps the clearest expression of this consensus is the repeated use – often unconscious – of terms such as 'we', 'us' and 'ours', usually coupled with a need for 'sacrifice'.[3] Writing shortly after the 1967 War, Yair Aharoni for example describes how 'we are required, and justly so, to demonstrate resilience and hold out against political and economic pressures', while 'our young are called for a long reserve service and blood-letting' (1969: 157). Although hinting that the Labour government of Golda Meir should re-evaluate its priorities, Aharoni is careful to add that this is 'not to doubt the need to devote whatever is necessary in order to assure our very survival' (p. 160). And once defence cuts are put out of the question, a 'belt-tightening' economist (with tenure) can step in to announce that 'if we want to enjoy this kind of growth in the future, we must begin immediately by rapidly reducing the standard of living' (Berglas 1970: 195). The only question is who are these 'we' whose belt the economists are so eager to tighten.

The 'Unique Case' of Israel

The adoption of statism by Israeli academics was greatly facilitated by the view of Israel as *sui generis*, or a 'special case'. The first reason for this uniqueness is exogenous. Unlike many other democracies, goes the argument, Israel has been in a constant state of war forced onto her by hostile, uncompromising neighbours. Thus, 'Insofar as Israel is concerned', writes Mintz (1984: 104), 'one cannot apply the concept of military-industrial complex to this Western-style democracy in the sense of a conspiracy by heads of the political, defense and economic establishment solely for the sake of furthering their own interests. After all, Israel's very survival has been threatened for many years.' Following a similar vein, Peri (1983: 1) writes that 'Since its establishment, and in fact even prior to 1948 Israel has been in a state of war' and that 'the all-encompassing nature of war in Israel and the centrality of security to national existence have created a situation whereby numerous spheres, which in parliamentary democracies are considered "civil", fall within the security ambit and are enveloped in secrecy'. And so, 'Beyond the ideological and political disagreements prevailing in the Israeli public', write Horowitz and Lissak (1988: 28), 'there was always a broad consensus regarding the threat for survival embedded in the Israeli–Arab dispute' (for a similar line, see also Horowitz and Lissak 1989, Ch. 6). The consequence was that Israel became a unique case. 'Unfortunately', writes Ben Dor (1977: 431), 'in the current state of the theoretical literature, Israel constitutes such an exceptional case of a "nation in arms" (a "barrack democracy"), that it is almost impossible to compare it to any other similar case'. And, 'In spite of the many references to Israel and the IDF in comparative works on civil–military relations, none of the existing conceptual frameworks in the field appear fully applicable to the case of Israel' (Horowitz 1982: 96).

3   On the concept of 'we', see Zamiatin (1924), and more recently, Barnet (1972: 7).

The second, and perhaps more important reason for the uniqueness of Israel stems from its own 'primordial sin'. The East European 'founding fathers', goes the argument, instituted an authoritarian 'socialist' culture, and it is this culture, at least according to the vast majority of Israeli social scientists, which lies at the root of 'Israel's malaise'. Beginning in the 1920s, the political system seized control of the economy, first through the Labour Party and the Histadrut (federation of labour unions), who then transferred their power to the government of the newly born state. The result was the institutionalisation of an authoritarian/statist culture. Shapiro (1975: 207–8), for example, believes that contrary to the basic individualistic-liberal principles of Western society, Israel has failed to maintain the necessary separation between economics and politics, and allowed the public-political domain to impinge upon the private-economic sphere (see also Shapiro 1977; Arian 1989; and Aharoni 1991). The consequences for Israeli society were detrimental. The petrifying of political dominance since the British Mandate era has created grave 'distortions', mostly associated with the evils of a 'socialist tradition' and excessive 'government intervention' (Halevi and Klinov-Malul 1968: 4). 'The socialist ideology', writes Ben-Porath (1986: 14), 'included a distrust of the market, a view of profits as mere rewards to parasitism, and (paradoxically) a view of services as unproductive.' And the curse lingers: 'The founding fathers of the state, and more precisely of the its labour movement', reiterates Kleiman (1996: 206), 'were disposed toward direct intervention and planning', policies which unfortunately 'continued well after their practical causes were long gone'.

The model, then, is fairly simple. Most broadly, it argues that a socialist tradition inevitably gives rise to a statist bureaucracy, which in turn depresses the spirit of private enterprise, draining society of its vitality, and ends up in chronic stagnation. From the new-right perspective of Sharkansky (1987: 5), 'the predominance of the government in Israel's economy makes it the most socialist country outside the Eastern Bloc. Along with a government budget that exceeds gross national product, there are numerous detailed controls on the activities of government officials, private-sector companies, and individual citizens.... It is Israel's fate to suffer the worst from the centrally controlled east and the democratic west.'

'Classless' Capitalism

In short, Israel – at least until recently – was like no other capitalist society. Its history was the result of 'the trilateral relationship between the settlement movement, the pioneering elite which exercised its control through the political parties and the bureaucratic stratum which recognised its hegemony' (Shapiro 1984: 45). It was 'a party state in which almost everything is determined by political parties' (Goldberg 1992: 16). According to Arian (1985), power, and hence the historical course of Israeli society, lay within the formal political sphere, in the hands of the political elites.

The 1990s seemed to have finally broken this mould. There is now a growing 'new literature' dealing with topics which until recently were off limit for academics wishing to keep their jobs. Many writers have finally discovered the wonders of political economy, and more and more of them speak freely about 'the politics of business groups', the 'military-industrial complex' and 'post-Zionism'. Yet this seemingly refreshing break from past practice is more apparent than real. A closer examination of such literature suggests it is mostly 'new wine into old bottles', as a recent review aptly put it, and that 'many of the so-called new works do not present anything very new' (Lochery 2000: 209). Israel, it turns out, is still run by omnipotent state officials, whose fight for 'survival' – against foreign 'enemies' and domestic 'actors' – continues to dominate the country's history.

Over the years, this convention about the primacy of politics and 'decision makers' served not only to separate the study of politics and economics, but also to divert attention from the class structure of Israel. Indeed, since control was in the hands of politicians and former army officers, and since these did not generally come from a capitalist background, class conflict was obviously irrelevant to the Israeli case. Israel, so it seemed, was a classless society in which the process of capital accumulation, the growth and consolidation of a ruling class, the ownership of resources, the distribution of income, the control of economic power, the methods of persuasion and legitimation, and the means of violence could all be safely ignored. Paradoxically, the few analyses of 'class struggle' which do exist pertain mostly to the pre-independence era – a period in which the society was hardly industrialised, in which there was barely any accumulation of capital or a meaningful working class, in which the most organised groups were the agricultural cooperatives, and in which the army and the police were those of a colonial power (Giladi 1973; Yatziv 1979). Since the 1970s, however, when these characteristics were long gone, replaced by a highly concentrated business structure, international economic integration, a developed industrial system of mass production, and an urban amalgamation of wage earners – there hasn't been even a single study about the Israeli ruling class or the process of accumulation, let alone the connection between them.

Toward a Global Political Economy of Israel

This book tries to offer an alternative. Although our story is by no means comprehensive, it deals with the three most essential processes which so far have been largely neglected: (1) capital accumulation; (2) ruling class formation; and (3) globalisation. Furthermore, it treats these not as separate phenomena, but rather as the integrated dimensions which together make the global political economy of Israel.

What do we mean by this term, 'global political economy'? The word 'global' here has two related connotations – one theoretical, the other geographical. First, it implies a universal approach. Our book is historical and therefore deals with much which is uniquely Israeli. Yet underlying the historical details, there are also more general processes and forces similar to those which have shaped other societies, and which suggest that Israel is in fact far from 'special'. The second meaning of global is spatial. The concept of 'globalisation' is commonly used in reference to the recent neoliberal phase of capitalist integration and interconnection on a world scale. But then Israel was *always* regionally and globally 'integrated'. We use inverted commas here since integration does not have to be 'positive' in the sense of trade, investment and ownership; societies could also integrate through conflict and war, and, as this book will amply demonstrate, Israel's outward interactions took both forms. For most countries, and especially smaller ones such as Israel, this global embeddedness defines the 'boundaries of the possible', and therefore should not only be recognised, but made the basis for the entire analysis.

Our interpretation of 'political economy' is also unconventional. As noted earlier, most writers prefer to treat its two components – 'politics' and 'economics' – as *independent* disciplines. Political economists tend to reject this separation; politics and economics, they argue, are inherently *connected*, and it is precisely the relationship between them which matters the most (see for instance, Caporaso and Levine 1992). In contrast to both of these views, our own aim is to transcend this divide in the first place. Politics and economics, we argue, are neither 'independent' nor 'connected' spheres of social life, but rather a consequence of a misleading dichotomy which has been imposed on what is essentially a *holistic* process, the process of social change.

The way to 'unify' the political economy of capitalism begins by focusing on its central process: the accumulation of capital. Our argument in this book is that capital is a power institution, and that power is both the means and end of accumulation. Because capital is a form of power, it should be understood in relative rather than absolute terms, hence our focus on what we call *differential accumulation*. Capitalists, we submit, are driven not to maximise profit as such, but to 'beat the average', and by so doing raise their ownership share. Furthermore, their ability to accumulate differentially reflects not 'economic' productivity or exploitation per se, but their broader power to restructure society and affect its overall development. The emphasis on differential accumulation suggests a particular research agenda, which focuses not only on 'capital in general', but also, and perhaps more so, on 'dominant capital'; that is, on the largest core corporations situated at the centre. This latter emphasis means that to study differential accumulation is also to study the emergence and formation of a ruling capitalist class. Indeed, the very existence of differential accumulation implies that a group of capitalist owners is able to control and shape more and more of the social process of reproduction. Analysing the origin of this group, the political-economic pattern of its evolution, the means by which it expands, the broader implications of its differential growth, and the limits and contradictions imposed on that growth, is therefore essential to the understanding of differential accumulation and capitalist development more broadly.

In sum, the global political economy of Israel is the process of domestic capitalist development, embedded in, and increasingly interconnected with the broader context of regional and global change. The central axis of this process is differential accumulation, which involves the rise and consolidation of Israel's ruling class, the dominant capital groups under its control, and their relationship, both conflictual and reinforcing, with the changing trajectory of world capitalism. Finally, the analysis of these key processes is significant not only in its own right, but also in helping to bring wider aspects of Israeli history into sharper focus.

Capital and Differential Accumulation

The theoretical framework of this book, introduced and developed in Chapter 2, is aimed at integrating capital and power. Although capital is the central institution of capitalism, there is surprisingly little agreement on what it means. The form, or 'shell' of capital, its existence as monetary wealth, is hardly in doubt. The problem is with the content, the 'stuff' which makes capital grow, and on this there is no agreement whatsoever. For example, does capital accumulate because it is 'productive', or due to the exploitation of workers? Does capital expand 'on its own', or does it need non-capitalist institutions such as the state? What exactly is being accumulated? Does the value of capital represent a material 'thing', 'dead labour' or perhaps something totally different? What units should we use to measure such accumulation? Despite centuries of debate, none of these questions has a clear answer. Yet they have to have answers. Capital is the essence of capitalism, and unless we can clarify what it means, our theories remain 'bagel theories', with a big hole in the middle.

Our own view is that capital should be understood as *power over cooperation*. Capital, we argue, is neither a material entity, nor a productive process, but rather the very ability of absentee owners to control, shape and restructure society more broadly. Although capital is by no means the only form of power, it has gradually become the most effective, flexible, and potentially most encompassing form of power. As an abstract financial magnitude, capital stands for the discounted value of future earning capacity. Such earnings are the consequence not of productivity as such, but of the control of productivity, which is in turn based not only on business arrangements, but on the entire spectrum of power institutions. To study accumulation therefore is to study the *commodification of power*.

From this perspective, every power arrangement which systematically affects the flow of profit is a potential facet of capital. This covers institutions and processes as diverse as military spending and managed stagflation in Israel, apartheid laws and democratisation in South Africa, the pendulum of inflation and corporate amalgamation in the United States, organised crime in Russia and IMF bailouts in Asia, or 'energy conflicts' and 'peace dividends' in the Middle East; it also covers more universal processes, such as the molding of consumer wants and preferences, patent laws, protectionism and the systematic use of violence. All of these bear on profit; and once their impact is 'discounted' by investors, they *become* capital.

This 'encompassing process' – the transformation by which capital increasingly 'commodifies' and therefore subsumes other forms of power – is perhaps the broader meaning of capitalist development. Examining this development requires that we place power at the centre of analysis, and that we do so from the very start. Once that is accepted, many 'political' and 'economic' phenomena anchored in accumulation no longer appear qualitatively different.

The commdification of power manifests itself through differential accumulation. Although capitalists exert their power over society, they measure it *relative to other owners*. Under modern conditions, capitalists are impelled not to maximise profit as such, but to 'beat the average'; they measure their differential accumulation as the *difference* between the growth rate of their own assets, and that of the average. This differential drive enables us to relate accumulation to the dynamic re-shaping of society: in order to accumulate differentially, leading capitalists have to constantly re-structure the underlying power institutions on which their relative profitability relies. Differential accumulation thus acts as a central axis for our story. In looking at phenomena such as stagflation, militarisation, corporate concentration, global finance, international conflict, or regional reconciliation, our aim is to articulate, both theoretically and historically, how *qualitative* power institutions are increasingly *quantified* into relative asset prices.

In its most simple form, the value of capital depends on two magnitudes: (1) the expected flow of future profit (or business income more generally), and (2) the normal rate of return used to discount this flow into present value. To beat the average, capitalists need to make their own profit grow faster than the normal, so that any understanding of differential accumulation requires an explanation of both. The first, most obvious question, therefore, is where does the normal rate of return come from? The answer, it turns out, is anything but simple.

Profit theory is perhaps one of the most unsettled branches of political economy. The basic problem is the apparent asymmetry between workers and capitalists – the former work for their wages, whereas the latter do no toil for their profit. Early mainstream thinkers offered a plethora of explanations for why the capitalist deserves compensation – ranging from Nassau Senior's 'abstinence', through Alfred Marshall's 'waiting', to Frank Knight's 'uncertainty' – but these have done little to calm the water. It was only with the work of John Bates Clark in *The Distribution of Wealth* (1899) that the issue seemed finally resolved. Clark made the income of capitalists a function of the productivity of their capital. And since capital, much like labour and land, was productive and therefore necessary, the income of its owner was clearly desirable and natural.

The theory offered robust ideological support for capitalism, and quickly became the conventional wisdom. Its logic, though, remained fatally flawed. The main problem was that in order to quantify the productivity of capital, we needed first to quantify capital itself. And yet, surprising as it may seem, this couldn't be done. The problem was fully exposed in a major debate among economists, known as the 'Cambridge Controversies'. As we'll see in Chapter 2, the debate showed that capital was not a 'material thing' with a definite 'physical quantity', and that it therefore couldn't have a clearly measurable productivity. But then, if capital wasn't productive, how could we treat its profit as being 'normal'?

Marx never tried to reason profit by the productivity of capital. On the contrary, profit, he argued, came through capitalist exploitation, which forced workers, the sole creators of the product, to accept only a portion of what they made. Yet, although Marx properly placed capitalist power at the very centre of his theory, his treatment of such power was incomplete, and ultimately inconsistent. Indeed, while he was the first to emphasise broader power processes, such as the concentration and centralisation of capital and the growing role of the state, these never found their way into the *analytical* formulation of his Labour Theory of Value – and nor could they; the latter theory depended crucially on the assumptions of free competition and the unfettered flow of capital and labour, and these assumptions would be quickly violated if power were allowed into the picture. In the final analysis, profit (or 'surplus value') in Marx's scheme was determined as a residual between the total output of labour and the 'socially necessary' cost of reproducing its labour power – an ingenious but dangerously circular concept.

The twentieth century rise of big business and big government brought a fuller recognition of the interplay between profit and power. New analyses of imperialism, 'imperfect competition', and the actual behaviour of modern firms served to cast doubts on the competitive model underlying the work of both Marx and the neoclassicists. By the middle of the century, these doubts gave rise to an alternative, 'neo-Marxist' school of Monopoly Capital, led by writers such Michal Kalecki, Josef Steindl, Paul Baran and Paul Sweezy. One of the principal claims of this school was that distribution was mostly a consequence of power, and hence potentially 'separate' from production as such. The result was to make normal prices, and therefore the ordinary flow of profit, theoretically indeterminate. The *actual* flow of profit of course remained both real and definite, but the theorist could no longer easily predict its magnitude.

This indeterminacy may be true in a strictly quantitative sense. In our opinion, though, the key challenge is not to find the quantitative determinants of profit, but rather to build a bridge between the quantitative and the qualitative. If capital is indeed a commodification of power, the task is to link the quantitative nature of profit and accumulation on the one hand, with the qualitative power institutions on which they are based on the other. This needs to be done at the differential level, by identifying the specific power institutions, arrangements and processes which shape the earnings of particular capital groups. And it is equally necessary at the general level, as a way of understanding the normal rate of return. From both perspectives, we could argue that the increasing normality of profit reflects the progressive universalisation and standardisation of power under capitalism. To expect profit to grow at some normal rate is therefore to expect the underlying power institutions to remain stable; the more stable these institutions, the more normal the rate of return, and vice versa.

The normalisation of profit is intimately related to the changing nature of the state. The growth of big government and the spread of bureaucratisation since the early part of the century gave rise to a heated debate regarding the connection between state and accumulation. Opinions on the matter of course vary greatly. The conservative, statist perspective sees the state as using capital to advance the 'national interest', defined materially and ideally by its own state officials. Liberals, taking a middle-of-the-road position, think of the state more as the battle ground, or negotiating arena for competing societal groups and demands. Finally, Marxists consider the state as having an inherent pro-capitalist bias, although they disagree on the extent to which it is 'autonomous' from the structural constraints of accumulation. Beyond the many differences, however, there is one thing on which most writers tend to agree, and that is that state and capital are essentially *distinct* entities. As such, they of course constantly interact with one another, sometimes through conflict, sometimes by reinforcement; but their essence remains separate – one anchored in production, the other in power.

Our own point of departure is different. The concept of 'state' is often used to denote the set of key political institutions and central governing organisations in society. Using this broad understanding, our argument is that *capital itself can be seen as an emergent form of state*. This, we acknowledge, is a radical departure from accepted wisdom, if only because the state is commonly defined as having a territorial dimension, whereas capital is inherently *a*-territorial. Note, however, that the territoriality of states is largely a historical fact, not a logical necessity. Many of today's transnational organisations and multilateral institutions transcend physical space, and if these were ever to develop into a global state, territory would clearly cease to be a defining feature.

But there is really no need to peek into the future. In fact, state and capital were always symbiotic, coalescent, and often fused. The modern nation state, from its very beginning, was highly dependent on capitalist finance, while capitalisation was similarly reliant on state power. Indeed, it was this fusion between them which gave rise to the first form of modern capital – the government bond – whose very essence was the *private ownership* of the *gov-*

ernment's power to tax. Since then, the overlap grew deeper and wider, with an increasing proportion of capital values depending on, and in turn dictating the nature of key political institutions and organisations. The fact that investors now increasingly 'discount' state policies and processes into asset prices indicates the extent to which these have become predictable, and hence far less 'discretionary'.

We therefore end up with a double-sided 'commodification of the state'. On the one hand, state institutions and organisations, through their systematic impact of profit, become facets of capital. On the other hand, differential power institutions are increasingly crystallised as capital, and by virtue of their social centrality emerge as 'a state' in their own right.

The gradual emergence of 'capital as state' is well illustrated by the political economy of Israel. On the one hand, the Israeli state was created and subsequently sustained by foreign capital inflows. These flows, extended by both private investors and foreign governments, enabled their owners to act as partners, and often as the real boss, in crucial local and regional matters, including economic policy, war, and peace. On the other hand, domestic capital was born from within this context. Initially weak and sheltered by the state, it eventually grew to transcend it, locally by taking over and controlling more and more state functions, as well as globally by integrating into the transnational structure of accumulation.

Regimes of Differential Accumulation

The 'commodification of the state' is of course highly conflictual and historically contingent. Our analysis of this changing capital–state symbiosis resembles to some extent attempts by the Social Structures of Accumulation approach (SSA) and the French Regulation school to link accumulation with its supporting 'complex of institutions' or 'modes of regulation' (for instance, Aglietta 1979; and Kotz et al. 1994). There is however a big difference: whereas the Regulation and SSA schools view accumulation as related to, but inherently *distinct* from wider social dynamics, our own research focuses specifically on the ways in which such social dynamics gradually become the *very essence of accumulation*.

The centrepiece of this framework is the notion of differential accumulation *regimes*. The basic idea is to identify the main avenues, or paths, through which differential accumulation can take place, and then examine their broader causes, interactions and ramifications. In principle, profit growth could be thought of as the sum of two components – the rate of growth of employment and the rate of growth of profit per employee. For dominant capital, a positive rate of differential accumulation could hence be achieved by following two distinct routes: either through 'breadth', by expanding employment faster than the average to increase market share, or via 'depth' by raising profit per employee faster than the average. Understood as broad social regimes, these two paths are

fundamentally different. Breadth is commonly associated with rapid proletarianisation, economic growth and corporate amalgamation, relatively low
inflation, more open political institutions and a certain easing of social conflict.
Depth, on the other hand, is typically characterised by stagflation, crystallisation of political institutions and intensifying of social conflict.

What is the relationship between breadth and depth? Can these two regimes
occur concurrently, or do they evolve 'counter-cyclically' to one another? What
are the reasons for their particular interaction? The answers are often as
surprising as they are revealing. For instance, the evidence from Israel and
elsewhere suggests that inflation is in fact negatively correlated with growth.
This inverse relationship is a serious anomaly for conventional economics, yet
is perfectly sensible when seen from the viewpoint of differential accumulation regimes. The latter perspective argues that inflation, which typically arises
in the depth phase, is the result of differential struggles among firms to raise
profit per employee. Such struggle requires institutional restrictions on breadth,
and therefore slower, not faster growth.

A second set of questions concerns patterns of political activity and social
conflict in the two regimes. Generally speaking, breadth thrives on the conquest
of new profit streams, and is therefore likely to be associated with the restructuring of power institutions. Depth, on the other hand, is based on deepening
existing distributional patterns, and hence on the consolidation of power and
a more explicit role for formal political arrangements. Of course, the precise
difference between 'new' and 'existing' profit streams, or between institutional
'change' and 'consolidation', is not always obvious. But given that depth is
commonly characterised by redistribution of a stagnating 'pie', whereas in
breadth the battle lines are often blurred by overall growth and expansion, we
can expect the former to be more conflict-ridden than the latter, if only in
appearance.

A third issue revolves around the 'choice' of regime. What structural forces
and conscious action favour one regime over another? Why and how does a
regime run its course? And what triggers a transition from one regime to
another? Most generally, we would expect the centrifugal forces of capitalism
– particularly the effect on competition of technological change, and the
perpetual lure of non-capitalist, 'virgin territory' – to make breadth the path of
least resistance. A stagflationary depth regime, on the other hand, is intensely
antagonistic, unstable, difficult to manage and often uncertain in outcome –
but it also has huge redistributional potential (shown most vividly during hyperinflation). The consequence is that when competition starts to seriously
undermine profit margins, and/or when proletarianisation and corporate amalgamation run into temporary barriers, dominant capital tends to gravitate, with
a mixture of fear and greed, toward depth.

This last hypothesis offers insight into the three-way interaction between
(1) the political economy of stagflation and growth; (2) the process of corporate
amalgamation; and (3) the broader forces of globalisation. As we show in

Chapter 2, over the past century, there has been a clear, negative correlation in the United States, the world epicentre of capital accumulation, between stagflation on the one hand, and corporate amalgamation on the other; uplegs in merger activity were invariably accompanied by easing stagflation, whereas a lull in mergers was always correlated with its intensification. Underlying this cyclical interaction, the *cumulative* effect of mergers and acquisitions was to progressively extend the reach of dominant capital – from its initial industry groupings during the so-called 'monopoly' wave of the 1890s and 1900s, through sectoral associations during the 'oligopoly' cycle of the 1920s, to national amalgamation in the 'conglomerate' cycle of the 1960s and, finally, to the global alliances in the current 'cross-border' phase. This pattern offers a broad framework for understanding the globalising nature of capital in relation to differential accumulation and its underlying political-economy processes. It also offers a setting for understanding the specific Israeli experience, which was deeply embedded in this global pattern of oscillating breadth and depth, and which also reproduced it internally.

The Rise and Consolidation of Israel's Ruling Class

By the end of the twentieth century, Israel's was a highly centralised, increasingly transnational and rapidly changing political economy. Ownership was tightly concentrated in the hands of a relatively small group of absentee owners. Some of these owners were Israeli by birth, others were foreign; a few were heads of wealthy families, while many were anonymous representatives of large institutions; some were long-term investors, others were in for the quick kill; most were 'legitimate', a few were criminal. Together, they formed the most powerful class ever to rule Israel. Their power came not only from what they owned and controlled domestically, but increasingly also from being part of a transnational capitalist class. Indeed, since the 1990s, Israel has emerged not only as a favourite destination for 'high-tech' investors, money managers, and illegal flight capital, but also as the source of much capital outflow, with locally based capitalists acquiring assets outside their country. As a result of this cross-fertilisation, it was no longer easy to distinguish 'Israeli' from 'foreign' investors, or for that matter to talk about 'Israeli capitalism' as such. Finally, the structure of ownership, although centralised and transnational, kept changing at an unprecedented pace, with mergers and acquisitions, divestitures and asset re-shuffling keeping power forever fluid.

 These features may not seem particularly startling at the dawn of the twenty-first century. But then, until recently, most people saw Israel not only as statist and socialist, but also as special and even unique. So why this sudden conversion to unregulated capitalism and transnationalism? Was this a historical accident? An externally imposed change? Was it a form of state 'self-preservation'? Or maybe it was simply that local elites finally saw the light, and decided to 'get their act together'? In our view, none of these explanations is satisfactory, if only since they all fail to see present developments as part of a broader capitalist history. As we show in Chapter 3 and reiterate throughout the rest of the book, the recent neoliberal phase was not at all a structural 'break', but rather the latest step in the long process of Israeli capitalist development; a process which began not in the 1990s, but almost a century earlier, with the initial Jewish colonisation of Palestine.

Indeed, the very notion that Israel 'moved' from statism to liberalism is to some extent misleading, particularly when presented in terms of a 'clash' between state officials and markets. First, the market is merely a mechanism. It has no 'will' of its own, and it certainly cannot 'act'. Indeed, this is one reason why liberals glorify the market, whose automaticity and anonymity they view as the best way to defuse power. Second, and more importantly, the crucial process here is not the elimination of power, but its transformation. Israeli state power was not nullified by markets, but rather taken over by capitalists. As we argued earlier, and as the real history of Israel amply demonstrates, state and capital did not really 'fight' one another, if only because they were never entirely 'separate'. Moreover, their very essence was gradually but profoundly altered by their mutual interaction, symbiosis and fusion: capitalist development has turned the Israeli state today into something different from what it was in the 1920s or in the 1950s, while governmental, military and judiciary processes have similarly changed the nature of capital.

In our view, the intertwined history of 'capital' and 'state', as well as the reason for their transformation, could be best understood as part of the broader analysis of class, and particularly of ruling class. In its early years, the Israeli state, while on the surface apparently subjugating capital to its own ends, was in fact the initial 'cocoon' within which capitalist institutions and organisations were allowed to develop. The cocoon analogy is useful in that both state and capital – like a cocoon and its larva – transmute via mutual symbiosis. During its short history, Israeli capital has not only outgrown the initial state structure from which it emerged, but also altered the very nature of that structure. Indeed, capital seems to have increasingly encapsulated the state, turning more and more of its public features into integral facets of private accumulation. Of course, this 'Cocoon Thesis' is by no means unique to Israel. The emergence and consolidation of European capitalism, for instance, began with omnipotent states providing the incubator for vulnerable capitalist interests, only to see these interests eventually grow to take them over. A similar process characterises the emergence of capitalism in colonial societies such as Latin America's, or more recently in East Asia and former Soviet bloc countries. Where Israel does stand out, though, is in the speed of its transition; whereas in most other countries the process required a few centuries, in Israel it took only a few generations.

During the earlier stages of this development, from the turn of the century until Independence in 1948, the main domestic power struggle was over immigration. The labour exodus from crisis-ridden Europe produced a breadth bonanza in Palestine. Yet, as a 'pre-emerging market', with a small, dispersed and relatively powerless private sector, the Holy Land did not have the capitalist infrastructure needed to turn this potential into expanding profit. The historical task of creating this infrastructure therefore had to be shouldered by the Zionist institutions, most notably the Jewish Agency, and by the Histadrut, or federation of labour unions. The package deal between them was simple: the Histadrut, after a bitter trench war with competing unions, gained the exclusive right to import, organise and discipline the labour force, whereas the Jewish Agency, through its quasi-state institutions, was responsible for raising the foreign capital needed to put it to work.

Much of Israel's hyped rhetoric of 'statism', 'socialism' and 'nationalism' originated during those years. Yet behind the ideological commotion, there was another, much more important process: *the formation of an Israeli ruling class*. Zionist and labour organisations not only cooperated from the very beginning, but their leaderships were also gradually integrating – through joint projects, revolving door nominations, kinship ties and converging ideologies – into a 'New Class', similar to the one described by Milovan Djilas (1957) in his account of communist society. The formation of this corporatist-socialist class, though, was inherently contradictory, and the results were quick to emerge in the Histadrut itself – an organisation which represented workers, while simultaneously acting as their biggest employer. Ben-Gurion, for example, who was concurrently head of the Histadrut as well as a Jewish Agency board member, openly declared that his organisation, the Histadrut, offered the best protection against wildcat strikes; he also fought zealously for the conquest of 'Hebrew Work' (over the indigenous Palestinian population), and rarely insisted on higher wages. Later on, as urbanisation progressed, the labour movement as a whole began to fracture, with its core MAPAI Party gradually shifting away from representing workers, and into manipulating them as electorates. In parallel, the 'private sector', although still small, began to consolidate, often in open collaboration with its official 'class enemy', the Histadrut.

Independence in 1948 established the apparent primacy of the state and the 'New Class', yet within this warm cocoon, the seeds of dominant capital and the institutions of its differential accumulation already began to develop. These institutions included the distribution of land confiscated from Palestinian refugees, the controlled proletarianisation of a rapidly growing immigrant population, and the allocation of unilateral capital inflow, primarily from world Jewry and foreign governments. The impact of these external stimuli was highly differential, contributing to the relative growth of several core firms, primarily Bank Leumi of the Jewish Agency, Bank Hapoalim and Koor which were owned by the Histadrut, and the privately held Discount Bank. Although only the latter was formally private, the others were rapidly 'commodified' into de facto capitalist enterprises. This broad capitalisation process was accompanied by a growing integration between the existing 'New Class' cadres on the one hand, and the emerging big bourgeoisie on the other.

The collapse of the statist model, which came during the 1970s, coincided with a massive shift, globally as well as in Israel, from a differential accumulation regime based on breadth, to one relying on depth. At home, the main drivers of the early breadth boom – population growth and foreign aid – had dried up. Moreover, by the early 1970s, the statist cocoon had already produced a core of very large dominant capital groups, whose magnitude relative to the small Israeli market was becoming self-limiting. If the latter's differential accumulation were to continue (which it did), the underlying regime had to change – away from relying on growth and merger which had subsided, and toward higher profit margins through redistribution, conflict and stagflation. The transition was greatly facilitated by the global intensification of stagflation (which, as we explain later, was itself propagated by growing conflict in the Middle East). Domestically, the result was a new order of 'accumulation-through-crisis', with differential accumulation depending increasingly on the twin engines of rising military spending and inflationary finance.

The essence of this new depth phase was a mutual transformation of both state and capital. On the surface, the state apparatus seemed to have 'lost its autonomy'. It got deeper and deeper into external conflict and an escalating arms race; it grew increasingly dependent on the United States; and it stood paralysed in the face of domestic recession and sprawling inflation. Under the surface, though, the real transformation was not the decline of the state, but its further 'commodification' as an integral facet of accumulation. And indeed, the dominant capital groups, all of which were by now operating as capitalist enterprises regardless of their formal ownership, had little to complain about. On the contrary, their profitability soared – absolutely, as well as relatively to smaller firms, who were typically hit hard by the stagflationary crisis.

Israeli economists tend to ignore this differential accumulation-through-crisis. A few acknowledge the redistributional process, although most deny it was purposeful, preferring to explain it as coincidental, or better still, as a 'policy mistake'. And they could be right. After all, mistakes do happen all the time. The only question is why were the 'errors' so systematic in their impact, and how could they last for more than a decade? The answer, we think, should begin with the very concept of 'state policy' here. In our view, if there was indeed a conscious foreign and domestic policy during that period, it was certainly no longer 'statist'; instead, it was the policy of dominant capital, to which the state apparatus became increasingly subservient. And indeed, by the 1970s, the disparate elites of Israel's 'ancient regime' had already been amalgamated into a single ruling class, whose end and tail were no longer easy to disentangle. Moreover, as we discuss in Chapter 5, the interests of this class were growing increasingly tied with those of large oil and armament firms based in the United States, whose own fortunes were in turn dependent on the continuation of conflict in the region as a whole. These latter corporations and their Israeli satellites not only benefited systematically from a regime of regional instability and militarised stagflation, but also managed to have their governments in Washington and Jerusalem sustain and support this regime against the wider interests of their underlying populations. Their ability to do so points out the extent to which *their rule* became *state rule*.

In this broader context, the 1977 dethroning of the Labour Party by the right-wing Likud bloc appears far from the 'political earthquake' observers often make it look like. Being increasingly subsumed by dominant capital, successive Labour governments found it increasingly difficult to deliver what their socialist rhetoric promised, and therefore grew vulnerable to new 'populist' competitors. More importantly, dominant capital itself was now interested not in a strong government, but a *large* one – which, paradoxically, was much easier to have with the 'liberal' Likud than the 'statist' Labour. The Likud's combination of right-wing foreign policy and hands-off economic policy, similar to the menu offered by the Reagan Administration in Washington, helped consolidate the new depth regime, securing higher military procurement and rising debt loads, as well as financial 'deregulation', a carte blanche for stock market rigging, and further stagflation.

Accumulation Through Crisis

At first sight, these external hallmarks of depth look highly perplexing. How could large firms benefit from raising their prices faster than the average rate of inflation? Won't this 'price them out of the market'? Can accumulation really thrive on stagflation and crisis? Aren't capitalists interested in the growth and tranquillity offered by 'business as usual'? Why should businessmen prefer war to peace? Do they have a say in this anyway? Surprisingly, these questions are not very difficult to answer, provided of course one is willing to first dispense with some basic preconceptions.

The first of these preconceptions is the myth of the 'aggregate', which by the end of the twentieth century has been perfected to a point of concealing the most fundamental tension of political economy – the contradiction between well-being and power. Take a standard concept such as the 'average standard of living'. Academic and popular media love to use this term, but what does it really tell us? To begin with, emphasising an average necessarily de-emphasises its distribution. For instance, if the standard of living of the poor fell, but that of the rich rose by much more (as was the case in both the United States and Israel over the past decade), the overall average could well go higher. Focusing on that average would clearly distort the picture of what actually happened to the vast majority of the population. The more fundamental problem, however, is the implicit assumption that well-being is the main engine of capitalism. The standard of living is of course very important to most people, but then capitalism isn't run by 'most people', but by a relatively small number of very large capitalists. For them, the main goal is not well-being, but power. What they are after is neither the size of the pie, nor the 'absolute' magnitude of their own income, but rather their distributive share. The latter can of course be augmented through overall growth, but it doesn't have too. Sometimes, a shrinking pie works much better, for example, when the large capitalists gain much of what the rest of society loses. In short, differential accumulation for dominant capital neither requires nor implies prosperity for all. During breadth periods, when dominant capital accumulates differentially through overall growth, the two appear mutually reinforcing. But during depth, when differential accumulation thrives on crisis and overall contraction, the aggregate myth breaks down.

The second misconception concerns the issue of 'instability'. The conventional view is that stability is good for business, and that there is nothing capitalists hate more than volatility and uncertainty. The usual reason given for this is twofold. In the short run, instability raises interest rates and risk premiums, and hence undermines asset prices, while in the longer run it jeopardises capitalist institutions and possibly the accumulation process itself. These observations, although correct, are incomplete and therefore misleading. Instability does raise interest rates and risk perceptions; yet, if these come together with even faster increases in expected profit – as was the case for instance in Israel during the early 1980s and in Latin America during the early 1990s – the overall impact on asset prices will be positive, not negative. Furthermore, those who benefit from instability are often different from those who foot up the bill. The link between crisis and accumulation was well expressed by a contemporary of Marx, J.P. Dunning, in a passage worth quoting:

> Capital is said by a Quarterly Reviewer to fly turbulence and strife, and to be timid, which is very true; but this is very incompletely stating the question. Capital eschews no profit, or very small profit, just as Nature was formerly said to abhor a vacuum. With adequate profit, capital is very bold. A certain 10 per cent will ensure its employment anywhere; 20 per cent will produce eagerness; 50 per cent, positive audacity; 100 per cent will make it ready to trample on all human laws; 300 per cent, and there is not a crime at which it will scruple, nor a risk it will not run, even to the chance of its owner being hanged. If turbulence and strife will bring a profit, it will freely encourage both. (cited in Marx 1909, Vol. I: 834)

This logic of public pain for private gain is evidently still in place. During the 1970s and early 1980s, for example, the oil companies and OPEC countries benefited greatly from a twelvefold increase in petroleum prices, while the rest of the world suffered the macro consequences of deep stagflation and monetary volatility. Of course, no dominant group can benefit from endless crisis and instability, but that is beside the point here since most capitalist crises eventually get 'resolved' (otherwise, capitalism would have been long gone by now). Similarly, although crises are not necessarily 'premeditated', that in itself is secondary. The key question is who benefit from a crisis, the extent to which they can and cannot affect its trajectory, and the broader conditions and contradictions within which they operate to enhance their interests.

Perhaps the best way to address such questions is to begin from the neoclassical ideology created to conceal them in the first place. The intellectual edifice of this ideology, conceived by the profession's grand priests, built and rebuilt by its numerous foot soldiers, financed by dominant capital and tax money, implemented as policy by state organs, and distributed for public consumption by the various media, is certainly impressive. It is also impenetrable. Most outsiders cannot decipher its complicated sign language and mysterious rituals, and even those who can are often left excluded by its professional barriers to entry. The reason, though, is not that the study of economics is somehow more difficult than other social subjects, but rather that it is *deliberately made to look that way*. Moreover, by depicting the economy as if it were 'natural', and therefore subject to 'objective' scientific inquiry, economists have effectively managed not only to stifle meaningful public discussion, but also to eliminate the need for such discussion in the first place. After all, laws of nature can be discovered, but they can never be changed; so what is the point of debating them? The fallacious application of this logic to society, which Marx called 'fetishism', is one of the greatest powers of capitalism: the power to control the minds of it subjects. Yet, this ideology seems omnipotent mostly from the outside. From the inside, it looks more like a house of cards, built on logical contradictions and pseudo-facts. For this reason, it is important to engage with neoclassical ideology on its own turf. The stagflation of the 1970s and 1980s provides plenty of opportunity for such an exercise, which we take on in Chapter 4.

According to received dogma, in Israel as elsewhere, inflation is the consequence of 'excess demand', or its mirror image, 'deficient supply'. Since this belief is generally accepted as an article of faith, the main task for the believer is to find the exact mechanism by which the excess or deficiency are translated into rising prices. This, though, is far trickier than it seems. At the most general level, both explanations (excess and deficiency) are reducible to the notion that when 'too much money' chases 'too few commodities', the result is extra 'liquidity' (relative to what is needed to buy and sell commodities at stable prices), and therefore inflation. The logic sounds intuitive enough, only that reality refuses to obey. For this causal chain to make any sense, liquidity must rise *before* inflation; and yet in Israel the sequence was always the reverse, with inflation leading and liquidity trailing!

As it turns out, such mismatch between universal theory and worldly facts is prevalent throughout the neoclassical treatment of inflation. To take another example, consider the government, which Israeli economists, like their counterparts the world over, love to blame for the disease. The usual suspect here is the budget deficit. Public spending, goes the argument, tends to be wasteful, in that it creates demand without a corresponding supply. This means excess; and excess, as every child knows, leads to inflation. But then here too the treacherous facts spoil the show. The Israeli deficit as a whole shows a changing relationship with inflation, sometimes positive, sometimes negative, and many of its individual components actually move in the opposite direction. The economists are not entirely in the wrong, however. A selected number of budget items – specifically, business subsidies and interest on the public debt – show a systematically tight positive correlation with inflation. Isn't this, then, the Holy Grail? A proof, however partial, that government spending is inflationary after all? Not really. The reason why these budget items rose and fell with inflation is in fact very simple: until recently they were indexed to inflation. In other words, the Israeli government acted here merely as an intermediary, translating higher inflation into higher corporate profit.

Another inflationary villain on the demand side are the workers, whose 'excessive' wages are usually seen as a source of wild and highly inflationary spending sprees. The most effective way to combat this danger is by raising unemployment. There is nothing like a good dose of layoffs to cool off workers' militancy; and with employees having less to spend, inflation has nowhere to go but down. The belief in this medicine gained much of its legitimacy during the late 1950s from the so-called Phillips Curve, which showed that inflation and unemployment were negatively correlated. The problem, though, was that the relationship not only broke down almost as soon as it was discovered, but also went into reverse; in many countries, Israel included, inflation and unemployment since the 1960s have become *positively* correlated!

The inversion of the Phillips Curve created a serious theoretical challenge. Recall the underlying neoclassical maxim, stipulated by supply and demand analysis, that prices rise as a consequence of 'shortage'. But if so, how could inflation occur when the economy is stagnating with unused resources and unemployed workers? Does this mean that neoclassical analysis was fundamentally wrong? Not at all, argued its adherents. Inflation in the midst of stagnation was still a consequence of shortage; only that the reason now was not excess demand, but deficient supply. The latter was created when 'unjustified' wage increases pushed cost beyond what it 'should' be, forcing firms to simultaneously 'restrict' supply and jack up prices. This line of reasoning also opened the door for bringing in new villains, such as the oil sheiks of the Middle East and the weather gods, who, by making energy and food more expensive, helped feed the stagflation demon. Most importantly, the lining-up of these culprits helped exonerate capitalists, who were excused from the list on technical grounds. Unlike workers or oil sheiks, whom the theory classified as 'price makers', capitalists were declared 'price takers'; competition, argued the neoclassicists, made them practically powerless, and therefore innocent of 'cost-push' stagflation. Fascinating theory, only that the evidence (or lack thereof) again failed to cooperate, leaving stagflation, as one neoclassical priest put it, as 'mysterious' as ever. But then, neoclassicists were never too concerned with evidence. After all, their real mission was always to conceal reality, not to reveal it; and so the facts, which usually made their job more difficult, could always be dispensed with when necessary.

Clearly, there is a lot to uncover in what the neoclassicists seek to hide. Our own premise is that inflation is neither a punishment for some social 'excess', nor a consequence of policy 'mistake', and it is certainly not the result of some 'autonomous' decision or 'external shock'. Inflation is not an alien macroeconomic phenomenon, but rather a central aspect of capitalist development in general, and of differential accumulation in particular. Moreover, contrary to the basic tenet of neoclassical logic, inflation tends to appear as stagflation – that is, *together* with slack. This hypothesis is examined in Chapter 4 against the rise and decline of Israeli inflation – from the relatively inflationless growth of the 1950s; through the heightened stagflation of the 1970s and 1980s; to the disinflation and renewed growth of the 1990s. The argument, based on our notion of differential accumulation regimes, is that during the 1970s and 1980s, after the breadth sources of population growth and capital inflow dried up, Israeli dominant capital pushed toward an alternative depth regime, based on stagflationary redistribution. The process worked mainly through the twin engines of militarisation and financial manipulation. Dominant capital became the main beneficiary of domestic military procurement, chiefly through its ability to raise armament prices faster than the overall rate of inflation. A similar process occurred in the realm of finance, where the large firms, supported openly by the government, manipulated stock prices so as to effectively 'print' their own profits. These two processes not only fuelled an inflationary spiral, but also sent the economy into deep recession and heightened instability. And yet, since the higher profits went primarily to dominant capital, whereas the cutbacks were suffered mainly in the rest of the business sector, the result was an unprecedented surge of differential accumulation. In short, stagflation, which to the macroeconomists appeared as an alienated riddle, was in fact a mechanism for a massive restructuring of power. This restructuring involved diverse processes, such as growing income inequality and heightened social tensions; the decline of the Labour Party and the rise of clericalism; the militarisation of production and the rise of finance; the intensification of the Middle East conflict; and the growing dependency of Israel on U.S. assistance. Most importantly, it was itself part of a broader depth regime, affecting the nature of global differential accumulation.

The Middle East and the Weapondollar–Petrodollar Coalition

Since the early 1970s, dominant capital groups in the developed countries shifted their emphasis from growth and amalgamation to stagflation and redistribution. The epicentre of this new depth phase was the Middle East, where Israel played an important role. So far, though, there has been no attempt to situate the political economy of Israel within this broader development. There are two basic reasons for this. The first one is methodological. The political economy of the Middle East, much like that of Israel, is usually examined from a 'system' perspective, which customarily separates politics from economics, and domestic from international developments. These different 'systems' supposedly interact with one another, although in practice they are rarely integrated into a grand historical narrative. The second reason is political. Such grand narrative, at least from a political-economy viewpoint, would have to deal with capital accumulation, which is precisely what most writers on the subject seek to avoid. Chapter 5, which focuses on the post-war history of the Middle East, tries to fill this void. The purpose is to understand this history not as a collection of 'systems' and 'levels of analysis', but rather as part of the broader evolution of global accumulation. Since the 1940s, the region's role in world accumulation was intimately linked to oil exports. From the 1960s onwards, this significance was further augmented by a newer flow of arms imports. The interaction of these two flows, and most importantly the *profits associated with them*, form the heart of our story.

Most works on the subject, written largely from a Western perspective, emphasise the tension between cheap energy on the one hand, and the conflict over access to such energy on the other. According to this framework, the indus-trialised economies have an interest in freely flowing, cheap oil. To secure this interest, however, they need to engage in international and regional *realpolitik*, which is often conflictual and sometimes destabilising. The result is an 'access vs. price' trade-off, in which occasional armed conflicts and periodic energy crises are seen as the necessary cost of enjoying continued access to cheap oil. The major drawback of this framework is its emphasis on aggregate, statist categories. The very notion that policies, events and processes are subservient to the so-called 'national interest' already precludes alternative explanations based on conflict and friction *within* societies, as well as cooperation and alliance cutting *across* different nations. In fact, in this context even the interest of the 'capitalist class' is potentially too broad as a basic unit of analysis, since it conceals crucial intra-capitalist struggles.

The problem is easy to illustrate against the backdrop of the 1970s and 1980s. During that period, Middle East conflicts and energy crises aggravated the processes of stagflation and monetary instability around the world, intensified the global arms race, and further undermined the ability of most developing countries to improve their meagre incomes. Clearly, these developments were detrimental to much of the world's population. They were also harmful to most firms, including many large ones, who suffered from the rising cost of energy, recession, soaring interest rates, and currency turmoil. And yet not everyone took a hit. The most publicised winners were of course the OPEC countries, but they weren't alone. The other winners were the large oil companies, military contractors, infrastructure companies and key financial institutions. For this group, which we label the Weapondollar–Petrodollar Coalition, the process spelled a massive differential accumulation bonanza. Of course, this coalition wasn't omnipotent to shape history as it pleased. At the same time, neither was it a lucky private bystander, who just happened to jump on a bandwagon driven by state officials. Instead, what seems to emerge from the broader contours and key details of this history is a radically different picture, in which the very distinction between 'state' and 'capital', 'government policy' and 'private action', 'international relations' and 'global business', is difficult and often impossible to pin down.

Perhaps the most remarkable illustration of this growing symbiosis is the dual process, involving the *commercialisation* of arms exports on the one hand, and the *politicisation* of oil on the other. Since the 1960s, the international arms trade was gradually 'privatised', turning from a foreign policy instrument into a counter-cyclical, life-support mechanism for the leading arms contractors. Military exports, which after the Second World War were financed mostly through grants and aid, were now increasingly paid for by their recipients. By contrast, the oil business, traditionally the stronghold of private interests, became subject to increasing political control. Oil producing countries gradually nationalised their oil reserves, while many industrialised countries moved to regulate the distribution, taxation and price of petroleum products. These two processes were intimately connected. The commercialisation of arms exports required that buyers had the money to pay for their purchases, and it is therefore not surprising that the major boost for this transition occurred during the early 1970s, when the Middle East took over from South East Asia as the world's leading market for imported weaponry. Now, the main reason why Middle East countries could pay for these weapons was the politicisation of oil, which enabled a twelvefold increase in oil prices, therefore massively boosting their revenues. The process also worked in reverse, from armament to oil. Indeed, the primary factor behind the rise of petroleum prices during the 1970s and early 1980s was the heightened regional conflict, which military imports helped sustain. And so emerged a cycle of Middle East 'Energy Conflicts', sustained by a new political realignment between the Weapondollar–Petrodollar Coalition, OPEC and key government officials in the Western countries. The cycle created havoc in the region, and helped destabilise the global economy. But it also provided the necessary fuel for the depth phase of differential accumulation, while enriching the key oil and armament interests which propagated it in the first place.

Like any other broad narrative, our emphasis here on accumulation in general and the Weapondollar–Petrodollar Coalition in particular, is of course contestable. Clearly, there could be other explanations for the region's history. What seems less open to dispute, is the robustness of our story. As it turns out, the differential financial performance of this coalition, examined in Chapter 5, was not only affected by the region's 'energy conflicts', but also seems to have anticipated them with remarkable accuracy. Every time the differential accumulation of this coalition (particularly the large oil companies) became negative, there followed an 'energy conflict'; once the conflict was under way, differential accumulation was restored into positive territory; and, finally, no energy conflict occurred without a prior differential accumulation crisis. These statistical findings are further corroborated by the foreign policy backdrop during that period, particularly that of the United States. Although U.S. public officials swore allegiance to the national interest, their actual policies toward the Middle East proved much more ambivalent. The ambiguity remained latent as long as the so-called national interest coincided with the differential interests of the Weapondollar–Petrodollar Coalition. But when the two collided, the policy stance almost invariably tilted in favour of the coalition. The result was that, during the 1970s and 1980s, the United States ended up promoting both instability and high oil prices, exactly the opposite of its openly publicised aims.

The Israeli elite, which endeavoured relentlessly since the early 1960s to become a U.S. satellite in the region, assumed a central role in this process, both by participating in the regional conflict, and by helping the Americans with various clandestine operations around the world. In return for these services, Israel was allowed to run a closed war economy, protected by high trade barriers, and bolstered by massive economic and military assistance. It was within this context of regional conflict and U.S. support that Israel's dominant capital was able to enjoy close to two decades of depth-driven differential accumulation. At the same time, these developments also set in motion a process of transnationalisation, which eventually 'denationalised' Israeli capital, integrating it into the larger process of global accumulation.

From Foreign Investment to Global Accumulation

Ever since its independence in 1948, and in fact from the early days of Jewish settlement in Palestine, Israel was dependent on foreign capital and assistance. This dependency and its impact on the country's autonomy have been the subject of numerous learned studies. Most economists agree that foreign funds were essential during the early years, when subsistence standards of living prevented sufficient savings. During the 1950s and 1960s, however, rapid economic growth significantly raised income levels, which should have both increased savings and reduced external dependency. This, though, hasn't happened, at least not until recently. And the reason, according to the experts, is simple. Savings did grow, but government profligacy, together with a greedy population unwilling to live by its own means, made spending grow even faster. This, in any case, is the official story.

The facts, though, tell a rather different story. If the trade deficit and corresponding capital inflow are indeed caused by 'excessive' spending, we should expect their size to be positively correlated with economic growth – either because growth generates excess imports and a need for more foreign currency; or because rising capital inflow allows for faster growth, and therefore a greater appetite for imports. In Israel, however, neither explanation seems persuasive, simply because, over the past half century, the relative size of the trade deficit was *negatively* correlated with growth. When the economy accelerated, excess imports, instead of rising, actually declined, and when the economy slowed down, excess imports began to soar. In other words, whether or not there was indeed a 'need' for more foreign capital, it had little to do with the country's shifting macroeconomic conditions.

The secret of capital flow lies elsewhere, in Israel's development as a capitalist society. The crucial aspects of this process, examined in Chapter 6, relate not to the country's consumption, saving or productive capacity, but to its ruling class and its progressive integration into the global political economy. A large part of the foreign inflow, particularly during the pre-independence period and the early years of the state, came as donations from the Jewish Diaspora. Contrary to popular perceptions, though, most big donors saw their contributions as political investments, on which many of them have since reaped enormous returns in the form of tax exemptions, special privileges, exclusive business rights, and privatised state assets at bargain prices.

From the 1950s, the Israeli elite also began a parallel love affair with inter-governmental transfers, initially from Germany in compensation for the Holocaust, and subsequently from the United States in return for various security and insecurity services mentioned earlier. The so-called economic part of this aid quickly became a target for the dominant capital groups, who fought viciously over its allocation. Eventually, most of this aid found its roundabout ways down to their bottom lines. Unlike economic assistance, military aid couldn't be pocketed by the domestic groups, at least not directly. The main reason was that the money itself never left the United States. Instead, it was transferred straight from the bank account of the U.S. government to the bank accounts of U.S. military contractors, who then shipped their hardware to Israel. The arrangement did not leave the Israeli groups empty-handed, however. The first impact of this aid, indirect but enormously powerful, was to boost local military procurement, which started rising in tandem with U.S. shipments and the consequent regional arms race. And there was more. Since the Israeli army retained the right to pick and choose its American weapons, each U.S. supplier had to hire its own local retainers to plead its case and hopefully share the spoils. Over the years, many of Israel's retired IDF generals and chiefs-of-staff, big businessmen and leading politicians – including ministers, prime ministers and state presidents – have been integrated as middlemen into this mechanism. In addition, numerous contracts were conditioned on re-purchase agreements from large Israeli contractors, creating yet another access to the precious flow of greenbacks. And so, while on the surface the inflow of capital looked largely a matter of philanthropy, humanitarian aid or foreign policy, under the surface it helped create and sustain a complicated international infrastructure of private accumulation.

From the late 1980s this pattern began to change. Differential accumulation in the developed countries was once more shifting from depth to breadth, and the superpower and regional conflicts which earlier linked Israeli and U.S. capitalist groups were coming to a close. Instead of disintegrating, however, the relationships between these two corporate groups became all the more intimate. Whereas earlier, corporate interaction had to be mediated through intergovernmental aid and loans, since the early 1990s the shift toward private capital flow rapidly altered the structure of ownership, causing Israeli accumulation to be directly assimilated into the global circuit of capital. Within less than a decade, many of Israel's leading firms, along with a growing part of its ruling class, have been transnationalised.

Until recently, the essence of this transnationalisation has been effectively concealed by a smokescreen of ideological hype. This hype, whose specific purpose is to promote the 'new world order' of neoliberalism, seems to rest on three related foundations: first, that 'states' have been declining relative to 'markets'; second, that as a consequence of deregulation, globalisation and technical change, the business world is now much more 'competitive'; and finally, that these two processes together work to defuse the direct power of agents (such as governments, unions, and firms), in favour of the structural dictates of the 'invisible hand' (which of course works for the common good).

All three foundations, however, are made out of sand. The 'decline of the state', for example, is a highly questionable proposition, particularly if the state is understood to denote the organised institution of social power and authority. Are these organised institutions really weaker now than before? Similarly with business competition. If we were to judge by U.S. corporate markups, for example, the overall power of capital would seem to have actually *risen* more or less continuously over the past half century, and most rapidly so since the surge of neoliberalism in the 1990s. Finally, direct power remains alive and kicking. Although the Weapondollar–Petrodollar Coalition of the depth phase has declined, a global Technodollar–Mergerdollar Coalition, based on a new breadth regime of high technology and corporate amalgamation, has emerged to replace it.

What happened in Israel during the 1990s is part and parcel of these global developments. The changes have been nothing short of profound. Dominant capital firms, along with thousands of startup companies, shifted rapidly toward high technology; economic policy switched gears from large spending to sound finance; the social outlook reverted from state paternalism to individualism; and the external stance moved from regional conflict to reconciliation. In less than a decade, the collectivist Zionist ethos which dominated the country for nearly a century, has been effectively challenged by the new 'Washington Consensus' of free market transnationalism. This 'new look' has been marketed by its dominant capital proponents as a sure bet, the ultimate success story. According to this view, the future lay with 'high technology', and if Israel continued to ride this bandwagon, its position as the Silicon Wady of the Middle East, complete with fabulous riches and perpetual growth, was all but assured.

But then, this wasn't the first time Israeli citizens heard about such magic bullets. During the 1980s, the same ruling class assured its subjects that 'living by their sword' was actually good business. Granted, a permanent war economy had its unfortunate downsides such as occasional wars; but that was a price worth paying, since by capitalising on its military expertise to sell its weapons abroad, Israel could export its way to prosperity. As we now know, that pipe-dream ended with a whisper only a few years later, when the end of the Cold War, along with decisive opposition from U.S. contractors, brought Israeli military firms down to their knees. The civilian 'high-tech' dream, although still alive, seems destined for much the same fate. Contrary to the neoliberal promise, privatisation and deregulation have led to the creation of the most concentrated corporate structure ever to rule Israel. 'High technology' has proliferated, but largely by eviscerating other parts of society. The average standard of living rose, yet not nearly as fast as one would expect from a 'technological revolution', and certainly far more slowly than during the 'low-tech' decades of the 1950s and 1960s. In recent years, overall unemployment has approached historical records, and income inequality soared to levels typical of Latin American dictatorships.

Of course, as before, not everyone suffered from this new turn of events. The most notable winners were the transnational segments of the ruling class. During the 1990s, Israel's dominant capital has been thoroughly integrated into the circuits of global accumulation. Many of the local groups, including some of the largest such as Bank Hapoalim and Koor, have been taken over by foreign investors, while foreign institutional investors have penetrated every corner of the Israeli stock market. The flip side of the process is that Israeli capital has begun, for the first time, flowing outward in quest of foreign acquisitions. Having taken over much of its own corporate universe, dominant capital can now expand only by going global, extending its reach *outside* the country.

This latter development may mark the beginning of the end of Zionism. Throughout its history, Zionism went hand in hand with capitalist development. As a dominant ideology, it acted as a cultural melting pot, helped proletarianise a highly heterogeneous immigrant population, and sustained one of the more effective garrison states in the Western world. Over the past century, these were the key structural processes on which differential accumulation and ruling class formation were based. During the 1990s, however, there emerged, perhaps for the first time, a major cleavage within the elite. On the one hand, there is the 'reactionary' Zionist faction which hopes to freeze the world of yesterday. On the other hand, there is an increasingly powerful, 'progressive' faction, which seeks to 'normalise' the country, yet whose commitment to such normalisation weakens as its investment outside the country increases. This ruling class conflict doesn't bode well for most Israelis, and for the Middle East as a whole.

Before getting to the current conjuncture, however, we need to come to terms with the past. We need to explore in some detail the key processes, forces and people that shaped the political economy of the twentieth century – in Israel, in the region, and in the world as a whole. The first step in this journey is the institution which almost everyone seems to ignore – capital.

2

Capital and Power: Breaking the Dualism of 'Economics' and 'Politics'

There is the word. It is the king of words – Power. Not God, not Mammon, but Power. Power is over your tongue till it tingles with it. Power.
— Jack London, *The Iron Heel*

To understand the global political economy of Israel is to understand its evolution as a capitalist society within a changing world. This chapter outlines our own theoretical approach for such an understanding. We start by arguing that capital is a strategic, power institution. We then examine the different ways, or regimes, through which capitalist power is accumulated, and what they mean for capitalist development more broadly. Finally, and embedded within this framework, we sketch the major phases of Israel's capitalist development, internally as well as in relation to the global political economy.

Capital Accumulation: Production or Power?[1]

As it stands, capital theory is besieged by serious methodological problems. The principal difficulty comes from trying to reconcile the *social* and *material* aspects of capital, or its essence as 'power' and 'wealth'. The neoclassicists, who have dominated the economic discourse for the past century, resolved the problem by eliminating it in the first place. For them, capital is material wealth, and only material wealth, a 'physical' amalgamate of capital goods.[2] The power

---

1 The issues dealt with under the first four headings of this chapter are elaborated more fully in Nitzan (1998), Nitzan and Bichler (2000), and Bichler and Nitzan (2001: Ch. 2).
2 The following examples are typical. Clark (1899: 116, 119) asserts that 'Capital consists of instruments of production', which 'are always concrete and material', and whose appearance as value is 'an abstract quantum of productive wealth'; Fisher (1906: 52) takes capital as equivalent to the prevailing stock of wealth; Knight (1933: 328) sees capital as 'consisting of non-human productive agencies'; while Pigou (1935: 239)

31

aspect of capital, if that is ever an issue, is an 'imperfection', a social dimension external to its existence as tangible wealth.

This materialistic view of capital was challenged early on by Thorstein Veblen, and later exposed as a logical impossibility by the Cambridge Controversies.[3] The main problem was the 'quantity' of capital. According to the critics, this quantity could not be measured independently of prices and distribution. And since prices and distribution were social phenomena, external to the underlying capital goods, it followed that capital was not a purely physical thing.

The gist of the argument goes as follows. The value of capital depends on the profit it generates. Now, for the neoclassicists, capital is a 'factor of production', much like labour and land. Each of these factors makes a distinct 'contribution' to the output, and each, or so we are told, is remunerated accordingly: the wage is equivalent to the contribution of labour, the rent to the contribution of land, and the profit to the contribution of capital.[4] In order to figure out these separate contributions, however, we first need to know the physical quantity of each factor, and here things turn dicey.

In contrast to labour and land, whose units, at least in principle, are relatively homogenous, capital is made up of *fundamentally different* 'capital goods'. A machine making integrated circuits is a qualitatively different thing from a one peeling potatoes, or another moulding wood. The only way to measure their overall quantity – that is, their quantity as 'capital' – is to sum up their individual dollar values. But then, bringing dollar values into the picture creates a problem, since these values depend on profit, and profit is what the theory is supposed to explain to begin with.... In other words, we end up going in a circle: in order to know the value of capital we need to know its quantity, but that quantity can only be determined by first knowing its value! Even the high priests of neoclassical economics had no choice but admit it: capital was *not* a physical thing.[5]

Contrary to the neoclassicists, Marxists do not see capital as a thing, but as a comprehensive process of social reification. For Marx, accumulation had two

---

conceives capital as a heterogeneous material entity, 'capable of maintaining its quantity while altering its form'. Summing it all up, Schumpeter (1954: 632–3) concludes that, in its essence, 'capital consisted of goods', and specifically, of 'produced means of production'. Even Böhm-Bawerk (1891), who tried to treat accumulation as a process characterised by time rather than material objects, remained caught in the boundaries of production and consumption.

3   The most important writings of Veblen on the subject are *The Theory of Business Enterprise* (1904), *Absentee Ownership* (1923), and two articles on the 'Nature of Capital' (1908a; 1908b). For reviews of the Cambridge Controversies, which began in the 1950s, see Harcourt (1969) and Howard and King (1992: Part IV).

4   The formal neoclassical argument is a little more refined, making the price of each factor equal to its *marginal* contribution. This difference, though, need not detain us here.

5   This admission, it must be noted, was largely a theoretical formality. The notion that capital was 'productive' and therefore worthy of profit, was too important to abandon. And so, in practice, neoclassical economists continue to 'measure' capital as if the debate never happened.

basic dimensions: a qualitative dimension involving the very commodification of social relations, and a quantitative dimension consisting of the progressive augmentation of capital measured in monetary terms. The problem was how to link the two. Marx's choice was to concentrate on production, particularly the labour process, whose commodification he considered the main manifestation of capitalist power, and whose quantification as 'dead labour' was therefore to be the underlying unit of accumulation. This, though, was easier said than done. In order to provide the 'quantitative code' of accumulation, the labour process *itself* must be objective, quantifiable and observable. Yet, as Marx himself anticipated and as the Cambridge Controversies would later demonstrate, once we go beyond the most simple production processes these requirements no longer hold. Indeed, the very tendency of capitalistic production to become ever more complex makes it practically impossible to identify the distinct 'contributions' to value of specific labour inputs. But if we cannot identify these contributions, even on paper, how can we measure the 'labour contents' of capital?

As we see it, the solution is to redefine accumulation not as an offshoot of production, but as a broader tension between productivity and power.

Perhaps the first attempt to develop an institutionalist theory of capital along these lines was offered at the turn of the century by Veblen. Criticising the prevailing consensus of his time, Veblen pointed out that, unlike economists, businessmen tended to think about capital and accumulation in *pecuniary*, not material terms. For the modern investor – the owner of corporate stocks and bonds – capital did not denote machines, structures or raw materials, and accumulation had little to do with the material augmentation of such articles. Instead, capital simply meant the monetary value of the owned securities, and accumulation was nothing more than the temporal increase in that value. The value of capital was of course not an independent entity. It was a capitalisation of anticipated business earnings, and its pace of accumulation therefore depended on the expected growth of such earnings.[6] Contrary to prevailing convention, however, Veblen argued that the *source* of these earnings was only partly and often not at all related to the underlying productivity of the owned machines as the neoclassicists claimed, or of the hired workers as the Marxists insisted. Profits, he maintained, were determined not by production, but by the *politics of production*.

What severed the conventional link between profits and productivity? The principal cause, according to Veblen, was the growing separation between 'industry' and 'business', or between productive activity and absentee ownership. Production was essentially an integrated communal process. Its output depended mostly on the complex *interaction* of its numerous social components, and only marginally, if at all, on their *individual* contributions.

---

6 Symbolically, the value of capital (K) is equal to expected earnings (Π^e) discounted to their present value by the normal rate of return (r), so that $K = \Pi^e / r$.

Indeed, for Veblen the very notion of separate 'factors of production' was meaningless. Production and productivity, he argued, were *inherently societal*. Humans, machines and raw materials – the traditional factors of production – were merely repositories of that knowledge, and as he bluntly put it, it 'seems bootless to ask how much of the products of industry or of its productivity is to be imputed to these brute forces, human and non human, as contrasted with the specifically human factors that make technological efficiency' (1908a: 349–50). From a Veblenian perspective, every product, be it a sophisticated microchip factory or a simple loaf of bread, was like a hologram, embodying within it the entire history of human knowledge, and therefore the entire social effort which made such knowledge possible.[7] But if that was the case, how could we know what 'portion' of that effort was responsible for what 'portion' of the product?

For contemporary theories of capitalism, the upshot was as simple as it was devastating. For unless we could identify and measure all inputs, we could construct neither a neoclassical production function (which required separate factors of production, including 'know-how'), nor a Marxist circulation scheme (which assumed we could reduce 'skilled' to 'simple' labour). And if we could not quantitatively describe the process of production to begin with, how could we use it to explain distribution?

For Veblen the answer was simple: we shouldn't even try. Distribution, he said, derived not from production, but from *power over production*.

Note that unlike the neo-Ricardians after him, Veblen never suggested that distribution was somehow 'independent' of production. On the contrary, the two were intimately connected, only that their relationship was complex and potentially non-linear. Production was of course necessary for profit, but 'too much' of it could be just as hazardous as 'too little'. The secret was to find the golden path between these two extremes – the path which 'calibrated' industrial activities to profitable ends.[8]

---

7   The hologram, an optical principle to record the interference patterns created by incident waves, was invented in 1948 by British physicist and future Nobel laureate Denis Gabor. The word comes from combining the Greek 'holos' ('whole') and 'gramma' ('message'). The idea could be illustrated with a simple example. If you threw two pebbles into a pond, the resulting waves, criss-crossing each other, will have spread to cover the entire water surface. If you were then to take any slice of that surface, however small, that slice would contain within it all the information needed to figure out the *entire* wave image of the pond. Psychologist Karl Pribram (1971) later suggested that the brain, and perhaps consciousness, had holographic properties. Veblen, although writing half a century before Gabor, was essentially making a similar argument about social production, whereby every bit of 'output' embodied the *entire* productive effort of humanity.

8   The Great Depression of the 1930s was clearly a crisis of 'too little'. The Asian crisis of 1997, on the other hand, was one of 'too much'. During the 1990s, the region had 'accumulated' massive productive capacity. But as we know, productive capacity is not capital, and when investors realised that this capacity was 'excessive', they pulled out, triggering a massive accumulation meltdown. The machines remained intact, but capital, precisely for that reason, had lost half its value.

To follow Veblen, the ultimate source of capitalist earning power rests with strategic business 'sabotage'. For the absentee owner, the modern investor of funds, profit derives not from their contributions to production, but from their ability to *limit such production below its full potential*. Under certain circumstances, the limitation remains latent. For instance, when rapid population growth far exceeds the pace of technical change, as was the case in the United States until the mid-nineteenth century, high profits could be earned merely through the *threat* of unemployment. Capitalism, however, tends to accelerate technical change and hence the spectre of excess capacity, and that can be offset only through *active* 'sabotage'. Under these latter circumstances, a certain degree of stagnation is not a menace, but a *prerequisite* for profit. The evidence for this is so obvious that we tend not to see it. Thus, in the United States, 'business as usual' during the twentieth century meant a rising income share for capital, *going hand in hand* with much unused capacity and an average unemployment rate of 7 per cent.

Over time, the means of achieving such sabotage have changed a great deal. During the 'competitive' nineteenth century, these means were mostly 'structural', confined largely to the impersonal and seemingly automatic mechanism of boom and bust. Other, more 'direct' methods were of course practised extensively, but their role was relatively secondary. It was only since the late nineteenth century, with the emergence of 'big business' and 'big government', that these mechanisms assumed the centre-stage, creating an increasingly complex and more deliberate system of sabotage. In the twentieth century, these means further expanded to rely on the broader political realm of the state, including aspects of policing, propaganda, taxation, tariffs, subsidies, patent laws and intellectual property rights, as well as on international institutions such as trade zones, regional investment agreements and global, government-backed corporate alliances.

Moreover, the object of sabotage – the process of 'production' – has long transcended the factory. Focusing on the plant, mill and workshop was perhaps adequate in Marx's time. But in our age, with capitalist society having become highly integrated and complex, it is clear that what was previously called 'production' now encompasses the *entire* spectrum of human activity, including science and ideology, culture and leisure, consumption and waste, formal politics and international relations. Nowadays, the power to strategically limit production is the power to control the *social process as a whole*.

Finally and crucially, power is not only the means of accumulation, but also its most fundamental aim. In this sense, large-scale business enterprise is driven by the same principal force which animated all previous power civilisations – namely, the quest to control nature and people. Indeed, according to Lewis Mumford (1967; 1970), the first 'machine' was not at all tangible, but social; made not of physical components, but of human parts. This was the 'mega-machine' of the ancient delta civilisations, the giant social organisation needed to build the pyramids, palaces and public works. Building things, however, was only a means to an end. The real purpose was to *exert power*. In assembling and commanding the mega-machine, Mumford tells us, the king was asserting his absolute power, mimicking the cosmic order in a vain quest for God-like immortality.

Modern capital accumulation is in many ways similar to a mega-machine. The leading capitalists of today, much like their royal predecessors, try to mechanise and automate society. Much like the sun kings, they try to have it march to their own command. And perhaps, deep down inside, they too hope that supremacy will make them live forever.

Accumulation of What?

Coming back to earth, the question is how to measure accumulation? If capital is not a 'tangible' thing, what is it? Surely, the mere augmentation of money values tells us little about power, particularly in the presence of inflation or deflation. So what exactly is being accumulated, and how does it get quantified?

To reiterate, in its form, modern capital is finance, and *only finance*. Its magnitude is the discounted value of expected earnings, and earnings are a matter of power – the power of capitalists, operating against opposition, to strategically shape the societal process to their own ends. From this viewpoint, the accumulation of capital represents neither material wealth, nor a productive amalgamate of 'dead labour', but rather the *commodification of power*. Capitalists accumulate not things carried over from the past, but vendible power titles projected into the future. In this sense, their capitalised profit represents a claim not for a share of the output, but for a *share of control over the social process*.

Now, whereas capitalist power is exerted over society, it is measured *relative* to the power of other owners. At first sight, this assertion may look strange. After all, isn't the goal of accumulators to get as much money as possible? Don't they try to 'maximise' profit? And given the 'absolute' nature of their aim, how does relative power come into the picture?

The answer has to do with assessing 'success' and 'failure'. In the shifting sands of capitalism, nothing seems permanent. 'All that is solid melts into air, all that is holy is profaned', observe Marx and Engels in their *Communist Manifesto*. In this context of chaos and flux, capitalists must have a benchmark. In order to act, they need a yardstick, a clear gauge to tell them whether they do well or fall behind. According to most economists, including many Marxists, this benchmark is the price level. If you divide the dollar value of profit by the price index, you bring it down to earth; you turn it from 'nominal' profit, to 'real' profit. But there is a catch here. Consciously or not, this procedure makes hedonic pleasure the ultimate purpose of profit. Capitalists, it effectively says, are never satiated, and regardless of how much they consume (or save for future consumption), they are relentlessly driven to 'maximise' their profits in order to augment their utility further and further.

The problem with this logic is twofold. First, capitalists are of course concerned with consumption, but beyond a certain level of wealth their consumption is only marginally affected by their rate of accumulation. Moreover, profit-induced consumption is usually conspicuous – that is, aimed at establishing a *differential* status. This is highly important, because once we move into the realm of conspicuous consumption, the notion of 'real profit' assumes an entirely different meaning: higher prices, which from a utilitarian perspective imply a lower real income, for the conspicuous consumer often mean the exact opposite, since they bestow a higher differential status.

The second difficulty is that, despite endless academic debates, the precise meaning of 'profit maximisation' is still unclear. Capitalists may of course wish to earn 'as much as possible', but since the maximum attainable profit is forever unknown, the principle remains problematic in theory and irrelevant in practice.[9]

Differential Accumulation

In reality, accumulators have long abandoned Archimedean absolutes in favour of Newtonian relatives. Modern capitalists benchmark their accumulation not against a price index, but against its own mean. They seek not to maximise profit, but to beat the average. Their yardstick is the 'normal rate of return', their goal – to exceed it. A 5 per cent profit growth during recession is success; a 15 per cent when others make 30 is failure.

In short, the real issue is not absolute accumulation, but *differential* accumulation. Unlike the elusive 'maximum', reference to the 'normal' and 'average' is everywhere. Large companies gauge their performance relative to listings published by periodicals such as *Fortune, Business Week, Far Eastern Economic Review, Euromoney* or *Forbes*; fund mangers are hired and fired based on whether

9 Conventional theory celebrates the iron law of profit maximisation, although it is not very clear why. For one, the concept holds little water in the real world. As Hall and Hitch (1939) showed more than half a century ago, few if any capitalists know what maximum profit means or how to achieve it, and as many studies before and since have suggested they instead use 'markup pricing' to achieve a 'target rate of return' (for instance, Brown 1924; Kaplan et al. 1958; and Blair 1972). The marginalists could not accept this heresy. Led by Machlup (1946), they lashed back, arguing that regardless of what businessmen said, in the end markup formulae were nothing more than real-world techniques for maximising profit – although they themselves were still unable to show exactly what that 'maximum' was (Robinson 1966: 78–9). Of course, many theorists cannot be bothered by such earthly debates, only that the situation is hardly better in the higher world of textbooks. As it turns out, maximum profit is indeed 'workable' in the extreme cases of perfect competition and monopoly. But then what about the entire range of 'imperfections' between these (non-existing) ideal types? The problem, first identified by Cournot (1838), is one of oligopolistic interdependence, which in its 'unrestricted' form makes maximum profit indeterminate, even in the mind of the economist. Of course, game theory has solved this problem a million times over, but only by assuming certain predetermined rules. Sadly, though, real firms are free to ignore such rules, so the enigma of maximum profit remains.

they exceed or fall short of their relevant benchmark; and stock performance is meaningless unless compared to aggregate or sector indices. In fact, the notion of normality as a benchmark for competitive achievements has been so thoroughly accepted in capitalist society, that it now dominates numerous non-business spheres, such as education, sports, the arts, and even foreign relations, where GDP per capita, growth rates and alike are constantly contrasted with regional or global averages.

The connection between differential accumulation and power should now become clearer. To accumulate differentially is to increase your share of total profit and capitalisation. And to increase your distributive share of these magnitudes is to increase your relative power to shape the process of social change. The source of such power is the ability of owners to strategically limit, or 'sabotage' the process of social reproduction.

This sabotage is carried out in two ways, *differential* and *universal*. At the dis-aggregate level, it is exercised through the differential practices of dominant firms or coalitions of firms. The aim of these practices is to redistribute the pie, but that almost always involves restricting its size, particularly by limiting the slices of others.[10] Now, given that these differential practices are carried out by all dominant groups, their aggregate consequence is a certain 'average level of sabotage' spread across society, along with a corresponding 'normal rate of return'. Clearly, this 'normal rate of return' is the manifestation not of productive contributions under perfect competition as the neoclassicists argue, but of sabotage and a complex structure of power. Indeed, the very existence of this 'normal' enables even the most insignificant actors to exercise their 'natural right' for universal sabotage. Since individual capitalists, however small, can always earn the normal rate of return by simply owning a diversified portfolio, they have no reason to produce at less than that rate. But in accepting the normal rate of return as a minimum yardstick below which production should not be extended, they effectively propagate sabotage – even when they themselves do not have the differential power to back it up. Sabotage becomes invisible, 'business as usual' as they say.

In this framework, if we take the total dollar value of capitalisation as a 'map' of capitalist power as a whole, any given fraction of this capitalisation represents a corresponding, undifferentiated part of that overall power. Individual capitalists, or groups of capitalists, constantly try to increase and secure these claims through particular power realignments, organisations and institutions, so the *contents* of their power are always qualitatively unique. But because this power is exercised over society as a whole, its *form* can be quantified into universal monetary units, claims on the entire process of social restructuring.

---

10 Think of the consequences of General Motors raising its output. If other companies, such as Ford, DaimlerChrysler, Toyota and Honda, do the same, GM's profit may not increase differentially, and may even contract absolutely due to overall glut. On the other hand, if GM is able to increase its own slice by reducing that of its competitors, its earnings are likely to rise both absolutely and relatively.

This then is perhaps the central 'link' between quality and quantity in accumulation – between the qualitatively different social conditions and processes of power on the one hand, and the identical units in which this power is measured on the other.

Notably, the link itself, the 'conversion' of *power as a quality* to *power as a quantity*, is not an objective process. First, capitalisation itself, although treated as an objective quantity, is at least partly based on the sanctity of profit and its surrounding rituals. Second, the magnitude of capitalisation, although readily observable, can never be 'inferred', so to speak, by simply observing the social scene. For instance, the fact that a certain corporation has been granted a patent cannot, in itself, tell us much about its differential accumulation. Similarly with things such as favourable government policies, the introduction of new production techniques, or the acquisition of a competitor. These arrangements all affect the qualitative nature of power, but their 'translation' into quantitative units of differential accumulation is inherently speculative. The way to understand this link is actually in reverse, moving from the quantitative process of differential accumulation to the qualitative institutions, organisations and processes on which it stands; from observing the numerical ups and downs of differential accumulation, to speculating about their social causes. Of course, any such attempt to bridge the gap between quantities and qualities involves a certain quantum leap, whose persuasiveness depends less on the rigour of science and more on our ability to tell a compelling story. But then, capitalism *does* try to quantify social relations, so it is crucial to try to understand how – even if the 'evidence' is forever circumstantial.[11]

Let's begin then with a simple, working definition of accumulation:

1. The 'differential power of capital' (*DPK*) possessed by a particular group of owners should be measured relatively, by comparing the group's combined capitalisation to that of the average capital unit. If this average is $5 million, a capital worth $5 billion represents a *DPK* of 1,000. It means that as a group, the owners of that capital are 1,000 times more powerful than the owners of an average capital.

2. With this definition, the pace of 'differential accumulation' (*DA*) is given by the rate of change of *DPK*; that is, by the rate of growth of the group's capitalisation less the rate of growth of the average capitalisation. Positive, zero or negative rates of *DA* imply rising, unchanging or falling differential power, respectively.[12]

11 In this sense, our logic here is similar to Kalecki's 'degree of monopoly' (1943a), which measures the *consequence* for relative profit margins of monopolistic institutions and forces (and which we use later in Chapter 6). Our own notion here, though, differs from Kalecki's in that it reflects not on the narrow question of monopoly versus competition, but on the entire dynamics of power under capitalism.

12 Strictly speaking, differential accumulation requires not a positive rate of growth, but a positive difference between rates of growth. A dominant group can therefore accumulate differentially even with its own capitalisation falling, provided that the average declines even faster. This understanding is assumed throughout.

3. Strictly speaking, only capitalists with a positive DA are said to 'accumulate'. The study of accumulation should therefore have them at its centre.

The next question, then, is who are these 'differential accumulators' and how should they be classified? Our own preference is to focus not on the individual owner, but on a group of owners. The reason is that the vendibility of capital creates centrifugal as well as centripetal forces, thus limiting the power of any single capitalist. In counteracting the centrifugal forces, the elementary solution is the *corporation*, and, eventually, the *corporate coalition*. Notwithstanding the long debate on the separation of corporate ownership and control, we concur with Veblen that the corporation, regardless of who runs it, was historically necessary for the survival of capitalism. Without this institution, which for Marx signalled the immanent 'abolition of capital as private property within the framework of capitalist production itself' (1909, Vol. III: 516), the centrifugal forces of competition and excess capacity would have probably killed the bourgeois order long ago. During the twentieth century, the corporation emerged as the basis for integrating accumulation and state; it became *the* entity around which both class consciousness and political power could be built. Any analysis of modern capitalism must therefore have the corporation as a central building block.

The underlying purpose of coalescing individual capitalists into a corporation, and corporations into corporate alliances, is *exclusion*. In non-capitalist systems, exclusion is usually embedded in relatively rigid customs, such as those preventing serfs from growing into kings, slaves from turning into masters, and untouchables from becoming Brahmins. Capitalism does not have similar customs. Commodification makes upward mobility possible, and in principle there is nothing to prevent a son of a wandering vendor of quack medicine from assembling the Standard Oil of New Jersey, or a university dropout from starting Microsoft. This, though, does not imply that capitalism has done away with exclusion. Far from it. Indeed, for John D. Rockefeller or Bill Gates to have acquired their own power, others had to give it up. Because of the constant threat of 'equal opportunity', such exclusion requires relentless formation and reformation of 'distributional coalitions', to use the language of Olson (1965; 1982). Moreover, as in other systems, the process of exclusion is inextricably bound up with state institutions, only that now, due to the 'liberal' appearance of capital, the symbiosis becomes invisible. The difference therefore is largely one of form: whereas in other power systems, exclusion is largely static, built into the social code and resulting in relatively stable groupings, under capitalism it must be dynamically recreated through ever shifting alliances.

The upshot is that the accumulation of capital in general depends on the accumulation of capital at the centre. It is 'dominant capital', the largest and most profitable corporate coalitions at the core of the social process, which are crucial. The periphery of capital, the many capitals outside the core, are in fact a constant threat to the viability of capitalist development as a whole. Subject to the strong centrifugal forces of competition, their behaviour is forever undermining the collusive essence of business 'sabotage', without which accumulation is impossible. Only to the extent that dominant capital is able to retain and augment its *exclusive* power against these lesser capitals, keeping them 'out of the loop', can the capitalisation process can be sustained.

Note, however, that there is no assumption here that the same group of capitalists will dominate the process throughout. On the contrary, the very essence of differential accumulation is an intra-capitalist struggle simultaneously to restructure the pattern of social reproduction as well as the grid of power. As an organised and often conscious power process, it involves purposeful action against opposition, so its outcome cannot possibly be automatic. The important point here is rather the progressive differential growth of big business *as a whole*, regardless of its shifting composition. As George Orwell aptly put it, 'A ruling group is a ruling group so long as it can nominate its successors.... *Who* wields power is not important, provided that the hierarchical structure remains always the same' (1948: 211, original emphasis).

Now, this is all very interesting, you may say, but so what? True, leading capitalists seek power, not utility. It's also true that investors try to beat the average rather than maximise profit. And yes, politics, culture, science and force are all crucial for understanding modern capitalism. But how does this change our concrete analysis of the world? Does it give us new analytical tools? And will it shed new light on the global political economy of Israel?

The answers to these questions are all positive. As we shall see throughout the book, capitalism, when viewed through the spectacles of differential accumulation, looks quite different, and sometimes very different, from the way it is portrayed by conservative and even Marxist writers. Let's turn to see how.

Accumulation Crisis or Differential Accumulation Boom?

Our exploration begins not with Israel, but with the United States. The reason is threefold. First, the United States has been the epicentre of twentieth century capitalism, so its experience is crucial for understanding the world in which Israel has developed. Second, U.S. differential accumulation directly affected the history of the Middle East and of Israel itself. And third, the U.S. accumulation 'model' has been replicated in many countries, including Israel, so it's worth studying more closely. It is therefore only at the end of the chapter, after having examined the broader forces at work, that we can tie the knots together, positioning Israel's specific experience within the Middle East and the global political economy at large.

As noted, differential accumulation is the rate at which the capitalised income of 'dominant capital' expands relative to the economy's average. Because this income includes both profit and interest, the proper capitalising aggregate is that of total assets. Given the forward-looking nature of capital, this could be measured by the market value of all outstanding equity and debt. However, this measure is often 'contaminated' by investors' 'hype' – that is, by swings of optimism and pessimism which respond more to the prospects of capital gain and loss than to a cool-headed assessment of future earnings and the likely course of the 'normal rate of return' (Nitzan 1995; 1996). Moreover, historical data for market value are often unavailable. The alternative, then, is to use 'book value' as reported in the financial statements. The latter is a somewhat 'lagging' indicator for capitalisation, reflecting earning expectations prevailing when the assets were first recorded. However, given that differential accumulation is about relative rather than absolute values, this shouldn't be much of a concern, particularly over the longer term.

Applying this definition to the United States, Figure 2.1 provides capitalisation indicators for a 'typical' corporation of the 'dominant capital' group, as well as for the average corporation in the economy. 'Dominant capital' is provisionally defined here as equivalent to the 500 largest U.S.-based industrial companies, listed annually since 1954 by *Fortune*. This group is limited to publicly traded companies with 50 per cent or more of their sales coming from

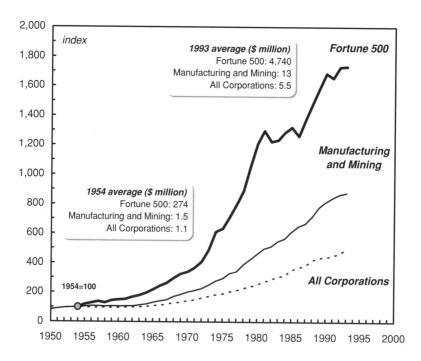

Figure 2.1 Average Firm Size in the U.S.A. (assets per firm)

SOURCE: Fortune; U.S. Internal Revenue Service.

manufacturing and/or mining. Diversified companies, those relying more heavily on other lines of activity, and private firms are excluded. (Since 1994, the Fortune 500 coverage has been expanded to the entire universe of publicly traded companies. For consistency, our series ends in 1993.) Based on these data, the average capitalised income of 'dominant capital' is given by the total assets of the *Fortune* list divided by 500. Two proxies for the economy's average are given by dividing total corporate assets by the number of corporate tax returns – first for the economy as a whole, and then for the combined mining and manufacturing sector, both using data from the U.S. Internal Revenue Service (for ease of comparison, all series are rebased with 1954=100).

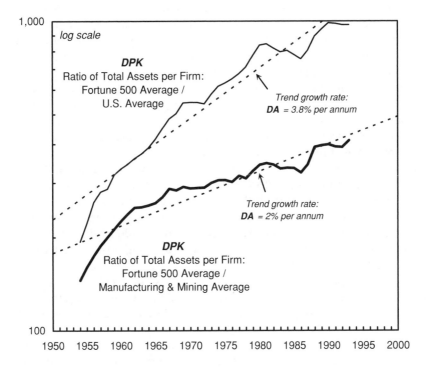

Figure 2.2   Differential Accumulation in the U.S.A.

SOURCE: Fortune; U.S. Internal Revenue Service.

Figure 2.2 charts two alternative measures for the differential power of capital (*DPK*) possessed by an average Fortune 500 company – one based on comparison with the average U.S. corporation, the other on comparison with the manufacturing and mining average. With a logarithmic scale, the slopes of the two *DPK* series indicate the difference between the rate of accumulation of a typical company in the 'dominant capital' group, and the average rate of accumulation in the broader corporate universe. These slopes therefore provide proxies for the rate of differential accumulation (DA) by U.S. 'dominant capital'. What do the figures tell us? Most generally, they suggest that U.S. differential accumulation has proceeded more or less uninterruptedly for the past half century, and possibly longer. Relative to the manufacturing and mining average, differential accumulation by U.S. 'dominant capital' has averaged 2 per cent annually (the slope of the trend line). The broader comparison against the economy's average suggests a far faster rate, averaging 3.8 per cent. In fact, even this higher rate may well understate the pace of differential accumulation. There are two reasons for this. First, our Fortune 500 proxy for 'dominant capital' is heavily biased toward manufacturing and mining which have tended to decline vis-à-vis the tertiary sector. As a result, the generally *faster*-growing service-oriented companies are excluded from our 'dominant capital' proxy but included in the economy's average. Also, over the years, some Fortune 500 firms became 'too' diversified and dropped from the list, although conceptually and practically they remained an integral part of 'dominant capital'. For these reasons, an alternative proxy for 'dominant capital', based solely on size and with no sectoral restrictions is likely to show an even faster rate of differential accumulation.

Seen as a *power* process, U.S. accumulation appears to have been on a sustainable keel throughout much of the postwar era. This conclusion is hardly intuitive. Indeed, according to the analysis of the Regulation and Social Structures of Accumulation (SSA) schools, the United States has experienced an accumulation *crisis* during that very period, particularly since the late 1960s.[13] How is this difference possible? In our view, the reason is rooted in the troubled definition of capital. The conventional wisdom which focuses on profit (rather than capital income as a whole) indeed suggests a crisis. Figure 2.3 shows that net profit as a share of national income has been on a downtrend; and given that profit is seen both as the principal source of investment finance as well as its major inspiration, it is only natural that accumulation (measured in material rather than power terms) should follow a similar downward path, as the figure patently confirms.

This notion of accumulation crisis lies in sharp contrast to the evidence based on differential accumulation. As illustrated in Figure 2.4, unlike profit, *total* capital income, measured as the share of profit and interest in national income, has in fact trended up since the end of the Second World War, reaching a record high during the 1980s. These data show no sign of lingering crisis; if anything, they indicate that capital income has grown *increasingly abundant*.

From a conventional viewpoint, this evidence presents a serious theoretical inconsistency: if capital income has indeed risen, why did it not fuel a 'real' investment boom? From a Veblenian viewpoint, on the other hand, the two developments are consistent: capital income depends not on the *growth* of

13   For instance, see Aglietta (1979), and Kotz et al. (1994).

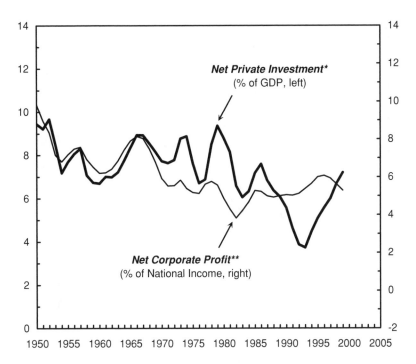

Figure 2.3   A U.S. Accumulation Crisis? ...

* Private gross capital formation less depreciation.
** After-tax corporate profit, including capital consumption allowance and
inventory valuation adjustment.
NOTE: Series shown as 3-year moving averages.
SOURCE: U.S. Department of Commerce through McGraw-Hill (Online).

industry, but on the strategic *control* of industry. Had industry been given a
'free rein' to raise its productive capacity, the likely result would have been
excess capacity and possibly a *fall* in capital's share.[14] From this perspective, it
is entirely possible that the income share of capital trended up precisely because
'real' investment declined.

To close the circle, note that the postwar uptrend in the income share of
capital coincided with the positive path of differential accumulation by
'dominant capital' (Figure 2.4). This relationship is hardly trivial, at least from
the perspective of economic orthodoxy. Neoclassical analysis, for one, suggests
that because of diminishing returns, accumulation (defined as rising capital
goods per head) should be associated with lower rates of returns and hence
downward pressure on the income share for capital. Marxist analysis is more

14   This point is articulated theoretically and demonstrated empirically in Nitzan and
       Bichler (2000).

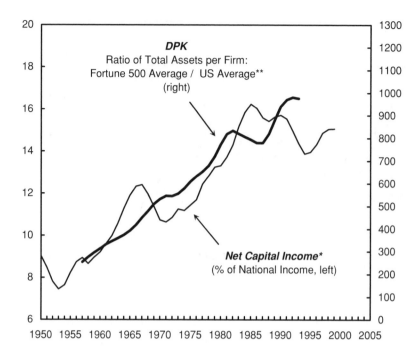

Figure 2.4   ... Or Differential Accumulation Boom?

* Net capital income is the sum of after-tax corporate profit (with capital
consumption allowance and inventory valuation adjustment) and net interest.
** U.S. average comprises all corporations.
NOTE: Series shown as 3-year moving averages.
SOURCE: U.S. Department of Commerce through McGraw-Hill (Online); U.S. Internal
Revenue Service; Fortune.

ambivalent on the issue, accepting on the one hand that distribution could
depend on power, but remaining hostage to the labour theory of value in which
a rising organic composition of capital is a depressant of surplus.

From a Veblenian viewpoint, however, the positive association between accumulation and capital's income share is exactly what one would expect.
Accumulation is a power process, not a material one. Defined in differential
terms, it involves the growing relative power of society's leading business
concerns, which in turn helps sustain or expand the overall income share of
capital.

We can therefore tentatively argue that, over the longer term, capital accumulation depends on two key conditions, and that the absence of one or both
of these conditions brings a threat of capitalist crisis:

1. *A non-negative rate of differential accumulation by the 'dominant capital' group.* This condition implies that the relative power of the largest absentee owners is either stable or growing, reflecting both the power drive of accumulation and its actual exercise which keeps 'industry' under effective 'business' control.

2. *A steady or rising capital share of income.* Although this is partly an indirect result of the first condition, it also reflects the overall balance of power between capitalists and other societal groups. Unless this condition is fulfilled, the very 'capitalist' nature of the system could be put into question.

Regimes of Differential Accumulation

Differential accumulation is a process of change, a dynamic power struggle to restructure society against opposition. This change has two dimensions. In form, it is a *quantitative* redistribution of ownership. In content, it is a *qualitative* transformation of social relations. Now, since qualitative change means novelty, and novelty is forever surprising, it follows that differential accumulation, despite its 'objective' appearance, is inherently unpredictable.[15] There is no point looking for 'equilibrium' here, since there couldn't be any; differential accumulation, by its very essence, defies both stability and harmony. Similarly, there is little prospect for discovering any 'laws of motion', particularly since differential accumulation may fail to happen in the first place. In short, like everything else in society, it is an open-ended journey, a story continuously rewritten by its own characters.

And yet, it is a particular story, following specific paths, and subject to some concrete limitations. These paths and limitations, the provisional 'rules of the game', are themselves created by humans, so they too can be altered. But such changes, being more fundamental in nature, always come with difficulty and never too quickly. To paraphrase Marx, 'man makes his own history, *as well as* the circumstances in which this history unfolds, but the latter are much more difficult to change than the former'. And as long as these circumstances, or 'structures', persist in their general form, their impact is to restrict action and 'limit the possible', as Fernand Braudel (1985) put it. It is in this latter sense that commodification and capitalisation gradually make the quest for differential accumulation a primary compass of social action, a structural constraint shaping

---

15 'The most important aspect of the economic process', writes Georgescu-Roegen (1979: 321), 'is precisely the continuous emergence of novelty. Now, novelty is unpredictable, but in a sense quite different from the way in which the result of a coin toss is unpredictable ... [it] is unique in the sense that in chronological time it occurs only once. Moreover, the novelty always represents a qualitative change. It is therefore understandable that no analytical model can deal with the emergence of novelty, for everything that can be derived from such a model can only concern quantitative variations. Besides, nothing can be derived from an analytical model that is not logically contained in its axiomatic basis.'

both ideology and behaviour. And insofar as this quest materialises – that is, insofar as dominant capital *does* grow faster than the average – its expansion tends to occur within certain boundaries and follow particular paths.

What are these paths? How are they related? And why are they important? Broadly speaking, the history of differential accumulation in the twentieth century can be characterised by three related patterns, which we examine throughout the remainder of the chapter. The first, secular feature is the gradual *spread* of differential accumulation as the principal driving force of capitalist development – both within a given society and into virgin territory previously untouched by vendible capital.

The second feature, also secular, is the increasing *integration* of separate differential accumulation processes. As capital becomes more and more vendible, its buying and selling transcends its original industry, sector, and finally home country, resulting in a progressive convergence of profitability benchmarks across these different universes. The social process underlying this convergence is the growing unification and standardisation of business principles, so that more and more societies find themselves responding to the roller coaster of differential accumulation elsewhere, and to an increasingly similar normal rate of return everywhere.

The final feature of this history is *cyclical*. Differential accumulation tends to move in long swings, alternating between the two distinct regimes of 'breadth' and 'depth'. A breadth regime is characterised by proletarianisation, growth and corporate amalgamation, tends to be structurally dynamic, and is commonly less conflictual. A depth regime, on the other hand, is marked by stagflation, tends to consolidate rather than change institutions and structures, and is usually more conflictual and often violent.

These three features of differential accumulation – its spread, integration and alternating regimes – are closely related: the first two work to reinforce one another, and as they advance, their effect is to make the breadth–depth cycles of different sectors and societies ever more interdependent and synchronised.

The other side of this process has to do with class. Ongoing differential accumulation means the centralisation of commodified power in the hands of an ever more cohesive group of dominant capital, whereas the spatial integration of the process makes this group increasingly transnational. The study of differential accumulation regimes is therefore a study of capitalist class formation. It tells us how this class comes into being, the methods it uses to build and consolidate its power, and of course, the conflicts and contradictions inherent in seeking ultimate hegemony.

In what follows we try to delineate the general boundaries and paths of these processes, characterise their features, examine their interactions, and assess their broader significance – for capitalist development in general, and for the global political economy of Israel in particular. The conclusions of this analysis then provide the framework underlying the rest of our story.

Breadth and Depth

How can dominant capital achieve differential accumulation? For the large corporation, the level of profit is the product of the number of employees, multiplied by the average profit per employee. This decomposition, although true by definition, is purposeful. Capitalists own the corporation not for its own sake, but as a vehicle of power over society as a whole. This power is codified through profit (inclusive of interest), which is in turn determined by both the 'size' of the corporate organisation and its 'elemental power', so to speak. The firm can therefore raise its profit in two ways. The first, which we call 'breadth', is to augment the size of its organisation by having more employees. The second, which we label 'depth', is to increase its elemental power, making its existing organisation a more effective appropriator of profit per employee.[16]

Applying the same logic at the relative level, the implication is that a large firm can accumulate differentially by (1) expanding its employment faster than the average, (2) raising its profit per employee faster than the average, or (3) some combination of the two.[17] Each avenue – breadth and depth – can be further subdivided into 'internal' and 'external' sub-routes, leading to a four-way taxonomy:

Table 2.1   Regimes of Differential Accumulation

	External	Internal
Breadth	Green-field	Mergers & Acquisitions
Depth	Stagflation	Cost cutting

1. *External Breadth: Green-field Investment.* A firm can achieve differential accumulation by building new capacity and hiring new employees faster than the average, so as to increase its market share. This method is labelled 'external', since, from a societal perspective, it involves a net addition of employees.[18] Its upper social ceiling is the extent of proletarianisation. The

16 Note that this decomposition differs from the common view of profit as the product of sales revenues multiplied by the profit margin. Although both decompositions are 'correct', the latter does not strictly correspond to our separation between the corporation's 'size' and its 'elemental power' to appropriate. To illustrate, sales revenues can be raised by increasing employment in order to produce more output ('size'), or by raising prices ('elemental power'). Likewise, profit per employee (which for us represents 'elemental power') can be raised by increasing prices and therefore sales revenues, or by widening the profit margin. Formally speaking, 'breadth' affects market share, but market share does not always involve 'breadth'. Similarly, profit margins affect 'depth', but 'depth' doesn't necessarily influence profit margins.

17 As before, the focus is on the *difference* between growth rates, so that differential accumulation could take place even when profits are falling.

18 For any given firm, green-field investment can of course draw on inter-firm labour mobility as well as on new employment. From an aggregate perspective, however, labour movement between firms is properly classified as internal breadth.

more immediate limit comes through the negative impact it has on depth: 'excessive' green-field growth creates a downward pressure on prices and hence on profit per employee.

2. *Internal Breadth: Mergers and Acquisitions.* Here, too, the purpose is differential accumulation through increased market share, but the method is different. Strictly speaking, internal breadth involves differential earnings growth through inter-firm labour mobility. This can happen when a firm adds new capacity and employment against cutbacks elsewhere, although such movements relate more to industrial restructuring (labour mobility between sectors) than to the size-redistribution of firms (employees moving from small to large firms). The situation is different with corporate amalgamation via mergers and acquisitions, where no new capacity is created. By taking over other companies, the firm increases its own profit relative to the average (which is virtually unaltered). We call this route 'internal' since it merely redistributes control over existing capacity and employment. Merger and acquisition activity is perhaps the most potent form of differential accumulation, serving to kill two birds with one stone: it directly increases differential breadth, while indirectly helping to protect and possibly boost differential depth (through relative pricing power). It is limited, however, both by the availability of takeover targets as well as by social, political and technological barriers.

3. *Internal Depth: Cost Cutting.* The purpose is to cheapen production faster than the average, either through relative efficiency gains, or by larger reductions in input prices. It is 'internal' in that it redistributes income shares within a given price. Although cost cutting is relentlessly pursued by large firms (directly as well as indirectly through outsourcing), the difficulty of both monopolising new technology and controlling input prices suggests that the net effect is commonly to meet the average, rather than beat it.

4. *External Depth: Stagflation.* Our emphasis on stagflation rather than inflation is deliberate: contrary to the conventional wisdom, inflation usually occurs with, and often necessitates, some slack. Now, for a single seller, higher prices commonly are more than offset by lost volume, but things are different for a coalition of sellers. Dominant capital, to the extent that it acts in concert, can benefit from higher prices since, up to a point, the relative profit gains per unit outweigh the relative decline in volume. Of course, for this to become a continuous process (inflation rather than discrete price increases), other firms must join the spiral. Yet, since small companies have little political leverage and are usually unable to collude, the result is to redistribute income in favour of the bigger ones which can. We refer to this method as 'external', since the redistribution occurs through a (pecuniary) expansion of the pie.

What are the implications of this taxonomy? In addressing this question, it is important to distinguish the case of an individual large corporation from the broader analysis of dominant capital as a group. A single firm may successfully combine different facets of breadth and depth. Not so for dominant capital as a whole. If we look at breadth and depth not as corporate strategies, but as *overall social regimes*, it quickly becomes apparent that broader conditions which are conducive to one often undermine the other. For the sake of brevity, we group our arguments here into eight related propositions:

- *Proposition 1. Understood as broad regimes, breadth and depth tend to move counter-cyclically to one another.* Breadth presupposes some measure of economic growth as well as relative political-economic stability. Depth, on the other hand, commonly implies political restrictions, social conflict, and stagflation. Although strictly speaking the two regimes are not mutually exclusive, they tend to 'negate' one another, with more breadth associated with less depth, and vice versa.
- *Proposition 2. Of the two regimes, breadth is the path of least resistance.* There are two reasons for this. First, it is usually more straightforward and less conflictual to expand one's organisation than it is to engage in collusive increases in prices or in struggles over input prices. Although both methods are political in the wide sense of the term, depth commonly depends on complex state and social realignments which aren't necessary for breadth. Second, breadth is relatively more stable and hence easier to extend and sustain, whereas depth, with its heightened social antagonism, is more vulnerable to backlash and quicker to spin out of control.
- *Proposition 3. Over the longer haul, mergers and acquisitions tend to rise relative to green-field investment.* While both routes can contribute to differential accumulation, as capitalism spreads geographically and dominant capital grows in importance, so does the threat of excess capacity. Mergers and acquisitions alleviate the problem whereas green-field aggravates it. The broader consequence of this shift is for chronic stagnation to gradually substitute for cyclical instability.
- *Proposition 4. The relative growth of mergers and acquisitions is likely to oscillate around its uptrend.* Corporate amalgamation involves major social restructuring and hence is bound to run into roadblocks. The result is a wave-like pattern, with long periods of acceleration followed by shorter downturns.
- *Proposition 5. The underlying logic of mergers and acquisitions implies progressive 'spatial' unification, and, eventually, globalisation.* For amalgamation to run ahead of overall growth, dominant capital must successively break its 'envelopes', spreading from the industry, to the sector, to the national economy, and ultimately to the world as a whole. In this sense, differential accumulation is a prime mover of spatial integration and globalisation.

- *Proposition 6. Cost cutting is not a real alternative to an amalgamation lull. The pressure to reduce cost is ever present, but its effect is more to meet than beat the average.* The principal reason is that productivity improvements are neither inherently related to corporate size, nor easy to protect. Similarly, reductions in input prices are seldom proprietary and often spill over to other firms.

- *Proposition 7. A much more potent response to declining mergers and acquisitions is inflationary increases in profit margins.* This is often facilitated by previous corporate centralisation, and although the process is inherently unstable and short-lived, it can generate very large differential gains. By its nature, though, such inflation is possible only through a vigilant limitation of production, with the result being that inflation appears as stagflation.

- *Proposition 8. Over the longer term, differential accumulation depends primarily on mergers and acquisitions. In the shorter term, it can benefit from sharp stagflationary crises.* The main engine of differential accumulation is corporate amalgamation, which thrives on overall growth and the successive break-up of ownership 'envelopes'. Occasional discontinuities in the process, however, push dominant capital toward an alternative regime of stagflationary redistribution. The result is a pendulum-like oscillation between long periods of relative political-economic stability accompanied by economic growth and low inflation, and shorter periods of heightened social conflict, stagnation, and inflation.

Let us now look more closely at the broader significance of these various propositions, focusing first on the United States and the global political economy, and later on the Middle East and Israel.

Green-Field

Employment growth is a double-edged sword for dominant capital, directly augmenting external breadth (differential employment per firm), while indirectly threatening external depth (differential pricing power). Consider first the direct impact. In general, overall employment growth augments the differential breadth of dominant capital, but the reason is largely due to the way it affects smaller firms. Large companies react to overall growth mainly by increasing their employment ranks. Smaller companies, on the other hand, respond by growing in number (through the birth of new firms), as well as in size (by hiring more workers). This is important since newborn firms, by their very nature, tend to be smaller than the average. The implication is that, even if green-field growth is spread proportionately between dominant capital and the rest of the business universe, as long as some of this growth results in the birth of smaller firms, the net impact is to reduce average employment per firm, thus augmenting the differential breadth of dominant capital. U.S. data, for instance, show that over the past 75 years, the number of corporations has risen 3.6 times faster than overall employment, causing average employment per firm to drop by 72 per cent.[19] Since the size of large firms in terms of employment has increased over the same period, we can safely conclude that overall employment growth worked to directly boost the differential breadth of dominant capital.

In contrast to this direct impact, the indirect effect, operating through depth, is more complex and harder to assess. On the one hand, the multiplicity of small firms keeps their own profit per employee low, partly by precluding cooperation and pricing discretion, and partly by undermining collective political action. This bears positively on the differential depth of dominant capital. On the other hand, unruly growth in the number of small firms can quickly degenerate into excess capacity, threatening to unravel cooperation within dominant capital itself. In addition, rapid green-field growth often works to dilute the 'coordinating' impact of direct government involvement in allocation and pricing, which in turn further aggravates the spectre of glut. The balance between these conflicting forces is difficult if not impossible to determine.

In sum, although green-field growth is tempting, particular in the presence of 'non-capitalist', 'proletarianisation-ready' populations in and outside one's own society, such growth is not necessarily a panacea for dominant capital. The process boosts its differential breadth, but it also has an indeterminate, and possibly negative effect on differential depth. The main way of counter-acting this latter threat is through corporate amalgamation, to which we turn now.

Mergers and Acquisitions

Our discussion in this section begins with Figure 2.5. In this chart we plot a 'buy-to-build' indicator for the United States, expressing the dollar value of mergers and acquisitions as a per cent of the dollar value of gross fixed investment. In terms of our own categories, this index corresponds roughly to the ratio between internal and external breadth. (The data sources and method of computing this index are described in the Data Appendix to the chapter.)

The chart illustrates two important processes, one secular, the other cyclical. First, it shows that, over the longer haul, U.S. mergers and acquisitions have indeed grown more and more important relative to green-field investment (Proposition 3). At the end of the nineteenth century, money put into amal-gamation amounted to less than 1 per cent of green-field investment. A century

19   See Nitzan (2001: 10–12).

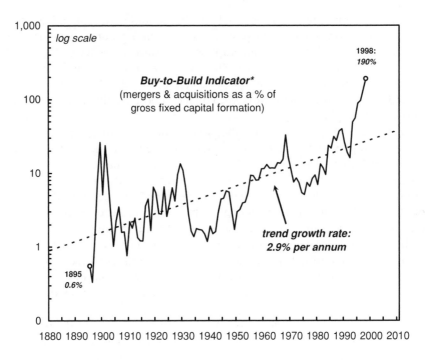

Figure 2.5   U.S. Accumulation: Internal vs. External Breadth

* Based on splicing of separate series.
SOURCE: See Data Appendix.

later, the ratio was approaching 200 per cent, and rising. The trend growth rate indicated in the chart suggests that, year in, year out, mergers and acquisitions grew roughly 3 percentage points faster than new capacity.

Now, whereas employment associated with new capacity is added by small and large firms alike, amalgamation, almost by definition, increases mostly the employment ranks of dominant capital. The net effect of this trend, therefore, is a massive contribution to the differential accumulation of large firms.[20]

The reasons for this tendency are not at all obvious. Why do firms decide to merge with, or take over other firms? Why has their urge to merge grown stronger over time? And what does it mean for the broader political economy?

20   The effect on relative employment growth is probably somewhat smaller than implied by the dollar figures. For one, amalgamated companies often end up shedding some workers, and two, merger and acquisition data include divestitures which reduce rather than raise employment. Correcting for these qualifications, though, would not likely alter the overall trend.

Needless to say, corporate amalgamation is a real headache for mainstream economics, whose models commonly rely on the assumption of atomistic competition. Alfred Marshall (1920) tried to solve the problem by arguing that firms, however large, are like trees in the forest: eventually they lose their vitality and die out in competition with younger, more vigorous successors. On its own, though, the forest analogy was not entirely persuasive, if only because incorporation made firms potentially perpetual. For the sceptics, therefore, Marshall had to offer an additional explanation. Even if large firms failed to die, he said, and instead grew into a corporate caste, the attendant social costs were still tolerable – first because such a caste tended to be benevolent and, second, since the costs were outweighed by the greater efficiency of large-scale business enterprise.

The rigorous spin on this latter argument was put by Ronald Coase (1937), who, in a Nobel-winning argument, stated that the size of firms was largely a matter of transaction costs. Inter-firm transactions, he asserted, were the most efficient since they were subject to market discipline. Such transactions, however, were not free, and therefore made sense only if their efficiency gains exceeded the extra cost of carrying them through. Otherwise, they were better internalised as intra-firm activity. Using such calculus, one could then determine the proper 'boundary' of the firm, which according to Coase was set at the point where 'the costs of organizing an extra transaction within the firm become equal to the costs of carrying out the same transaction by means of an exchange on the open market or the costs of organizing in another firm' (p. 96).

The ideological leverage of this theory proved immense. It implied that if companies such as General Electric, Cisco and AOL-Time Warner (or like IDB and Clal in Israel) decided to 'internalise' their dealings with other firms by swallowing them up, then that must be socially efficient, and that their resulting size – no matter how big – was necessarily 'optimal'. In this way, the non-existence of perfect competition was no longer an embarrassment for neoclassical theory. To the contrary, it was the *market itself* which determined the right 'balance' between the benefits of competition and corporate size, and what's more, the whole thing was achieved automatically, according to the eternal principles of marginalism.

The argument is hard to refute, although that is by no means a blessing. The problem is that marginal transaction costs – much like marginal productivity and marginal utility – are unobservable, so reality can never be shown as being at odds with the theory. For instance, one can use transaction costs to claim that the historical emergence of 'internalised' command economies such as Nazi Germany or the Soviet Union means they were more efficient than their market predecessors. The obvious counter-argument, which may well be true, is that that these systems were imposed 'from above', driven by a quest for power rather than efficiency. But then, can we not say the exact same thing about the development of oligopolistic capitalism? Hasn't big business in the United

States, Japan, South Africa and Israel – indeed, in all capitalist countries for that matter – evolved largely as a vehicle of power?

In fact, if it were only for efficiency, corporations should have become smaller, not larger. According to Coase's theory, technical progress, particularly in information and communication, reduces transaction costs, making the market look increasingly appealing and large corporations ever more cumbersome. And indeed, using this very logic Fukuyama (1999) recently announced the 'death of the hierarchy', while advocates of the 'E-Lance Economy' (as in freelance) argue that today's corporate behemoths are anomalous, and will soon be replaced by small, 'virtual' firms (Malone and Laubacher 1998). So far, though, these predictions seem hopelessly misplaced: amalgamation has not only continued, but accelerated, including in the so-called high-technology sector, where transaction costs supposedly fell the most.

How can that be true? Why do firms give up the benefit of market transaction in pursuit of further, presumably more expensive internalisation? Are they not interested in lower cost? The riddle can be solved by using Veblen's distinction between 'industry' and 'business'. Improved technology can certainly reduce the minimum efficient scale of production (MES), and indeed today's largest establishments (plants, head offices, etc.) are often smaller than they were a hundred years ago. Firms, on the other hand, are business units, and since they can own many establishments, their boundary need not depend on production as such. The real issue with corporate size is not efficiency but differential profit, and the key question therefore is whether amalgamation helps firms beat the average, and if so, how?

The conventional wisdom here is that mergers and acquisitions are a disciplinary form of 'corporate control'. According to writers such as Manne (1965), Jensen and Ruback (1983) and Jensen (1987), managers are often subject to conflicting loyalties which may compromise their commitment to profit maximisation. The threat of takeover puts them back in line, forcing them not only to improve efficiency, but also to translate such efficiency into higher profit and rising shareholders' value. The logic of the argument, though, is problematic. Mergers may indeed be driven by profit, but that in itself has little to do with productivity gains. To begin with, there is not much evidence that mergers are either prompted by inefficiency, or that they make the combined firms more efficient (Ravenscraft and Scherer 1987; Caves 1989; Bhagat et al. 1990). Indeed, as we argue below, the latent function of mergers in this regard is not to boost efficiency, but to *tame* it, by keeping a lid on overall capacity growth. Moreover, there is no clear indication that a merger per se makes the amalgamated firms more profitable than they were separately, although here the issue is somewhat more complicated.

First, there is a serious methodological difficulty. Most attempts to test the effect of mergers on profitability are based on comparing the performance of merged and non-merged companies (for instance, Ravenscraft 1987; Ravenscraft and Scherer 1989; and Scherer and Ross 1990, Ch. 5). While this method may offer some insight in the case of individual firms, it is misleading when applied to dominant capital as a whole. Looking at the amalgamation process in its entirety, the issue is not how it compares with 'doing nothing' (that is, with not amalgamating), but rather how it contrasts with the alternative strategy of green-field investment. Unfortunately, such a comparison is impossible to make, since the very purpose of mergers and acquisitions is to avoid creating new capacity. In other words, amalgamation removes the main evidence against which we can assess its success. Perhaps a better, albeit unscientific way to tackle the issue, is to answer the following hypothetical question: What would have happened to the profitability of dominant capital in the United States, if instead of splitting its investment one-third for green-field and two-thirds for mergers and acquisitions, it were to plow it all back into new capacity? As Veblen correctly predicted, such a 'free run of production' is not going to happen, so we cannot know for sure. But then the very fact it has not happened, together with the century-long tendency of moving in the opposite direction, from green-field to amalgamation, already suggest what the answer may be....

The second important point concerns the meaning of 'profitability' in this context. Conventional measures such as earnings-to-price ratio, return on equity, or profit margin on sales, relevant as they may be for investors, are too narrow as indicators of *capitalist power* when such power is vested in and exercised by corporations rather than individuals. A more appropriate measure for this power is the distribution and differential growth of corporate profit, and from this perspective mergers and acquisitions make a very big difference. By fusing previously distinct earning streams, *amalgamation contributes to the organised power of dominant capital*, regardless of whether or not it augments the more conventional rates of return. In our view, this 'earning fusion', common to all mergers, is also their ultimate reason.

And indeed, by gradually shifting its emphasis from building to buying, from competing to colluding, and from private to state-backed coalitions, corporate capitalism in the United States and elsewhere has been able not only to lessen the destabilising impact of green-field cycles pointed out by Marx, but also to reproduce and consolidate on an ever growing scale. Instead of collapsing under its own weight, capitalism seems to have grown stronger. The broader consequence of this shift has been creeping stagnation (Proposition 3), yet as Veblen suggested earlier in the century, and as we shall see throughout the book, the large accumulators have learned to 'manage' this stagnation for their own ends.

Breaking the Envelope

Now, this general rationale for merger does not in itself explain the concrete historical trajectory of corporate amalgamation. Mergers and acquisitions grow, but not smoothly, and indeed the second feature evident in Figure 2.5 is the cyclical pattern of the series (Proposition 4). Over the past century, we can identify four amalgamation 'waves'. The first wave, occurring during the transition from the nineteenth to the twentieth century, is commonly referred to as the 'monopoly' wave. The second, lasting through much of the 1920s, is known as the 'oligopoly' wave. The third, building up during the late 1950s and 1960s, is nicknamed the 'conglomerate' wave. The fourth wave, beginning in the early 1980s, does not yet have a popular title, but based on its all-encompassing nature we can safely label it the 'global' wave.

This wave-like pattern remains something of a mystery. Why do mergers and acquisitions have a pattern at all? Why are they not erratic, or alternatively, why do they not proceed smoothly? So far, most attempts to answer these questions have approached the issue from the micro perspective of the firm, which is precisely why they usually run into a dead end.

One of the more famous explanations is based on the work of Tobin and Brainard (1968; 1977). According to this explanation, if green-field capacity is cheaper, a firm will build it from scratch; if existing capacity is cheaper, the firm will buy it from others. Extending this logic to the economy as a whole, we should therefore expect the buy-to-build ratio to be inversely correlated with the ratio of market value to replacement cost, now known as *Tobin's Q*: the less expensive existing assets are relative to new ones, the greater the proportion of 'financial' to 'real' investment, and vice versa. This seems sensible, except that in reality things happen to move in the opposite way. Since the 1950s, the correlation between *Tobin's Q* and the buy-to-build ratio in the United States was not negative, but positive.[21] In other words, instead of investing in what is cheap, U.S. capitalists systematically overspent on the expensive!

This looks anomalous, but only because we are using neoclassical microeconomic logic to explain a complex power process. New capacity may indeed be cheap if you are the only one adding it. But if your competitors all do the same it is a different matter altogether. Under the latter circumstances, the threat of glut and falling profit makes buying existing assets much cheaper than it looks on paper. As we explain below, large firms understand this all too well and act accordingly.[22] In short, mergers and acquisitions, although pursued by individual firms, occur within a broader and ever changing political-economic context. It is only when making this restructuring process the centre of our analysis that the general pattern of amalgamation begins to make sense.

Seen from a differential accumulation perspective, amalgamation is a power process whose goal is to beat the average and redistribute control. Its main appeal to capitalists is that it contributes directly to differential breadth, yet without undermining and sometimes boosting the potential for differential

21 See Nitzan (2001, Figure 3, p. 243).
22 In this context, *Tobin's Q* turns from a cause to a consequence, with mergers and acquisitions driving up asset prices and therefore the ratio of market value to replacement cost.

depth.[23] Thus, everything else remaining the same, it makes more sense to buy than to build. But then everything else does not, and indeed *cannot* remain the same. The reason is simple: amalgamation transforms the very social conditions and power institutions on which it is based.

Three particular transformations need noting here. First, amalgamation is akin to eating the goose that lays the golden egg. By gobbling up takeover targets within a given corporate universe, acquiring firms are depleting the pool of future targets. Unless this pool is somehow replenished, mergers and acquisitions eventually lead to a highly centralised structure in which dominant capital owns everything worth owning. From a certain point onward, the pace of amalgamation therefore has to decelerate. Although further amalgamation within dominant capital itself may be possible (large firms buying each other), the impact on the *group's* differential accumulation relative to the average is negligible: by this stage, dominant capital has grown so big, it *is* the average.

Green-field growth, by adding new employment and firms, works to replenish the takeover pool to some extent. But then, and this is the second point worth noting, since green-field growth tends to trail the pace of amalgamation in both employment volume and dollar value, its effect is mostly to slow down the depletion process, not stop it. Indeed, the very process of amalgamation, by directing resources away from green-field investment, has the countervailing impact of reducing growth, and hence hastening the depletion process. Thus, sooner or later, dominant capital is bound to reach its 'envelope', namely the boundaries of its own corporate universe, with few or no takeover targets to speak of.

Finally, corporate amalgamation is often socially traumatic. It commonly involves massive dislocation as well as significant power realignments; it is restricted by the ability of broader state institutions to accommodate the new corporate formations; and it is capped by the speed at which the underlying corporate bureaucracy can adapt (this last point is due to Penrose 1959). The consequence is that as amalgamation builds up momentum, it also generates higher and higher roadblocks, contradictions and counter-forces.[24]

Taken together, the depletion of takeover targets, the negative effect on growth associated with lower levels of green-field investment, and the emergence of counter-forces, suggest that corporate amalgamation cannot possibly run smoothly and continuously (Proposition 4). But then, why should amalgamation move in cycles? In other words, why does the uptrend resume after it stumbles? And what does this resumption mean?

23 Note that the act of merger itself has no effect on depth. Its impact works only indirectly, through increasing corporate centralisation, and even that is merely a facilitating factor. Consolidation makes it easier for firms to collude, but that does not imply that collusion will actually take place, or that it will be effective.
24 The 1933 Glass-Steagall Act, for instance, barred U.S. banks from making industrial investments, a restriction which is only now being relaxed. Similar effects were brought on by the postwar dismantling of the Japanese *Zaibatsu*, the unbundling of South African holding groups during the 1990s and the recent divestment of Israeli banks of their 'non-financial' holdings as detailed in Chapter 6.

From the perspective of dominant capital, amalgamation is simply too important to give up. And while there may be little worth absorbing in their own corporate universe, *outside* of this universe targets are still plentiful. Of course, to take advantage of this broader pool, dominant capital has to break through its original 'envelope', which is precisely what happened as the United States moved from one wave to the other (Proposition 5).

The first, 'monopoly' wave marked the emergence of modern big business, with giant corporations forming within their own original *industries*. Once this source of amalgamation was more or less exhausted, further expansion meant that firms had to move outside their industry boundaries. And indeed, the next 'oligopoly' wave saw the formation of vertically integrated combines whose control increasingly spanned entire *sectors*, such as in petroleum, machinery and food products, among others. The next phase opened the whole *U.S. corporate universe* up for grabs, with firms crossing their original boundaries of specialisation to form large conglomerates with business lines ranging from raw materials, through manufacturing, to services and finance. Finally, once the national scene has been more or less integrated, the main avenue for further expansion is across international borders, hence the recent *global* merger wave. This process, whereby dominant capital breaks through its successive envelopes, is of course hardly unique to the United States. It occurred in many other countries, and was repeated, almost to the letter, in Israel.

The pivotal impact of mergers is to alter not the structure of production per se, but the *broader structure of power*. The reason is rooted in the double-sided impact of amalgamation. By constantly pushing toward, and eventually breaking through their successive social 'envelopes' – from the industry, to the sector, to the nation state, to the world as a whole – mergers create a strong drive toward 'jurisdictional integration', to use Olson's terminology (1982). Yet this very integration pits dominant capital against new rivals under new circumstances, and so creates the need to constantly restructure the wider power institutions of society, including the nature of the state, interstate relations, ideology and violence.

These power dynamics of mergers, neglected by those who distinguish 'accumulation' from 'society', will prove crucial for understanding the evolution of Israel's political economy. And given Israel's chronic thirst for foreign capital, the first step toward such understanding is the broader process of globalisation.

Amalgamation and Globalisation

The gist of capitalist globalisation is the spatial spread of *accumulation as power*, whose main vehicle is *the movement of capital*.[25] Most analyses of the process

---

25 Globalisation of course has other dimensions, but these are secondary for our purpose here.

concentrate on its alleged cyclicality. The common view is that although the international flow of capital has accelerated since the 1980s, the increase is part of a broader recurring pattern whose peaks were in fact recorded during the late nineteenth and early twentieth centuries (Taylor 1996). The standard approach to these ups and downs in capital mobility is the so-called 'Unholy Trinity' of international political economy. According to this framework, there is an inherent trade-off between state sovereignty, capital mobility and international monetary stability, of which only two can coexist at any one time (Fleming 1962; Mundell 1963; Cohen 1993).[26]

Thus, during the liberal Gold Standard which lasted until the First World War, limited state sovereignty allowed for both free capital mobility and international monetary stability; during the subsequent, inter-war period, the emergence of 'state autonomy' along with unfettered capital flow served to upset this monetary stability; after the Second World War, the quasi-statist system of Bretton Woods put a check on capital mobility, so as to allow domestic policy autonomy without compromising monetary stability; this 'Golden Age' didn't last long, however; since the 1970s, the rise of neoliberalism has again unleashed capital mobility, although it is still unclear which of the other two nodes of the Trinity – state sovereignty or monetary stability – will have to go.

Why has the world moved from liberalism, to instability, to statism and back to (neo)liberalism? Is this some sort of inevitable cycle, or is there an underlying historical process here which makes each phase fundamentally different? The answers vary widely. Liberal interpretations emphasise the secular impact of technology which constantly pushes toward freer trade and greater capital mobility, with unfortunate setbacks created by government intervention and distortions. From this perspective, post-war statism, or 'embedded liberalism' as it came to be known, was largely a historical aberration. After the Second World War, governments took advantage of the temporary weakness of capitalism to impose all sorts of restrictions and barriers. Eventually, through, the unstoppable advance of information and communication forced them to succumb, with the result being that the rate of return rather than political whim once again governed the movement of capital. Critics of this 'natural-course-of-things' theory tend to reverse its emphasis. Thus, according to Helleiner (1994), the key issue is neither the expansionary tendencies of technology and markets, nor their impact on the propensity of capital to move, but rather the willingness of states to let such movements occur in the first

---

26 The rationale is based on the external account identity between the current and capital balances. If the international monetary system were to remain stable while states retain domestic sovereignty over exports and imports, capital movements must be controlled in order to accommodate the resulting current account imbalances. In the absence of such capital controls, states would have to give up their policy autonomy, for otherwise the mismatch between the current and capital balances would upset international monetary stability.

place. From this viewpoint, state regulation is not an aberration but rather the determining factor, which governments remain free to switch on and off. One of the reasons for such cyclical change of heart, suggests Frieden (1988), is the shifting political economy of foreign debt. According to this view, during the Gold Standard Britain became a 'mature creditor', and was therefore interested in liberalisation so that its debtors could have enough export earnings to service their foreign liabilities. The United States reached a similar position during the 1970s, and used its hegemonic power to re-impose liberalisation for much the same reason. According to Goodman and Pauly (1995), this second coming of liberalism was further facilitated by the desire of governments to retain the benefits of transnational production. The latter required that they also opened the door to transnational financial intermediation, hence the dual rise of portfolio and foreign direct investment.

Plus ça change, plus c'est pareil? Perhaps, but only because much of this discussion focuses on the cyclicality of capital flow. As it turns out, though, this preoccupation, convenient as it may be for those sceptical of globalisation, is not entirely warranted. First, although the *pace* of globalisation as indicated by the ebb and flow of capital movement has indeed oscillated over time, its impact on the *level* of globalisation tends to be cumulative (Magdoff 1969). Thus, while sceptics such as Doremus et al. (1998) are correct in pointing out that most companies are still more national than global, the rapid pace of globalisation suggests that the situation may not stay that way for long.[27] A second, related point is that most analyses of capital flow concentrate on *net* movements – namely, on the difference between inflow and outflow. This choice is inadequate and potentially misleading. Capitalist integration and globalisation can move both ways, which means that the proper measure to use here is the *gross* flow – that is, the sum of inflow and outflow (Wallich 1984). The net and gross magnitudes are the same when capital goes in only one direction, either in or out of a country. But when the flow runs in both directions, the numbers could be very different. And indeed, since the early 1980s, the relative increase of gross flows was both powerful and secular, whereas that of net flows was more limited and cyclical.[28] Although lack of historical data on gross movements makes it difficult to compare current developments with conditions prevailing at the turn of the century, the fact that two-way capital mobility is a relatively recent phenomenon suggests that the current pace of globalisation may well be at an all time high.

---

27 According to the *World Investment Report*, the share of transnational production in world GDP has risen from 5.3 per cent in 1982, to 6.6 in 1990, to 10.1 per cent in 1999, while the average 'transnationality' of the world's top 100 transnational corporations increased to 54 per cent in 1998, up from 51 per cent in 1990 (United Nations Conference on Trade and Development 2000: Table I.1, p. 4 and Table III.2, p. 76). (UNCTAD's 'Transnationality Index' is defined as the average of the ratios of foreign to total assets, foreign to total sales, and foreign to total employment.)

28 See Nitzan (2001, Figure 4, p. 248).

The other common thread going through most analyses is that capital flow is largely a response to the more 'primordial' forces of production and trade. To us, this is akin to putting the world on its head. The global movement of capital is ultimately a matter of ownership and hence power. Note that, on its own, the act of foreign investment – whether portfolio or direct – consists of nothing more than the creation or alteration of ownership titles.[29] Note further that the magnitude of such titles is equal to the present value of their expected future earnings. Now, since these earnings can fall as well as rise with output, and given the many 'political' factors at play, it seems clear that the dollar value of cross-border flows of capital, both private and public, reflect the restructuring not of global production as such, but of the global *politics* of production.

One of the first to approach international capital mobility as a facet of ownership and power was Hymer (1960), who argued that firms would prefer foreign investment over export or licensing when such ownership conferred differential power, or 'ownership advantage' as it later came to be known. Based on this interpretation, the power of U.S.-based foreign investors rose exponentially over the past half century. According to U.S. Department of Commerce data, the share of export in GDP during that period expanded at a trend growth rate of 1.3 per cent, but the share of foreign operations in overall net corporate profit rose more than twice as fast, at a trend growth rate of 2.8 per cent. The result is that foreign operations now contribute to accumulation roughly twice as much as exports, up from par in the 1950s. The difference seems all the more perplexing since, even with the recent resurgence of capital mobility, gross U.S. trade flows are still roughly three times larger than gross capital flows. But then, unlike trade, investment tends to accumulate, eventually causing overseas earnings to outpace those coming from export.

This divergence serves to heighten the *power* underpinnings of trade liberalisation. Advocates of global integration, following in the footsteps of Adam Smith and David Ricardo, tend to emphasise the central role of free trade. Unhindered exchange, they argue, is *the* major force translating greater efficiency into lower prices. And as it stands their claim may well be true. Indeed, this is one reason why dominant capital is often half-hearted about indiscriminate deregulation, particularly when it allows competitors to undermine its differential margins. Yet despite this threat, over the longer haul

---

29 The popular perception that direct investment creates new productive capacity, in contrast to portfolio investment which is merely a paper transaction, is simply wrong. In fact, *both* are paper transactions whose only difference is relative size: investments worth more than 10 per cent of the target company's equity are commonly classified as direct, whereas those worth less are considered portfolio. Conceptually, both direct and portfolio investment occur on the liabilities side of the balance sheet, whereas the creation of capacity affects the assets side. Although total liabilities are by definition equal to total assets, there is no one-to-one correspondence between their underlying components. In this way, the proceeds from a public offering sold to portfolio investors can end up financing a new factory, while direct investment may be used to pay dividends or buy government T-bills, for instance.

large firms have tended to support freer trade, and for a very good reason. For them, it is a means to something much more important, namely free investment – or more precisely, the *freedom to impose and commodify power*. In this sense, and as we shall see later in the book, private capital flow is similar to government aid and loans, in that they all work to reshape social relations and restructure power.

Although difficult to ascertain with available data, the cumulative (albeit irregular) build-up of international investment has probably contributed greatly to the differential accumulation of U.S. dominant capital. The reason is that whereas exports augment the profits of small as well as large firms, the bulk of foreign earnings go to the largest corporations. It is therefore the *globalisation of ownership*, not trade, which is the real prize. While free trade could boost as well as undermine differential accumulation, free investment tends mostly to raise it. But then, since free investment can come only at the footsteps of liberalised trade, the latter is worth pursuing, even at the cost of import competition and rising trade deficits.

Foreign investment, like any other investment, is always a matter of power. The nature of this power, though, has changed significantly over time. Until well into the second half of the nineteenth century, the rapid spatial expansion of capitalism enabled profitability to rise despite the parallel increase in the number of competitors.[30] As a result, there was only limited need for collusion, and indeed most capital flows were relatively small portfolio investments, associated mainly with green-field expansion (Folkerts-Landau et al. 1997, Annex VI). Eventually, though, excess capacity started to appear, giving rise to the progressive shift from green-field to amalgamation described in the previous sections. Yet for more than half a century the shift was mostly domestic, with mergers and acquisitions initially breaking through the various national 'envelopes'. It was only since the 1970s and 1980s that the process started to become truly global, and when that happened the character of capital flow itself started to change. The need to exert control has gradually moved the emphasis toward larger, 'direct' foreign investment, while the threat of excess capacity pushed such investment away from green-field, with over 75 per cent of the world total now taking the form of cross-border mergers and acquisitions (United Nations Conference on Trade and Development 2000: Figure IV.9, p. 117). From a power perspective, therefore, one could say that whereas during the late nineteenth and early twentieth centuries capital mobility was largely a 'choice', by the end of the twentieth century it became more of a 'necessity', mandated by the combination of excess capacity and the cumulative build-up of giant firms, for whom profitable expansion increasingly requires global amalgamation.

---

30   For evidence to this effect, see Veblen (1923, Ch. 4); Josephson (1934); Hobsbawm (1975, Chs 2–3); and Arrighi et al. (1999).

In summary, there is a long but crucial link leading from capitalism, to differential accumulation, to amalgamation, to capital mobility (Proposition 5). From this perspective, the present process of globalisation is inherent in capitalist development and therefore not easily reversible without altering capitalism, or moving away from it altogether. Moreover, contrary to popular perception, the underlying force here is not greater efficiency, but the control of efficiency, and the purpose is not aggregate but differential gain. Over time, and particularly since the 1980s, foreign investment has come to rely less on green-field and more on cross-border mergers and acquisitions, as firms increasingly break through their national 'envelope'. The big winners are the large 'distributional coalitions' of dominant capital. For society as a whole the picture is less cheerful, as the emphasis progressively shifts from green-field to amalgamation, causing growth to recede and stagnation to creep in (Proposition 3).[31]

Cost Cutting

Although mergers and acquisition are the most effective engine of differential accumulation, they are not always feasible (Proposition 4). And when merger activity recedes, dominant capital has to resort to other means – or risk differential *de*cumulation (which, to repeat, is always possible). In principle, this can be done through either relative cost reduction (internal depth), or differential stagflation (external depth). In practice, though, the latter is much more effective (Propositions 6 and 7).

Consider cost cutting first. The conflictual dynamics of capitalism, persistent even in the presence of oligopoly and monopoly, imply a constant pressure on firms to improve productivity and reduce input cost. This pressure, identified by the classical economists and reiterated by all subsequent schools, radical as well as conservative, seems beyond dispute. From the perspective of differential accumulation, however, cutting cost is much like 'running on empty'. It helps dominant capital meet the average rather than beat it.

This claim is difficult to test directly, since data on productivity and input prices are rarely if ever broken down by firm size. The indirect evidence, though, seems to support our view here, if only provisionally (the numbers in this section are computed on the basis of data from *Fortune*, the U.S. Internal Revenue Service, and the U.S. Bureau of Labor Statistics). The logic is straightforward: output per employee, taken as a broad measure of 'productivity', is given by the ratio of sales per employee divided by unit price (abstracting from inventory changes). Now, over the past half century, dollar sales per employee in large firms (the Fortune 500) have changed little relative to the comparable

---

31 Economic growth is of course hardly an end in itself. It's only that, under capitalism, such growth is crucial for the livelihood, employment and personal security of most people.

figure for the average firm: the ratio between them was 1.4 in 1954, fell gradually to 1.1 by 1969, and then rose steadily, reaching 1.7 by 1993 (although the latter increase is probably overstated due to the growing significance of outsourcing by large firms). We can also reasonably assume that prices charged by larger firms have not fallen relative to those of smaller ones, since, as we show in the next section and in Chapter 4, inflation has historically worked in their favour. These conjectures, along with our above definition, imply that productivity gains by dominant capital have probably been roughly equal to the economy's average.

The difficulty of achieving systematic differential cost-cutting is really not that surprising. First, even the largest firms have only limited control over their input prices, particularly with the proliferation of outsourcing; and when they do exercise such control, the benefits often spill over to other firms (a wage freeze by dominant capital groups would empower smaller firms to do the same; political pressure on OPEC by car companies to reduce oil prices would benefit all energy users; an importer winning a tariff reduction gives competing importers a free ride, etc.).[32] Second, there is no inherent reason why large firms should be better than small ones at developing new production technologies. For instance, much of the recent advances in bio-technology, information and communication have been driven by smaller companies, some with only a handful of workers. Dominant capital was often unable to match this flurry of innovation, and in many cases found it cheaper to let smaller companies incur the R&D cost and then buy the more promising startups, sometimes just to keep their technology from spreading too quickly (this point is particularly crucial for understanding Israeli developments in the 1990s, and we return to it in the last chapter). Finally, production techniques, by virtue of their integrated *societal* nature, are notoriously difficult to monopolise. Unlike new products which could often be protected through patents, copyrights and other threats, improvements in the social organisation of production tend to proliferate easily, undermining the initial advantage of whoever implemented them first.

Stagflation

Unlike cost cutting, stagflation is a highly effective means of differential accumulation. At first sight, this seems a strange claim to make. How could large firms benefit from a crisis of rising prices, stagnating output, and falling

---

32   The challenge to differential accumulation of 'universal' cost was summarised neatly by Andrew Grove, chairman of Intel: 'How do you build a company', he asks 'when your buyers are infinitely knowledgeable and where your suppliers maintain a level playing field for your competitors? What remains your competitive differentiator or your source of value or whatever academic cliché you want to wrap around it?' (*Business Week*, 28 August 2000).

employment? And if stagflation is indeed so 'accumulation friendly', why does it not continue indefinitely? These questions are explored more fully in Chapter 4, but it is important to deal with them briefly here, so as to complete our general framework.

The impact on profit of raising prices and lowering volume is of course non-linear (think about the consequence for profit of moving along a downward-sloping demand curve). But recall that our concern here is not prices, but *inflation*. Furthermore, we are interested in the impact of inflation not on profit, but on *differential* profit. These two qualifications make a big difference.

In contrast to mergers and acquisitions, which are commonly pursued only by a subset of firms (the larger ones), a strategy of inflationary redistribution can succeed only within a broader inflationary context in which *all* prices tend to rise. That being said, it is also true that inflation is never uniform and hence never 'neutral'. Indeed, this is the whole point: inflation exists precisely because it redistributes. Paraphrasing Milton Friedman, we can safely state that 'Inflation is always and everywhere a redistributional phenomenon.' The key question is who benefit from such redistribution, and this cannot be answered *a priori*. The essence of inflation is a comprehensive destabilisation and restructuring of all market relations, and although there is good reason to expect the more powerful groups to come out on top, the identity of such groups cannot be determined up front. It can only be decided in hindsight, based on the distributional outcome.

In the case of the United States, this outcome, illustrated in Figure 2.6, leaves little doubt as to who the winners are. The data in the figure contrast two series. The first is the rate of inflation, measured by the annual per cent change of the wholesale price index. The second is the profit-per-employee ratio, computed by dividing profit per employee in the Fortune 500 group of companies by profit per employee for the economy as a whole. The latter index corresponds to our notion of differential depth, its fluctuations measuring the extent to which dominant capital – approximated here by the Fortune 500 – is able to raise its profit per employee faster than the average.

As the figure shows, the success of dominant capital here has been tightly and positively correlated with the overall rate of inflation. In other words, higher rates of inflation have played into the hands of the big players, allowing them to raise their profit per unit of organisation faster than their smaller counter-parts. (Further analysis reported elsewhere suggests that the link between inflation and differential depth is positively related to firm size: the larger the firm, the greater and more systematic the differential gains from inflation. See Nitzan 1992.)

But if the chart shows that dominant capital clearly benefited from inflation, it also suggests that this benefit was always short lived, lasting only as long as the underlying bout of inflation. Indeed, the only way to keep such gains coming is to keep inflation going; and if the gains are to be raised, inflation needs to be accelerated. Although such increases occasionally happen, and often with the desired impact on differential accumulation, they cannot last

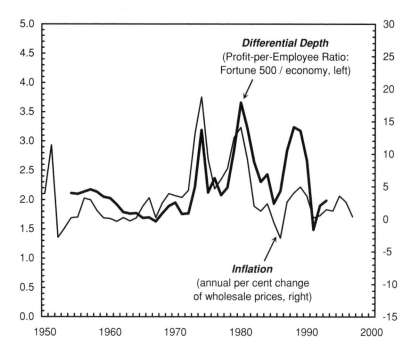

Figure 2.6   Differential Depth and Inflation in the U.S.A.

NOTE: The economy's profit per employee is computed by dividing corporate profit with inventory valuation adjustment and capital consumption allowance, less taxes, by the number of non-agricultural employees. Fortune's profit per employee is computed by dividing net profit by the number of employees.
SOURCE: Fortune; U.S. Department of Commerce through McGraw-Hill (Online).

indefinitely. As illustrated repeatedly throughout history and across the world, including in Israel, inflation is a risky business. It is difficult to 'manage' and often degenerates into an uncontrollable spiral whose consequences – for differential accumulation and more broadly for the structure of capitalist power as a whole – are difficult to predict.

For this reason, inflation is more of a stop-gap option for dominant capital. In contrast to breadth, whose differential impact is slower to develop, the differential gains from inflation, which has no upper 'technical' limit, are potentially huge. These gains, however, come with considerable risks, which under normal circumstances are deemed too high. It is only when the gains from breadth dry up, that dominant capital, seeing its differential accumulation undermined, moves reluctantly toward inflationary redistribution.

The connection between inflation and power here cannot be overstated. Mainstream theory, built on the belief in competitive markets, insists that inflation and growth should go hand in hand.[33] This belief, though, is usually based on a cyclical argument about supply constraints, which, valid or not, is meaningful only in the short term. Over the longer haul, capacity can be increased as needed so material bottlenecks are largely irrelevant.

The real key then becomes power. Since production provides no 'natural' bottlenecks, these have to be created institutionally, through collusive and other arrangements among the key players. Regardless of their particular form, the purpose of all such arrangements is to keep overall capacity from growing too fast. The emphasis here on *overall* capacity is crucial; dominant capital may be able to keep its own production stable or even growing, but unless it manages to cap overall growth, coordination is bound to disintegrate into a price war, leading to disinflation or even outright deflation.

The upshot is simple: over the longer haul, we should expect inflation and growth to be *inversely* related. Long-term growth, far from stoking the inflation fire, works to cool it off by undermining collusion. Inflation, on the other hand, requires slack and therefore tends to appear as stagflation.

Before testing this proposition, however, it should be noted that the term stagflation has more than one interpretation. The 'weak' version, due to Samuelson (1974: 801), views stagflation as inflation together with unemployment and under-capacity utilisation. The 'moderate' version, found for instance in Baumol et al. (1986: 83), defines it as inflation combined with slow growth or recession. Finally, the 'strong' version, adopted for example by Parkin and Bade (1986: 618), limits stagflation only to instances in which inflation occurs with falling output.

For our purpose here, the 'weak' version is too broad: twentieth century capitalism has been characterised by some measure of unemployment and unused capacity throughout, so its inflation was invariably stagflationary according to this definition. The 'strong' version, on the other hand, is too narrow, since falling overall output is relatively rare. The most useful of the three is the 'moderate' version, particularly when understood as a relationship. If growth is positively related to inflation, stagflation is clearly an anomaly. On the other hand, if the relationship is negative, stagflation must be seen as a 'normal' phenomenon, intensifying as growth declines and inflation rises, and receding when growth increases and inflation falls.

As it turns out, the long-term relationship is almost invariably negative. Indeed, the evidence on this is nothing short of overwhelming (although systematically ignored by most economists). Figures 2.7 and 2.8 illustrate respectively the case of the United States over the past century or so, and of the industrialised countries as a group since the late 1960s. The data contrast inflation and growth, both smoothed as 20-year moving averages to accentuate

---

33 Supply-shock explanations, in which stagflation is typically blamed on 'autonomous' price increases by labour unions or oil sheiks, are in this sense outside the mainstream, since they acknowledge, if only half-heartedly, the existence of market power.

their long-term pattern. Although neither relationship is very tight, in both cases it is clearly negative. (In Figure 2.7, the relationship seems to have changed since the early 1990s, perhaps due to the impact of greater global integration which we discuss in the next section.) Furthermore, these charts are by no means exceptional. In fact, the negative long-term pattern seems to repeat itself in numerous individual countries, both developed and developing, with one of the tightest negative correlations offered by none other than Israel (see Figure 3.1 below).

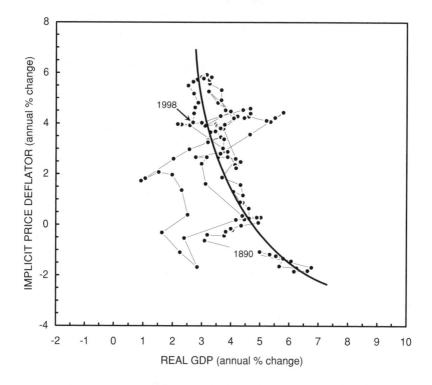

Figure 2.7   U.S.A.: Long-Term Inflation and Growth

NOTE: Series are shown as 20-year moving averages. The smooth curve running
    through the observations is drawn freehand for illustration purposes.
    SOURCE: U.S. Department of Commerce through McGraw-Hill (Online).

The negative long-term correlation between growth and inflation also helps explain the post-war schizophrenia of policy makers in capitalist countries. Their stated, eternal purpose is to promote growth and assure price stability. Their unstated commitment, though, has progressively drifted in favour of dif-

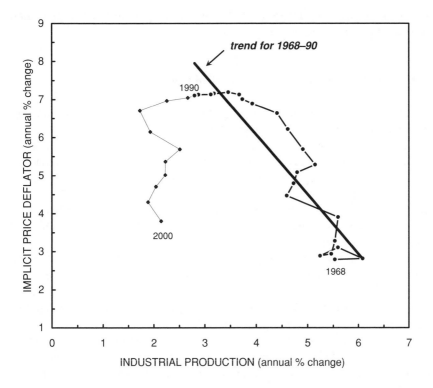

Figure 2.8   Industrialised Countries: Long-Term Inflation and Growth

NOTE: Series are shown as 20-year moving averages. The trend line represents
an OLS regression for the 1968–90 period.
SOURCE: IMF through McGraw-Hill (Online).

ferential accumulation. During breadth periods, the stated and latent goals are
consistent, with high growth and low inflation allowing policy makers to do
little and claim success. The problem arises when differential accumulation
moves into depth, and the macroeconomic scene turns stagflationary. Then
the two commitments clash, and the winner is almost invariably dominant
capital. Policy is tightened, presumably in order to rein in inflation, but the
consequence is exactly the opposite: the economy slows, which is precisely
what dominant capital needs in order to keep inflation going!

Occasionally, policy tightening claims a big victory – for instance, during
the early 1980s, when higher interest rates were eventually followed by disinflation. But was tighter policy here indeed the *cause* of lower inflation? As
illustrated in Figure 2.3, during the early 1980s dominant capital began shifting
back to breadth, with a new merger wave gathering momentum. Under these
circumstances, both the need for inflation and the ability to coordinate it tend
to decline. If this interpretation is correct, the real cause of disinflation was

resumed breadth, with restrictive policy in fact keeping inflation higher than it would have been otherwise.

Differential Accumulation: An Historical Outline

To recap, our discussion so far suggested that differential accumulation, although never predetermined, does follow certain general patterns, or regimes. We identified four such regimes, of which the more important were internal breadth through mergers and acquisitions, and external depth via stagflation. Internal depth, we argued, was the most potent in the long run, whereas external depth, although equally powerful, was less sustainable. Finally, we claimed that the underlying logic of these two regimes was mutually contradictory, so that more mergers and acquisitions implied less stagflation, and vice versa (Proposition 8).

Figure 2.9 illustrates these general patterns with respect to the United States. The chart contrasts our amalgamation index (the buy-to-build indicator), with a composite stagflation proxy, both smoothed for easier comparison. The latter proxy is constructed first by expressing unemployment and inflation as relative per cent deviations from their respective historical means, and then averaging the two series into a combined stagflation index. (The purpose of including both inflation and unemployment is to accentuate the broader crisis aspects of depth, although the pattern would have been similar had we used inflation only.)[34]

The chart shows that, over the long haul, mergers and acquisitions were indeed the path of least resistance (Proposition 2). Whereas stagflation moved sideways, oscillating around its own stable mean, mergers and acquisitions rose exponentially relative to green-field investment (note the logarithmic scale). It also shows that since the turn of the century, following the initial emergence of big business in the United States, internal breadth and external depth tended to move counter-cyclically. Temporary declines in mergers and acquisitions were invariably 'compensated' for by sharp increases in stagflation; and when amalgamation resumed, with dominant capital breaking through its existing envelope and into a broader universe, stagflation promptly abated (Propositions 1 and 8).

The *very existence* of this counter-cyclical pattern is quite remarkable, particularly since, as we have repeatedly emphasised, differential accumulation does not have to happen and can as easily go into reverse. Also significant is the fact that the inverse correlation between breadth and depth has *grown tighter* over time, perhaps as a consequence of the ascendancy of dominant capital

---

34 Inflation fluctuates much more than unemployment, and therefore dominates the combined stagflation index. The correlation coefficient between the combined index and its inflation component, both expressed as five-year moving averages, is 0.93.

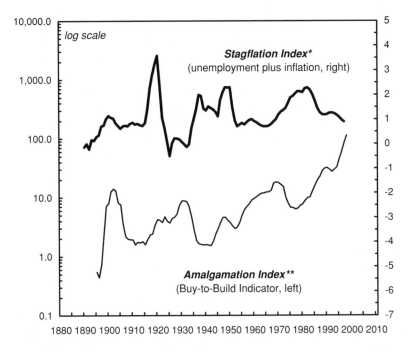

Figure 2.9 Amalgamation and Stagflation in the U.S.A.

* Average of standardised unemployment and standardised GDP Deflator
Inflation (per cent deviations from mean).
** Mergers and acquisitions as a per cent of gross fixed capital formation.
NOTE: Series are shown as 5-year moving averages (the first four observations
cover available data only).
SOURCE: U.S. Department of Commerce through McGraw-Hill (Online), and
sources listed in the Data Appendix.

and the spread of differential accumulation.[35] The progression is clear from
the chart. During the last decade of the nineteenth century, when big business
was only starting to take its modern shape, the two series still moved in the
same direction. By the first decades of the twentieth century, however, with
dominant capital having assumed the centre-stage, the relationship turned
clearly negative, although still somewhat loose. And from the 1930s onward,
as differential accumulation became increasingly entrenched, the negative fit
grew tighter and tighter.

The progressive move from loose to tighter correlation is not surprising.
Differential accumulation, understood as a broad historical process, is relatively

35 The 30-year moving correlation between the stagflation and amalgamation indices
(with the latter expressed as deviations from trend), rose gradually from a negative
0.11 in 1927, to a negative 0.9 in 1998.

new, rising to prominence only at the end of the nineteenth century when corporations grew large enough to administer strategic sabotage. The process first became important in certain sectors in the United States and Europe, from where it subsequently spread domestically and internationally. However, the spread was highly uneven, and so despite high capital mobility, the cyclical regimes in different sectors and countries were initially disjoined and out of step with one another. It was only later, with the gradual proliferation and deepening of business principles, the progressive breaking of sectoral envelopes, and the growing globalisation of ownership, that differential accumulation became the compass of modern capitalism. And it was therefore only toward the middle of the twentieth century, when the combined effect of these processes began to be felt, that breadth and depth grew stylised and more synchronised.

Now, since differential accumulation is a process of social transformation, its specific regimes are important for understanding the broader nature of institutional and structural change under capitalism. Perhaps the most important of these changes concerns the pattern of conflict. Although dominant capital always struggles to increase its power relative to other capitalists, in breadth this is done directly, whereas in depth the path is indirect. When expanding through breadth, capitalists fight each other to control existing and new employment. Their inner struggle is commonly associated with overall growth and ongoing institutional change, which in turn partly conceals the conflict between capitalists and society at large. In depth, on the other hand, the inner capitalist struggle is 'mediated' through a redistributional conflict between capitalists and the rest of society. Moreover, in contrast to breadth, this process thrives on stagflation, not growth. Obviously, sustaining such accumulation-through-crisis requires entrenchment, fortified power arrangements, and greater use of force and violence.

These distinct features of breadth and depth provide a framework for the global political economy of Israel. They help us periodise the evolution of differential accumulation in the core countries, illuminate the way this accumulation affected developments in the Middle East, and understand the history of Israeli capitalism itself – internally as well as in relation to these broader process.

The Global View

At the global level, we can identify several broad phases of differential accumulation, whose initially blurred contours gradually sharpen into focus. From the perspective of dominant capital groups in the core industrialised countries, these phases include: (1) a mixture of breadth and depth until the 1910s; (2) a partial breadth regime during the 1920s; (3) the depth regime of the 1930s; (4) the breadth regime between the 1940s and 1960s; (5) the return to depth in the 1970s and early 1980s; and (6) the re-emergence of breadth in the 1980s and

1990s. During the first years of the twenty-first century, the sustainability of breadth was again called into question, although, so far, there are no clear signs of resumed depth.

The period from the 1890s until the 1910s was one of rapid and accelerating economic growth, coupled with relatively low inflation and the beginning of corporate transnationalisation, particularly by large U.S.-based companies. Internationally, differential accumulation was still cloaked in 'statist' clothes, with American and European companies often seen as imperial agents as well as pursuers of their own interests. Their competitive expansion, however, was largely uncoordinated, and soon led to the creation of massive imbalances of excess capacity. Left unattended, such imbalances would have spelled business ruin, so there was growing pressure to 'resolve' the predicament via depth. And indeed, since the mid-1900s, U.S. merger activity has collapsed, followed in the 1910s by war in Europe and the spread of economic crisis and inflation around the world.

The 1920s offered a brief break. In the United States, merger activity soared while stagflation subsided sharply. In Europe, however, the reprieve was short and stress signs were soon piling up again. Protectionist walls, both between and within countries, emerged everywhere; stagflation spread through a cascade of crises; and before long the world had fallen into the Great Depression of the 1930s.

By that time, the counter-cyclical pattern of breadth and depth had become more apparent, with declining merger activity accompanied by rising stagflation.[36] The new depth regime was marked by the massive use of military force, in which the global power impasse was 'resolved' through an all-encompassing world war. This use of violence was painted and justified largely in statist terms: it was a war of sovereigns, waged over territory and ideology. But it was also highly significant for differential accumulation. Most importantly, it accelerated the relative ascent of U.S.-based corporations, as well as the global spread of the normal rate of return.

After the war, the world again shifted to breadth. The counter-cyclical regime pattern was sharpened even further, while the inverse correlation between inflation and growth became increasingly apparent. Now, on the surface, it looked as if developments during that period, which lasted until the end of 1960s, should have *undermined* breadth. For one, superpower rivalry, decoloni-

36 Strictly speaking, and contrary to our stylised characterisation of depth, the Great Depression brought deflation, not inflation. This observation, however, is true only from an aggregate viewpoint. As Gardiner Means (1935) showed in his innovative study of the United States during that period, the nature of the crisis was highly uneven. For smaller firms with little market power the crisis was largely one of sharply falling prices and only a moderate drop in output. The large firms, on the other hand, were able to keep their prices relatively stable, letting their output fall by as much as 80 per cent. In other words, stagflation, although invisible in the aggregates, was already very much present, if only in embryonic form.

sation, and the non-alignment movement, limited the geographical expansion of Western dominant capital. In addition, many developing countries, previously open to foreign investment, adopted 'import substitution' policies which favoured domestic over foreign producers.

And yet, for much of the 1950s and 1960s, these barriers on breadth were more than compensated for by two powerful counter-forces. The first of these was the post-war 'baby boom', which boosted population growth. The second was the post-war rebuilding of Europe and Japan which was in some sense equivalent to the re-proletarianisation of their societies. The result was a powerful breadth engine, particularly for the large U.S. firms which saw their profit soar during that period. The macroeconomic result – anomalous from a conventional viewpoint but consistent with differential accumulation – was rapid economic growth averaging 6 per cent, combined with low inflation of only 3 per cent.

This picture was inverted in the 1970s. The German and Japanese miracles were running out of steam, Western rates of population growth dropped sharply, and foreign outlets for investment in periphery countries remained hindered by communist or statist regimes. Faced with rising obstacles to breadth, dominant capital groups in the developed world were again driven toward depth, with the average rate of inflation rising to 8 per cent and economic growth dropping to 3 per cent. And, as before, the new depth regime was accompanied by heightened conflict and violence. This time, though, the conflict was played out mostly in the outlying areas of the developing world, particularly in the Middle East.

The Middle East

Until the late 1940s, the region was 'out of sync' with the global cycle of differential accumulation. Its energy resources were parcelled out by the international oil companies already in the 1920s, but with the world being awash with oil, these companies mostly 'sat on their concessions' and produced little. As a result, the Middle East remained relatively isolated, and when Europe slipped into stagflation and conflict during the 1920s and 1930s, Palestine and the rest of the region prospered. After the war, though, the tables turned. The Middle East, which until then was a true 'outlying area', suddenly became a centre-stage for the global drama of differential accumulation.

Initially, the link was pretty simple, with oil from the region helping sustain the growth underpinnings of global breadth. During the early 1970s, however, when differential accumulation shifted into depth, things became more complicated. The background for this latter shift is illustrated in Figure 2.10. The chart shows a positive long-term correlation between inflation in the industrialised countries on the one hand, and the global arms trade on the other (expressed as a share of world GDP). Conventional economics would probably treat this relationship as accidental and largely irrelevant. From the viewpoint of differential accumulation, however, it is both central and meaningful.

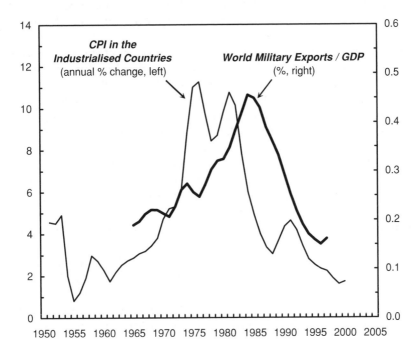

Figure 2.10   Inflation and Arms Exports

NOTE: Series are smoothed as 3-year moving averages.
SOURCE: IMF through McGraw-Hill (Online); U.S. Arms Control and
Disarmament Agency.

As we noted earlier, the inflationary depth regime of the 1970s and 1980s was largely the response for Western dominant capital having 'run out of breadth'. This exhaustion was in turn partly the consequence of bipolar geopolitics, which prevented capitalist expansion into outlying areas contested Western control over strategic regions, particularly the Middle East. One key consequence of this antagonism was an intense arms race, and it is hence not surprising that arms exports roughly follow the periodicity of Western inflation: the first provided the antagonism and violence of depth, the second its redistributional mechanism. Both arms exports and inflation rose until the mid-1980s, peaked as the Cold War began to weaken, and went into a free fall with the disintegration of communism and the onset of global breadth.[37]

37   The data for military exports here are based on the value of *deliveries*; if we were to display military *contracts*, which lead deliveries by roughly 3 years, the correlation would have been even tighter.

Moreover, the two were causally connected, with military conflict, especially in the Middle East, contributing to higher inflation. As we shall see later in the book, much of this cycle of militarisation and demilitarisation was played out in the Middle East, with massive consequences for the various participants, including Israel.

The late 1980s seemed to mark the beginning of yet another breadth phase, this time at the global level. On the surface, the new breadth regime was somewhat anomalous according to our criteria. The reason, illustrated in Figure 2.8, is that while inflation in the industrial countries dropped sharply, growth hasn't revived. But there is more here than meets the eye. First, with the collapse of the Soviet Union and the wholesale capitulation of statism, the entire world economy has finally been open for capitalist expansion and differential accumulation. The result was that although external breadth for dominant capital fizzled in the industrial countries proper, it remained strong outside of these countries, particularly in developing Asia. Moreover, cheap imports from Asia helped keep inflation in the industrial countries low despite their domestic stagnation. Second, the ideological demise of public ownership and the 'mixed economy' opened the door for privatisation of state assets and government services, which, from the viewpoint of dominant capital was tantamount to green-field investment. And third, the decline of statist ideology weakened the support for 'national' ownership, thus contributing to the spread of cross-border mergers and acquisitions. Together, the combination of expansion into less developed countries, privatisation and corporate amalgamation helped sustain a powerful breadth drive for large Western corporations, despite the lacklustre growth of their 'parent' economies.

This global shift from depth to breadth has fundamentally altered the role of Middle East militarisation and war. Regional 'energy conflicts', which previously helped fuel the inflationary fire of global depth, have now become a menace to global breadth. And indeed, before long, local rulers found themselves embroiled in a sudden 'peace blitz', sponsored by no other than their largest weapon suppliers, the United States and Europe. A new order of 'peace dividends' had dawned on the region.

Israel

It is within this broader global and regional context that the evolution of Israeli differential accumulation must be understood. To begin with, the starting point of Israeli capitalism differed markedly from other countries. The reason is illustrated Figure 2.11, which contrasts two fundamental processes – population growth and the growth of per capita GDP (measured in constant prices). The chart shows that, until the 1960s, Jewish Palestine and then Israel experienced rapid population growth, coupled with an even *faster* rate of productivity growth (averaging 3 and 5.4 per cent, respectively). This combination is highly unusual for a developing country. In the United States, for instance, high population growth was until the 1860s accompanied by *little* productivity gains; similarly in developing Asia, where overall growth was until recently fuelled almost exclusively by proletarianisation.[38] The reason is that, unlike in the United States where immigration was initially absorbed mainly in the rural sector, Israel had no 'frontier', so most immigrants ended up the cities and towns.[39] In this sense, Israel appears to have 'skipped a stage'. Whereas most developing countries require significant improvements in agricultural productivity to underwrite urbanisation and proletarianisation, in Israel this seemed unnecessary. The

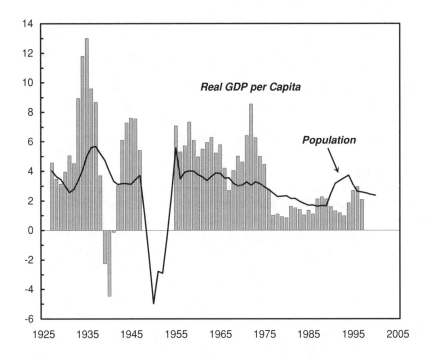

Figure 2.11 Israeli Growth Trends (annual % change)

* Series are expressed as 5-year moving averages.
SOURCE: Israel's Central Bureau of Statistics; Gross and Greenberg (1994).

38 For U.S. productivity in that period, see Nitzan (1998: Figure 1, p. 190). For the Asian experience, see Krugman (1994).
39 For comparison, in 1948, before the big push toward industrialisation, Israel already had less than 10 per cent of its population in agriculture (*The Hebrew Encyclopaedia*: Vol. VI, p. 731). In the United States circa 1900, on the other hand, after four decades of rapid industrialisation, 38 per cent of the workforce were still in agriculture (U.S. Department of Commerce. Bureau of the Census 1975: Vol. I, pp. 140–5).

country not only experienced 'miraculous' growth rates, but also achieved them with practically no transfer of surplus from the primary sector!

But then, urbanisation could not start on its own, even in the Holy Land. In fact, although uncommon, Israel's is not the only case where industrialisation was independent of rising agricultural surplus. A similar process happened in Hong Kong and Singapore, for example, and in all cases the explanation was the same: foreign capital inflow. While Israel had little agriculture surplus, this was more than compensated for by abundant, and for the most part gratuitous capital coming from the outside. This inflow enabled it to immediately expand the secondary and tertiary sector where productivity gains are commonly much higher than in agriculture, hence the 'miracle'.

The implications of this 'leap' were twofold. First, it meant that Israeli capitalism entered its 'maturity' stage more quickly than elsewhere, and that it was faced, almost from the very start, with the problem of excess capacity. Indeed, unlike in the United States, where until the mid-nineteenth century markets expanded much faster than capacity, in Israel the situation was exactly the opposite, making profit dependent on restrictive power institutions from the very start. The initial lack of business infrastructure, however, implied that these power institutions had to be built by the state, which in turn serves to explain why class conflict was for long buried under the guise of national-ethnic struggles.

The second implication was that the domestic cycle of breadth and depth was initially out of step with the rest of the world. This is provisionally illustrated in Figure 2.12, where we contrast the GDP growth rate in Israel with that of the four leading world economies (the United States, Japan, the UK and Germany). Although economic growth is not in itself a measure of differential accumulation, its ups and downs give us an indirect indication as to whether such accumulation proceeds through breadth or depth.

From this perspective, the most striking feature here is Israel's gradual shift from divergence to convergence. Until the mid-1960s, domestic growth was almost a mirror image of global growth, although its pace was nearly three times faster (notice the dual scale). During that period, Israeli differential accumulation was making its first steps, with the local dominant capital groups expanding their differential breadth – initially through green-field investment and subsequently via mergers and acquisitions. By the early 1970s, however, the domestic sources of breadth had dried out. Moreover, Israel had become increasingly integrated globally and entangled regionally, so its underlying regimes were no longer disjoined from what happened elsewhere. And so, during the 1970s and early 1980s, Israel, along with the rest of the world, entered its depth phase. Inflation soared, stagnation set in, and productivity growth – for the first time since the 1920s – dropped below the growth rate of the population (Figure 2.11). Internal redistributional conflict, massive military spending and intensified regional hostilities besieged most of the population,

Figure 2.12 Real GDP

* Annual GDP growth for Israel in 1948–50 are interpolated.
** Germany, Japan, UK and United States.
NOTE: Series are smoothed as 10-year moving averages.
SOURCE: Israel's Central Bureau of Statistics; Gross and Greenberg (1994); Maddison (1991); IMF through McGraw-Hill (Online).

while contributing massively to differential accumulation by the country's dominant capital groups.

This situation, though, was largely dependent on global conditions; and, when, during the 1990s, the world moved back to breadth, so did Israel. The end of superpower confrontation, the opening to business of developing countries, and the move toward global corporate amalgamation made it both impossible to sustain local stagflation and lucrative to expand outside the country. A new, transnational phase had opened up for Israel's leading capitalists.

Back to Depth?

Developments during the first years of the twenty-first century have seriously shaken capitalist optimism. First, in late 2000, world stock markets went into a tailspin, pulling the rug from under a decade-long surge in merger activity.

Second, the global economy, perhaps for the first time since the Great Depression, has fallen into a *synchronised* recession involving all major countries. And third, after a decade of 'peace dividends', attacks on the World Trade Center and the Pentagon, followed by retaliation against Afghanistan, have rekindled the ghost of violence and 'war profits'.

Was the world running out of breadth? Were these developments the beginning of a new depth phase? Or maybe they were merely minor ripples, soon to be forgotten, on the tidal wave of globalisation and amalgamation? Clearly, it is too early to tell. On the one hand, mounting barriers on corporate centralisation, both domestic and cross-border, have made the recent pace of internal breadth difficult to sustain. And if the lull in mergers continues, pressures to move back to depth may well intensify, along with stagflation, rising conflict and mounting violence. On the other hand, global accumulation is still far from being fully integrated, with half of the world population waiting to be proletarianised, and with takeover targets still more than ample. If these temptations of breadth remain strong and accessible, we may soon see the threat of conflict recede, growth resume, and the merger wave rekindled. And there is yet a third alternative, namely that dominant capital will fail to achieve either breadth or depth, falling into a differential accumulation crisis. But then, these speculations belong at the end of our story. To get there, we have to start from the beginning.

Data Appendix

There are no systematic historical time series for mergers and acquisitions in the U.S. (other countries have even less). The series constructed in this chapter and plotted in Figures 2.5 and 2.9, is computed on the basis of various studies, which often use different definitions, covering different universes of companies.

The dollar values of mergers and acquisition for the 1895–1919 period are taken from Nelson (1959, Table 14, p. 37), whereas those covering the 1920–29 period come from Eis (1969), as reported in *Historical Statistics of the United States* (US Department of Commerce. Bureau of the Census 1975, Vol. II, Table V38–40, p. 914). Both data sets cover manufacturing and mining transactions only, and thus fail to reflect the parallel amalgamation drive in other sectors (Markham 1955).

Data for the 1930–66 period are from the US Federal Trade Commission, reported in *Historical Statistics of the United States* (1975, Vol. II, Table V38–40, p. 914). These data, again covering only manufacturing and mining, pertain to the number of transactions rather than their dollar value. Significantly, though, the number of mergers and acquisitions correlates closely with the value ratio of mergers and acquisitions to green-field investment, during previous and subsequent periods for which both are available (the 1920s and 1960s–1980s). In our computations, we assume a similar correlation to have existed during

1930 to 1966, and hence use the former series (with proper re-basing) as a proxy for the latter ratio.

From 1967 onward, we again use value data which this time cover all sectors. Figures for 1967–79 are from W.T. Grimm, reported in Weston (1987, Table 3.3, p. 44). For 1980–83, data are from Securities Data Corporation, comprising transaction of over $1 million only. The last batch, covering the period from 1984 to the present and coming from the same source, consists of transactions of $5 million or more. The latter two data sets are reported regularly in the U.S. Department of Commerce's *Statistical Abstract of the United States* (Annual).

In constructing our indicator for the ratio of mergers and acquisitions to gross fixed investment, we divided, for each year, the dollar value of mergers and acquisitions by the corresponding dollar value of gross fixed capital formation (taken from the *Historical Statistics of the United States* (1975) and from various issues of the *Statistical Abstract of the United States*). For the 1930–66 period, we spliced in the number of deals, linking it with prior and latter value ratios.

3

The History of Israel's Power Structure

> ... races condemned to one hundred years of solitude did not have a second opportunity on earth.
>
> – Gabríel Garcia Márquez, *One Hundreds Years of Solitude*

For neoliberal ideologues, the 1990s marked the beginning of a new era in Israeli capitalism. After decades of imperfections, resource misallocation and excessive government intervention, 'the market' is finally having its say. The victory is not yet complete. State officials and other interest groups still cling to their perks, but not for long. Their opponent now is the global market itself, and against this white knight of freedom, even Leviathan – the omnipotent Israeli government – seems feeble, its resistance futile. 'The markets are much smarter than we think,' explains former Governor of the Bank of Israel, Jacob Frenkel, 'the secret is to know how to talk to them'. Of course, it was he, Frenkel, a faithful Chicago-trained storm-trooper of neoliberalism, a non-resident Israeli for most of his professional life, who brought this secret home. Retiring to the private sector after eight years at the helm of the central bank, he could proudly announce: 'we passed power from politicians to the market, the ultimate stick, the judge of bad behaviour' (*Ha'aretz*, 2 January 2000).

That this type of rhetoric could still sell so many copies at the end of the twentieth century is indeed a victory, but it is certainly no victory of 'the market'. The market is forever a mechanism, and mechanisms can neither win nor lose. The real victors are always real people. Who, then, are the people for whom neoliberalism is such a triumph? What is their secret? How did they manage to pass power into their market hands? Are they new in the game, or maybe what we see here are the same actors in a different guise? The answers to these questions make up the story of Israel's ruling class – how it emerged, consolidated and shaped the history of its society. Their story is the subject of the present chapter.

Transnational Dominant Capital

On the eve of the twenty-first century, power in Israel was best described in two words: absentee ownership. The three principal hallmarks of this ownership

84

were (1) high corporate centralisation and integration, perhaps the highest the country has ever known; (2) increasing transnationalisation; and (3) incessant restructuring of vendible assets. What did this structure look like?

Centralisation

The first feature, as indicated, was high corporate centralisation. At the centre of it all was dominant capital, composed of a handful of giant conglomerates, along with several big but more focused companies, and a large but self-liquidating group of government-owned firms on their way to privatisation. Although the main constituents of this core are well known, its structure can only be described in fairly general terms. One reason is that many of its firms were linked through complex and often circular cross-ownership ties, and even when these ties were conceptually straightforward, their origins were often concealed by long ownership chains leading to offshore shell companies. The other reason is that the core was changing so rapidly, that even the most accurate description quickly became outdated. The general contours of the core, though, were clear enough, and are illustrated in Tables 3.1 and 3.2.

Table 3.1 lists the principal domestic holdings of the country's five biggest private groups and the government. Of these, the largest in terms of market capitalisation was Israel Discount Bankholdings (IDB), controlled by the Recanati family, along with the Carasso family, Goldman Sachs and William Davidson. In March 1999, IDB had a net market value of nearly $11 billion, equivalent to roughly 22 per cent of the entire Tel Aviv Stock Market. The group had majority and minority stakes in hundreds of companies spanning the entire business spectrum, from banking, through finance, to high technology, industry, real estate, retail, services and transportation. The second largest group, valued at $3.5 billion (7.4 per cent of the market), was the Ofer group, owned by Ofer brothers. Its holdings included numerous companies in banking, finance, raw materials, high technology, real estate and transportation. The Ofers also had a minority stake in the third largest group, Koor, whose principal owners were the Bronfman and Kolber families, along with the Arison, Nechama and Dankner families, as well as Goldman Sachs (through Bank Hapoalim). Koor, whose value of $2.8 billion accounted for close to 6 per cent of the market, was more focused than the previous two groups, with holdings primarily in high technology, raw materials and real estate. The Dankner group, owned by the Dankner family, ranked fourth, with a value of $1.2 billion (2.6 per cent of the market). It had partial control of Bank Hapoalim, as well as stakes in high technology, chemicals, energy and real estate. It also had a share, through its ownership in Bank Hapoalim, of Koor and Clal (the latter being part of the IDB empire). The fifth ranking group, Arison Holdings, was owned by the Arison and Nechama families, with a value of $1.1 billion (2.3 per cent of the market). Its main assets were Bank Hapoalim (which gave it stakes in

Table 3.1   Israel's Dominant Capital, circa 1999

Group (controlling family/ interest)	MCAP* $ billion (1999)	Principal Holdings (majority and minority control)
Israel Discount Bankholdings (IDB) Recanati family Carasso family Goldman Sachs William Davidson	10.8	*Banking*: Discount Bank, Discount Mortgage Bank, Industrial Development Bank, Mercantile Discount Bank *Finance*: Ilanot-Batucha, Albar-Mimunit, Visa, Y.L.R. Capital Markets *High technology*: Barak, Celcom, ECI Telecom, Elbit, Elron, Gilat, Liraz, Nice, R.D.C. Rafael Development, Scitex, Telad, Tevel, United Pan European Communications *Industry*: American Israel Paper Mills, Gadot Chemical, Granit Hacarmel, Kitan, Klil, Nesher, Ormat, Polgat, Sonol, Tambour *Provident funds*: Tamar *Real estate*: Azorim, Property and Building Corp *Retail, services & transportation*: Clal Insurance, Clal Tours, El-Yam Ships, Supersol, Overseas Shipholding Group, Zannex Securities
Ofer Ofer family	3.5	*Banking*: Bank Adanim, Bank Tefahot, United Mizrahi Bank *Finance*: Melisron, Almog Beach *High technology*: Tower Semiconductors *Industry*: Dead Sea Bromine, Dead Sea Periclase, Dead Sea Works, ICL-Israel Chemical, Koor Industries, Ofer Development, Oil Refineries, Omni, Priclass *Provident funds*: H.L. Finance *Real estate*: Elram, Ofer Development *Retail, services & transportation*: Judea Hotels, Ofer Trading, Royal Caribbean, Tanker Pacific Shipmanagement, Zim Lines, Zodiac *Cross-holdings*: Koor
Koor Bronfman family Kolber family Bank Hapoalim	2.8	*High technology*: ECI Telecom, Tadiran, Telrad Machteshim-Agan, Mash'av, Middle East Tubes, United Steel Mills *Real estate*: Koor Properties *Retail, services & transportation*: Knafaim, Sheraton Moriah
Dankner Group Dankner family	1.2	*Banking*: Bank Hapoalim *High technology*: Matav *Industry*: Carmel Chemicals, Dor Chemicals, Dor Energy, Israel Salt Industries *Real estate*: Dankner Investment *Cross-holdings*: Koor, Clal (IDB)
Arison Holdings Arison family Nechama family	1.1	*Banking*: Bank Hapoalim *High technology*: Biomedical, El-Ar, Eurocom, Euronet Gold, Hamlet, Medsim, Mirabilis, Partner, Polaris, Steps, V-CON *Real estate*: Herouth, Housing and Construction Holdings (Shikun Ubinui), Lime and Stone, Orbond, Or-Yam, Secom, Shikun Ovdim, Solel Boneh *Cross-holdings*: Clal (IDB), Koor
Israeli Government	7.2	*Banking*: Bank Hapoalim, Bank Igud, Bank Leumi, Discount Bank, Industrial Development Bank *High technology*: Bezeq, Israeli Aircraft Industry *Industry*: Ashot, RAFAEL, Israeli Military Industries, Oil Refineries *Retail, services & transportation*: Coal Supply Company, El-Al, Israel Electric Corporation, Mekorot, Shekem

* Market capitalisation comprises only domestic holdings, and includes the total value of majority holdings (including what is held by minority owners and the public) and the pro-rated value of minority holdings.

SOURCE: Authors' archive; Dun & Bradstreet Israel, *Israel's Largest Enterprises 1999*; Standard & Poor's *Israel's Leading Public Companies* (http://www.standardpoor.co.il/bankhapoalim/); the U.S. Securities and Exchange Commission (http://www.sec.gov/); Moody's (Online); and Abramov and Zuk (1999).

Koor and IDB), 'high-technology' companies, and a wide array of real estate and construction firms.

The sixth group in Table 3.1 is the government, with holdings in many sectors, including banking, telecommunication, military production, energy, infrastructure and transportation. The government's stake in publicly traded companies was valued at $7.2 billion, or 14.8 per cent of the market (some of the companies listed in the table were not publicly traded when these lines were written). Although the value of its holdings ranked the government second only to IDB, we placed it at the end of the list since it operated mostly as a 'night watchman', with many of its assets destined for privatisation.

Of the 652 companies listed on the Tel Aviv Stock Exchange in March 1999, 82 were wholly or partly controlled by these five private groups (92 with the government). The relative value of these companies, however, was far larger than their relative number; together, they accounted for as much as 41 per cent of the market's overall capitalisation (55 per cent with the government). The remaining half of the market was also highly concentrated. According to analysis published by the Tel Aviv Stock Exchange, the next five groups, following the top five and the government, accounted for another 7 per cent of the market (Abramov and Zuk 1999). These groups included the Fishman family (1.8 per cent of market capitalisation); Migdal, owned by the Italian Generali group (1.6 per cent); the Tshuva family (1.3 per cent); Elco, owned by the Zelkind family (1.3 per cent); and the Land Development Company (Hachsharat Hayishuv), controlled by Nimrodi (1 per cent). Altogether, 34 ownership groups controlled up to 77 per cent of the market value, with much of the rest held by several large firms – specifically Teva (widely held, mainly by U.S. investors), Blue Square (a cooperative on its way to privatisation), Osem (controlled by Nestlé and the Propper family), Elite (owned by the Federman family), Harel Investment, Delta, and Agis.

Table 3.2 provides selected summary indicators on the aggregate power of the five largest groups and the government. Data include the number of firms controlled (through majority or minority stakes), along with their combined sales, net profit, and employees, and are broken down by different corporate segments. (Note that the different segments are not mutually exclusive – for instance, conglomerates have stakes in industrial or service companies, while some companies listed abroad are included in other segments.) The picture, however cursory, is highly revealing. It shows that, together, these groups dominated much of the conglomerate, banking, finance and industrial segments. Their stranglehold over the service sector appeared somewhat looser, but this is only because their power here was shared with several large retailers, such as Tnuva and Blue Square. An increasing number of Israeli companies, primarily in the 'high-technology' sector, are listed in the United States and Europe. Yet, as the bottom row of Table 3.2 shows, here too, despite the much bigger pool of investors, the presence of the leading Israeli groups is significant.

Table 3.2   Control Indicators by the Five Largest Groups and the Government, 1998

SEGMENTS (No. of top firms)	NUMBER (% of segment)		SALES ($BN) (% of segment)		NET PROFIT ($M) (% of segment)		EMPLOYEES (% of segment)	
	Top 5	Top 5 & Gov't	Top 5	Top 5 & Gov't	Top 5	Top 5 & Gov't	Top 5	Top 5 & Gov't
Conglomerates (17)	12	13	9.2	9.5	619	621		
	(70%)	(76%)	(79%)	(82%)	(89%)	(90%)		
Commercial banks (19)	10	13			375	609	26,103	39,876
	(53%)	(68%)			(56%)	(91%)	(60%)	(92%)
Mortgage banks (9)	3	4					942	1,295
	(33%)	(44%)					(48%)	(66%)
Provident funds (10)	6	10						
	(60%)	(100%)						
Industrial (100)	30	31	11.4	15.4	226	301	56,320	86,495
	(30%)	(31%)	(38%)	(52%)	(33%)	(45%)	(32%)	(50%)
Service (100)	17	22	5.4	8.9	47	278	16,407	30,742
	(17%)	(22%)	(22%)	(36%)	(12%)	(70%)	(15%)	(29%)
Listed abroad (94)	23	23	8.1	8.1	157	157		
	(24%)	(24%)	(51.9%)	(51.9%)	(23%)	(23%)		

NOTE: The Top 5 groups comprise IDB, Ofer, Koor, Dankner, and Arison. All companies under direct or partial ownership of the Top 5 and/or the government are counted, and their data are measured in total, rather than on a pro-rated equity basis. Companies under the joint control of more than one of the Top 5 and the government are counted once. Profit data are based on incomplete reporting and should be interpreted as rough estimates. Analysis for each segment is focused on the largest firms, whose number is indicated in parentheses in the first column. Segments are not mutually exclusive.

SOURCE: Computations by the authors bases on data from Dun & Bradstreet Israel, *Israel's Largest Enterprises 1999*; K. Abramov and Y. Zuk (1999); *Standard & Poor's Israel's Leading Public Companies* (http://www.standardpoor.co.il/bankhapoalim/); the U.S. Securities and Exchange Commission (http://www.sec.gov/); authors' archive.

Transnationalisation

The second hallmark of the Israeli power structure was its increasing transnationalisation. By 1998, foreign ownership had risen to 14.4 per cent of the Tel Aviv market, up from 3 per cent only five years earlier (Bank of Israel. Monetary Department 1998: Table 3-4, p. 85). In less than a decade, Israel has been invaded by hordes of foreign investors, both private and institutional, conservative and adventurous, respectable and criminal, who were all lured by the prospects of peace and the smell of peace dividends. This invasion – which Israel's dominant capital welcomed wholeheartedly – has fundamentally altered the nature of power.

To begin with, many of Israel's leading domestic firms were by now controlled, partly or wholly, by foreigners. At the end of the century, the list included, with foreign owners/partners in parentheses, companies such as Barak (Sprint, Deutsche Telekom and France's Télécom), Cellcom (Bell South), Class Data, InfoGear and Scoia Fund (Cisco), Coca Cola (Coca Cola), Cromatis and

Elron (Lucent), FIBI (Safra family), Dead Sea Magnesium (Volkswagen), Gilat (General Electric and Microsoft), Golden Lines (the Italian state-owned Stet and Southwestern Bell), Indigo, Geotek and Scitex (George Soros), Intel Israel (Intel), Jerusalem Economic Corporation (Bear Stern), Libit (Texas Instruments), Medinol (Boston Scientific), Biosense (Johnson & Johnson), Mirabilis (AOL-Time Warner), NDS (NewsCorp), Nicecom (3COM), Orbotech and Opal (Applied Materials), Ornet (Siemens), Osem (Nestlé), Partner (Hutchison Whampoa), Paz (the Liberman family from Australia) and Telrad (Nortel). In addition to these direct foreign holdings, foreigners have also increased their indirect ownership, mainly through diversified portfolio investments by pension, mutual and hedge funds.

Some of the most rapidly growing Israeli firms – primarily in high technology – were listed abroad, mainly in New York, and were held almost entirely by foreigners. The most noted of these were the pharmaceutical giant Teva (with 1999 sales of $1.2 billion, net income of $134 million and a market capitalisation in excess of $3.5 billion); Comverse, the world's leading supplier of cellular voice cells and the first Israeli-based company to make it to the Standard & Poor's 500 index (with $850 million in sales, $150 in net income and a market capitalisation of over $10 billion); the cellular billing company Amdocs (with $620 million in sales, $97 million in net income and a market capitalisation of over $7 billion); and Check Point Software, inventor of the 'Firewall' (with 1999 sales of $215 million, net income of $92 million and a market capitalisation in excess of $4.5 billion) (data in this section from corporate reports and Moody's).

The most important aspect of this process, however, was the transnationalisation of dominant capital itself. By the late 1990s, two of the five top groups – Arison and Koor – were effectively in foreign hands. Arison Investment was founded by the late Ted Arison, an Israeli emigrant who made his fortune in the leisure business, through his 47 per cent controlling share in Carnival Cruise, the world's largest ocean leisure firm (1999 sales of $3.5 billion, net income of $992 million and market capitalisation of $27 billion). Koor Industries was controlled by Charles Bronfman and his partner Jonathan Kolber. Until 1999, the former was co-chairman and owner (9.5 per cent) of Seagram, a global beverage, entertainment and investment giant, with sales of $15.3 billion and market value of $16 billion. In 2000, Seagram merged with France's Vivendi in a $34 billion share swap, creating a global entertainment and infrastructure giant with sales in excess of $53 billion, in which Charles Bronfman now had an equity stake of over 3 per cent. Compared to the Bronfmans, Kolbers and Arisons, the Ofer brothers, owners of Israel's second largest group, look like true 'sabras', but the appearance is deceiving. They too made their fortune abroad, and in no other than the leisure industry. As it turns out, their principal asset was a 20 per cent stake in Royal Caribbean Cruises, another leisure giant with 1999 sales of $2.6 billion, net income of $384 million and market value of $9.1 billion. The Ofers shared their ownership in Royal

Caribbean with Pritzker, a former Israeli contractor who now owned the Hyatt chain, and with Wilhelmsen, a Norwegian shipping firm. In 1997, the Ofers and the Arisons competed over the purchase of a third leisure company, Celebrity Cruises, which the Ofers eventually won and merged into their Royal Caribbean. The sellers of Celebrity were no other than the Recanati family, owners of IDB, who held 50 per cent of Celebrity's shares through their Overseas Shipholding subsidiary. (And perhaps this is how it was destined to be. After all, capitalism got its first global push in the sixteenth century with the plundering of Caribbean gold, while the United States reached its global economic peak with a bootlegger family in the White House; so it seems only fitting for Israeli transnationalisation to be led by heirs of a famous alcohol smuggler and by cruise ship owners registered in the Caribbean....) Like the Ofers, the Recanatis themselves were no foreigners, having immigrated to Palestine from Greece in 1936. However, over the years, the family not only expanded its foreign business, but also aligned itself with an impressive battery of overseas partners. By the end of the century, these included Goldman Sachs and William Davidson (who had direct stakes in IDB), Bell South and the Safra family (partners in Cellcom), General Electric and Microsoft (partner in Gilat Satellite and General Engineers), Kimberly Clark (in American Israeli Paper Mills), Praxair (Maxima), International Paper and George Soros (Scitex), Shamrock Holdings (Tel-Ad), TCI and UPC (Tevel), and Prudential Securities (YLR), to name only a few (data in this section are from company reports, the U.S. Securities and Exchange Commission, Moody's, and newspaper clippings).

The other facet in the transnationalisation of ownership was outward foreign investment by Israeli dominant capital. Over the past decade, direct outflows have risen to over 1 per cent of GDP, from virtually nothing in the 1980s, with funds primarily earmarked for foreign acquisitions. The forerunner in this movement was Koor, followed closely by the other major groups.

Restructuring

Together, the two processes of centralisation and transnationalisation made the ownership scene dynamic to an extent never seen before in Israel. And indeed, incessant restructuring was now the third hallmark of the Israeli power structure. What was until a decade ago a very rigid structure, has turned into one of permanent flux. For instance, during the first 50 years of its existence, Koor was under the joint ownership of the Histadrut and Bank Hapoalim. And then, in a matter of ten years, the company was sold and bought several times, first to Shamrock, an investment arm of the Disney family, who then sold it to Bronfman and Kolber, who in turn dismembered it by selling off unwanted assets and buying new ones. Similarly, state assets, once privatised, began rotating between the different actors. The Israel Corporation and Israel Chemical Industries, for instance, were sold to one of Israel's biggest foreign investors, Saul Eisenberg. When Eisenberg died in 1997, his family resold the companies to the Ofer brothers, who then proceeded to chop it to pieces, keeping the parts they liked and selling those they didn't. The investment company Clal, which since its inception in 1962 was held jointly by IDB, Bank Leumi and Bank Hapoalim, was taken over by IDB and merged into its operation through massive reorganisation. All in all, the ownership structure remains as concentrated, complicated and interlinked as before; but now it was also constantly changing.

Evidently, then, Israel has changed a great deal, but the nature of this change had little to do with the market fairy tale of Jacob Frenkel and the like. The rigid power of state capitalism is certainly gone, but replacing it we see emerging the even more powerful hand of global capital. What caused this shift? How did a small colonial society turn transnational? Was this a historical coincidence? A consequence of narrow-sighted politicians and a spineless, indifferent public? Or perhaps there is logic to it after all – not inevitable as Marx's 'laws of motion', but nonetheless clear in its pattern? Let us then start at the beginning.

The Pre-Independence Sectors

Writers on the subject usually describe the Jewish settlement in Palestine of the 1920s in terms of three pluralistic sectors, separated along political and ideological lines: the 'national sector', comprising a network of financial organisations established since the turn of the century by German and British Zionists; the 'Histadrut sector', which combined the various political and economic organisations of the labour movement; and the private, or 'civil sector', a relatively loose political alliance made of citriculturists, importers, merchants, landlords and city mayors. Like other colonial societies of the time, Palestine also had its share of foreign investors and multinational subsidiaries operating alongside and in cooperation with domestic groups. Finally, until Independence in 1948, the whole process was embedded in a vibrant Palestinian society which was itself starting to industrialise (Gozansky 1986).

The first to emerge was the national sector. The decline of the Ottoman Empire at the turn of the century had spurred various colonial companies, usually under the auspices of European governments, into investing in Middle Eastern banking, railroads, agriculture and the like. Riding this wave, Jewish organisations in Great Britain and Germany had tried to channel into Palestine capital from Europe and America, along with Jewish labour seeking to escape Europe's unemployment and pogroms. One of these organisations was the Jewish Colonial Trust, registered in London in 1889. A subsidiary of the Trust, the Anglo-Palestine Company, or APC, which would later become Bank Leumi, had been specifically set up in 1902 in order to finance 'land redemption' for

Jewish settlement.[1] Another investment group, the Palestine Land Development Company (Hachsharat Hayishuv), was established in 1908. The company, headed by Arthur Ruppin, tried to reproduce in Palestine an East Prussian model of agricultural plantations manned by propertyless peasants. Perhaps the most famous undertaking of this type was Edmund Rothschild's £5 million vineyard investment on the coastal plain. Until the British conquest of 1918, however, most of these attempts failed, usually for lack of immigrants, who generally preferred the New World to the Holy Land. And yet, while the ventures themselves faltered, their pattern of mixing business with Zionism was clearly a winner. The Jewish Foundation Fund, for example, which would later become the financial arm of the Jewish Agency, was founded in 1921 by venture capitalists, while its partner in many an undertaking, the Palestine Economic Company (PEC), was similarly set up by American and Canadian investors headed by U.S. Supreme Court Justice Louis Brandeis. Patriotism and nationalism had proven profitable around the world, and their Zionist version was scarcely an exception.

The twin engines of growth during that period were Jewish capital inflow and British infrastructure spending. Naturally, many groups were fighting for a share of the spoils, and, initially, their struggles were mostly political. The reason was threefold. First, the business infrastructure was undeveloped; accumulation was relatively slow and disjoined, most business units were tiny, capital was hardly vendible, and absentee ownership had yet to emerge. Second, the means of coercion and violence were monopolised by the British Empire. And, finally, many of the more important social formations, such as agriculture cooperatives, credit unions, city councils, and interest groups, were voluntary. In this loose context, formal politics was by far the best vehicle for action, and, indeed, the important organisations of the time were initially set up as pressure groups.

The first to grasp the historical opportunity were activists of two small political parties: Hapoel Hatzaier (The Young Worker) headed by Haim Arlosoroff, and Ahdut Ha'avodah (Unity of Labour) headed by David Ben-Gurion and Berl Katznelson. These politicians expected British recognition of Palestine as a Jewish homeland to attract masses of impoverished East European Jews. They also realised that whoever controlled this immigration may well control the political destiny of the country. This realisation led to the establishment in 1920 of a superstructure labour organisation, the Histadrut, and in 1921, of its economic arm, Hevrat Ovdim (Workers' Company). Ben-Gurion was quite explicit about his intentions: 'Without a single, general authority combining all the partial bodies of the working class', he declared, 'we cannot

1   On the surface, the redemption seemed to run smoothly since most of the lands belonged to absentee Arab owners. However, the acquired properties were almost never empty, which meant that their direct cultivators, the peasants who lived and worked on them for centuries, had to 'relocate'. This is how the 'Palestinian Problem' started (Laqueur 1972: Ch. 5).

succeed.... The organisational and political unity [of the Histadrut] must be complemented by economic amalgamation. We must establish "Hevrat Ovdim" that will consolidate all rural and urban aspects of workers' production and supplies for the purpose of self-sufficiency of the entire working class' (Ben-Gurion 1933: 129). The resulting arrangement combined large-scale business enterprise with social care-taking, providing its workers' cradle-to-grave needs – from jobs, to transportation, to housing, credit, education, and cultural activities (Arlosoroff 1934: Vol. IV). As part of this grand scheme, the Histadrut then moved to establish Bank Hapoalim (Workers' Bank) in 1921, the construction company Solel Boneh (Office for Public Works) in 1923, and the insurance company Hasneh in 1924; in addition, it began integrating the various activities of the Kibbutzim and cooperative townships into a single national network.

The key to these endeavours was exclusion – and, if that didn't work, then co-optation and takeover. Ben-Gurion, for example, fought nail and tooth, often in coalition with employers, against competing labour organisations such as Jabotinsky's National Workers Federation (Histadrut Ha'ovdim Hale'umiym), in order to retain his monopoly over the labour force. He also pushed for relentless green-field expansion in both production and politics, usually with total disregard to profit, just to keep competitors at bay. In this sense, the 1930 merger between the political parties Hapoel Hatzeir and Ahdut Ha'avoda into MAPAI was largely a predatory move, designed to both ward off contenders in the labour market, as well as to set the stage for taking over the Jewish Agency itself. This constant need to overcome the strong centrifugal forces, inherent in any pluralistic structure, serves to explain the centralised-hierarchical world view of MAPAI and the Histadrut, as well as their legacy of intrigue, coercion, financial strangling, defamation and slander.

Many plantation owners, bankers, industrialists, traders, landlords and contractors were alarmed by these strong-hand tactics, and responded by forming their own 'civic' organisations and institutions. Part of their concern was the Histadrut's attempt to monopolise the labour force, and replace docile Arabs with more expensive Jewish workers (the so-called 'conquest of Hebrew work'). Their other main worry was getting a 'fair share' of the capital inflow and British contracts. And, indeed, many of their organisations – such as the Association of Industrialists and Employers in Tel-Aviv Jaffa (1921), the Farmers' Association (1922), and the General Association of Merchants and the Middle Class (1925) – were set up as pressure groups largely for that purpose.

During the 1920s, the national, Histadrut and civil sectors were engaged in heroic 'ideological struggles' over who 'contributed' the most to the Zionist cause. Much of their 'class' rhetoric, however, was imported wholesale from Russia and Europe, with their hyperinflation, unemployment and severe social crises. The situation in Palestine was completely different – so much so, that Ben-Gurion, a socialist, had this to say to his friend Krinitzi, a businessman and mayor in the civil sector: 'The capitalists must understand that their own interest requires dealing with an organised and responsible Histadrut and not with private individuals.... Only this will bring anarchy to an end' (Tevet 1980: 302). And, indeed, soon enough, and despite lingering squabbles, the sectoral elites started to cooperate. The most important arrangement was the 'package deal' between the Jewish agency and the Histadrut, in which the former supplied the foreign capital while the latter imported, organised and disciplined the labour force. This broad understanding, perhaps more than anything, helped give rise to a 'New Class' in the national and Histadrut sectors, a bureau-cratic cadre, which together with the local bourgeoisie and foreign investors, ruled Israel's 'mixed economy' of private and public enterprise.[2]

Collaboration between the different sectorial elites increased during the 1930s. Joint supervision of various 'national' organisations, participation in the distribution of inflowing capital, common negotiations with the British authorities, and the coordination of different pre-state militias, all contributed to mutual recognition and growing economic and political ties. These were boom times in Palestine. The global depression and the rise of fascism in Europe sent capital and people fleeing to safer havens. Whereas capital in the core countries was often decumulating, rates of return in the 'emerging market' of Palestine reached 15 per cent, attracting hordes of foreign institutional investors and tens of thousands of Jewish immigrants (profitability estimate from Giladi 1973: 79). The financial sector developed in leaps and bounds, and by 1936 had about 100 credit unions and 70 banks, including the newly founded Discount Bank, later to become Israel's largest holding group. The expansion was particularly beneficial for the pro-British, right-wing citriculturists, such as Rokakh (Mayor of Tel Aviv), Sapir (Mayor of Petah Tikva), the Dankners (future owners of Bank Hapoalim) and Ben Ami (mayor of Natanya and future owner of *Ma'ariv*). For a while, this contributed to inter-elite friction, since the high profit margins of these citriculturists made them independent of Jewish capital inflow, thereby strengthening their opposition to the Histadrut.[3] The conflict, however, was greatly mitigated by the economic crisis of 1937. The

2   The concept 'New Class' was coined by Milovan Djilas to denote the emergence of a non-capitalist ruling class in the Soviet bloc. '[A]s the new class becomes stronger and attains a more perceptible physiognomy', he wrote, 'the role of the party diminishes. The core and the basis of the new class is created in the party and at its top, as well as in the state political organs. The once live, compact party, full of initiative, is dis-appearing to become transformed into the traditional oligarchy of the new class....' (Djilas 1957: 40). By monopolising violence, ideology and communication, argued Djilas, this new class controlled the surplus pretty much like the classical bourgeoisie, using it for its own luxury consumption, as well as for investment and institution-alised waste, including military build-ups. The main difference was that here the whole thing was done in the name of the 'working class'. This certainly created confusion, but the evidence of power was nonetheless revealed through growing income inequality. According to Djilas, by the 1950s, a mere decade after the 'liberation' from capitalism, a manager of a Yugoslav regional committee already earned 25 times the income of an average worker.
3   On the right-wing world view and politics of the citriculturists during the 1930s, see the memoirs of Ileen (1985).

Mediterranean citrus market collapsed in the wake of Italy's invasion of Ethiopia, and the local citrus growers, battered by a deep recession, were more or less forced to accept the emergent political coalition headed by MAPAI, along with its associated pattern of allocation and distribution. Solidarity among the different elites was further boosted by the Arab Revolt of 1939, which heightened the 'national' conflict between Palestinians and Jews, as well as between the latter and the British.

The Second World War brought additional concentration and consolidation. Reversing their earlier colonial policy of balanced budget and *laissez-faire*, the British began to spend heavily and intervene deeply in the economy. Those close to the process found it difficult not to make money. Solel Boneh, for instance, quickly became the largest company in the Middle East. Recalls Hillel Dan, a company manager:

> No matter how much glass we wanted to produce and sell, the army needed more. The local market was irrelevant. The British Army was the main customer. We let the military authorities buy directly at the factory gate. We set up four marketing companies abroad, in partnership with local merchants. We sold these companies a squared foot of glass for 3.5 Liras. The companies sold it for 7.... In less than three years we recovered our investment plus a net profit of 75 thousands Liras. (Dan 1963: 236–7)

Another winner was the Central Company for Trade and Investment (later absorbed by Clal). The company merged the country's leading suppliers of construction materials, who realised that one firm was more effective than loose cooperation through pools and trusts, and that in this way they could properly split the market with Solel Boneh. For these and similar groups, such as Hamashbir (wholesaler), Nesher (cement), APC, and the Discount Bank (whose equity according to its owner rose tenfold during the war), the boom spelled massive differential accumulation, working through both green-field and takeover (Recanati 1984: 38–9).

The process also helped transform the very nature of power. First, the leading firms grew less dependent on their parent political organisations, while cooperating more closely among themselves – often in gross violation of the 'class divide'.[4] Second, the sectors themselves became more concentrated. The left-leaning segments of the labour movement were undermined by the political split between Mapam and Ahdut Ha'avoda; the cooperative system, which flourished during the 1930s, was beginning to decline; and income disparity between the Histadrut management and workers was widening. Similarly in the

---

4 One of the more sensational collaborations was the joint acquisition of Nesher, the region's largest cement factory, by Solel Boneh of the Histadrut on the one hand, and the Central Company for Trade and Investment from the civil sector on the other. Today, such a deal would scarcely raise an eyebrow, but during the 1940s, when the business ethos was still undeveloped, it was vehemently attacked by newspapers and politicians from both sides of the spectrum.

civil sector, the petty bourgeoisie, especially landlords hit by rent control during the war, was weakened relative to the larger corporate owners. This, together with the rising power of the military militias toward the 1948 conflict, signalled the coming end of the 'mixed economy' and the beginning of state capitalism.

The State Cocoon

The first few years of the state proved crucial. Many of the key institutions, allocation patterns, and dominant ideologies, which for most Israelis today seem 'natural' and unquestionable, were formed during those fateful years, roughly between the *Tsena* (Austerity) of 1949–51, and the beginning of the German Holocaust restitution payments in 1955. The subsequent structure of power, the division between rulers and ruled, the regional conflict and dependency on Western superpowers, all bear the mark of this critical historical moment. On the surface, the state reigned supreme. The MAPAI government controlled the process of capital formation, allocated credit, determined prices, set exchange rates, regulated foreign trade and directed industrial development. However, this very process also set in motion its own negation, so to speak, by planting the seeds from which dominant capital was subsequently to emerge. In this sense, the state acted as a cocoon for differential accumulation. The budding corporate conglomerates were initially employed as national 'agents' for various Zionist projects. Eventually, though, their increasing autonomy helped them not only shed off their statist shell, but also change the very nature of the state from which they had evolved. Most importantly, there was never a clear separation between 'politics' and 'economics' in this process. As we shall see, state and capital, or sovereignty and ownership, did not stand *against* each other, but rather developed as part of a single power process: the evolution of Israel's ruling class.

The overall context was clearly one of breadth. Following the annexation of Arab lands conquered in the 1948 War, the country's territory increased by over a third, green-field investment advanced in leaps and bounds, and the population increased threefold within the first decade. Economists like to think of these items as land, capital and labour – 'factors of production' whose combination generates growth and prosperity. For the ruling class of Israel, though, they were mostly levers of power, and the decisions as to who would control these levers, how, and to what ends, were made in the first few years of the state.

Land

Very little is known about the distribution of Palestinian land and property. The basic background is as follows. The 1949 truce agreement had Israel annex close to 6,000 square kilometres captured in the fighting. About 700,000

Palestinians who lived on those lands were deported or escaped, leaving behind them cultivated fields, livestock, houses, businesses and industrial equipment. The UN Commission for Refugees estimated the value of this property at about $330 million.[5] Assuming a 3 per cent real rate of return and taking into account U.S. dollar inflation, this would amount to over $10 billion in today's prices.

Who got this property? As is often the case with such instances of 'primitive accumulation', nobody seems to know. Moshe Sharet, Israel's first Foreign Minister, hoped to resolve the Arab–Israeli conflict, perhaps with some compensation and partial resettlement of Palestinian refugees. To prepare for this he instructed David Horowitz, then general director of the Finance Ministry, to draft a report estimating the abandoned properties of the refugees (Sharet 1978: 386). And indeed, such a report is listed in the government archive, as well as in the foreign ministry. The actual document, however, has conveniently disappeared. Unlike the case of Brazil, whose government set its entire slavery archive on fire after slavery was abolished, here there was no need for big drama. One little report gone and the entire process of 'initial endowment' goes up in smoke. And yet, as the following cryptic passage from Sharet's diaries suggests, there was clearly order in the chaos:

> Stage A is completed. 1,200,000 dunam were transferred to the Development Authority. Compensation on 300,000 dunam, including the *Wakf*'s, comes to £400,000 for those willing to emigrate.... So far we paid 300,000 Israeli Liras in compensation for 3,500 dunam ... the problem of compensation for 150,000 dunam in the northern Negev and 81,000 dunam and there is no problem [sic].... (Sharet 1978: 481).

Based on evidence from different sources, it seems that the land area held by Keren Kayement (Jewish National Fund) rose to 3.3 million dunam in 1953, up from 900,000 on the eve of the 1948 War. Roughly 1 million dunams of the added Arab land were distributed to Jewish organisations and individuals, helping them double their cultivated area. The lion's share probably went to the kibbutzim, whose holdings rose to 1.3 million dunam (Israel Central Bureau of Statistics, 1953, No. 19; and Sharet 1978: 357, 481, 509). These back-of-the-envelope calculations suggest that redistribution was massive and probably highly differential. And, yet, till this very day there is not even a *single* empirical study, Zionist or post-Zionist, to tell us who got what, when, and how. As C. Wright Mills put it: 'Methodologists! Get to Work!' (Mills 1959: 123).

Capital

The situation regarding the allocation of foreign capital inflow, mostly aid and loans, is not much better. The main reason, again, is official secrecy, although,

---

5 For other details and estimates, see Lustick (1980: Ch. 5) and Segev (1984: 83–91).

admittedly, the general statistical chaos of the time would have made even the best picture partial.[6] What we do know, however, is that capacity formation during the 1950s and early 1960s followed a fairly stable pattern: roughly 50–60 per cent was done by the private sector, 20–25 by the Histadrut and 20–25 per cent by the government (Lubell et al. 1958; and Barkai 1964). Since this investment was financed almost entirely by foreign inflows, and given that both were controlled by the government, it seems reasonable to assume that the inflows were distributed more or less proportionately to capacity formation as done by the sectors.

The process assumed two principal forms. The first, direct method, on which there is no statistical information, was subsidised credit. The arrangement was particularly profitable since the government refused to admit the existence of inflation during those years, charging interest rates often as low as one-tenth of the going black market rate, thereby creating an enormous spread for its fortunate debtors. The other, indirect method worked through the selective handout of exclusive concessions, certificates and licences. In a context of severe foreign currency shortages and tight import-substitution policies, these property rights quickly turned into gold mines for those lucky enough to get them.[7]

Much of this allocation process took place in the Knesset (parliament). Unlike today, when the rhetoric in the legislature is often difficult to sort out (perhaps because the real business has already moved elsewhere), during the 'ideological' era of the early 1950s the battle lines were surprisingly clear. As long as the distribution of abandoned Arab properties, American loans, and government concessions proceeded according to the implicit sectoral key, the house remained calm. But when new property – tangible or otherwise – was up for grabs, the 'class struggle' quickly flared up.

For instance, when Finance Minister Eliezer Kaplan refused to ratify Solel Boneh's attempt to take over the oil refineries left by the British, the company's representatives were up in arms defending the 'working class' against a government set on enriching capitalist fat cats. The private sector was of course equally adamant. A typical challenge to Kaplan from a General Zionists member: 'Private merchants have been avoiding contacts with Germany. Only Solel Boneh is buying complete factories there, moving them to Israel, sometimes guised as immigrant properties....' (*The Knesset Record 1* 1949, Vol.

---

6 For instance, according to Don Patinikin who constructed national account estimates for the first decade, the total amount of government loans and grants in 1952–53 exceeded the gross fixed investment by their recipients (Patinikin 1965: 80).
7 Particularly popular were bank charters. In this way, the Union Bank was given to Willie Cohen, a British millionaire associated with MAPAI; Hapoel Hamizrahi Bank was handed as a coalition dowry to the National Religious Party; the Industrial Bank was given to industrialists linked to the Liberal Party; the Export Bank to British millionaires Wolfson and Klor and to the Meir brothers; the Foreign Trade Bank to owners of the Central Company for Trade and Investment associated with the General Zionists Party; General Bank to Baron Edmund de Rothschild; and so on and on.

III: 450). On another occasion, the same speaker charged that 90 per cent of the abandoned Palestinian property was going to MAPAI members: 'The custodian does with these enemy properties as he sees fit, for the good of his own party and friends ... the whole country is becoming one politburo....' (p. 40). Ideology was also quickly invoked upon suspicion of any deviation from pre-set distributional patterns. For instance, at one point Hamashbir, the symbol of 'Bolshevism' in the eyes of the civil sector, broke ranks by leaving the Trade Association through which it cooperated with private merchants since the British Mandate. In theory, this should have increased competition, and yet instead of extending his blessing, Israel Rokakh of the General Zionists jumped to denounce the plot: 'This bizarre move by Hamasbir symbolizes the sorry state of affairs in which one sector is preferred over another....' Dov Yossef, the Minister of Rationing, had to calm him down, assuring him that there would be no discrimination in import licences and that 'free trade' would continue getting its fair share (p. 1023). The checks and balances between the different sectors were often less than subtle:

– Abba Khushi [Mayor of Haifa]: The Jewish Agency is the largest importer of building materials. It gives these to the kibbutzim in lieu of a budget, and they sell them on the black market. We have evidence regarding twenty one cases....
– Dov Yossef [Minister of Rationing]: The owners of Liber as well as those of Z.D. [affiliated with the General Zionists] are already on trial. Another file was opened against Elite [close to Herut].
– Ben-Gurion [Prime Minister]: How could they deal in the black market? Aren't they millionaires?
– Abba Khushi: They made their fortune from such activity already during the time of the English....
– Ben-Gurion: Can Mr. Liber be fined 20,000 Liras?

(cited in Segev 1984: 294)

Or a similar exchange between private coffee and tobacco importer Eliyahu Elyashar, and Rationing Minister Dov Yossef:

– Dov Yossef: I have a list of examples how they [the coffee manufactures and merchants] defraud the public....
– Elyashar: We are not talking against this particular regulation.
– Dov Yossef: I know my own people, and I know your specific concern is only for controls which affect you, and that you have no objection to those controls which hurt others....

(*The Knesset Record 1* 1950: 690)

The Herut Party, headed by Menachem Begin, was terrified of being sidestepped in the distribution process. Its representatives anxiously hammered the virtues of 'liberalism', 'civil rights' and 'democracy', particularly regarding the budget and foreign capital, insisting that the legislature rather than the government should run the country, and that allocation be done through 'public committees'. Their greatest hope was that the U.S. administration of the Cold War would refuse to do business with the Bolsheviks from MAPAI; after all, who, better than Begin and Herut, could represent the 'free market' in this part of the world? When the first American loan arrived in 1949, their eyes almost popped: 'How and in what way will the money be distributed between the economic sectors?' demanded Herut member Ben Eliezer. 'What guarantee do we have that it will be properly allocated in the collective sector and how do we know it will go to the private sector? Finally, what guarantee can we give to the "other public" in whose name I have the right to speak ... this public demands full participation ... and just as it didn't give up in other areas, it won't give up in this one....' (*The Knesset Record 1* 1949: 150). The 'other public' he referred to were the immigrant masses who came after 1948 from North Africa and the Middle East. Growing corporate concentration and income inequality left most of them with the short end of the stick, giving Begin, who at one point contemplated leaving politics, the opportunity for a big comeback as the leader of the underdog. And, indeed, as this 'other public' grew from election to election, the allocation of foreign capital turned into an effective populist weapon. In one of his public speeches, Begin pointed to a man in the audience: 'Did you receive ten thousand Liras from the government?' he asked. 'No, I didn't', replied the embarrassed man. 'Of course you didn't!' cried the triumphant Begin, 'But the Jewish Agency did! It received in your name tens of thousands of Liras, which it went on spending without giving you your fair share....' (Almogi 1980: 173–4).

Herut politicians and activists, it must be noted, were usually much more fortunate than their voters. Ya'acov Meridor, for instance, for whom Prime Minister Begin would later create a special Economy Ministry, began his illustrious business career during that period, usually with generous financial support from the 'socialist' government and in surprisingly close cooperation with the 'establishment'. Meridor's brother-in-law and Herut's future Controller, Yossef Kremerman, received an import concession, which he of course put to good use, setting up, together with Solel Boneh, Hamashbir and the Saharov family from the General Zionists, a national cartel for pressed wood. Another Herut winner was Reuven Hecht, a gun runner for Begin's para-military Irgun Zva'i Leumi, who got the exclusive certificate for grain imports (Almogi 1980: 137).

Particularly revealing in this regard were the shifting positions of Herut member Avraham Recanati, whose brother, Leon, founded the Discount Bank. Most of the time Recanati fought fiercely for 'free trade' and the 'small citizen', usually against the Histadrut and government intervention. When the first U.S. loan arrived, however, his stance quickly changed. Part of the loan was earmarked for the citrus plantations, and Recanati, whose family had recently taken over the orchard holding group Pardes Syndicate, was suddenly in favour of careful government planning, insisting that the process be centrally controlled by the MAPAI government, and that the money be orderly distributed among the large citriculturists. This preference was not carved in stone, of course. Another part of the loan was put into shipping, a future specialisation of the Discount group, and here Recanati was all for free markets and equal opportunity:

> I approve the loan legislation, on condition that there is one law for all, and that all companies are treated equally with [government owned] Zim Shipping.... Zim has privileges which private companies don't.... This is the same monopolist, imperialist approach we know from other areas, and which pushes us down hill. Only if Mr. Remez [Transportation Minister] has the courage to translate talks into deeds for the benefit of private shipping ... will there be hope for improvement.... (*The Knesset Record 1* 1950: 1084)

Notably, these concerns for a level playing field were brand new. A year earlier, when the Recanatis were still partners with Zim, Ampal and PEC in Israel-America Line, a joint venture with the exclusive right to commercial sea transport between the two countries, they seemed perfectly happy with the status quo. It was only when the partnership broke up, with Discount setting up its own shipping subsidiary El-Yam, that they rediscovered the evils of monopoly.

Labour

The most important prize of the time, however, was the labour force itself. The local elites did not have to read Marx, Veblen or Kuznets to know that without this ultimate commodity there was no economic growth, no profit, no capital and, indeed, nothing to rule over. Ben-Gurion hoped to have this labour supplied by Europe's Jewry, but the Holocaust left his plan in shambles. 'For thousands of years', he lamented, 'we were a nation without a state. Now there is a danger that Israel will be a state without a nation' (cited in Segev 1984: 97). The substitutes were the Jews of North Africa, the Middle East and the remnants of Eastern Europe. Ben-Gurion viewed them with disdain; 'human dust', he called them, comparing them to the black slaves brought to America (p. 157). And yet there was no other choice. As Berl Locker, chairman of the Jewish Agency Executive, told Henry Morgenthau, Roosevelt's Treasury Secretary: 'In our opinion the Sephardi and Yemenite Jews will play a considerable part in building our country. We have to bring them over in order to save them, but also to obtain the human material needed for building the country' (cited in Segev 1984: 172).

Often penniless, culturally fragmented, and without knowledge of Hebrew, the new immigrants were easy prey for manipulation. The magic word was 'immigration absorption', with all key players fighting for a share in the lucrative trade. The most effective, by far, were the various social and cultural organs of MAPAI, although others, including its religious coalition partners and their educational institutions, were in close pursuit. The principal technique of commodifying this Tower of Babel into a standardised, cohesive and obedient labour force was nationalist rhetoric buttressed by common enemies. Indeed, the heating up of the Israeli–Arab conflict during the 1950s was conceived, at least partly, with this very purpose in mind. According to Moshe Sharet, who objected this type of manipulation, Ben-Gurion and his 'officer junta', as he called them, believed that only a permanent state of war could turn the immigrant rubble into a 'new Hebrew man'.[8]

State Capitalism and Corporate Centralisation

The growing contrast between the process of proletarianisation and the consolidation of power is well illustrated by the period's memoirs. For David Horowitz, then general director of the Finance Ministry, 1951 was a very bleak year:

> As the immigration wave rose, the economic problems imposed themselves on us with enormous might, forceful enough to break the backs of those in charge of the immigration absorption. Tens of thousands of people were crowded in the *ma'abarot* [transit camps] and the camps for the ailing. They were grieved by war, tormented with the horrors of the Holocaust and often burdened with large families. Within a short while, 60,000 people, or 10 per cent of the [Jewish] population, were congested into the camps. A similar number stayed in decaying buildings of abandoned Arab towns and villages. The tent and hut camps were damp and cold during the winter and burning hot through the summer. The congestion, filth, and stench exhausted their

---

8 In the mind of Ben-Gurion and the officers, wrote Sharet, 'Israel has no worries, neither international nor economic. The question of peace does not exist. What happens in the region and in the world is irrelevant. In their view, [the state] should see war as the principal and perhaps only means of increasing welfare and keeping the moral tension.... [The retaliatory operations] are the elixir of life.... They help us keep the civil and military tension. Without them, we wouldn't have a fighting nation, and without a fighting regime we are lost.... For this purpose, we can concoct dangers; indeed, we are obliged to. Give us a war with the Arab countries and all our troubles will be over.... Ben-Gurion himself once uttered that we should take an Arab and pay him a million Liras to finally start a war' (Sharet 1978: Vol. III, pp. 1021–2). Unaware of Sharet's yet unpublished *Personal Diaries*, Aronson and Horowitz (1971) speculated in this very spirit, arguing specifically that the latent function of the retaliatory operations were to both help integrate the immigrant masses and increase their support for Ben-Gurion and his government.

strength and shook their souls.... The *ma'abarot* ... turned into sites of filth, desperation and forced idleness. Family ties began to loosen, the foundations of traditional society to collapse.... (Horowitz 1975: 23–4, 110)

Unlike Horowitz, for whom the period was marked by misery and despair, for Harry Recanati, then owner and director of the Discount Bank, it was an epoch of great business success: 'By 1951, I had good reason for being satisfied with the completed task. The bank left to us by our father had prospered and constituted the base for a first-rate Israeli financial group' (Recanati 1984: 71).

How did this rapid expansion come about? What was it that enabled a small financial institution, established only 15 years earlier by tobacco merchants and realtors, to become the country's second largest bank and fifth largest industrial conglomerate? How did the owners of this bank, who had no prior experience in finance or manufacturing, all of a sudden become experts in areas such as rubber, paper, energy, shipping, aluminium, insurance, construction, mortgage banking, citrus orchards and electric equipment? Part of their success was of course due to rapid immigration, which, even in the absence of per capita growth, expanded the overall economy, lifting all boats large and small. But then Discount's own expansion was much faster – indeed, so much faster that, by 1951, the group was already pushing against the national 'envelope': 'I had striven thinking about new initiatives', wrote Recanati, 'but in vain. We already had in our group all the subsidiaries appropriate to our basic operations....' (1984: 71). Clearly, this type of differential accumulation, experienced also by several other groups, could have occurred only with consistent government backing and through increasing reciprocity and cooperation among the different elites.

The dual rise of state capitalism and corporate concentration spelled the end of the pre-Independence sectors. The disintegration was most visible in the civil sector. In the 1951 elections, the Liberal Party, the self-proclaimed representative of the 'the bourgeoisie', still managed to win almost 20 per cent of the votes on its *laissez-faire* ticket of 'let us live in this country'. But this was a dead-cat bounce. By the mid-1950s the big bourgeoisie was already aligning itself with the New Class, its interests rapidly diverging from and often contradicting those of the small economy and rentiers. And once the process was under way, it was only a matter of time before the Liberals were swallowed by Begin's nationalist Herut, and eventually amalgamated into his populist Likud bloc.

The Histadrut sector was also disintegrating, although here, due to MAPAI's stranglehold over the press, the process was harder to detect. The most visible sign was the emergence of multiple struggles within and between its various organisations: Pinchas Lavon and Moshe Sharet against Ben-Gurion; the 'old guard' against the 'young'; the 'bloc' (party machine) against the technocrats; conflicts between MAPAI ministers and the Histadrut's Executive; between the latter and Hevrat Ovdim; and between the cooperative sector and Hevrat Ovdim companies.

Underlying these numerous conflicts was the basic contradiction of the Histadrut: an organisation whose mandate was to *both* accumulate capital and represent workers. Initially, much like in the Soviet Union and Fascist Italy, the contradiction was 'eliminated', first by elevating the workers 'from a class to a nation' (as Ben-Gurion put it), and then unleashing against them an endless battery of enemies – from citriculturists, through Jewish and Arab capitalists, to cheap Arab labour, oriental feudalism, Arab nationalism, British imperialism and Jewish fascism. The real battle lines were further blurred by the high economic growth associated with the breadth regime. Indeed, in this sense Israel was not alone. After the Second World War, many in the West were tempted to believe that the world had entered a new era of prosperity. They gave it various names – the 'end of ideology', the 'end of capitalism', 'post-industrial society', the 'welfare state' – all suggesting a new, conflict-free future. And yet, under the surface, power continued to concentrate.

Within the Histadrut, the contradiction of capital accumulation and labour representation was politicised through the struggle between the Executive and local workers' councils, which until the early 1950s enjoyed considerable autonomy. The Executive's assault was fully backed by the MAPAI government, which nationalised the councils' employment offices, used the central bank to undermine their credit unions with high liquidity requirements, and consistently supported employers in labour disputes. For example, when sailors in the merchant fleet launched a big strike in the early 1950s, Ben-Gurion took the opportunity to show the Americans his true loyalties, sending a large police force to crush the 'communist plot', as he called it. On another occasion, he tried to have the army settle a railroad labour dispute. And when Hans Moler, owner of the largest textile factory Ata, refused to recognise a strike by an elected union, Ben-Gurion took his side, demanding that the workers surrender, just as he did when workers went on strike in Rotenberg's Electricity Company in Haifa. The Labour government also moved to nationalise the workers' education system, effectively eliminating the risk of contending ideologies (the autonomy of religious education, though, was left intact).

The effect of these various assaults was accelerated by the emergence of two parallel stratifications: an ethnic stratification between the Ashkenazi who came from Europe before 1948 and the Middle Eastern Sephardi who arrived after, and another, national stratification between Jewish workers and Palestinian labourers from the territories occupied in 1967 (Rosenfeld and Carmi 1979). The pecking order created by these strata and the associated rise of a 'middle class' sounded the death knell for workers' autonomy in Israel.

By the middle of the 1950s the sectoral structure was gone, replaced by a statist regime whose control over capital formation, nationalism and militarism helped nourish the embryos of dominant capital. Perhaps the best summary of this capital–state symbiosis can be found in the memoirs of Harry Recanati who headed the Discount group during the 1950s. Ousted from his position by a family feud, Harry spent the next quarter of a century outside the country, so his reflections remain authentic, uncorrupted by subsequent events:

> I said to myself that our bank had completely changed. It was no longer the family bank founded by my father. My brothers turned it into an industry, against my will. There were other things that caused me anguish: the flattering advertisement, much of which was created under our own aspiration, the charity organisations and institutions established under our auspices with tax deductible donations, the indiscriminate support of all political parties, left and right, to acquire the friendship of each and every one, and the stock market manoeuvres where share prices were jointly determined in collusion among several banks. Even less cherished was our mangers' friendship with government officials in Jerusalem. I resented their constant striving for government benefits of every kind, all under the pretext of the national interest. Our group was a private business, not a public institution. It was unjust and undignified to bank on government grants for the benefit of shareholders who were mostly affluent capitalists. I was well aware that my views were uncommon in Israel. This was a country where too many financiers and businessmen enjoyed the allocation of public wealth and were continuously nourished by German payments, U.S. grants and donations from the Jewish Diaspora. (Recanati 1984: 92–3)

In Israel, they called this symbiosis the 'Sapir Method', named after MAPAI's Finance Minister of the time. But the principle was hardly original. In 1940s Brazil, for instance, where President Kubitschek called for 'fifty years of development in five', a similar arrangement, the *entreguista* (collaborator) state, was set up, whereby the administration socialised the less profitable investments, supported joint ventures with private enterprise, and subsidised capitalists left and right so as to encourage them to 'take the initiative' (Hewlett 1980). Perhaps this, rather than Keynes's 'animal spirits', is the real secret of 'primitive accumulation'. It is not the setting up of new factories which leads to accumulation, but the setting up of new *power institutions*, and here the government is often crucial. By creating the institutional context with its various allocation rules, social arrangements, ideological conventions and disciplinary means, it helps generate and regulate profit expectations, which can then be discounted into capital.

The Socio-Ideological Basis

The 'Class Struggle'

Growing business and political cooperation among the different elites was accompanied by increasing ideological cohesion, so that, by the 1920s, MAPAI activists and Histadrut managers were already closer in their thinking to the private sector than to the workers they represented. This is not commonly recognised, of course. Subsequent historians did a great job of painting this period as an epic class struggle for the 'conquest of Hebrew work'. How and why this 'conquest' – which essentially consisted of displacing poor Arab day workers by propertyless Jewish immigrants – was a 'class struggle', is a question best left for terminologists. What does seems clear, though, is that the struggle, regardless of its name, was fought largely on the backs of the workers rather than for them.

Take the famous 1927 'battle' for Hebrew work in the orchards of Ness Ziona, a small township on the coastal plane, in which the Histadrut fought the citriculturists to have them employ Jews in lieu of Arabs. In the Zionist mythology, this was a defining moment in the fight between labour and capital. The reality, though, was more of a showoff, a spectacle staged by Ben-Gurion and Katznelson of the Histadrut as part of their effort to gain control over the Jewish Agency. A little earlier, a committee of 'experts' set up by the Agency recommended that the organisation cut its funding to the 'inefficient' Histadrut, in favour of private enterprise and 'free' labour. Unlike today, when most labour leaders would find themselves powerless in the face of similar IMF dictates, Ben-Gurion retaliated swiftly, sending the unemployed of Tel-Aviv to 'conquer' Hebrew work at the orchards of Ness Ziona. The ensuing chaos, in which plenty of heads were cracked open by the British police, put the Jewish Agency's board, many of whom were themselves private investors, in the awkward position of undermining Zionism. They retreated hastily, and the citriculturists were forced to accept the Histadrut as their exclusive supplier of workers (Tevet 1980: 436).

Here, as in many similar 'struggles', the key issue was the interests not of workers, but of their 'leaders'. The political power of MAPAI and the Histadrut was dependent entirely on their ability to control the labour force. Without this monopoly over jobs, social services, culture and ideology, they were irrelevant. In this context, the use of proto-Marxist rhetoric seemed entirely appropriate. Keynesianism was still a generation away and the only broad alternative to liberal capitalism was Soviet-style planning. Like the elites of other developing countries of the time, the Jewish labour movement tended to see international inequality as a consequence of class division, and thought that socialism was the most effective way of organising large-scale immigration for nationalist projects. Their actual policies, though, were often closer to the bureaucratic model of imperial Germany, and indeed, some, such as Arlosoroff who preferred the German sociology of Weber, considered Ben-Gurion's 'class struggle' a relic of history (Arlosoroff 1934: Vol. III, pp. 121–32).

The view of labour as a means rather than end is also evident in attitudes towards wages. In contrast to issues of employment, where 'labour leaders' rarely gave an inch, when it came to income they were surprising flexible, usually downward. Here, their view, much like that of the Jewish Agency and the civil sector, was strictly neoclassical: if wages were to become too high, they warned, demand for workers would fall, immigration would stop, and the entire Zionist project would be put at risk (Ben-Gurion 1933: 198–211). It is therefore hardly surprising that the memoirs of these 'labour leaders' overflow with complaints about the workers' uncontrollable 'greed' and unquenched thirst for various 'raises'.[9] Their own incomes, though, usually didn't fair too badly. For instance, during the 1930s, at the height of the 'class war', Ben-Gurion already earned 80 liras (excluding his generous travel expenses), roughly ten times the income of a full-time orchard worker, and one-third of the profit of a large citriculturist.[10]

In any event, by that time Ben-Gurion had already become a board member of the Jewish Agency, and naturally began emphasising the primacy of statist over labour organisations. Although this ideological shift may seem instrumental, Ben-Gurion himself was probably sincere. After all, since public capital was in his view more efficient than private, it took only a small step to conclude that MAPAI's nationalism had to be the local manifestation of socialism, and that blocking the General Zionists from Jewish Agency funds was therefore part of the class struggle (Ben-Gurion 1933: 26–9; Gorani 1973: 154–64). Whatever the case, the important point is that this ideological shift was itself part of the changing nature of capitalism. The bourgeois model of the late nineteenth century was giving way to the state cocoon of the early twentieth century, and in this context, with accumulation being promoted, yet hidden, by the government's warm embrace, it was only fitting for 'labour leaders' to start viewing themselves as 'statesmen'.

And indeed, upon his promotion to the Jewish Agency Executive, statesman Ben-Gurion began contemplating broader, cosmological theories. One of these was the 'theory of political time'. 'In this game of historical forces', he observed, 'there sometimes arises a big historical chance ... one big moment in a year when the skies open up and you can get all that you wish.... A [political] movement has to have the sense to capture this moment....' (cited in Tevet 1987: 9, 12). 'They [the Arabs]', he continued, 'ignore the internal and external obstacles and the time factor.... Alas and alack if we don't know how to exploit this time in order to grow and fortify....' (cited in Aronson 1994–95: Vol. I, p. 22). In other words, high politics, like modern business, was a matter of 'timing', the ability to seize the moment and beat your competitors in the historical bourse. This ability, or 'vision', was what differentiated a real statesman from an ordinary politician. The only problem was that, much like in business, the historical cycles kept getting shorter and trickier, the competitors were forever breathing down your neck, and unless you constantly came up with 'new and

---

9   See for instance Horowitz (1975: 30–1, 108–9, 247–9), Almogi (1980: 95–6, 149–50, 153–4), Dan (1963, Ch. 35), and Yadlin (1980: Ch. 15).
10 Ben-Gurion's income is based on Tevet (1980: 354–64) and Greenberg (1988). Other incomes are from Giladi (1973: 79, 181, 195), Horowitz (1944: Ch. 4), the *Hebrew Encyclopaedia* (Vol. VI, p. 835); and Gozansky (1986: Chs 4–5).

improved' visions, you in turn became history. And so, during the 1920s, the key was to quickly amalgamate the 'working class' parties in order to capture the labour market and the Jewish Agency before the competitors had a chance to organise. Then, in the 1930s and the 1940s, it was necessary to unite the 'Jewish world' in order to bring in enough immigrants, before Arab nationalists got their act together and stopped the Jewish colonial project dead in its tracks. In the 1950s it was crucial to have the 'Jewish genius' develop nuclear weapons to keep the Arabs states at bay. And in the 1970s and 1980s the call of the day was to import Russian immigrants for the settlements before the end of the Cold War caused Israel to lose its historical tempo. Unfortunately, as the statesmen got older, the race looked more and more like a treadmill, with the epochal jackpot becoming increasingly elusive, and the public, as always, totally oblivious to the grandeur of historical timing.

The Dynasties

Over the years, the business, political and ideological affinity among the elites was fortified by intricate kinship ties. In contrast to popular belief, most of these elites, including the cadres of the New Class, came from affluent bourgeoisie backgrounds, and even those who didn't, such as Ben-Gurion, Ben-Zvi, Peres and Lavon, were commonly of petty bourgeois origin. Only a few were working class. The genealogy of Israel's ruling class rests on a surprisingly small number of family trees – primarily Hacohen, Ruppin, Shertok (later Sharet) and Elyashar – whose thick trunks and multiple branches are intimately interlaced with one another, as well as with many other dominant families. The resulting octopus-like structure makes the spheres of government, business, military, culture and opinion-making so entangled, that 'state' and 'capital' can longer be clearly separated.

One of the key figures of this structure is David Hacohen, a descendant of Russian Jewish wood merchants who became chairman of Solel Bonhe. His father, Mordechai Ben-Hillel Hacohen, was one of Palestine's biggest importers of construction materials, and a founder of Jewish Haifa. His uncle from his mother's side, Shmuel Pevsner, married the daughter of Asher Ginzberg, also known as Ahad Ha'am (in Hebrew, 'one of the people'). Ginzberg himself managed the London office of Russian tea baron Wisotsky, and is considered to be the father of 'cultural Zionism', an alternative to the 'political Zionism' of Herzel and Nordau. David Hacohen, Ginzberg's nephew, grew up among the inner circle:

During that time, I was very close to the Zionist high echelon in London. There were the family ties with Ahad Ha'am, the personal contacts in his London home and in the Jewish movement offices with Dr. Chaim Weitzman and Nahum Sokolow, and with the entire leadership of the Jewish movement which had come from the continent to London. Almost all of them were long-time friends of my father, and visited us when they came to Israel.... My parents' house was a meeting place for visiting VIPs: Weitzman, Jabotinsky, James Rothschild, Professor Friedlander from the U.S.A, Dr. Eider, council members, high ranking British officers and members of important British families.... (Hacohen 1981: 18, 20–1).

David Hacohen's cousin from his father's side was Rosa Cohen, a key Histadrut functionary. Rosa Cohen's son was Yitzhak Rabin, a man who would later become the IDF's chief-of-staff, twice Defence Minister, and twice Prime Minister. Her daughter would marry Avraham Yaffe, a general in Rabin's army. Rabin's own daughter, Dalia, would marry Avi Philosoph, a scion of the Sephardi bourgeoisie and one-time owner of the coffee monopoly Elite.

David Hacohen's sister, Rosa, married another key figure in our story, Arthur Ruppin, who headed the Land Development Company (Hachsharat Hayishuv), the investment arm of the Jewish Agency. Rosa and Arthur had three daughters. One of them married Dr Zvi Dinshtein, deputy Defence Minister in Eshkol's 1960s government, head of the economic mission to the United States, a member of Knesset, and chairman of the Industrial Development Bank, the key government source for subsidised credit. Dinshtein studied law in Switzerland with Rami Tiber, owner of the insurance company Zion and partner in the Central Company for Trade and Investment. While in Switzerland, the two lads filled their days by buying weapons for Israel under the supervision of Pinchas Sapir, then General Director of the Finance Ministry. Dinshtein eventually became a retainer for foreign investors, particularly those dealing in oil and peace-related ventures. The second daughter of the Ruppins married Yigael Yadin, the IDF's second chief-of-staff, an archaeology professor and Deputy Prime Minister in Begin's government of the late 1970s. Their third daughter, following a similar path, married army general Uzi Narkis, whom the Zionist mythology considers 'liberator of Jerusalem', and who later became a manager in the Jewish Agency. David Hacohen's nephew, Carmel Hacohen, was a vice-president at the government-owned Zim Shipping.

And the story continues. David Hacohen's daughter married Aharon Yadlin, a political commissar in the 1948 war, Education Minister in Rabin's government of the mid-1970s, and general secretary of the Labour Party. Aharon's cousin was Asher Yadlin, leader of the Histadrut during the 1960s, and Managing Director of Kupat Holim (the Histadrut's medical arm). He was groomed to become governor of the central bank, but eventually got convicted on embezzlement and corruption charges, landing instead in Ma'asiahu, Israel's penitentiary for white-collar criminals. Asher Yadlin's wife was the daughter of Eliahu Golomb, a leading MAPAI figure and head of the Hagana, the pre-state paramilitary arm of the Histadrut. Golomb's wife, Ada, was sister of Moshe Shertok (Sharet).

Moshe Sharet was editor of the Histadrut's daily, *Davar*. Later, like Ben-Gurion and others in the organisation, he moved to the Jewish Agency, where he became head of the 'foreign department' – just as his brother-in-law, Eliyahu Golomb, was running the pre-state 'army', Hagana. When Israel became independent, Sharet was made the official Foreign Minister, and in 1953–55, the Prime Minister. Although nominally a 'labour leader', Sharet was by no means a socialist and harboured little sympathy for workers. As a child, he very much preferred the docility of Arab labourers over Jewish employees, particularly after the latter staged a violent strike in his family's sawmill. Upon reaching adolescence, he was sent, along with his future relatives Golomb and Hachoen, to the Herzlia high school, Israel's 'Ivy League' academy for offsprings of the pre-state elites. Like many others in the Histadrut sector, Sharet's ideology was influenced largely by strategic considerations. During the early part of the century, the Histadrut and Zionist leadership hung their hopes on the bourgeois nationalism of the Young Turks, whom they expected to overthrow the Ottomans and establish parliamentary autonomy in Palestine. These hopes were dashed by the First World War, forcing Sharet and his friends to look for a new direction. It was then that many activists of bourgeois origins suddenly decided to 'go socialist', as David Hacohen put it, joining MAPAI and the Histadrut (Hacohen 1981: 14–25). This decision, once again, was mainly strategic. The inter-war crisis in Europe convinced them that capitalism was on its last leg, and that the future lay in central planning based on British Fabianism. And since the best way to prepare for this eventuality was to study in England, Sharet, Hacohen and others headed for the London School of Economics.

As we now know, their bet on British socialism, like the earlier Turkish gamble, proved erroneous, and when the British Empire declined, Israel's New Class had to, once again, reorient. This time, their Mecca was the American academies of 'free enterprise' and 'scientific management'. One of the first pilgrims to this new world of learning was Asher Yadlin, Golomb's son-in-law. As a youngster, Yadlin learned from his father, a teacher to children of wealthy citriculturists, that strikes were a bad thing (Yadlin 1980: 90). Instead of going to school in the 'worker stream', he was sent to a proper institution, Herzelia, where he could socialise with the future elites. The mingling proved fruitful and Yadlin married into the Golombs. The only missing ingredient was a technocratic seal of approval, and so the government (or the party, it is not clear which) sent him to study in America. Coming from a country suffering from austerity and shortages, Yadlin was awestruck by what he saw:

I devoted my time to getting acquainted with the world's most advanced economy and the exemplary democracy of the U.S.A. I started my studies of economics and labour relations in the University of California, and completed my first degree in economics in the New School for Social Research in New York. There I also met Shimon Peres, who studied in the same school, while representing the Defence Ministry. Undoubtedly, my political and economic worldview was shaped through the combination of my Kibbutz experience and the reality in the land of unlimited opportunities. According to this view, a society in which everyone is given an equal opportunity, and in which production is efficiently managed by able and creative minds, is a society which can sustain itself, conquer poverty and bring prosperity [i.e., the American dream]. This view, of course, stands in contrast to the parasitical perception of 'I deserve it' without work, the perception of a social and economic system in which your job depends not on your abilities, but on your connections [i.e., the Israeli reality]. (Yadlin 1980: 98)

In short, ideology is a relic of ignorance and poverty. In a modern society, there are no more capitalists (everyone can be an 'investor'), there are no more workers (they are all 'middle class'), and knowledge and mass consumption eliminate the need to fight over ideas (the 'end of ideology'). The lesson for Israel is crystal clear. Since prosperity is equal to technology plus management, all that the country needs is to infuse some 'knowledge' into MAPAI's socialism, bringing the 'management' of Zionism up to American standards. (Incidentally, after serving his time in the Israeli prison, Yadlin hurried back to America, where, as Anatole France once observed, everyone had an equal opportunity to sleep under the bridge. There, without any connections and relying exclusively on his own ability and creativity, he managed to lose in the commodities market all the money he had made through the 'I deserve it' method back home. Luckily, his family's intervention saved him from another imprisonment, this time in an efficient U.S. jail.)

Yadlin's brother-in-law, son of Eliyahu Golomb and Ada Shertok, was David Golomb, a manager in Koor Industries, the industrial arm of Solel Boneh set up in 1944. David was also a Dash member of Knesset, a party founded in 1976 by a coalition of financiers, industrialists and retired IDF officers headed by his relative, former chief-of-staff Yigael Yadin. Another family connection in the party was retired general Avraham Yaffe, Rabin's brother-in-law. Together with them at Dash were also other dignitaries, such as Meir Amit, a retired general who previously headed Koor Industries; Amnon Rubinstein, whose family, like Solel Boneh and Koor, took off during the Second World War; and Shmuel Tamir, whose mother, Bat-Sheva Katznelson, was a MAPAI member of the first Knesset and relative of the country's third President, Zalman Shazar.

Another student at the London School of Economics during the 1920s was Yitzhak Schwartz, the future legal adviser of the Jewish Agency. Schwartz, an Ashkenazi, married into the Elyashars, a key clan of Palestine's Sephardi gentry. The Schwartz–Elyashar couple had two daughters, Ruth and Reuma. Ruth married Moshe Dayan, the IDF chief-of-staff during the MAPAI era, a Labour Minister of Defence, and Foreign Minister in Begin's government. Moshe Dayan's father, Shmuel Dayan, was a MAPAI member of the first Knesset, while his mother, Deborah, was the sister of Joshua Zatolkowsky, a manager of Solel

Boneh and later head of the state-owned Israel Military Industries. Moshe Dayan's second cousin was Yigal Hurwitz, owner of Tene-Noga Dairies, Begin's Minister of Industry and Trade during the late 1970s, and Minister of Finance during the early 1980s. Schwartz's other daughter, Reuma, married Ezer Weitzman, Israel's future President and nephew of its first President, Chaim Weitzman. Ezer's father was a wood merchant and realtor who represented British firms in Palestine. One such firm was Imperial Chemical Industries (ICI), whose owner, Lord Mund, was among Palestine's largest orchard investors and, naturally, a board member of the Jewish Agency. David Hacohen's first wife was a manager at Mund's ICI subsidiary.

Before entering politics and business, Ezer Weitzman was head of the Israeli air force, a post to which he was nominated by his brother-in-law, chief-of-staff Moshe Dayan. Weitzman's predecessors in the air force were also part of the family. Before him, the force had been commanded by Dan Tolkowsky, who would later join Recanati's Discount group, and whose father, Shmuel Tolkowsky, was a rich citriculturist close to the Zionist elite and the Weitzmans. Tolkowsky's own predecessor in the air force was Aharon Remez, the son of David Remez, who chaired Solel Boneh during the 1920s and held the transport portfolio in the MAPAI government of the 1950s. Upon leaving the military, Ezer Weitzman became Transport Minister in the national unity government of the 1960s, where his brother-in-law, Moshe Dayan, was by then Defence Minister. In the late 1970s, when Begin came to power, the actors again switched chairs – Dayan took the Foreign Ministry while Weitzman got the Defence portfolio. The third family representative in that government was Yigal Hurwitz, who was nominated Industry and Trade Minister and later Finance Minister. During the early 1980s, the three abandoned ship, convinced that Begin was becoming senile, and that Labour, led by Peres, was set for a comeback. They were wrong, and when Begin won the 1981 elections, he brought with him Ya'akov Meridor, a compatriot from their pre-state right-wing militia Irgun Zva'i Leumi, for whom the government now created a brand new portfolio of 'Economy Minister'. During the 1960s and 1970s, Meridor was partner, together with Mila Brenner, in a commercial shipping line, the Maritime Fruit Transport Company. One of the company's directors was MAPAI member of Knesset, David Hacohen, who had by then retired from Solel Boneh. The company's sales manager was Ezer Weitzman, who took the job after his party left the government of national unity. Ezer's cousin, Michal, married Mila Brenner, the company's joint owner. Brenner and Meridor were also partners in two fishing companies, Jonah and Atlantic, whose chief executive at the time was Ezer Weitzman's brother-in-law, Moshe Dayan. A third partner in the companies was Hevrat Ovdim, headed by none other than Asher Yadlin....

By now, our reader must find it a little difficult to make head and tail of this complicated genealogy of the military, politics and business – and yet the plot continues to thicken. The Elyashar clan, with which these figures were inter-married, dates back to the Ottoman period. The family represented various

European business interests and Zionist organisations, and generally got along well with the regional superpower of the day, supplying food to the Turkish army during the First World War (in partnership with the famous Palestinian Hussaini family), and to the British forces during the Second World War. From this perspective, Israel's independence in 1948 was somewhat of a setback, particularly since the Israeli Defence Ministry seemed to favour 'Ashkenazi' suppliers like Saul Eisenberg and Marcus Katz, over 'Sephardi' dealers such as the Elyashars. And, indeed, Elyashar's memoirs, *To Live with Jews*, are replete with nostalgia for the good old days, before the Ashkenazi took over the country, destroying the beautiful coexistence between Sephardi nobility and local Palestinians. Of course, by the 1980s, when these memoirs were written, the Elyashars were so deeply intertwined with other Israeli ruling families, Ashkenazi as well as Sephardi, that the ethnic line sounded a bit hollow.

Some of these family ties included the Navons, founders of the Jaffa–Jerusalem line, Palestine's first railroad; the Amzalegs, who represented the British Lloyds, and the Valeros, who were among the first Jerusalem bankers. All of these families were in turn connected through marriage with the affluent Moialle, Kookia and Shlush families. The Moialles themselves were linked to Israel Rokach, who, when acting as Interior Minister in Sharet's government, nominated his cousin, Aharon Moialle, as his general manager. Yossef Kookia, whose family was Jerusalem's biggest landlord in the 1930s and the Recanati's first big depositor, became General Manager of the Justice Ministry during the Austerity period. The Shlush family had intimate business links with the Carassos, Recanati's partners in Discount, as well as with the Saharovs with whom they also intermarried.

Like many of its contemporaries, the Saharov family started its career in the wood business, from which it ventured into new areas such as insurance, banking, weaponry and, of course, public service. Their eldest son, Yekhezkel, was Chaim Weitzman's bodyguard and Israel's first chief-of-police. His deputy in the force was Amos Ben-Gurion, who was nominated for the post while his father, David Ben-Gurion, was Prime Minister. In their infinite wisdom, both Chief Saharov and Deputy Ben-Gurion were hectically mixing public duty with private business, and eventually, after dozens of scandals, were forced to quit their posts. Both were given a second chance. Amos Ben-Gurion was made manager of Israel's largest clothing company, Ata, which belonged to Swiss financier Tibor Rosenbaum, and whose Israeli representative at the time was Amos Manor, former head of Shin Beit (Israel's internal security service). When Rosenbaum's Banque de Crédit Internationale collapsed with much fanfare in the mid-1970s, Ata was passed on to Saul Eisenberg, who replaced Amos Ben-Gurion with Yossef Hermelin, another former head of the Shin Beit. Yekhezkel Saharov didn't fare any better. After leaving the police he became Israel's ambassador to Austria, but was ousted on convictions of false testimony; later, he also got entangled in scandalous land deals in the West Bank. His brother, Liberal Party controller Israel Saharov, had a less illustrious but perhaps more productive career. When Ezer Weitzman became Minister of Defence in Begin's government, he nominated him to manage the state-owned Israel Aircraft Industries, the country's largest industrial company. As it turned out, his main job was less to manage and more to privatise, a task to which he devoted himself with much zeal. The news of his success spread quickly, and when Yigal Hurwitz, Weitzman's second cousin, became Minister of Industry and Trade, he moved Saharov to the helm of another government-owned firm, Israel Chemical Industries, for much the same purpose. Incidentally, the earlier nomination to Israel Aircraft Industries was also motivated by Weitzman's own business dealings. As it turns out, Saharov's daughter was married to a family friend of the Begins, David Koolitz, who, together with Ezer Weitzman and Michael Albin of the Eisenber group, were among the first Israelis to deal openly in arms. Their company, Elul Technologies, represented the U.S.-based General Dynamics. When American weapon shipments started flowing into the region during the 1970s, the three partners were making commission on every F-16 fighter jet delivered to the IDF.

One of the many associates of the Weitzmans was Shmuel Tolkowsky, father of Dan Tolkowsky, Weitzman's predecessor at the air force. Shmuel Tolkowsky himself was the son-in-law of Yitzhak Goldberg, a founder of the Jewish Foundation Fund, the holding company of Bank Leumi. Tolkowsky's business network was cast far and wide. Besides being Israel's council in Bern, Switzerland, and a partner in one the country's largest citrus groups, Pardes Syndicate (later part of the Recanatis' empire), he was also a board member of various companies. One of these was Migdal, Israel's second largest insurer (Migdal itself was a subsidiary of Africa-Israel, a joint venture of South African investors, which was later taken over by Bank Leumi, and recently sold to Russian-born investor Lev Leviev). Another Migdal director was Alfred Foictwanger, one of the 'German bankers' of the British Mandate period. Foictwanger was an uncle of Ernest Yaffet, who later became the autocratic head of Bank Leumi, and whose own family outlet, the Yaffet Bank, was taken over by Bank Hapoalim, headed by Ya'akov Levinson, the quintessential New Class member to whom we will return later in the chapter. The board also included former Minister of Trade and Industry Jack Garry, who now represented the company's majority owners from South Africa, as well Arie Shenkar, owner of the textile company Lodjia and head of the Industrialists Association. When Dan Tolkowsky, Shmuel's son, left the air force in the early 1950s, he went to work for the Recanatis' Discount Investment Corporation, where he eventually rose to position of Chief Executive Officer.

The Recanatis never regretted nominating Tolkowsky, whose family and military connections helped them make Discount Investment one of the country's leading armament conglomerates. However, during the 1950s, when transportation, trade and agriculture were still better business than weapons, they were looking for somewhat different qualifications. Their first choice was Felix Shin'ar, Israel's foreign currency controller during the Austerity. To their great chagrin, Shin'ar was snatched by Nahum Goldmann of the World Jewish Congress to head the country's Restitution Mission to Germany. Of course, this was hardly the end of the world, since their connections with Shin'ar helped them keep an eye on this crucial process. As Harry Recanati later put it, 'luck had it that we could follow closely the unfolding of negotiations regarding these reparation payments....' (1984: 65). And indeed, the subsequent distribution of these payments as subsidised credit gave Israel's dominant capital, including the Discount group, a major differential boost.

Their second choice for the job, at least according to this candidate's claim, was Herman Hollander, general director of the Ministry of Trade and Industry during the Austerity, and a board member of Discount's subsidiary Pardes Syndicate (Hollander 1979: 226–7). Hollander refused the offer. He got a far better one from his own family business, the Hollander leather and fur group based in Sweden, complete with a $40,000 salary, roughly 30 times the average Israeli wage. Not that the family business was neglected when Hollander was still serving the public. According to his memoirs, during the 1950s, when Israel was short on foreign exchange, he was sent by Finance Minister Kaplan and Foreign Minister Sharet to cut barter deals with Argentina. Upon his arrival to Buenos Aires, the furrier-cum-director was greeted by a small entourage. One of them was Berl Locker, a long-time functionary of the Jewish Agency and the Hollander Group's retainer in South America. The second was Benno Gitter, the Hollanders' local business competitor. Gitter, who in 1947 founded Arpalsa (Argentina-Palestine), a meat-exporting venture intended to tighten trade relations between the two countries, was now worried he might lose his patriotic exclusivity. (Later, Trade and Industry Minister Pinchas Sapir would nominate Gitter as chairman of Clal, a concession-loaded firm with which he hoped to entice foreign investors into Israel.) The third member of the entourage was Israeli ambassador Ya'akov Zur, whose daughter married Aharon Dovrat, son of a small Argentinean leather merchant. (Dovrat himself became a protégé of Sapir, who in the late 1960s nominated him as Gitter's successor at Clal.) The group's negotiations with the Argentineans were highly successful. As in the mythical Pareto Optimum, 'everyone' came out better off: Israel got itself a stable source of meat; the Rabbis got their Kosher commissions; the haciendas boosted their sales; Eva Peron was promised to have the 'Jewish Lobby' plead on her behalf for U.S. aid; Israeli exporters got promises for offsetting orders; and Gitter got to keep his monopoly on meat shipments plus a 1 per cent commission to boot (Hollander 1979: 197). Needless to say, this Pareto Optimum was greatly facilitated by the infinite number of indifference curves, representing Israel's silent consumers.

Upon leaving the government in 1951, Hollander found his way to Migdal, where he bought the equity share of Dov Yossef, former Minister of Rationing, and later Minister of Trade and Industry. His colleagues on the board were by no means strangers. Among others, they included the consul from Bern Shmuel Tolkowsky, his former boss at the Ministry of Trade and Industry Jack Garry,

Arie Shenkar from Lodjia, and Alfred Foictwanger, whose Yaffet Bank was incidentally employing Hollander's brother, Yitzhak-Ernst Neventsel, who would later become Israel's most tolerant State Controller. Hollander also had other going concerns. One of these was a cattle slaughter house in Ethiopia, called Incoda, built in partnership with would-be Economy Minister Ya'akov Meridor, and with Arthur Ben-Nathan, Israel's future ambassador to France and Germany, and adviser to Defence Minister Shimon Peres. Like many similar highbrow ventures, this deal too had a silent partner – the Israeli government, whose deep pockets helped save it from bankruptcy.

During this adventurous epoch, when Ben-Nathan and Meridor were exploring Ethiopia, and Yadlin and Peres were learning in America how to 'technologise' society, Gideon Persky, Shimon Peres' brother, was setting up shop in Geneva. Israel was short of foreign exchange, and Persky's contribution to the Zionist cause was to found Swiss-Israel Bank, whose commissions were earmarked for the Defence Ministry's clandestine operations in Europe. The business, though, didn't go well. Its clandestine aspects were eventually assumed by Tibor Rosenbaum's infamous Banque de Crédit Internationale, while Swiss-Israel itself was taken over, with government assistance of course, by the Central Company for Trade and Investment. The new head of Swiss-Israel was Akiva Persitz, whose daughter married Gershom Schocken, owner of the daily Ha'aretz (curiously, the newspaper was given to Gershom as a wedding gift from his father, who bought it from Dan Tolkowsky's grandfather). Persky himself, now out of a job, headed back to Israel, where he embarked on a new initiative to produce batteries for the army. The business again faltered, and when Shimon Peres got the defence portfolio, his ministry bought it out from his brother. Eventually, though, military spending started to pick up, and Persky's company, now known as Tadiran, grew into a thriving electronics conglomerate (later absorbed into Koor).

During the 1950s, however, it was still oranges rather than guns that made you money. And so Hollander, our civil-servant-cum-businessman, naturally decided to further expand his citrus portfolio by investing in Netiot Hadarom, a plantation subsidiary of the Discount group. One of his fellow board members in the company was Egyptian-born Avraham Ambash, an old-time Discount investor. Mr Ambash had two daughters. One of them, Suzie, married Abba Eben, who was Israel's ambassador to the UN and the United States, and Foreign Minister under Golda Meir. His other daughter, Ora, married Chaim Herzog, another long-time board member of the Discount group. Herzog's father, Yitzhak Herzog, was Palestine's 'Chief Rabbi', a position created by Ben-Gurion as a coalition dowry to the more 'modern' religious parties, such as Hamizrahi and Hapoel Hamizrahi. Chaim's brother, Ya'akov Herzog, also served the public, acting as general director of the Prime Minister's office under both Ben-Gurion and Eshkol. Herzog himself was head of army intelligence during the 1950s, military attaché to Washington, and Israel's President in the late 1980s. He was also partner of the Herzog Fox & Neeman law firm, a key political power broker among the elites, whose clients were mainly heavy business interests, including the Recanatis. Herzog's partner in the firm, religious-nationalist Yaakov Neeman, was general director of the Finance Ministry in Begin's government, and Finance Minister under Netanyahu. Herzog's own sons followed a similar path. One of them, Yitzhak, also a lawyer at Herzog Fox & Neeman, was Government Secretary under Ehud Barak. The other son, Joel, married the daughter of Swiss financier Nessim Gaon and moved to Geneva, from where he managed his father-in-law's sprawling armament business.

And indeed, by the late 1960s, with the post-war breadth regime about to give way to a new depth phase of conflict and inflation, this was the right business at the right time. Soon enough, much of the Israeli elite would be busy producing weapons, peddling arms, and making sure the Arab–Israeli conflict remained alive and kicking. Before turning to examine this next phase, however, it is useful to stop the roller coaster for a moment, and take stock.

The Dual Political Economy

By the early 1970s, after several decades of relentless differential accumulation, Israel's statist cocoon was finally shed off, replaced by a powerful bloc of dominant capital towering over the rest of society. The new structure resembled in many ways the 'dual economy' of the United States, in which big business and organised labour were seen as bifurcated from the small economy and unorganised workers, each with its own unique organisation and modus operandi (see for instance, Steindl 1945; Averitt 1968; Edwards 1979; and Bowring 1986). Although the Israeli divergence was similar, we prefer to describe it not as a dual economy, but as a dual *political economy*, since it concerned the entire regime.

This dual structure characterised the turbulent depth period of the 1970s and 1980s. At its zenith, during the early 1980s, its corporate formation could be divided into a 'big economy' made of several dozen very large firms, surrounded by a 'small economy' comprising thousands of minor companies. Within the big economy itself, one could further distinguish between a core of five corporate conglomerates, which we consider as Israel's dominant capital, and a perimeter of more focused firms, usually monopolies or oligopolies in their respective industries.

The Business Sector

The five dominant capital groups, whose names should by now ring familiar, were Leumi, Hapoalim, Israel Discount Bankholding (IDB), Koor, and Clal (the latter being controlled by the first three). To recap: Bank Leumi was established in 1902 as the Anglo-Palestine Company, with a mandate to finance colonial settlements of the Zionist movement; Bank Hapoalim was formed in 1921 in order to finance cooperative activity in agriculture, construction and industry; IDB began as a private bank in 1936, when capital flight from recession-hit Europe and British preparations for the Second World War fuelled an economic boom in Palestine; Koor was established in 1944 as the industrial subsidiary of Solel Boneh, after war spending had turned the latter into the largest contractor in the Middle East; and Clal was set up in 1962 by Finance Minister Pinchas Sapir as a way of luring foreign investment through tax incentives and subsidies, eventually becoming a 'gravity centre', owned by the domestic core groups in partnership with several foreign investors and the government. During the 1950s, there were several other large groups, but these either declined or got absorbed by the five core conglomerates. Intertwined in this structure was a sixth 'group' of state-owned firms, although by that time it already functioned more as a storage facility for privatisation targets, than as an accumulation-driven organisation.

The five core conglomerates came to dominate almost every significant business activity – from raw materials, through finance, to consumer-good and investment-good industries, services and merchandising, communication and advertising – usually with the backing and cooperation of the government. According to Dan & Bradstreet (1984), the core groups and the government together controlled 14 of the top 20 industrial firms, 28 of the top 50, and nearly half of the top 100 – 23 by Koor, 8 by IDB, 8 by Clal and 9 by the government. A similar picture emerges in the banking sector, where, according to central bank data, Leumi, Hapoalim and IDB together controlled 80 per cent of all assets, employment and branches, and 70 per cent of all net profits (excluding foreign subsidiaries). The core groups also dominated many of the non-industrial sectors, such as fuel and gas, merchandising, construction, insurance, shipping and real estate. Although often fiercely 'competitive', at least on paper, the five groups were in fact closely intertwined through formal and informal structures and institutions, including cross-ownership, reciprocal business dealings, family and ideological ties, as well as through strong links to various state organs, the media, and increasingly also to transnational corporations. Their socio-political cohesion was reflected in the very high correlation between their individual performance indices, including sales, value added, subsidies, taxes, executive compensations, and above all, net profits (for detailed analyses, see Rowley et al. 1988; Bichler 1991).

The perimeter of the big economy included a collection of lesser private firms, foreign subsidiaries and government-owned companies, who were themselves often associated with the core through various ownership, trade, credit, kinship and other social ties. Some of the private groups (with family owners in parentheses), included Strauss Dairies (Strauss), Pecker Steel (Pecker), the food company Elite (Federmann), Zion Insurance (Tiber), Sahar Insurance (Saharov), Land Development (Nimordi), Delta Textile (Dov Lautman), Caesarea-Glenoit Carpets (Shapira), and the daily *Yediot Aharonot* (Moses), as well as remnants of the cooperative-Histadrut sector, such as the food company Tnuva and the wholesaler Hamashbir, whose effective ownership was somewhat ambiguous. The main foreign investors and corporations whose subsidiaries operated in Israel during the time were Eisenberg, Wolfson, Bronfman, Abramson, Rothschild, Azrieli, Maxwell, TRW, GTE, Intel, Motorola, Loral, CDC, IBM and Hewlett Packard. Finally, and as already noted, the government still owned several large firms, such as Israel Aircraft Industries, Israel Shipyards, RAFAEL (military R&D), El-Al Airlines, Israel Chemical Industries and the telephone monopoly Bezeq. Most of these, though, were destined for privatisation, following the earlier dispensation of companies such as Rasko (construction), Paz (energy), Arkia (airline), Shekem (consumer distributor), Oil Refineries, Maritime Bank and the Jerusalem Economic Corporation (real estate).

The true face of this cohesive power bloc was usually concealed by a thick conspiracy of silence. Although there was nothing inherently secret about this power, the academia and much of the media went out of their way to obscure its existence, discourage research into its functioning, and make sure the discourse remained focused on more fruitful questions, such as the evils of 'government intervention', the greediness of 'labour unions' and the merits of 'free enterprise'. On rare occasions, though, mainly as a consequence of intra-elite struggles, the common front would be breached, revealing, if only for a moment, some of the actual mechanisms and institutions which made Israel's political economy tick.

One such occasion, which we examine more closely in Chapter 4, was the redistributional struggle preceding the 1983 stock market crash. After the collapse, the Bejsky Commission nominated to investigate the scandal 'suddenly' discovered that the large banks had for years cooperated, and rather tightly, in many of their diversified activities. Among other things, their managers collaborated in manipulating share prices and predetermining their real rates of return, concealing information, window-dressing their financial reports, and transacting illegally in foreign exchange (Bejsky et al. 1986). The report also revealed that the government, having lost its earlier primacy, acted as a silent accomplice to this elaborate scheme. From time to time, some of its officials made feeble attempts to regain the 'initiative' – for instance, when, on the eve of the 1984 elections, Likud Industry and Trade Minister Gideon Pat suddenly decided to charge the banks for colluding in setting interest rates – but these 'challenges' were few and far between, and commonly ended in nothing. It was only in the early 1990s, when the dual structure was already giving way to transnationalism, that 'monopoly busting' again looked fashionable; but then that puts us ahead of our story.

In contrast to the big economy which in many ways acted like a single bloc, the small economy continued to behave as a 'free market'. Consisting of small firms, usually owning a single establishment, it displayed wide business fluctuations, significant inter-company disparities, and little correlation across sectors. Furthermore, unlike in the big economy, where the separation between 'politics' and 'economics' was practically meaningless, here the two were linked mostly indirectly, through loose professional associations and pressure groups. Not surprisingly, this sector remained a bastion of nineteenth century ideals of 'competition' and 'free enterprise', coupled with suspicion and hostility toward big government and big business.

The Bifurcation of Labour

The period after the 1967 War saw a parallel duality developing in the labour market. The first to analyse this process was Farjoun (1978; 1980; 1983), who emphasised the unequal exchange between the developed Israeli economy and the underdeveloped Palestinian one. Attempts to create a dual labour market, he argued, began even before Independence in 1948, with the Israeli elite striving for a separate agricultural economy based solely on Jewish labour. However, after the 1967 occupation of the West Bank and Gaza Strip and the concurrent militarisation of the 'big economy', the emphasis shifted. From then on, writes Farjoun (1978: 4), there was a growing need 'for a cheap, mobile labour force, with no social rights; a free labour force in the classical meaning of the term'. This was achieved by the proletarianisation of the Palestinian population, which was rapidly becoming the main labour pool for a growing number of 'small economy' sectors, such as agriculture, construction, services, and low-technology civilian manufacturing. At the time of the study, wages in the small economy were only half of those paid in the big economy and, according to Farjoun, the survival of this sector was more or less contingent on the availability of Palestinian workers.[11] The other side of this process was that the 'big economy', particularly its financial and military branches, came to rely solely on Jewish, unionised workers, with much higher earnings and relatively extensive social security (p. 17).

Needless to say, this view did not sit well with Israel's mainstream economists. For most of them, the occupied territories represented a net burden on Israel – first, because the availability of cheap Palestinian labour reduced the incentive to invest in new technologies; and, second, due to the need to spend heavily on security. Tuma (1989: 594), for instance, estimated in a symposium on the issue that the occupation had reduced Israel's annual economic growth by roughly 1 per cent between 1967 and 1982, whereas others, such as Eitan Berglas and Ephraim Kleiman, argued that the forced integration between the two economies contributed a mere 2 per cent to Israel's

---

11 This dependency became clear during the first Palestinian *Intifada* (uprising) of the late 1980s and early 1990s, when repeated closures of the occupied territories paralysed segments of the small economy. The problem was eventually 'solved' with the importation of foreign workers, mostly from Eastern Europe and Asia, so that by the second *Intifada* of the 2000s, labour supply to small business remained ample despite the hostilities.

GDP. According to their computations, the real winners, in terms of their standard of living, were none other than the Palestinians. Now, for the sake of fairness, it must be noted that Israeli economists are not alone in using such peculiar reasoning. On the contrary, many a fine scholar has claimed for example that the United States, particularly the south, 'lost' from slavery, or that the British 'suffered' from their empire building (for instance, Kennedy 1987). But, then, if occupation and domination are indeed so costly, why don't the rulers simply give them up?

In the case of Israel, the economists' error is twofold. First, the computed 'losses' are based on the dubious neoclassical assumption of 'equal exchange'. This assumption implies that the productive contribution of Palestinian workers to the Israeli economy was equal, by definition, to their low wages. Now, given that 'productive contribution' is both dubious conceptually and unobservable empirically, such assumption cannot be verified. But if we nonetheless want to stick to such calculus, why insist on equal exchange? Emmanuel (1972), for instance, offered an alternative framework of *unequal* exchange between core and periphery. In this latter scheme, with the Palestinians being paid less than their 'worth', the big winner would clearly be Israel. Moreover, the entire calculation is based on holding everything else constant. And yet, without the occupation, which prevented Palestinian industrialisation, forestalled the creation of monetary and fiscal systems, confiscated land and water, hindered technological education, and encouraged emigration of skilled workers, the historical evolution of Palestine (and for that matter of Israel and the Middle East as a whole) would surely look very different. This 'alternative' history, of course, will never be known. But, then, how could we possibly compute the net gain or loss?

The second, and perhaps more important error is the very use of aggregates. Only in the fictitious world of Pareto can an *entire* society lose or gain. In the real world of occupation and domination, 'average' losses always conceal some differential winners. And, indeed, what the narrow economic interpretations fail to account for is the deeper social impact of the occupation. As Farjoun (1978) perceptively pointed out, the ethnic discrimination against Arabs and in favour of Jewish workers helped the Israeli bourgeoisie divide and conquer *labour as a whole*. Until the 1960s, the Histadrut was still able to and interested in keeping its key asset – the workers – in relatively good shape. The occupation of 1967, however, changed this for ever. By reintroducing 'free' Arab labour into the picture, it broke the Histadrut's monopoly, helping establish the unquestioned superiority of the big bourgeoisie. This superiority was further hastened by the emergence of a Jewish 'labour aristocracy' and a new 'middle class'. Easily swayed into supporting both militaristic nationalism and 'free markets', these groups contributed, unsuspectingly, to the rapid growth of big business. In this way, the ethnic segmentation of the labour market helped consolidate the dual structure of the business sector, while simultaneously bolstering the broader political hegemony of dominant capital.

Until the early 1970s, standard analysis of Israeli society managed to effectively mask this process. Using macroeconomic and macropolitical spectacles, it portrayed the nation state as inhabited by an amorphous body of 'private' and 'governmental' agents, subject to the 'equilibrating' forces of economics and the 'distorting' impact of politics. The key purpose of this aggregate scheme was to maximise 'societal' welfare, which in the case of Israel boiled down to a basic trade-off between economic prosperity and national security. By the mid-1970s, however, that macro picture began to melt. First, the 'prosperity vs. security' trade-off no longer seemed to work. With depth substituting for breadth, growth plummeted, inflation soared and the external accounts plunged into crisis; and, yet, despite the economic 'sacrifices', Israel's military superiority and sense of security seemed to deteriorate rather than improve. Second and no less importantly, there emerged a problem of disaggregation: while the majority of the population, Jews as well as Arabs, were hard hit by the crisis, dominant capital actually thrived, making a mockery of aggregate notions such as 'societal welfare' and the 'national interest'.

From Breadth to Depth: War Profits and Inflationary Finance

The transition from breadth to depth was rather dramatic. Until the late 1960s, the economy was growing in leaps and bounds, expanding by 11 per cent annually during the 1950s, and by over 8 per cent during the 1960s. The expansion was driven by two main forces: population growth and foreign aid. The impact of the first force is illustrated in Figure 3.1, which charts the growth of population and productivity (GDP per capita) over the past half century (series are smoothed for ease of comparison). The positive correlation between the two indicators is particularly significant since productivity is generally viewed as a facet of knowledge rather than procreation. And yet there is obviously more here than meets the eye. As Thorstein Veblen pointed out, productivity is largely a matter of *societal* organisation, and that seems to be greatly affected – in Israel and elsewhere – by the pace of demographic change.[12] Fed by continuous immigration, population growth during the early years of the state was remarkably rapid, running at an annual pitch of 4.7 per cent during the 1950s, and 3.5 per cent in the 1960s (for comparison, the population of the industrialised countries during those years grew at an annual rate of only 1.1 per cent). This extremely rapid expansion necessitated massive social changes in the organisation of production, and as the chart clearly illustrates,

12 The correlation coefficient between the two variables in Figure 3.1 is 0.79. For comparison, in developing Asia, the same coefficient for 1967–96, with both growth series expressed as 10-year moving averages, is 0.85. For the industrialised countries, the correlation coefficient between the growth of industrial production and the growth of population during 1951–97, again expressed as 10-year moving averages, is 0.86 (based on IMF and World Bank data).

the process was indeed accompanied by rapid increases in GDP per capita. The second force boosting the breadth phase in Israel was massive intergovern-mental transfers, roughly $500 million, or 2 per cent of GDP, which arrived between 1955 and 1965 from Germany in restitution for the Holocaust. During this period, the annual additions to GDP were almost identical to the yearly capital inflow, although as already noted, the distribution of these funds was highly differential, with the bulk going to the big economy. The broader social impact of this twin engine of population growth and foreign capital inflow was to keep political conflict and class antagonism relatively muted. On the one hand, population growth and green-field expansion served to extend the national 'envelope', so as to allow large firms to take over smaller rivals without much fuss, while on the other hand, rising standards of living helped defuse resentment toward corporate concentration and the centralisation of power.

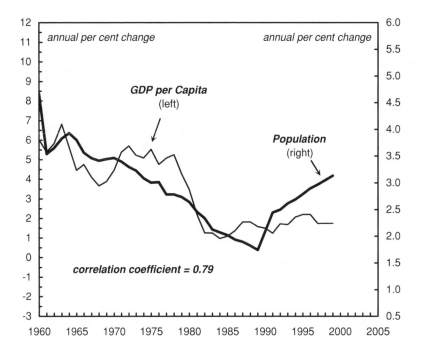

Figure 3.1   Israeli Population and GDP per Capita

NOTE: Series are smoothed as 10-year moving averages.
SOURCE: Israel's Central Bureau of Statistics.

By the mid-1960s, however, the breadth process approached its internal limits. Population growth started its long-term descent, and with the ten-year German gratuity coming to a close, the government got cold feet. Fearful of being unable to finance its current account deficit, it pressed on the policy brakes, sending the economy into a deep slump, known in Israel as the *Mitun*, or recession. This would have probably sounded the death knell for breadth, but then came the 1967 War. Although demographic growth in Israel itself continued to decelerate, the shortfall was more than compensated for by the economic annexation of over 900,000 Palestinians who lived in the newly occupied territories. The 'merging' of this population was tantamount to a massive injection of breadth, equivalent to one-third of the overall market. Moreover, the social reorganisation mandated by the merger, the proletarian-isation of the agrarian Palestinians, and the rapid incorporation of their cheap labour into Israel's small economy – up to 140,000 workers, or 14 per cent of the overall labour force – helped rekindle productivity as illustrated in Figure 3.1, causing overall growth to soar. The euphoria, however, proved short lived, and by the mid-1970s, with the integration complete, growth again plummeted.

The renewed recession, of course, was part of an emerging global deceler-ation. As we described in Chapter 2, dominant capital in the Western countries

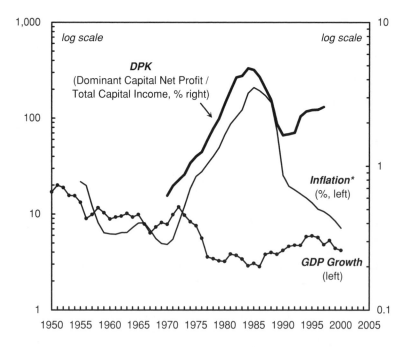

Figure 3.2   Israeli Stagflation and Differential Accumulation

* Based on the GDP implicit price deflator.
NOTE: Series are shown as 5-year moving averages. Dominant capital includes Leumi, Hapoalim, IDB, Koor and Clal. Data for 1996–97 are preliminary.
SOURCE: Corporate financial statements. Israel's Central Bureau of Statistics.

was itself shifting into depth, and Israel, which was by now much more synchronised with the global cycle, followed suit (see Figure 2.12). Part of this growing synchronisation was due to the heating up of the Middle East conflict, which on the one hand supported the global depth regime, and on the other provided dominant capital in Israel with the conflictual setting necessary for its own redistributional mechanism. It was in this global/local context that differential accumulation in Israel entered its stagflationary phase. The gist of the new regime, whose intricacies are examined more closely in the next chapter, is highlighted in Figure 3.2, which contrasts the macroeconomic picture of growth and inflation with the power process of differential accumulation. As the chart shows, the situation until the late 1960s was clearly one of breadth, with growth running high and inflation relatively low. This picture was inverted in the 1970s. Growth sank and inflation soared, a typical depth combination. For dominant capital, though, the macro crisis was differential accumulation manna. The thick line in the figure traces the differential power of Israel's five dominant capital groups, or the *DPK* as defined in Chapter 2, measuring their net profit as a share of the total after tax capital income of the business sector.[13] Contrasting this indicator with both growth and inflation shows clearly that as the overall crisis got deeper and deeper, differential accumulation soared higher and higher. (In the mid-1980s, the macro picture again started to invert, and since the early 1990s differential accumulation itself was no longer dependent on stagflation; but then, that belongs to a later part of our story.)

Finance

During the depth period, differential accumulation centred around two related poles: finance and armament. The financial sector was by now well developed, having seen its 'envelope' stretched rapidly during the preceding breadth phase. The main force underlying that expansion was the introduction of mass banking, which brought more and more people into the warm embrace of mother credit. The idea of amalgamating workers' savings into a concentrated power leverage wasn't new, of course, having been implemented half a century earlier by Amadeo Giannini, the innovative owner of Bank of America (Sampson 1981: 56–8); in Israel of the 1940s, however, it was still a big deal. The first to introduce it locally was the Discount Bank. 'In 1948', recalls Harry Recanati, 'I decided there was a need to create a network of urban branches in order to set root in the workers' neighbourhoods. This was an entirely new initiative in Israel, with Bank Leumi having only two small urban branches in Tel Aviv.... It was then that we came up with our famous slogan "Discount Bank, the people's bank"' (Recanati 1984: 66). The other two frontrunners, Leumi and

---

13   Complete data for all five core conglomerates are available only from 1966 onward. Detailed definitions and sources are provided in Chapter 4.

Hapoalim, were soon doing the very same thing, and before long the credit system was taking over the older, money-based economy. One of the key impacts of this 'larger use of credit', as Veblen (1923) called it, was to change the nature of private ownership, which increasingly shifted from family control to absentee ownership. And indeed, during the late 1960s, after a major family feud, the Discount group finally became a public corporation. 'What saddened me most', bemoaned Recanati, 'was that my brothers let me understand that I was an old-fashioned proprietor, and that as long as we controlled the business, our equity share was immaterial. For them, the only important thing was the price of the stock. They failed to realise that they would become public servants to an ever more critical and greedy public....' (Recanati 1984: 84).

The structure of Bank Leumi, then the country's largest bank, was also changing. Previously an instrument of the Zionist movement, the bank has grown into a 'managerial corporation' whose defused public ownership has left effective power in the hands of its executive. The dominant figure in the bank was Ernest Yaffet, a descendant of the so-called German bankers, who, after becoming chief executive officer and chairman in 1970, ran the bank pretty much as his personal fiefdom. Yaffet was the first to import into Israel the American business ethic of 'aggression'. In his speeches, he would encourage his top managers to attack like 'hungry leopards', to fight nail and tooth over every large client, and to treat competitors as 'sworn enemies'. To consolidate his own power, Yaffet packed Leumi's management and board of directors with yes-men from politics and business, who rubber-stamped his internal decisions, while extending his external reach into government policy and his clients' business.[14]

The politicisation of finance was perhaps most visible in Bank Hapoalim of Ya'akov Levinson. Like Yaffet of Leumi, Levinson did not own Hapoalim; at the time, the bank still 'belonged' to the working members of the Histadrut, at least on paper. But very much like Yaffet, Levinson also reigned supreme, turning his bank into a hyper-aggressive accumulation machine. Levinson, again much like Yaffet, filled his management and board with loyalists, whom he ruled through a close-knit cadre of lieutenants. His reign was as secretive as it was ruthless. 'Power is a function of information', he once explained to Asher Yadlin in a twisted paraphrasing of Sir Francis Bacon. 'The one who holds more information holds everybody else. No one could touch him' (Yadlin 1980: 133–9). And Levinson certainly knew how to use his knowledge effectively, manipulating the media to smear his opponents on the one hand, while bribing

---

14   The strategy was naturally prone to scandals. One of these happened when Yossef Pecker from Pecker Steel and Eli Horowitz from Teva Pharmaceuticals were forced to resign from Leumi's board, having been accused of approving generous compensation to the bank's top management, in return for cheap credit to their own companies (Ha'aretz, 7 January 1987).

15   For more, see for example, Yadlin (1980); Kotler (1984); Amit (1999); and Ha'olam Hazhe, 1 February 1984, 24 February 1984.

politicians to help his takeover campaigns on the other.[15] His success was undeniable. Hapoalim, which during the late 1960s was only half the size of Leumi, grew so rapidly, that by the early 1980s the two institutions were already running neck and neck.

Levison's most important coup was taking over the Histadrut's retirement funds, a move which put another long nail in the coffin of worker autonomy in Israel. During the recession of 1965–66, these pension and provident funds, which were previously managed by various organs of the Histadrut, were brought under one roof. The immediate purpose was to boost the ailing finances of companies such as Solel Boneh, Koor, and Teus, which were hurt by the slowdown. The plan was backed by Labour Minister of Finance Pinchas Sapir, and the man in charge of the operation was Levinson. In a typical manoeuvre, Levison, who had no intention of having the Histadrut Executive looking over his shoulder, merged the previously separate funds into a single pool named Gmool, which he then turned into a department of his bank, far from the peering eyes of the Histadrut Controller. Gmool's deal with the government was sweet and simple. Half of its funds had to be kept in government bonds. The other half was earmarked for investment and subsidised credit, with the interest rate spread financed by the government's development budget. The beauty of the deal was that the precise allocation of these funds was up to Gmool's managers to decide – that is, for Levinson. In this way, Levinson crafted for himself an enormous leverage, far greater than any of his competitors, and one which he quickly put into use. The mechanism worked more or less as follows. Workers and employers would make monthly contributions to Gmool. After putting half of these in government bonds, the rest was up for discretionary investments. Of that half, part would be earmarked for buying new stocks issued by Hapoalim and its subsidiaries; this part provided Levinson with 'free money' (since Gmool had no ability to exercise 'control'), as well as a powerful vehicle for manipulating stock prices (since it enabled him to control both supply and demand). The other part would be invested in, or lent to Histadrut companies; in order to get these loans and investments, however, the companies had to mortgage their assets to Hapoalim, open their books to Levinson's peering eyes, and accept his representatives as directors on their boards.

And so, by plundering the workers' savings, Bank Hapoalim, which in Hebrew means literally 'the workers' bank', was turned into a massive instrument of differential accumulation, standing against the very workers who officially owned it. By the 1980s, the bank had become the country's most diversified conglomerate, with equity stakes, outstanding loans, and board representatives in hundreds of companies. Ironically, Levinson himself didn't survive the power game he so excelled at. In his zeal, he devised an elaborate plan to siphon assets from Bank Hapoalim to U.S. investment companies controlled by his associates. The plan was eventually uncovered, and Levinson committed suicide. The power game itself, of course, continued unabated, with new unsuspecting heroes eager to jump on the differential treadmill, in quest of the ever illusive 'more'.

The centralisation process was by no means limited to finance. The industrial sector was also consolidating rapidly; although, as we noted, during the 1950s and 1960s the process was partly obscured by the simultaneous green-field expansion. It was only during the policy-induced recession of the mid-1960s, that the full impact of this consolidation came into view. Although the severe slowdown hurt dominant capital, its negative effect on lesser firms was much stronger and often terminal, particularly since the government moved to bail out the larger companies, such as Koor and Solel Bonhe, while leaving their smaller counterparts at the mercy of the 'market'. Not surprisingly, many of these latter firms became easy prey. Some of the larger corporate casualties included Africa-Israel, which was taken over by Bank Leumi; PEC, which was absorbed by IDB; and a list of companies which were merged into Clal – including the Central Company for Trade and Investment, Gass-Rasko (which belonged to the Jewish Agency), and Israel Holdings (whose previous owner, the famous Herman Hollander, got entangled with the law).

Armament

Since the late 1960s, the concentration process was intimately linked to the changing role of government, which gradually withdrew from direct involvement in capital formation, curtailing its development budget, and selling off state-owned assets. Government 'intervention', however, remained large. The difference was that now it acted indirectly, through fiscal and monetary policies. A key facet of this new role was the defence budget. The regional conflict was heating up, the arms race was gaining momentum, and with domestic military spending rising sharply, the armament business became a key pillar of differential accumulation. The growing significance of militarisation is illustrated in Figure 3.3, which shows the evolution of three spending indicators, expressed as a per cent of GDP: overall military spending (domestic and imports), domestic spending (purchases and salaries), and domestic purchases alone. All three indicators began to rise in preparation for the 1967 War, reaching a cyclical peak during the 1970 War of Attrition, and their highest levels around the 1973 War. After that, there was some decline, but the overall levels remained high for another decade, with cyclical increases toward the first invasion of Lebanon in 1978, and then again during the second invasion in 1982. The magnitudes involved were huge. Over the two decades between the mid-1960s and mid-1980s, total military spending amounted to 23 per cent of GDP, domestic spending to 14 per cent, and domestic purchases to 9 per cent (for comparison, at its post-war peak in the 1950s, total military spending in the United States amounted to 10 per cent of GDP). Another important development during the period, not illustrated in the chart, was the parallel growth of arms exports, mainly to dictatorships and peripheral countries such as South Africa, Panama, Taiwan, Ecuador, Zaire, Thailand, Nigeria and Iran.

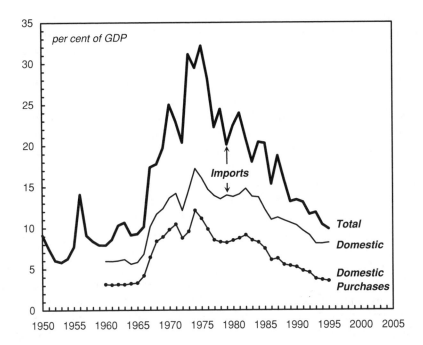

Figure 3.3   Israeli Military Spending

SOURCE: Israel's Central Bureau of Statistics.

Taken together, these processes worked to create a persistent 'military bias' in the business sector, giving dominant capital plenty to chew on.

The marriage of militarisation and finance worked well for the large conglomerates. On the one hand, they profited from the arms build-up, subsidies, and protectionism of a closed war economy, while on the other hand they reaped the benefits of the associated financial explosion, which they in turn helped inflame and manipulate. The combination was typical to all core firms. IDB for its part joined the military business during the late 1960s. Rising superpower confrontation in the region convinced its owners that there were profits to be had here; and, so, after the 1967 War, they nominated Dan Tolkowsky, the well-connected former commander of the Israeli air force, as head of their newly reorganised industrial subsidiary, Discount Investment Corporation. Tolkowsky, with his multiple links to the bourgeoisie, the Labour Party leadership and the military establishment, was well situated for the job. And as his company expanded, he drew on these connections to bring on board many of his friends from the army, Shin Beit (security service) and Mossad (spy agency). One of these was Benjamin Peled, also a former head of the air force, whose extreme right-wing and racist overtones did little to hinder his nomination as head of Elbit, a key weapon-making subsidiary of Discount

Investment. Tolkowsky's company acquired numerous holdings in the military sector, usually in association with tax exempt foreign partners, and within a few years began accounting for a rising share of IDB's overall profits.[16] The main outlet for these profits was the flourishing stock market, where IDB's mutual and pension funds were increasingly active in stock manipulation, which of course further contributed to the group's profit.

Much like IDB, Koor too was transformed by the militarised boom. The group's losses turned into profits, while its workforce more than doubled to 22,000 by 1974, up from only 10,000 in 1967. Financial decisions were centralised, and the company's numerous business activities, which until then had no coherent structure, were organised into 13 'brigades', along military-bureaucratic lines. Management, too, was increasingly militarised. In 1968, Meir Amit, a former head of both army intelligence and Mossad, was made Chief Executive Officer, and like Tolkowsky in Discount Investment, he started bringing into Koor his friends from the army.[17] When Amit himself left to become Transportation Minister in Begin's government, his successor at the helm was another former general, Ysha'ayahu Gavish. When Gavish took office, Koor, although still nominally owned by its own workers (as well as by all other members of the Histadrut), was already behaving to all intents and purposes like a large capitalist enterprise. Executives were earning incomes many times higher than their workers, and their eagerness to have their company 'beat the average' was as strong as anyone's. Strategically, Koor concentrated on taking over firms rendered vulnerable by the 1965–66 recession, of which it acquired dozens in areas such as chemicals, steel, edible oil, pharmaceuticals and automotives. Its biggest incursion, however, was into defence – particularly through Koor

16   The foreign partnerships included Elron (jointly owned with TRW); Elbit (with Control Data); and Iscar and Iscar Blades. Investment in the latter two companies was shared with Stef Wertheimer, a former member of Knesset and a leading advocate of Ayn Rand's *laissez-faire* philosophy, who skilfully combined the benefits of massive government contracts with the glory of 'free enterprise'.

17   'Naturally', explains Amit, 'many of my nominations in Koor were high-ranking army officers; I called to arms people whom I knew closely, and whose qualifications, honesty and loyalty I could trust.... I was immediately accused of resurrecting a "mini" central command in Koor' (Amit 1999: 269). Amit's own nomination to the job was also typical of the times: 'In the spring of 1968, five years after I joined the Mossad, I began thinking about retiring.... I went to [Prime Minister] Eshkol and told him what was on my mind.... There was no shortage of offers: to manage El Al Airlines, Zim Shipping, and others.... In the end, I took the offer of Asher Yadlin, then chairman of Hevrat Ovdim, to manage Koor. I made this decision after a series of meetings with friends: the retiring chairman of Koor, Yitzhak Eilam, and my brother-in-law Moshe Kalman, who was a member of Koor's top management. I remember vividly my meeting with Yadlin in the home of our mutual friend, retired general Moshe Goren, who was then manager of Hamashbir, where I agreed to take the job.... I have to mention that the Secretary General of the Histadrut, Aharon Becker, who was by the way a close friend of my parents, did not stand in my way....' (ibid.: 266–7).

Trading which exported arms, and through Tadiran which became Koor's principal weapon maker.[18]

Clal also began growing rapidly during the 1960s. After a few difficult years, in which losses were covered by the government, the group was taken over by Bank Hapoalim (42 per cent) and IDB (33 per cent). From 1969 onward, Clal expanded via mergers and acquisitions, financed largely by subsidised government loans (Aharoni 1976: 299). Similar to the cases of IDB and Koor, the expansion brought Clal into every corner of the economy, with holdings in diverse areas such as textiles, cement, frozen food, paper and rubber. Most significantly, Clal has developed into the 'gravity centre' of the big economy – both by virtue of its ownership structure and through a dense network of joint ventures with the other core conglomerates. For instance, it was a joint owner with Discount Investment of the paper monopoly Hadera Paper; it controlled, together with Koor, the cement monopoly Nesher; and, with Elron from the Discount group, it controlled the electronic imaging company, Scitex. Finally, much like the other groups, Clal too was becoming dependent on both the military and finance. For instance, its Urdan subsidiary manufactured land platforms for the army, including Israel's main battle tank Merkava; its automotive subsidiary supplied armoured vehicles and trucks; while its ECI subsidiary provided military communication gear. (Needless to say, these contracts brought numerous top brass into managerial positions in the companies, including the nomination of former chief-of-staff Zvi Zur as head of Clal Industries.) In the financial branch, Clal entered the insurance sector

---

18   Tadiran was previously owned jointly by Koor, the U.S.-based GTE, and the Israeli government. In 1969, when Elkana Caspi, former deputy of the army's Communication Corps, became Tadiran's manager, the government transferred its shares to GTE, which itself left the partnership in 1987, leaving Koor as the sole owner. The company owed its business success to two clients – the IDF, and the U.S. Defense Department, with which Israel had reciprocal repurchasing agreement. Not surprisingly, this dependency greatly affected the composition and modus operandi of the company's management. A newspaper article from the mid-1980s provides insight into the murky political–military–business linkages within Tadiran: 'After the chief executive officer, the strong man in Tadiran is the head of international trading, Itzhak Raviv. Raviv recently moved into arms exports, a change which caused some uproar in the company. The main reason is the pending retirement of Yehoshua Sagee [a former head of military intelligence who was dishonourably discharged after the 1982 Lebanon War]. Sagee was brought to Tadiran for his connections and was put at the helm of a special marketing unit of 16 people. Raviv now wants to replace him with Eli Halakhmi, who served in the army under Sagee and was [also] dishonourably discharged under humiliating circumstances. After leaving the army, Halakhmi was nominated head of police intelligence, but was dismissed after revelations regarding his involvement with companies convicted of criminal offences. Halakhmi was also entangled in the sale of forged Bank-of-Israel certificates; his partner in the central bank was sentenced to six years in prison, though Halakhmi himself was not charged. Halakhmi's girlfriend during that time was Leah Levi, deputy senior prosecutor at the Tel-Aviv district attorney's office where the charges were laid. She was forced to resign after being convicted for falsifying receipts.... After leaving the district attorney's office, Halakhmi brought her to work in Tadiran....' (*Hadashot*, 22 March 1985).

where, after taking over many of its mid-size competitors, it became the leading company.

Accumulating Through Crisis

The interaction between military and finance in Israel was not incidental. The country's large military-related deficits were financed partly by grants and loans from the United States, but mostly by a bulging domestic debt. Capitalists often object to large government deficits, on the ground that these serve to 'crowd out' private investment. In the protectionist war economy of the 1970s and early 1980s, however, the larger Israeli capitalists found the arrangement rather lucrative. Indeed, for the core conglomerates, the arrangement was doubly beneficial, since they enjoyed not only the benefit of massive military spending, but also the ability to invest in inflation-indexed government bonds issued to pay for such spending. True, massive government borrowing contributed to three-digit real rates of interest, but these hardly hurt the core conglomerates. First, their virtual monopoly over credit helped them maintain the real spread between lending and borrowing rates at 20–50 per cent; and, second, the effect on their profit of a high interest-rate regime was more then offset by political ties, which ensured cost-plus government contracts, subsidised credit, and tax exemptions. Moreover, to the extent that monetised deficits contributed to inflation, the positive effect of such inflation on profits and on the value of financial assets far outweighed its impact on rising wages.

And yet, despite these benefits, since the 1970s there was growing pressure for 'liberalisation' in the capital market. Government intervention, went the argument, was distorting the 'efficient allocation' of resources, and should therefore be stopped, or at least curtailed. Surprisingly, though, when the government began doing just that, reducing its directed loans in favour of private lending, the impact was rather the opposite from the one the neoclassicists would have us expect. Instead of rising, gross investment dropped like a stone, falling to about 15 per cent of GDP in 1985, down from 30 per cent ten years earlier. But then, for dominant capital, whose differential accumulation was now in a depth mode, this was hardly a bad thing. On the contrary. Redistribution worked through inflation; inflation in turn necessitated stagnation; and stagnation required not increasing capacity, but cutbacks. Moreover, liberalisation meant that dominant capital was now given a free hand to run the stock market, the main mechanism of inflationary redistribution. Tight collusion, particularly among the large banks, enabled them to manipulate the price of their own shares – as well as those of many others – to the point of guaranteeing investors a predetermined real rate of return. In the words of the Bejsky Commission (Bejsky et al., 1986: 59), the banks were able to create a 'new type of security' combining the properties of shares and indexed bonds in the same paper. This 'privately issued money' enabled dominant capital to run its own 'monetary policy', so to speak. On the one hand, systematic stock manipulation by these groups was tantamount to printing money; while on the other, the consequent market buoyancy allowed them to 'absorb' much of this newly created money from the unsuspecting 'public', in return for newly issued securities. In order to maximise the differential benefit of this invention, however, the government had to be pushed out, hence the pressure for 'liberalisation'.

In summary, since the 1970s, Israel was increasingly characterised by a dual political economy, dominated by several large core conglomerates. The differential accumulation of these groups was sustained mainly through depth, buttressed by a bifurcated labour market. The principal vehicles of differential accumulation were armament and finance – the first supported by the accelerated Israeli–Arab conflict and the growing superpower involvement in the region, the latter by intensifying stagflation. The Israeli government was getting deeper and deeper into debt. The servicing of this debt, though, was greatly beneficial for the local big economy, which owned much of its domestic components, and to U.S.-based military contractors, whose armament sales were intimately tied to Israel's foreign obligations. Finally, the process has fundamentally transformed the structure of power. The core conglomerates grew increasingly intertwined through a web of cross-ownership, business, political and kinship ties, while the government's role was gradually reduced to that of a mere intermediary, 'absorbed' so to speak into an increasingly encompassing process of accumulation.

From Dominant Party to Dominant Capital

The changing role of government in Israel has often been linked to the surprise rise to power of the Likud Party, which in 1977 swept into office, leaving the pundits gasping for an explanation. Most observers have interpreted the change, popularly known as the *Mahapakh*, or 'reversal', in purely political terms. The standard argument emphasises the cumulative impact of demographic, ethnic, cultural, religious and national changes. These changes, it is argued, have over the years altered the structure of the electorate, modified its ideological makeup, and even caused voters to skip from one camp to another (see for instance, Horowitz and Lissak 1977; Shamir and Arian 1982). In addition, global changes, goes the argument, particularly the spread of American ideals of 'competitive' politics, made Israel's 'dominant party' regime, along with its socialist-authoritarian culture, look inadequate and unsustainable (Arian 1977; 1985; and Shapiro 1977; 1980). In this context, with voters increasingly disenchanted with an outdated system, the *Mahapakh* from Labour to Likud was just a matter of time.

These narrow political considerations are not in themselves wrong. Making them the focus of analysis, however, serves to obscure a broader and potentially more important development, which is the *declining importance of formal politics altogether*. The rise of Likud certainly shattered the 'dominant party' model. But power, rather than shifting from politicians and party machines to the electorate, has been increasingly appropriated by 'dominant capital'.

Perhaps the most visible evidence of this transformation was the *simultaneous* emergence of liberalisation and big government. In its 1977 election platform, the Likud promised nothing short of an economic overhaul:

> During its long years in power, the Labour party created a rather unsuccessful combination of capitalism, socialism and anarchy, whose main purpose was to perpetuate the ruling party.... Likud will strive to establish a free market, based on efficiency, enterprise and competition. Likud will curtail the intervention in economic activity by government and public institutions, will gradually reduce government controls in the market, and will cut public spending earmarked for that purpose.... (cited in Ben-Porath 1989: 327–8)

And yet, much like in the United States of the Reagan era, as liberalisation started to kick in, the government budget, instead of falling, only grew bigger. During the 1977–84 period, at the heyday of Likud, it averaged 105 per cent of GDP, more than twice its level during the dominant-party era of 1950–76, when the average was a modest 50 per cent.

The puzzle of how a professedly liberal government ended up creating the country's biggest public debt burden elicited numerous explanations. One line of argument invoked Huntington's 'government overload' theory (Huntington 1975). According to this view, the Likud got entangled in multiple commitments, ranging from populist promises to its voters, through burning security needs, to blackmail from coalition partners. In addition, went the explanation, the Likud was also faced with the lingering legacy of bureaucratic petrifaction, a remnant of many years of Labour rule. And, so, despite the government's best intentions, its excessive commitments on the one hand and stifled initiatives on the other left the deficit and debt nowhere to go but up.

Another line of reasoning was the 'march of folly' argument, à la Barbara Tuchman (1984). Israel's founding fathers, explained the experts, failed to build up their own succession; the leadership was eventually taken over by less than mediocre politicians; and these politicians, when faced with big challenges, naturally got into trouble (Shapiro 1984). Now, on the surface, the evidence of their folly indeed seems overwhelming. During the period between the late 1970s and early 1980s, the various Israeli administrations appeared to be marching from blunder to blunder. Some of the period's highlights include the hasty peace negotiations with Egypt; the scorched-earth withdrawal from the Sinai peninsula; the first Palestinian 'autonomy' and Sharon's 'civil administration' in the occupied territories; the first invasion into Lebanon (1979); the second invasion into Lebanon (1982); the land plunder and settlement in the occupied territories; attempts to 'quell' the Palestinian *Intifada*; the botched withdrawal from Lebanon; the faltering 'balanced-budget' and 'anti-inflation' policies of the 1980s; the heroic 'export subsidy' programmes; the pathetic attempts to 'regenerate growth'; and so on. There were also endless scandals: the rise and demise of the 'Lavi' fighter aircraft; the manipulation and crash of the stock market; the technological hallucinations of Ya'acov Meridor (who, among other things, promised to solve the world's energy problems with one of his 'inventions'); the more modest proposal to build the Tunnel of the Seas (which, by linking the Mediterranean and the Dead Sea, pledged to give Israel more energy than it could ever use); Menachem Begin's scheme to use gold speculation in order to solve (once and for all) Israel's housing problem; and so on. It should be noted, however, that many of the politicians, civil servants and managers involved here, while indeed lacking in personal qualifications, were hardly inferior to, and sometimes better prepared for their job than their counterparts of the 1950s and 1960s. The question, therefore, is what made them all of a sudden embark on this march of folly? Why had government become so much more inefficient and impotent? And why did its failures look so *systematic*? Was this a mere historical fluke, or was there some logic in the chaos?

There was of course no open conspiracy here. When preaching economic liberalisation, Likud members usually meant exactly what they said. Most of them were socialised during the British Mandate era, and many of them, even today, remain locked into the petty bourgeois mentality of 'free markets' and 'small government'. But that is precisely the point. In their imagination, they were merely removing the shackles of government from an otherwise competitive economy. What they did in practice, though, was deregulate an oligopolistic war economy, effectively inviting dominant capital to take the lead. Viewed from this perspective, their 'political folly' no longer seems senseless. On the contrary, it looks as if their actions, unbeknown to them of course, were in fact serving a broader 'latent function'. For Israel's dominant capital, stagflation, rising military spending, growing dependency on the United States, and a ballooning debt, were the basic ingredients for successful differential accumulation. These very policies were also consistent with the interests of dominant capital groups in the United States, particularly those related to armaments and oil, which benefited from the escalating regional conflict, and which played an important role in shaping U.S.–Israeli relations. The most promising political platform for achieving these results was a combination of *laissez-faire* economics and racist militarism; and the party which believed in these principles, was ready to implement them, and, most importantly, *was to never fully understand their consequences*, was Likud.

Now, although such a 'latent function' could only be articulated in hindsight, political pressures to move in that direction were already evident in the late 1970s (for a detailed analysis see Bichler 1994–95). Toward the 1977 elections, the Labour government found itself between a rock and a hard place. On the labour front, unemployment started to rise after a long period of decline, real wages began to stagnate after growing continuously since the early 1960s, and the government, in its attempt to 'redress' the problem, implemented regressive taxation and a contractionary economic policy. Previously, such a predicament, although serious, would have been insufficient for an opposition victory. This time, though, the discontent ran much deeper, touching the very heart of Israel's power structure. Between 1974 and 1976, the leading core conglomerates saw their earnings drop by an annual average of 9 per cent. Much of the previous rise in their profits was fed by the armament build-up of the late 1960s and early 1970s. Now, however, with military expenditure already at record highs, the Labour government, although sympathetic, found it difficult to raise spending further. These limits could have been stretched by seeking higher military assistance from the United States, so as to free up resources for domestic contracts and subsidies. But, then, instead of courting its American patron, the Labour government got entangled in a dispute with Washington over peace talks with Egypt and over Palestinian self-rule, prompting the Americans to 're-evaluate' their military assistance (Gazit 1983a). The consequence of these developments was that, although dominant capital and the majority of the population continued to have conflicting interests, there emerged for first time in Israel a broad 'dissatisfaction consensus' against the Labour government. And once the heavy rhetoric of this negative consensus percolated down to the electorate, Likud was on its way to victory. The depth regime finally received its proper political shape, and the rest is history.

Or rather, the rest *should* have been history. As it turns out, the nature of this regime has never been fully articulated. The next two chapters are devoted to filling this void, with Chapter 4 dealing with stagflation, and Chapter 5 examining the role of militarisation and conflict.

4

The Making of Stagflation

... all our science is just a cookery book, with an orthodox theory of cooking that nobody's allowed to question, and a list of recipes that mustn't be added to except by special permission from the head cook.

– Aldous Huxley, *Brave New World*

The Israeli literature on inflation and stagflation is conspicuously unoriginal, owing much of its deep insight to conventional economic theory. With only few exceptions, its framework is entirely macroeconomic, dealing with aggregates. There is little discussion of the underlying political economy, and practically none of its central process of capital accumulation. The usual assumption, regardless of overwhelming evidence to the contrary, is that the economy is perfectly competitive. And when facts such as government involvement, corporate concentration, unions, war, conflict and ideology are acknowledged, they are usually treated as 'imperfections', deviations from how the world 'ought to be', and therefore justifications for why the model does not work when it should. None of this is acceptable, however. According to positivist guru Milton Friedman (1953), the assumptions of a theory are of little significance as long as the theory yields correct predictions; but then the predictive record of the Israeli literature is so poor, that even a positivist would suspect something must be wrong with the assumptions. And, indeed, as we examine some of the Israeli macroeconomic writings of the past three decades, what we find is that the assumptions – whether reasonable or nonsense – are never 'value free'. They are always useful for some, harmful to others. The study of mainstream economic theory, therefore, like the study of any other dominant ideology, is an integral part of political economy. It helps us not only delineate the patterns of social conflict, but also decipher the methods by which such conflict is concealed and camouflaged.

The 'basic mystery' facing Israeli economists, write Razin and Sadka (1993: 3), is 'what caused the change from exceptionally rapid growth in the early years of the state, and even before, to exceptionally slow growth in more recent years?' Even more seriously, how could it be that despite rapid growth and heavy government intervention in the earlier period, inflation remained so low, whereas in the second period of stunted growth, and particularly after the economy was 'liberalised' in 1977, inflation began to soar? As we saw in

Chapter 2, conventional thinking suggests that inflation should be positively related to the rate of economic growth. The argument, popularly known as the Phillips Curve (named after the British economist A.W. Phillips who first formalised this relationship), is that a 'heated' economy causes prices to rise, while a 'cooling' economy pulls them down. And yet in Israel, as in most other countries, the long-term Phillips Curve appears to be inverted. This negative relationship, illustrated in Figures 2.7 and 2.8 for the United States and the industrialised countries, is also evident in Figure 4.1 for the Israeli case. In all three charts, the general pattern has been for inflation to accelerate as the economy slowed, and decelerate when it grew – exactly the opposite of what the Phillips Curve says.

Regardless of this basic anomaly, most Israeli economists continue to hum the mantras of standard macroeconomic models. Inflation, they maintain, is the outcome of excess demand (or insufficient supply). The principal debate is

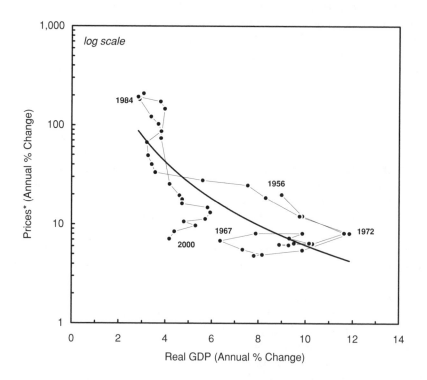

Figure 4.1   Israeli Growth and Inflation

* Prices are measured by the GDP Deflator.
NOTE: Data are shown as 5-year moving averages. The curve drawn
through the observations is a power regression line.
SOURCE: Israel's Central Bureau of Statistics.

over who is to blame. On the demand side, the villains are the government and the workers. On the supply side, there are the oil sheiks and, again, the workers. When standard demand and supply analysis does not work, there are expectations. And above all, inflation is an 'autonomous' phenomenon. It is created at will – by greedy workers or foreigners, and particularly by stupid or weak politicians – and it can therefore be stopped at will, by having visionary politicians listen to professional economists and implement bold (albeit) orthodox policies. Let us look at each of these explanations more closely.

Demand Side: Money

Theory

The mainstream literature, in Israel as elsewhere, takes as gospel Milton Friedman's famous maxim that 'inflation is always and everywhere a monetary phenomenon'. The theoretical justification comes from the Quantity Theory of Money, first articulated by the eighteenth century thinker David Hume, and later popularised by the American economist Irvin Fisher (1911). In its simplest form, the quantity-of-money equation could be written as:

(1) $\quad M \cdot V \equiv P \cdot T$

where (M) is the quantity of money, (V) is the velocity of money (that is, how many times each unit of money is used during a given period), (P) is the price level and (T) is the overall number of transactions. The right-hand side of the equation represents the monetary value of transferred goods and services, and is equal, by definition, to the left-hand side which denotes the corresponding transfer of money (Friedman 1970: 4). The tautology is turned into a price theory by rearranging equation (1), and then ascribing causality from right to left:

(2) $\quad P = (M / T) \cdot V$

so that price is determined by money, transactions and velocity. Turning this price theory into an inflation theory is then straightforward. All we need to do is express the variables of equation (2) as rates of change using lower case variables, and replace division and multiplication signs by subtraction and addition, respectively:

(3) $\quad p = (m - t) + v$

so that inflation (p) is a function of the rate of growth of money (m), the rate of change of transactions (t), and the growth rate of velocity (v). Because velocity is assumed to be changing only slowly (so v is roughly zero), equation (3) could be further simplified as:

(4) $p \approx m - t$

The difference between (m) and (t) is often referred to as 'liquidity', denoting the growth of money 'in excess' of what is needed to lubricate the economic machine at stable prices. The implication is simple. Inflation is the consequence of two principal variables – the money supply in the 'nominal sphere', and the level of economic activity (or transactions) in the 'real sphere'. If the money supply grows faster than the level of economic activity, the inevitable consequence is inflation. If it rises more slowly, the result is deflation.

Now, unfortunately for policy makers, goes the orthodox wisdom, economic policy has little impact on the pace of real economic growth, and, by extension, on the growth of transactions. In the long run, we are told, these are determined by the underlying parameters of productivity and factor endowments. The conclusion is that economic policy should hence be limited to 'sound finance' – that is, to letting the quantity of money expand as fast as the long-term trajectory of the real economy. No more, no less. Because the short- and medium-term growth path will cycle around the economy's long-term trend, the consequence will be a cyclical alternation between periods of inflation and deflation. But these will be mild and, in the long term will average out around price stability.

Underneath all the many layers of complicated reasoning, this belief in the classical dichotomy between the 'nominal' and 'real' spheres is the basic credo of Israeli economists. The conviction was hammered into their minds early on by Don Patinkin, a Chicago-trained economist who is credited for educating a cadre of followers, fondly known as the 'Patinkin boys'. 'Anyone who studied macro even at the introductory level', romanticises former Governor of the Bank of Israel Michael Bruno, 'would remember Patinkin saying: "Multiply the quantity of money, the wages, the prices ... and the real system will have remained unchanged"' (Bruno 1995: 581). As if by magic, the resulting inflation is 'neutral':

> Don drilled this theory into us until it was thoroughly assimilated, though it remained a theoretical principle. In 1981, when you suddenly see that prices really double or more within a year, and that all monetary aggregates similarly multiply *without a change in the real system*, you realise that this is what you learnt from Don Patinkin twenty years ago. This is his great achievement. (p. 581, emphasis added)

Indeed. Making your students look but not see is certainly somewhat of a triumph. For otherwise, how on earth could Bruno believe that the Israeli inflation came and went 'without a change in the real system'? Were rising income inequality, collapsing investment, chronic stagnation, and the growing unemployment which marked this period all 'unreal'? Or perhaps they were simply unrelated to inflation? Where was Bruno hiding during those turbulent years? Was chairing the economics department at the Hebrew University so time consuming that he missed all the action? Of course not. But then admitting that inflation may have anything to do with such developments is to deny the classical dichotomy between the real and the monetary, and that is heresy. It is better to stick to Don's drill and avoid the problem altogether.

The fundamental belief in the classical dichotomy and the Quantity Theory of Money is so entrenched, that the Bank of Israel has two departments – one for the 'real sector', the other for the 'nominal sector'. These departments, properly situated on two separate floors, have developed distinct 'philosophies' (as they call them) and engage in constant squabbles. And in the 1980s, that only seemed appropriate, since, according to Bruno, who governed the central bank between 1986 and 1991, Israel's 'inflation appears to have accelerated independently, with a nearly complete de-linking between the real and monetary realms' (Bruno 1989: 371). The same logic also works in reverse: 'In all the countries where inflation decelerated in recent years', writes Levhari, an economics professor at the Hebrew University, 'this was achieved by active monetary policy of proper absorption.' And why? Because 'inflation is a nominal phenomenon of a relationship between the quantity of money and commodities' (Levhari 1984: 839). According to Moshe Sanbar, the central bank's Governor in 1971–76, the 'dominant approach in the Treasury and the Bank of Israel has always linked the rise in the means of payment to infla-tionary pressures' (Sanbar and Bronfeld 1973a: 11). This, he admits, was 'a somewhat naïve application of the Quantity Theory of Money' (since it ignored other monetary aggregates), though 'notwithstanding the theoretical simplifi-cation, this approach reflects sound economics and the right way to conduct monetary policy' (ibid.). In practice, of course, Israel followed not the 'right way', but rather the bad example of Latin America, which eventually made inflation 'endogenous' (that is, inherent in the economic system itself rather than inflicted from the 'outside'). Yet, even then, the culprit was still liquidity. According to Bruno and Fischer (1989: 393), since the 1977 liberalisation, governments lost their ability, and often their will, to control monetary aggregates, pushing the economy into a 'new stage, in which inflation got a permanent hold and can seemingly move only up'. *Perpetuum mobile.*

Evidence?

There is only one little problem and that is the evidence. According to the Quantity Theory of Money, inflation is the *consequence* of liquidity. This means, first, that the two should be positively correlated; and, second, that inflation should coincide with, or lag after – but not lead – the movement of liquidity.

And yet, as we can see in Figure 4.2, that is not at all what happened in Israel. Using monthly data, the chart contrasts the development of liquidity and CPI inflation since the mid-1960s. Liquidity is measured here as the difference between the annual rate of growth of M1 (which represents the aggregate value of cash and demand deposits in the banking system, and corresponds to (m) in equation (4) above), and the annual rate of growth of industrial production (which approximates (t) in the same equation).[1]

Until the late 1970s, the correlation between the two variables was at best weak. The relationship was positive in 1965–67, negative in 1968–69, positive in 1970–74, negative in 1975, positive in 1976–77, and negative in 1978–79. Does this mean then that money during that period had no impact on inflation? Not necessarily, answer the monetarists. You see, money works with a lag. It can go on expanding with seemingly no effect on inflation, and then, bang, prices start rising to catch up. There is really nowhere to hide. Sooner or later you have to pay for your monetary sins. But, then, *how soon*? Economists try to put on a brave face when answering this question (see for instance Kleiman 1973). But the fact is that they don't really know. The problem is that the lag pattern is not fixed, so even if you 'discovered' it once, it can change on you without warning – two months, twelve months, three years – anything goes. Moreover, how can we know that what we discovered is in fact the 'right' lag? Perhaps we are just fitting the right data to the wrong theory? Finally, since the lag structure is visible only in retrospect, the theory can make no concrete future prediction other than saying that, 'eventually, more liquidity means higher prices'.

Now this may be good enough for the science of economics. But, then, in the 1980s, there emerged, at least in Israel, a far more serious problem. As we can see in Figure 4.2, inflation and liquidity, unlike previously, were now tightly

1 Note that we use a narrow definition of money. This is appropriate for two reasons. First, the notion of money supply is itself ambiguous. The definition of money as a means of payment and as a store of value is applicable to a very wide range of financial assets, from cash all the way to stocks and bonds. However, money in this sense is not synonymous with the *money supply*. The reason is rooted in the way money is created. When the central bank prints money banknotes, they exist as money irrespective of the demand for them; that is, they could be treated as a strictly supply magnitude. However, when money is created by the private banking system, which generates most of the money in the economy, the process depends on demand as well as supply. For instance, when a bank loan is cashed out and then put into a term deposit, the result is counted as new money, but the existence of such new money depends on the willingness of depositors to hold it no less than on the decision of the bank to lend out the money in the first place. For this reason, any money aggregate other than the 'monetary base' (i.e., banknotes and coins) is not a 'pure' supply variable. The second reason for using a narrow money definition is that the printing of banknotes is the only *direct* way of changing the money supply. Every other means – for instance, changing reserve ratios, open market operations, or setting the bank rate – affect the quantity of money only indirectly through changes in both the demand and supply for money. For this reason, the only unambiguous measure of money supply is the monetary base. The category of M1, which we use here since it is available for a longer period, includes the monetary base as well as chequeing accounts, but is sufficiently narrow for our purpose.

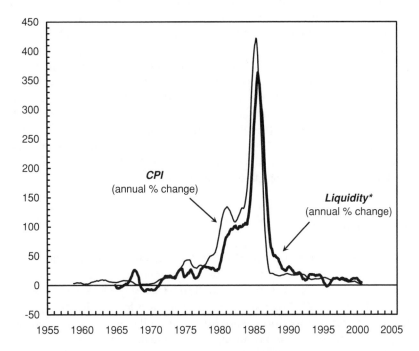

Figure 4.2   Liquidity and Prices

* M1 divided by the industrial production index.
NOTE: Series are based on monthly data expressed as 12-month moving averages.
SOURCE: IMF through McGraw-Hill (Online).

correlated. And yet, lo and behold, the lag had become *negative*! Liquidity, instead of leading inflation, was now systematically *trailing* it! This happened throughout the period until 1985 when inflation was rising, as well as subsequently when it was falling. Obviously, Israel was playing tricks with the holy scriptures of cause and effect. For the local profession, though, that was no more that a minor glitch. As long as the theory said that excessive money growth caused inflation, that must be true regardless of the evidence (or lack thereof). And once this minor problem was settled, the next stage was to determine what caused money to grow faster than it should.

Demand Side: Government Policy

The first villain of the lot was Leviathan. The conventional wisdom, in Israel and elsewhere, is that large government deficits cause inflation. 'The biggest problem of the economy', writes Michael Bruno, 'is the size of the public sector'

(1984: 846). 'The budget deficit', he states unequivocally, 'is the primordial sin' (1995: 582). According to Assaf Razin, this means that the inflationary acceleration of the early 1980s was by no means incidental: 'During that period', he observes, 'drastic changes in the government deficit have led, among other things, to inflationary spiral' (1984: 835). For Stanley Fischer, who later became Chief Economist of the World Bank and First Deputy Managing Director of the IMF, and for Jacob (Ya'akov) Frenkel, who was the IMF Research Director before becoming Governor of the Bank of Israel, there is hence 'no doubt that the primary factor in stopping [Israel's] inflation is a substantial cut in this deficit' (Fischer and Frenkel 1982: 248). Much like in the case of money, then, Israeli economists seem united in their conviction that the deficit causes inflation, and that it has to be cut if inflation is to be curtailed.

The Ghost in the Deficit

As we shall see shortly, the evidence – again, much like in the case of money – is dubious. But since we are dealing here with theoretical sacrosanctness, the facts are secondary. The key justification is the theory itself. What, then, is the anti-deficit argument? The parable goes more or less as follows. In the beginning, there was perfect competition, equilibrium and full employment. Then came the government and started running budget deficits – that is, spending more than it collected in taxes. Since the economy was assumed to be already at full employment, the consequence was 'excess demand', and therefore inflation. This of course is only a parable. In the real economy, as most neoclassicists readily admit, there certainly is unemployment, and therefore room for a non-inflationary expansion. But even then, government spending is inflationary.

The first reason is that government expenditure is wasteful. Private spending is driven by utility maximisation. Such spending, particularly on investment, generates greater capacity and rising efficiency. Public expenditure, on the other hand, is politically motivated. It distorts economic outcomes, undermines efficiency, and in general hampers the economy's growth potential. Large governments hence tend to 'misallocate' resources (relative to the ideal world of perfect competition), so the result is not only to augment demand, but also to limit supply.

The second and equally important reason, is that the government is often tempted to monetise its deficit. Instead of financing the deficit by borrowing from the private sector (which is already bad enough, since wasteful public spending tends to 'crowd-out' productive private spending), it borrows from the central bank. The government does this by selling bonds to the central bank, for which the latter pays with freshly minted money. Because there is no technical limit on the amount of money the central bank can print, monetised deficits tend to grow quickly, and so does the level of liquidity. And as every child knows (even if the facts sometimes show otherwise), liquidity growth is inflationary.

The grave pitfalls of this mechanism are described by Moshe Sanbar, who governed the Bank of Israel between 1971 and 1976 (Sanbar and Bronfeld 1973a; 1973b). The role of the central bank, he explains, is to control overall liquidity. The government, though, repeatedly compromises this role by caving in to 'interest groups'. The breach takes two principal forms. The first is 'directed credit'. The government, 'whose political considerations conflict with the needs of economic policy', allocates this credit by allowing private banks to lend in excess of their reserve requirements, as set by the Bank of Israel (Sanbar and Bronfeld 1973b: 227).[2] The second villain is the government's interest rate policy, which keeps lending rates deliberately low. The official purpose here is to induce growth, but the actual impact is excessive borrowing and undue monetary expansion. Sanbar's conclusion reiterates the traditional complaint of central bankers: 'monetary policy alone cannot stand against the inflationary deluge' (p. 235). Politicians must realise this, he says, and instead of letting the deficit flood gates open, strive for coordinated fiscal, income and foreign exchange policies in pursuit of 'common goals' (p. 235).

But then, if that is so simple, why don't they? Don't Israeli politicians realise that their policy is inflationary and that they should cut rather than raise the deficit? The usual answer is that most of the time they actually don't, and even when they do, their options are rather limited. Israeli politicians, like all other politicians, have to be re-elected; and deficit reduction, with its accompanied cuts in spending, wages and employment, is not the best recipe for an incumbent administration. In short, for governments, deficits are 'in their nature'. This view seems beyond debate – so much so, that Bruno and Fischer (1989: 393) make it their 'point of departure, that governments do not like to reduce inflation by contractionary means which could lead to deep recession'. According to Leviatan and Piterman (1989: 437), this makes governments prone to sacrificing their nation's long-term welfare for their own short-term political gains. In their view, 'one can say that the long-term inflationary acceleration was the consequence of policy which tried to achieve temporary goals by "putting out" fires in the balance of payments'. And why? 'Because the implementation of the classical principles of a fixed exchange rate regime (or crawling peg) would have been accompanied by higher unemployment and a bitter political struggle' – a tough medicine which all politicians prefer to avoid. In the opinion of Fischer (1993: 7), until the stabilisation plan of 1985, Israeli macroeconomic policy was not only faltering, but 'reckless'. Given that the government could easily monetise its deficit, it faced only a 'soft budget constraint' – that is, one based on politics rather than the 'hard' lack of cash. This access to the printing press, he continues, caused it to fall prey to various

---

2   The required reserve ratio refers to the minimum ratio of cash to loans banks have to maintain. This requirement is designed for two purposes – first, to enable banks to meet their day to day liquidity needs, and second, to put a maximum limit on lending and hence a ceiling on the overall amount of money in the system.

'pressure groups', with the end result being the 'large and growing role of the state'. The climax came in the early 1980s, when, in his words, the Israeli government 'conducted a populist economic policy in the worst sense of the word, a fundamentally faulty policy'. Of course, neither the folly nor its consequences were unique to Israel. Populism, as Fischer reminds us, 'was conducted all over Latin America where it resulted in the infamous debt crisis and a lost decade of economic development' (1993: 14).

And yet, Israeli politicians were not *always* short-sighted, half-witted, incompetent and selfish. According to Fischer himself (1993), during the 1950s and 1960s, at the height of their 'socialist period', Israeli policy makers were actually 'conservative' and their policy more 'responsible', as he puts it. Moreover, during the mid-1980s, the government again changed gears. As Razin and Sadka (1993: Ch. 2) point out, in contrast to the 1974–85 period, when instability was largely the consequence of a 'weak government' and a 'misunderstanding of the economic problem', in 1985 the 'pillars of the political system' all of a sudden started showing 'leadership', implementing a decisive, 'bold' policy. And surprising as it may seem, the public actually liked the bitter medicine, or at least that is the opinion of Shimon Peres, the Prime Minister of the time:

One of the fascinating lessons from the stabilisation programme was that the more we cut and harmed, the more popular we became. I could not believe my own eyes. We expected a revolt in the branches of the banks, but instead, the exact opposite happened. It seems that when people see you are serious about what has to be done, even when you think it is dangerous or unpopular, you win their support. I say it and advise not to be scared of strong economic measures. (Peres 1995: 573)

But then, all of this flip flop creates somewhat of a quandary, for how could politicians be locked into a predetermined path one day, while exercising free will the next?

To answer this question we need to look beyond the narrow boundaries of formal politics. Not that policy does not matter, or that politicians cannot make a difference. It is rather that these individuals and their actions cannot be understood in isolation from the broader structure of society, and particularly from the process of accumulation. Politicians are of course far from foolproof and they often make mistakes. But operating within an overall regime of accumulation, their policies cannot be *systematically* misguided.[3] In this context,

---

3 Ironically, the zeal to demonise government intervention got mainstream economists into a paradox. Individual economic agents, as long as they act like automatons and obey the iron laws of utility and profit maximisation, are considered 'rational'. Governments, on the other hand, with their freedom to choose, end up acting irrationally. The result is liberalism turned on its head, with rational determinism and irrational freedom.

notions like 'lost years', or 'lost decades' are at best meaningless and at worst misleading. Loss is never total and in every 'lost decade' there are usually very big winners. The populist regimes of Latin America, to whose 'recklessness' the Israeli polity of the 1970s and 1980s is often compared, were crucial for capitalist development. The *entreguista* (collaborator) state in Brazil, for instance, helped co-opt and 'de-class' organised labour, underwriting foreign direct investment, and promoting the domestic bourgeoisie. Similarly in Israel. In the opinion of Stanley Fischer, government populist policies were 'unnecessary and wasteful, pure and simple, a result of stupid and irresponsible policy' (1993: 15). But then *some groups have systematically gained from these 'wasteful' and 'irresponsible' policies.* And as we shall see later in the chapter, it was precisely when these particular gains were no longer evident, that the 'stupid' politicians miraculously became 'visionary' and 'bold', and that their policy stance suddenly turned 'responsible'.

Do Deficits Cause Inflation?

Now, up to this point we concentrated on the government's presumed tendency to generate deficits, taking as given that such deficits were inflationary. But are they? Israeli macroeconomists, as we have seen, tend to treat their theories as self-evident, sometimes irrespective of the facts; so it is perhaps a good idea to check the actual data, just to be on the safe side. Figure 4.3 shows the relationship between the domestic government balance as a share of GDP, and the rate of inflation measured as the annual per cent change of the GDP deflator (note the inverted scale for the budget balance).[4] And sure enough, the picture is not as simple as the theorists would have us believe. The data could be broken into three distinct periods. Until the early 1970s, the relationship between the deficit and inflation was clearly inverse – that is, the opposite of what the conventional wisdom suggests. In the early 1960s, there was a budget surplus, and as this surplus grew, so did inflation. In 1965, as the economy was heading into recession, the surplus started to shrink, giving way to a growing deficit. Inflation, however, fell sharply. After the 1967 War and until the early 1970s, the ensuing economic boom brought higher government revenues and lower deficits, but instead of moving down, inflation headed higher. So up to this point, the notion that Israeli budget deficits caused inflation seems baseless.

Most of the ammunition for the budget hawks comes from the next period. Between 1971 and 1984, the deficit was generally climbing and so did inflation.

---

4   The main reason for focusing on the domestic rather than overall balance, is that in Israel the difference between them – the foreign government balance – is financed mainly by foreign loans and grants, and in that sense does not contribute directly to inflationary pressures, at least according to mainstream logic. That being said, it should be noted that the overall budget balance, with only the brief exception of 1968–75, has been *inversely* related to inflation.

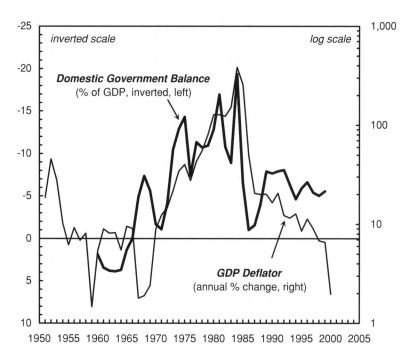

Figure 4.3   Government Deficit and Inflation

SOURCE: Bank of Israel; Israel's Central Bureau of Statistics.

In 1985 and 1986, the deficit dropped sharply, and as the pundits would have predicted, so did inflation. Moreover, the cyclical fluctuations of the two series over the 1971–86 period seem positively correlated. From the mid-1980s onward, however, the relationship again became inverse, with the deficit trending mildly upward and inflation sharply downward.

So far, then, the picture is somewhat ambiguous. To sharpen the image, let us take a step forward and look at the relationships between inflation and the different *components* of domestic spending, plotted separately in Figures 4.4, 4.5 and 4.6. Consider first the sum of civilian spending, transfer payments and public investment, charted in Figure 4.4. The relationship between these spending components and inflation was for the most part negative – the only exception being the 1970s, when they moved together. The relationship between domestic defence spending and inflation, illustrated in Figure 4.5, was more irregular: positive until 1965, negative until 1967, positive again until 1974, negative until 1984, and positive from then on.

Taken together, these observations suggest that although civilian spending, transfers, government investment and domestic military expenditures all affect

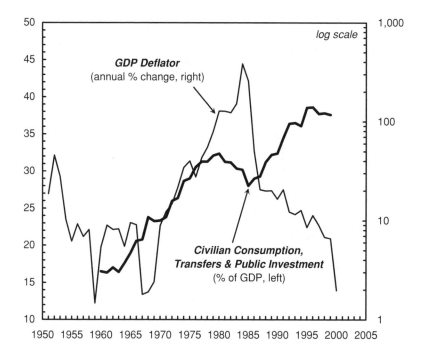

Figure 4.4　Civilian Consumption, Transfers and Public Investment

SOURCE: Bank of Israel; Israel's Central Bureau of Statistics.

the budget deficit, their relationship to inflation is anything but systematic. And there is really no compelling reason why it should be – that is, unless we insist the economy is in full-employment equilibrium to begin with. In fact traditional Keynesian theory argues that this kind of loose relationship is exactly what we should expect as long as the economy displays considerable slack.

But then, not all budget components are born equal. Figure 4.6 plots the rate of inflation against the combined GDP share of three items: government interest payments on the domestic public debt, capital grants, and subsidised credit. In contrast to the two previous charts, the correlation here is positive, apparent and consistent. Hence, if Michael Bruno is right, and the budget deficit is indeed the 'primordial sin' of inflation, its root cause must lie in these later components rather than in the former.

'Policy Errors'?

But then even that does not really vindicate the budget hawks. Suppose there is indeed a causal relationship here, why should we assume it runs from the

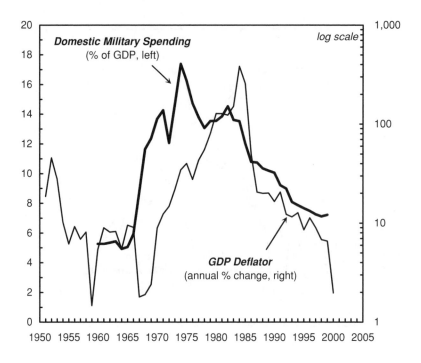

Figure 4.5   Domestic Military Spending

SOURCE: Bank of Israel; Israel's Central Bureau of Statistics.

deficit to inflation and not the other way around? Is it not possible that interest payments, grants and subsidised credit, rather than causing inflation, are in fact a *consequence* of inflation? In our view, this is a much more reasonable explanation. Consider the following facts. Since the early 1950s, Israeli governments issued an increasing number of indexed bonds, tied either to the U.S. dollar or to the level of consumer prices, so as to protect lenders against inflation. Naturally, the budgetary cost of servicing this debt was tightly correlated with inflation – but that cost was a *result* of inflation, not a cause. Similarly with capital grants. These were not formally indexed to inflation, but the rigid institutional arrangements underlying their allocation amounted to de facto indexation. Finally, subsidised credit was given at a fixed rate of interest, with the difference between this rate and the ongoing market rate picked up by the government. When inflation rose, the market rate rose with it, but the fixed rate did not. In this way the government's contribution became linked to the ongoing rate of inflation.

Now, on the face of it, one could argue – as many in fact did – that the government was evidently a victim of inflation. And indeed, according to Kleiman (1974), the government has unintentionally locked itself into a vicious

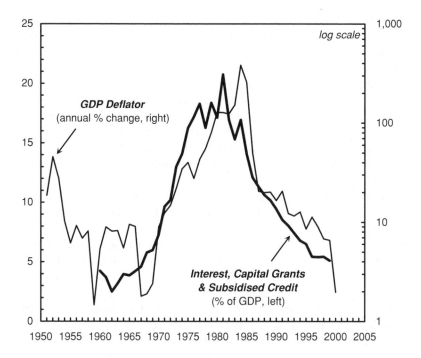

Figure 4.6   Interest, Capital Grants and Subsidised Credit

SOURCE: Bank of Israel; Israel's Central Bureau of Statistics.

cycle of inflationary losses. The logic goes something as follows. Because the rate of inflation cannot be predicted with certainty, inflation means risk. Savers who lend their funds at a given rate of interest may end up losing if inflation rises. Investors who borrow at a fixed rate, on the other hand, will lose if inflation falls. Because most economic agents are assumed to be 'risk averse', the implication is that inflation will tend to reduce both saving and borrowing, causing the economy to suffer from less capital formation and lower growth.[5] This unhappy outcome could be prevented, however, if agents are 'compensated' for their risk, and this is where the Israeli government came into the picture. In order to isolate the real economy from the nominal caprices of inflation, goes the argument, the government indexed its debt, so savers no longer had to worry about the attendant risk. In parallel, it also began

5   Risk-averse agents will prefer a sure level of income to a probabilistic combination of the same income. For instance, a guaranteed $1,000 would be deemed better than a 'gamble' with a 40 per cent chance of getting $400 and a 60 per cent chance of getting $1,400 (which 'on average' should yield exactly $1,000). A risk-loving agent would prefer the probabilistic outcome, while a risk-neutral agent would be indifferent (see Friedman and Savage 1948).

subsidising its loans, fixing its lending rate at 3–4 per cent, well below the ongoing market rate. In theory, this double indexation was supposed to compensate lenders and investors for their risk aversion, helping keep real investment intact. But then things turned dicey.

According to Kleiman, although the government took it upon itself to subsidise its loans to some extent, 'the acceleration of inflation raised this subsidy to a level which the government presumably *never meant to grant*' (1974: 238, emphasis added). The rate of 3–4 per cent, he says, was 'a proxy for the government's prediction of long-term inflation ... but that prediction was unduly influenced by the deep 1966–67 recession ... and the consequence of this error in prediction was severe' (p. 245). The main predicament was 'excess demand' for loans (since rising inflation made credit progressively cheaper), which in turn misallocated resources, distorted the budgeting process, and of course inflated the deficit (p. 246).

Maybe. But if so, why did this 'error' persist until the late 1980s? Didn't the government realise that inflation had risen well above its 3–4 per cent benchmark, and that its trend was clearly positive? And when the realisation finally came, why did the government wait for so many years, until *after* inflation had fallen drastically, in order to change the rules? Economists like to talk about the 'cost' of government 'errors'. In 1984, for instance, Michael Bruno suggested that 'the Aridor Era [1981–83, when Yoram Aridor was Finance Minister] cost the *economy* a loss of two to three valuable years.... Inflation rose and the growth rate declined. This puts *us* today in a much worse position than *we* stood three years ago' (1984: 844, emphases added). But then, these dark years were arguably some of the best for Israel's dominant capital, so Bruno's aggregates – the famous 'us', 'we', the 'economy' – are by no means all inclusive. And if some groups are excluded, how could the government work systematically, albeit inadvertently, *against everyone*? Finally, if the government is so omnipotent, which is what the relentless focus of its policies seems to suggest, how could so many of its decisions be 'erroneous' or 'unintentional'?

Perhaps what we need here is a closer look at who benefited from the 'unintentional' policies and repeated 'mistakes'. And that shouldn't be too difficult. A simple list of who-got-what will suffice. Of course, this list was never made public and probably never will. But we can certainly speculate, and our guess is that at the top of this list we would find the core conglomerates and their surrounding satellites. If this conjecture is correct – and we will be happy to learn otherwise – the implication is that Israel's dominant capital benefited greatly from the inflationary process; it also means that the gains came mainly through those components which until the mid-1980s bloated the budget deficit – namely, interest payments on the public debt, grants and subsidised credit.

Now, assuming there was indeed a link between government spending and the profit of dominant capital, this link must have surely compromised the government's 'fight' against inflation. After all, the benefit for the big economy from the government's 'erroneous' lending rate was proportionate to the rate of inflation, and if the government chose *not* to correct this error despite the overwhelming 'cost for the economy', why should we expect it to vigorously fight inflation? Of course, individual politicians and public servants whose own reputation was on the line – for instance the Finance Minister and the Governor of the central bank – may have been truly keen on combating the 'beast'. But these officials didn't act in a vacuum, and unless backed by a decisive elite consensus, their efforts were doomed to fail.

To sum up, the deficit does not 'cause' inflation, at least not in the way Israeli economists argue. A significant portion of government spending displays no particular relationship to inflation. Some components – specifically transfer payments to the big economy – are correlated with inflation, but that in itself does not imply causality. In our view, these spending components, and hence the deficit, are *derivatives* of inflation rather than its cause. Moreover, their size and direction is not compelling evidence of government incompetence, errors and short-sightedness. Instead, the growth and persistence of these particular budget components should be understood as part of a specific context of accumulation. During the 1970s and 1980s, these spending items most probably contributed to the differential growth of Israel's dominant capital. It is for this reason, we suggest, that 'deficit cutting' and the 'fight against inflation' in those years had little chance to succeed, despite their overwhelming cost for most Israelis.

Demand Side: Wages

Another most dangerous threat to the macroeconomic stability of Israel is rising wages. Indeed, besides government spending, nothing seems to stoke excess demand more than the income of workers. And since excess demand is inflationary, the battle against inflation is never complete unless it brings wages 'under control'. QED.

Demonising Workers

In a nutshell, the conventional premise is that because capitalists need to invest, they have a relatively high propensity to save. Workers, on the other hand, like to consume. Most of their income is spent immediately on non-durable goods. Some is saved, but only temporarily in order to buy big-ticket items – durable goods such as appliances, automobiles and houses. On the whole, therefore, workers have a lower tendency to save than capitalists. The implications for inflation are straightforward. When the income of capitalists rises, some of it is spent on consumption but most goes to investment. The consequence is higher productive capacity which boosts supply and eventually eases inflationary pressures. The opposite thing is supposed to happen when the income of workers rises. Most of this extra money goes to consumption, and since demand rises without a parallel increase in supply, the result is higher inflationary pressures.

As we shall see shortly, this logic has little to do with the Israeli reality. It does serve, however, the crucial ideological function of demonising workers. The assault begins with language. Zvi Zusman, for instance, one of Israel's leading labour economists, titled his 1974 article: 'The National Policy for *Restraining* Wages' (Zusman 1974, our emphasis). In other words, from the very start, workers are portrayed as raging bulls, creatures who know no limits, and whose behaviour must be tamed. With the onset of the post-1967 boom, Israeli industrialists were increasingly concerned that workers would demand a boost to their sagging income share. In 1970, the government, employers and the Histadrut (speaking for the workers) signed a 'package deal' designed to prevent this from happening; but capitalists remained worried. The 1965–66 recession was already a distant memory, and with unemployment at 3.8 per cent, down from its 1967 peak of 10.7 per cent, the economy looked 'over-heated'. For Ephraim Dovrat, economic adviser to the Ministry of Finance, the implication was obvious: 'As far as the package deal is concerned, one should not rely on the goodwill and promises of workers and employers' (1970: 21). In his opinion, 'only by limiting the overall level of economic activity and adjusting the labour market to eliminate over-employment will it be possible to assure that workers will maintain their part of the deal'. Although Dovrat did not bother to explain the meaning of 'over-employment', his message was clear: Israeli workers had to be punished for their own good. And time has done little to change the paternalistic tune. Preparing for the 1985 New Economic Plan (NEP), Michael Bruno announced that the real wage was 'out of equilibrium', and that if workers wanted to prevent unemployment they should accept a reduction (temporary, of course) in their real income (1984: 844, 846). Another decade had passed, but the song was still the same. According to Fischer (1993), the Israeli Dutch Disease could be blamed squarely on U.S. grants. These grants, he explained, have 'softened' the government's budget constraint, allowing it to pay workers 'too much', thus making exports uncompetitive and everyone worse off.[6]

The Histadrut Contra Workers

Given the importance of the issue, the obvious question is what makes Israeli wages so 'excessive'? In the opinion of Galin and Tab (1971), the reason is the 'clear imbalance' of Israel's labour relations between powerful workers and feeble capitalists: 'On the one hand there is a strong centralised labour union.

6   The Dutch Disease refers to the 'curse of excessive endowments'. The idea is that an injection of income from the discovery of a new resource tends to divert economic activity from the tradable to non-tradable sector, eventually causing the balance of payment deficit to widen. Among other things, this 'disease' has been blamed for the decline of Spain after the discovery of New World silver, of Britain after the discovery of North Sea oil, and now of Israel after its workers discovered Uncle Sam.

On the other – numerous, small, disparate, and weak employers associations' (p. 109). Now, to be fair, this naïve view, written as the core conglomerates were just beginning to take shape, perhaps shouldn't be judged too harshly. The interesting point, though, is that most economists who shared this perception, actually recommended not to curtail the power of the Histadrut, but to *boost it even further!*

This sounds perplexing to say the least. Why would the Israeli elite want a more powerful Histadrut? Who stood to gain from such strength? As we pointed out already in Chapter 3, the Histadrut was torn, from its very beginning, between accumulation and labour representation. And indeed, browsing through articles on the issue from the 1960s and 1970s, there is a clear sense of an organisation seized by acute schizophrenia. Although Galin and Tab recommended to strengthen the bargaining power of employers, they also admitted, quite openly, that 'as a consequence of its special nature and the relationships it has with the country's leadership, the Histadrut considers and helps resolve national economic problems'. And because 'at this time a general wage rise would definitely harm the Israeli economy, the Histadrut faces conflicting pressures – to fulfil workers expectations on the one hand and to care for the economy on the other' (p. 109). And indeed, most economists embarrassingly agree that the Histadrut has traditionally been more true to its role as an 'encompassing coalition' (to use Mancur Olson's terminology), than to its function as a labour union. 'Because of government pressure and the recognition that the Histadrut is too big to act irresponsibly', writes Zusman (1974: 51), 'the wage policy of the Histadrut – or more precisely, of the higher echelon of the Histadrut: the central committee, the Vaad Hapoel [Acting Committee] and the department for trade union – has accepted its role as a restraining factor in the labour market.'

This then should perhaps solve the riddle. Attempts to boost the central power of the Histadrut were aimed not to empower workers, but to *weaken* them. In theory, labour should be stronger if united; but, as we know, the Histadrut was never a traditional labour confederation like the AFL-CIO in the United States, for instance. Instead, it was more like the state-sanctioned unions of Brazil and Argentina during their populist eras. Presidents Vargas in Brazil and Peron in Argentina supported and manipulated the unions as a means of 'co-opting' and 'de-classing' their urban working classes. The result was the emergence of a 'labour aristocracy', which enjoyed a wide range of social services beyond reach for the non-organised sectors. In return, these workers have given up their autonomy, becoming peons in the process of capitalisation.[7] Since the 1970s, the anti-labour alliance between the Histadrut and the government has been evident from their combined front against sectoral wage

---

7 The significance of this reciprocity became all the more clear after the collapse of communism in the late 1980s. Over the subsequent decade, with dominant capital feeling much more secure, state-supported unions in Argentina, Brazil, Israel, and many other countries, have come under unprecedented assault, and have been rapidly disintegrating.

negotiations. Although the Histadrut has long been vilified as a 'monopoly', it was in fact the *competitive* model of separate negotiations which was feared the most. In this context, the best way to suppress wages was to consolidate the Histadrut's central monopoly even further.

Do Wages Cause Inflation?

The final, and perhaps most ironic twist in this saga, is that 'restraining' the wage share had little to do with fighting inflation, and for a very simple reason: most of the time, the relationship between the two processes was actually *negative*. And not that Israeli economists knew something we don't. Indeed, the issue seemed hazy from the very beginning. 'It is no secret', confessed Zusman (1969: 332), 'that our knowledge of interactions in the Israeli economy: how wage increases affect aggregate demand, prices, investment, etc., is rather limited.' Written in the late 1960s, when there were still only limited data to work with, these lines read as a genuine admission of ignorance. But then why would economists continue to see workers as the inflation culprit three decades later, when there was now ample evidence to show the opposite?

The relevant facts are outlined in Figure 4.7, which contrasts the rate of inflation with the wage share in GDP. The latter is measured twice, using the gross wage bill, as well as net wage bill (after income taxes). The reason is that, for workers, tax brackets are not fully indexed to inflation, so that their effective tax rates tend to rise and fall with inflation. The impact of this mechanism on the workers' tax burden – and by extension on their net wage share – is rather striking. During the relatively low inflation years of 1966–69 workers paid taxes equivalent to 15.8 per cent of GDP. In the subsequent period of 1970–85, when inflation soared, their contributions jumped by a third, to 20.5 per cent of GDP. And when in 1986–98 inflation decelerated, their tax burden fell back again, to 15.9 per cent of GDP (based on Bank of Israel data).

The conventional view that inflation works as a quasi-income tax therefore seems fully applicable to Israeli workers. Notably, the same cannot be said for Israeli corporations and the self-employed, whose effective tax rates actually tended to *fall* with inflation. Because capital gains are tax exempt (and real-estate investment even subsidised), and because interest payments were deducted nominally (rather than in inflation-adjusted terms), inflation contributed to a massive reduction in the business tax bill. This burden was further alleviated by the ability of business (but not labour) to delay tax payments until their value was significantly eroded by inflation. According to Sadka and Razin (1995: 631), the consequences were no less than dramatic. The average effective income tax on wages during the early 1980s rose to about 31 per cent. The corresponding rate for capital income, on the other hand, dropped –4.4 per cent in 1980, and as inflation accelerated, this fell further to –34.8 per cent by 1985. In other words, in that happy year, for every 100 shekels of business

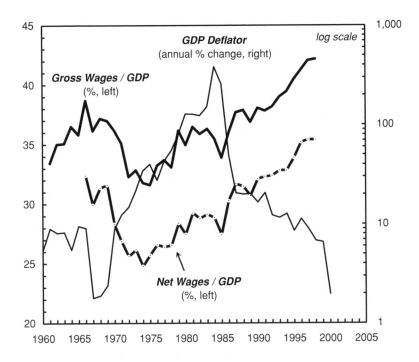

Figure 4.7   Inflation and the Wage Share

SOURCE: Bank of Israel; Israel's Central Bureau of Statistics.

income, capitalists got another 34 shekels from the taxman. Not bad for a so-called 'national-unity government'. Even Razin and Sadka had to admit that, in this case at least, 'economists should abandon the traditional concept of the "inflation tax" in favour of the more realistic "inflation subsidy"' (1993: 140).

Now, because our discussion here concerns the issue of demand pressures, the focus should be on net rather than gross wages (the latter is more relevant when discussing cost pressures). One way or the other, the relationship between the wage share and inflation has generally been *negative*: with the exception of the latter half of the 1970s, the two moved in opposite directions. (Note that, due to benign neglect, Israeli wage data include managerial salaries, which tend to move more closely with profit than with the average wage, and which have risen more than proportionately during the inflationary 1980s. If these salaries were factored out, the negative correlation between inflation and the wage share would most likely be far tighter.)

For our purpose, this evidence could mean one of two things. Either that labour income somehow generates less excess demand than the income of other factors, so when their share rises, demand pressures actually ease. Or else, that the neoclassical ritual of demand and supply is itself inadequate for under-standing inflation. Let us consider both of these heresies more closely.

A Disaggregate Perspective

One of the few innovative attempts to deal with Israeli stagflation was that of Esther Alexander (1975; 1990). The basic premise of Alexander is a disaggre-gation of income and demand in a quasi-Kaleckian model.[8] Her starting point is to divide society into two principal groups – those who gain from inflation (mostly capitalists) and those who lose from it (mostly workers), with gains and losses measured in distributional terms. She further differentiates between the 'price effect' and 'income effect' of inflation. The 'price effect', which is always negative, refers to the direct impact of inflation on consumption (assuming income remains unaltered). This is simply saying that the demand curve is negatively sloped, so the higher the price, all other things equal, the less the quantity demanded. The 'income effect' is the indirect impact inflation has on consumption, through changes in the income of the buyer (keeping prices unchanged). This effect can go either way. If the buyer benefits from inflation, the income effect is positive. Rephrased in standard economic terminology, it means that inflation shifts his or her demand curve up and to the right. For a buyer who loses from inflation, the income effect is negative, causing the demand curve to shift down and to the left. The overall effect inflation has on consumption (direct and indirect) is hence different for the two groups. Those who lose from inflation will see their consumption fall, since, for them, the price and income effects are both negative. For those who gain from inflation, on the other hand, the outcome depends on the relative magnitudes of the two effects. If the income effect is smaller than the price effect, their consumption too will fall (though by less that that of the first group). But if their income effect is stronger – and this, claims Alexander, is the usual case – their consumption will end up rising.

The next step is a similar separation between mass commodities (which are largely consumed by workers) and luxury goods (where capitalist demand is paramount). Now, inflation, according to Alexander, causes a *systematic* redis-tribution of income from workers to capitalists (1990: 98). The decline in workers' demand causes stagnation in the mass commodity market. The luxury-good market, on the other hand, is booming, since the income loss of workers is the income gain of capitalists. Excess demand for luxury goods then causes both output and prices to rise in the luxury-goods market. Because profit rates tend to equalise across the two sectors, companies in the depressed mass

---

8   Michal Kalecki was probably the first to introduce the distribution of income as a central force in macro-dynamics. See Kalecki (1971) for a collection of his essays from the 1930s onward.

commodity market are 'forced' to raise their prices in order to compensate for lower volumes, which in turn further curtails workers' purchasing power and demand. The aggregate result is generalised inflation. Output in the luxury market is rising, but this is more than offset by stagnation in the mass commodity market, so the economy as a whole remains sluggish.

Alexander's conclusion is simple: a policy of wage-restraint, instead of cooling inflation, will only fuel it further. A lower wage share will indeed cause stagnation, but that will actually *boost* inflation as the lost income of workers ends up being spent by capitalists. Attacking workers is therefore a sure recipe for stagflation. Although Alexander provided no systematic empirical evidence, her thesis seems to be corroborated, if only indirectly, by the negative relationship between the wage-share and inflation plotted in Figure 4.7.

However, Alexander's theory suffers from two related limitations. First, the framework is still based on 'excess' demand and supply, and, as Alexander herself admits, over time these tend to be self-adjusting. The consequence is that the model cannot account for *long-term* swings in inflation or stagflation. And, indeed, the second problem is that Alexander does not satisfactorily explain why inflation rises in the first place, and under what conditions should it decline. Part of the reason comes from an apparent confusion between the level and share of profit. She claims that stagflation is a regime of maximum *profit*, but that misrepresents her own formulation which is based on a maximum *profit share* (or markup). Profit is the product of sales multiplied by the profit share. Furthermore, as we have shown elsewhere, the relationship between them is usually non-linear, with the profit share initially rising with capacity utilisation, and then declining (Nitzan and Bichler 2000). The question, therefore, is under what conditions will capitalists prefer stagflation and a high profit share over growth and low inflation. Our own answer, related to differential accumulation rather than profit maximisation, and based on evidence from the United States and Israel, is that stagflation and rising markups tends to take hold when differential green-field and corporate amalgamation run into barriers. Alexander, on the other hand, seems to assume that profit-maximising capitalists always prefer stagnation over growth.

The institutional root of stagflation, she argues, globally as well as in Israel, is the rising power of 'financial' vis-à-vis 'productive' capital. The former, particularly the banks, are said to be interested merely in their maximum profit, at the cost of whoever may be concerned. Over time, as their political leverage strengthens, they are increasingly able to stir governments toward a monetarist regime of high interest rates, which tilts redistribution in their favour, setting in motion a stagflationary spiral. In this context, the road to prosperity depends on curtailing the power of the banks (1990: 133, 135). This, argues Alexander, will bring lower rates of interest, increase profits and wages in the productive sector, and restore high growth and lower inflation. But then, these are precisely the things which happened since she wrote her book – though *without* an apparent decline in the power of 'finance capital'.

The problem here is twofold. First, the very meaning of 'financial' as opposed to 'productive' capital is theoretically ambiguous and empirically non-operational. As we argued earlier in the book, capital is a financial and only financial magnitude. Its value is a claim over future income flows, and this claim is always based on the institutions of power, irrespective of whether the claim is made by a 'bank', a 'manufacturer' or a 'retailer'. The second, related problem, is the assumption that banks can set interest rates at will, or have the government do it for them. Even during the period of capital controls, the Israeli central bank could affect only very short-term interest rates, and even here its discretion was fairly limited. Medium and longer term rates are determined by a complex set of circumstances, and in the final analysis, by what the aggregate of investors sees as the 'normal rate of return'. This suggests that the rate of interest is itself a function of the rate of profit in the economy, and cannot be understood in isolation from it. In this sense, even in countries such as Israel, where the capital market is supposedly monopolised by the government and the large banks, the rate of interest is not independent of the broader power structure. It is the outcome of an overall regime of accumulation, not the fancy of influential bankers and their puppet politicians.

Supply Shocks: The Emperor's New Clothes

Because inflation is supposedly a consequence of excess demand, its cause could be insufficient supply as well as too much demand. And indeed, when inflation started to appear as stagflation during the 1970s, many baffled macroeconomists moved to endorse the new mantra of 'supply shocks'. Such shocks, we are told, are delivered in two forms: either by foreigners who manage to improve their relative terms of trade vis-à-vis the economy in question, or by workers who succeed in 'autonomously' pushing up their wage rates, and in the process upset the economy's delicate equilibrium. The model, needless to say, is universal, applicable to Israel as well as any other country.

In this section, we take a closer look at two, somewhat technical articles on the subject, written by Michael Bruno and Stanley Fischer. Readers who feel they have already had enough and are ready for an alternative, may wish to skip directly to the next section (Inflation and Accumulation). But for those who have the patience for a little extra, the effort should hopefully prove rewarding. Our purpose is not only to examine the validity of supply-shock theory, but also to demonstrate how dressing economic ideology in scientific clothes can help stifle public debate and justify the status quo. The articles we examine are 'state of the art' research; they were written by eminent economists with world reputation in both theory and policy; they use sophisticated statistical techniques; and they are repeatedly cited as a basis for policy making. Their language, though, is inaccessible, complicated by special terminology, Greek symbols and mathematical formula which most people cannot read, let alone understand. This combination of inaccessible sophistication helps economics sustain its aura of 'truth', the truth of a 'dominant ideology' whose intricacies have been fully worked out by the experts, all for the benefit of the unsuspecting public.

It is therefore important to remove the mathematical veneer, and look into the essence of what Bruno and Fischer actually say. Economists are not saintly carriers of some heavenly gospel, and regardless of claims to the contrary, their theories are *always* ideological. So what exactly is their message? How compelling is their logic? And does it correspond to reality? These are important questions, and readers patient enough to struggle through the details will soon find out that the emperor has little clothing. Plainly put, the theory which Bruno and Fischer espouse is not only logically feeble, but it also has nothing to do with the facts.

Sorting Out the Blame

We begin with an article by Michael Bruno, written while governing the Bank of Israel, and titled 'External Shocks and Internal Responses' (1989). Compared with the experience of the 1970s and 1980s, he writes, the earlier decades were a 'Gilded Age'. Israel enjoyed high growth and low inflation. Distortions were limited and were resolved with acceptable institutional arrangements; the balance of payment deficit was manageable and easily financed; and rising immigration and the incorporation of Palestinian workers have 'softened' labour markets, enabling rapid export-oriented growth. In short, a macroeconomic bliss. But then storm clouds began to gather. The initial reason was the bulging budget deficit, caused by accumulated social obligations which politicians found difficult to undo. And then came the external shocks of the 1973 War and the energy crises, and all hell broke loose.

The purpose of Bruno's article is to sort out the blame: to what extent can we accuse 'exogenous factors', and what can we attribute to 'internal Israeli factors' – that is, to workers and politicians.

The analytical framework is a standard textbook setup of aggregate demand and supply, with the overall price level on the vertical axis and the general level of economic activity on the horizontal axis. The aggregate demand curve is downward sloping. There are two basic reasons for this. One is that higher prices, everything else remaining equal, reduce real wealth and income, causing economic agents to spend less. The other is that higher prices, again keeping everything else constant, make imports relatively cheaper than exports, causing net exports to fall. The position of the demand curve is determined by three basic factors: the stance of fiscal and monetary policy (with expansionary policy shifting the curve up and to the right, and contractionary policy down and to the left); by the real cost of raw materials (with higher cost undermining purchasing power and hence causing the curve to shift down and to the left);

and by global demand (which, as it rises, increases net exports, pushing the curve up and to the right).

The aggregate supply curve is upward sloping, with rising prices causing an increase in desired output. The reason is rising marginal cost, meaning that after a certain point, each additional unit costs more to produce than the previous one, so higher output will remain profitable and forthcoming only at higher prices. The position of the supply curve is positively related to the level of capital stock and the state of technology: when these increase, production becomes less costly and the curve shifts down and to the right. Real wages and the real price of imported raw materials have the opposite effect on supply – as these rise, output becomes more costly, less can be produced at each price, causing the curve to shift up and to the left. (Note that unlike wages and rent, profit does not affect the position of the curve, and hence is not even mentioned by Governor Bruno. The reason is that, contrary to workers and owners of raw materials, capitalists are assumed incapable of deliberately affecting their own income. Their profit, we are told, is determined solely by productivity and free market forces.)

This framework, overly familiar to students of economics, comes to equilibrium at the point where the downward-sloping demand curve intersects the upward-sloping supply curve. In this context, writes Bruno (1989: 373), the 'essence of a stagflationary shock' comes from a shift of the supply curve up and to the left, causing output to fall and prices to rise. The shift in supply, he explains, is caused either by an 'external price shock' (for instance, when the weather or the oil sheiks make raw materials more expensive), or by an 'autonomous real wage push over and above productivity gain' (when workers suddenly decide to raise their wages faster than their output). The shock can be mitigated if 'wages are elastic in the downward direction' (that is, if workers can be made to accept lower income). This, according to Bruno, will limit the downward pressure on profit and bring a compensating move of the supply curve down and to the right. However, if workers stubbornly keep their wages 'rigid' – as they usually do – the consequence is a stagflationary combination of higher prices and lower output, followed in the longer run by less investment and a stagnant capital stock.

Shocks? What Shocks?

To apply this model to the Israeli case, though, seems a bit strange. For a start, the model suggests that a rising real wage should cause higher inflation. And, yet, in Israel inflation has had no connection whatsoever, either to the level of real wages, or to the rate of change of real wages. There is a link, of course, and that is between inflation and the wage *share* (measured in gross terms since we are concerned here with production costs). But, then, as we saw in Figure 4.7, this relationship has been mostly *negative*. And since a falling wage share mirrors a rising profit share, shouldn't we conclude that Israeli inflation was in fact the consequence of a 'profit shock'? No way, say the supply-siders. Remember that capitalists, by assumption, have no control over their own income, so that unlike workers and the oil sheiks they couldn't 'autonomously' shift their own supply curve.

The second problem is that the model says that inflation should move inversely with the terms of trade (the ratio of export prices to import prices). When these improve, goes the argument, the economy can buy more imports for its exports, causing the overall national pie to grow and inflationary pressures to abate. But then here too the evidence is far from convincing. Figure 4.8 relates the GDP deflator to the terms of trade, both measured in rates of change and smoothed. The relationship is at best weak. Wide swings in the terms of trade have tended to affect domestic prices, but the impact was anything but systematic. Furthermore, over the long term, the relationship between the variables actually appears to be mildly positive.

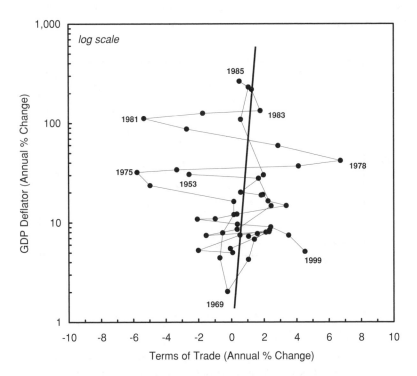

Figure 4.8 Israel's Terms of Trade and Inflation

* Ratio of export prices to import prices.
NOTE: Data are shown as 3-year moving averages. The straight line going through the observations is drawn freehand.
SOURCE: IMF through McGraw-Hill (Online)

The softness of this evidence is not surprising and, in fact, hardly unique to Israel. During the 1970s and early 1980s, many observers expected resource scarcity to create an indefinite 'commodity price-shock' and ever rising inflation. This doomsday scenario, though, failed to materialise. Inflation indeed continued, but not because of raw materials. The process is illustrated in Figure 4.9, where we contrast the movement of three price indices: consumer goods and services, oil, and raw materials (note the logarithmic scale). During the 1950s and 1960s, inflation could have had little to do with commodity supply-shocks, simply because prices of raw materials actually lagged those of finished consumer products. Then came the infamous 1970s. As the data show, raw material prices in general and oil prices in particular shot up, accompanied by accelerating consumer prices and the growing popularity of 'supply shock' explanations. By the early 1980s, however, raw material prices stabilised, while oil prices began to collapse. In the economist's jargon, this was tantamount to a *negative* supply shock. Contrary to the model, though, final consumer prices did not follow suit. In fact, not only did they continue to rise, but for the next 15 years, their rate of increase actually accelerated. It is only since the mid-1990s, that global inflation began to decelerate.

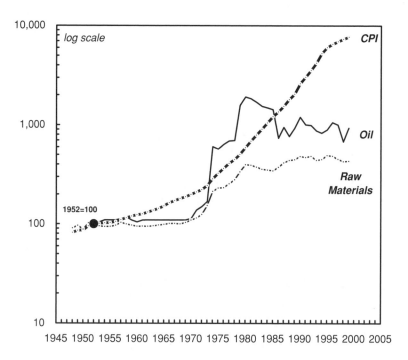

Figure 4.9   World Prices

SOURCE: IMF through McGraw-Hill (Online).

In retrospect, the 1970s episode of input and consumer prices rising together is clearly the exception, not the rule. Since the turn of the century, raw material prices have been falling in real terms, whereas consumer prices have been rising. In the final analysis, one could safely argue that raw material exporters – including the oil sheiks after 1980 – have been the victims, not the villains in the inflation story. And in fact, there is little here that should surprise our reader. In a world of large-scale business enterprise, relative prices reflect differential power no less than demand and productivity. The extent to which price setting is 'autonomous' depends not on the owner's nationality but on his or her differential power, and in this sense there is little difference between domestic firms and oil sheiks. Sometimes such firms act at cross-purposes which causes their profit margins to shrink, while at other times they move in unison and then profit margins widen. To argue, then, that the sellers of final goods and services passively 'adjust', in contrast to workers and raw material owners who actively 'initiate', is to be ideologically fixated. And, indeed, judging by the evidence in Figure 4.9, it seems clear that the balance of power between final sellers and raw material producers has been changing in both directions, although over the longer haul the former have so far had the upper hand.

Greek Symbols and the Naked Truth

Of course, such simple-minded logic and trivial facts are no match for the elegance of eternal theory, and so Bruno, undeterred by evidence, moves on to apply his universal model to Israel's industrial sector, beginning with an output regression:[9]

(5) $q - k = \alpha_0 + \alpha_1 w + \alpha_2 \pi_{t-1} + \alpha_3 d + \alpha_4 x$

where (q) is output growth, (k) is the rate of change of the capital stock (so $q - k$ is the rate of growth of output per unit of capital), (w) is the deviation of wage growth for its trend, (π_{t-1}) is the previous period's deviation of the rate of change of real input prices from their trend, (d) is the growth rate of demand (government spending and private investment) expressed as a deviation from

---

9 Regression analysis is a way of giving empirical 'content' to an analytical model. It comprises *variables* which can be observed, such as prices, output and employment, and *parameters*, which act as 'weights' in combining the different variables, and which need to be estimated based on the empirical data. The way this works is by figuring out (now with the aid of computers), what parameter values will create the 'best fit' between the data and the model. Regression analysis is a common way of 'testing' theoretical propositions – good fits are taken as tentative confirmation, bad fits as a basis for rejection. The methodological meaning and validity of such 'tests', however, have been seriously questioned. For an early commentary on the issue, conveniently ignored by most practitioners but valid as ever, see the debate between John Maynard Keynes (1939) and Jan Tinbergen (1940).

trend, and (x) is the growth rate of global income, again as a deviation from trend. The $(\alpha_i's)$ are parameters, whose relative size reflects the significance of their associated variables.

Now, recall that the purpose of combining supply and demand factors into a single framework was to sort out their relative blame for inflation. This, though, is easier said than done. The first problem is conceptual. Bruno's designation of $(q-k)$ as a 'supply variable' and (d) and (x) as 'demand variables' is axiomatic and unsubstantiated. Demand and supply are so-called 'notional' functions. They represent the *desire* to spend and sell rather than the *actual* levels of spending and production. Accepting for the moment that the world is indeed moving from one equilibrium position to the next (which is what regression analysis implicitly assumes), all measured variables – be they output per unit of capital, spending by consumers, or investment by firms – represent intersections of *both* supply and demand. But, then, if the two can only be observed together, how can Bruno hope to differentiate them?

This is not nit-picking. In fact, the problem touches the very heart of mainstream economics, as some Israeli economists are honest enough to admit. Michaeli (1981: 115), for example, readily concedes that although 'inflation can be generally explained by factors operating on demand or supply, identifying such factors, and particularly the distinction between the demand and supply sides, is at best a challenging and uncertain endeavour'. Indeed,

> even conceptually, the distinction is not cut and dry. A change in demand, for instance, could cause input and final prices to rise in a certain sector, which will in turn cause prices in another sector to rise in an apparent cost-push inflation. It is also possible to think of circumstances in which the expectation for rising demand can itself trigger an instantaneous rise in cost and prices (including key prices such as exchange rates); and here too it is difficult to say unequivocally whether this was demand or supply driven. (pp. 115–16)

And then there is the empirical side. Even if we ignore the conceptual problems, the actual results presented by Bruno are far from impressive. To be blunt, they suggest his model is in fact useless. Note that Bruno began with a very limited task, focusing not on the variables themselves, but on their deviations from long-term trends. As a consequence, his analysis can at best tell us why economic growth fell from 4 to 2 per cent, or why inflation rose from 200 to 250 per cent, but not why growth was 4 per cent and inflation 200 per cent to begin with. Yet, even this proves too much for the model.

Bruno's estimates, reported in Table 5 of his article, seem to explain very little of what his model promises to do. One common proxy for 'explanatory power' is R^2, a measure which describes the extent to which the regression accounts for variations in the variable of interest ($q-k$, in our case), ranging between 0 (no explanatory power) and 1 (100 per cent explanatory power).

The R^2 for equation (5), therefore, should reflect the extent to which wages, raw material prices, domestic and foreign demand help explain the output/capital ratio (all measured in rates of change and expressed as deviations from trend).[10] Bruno's measures of R^2 are very low: 0.37 when the model is applied to the 1964–79 period and a mere 0.26 when estimated for the entire 1964–82 period. Obviously, since up to 75 per cent are left unexplained, something very important must be missing from the model. Another measure of validity is the so-called t-statistic, which accompanies each estimate of the (α_i's). A high t-statistic (usually above the standard threshold of 1.96) indicates that the associated variable is probably important for the model, whereas a low value (below 1.96) suggests this variable is probably irrelevant and should be ignored.[11] Now, in Bruno's model, the t-statistics range from a low of 0.1 to a high of 0.36. In other words, according to standard statistical ritual, all of them are insignificant and should be ignored.

And the problem is hardly limited to a single equation. Moving to the nominal sphere of money, wages, prices and exchange rates, Bruno adopts the following 'standard' price and wage equations:[12]

(6) $p = \alpha_0 + \alpha_1 w + \alpha_2 p_n + \alpha_3 (m - y) + t$

(7) $w = \beta_0 + \beta_1 p + \beta_2 (1/u_{-1}) + \beta_3 (l_a)^2 + \beta_3 d$

where (p) is the rate of change of the CPI, (w) is the rate of change of nominal wages, (p_n) is the rate of change of import prices, (m) is the rate of change of narrow money (M1), (t) is the rate of change of indirect taxes, (u_{-1}) is the rate of unemployment in the earlier period, (l_a) is the proportion of Palestinian workers in the labour force, and (d) is a so-called 'dummy variable', with a value of one for periods of wage freeze and zero otherwise.

Estimated for the period between 1955 and 1974 (before inflation became 'independent', in Bruno's words), these equations yield a high explanatory power (R^2 of 0.95) – but then with so many nominal rates of change on the

10 R^2 is a rather biased measure of 'fit', since it tends to rise with the number of independent variables thrown into the model, even if these variables have no theoretical reason to be there. A better measure which corrects for this 'bias' is the one based on the F-test, but Bruno does not report these results in his article.

11 Tests based on t-statistics become problematic when the different variables on the right-hand side of the equation are highly correlated – for instance, prices and wages during times of high inflation. In such cases, t-statistics often end up being small not because the variables are unimportant, but since the regression is unable to differentiate between their separate impacts. Simple ways to bypass this problem are to drop one of the correlated variables, or to combine them into a composite variable. Bruno does neither.

12 Habituation, as Veblen observed, is a very strong social force, often much more potent than logic. Labelling a model as 'standard', 'conventional', 'traditional' or 'normal' seems to convey much more authority than alternative adjectives such as 'true', 'correct' or 'appropriate'.

right-hand side, it is in fact surprising that the explanatory power is not even greater. The trouble again is with the t-statistics. With the exception of the (β^3) none of the estimates is significant (the highest t-statistic is a mere 0.11, against the standard minimum of 1.96). Thus, much like the case of equation (5), here too the underlying theory receives no clear blessing from the canons.

Obviously, Bruno is having difficulties delivering on his initial promise. So far, his regressions told us nothing persuasive about the respective roles of supply and demand, leaving inflation mysterious as ever. But, then, Bruno is not a man to fuss over such trivialities. Keeping a straight face, he proceeds to combine equations (6) and (7) into a single expression, such that:

$$(8) \quad p = \gamma_0 + \gamma_1 (1/u_{-1}) + \gamma_2 (l_a)^2 + \gamma_3 d + \gamma_4 p_n + \gamma_5 (m - y) + \gamma_6 t$$

The estimates of this equation, however, are accompanied by no diagnostic statistics (R^2 or t-statistics) – perhaps they were too good to be true? Another problem, of which we learn only in passing, is that equations (5) to (7) were estimated only for 1955–74, because a longer coverage, extending beyond 1974, made the model 'less efficient'. But then how much less efficient can this model get? And why would Bruno not report, as scientists should do, his failures as well as successes?

The reason is that there is a better way out, and that is to announce – as Bruno ceremonially does – that after 1974, Israel's nominal and real sectors became 'separated'. The famous 'classical dichotomy' finally took hold in the Holy Land. The implication is that there is no longer any need to deal with real variables, which in turn means that the original goal of the paper – separating demand from supply – can now be conveniently ignored.

And while we are renovating, why not change also what we try to explain? Instead of dealing with inflation, Bruno now decides to concentrate on *changes* in inflation.[13] Trying to come up with some sort of explanation, he specifies equation (9):

$$(9) \quad \Delta p = \delta_0 + \delta_1 \Delta p_{-1} + \delta_2 \Delta p_{-2} + \delta_3 \Delta p_{-3} + \delta_4 \Delta e^+ + \delta_5 \Delta e^-$$

In this equation, the *acceleration* of inflation ($\Delta p = p - p_{-1}$) is explained in terms of its own lagged values (Δp_{-1}, Δp_{-2} and Δp_{-3}), and two variables representing acceleration (Δe^+) and deceleration (Δe^-) of the exchange rate. And so, in the end, we get a quasi-expectational model, in which inflation persists simply because people, looking at its past pattern, expect it to persist! Of course, with

---

13 Once upon a time, economists had something to say about prices. But then, as prices became inflationary, the focus moved to their first derivative, the rate of inflation. And when that too became difficult to explain, attention promptly shifted to second derivatives, the rate of change of the rate of inflation. Who knows, perhaps the next bout of inflation will send economists looking for third-derivative explanations.

an intrinsically auto-correlated process like inflation (in which successive observations of the same variable are highly correlated), this amounts to no explanation at all. In simple language, Bruno is telling us that we have inflation now simply because we had it in the past. Once started, inflation behaves like all other heavenly bodies, following its own 'inertia'. And yet, even here, with a nearly tautological model, the explanatory power is feeble. The R^2 is 0.55 and the highest t-statistics is 0.01 (against a conventional minimum of 1.96).

Aware of the model's failings, Bruno chooses to blame reality: 'Inflation in the Israeli case', he declares, 'seems to have acquired an independent momentum of its own [?!], with an almost complete separation between the real and nominal spheres' (1989: 371). Invoking the omens, he announces that 'one can consider the inflation since the end of 1977 as an independent process derived from the change in the monetary regime'. In fact, 'it looks as if there is no connection between this process and global shocks, or between this process and real developments in the economy' (ibid.). In short, an extra-terrestrial mystery. And this insight comes from the Governor of the Bank of Israel, the man in charge of monetary policy.

Tough life, but, then, maybe joining forces with another big name, Stanley Fischer, could help. And so, in a co-authored paper, Bruno and Fischer (1989) try to take yet another shot at the elusive alien. In a section entitled 'inflation dynamics', they have the acceleration of inflation ($\Delta p = p - p_{-1}$) written as a function of wage inflation (w), import prices (p_n), and its own lagged value (p_{-1}), such that,

(10) $\quad \Delta p = \delta_0 + \delta_1 (w - p_{-1}) + \delta_2 (p_n - p_{-1})$

And as the reader can by now guess, the explanatory power is again very weak – and this despite the fact that we are dealing here with first difference of nominal variables (Δp), and that the dependent variable is itself an explanatory variable (so it appears on both sides of the equation). The low t-statistics (the highest is 0.09) suggest that none of the independent variables has significant impact on (Δp). The implication is simple: whatever the results, they could be safely ignored.

Bruno and Fischer (1989: 411) admit that 'while our approach to inflation dynamics must explain short term variations in inflation, in itself this does not explain the underlying factors affecting inflation in the long run'. But then, this is hardly a reason to give up. After all, if the model does not work, something may be wrong with the facts. And sure enough, we come back full circle to the safest culprit of all, excess liquidity:

... the shift of inflation from one step to the next may be linked to three important developments: the increase in the budget deficit between the two wars (1968–1973), the declining growth rate after the crisis in 1973–1974, and the decline, which appears to have happened in the demand for money after 1977.... (ibid.)

Translation: given that GDP is growing only slowly and people want to hold less and less money (since it no longer stores value as it should), the government printing machine only adds liquidity, which in turns stokes inflation. The authors, however, are decent enough to warn us that 'since the monetary base ratio is itself a function of inflation, and since the decline in GDP growth could be partly related to the acceleration of inflation, one should not interpret our comparison in purely causal terms' (ibid.).

So that was it. Money was the cause *as well as* the consequence of inflation. And for this snake oil we needed to go through two convoluted articles, whose analysis tries to evade reality, and whose results are worthless by the authors' own criteria. Couldn't the bad news be delivered in two sentences?

But then that is the beauty of it all. In fact, it is precisely this hocus-pocus which made Israel's mainstream macroeconomics such a smashing success. Much like in *The Emperor's New Clothes*, the discipline's tailors are held in the highest esteem, their advice is sought by government and the media, and their basic ideological assumptions remain unchallenged. True, their hyperinflation of words taught us little about inflation, but as the reader should by now realise, that was never the purpose anyway. The real goal was to make the issue illegible and inaccessible, and here their victory was undeniable. Over the years, the establishment's economists used the mantra of competition and efficiency to conceal the political and class reality, while at the same time abusing their own academic monopoly to stifle and block competing explanations and alternative theories. It's high time to leave them behind. We need to understand what really happened, not how to hide it.

Inflation and Accumulation

Inflation is neither the consequence of market imperfections, nor the result of misguided policies, but rather part of an ongoing restructuring of capitalist society. A central facet of this restructuring, we argue in this book, is the process of differential accumulation – that is, the progressive redistribution of ownership claims in favour of dominant capital groups. Over time, this redistribution tends to follow the alternate paths of breadth and depth, the latter of which relies heavily on inflation. Seen from this perspective, there could be no theory of inflation separate from a theory of accumulation. Furthermore, since accumulation, particularly when understood as a power process, has no predetermined trajectory, neither does inflation. Like other macroeconomic phenomena, inflation is in fact a mirror of changing social relations, a projected image of the underlying struggle to reshape the broader structure of power. But the reflection, due to its *aggregate* definition, is inherently opaque. Moreover, its focus on totals and averages actually diverts attention from the redistributional process which makes it happen in the first place. To understand inflation, therefore, we need to go in reverse, disassembling the macro picture down to the elemental power process from which it originates.

In the remainder of this chapter, we extend and develop for the Israeli case our framework of differential accumulation regimes outlined in Chapter 2. Our purpose is to identify, conceptually as well as empirically, the principal redistributional processes: who gains, who loses, how, and why. The goal of the exercise is not to give a universal theory of inflation – which in our view is impossible – but rather to demystify the process, showing that the macroeconomic 'paradoxes' are not paradoxes at all, provided we are willing to dispense with the aggregate veil, and look at its underlying essence.

The Analytical Framework

Recall that, by definition, profit is the product of the number of employees (breadth), and the level of profit per employee (depth). In Chapter 2, we divided each of these further into internal and external routes. In the case of depth, profit per employee was thought of as a *difference* between price and cost: raising price constituted external depth, lowering cost made for internal depth. In what follows, we adopt a somewhat different decomposition, more amenable to the analysis of inflation. We write profit per employee not as a difference, but as a *product* of three components: the markup expressed as the profit share of sales, the price level measured as the ratio between nominal sales and output volume, and output per employee (assuming all output is sold).[14] Conceptually, we can write:

(11)   *Profit = Breadth · Depth*
        = (Employment) · (Profit per Employee)
        = (Employment) · (Markup · Price · Output per Employee) [15]

Expressing equation (11) in differential terms, that is, as a ratio between a typical dominant capital firm and the average firm in the corporate universe, we get:

14 In terms of our formulation in Chapter 2, external depth would then involve raising price (possibly but not necessarily with an accompanying increase in the markup), while internal depth would require either increasing output per employee, and/or widening the markup by lowering wages.

15 Symbolically, we can write:

(11a) $\Pi = L \cdot (\Pi / L) = L \cdot (\Pi / V) \cdot (V / Q) \cdot (Q / L) = L \cdot K \cdot P \cdot A$

where (Π) is profit, (L) is employment, (V) is sales, (Q) is output, (K) is markup expressed as the profit share in sales (Π / V), (P) is the price level (V / Q), and (A) is output per employee (Q / L).

(12)   *Differential Profit = Breadth · Depth*
  = (Differential Employment) ·
  (Differential Profit per Employee)
  = (Differential Employment) · (Differential Markup
  · Differential Price · Differential Output per Employee)[16]

Now, looking at a financial asset as the present value of a profit stream, its rate of accumulation is given by the rate of growth of profit, less the rate of growth of the discount factor.[17] When we measure *differential* accumulation, though, the discount factor, which is common to all assets, drops out. The result is to make the rate of differential accumulation (*DA*) – in our case, the extent to which a typical core firm accumulates faster than the average firm – depends solely on the difference between their respective profit growth rates. Using equation (11), this can be further decomposed, such that:

(13)   *DA = Breadth + Depth*
  = (Differential Employment Growth)
  + (Differential Growth of Profit per Employee)
  = (Differential Employment Growth) +
  (Differential Markup Growth + Differential Inflation
  + Differential Growth of Output per Employee) [18]

As noted in Chapter 2, this framework for differential accumulation can be used at various levels of analysis, from the individual core corporation, through corporate coalitions, to dominant capital as a whole. At every level, it enables us to examine accumulation and power not as distinct processes which need to be related, but as two sides of the same process of capitalist development. The abstract crystallisation of power appears on the left-hand side of our equations

16 Using stand alone notations for dominant capital and the $(_a)$ subscript for the average firm, this can be written as:

(12a) $(\Pi / \Pi_a) = (L / L_a) \cdot [(\Pi / L) / (\Pi_a / L_a)] = (L / L_a) \cdot (K / K_a) \cdot (P / P_a) \cdot (A / A_a)$

where (L / L_a) is differential employment, $[(\Pi / L) / (\Pi_a / L_a)]$ is differential profit per employee, (K / K_a) the differential markup, (P / P_a) is differential price, and (A / A_a) is differential output per employee.

17 The rate of accumulation is also affected by different perceptions of risk, but these can be incorporated into profit expectations, and need not concern us here. We also abstract here from the difference between expected and realised profit for reasons explained in Chapter 2.

18 With lower case notations denoting rates of change, stand alone variables for dominant capital and the subscript $(_a)$ for the average firm, the rate of differential accumulation (*DA*) is given by:

(13a) $DA = \pi - \pi_a = (l - l_a) + [(k - k_a) + (p - p_a) + (a - a_a)]$

where $(l - l_a)$ is differential employment growth, $(k - k_a)$ is differential markup growth, $(p - p_a)$ is differential inflation, and $(a - a_a)$ is the differential growth of output per employee.

in the form of differential accumulation, while the concrete political-economic processes through which this power is formed and reformed appear on the right-hand side, as components of breadth and depth.

Reiterating briefly, depth and breadth, when viewed as broad social regimes, involve different and often conflicting processes. When expanding through breadth, dominant capital groups could achieve differential employment growth either by adding new, green-field capacity faster than the average, or through amalgamation (which raises their own employment but not total employment). The preconditions for a sustained breadth regime are overall employment growth, or expansion into new territory where dominant capital does not yet operate. Otherwise, added productive capacity is bound to become excessive, while the supply of new acquisition targets dries out. Politically, a breadth regime necessitates some measure of openness and stability, in the absence of which growth is undermined and capital mobility runs into barriers. The combination of high growth, capital mobility and relative political stability works to mitigate pricing power, as well as the pressure to use it. The result is that a breadth regime is commonly characterised by relatively low inflation. A depth regime is far more conflictual. It involves one or more of the following: differential growth of output per employee (so-called 'labour productivity') which necessitates the erecting of barriers so as to prevent competitors from using the same technology; differential inflation, which is self-propelling and potentially destabilising; or differential markup growth which implies competitive redistribution and hence a heightened capital–labour conflict. Seen from a Veblenian perspective, all three depth mechanisms are based on 'strategic limitation' by dominant capital groups, who are able to politically 'sabotage' society's productive effort for their own differential gain. The broad economic feature of the depth route is therefore stagflation: stunted growth, combined with relatively high inflation.

Generalised as regimes, breadth and depth are unlikely to take place simultaneously. Breadth involves a competitive capitalist race to grab new profit streams in the context of growing production and employment. It hence weakens the ability and resolve of large firms to act in concert, openly or tacitly, toward capital–labour redistribution, which is the main venue of depth. Conversely, differential accumulation through depth, because it thrives on limitation and 'sabotage', ends up hampering growth and spoiling the benign political climate necessary for unfettered corporate amalgamation. It thus undermines the very preconditions of breadth.

Among the two regimes, breadth is the path of least resistance. Although growth may loosen business cooperation among the dominant capital groups and hence erode their pricing power, this is commonly tolerated in the expectation that such power will eventually be restored through amalgamation. In addition, growth tends to obscure the underlying capital–labour conflict, thus helping to consolidate the social hegemony of business institutions. Differential expansion via breadth is not always feasible, though, and when circumstances undermine green-field investment and/or amalgamation, dominant capital reluctantly gravitates toward depth. Compared with breadth, the depth route is far more contentious in method, risky in application, and uncertain in outcome. But the differential gains, at least in the short run, are potentially huge. The reason is that, contrary to breadth, where expansion is counted in employees, depth is counted in the much more 'flexible' monetary units of profit. Unlike the rate of growth of the former, that of the latter has no inherent limit. The spoils, therefore, are commensurate with the risk, and when dominant capital is pushed to the wall, with no breadth left, the temptation and imperative to dive into depth are difficult to resist.

Finally, it is worth repeating that this framework is not deterministic. We do not need to have *either* differential breadth *or* differential depth. Dominant capital my be unable to achieve a positive rate of differential accumulation, in which case one or both regimes will have been operating in 'reverse', with the core companies trailing rather than beating the average. But if dominant capital does expand differentially, our framework suggests its expansion will likely occur through one of these regimes, not both.

The Israeli Case: A Bird's-Eye View

Applying this framework to the Israeli case, our purpose is first to relate the country's broad political-economic development with the differential profitability of its dominant capital, and then use this framework as a basis for understanding the rise and decline of inflation. The task, though, is hardly simple. The main problem is lack of disaggregate data, particularly on the income side. Due to benign neglect, the national accounts conveniently contain no specific breakdown of capital income by category (such as profit, rent and interest), and there are no sectoral income accounts. Furthermore, there is no systematic tracking of employment, production and finance by corporate size. This neglect is of course politically motivated. Israel was one of the first countries to develop national accounting statistics, it is small in size and concentrated in structure. Collecting detailed income data under these circumstances should have been a relatively straightforward task. And yet, these basic facts remain more elusive than the country's nuclear secrets. Apparently, there is plenty to hide. Try looking for the numbers and in no time you'll find yourself running into invisible walls. In the Bank of Israel, in the Central Bureau of Statistics, in the Institute for Social Security, in the Tax Authority, in the Registrar of Companies – the data do not exist, are inaccessible, or are simply kept confidential. Fortunately for our purpose here, though, these hurdles are not entirely insurmountable. We bypass them by using roundabout estimates, which although inaccurate, are nonetheless sufficiently robust for our purpose of tracing overall trends.

Let's begin then with a bird's-eye decomposition of differential accumulation into breadth and depth. As the reader may recall from Chapter 3, we define

Israel's dominant capital as comprising the five largest corporate groups during the mid-1980s: Bank Hapoalim, Bank Leumi, Israel Discount Bankholding (IDB), Koor, and Clal. Aggregating these five groups into a single bloc, we approximate three ratios based on equation (12): differential profit, differential employment (breadth) and differential profit per employee (depth). For differential profit, the numerator is given by overall net profit of the core companies divided by five.[19] The denominator, average profit per firm, is approximated indirectly. Although there are no national accounting data for overall profit, existing data could be used to derive a useful if rough proxy. This is computed by subtracting from net national income the sum of wages and salaries, corporate taxes and income tax paid by unincorporated businesses. The result is a measure of non-labour income, which includes in addition to net profit also the net income of unincorporated business, rent and interest. Because profit is the most volatile component, its fluctuations (although not levels) are likely to dominate and hence correlate with those of non-labour income as a whole. This aggregate measure of non-labour income is then divided by the overall number of industrial establishments – a proxy for the number of firms – yielding a rough index for the economy's average net profit per firm.[20]

Next, consider breadth, measured by differential employment. Ideally, this could be observed directly by dividing average employment in the core by average employment per firm in the corporate universe as a whole. Neither of these figures is available, though, and both must be approximated indirectly. Here too, we rely on data for industrial establishments. Specifically, we use the ratio between *aggregate* employment by all large establishments (each with 300 or more employees), and the *average* employment per establishment in the industrial sector as a whole. Although this ratio is limited to the industrial sector, and is based on establishments rather than on firms, its temporal movements should provide a good proxy for changes in differential employment by the core.[21] Finally, the depth side, measured by differential profit per employee, is given by dividing differential profit by differential employment.

19 Systematic historical data on these groups are not publicly available, and were painstakingly collated by the authors from individual financial reports. See Rowley et al. (1988), Bichler (1991) and Bichler and Nitzan (1996).
20 Establishments are physical production locations, unlike firms which are legal entities. However, the vast majority of firms own a single establishment, so the overall number of firms tends to fluctuate together with the overall number of establishments. Similarly, although the industrial sector per se accounts for only part of the corporate universe, cyclical changes in the number of firms due to incorporation, bankruptcy and amalgamation tend to move in tandem across sectors.
21 The rationale is threefold. First, the vast majority of industrial firms are small, single-establishment outfits, so changes in average employment by firm and average employment by establishment will tend to fluctuate in tandem. Second, most large establishments are owned by dominant capital, and since the number of core firms is assumed fixed (five), fluctuations in the aggregate employment of large establishments should mirror those of an average core firm. Third, although industrial sector employment tended to decline relative to the service sector over the long haul, its cyclical fluctuations are similar to those of the economy as a whole.

Figure 4.10 plots all three indices on a logarithmic scale (smoothed and normalised for easier comparison). The data seem to confirm our claim that the early 1970s marked a watershed in Israeli differential accumulation. Until then, differential depth was dormant, with the core's profit per employee expanding roughly in line with the economy's average. Most of the action was in differential breadth, with dominant capital expanding its employment relative to the average – through differential absorption of newly proletarianised workers, as well as via mergers and acquisitions. Although prior data are unavailable, it is likely that breadth was the major source of differential accumulation through much of the 1950s and 1960s. Rapid economic growth, ushered first by massive immigration, then by German Holocaust restitution payments, and finally by the incorporation of the Palestinians into the Israeli economy, meant that the 'envelope' of the corporate universe was constantly expanding. This, combined with the fact that during this initial phase the large

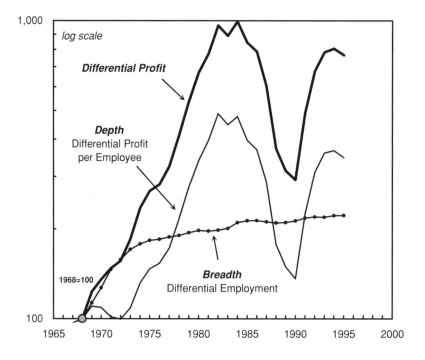

Figure 4.10   Sources of Differential Accumulation

NOTE: Indices express the ratio between a typical dominant capital.
corporation and the average firm. Series are shown as 3-year moving averages,
and are rebased with 1968=100.
SOURCE: Financial reports; Bank of Israel; Israel's Central Bureau of Statistics.

companies were still relatively small, implied an ample supply of takeover targets. Inflation in that period was relatively low, suggesting that the struggle over profit per employee was muted. Whatever differential accumulation occurred in that period should therefore be attributed largely to breadth.

The situation changed drastically in the early 1970s. Pent-up demand from the earlier immigration wave was receding, the inflow of cheap capital had ended, and the proletarianisation of the Palestinians was coming to a close. Moreover, with the core groups already having gained control over large segments of the economy, further amalgamation was becoming increasingly difficult. And as the breadth regime was reaching a dead end, pressures to shift into depth were building up.

Armament and Finance

Because differential employment growth was negligible during much of the 1970s and 1980s, our analysis of that period can safely focus on depth only, so that:

(14) DA ≈ Differential Growth of Profit per Employee
              ≈ Differential Markup Growth + Differential Inflation
              + Differential Growth of Output per Employee

The third components of depth – differential growth of output per employee – cannot be examined with available data, although that should matter little for the period at hand. The reason, illustrated in Figure 3.1, is that during the late 1970s and 1980s, GDP per capita grew by a meagre 1.4 per cent annually, compared with nearly 6 per cent during the previous quarter century, suggesting that *differential* growth in output per employee, if there was any, must have been negligible and could be ignored. For our purpose here, therefore, we can simplify further, approximating differential accumulation as a sum of two main components:

(15) DA ≈ Differential Markup Growth + Differential Inflation

This equation, too, cannot be observed directly since there are no separate data on the core's markup and rate of inflation. It could be deciphered, however, if only tentatively, by roundabout means.

Figure 4.11 shows the relationship between the overall rate of inflation (measured by the annual per cent change of the GDP deflator) and our depth index of differential profit per employee. The two series moved tightly together until the late 1980s, and then broke apart. The positive correlation of the earlier period could have direct and indirect reasons. The obvious, direct link is that when overall inflation is on the rise, dominant capital's own rate of inflation rises even faster, culminating in differential inflation (and vice versa when

overall inflation is falling). But inflation can also affect the overall rate of differential accumulation indirectly, even in the absence of differential inflation.
This will happen if inflation is positively correlated with differential markup
growth, so when inflation rises the core groups are able to raise their profit
share in sales faster than the average (and vice versa when inflation falls). Of
course, both mechanisms could operate simultaneously, and, indeed, our
analysis below suggests that this was probably the case in Israel.

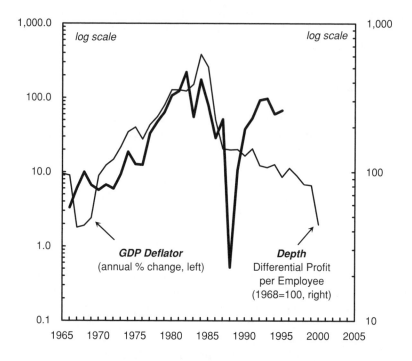

Figure 4.11   Inflation and Differential Depth

SOURCE: Financial reports; Bank of Israel; Israel's Central Bureau of Statistics.

As we pointed out in Chapter 2, the impact on differential accumulation of
differential inflation depends crucially on the relative power of dominant
capital. If this power is limited, raising prices faster than the average on the
depth side is likely to be more than offset by lost market share on the breadth
side, leading to net differential *de*cumulation. But in the Israeli reality of the
1970s and 1980s, there were two key sectors where dominant capital was pretty
much unchallenged: armament and finance. In both sectors, the large firms
enjoyed something akin to a near monopoly – not so much that they literally
dominated the entire business, but in the sense of facing little profit

competition. Moreover, since the 'product' or 'service' of these sectors had no close substitutes, their providers faced practically no inter-sectoral competition. Under such circumstances, differential inflation could work to boost depth with minimal or no impact on breadth.

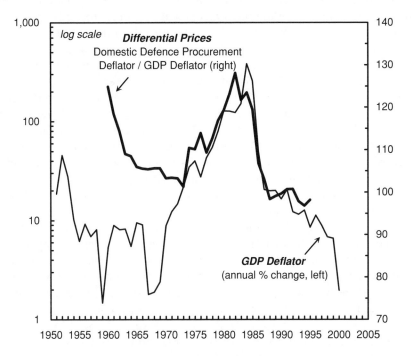

Figure 4.12   Differential Inflation

SOURCE: Israel's Central Bureau of Statistics.

Consider first the military sector. Figure 4.12 correlates the overall rate of inflation (based on the GDP deflator), with the *relative* price of military procurement (the so-called 'real price'), measured as the ratio of the GDP deflator for military procurement and the overall GDP deflator. The evidence from the chart is rather remarkable. Until the early 1970s, military price inflation was lower than overall price inflation, causing the relative price of military procurement to fall. One possible reason is of course mismeasurement.[22] But there could be another, substantive explanation: during that period,

22   A price deflator is a quotient given by dividing nominal output by 'real' output. The measurement of the latter is based on highly dubious assumptions regarding the link between quality/quantity and price. This problem, serious already under the best of circumstances, is amplified manifold when dealing with military artefacts, whose 'quality' or 'quantity' are conceptually unclear and shrouded in secrecy.

military production was not yet privatised, so there was greater concern with productivity improvements, as well as an effort to translate productivity gains into lower relative prices.

One way or the other, the honeymoon ended by the mid-1970s. With dominant capital rapidly displacing state companies as major players in the field, the relative price of military procurement not only stopped falling, but also became closely correlated with inflation. The intensification of the Israeli–Arab conflict made the military sector a captured market for the core firms, and with little foreign competition (military imports were financed by U.S. aid), the road for differential inflation was wide open.

Since the late 1980s, the situation has reversed. Overall inflation dropped sharply (for reasons to which we return later), putting downward pressure on military price inflation. Indeed, the downward pressure in the military sector was much stronger than elsewhere in the economy: militarisation came under growing public scrutiny and calls for domestic spending cuts mounted. Under these political circumstances, the *relative* pricing power of the core firms deteriorated rapidly, contributing, as the data suggest, to a negative differential inflation in that period.

A similar picture emerges from the financial sector. Here, too, the core groups reigned supreme, with a government 'licence' against domestic competition, complemented by capital controls which effectively eliminated external competition. Before examining this case, however, an important clarification is in order. The notion of 'price' in the financial sector is somewhat ambiguous. Note that financial intermediaries sell not a product, but a service: a 'linking' of those who have capital with those who wish to use it. Seen in this light, financial intermediation is one of the most standardised services, having changed little over the past millennia. The cost of providing it, though, has dropped a great deal. The spread of universal accounting standards, of asset markets and of new communication technologies must have contributed to a huge productivity improvement. On the face of it, then, the real cost of intermediation should have trended down. Moreover, since we are dealing with *relative* prices, this tendency should have been independent of inflation.[23]

But that is not what happened in Israel. In Figure 4.13, we contrast the rate of inflation with the real interest rate spread between lending and deposit rates.

---

23   For the mathematically inclined, let (P) be the price index, (LR) the nominal lending rate into the next period, (DR) the nominal deposit rate into the next period, and (RPI) the real price of intermediation. For any period t:

$$RPI_t = (LR_{t-1} - DR_{t-1}) / (P_t / P_{t-1})$$

In other words, the ex-post real price of intermediation is determined by the nominal interest rate spread set in the previous period, divided by the ratio between the current price index and the price index prevailing in the previous period. As defined in the above expression, (RPI) is already corrected for, and should therefore be independent of price inflation.

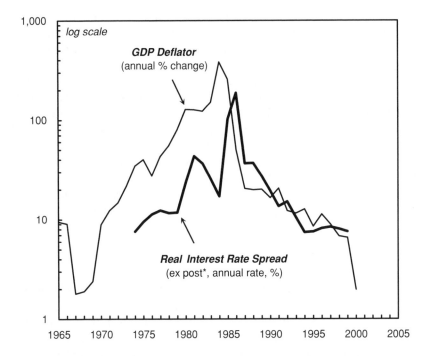

Figure 4.13   Inflation and the Price of Financial Intermediation

NOTE: Annual data.
* (lending rate$_{t-1}$ – deposit rate$_{t-1}$) / (price index$_t$ / price index$_{t-1}$).
SOURCE: Israel's Central Bureau of Statistics; Bank of Israel.

Expressed in percentage terms, the latter index measures the proportionate 'cut', adjusted for inflation, which financial institutions took from the money they moved between savers and borrowers. In Israel, this spread, instead of remaining fixed or falling, has actually moved up and down together with inflation.

The consequence was that instead of remaining stable as it should according to mainstream theory, real income from intermediation rose more than tenfold (!) during the 1975–85 period (approximation based on interest rate spreads and the volume of outstanding credit measured in constant prices, both from the Central Bureau of Statistics). Remarkably, this rise occurred while the 'real' volume of intermediation remained relatively stable. It was only in the late 1980s, when inflation started to decline, that intermediation activity began picking up again – but then, instead of increasing, the real income from intermediation actually went down! In other words, we have here a classic case of 'Veblenian sabotage', with the income of absentee owners rising as they tighten their grip through 'industrial limitation' and stagflation, and falling when their power loosens, growth resumes and inflation subsides.

In sum, the core groups, by dominating the military and financial sectors, were able to enjoy differential inflation during the 1970s and early 1980s. Faced with no meaningful rivalry, they kept their inflation in these sectors higher than the average, without any repercussions on the breadth side. In this way, even with no significant changes in differential markups, inflation for them was a principal engine of differential accumulation. Moreover, because of the leading role of military and finance in the Israeli economy at the time, differential inflation by the core firms was not only a consequence of overall inflation, but also one of its principal causes. During the 1970s and 1980s, it fuelled an upward price spiral as other income groups tried to keep up. And when these two sectors nearly collapsed – first the financial sector in the early 1980s, and then the military sector a few years later – their lower differential inflation was a major force pulling the overall rate of inflation down.

Wage Income and Capital Gains

The other component of depth – differential markup growth – is considerably more difficult to assess, since there are no markup data for either dominant capital or the average firm. But here too, a roundabout inquiry can still be instructive. Changes in markup are affected largely (although not only) by the redistributional struggle between workers and owners (the other key participants being the government and foreign owners). The analysis of *differential* changes in markups therefore requires that we examine this struggle at both the level of dominant capital and the average firm.

As illustrated in Figure 4.7 above, labour generally lost when inflation rose, while benefiting when it fell. Inverted, this relationship suggests that the overall income share of capital was positively related to inflation, although that alone still does not tell us about the markup, which measures specifically the *profit* share of income. Insight into this latter ratio could be gained by looking at the relationship between inflation and the stock market.

From an investor's viewpoint, inflation affects equity prices in two conflicting ways: it increases expected profit, while simultaneously raising the rate of interest used to discount this profit down to its present value, leaving the net impact hanging on the balance of the two. During the Gilded Age of the Israeli stock market, between the early 1970s and early 1980s, the first effect clearly dominated. Rising inflation brought soaring interest rates, but the stock market rose even faster, suggesting a spectacular, if only implicit rise in expected profit. There are two possible reasons for this. One is that investors expected inflation to generate massive earning gains through redistribution. The other is that they were simply manipulated into buying increasingly 'overvalued' stocks. We consider them in turn.

Redistribution

Figure 4.14 contrasts the evolution of CPI inflation with that of an index of redistribution between owners and workers. The index is computed as a ratio between the monthly capital gain from investment in equities (calculated as first

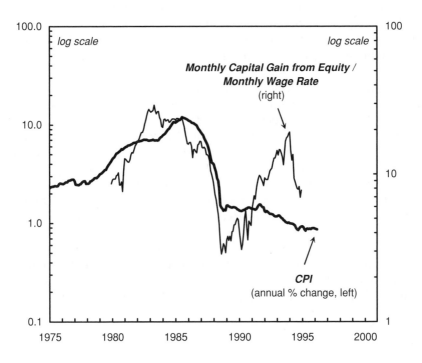

Figure 4.14 Inflation and Redistribution

NOTE: Series show monthly data expressed as 3-year moving averages.
SOURCE; IMF through McGraw-Hill (Online); Tel Aviv Stock Exchange;
Israel's Central Bureau of Statistics.

differences between monthly observations of the general stock market index), and the average monthly pre-tax wage rate, with both series smoothed for easier comparison. Movements in this index reflect the relative pecuniary benefit from owning assets as opposed to owning labour power.[24] The chart suggests that until the early 1990s, equity investors tended to gain relative to workers when inflation was rising, and lose relatively when it was falling. In other words,

24 This measure ignores the differential effect of taxes, which in Israel are levied on wages but not on capital gains, and which therefore further intensify the redistributional impact of inflation.

inflation helped redistribute earnings not only in favour of capital income in general, but also in favour of profit in particular. Between the late 1970s and mid-1980s, capital gains rose roughly five times faster than the average wage rate. From the investors' viewpoint, at least some of this relative appreciation seems justified – first, given the negative correlation between the wage share and inflation shown in Figure 4.7; and, second, since the wage bill is larger than total profit, so when it falls, the relative effect on profit is much larger.

The next question concerns specifically the markup of dominant capital. Was the core's own profit share positively correlated with inflation, and if so, was the redistributional impact *greater* than in the rest of the business sector? In other words, was inflation helping the core groups more than the average firm, hence generating differential markup growth? In principle, inflation could be associated with a differential decline, as well as growth in the markup. (For instance, if workers in the core firms are better able to maintain or even raise their wage share of sales relative to workers in smaller companies, the profit share in the core will fall relative to the average.) Although we cannot know for sure, this was probably *not* the case in Israel. The reason is that since the early 1970s, dominant capital accounted for an increasing share of the stock market's overall capitalisation, with the three largest banks alone making up 44 per cent of the total by 1982, up from a mere 7 per cent a decade earlier (Bejsky et al. 1986: 61). In other words, if the rising stock market indeed reflected a general redistribution in favour of profit as we argue, *a growing share of this redistribution must have been enjoyed by the large core firms*. We can therefore tentatively conclude that until the mid-1980s, dominant capital benefited from both components of equation (15) – differential inflation as well as differential redistribution.

Hype

The major caveat in this analysis is that during this Gilded Age, stocks became increasingly 'overvalued', with investors 'discounting' an income redistribution far in excess of what was possible in practice. That in itself of course would be hardly unique to Israel – equity prices everywhere are subject to 'hype cycles' of excessive optimism and pessimism, driven primarily by self-fulfilling expectations about asset prices rather than their underlying profit (Nitzan 1995; 1996). What makes the Israeli bubble interesting for our purpose here is first the mechanism by which hype was inflated and maintained and, second, the impact this had on differential accumulation.

As noted in Chapter 3, until 1982 investor's hype was fuelled through an elaborate stock-rigging scheme, popularly known as 'regulation' (*visut* in Hebrew). The largest players were the core groups, whose game-plan enjoyed the tacit backing of the government and the central bank. The general idea, gradually articulated into a full-fledged conspiracy, was to convince the mass of middle- and working-class retail investors that they could legitimately expect a predetermined real capital gain, and that this gain would *rise with inflation.* And for a long time, the promise was kept with 'everyone' seemingly becoming better off. But then the gains were hardly even, and what on the surface seemed like a societal panacea of 'wealth creation', was in fact a smokescreen for massive redistribution.

The process assumed two principal forms. The first was the ongoing re-rating of relative stock prices. The alchemy was fairly simple. Every morning the banks, who also acted as the largest brokers, would begin by offsetting among themselves the 'buy' and 'sell' orders received from clients. The remaining difference would then be thrown onto the perfectly competitive floor of the Tel Aviv market, where it would meet the banks' counter orders. Needless to say, these latter orders were carefully measured so that demand would typically beat supply, all to the standing ovations of the investing public. In this way, the banks and other large players managed to rig not only the overall market, but also individual stocks whose prices often soared by hundreds of per cent a month, usually without any connection to their actual or expected profits.

The other redistributional mechanism worked through public offerings of new shares (POs). According to received economic doctrine, the stock market is where entrepreneurs (who make 'real investment') meet savers (who supply the 'finance'). Their PO marriage contract, in principle at least, is for the former to take the money of the latter in return for new ownership certificates (shares), put it to productive use, and once the investment comes to fruition, split the spoils. Since POs are based on expectations for additional profit, they should correlate positively with net investment (leaving replacement investment to be financed through depreciation allowances). Now, intuitive as it may sound, this explanation must be missing something – at least in the case of Israel. Between 1973 and 1982, net investment dropped – from 21 per cent of GDP to less than 7 per cent, yet the ratio of POs to GDP, instead of falling, rose tenfold! (POs estimated based on first differences in market capitalisation deflated by stock prices.)

Impossible? Not really. While POs are indeed driven by expectations for more profit, that in itself does not mandate new productive capacity. As we explained in Chapter 2, under certain conditions, such as those prevailing in Israel at the time, the only way to increase profit expectations is to *curtail* productive capacity. During the 1970s and early 1980s, differential accumulation depended on rapid increases in depth (and on expectations for further increases in the future). Since these increases hinged on limiting breadth, any attempt to plow PO funds back into production would have spelled an excess-capacity disaster, and the possible collapse of differential accumulation altogether. It was much better to channel the money back into the financial market.

Needless to say, the *visut* mechanism was enthusiastically endorsed by the establishment's inner circle: the 'policy makers', who pretended not to see the criminality of it all, while insisting that the stock market must be kept tax free so that capital would continue to be allocated 'efficiently'; the big accounting firms, who collaborated in beautifying and falsifying corporate reports; and of course the 'free press', whose objective analysts were all too happy to issue passionate buy recommendations (alongside advertisements paid for by the same companies they endorsed). To celebrate their victory, the banks composed a happy jingle, broadcast endlessly through the various media. The banks, went the jingle, were the 'oxygen of the country', and the people were humming.

The eventual 1983 collapse of the stock market demonstrated the extent to which the process was driven by hype; but as long as it lasted hype was itself a powerful mechanism of redistribution. Established capitalists – mostly the core groups – had the market on their side. Systematically rising stock prices acted as an irresistible magnet, luring fresh liquidity into POs from 'aspiring capitalists', many of whom were workers whose life savings were thrown into the pit. This enabled the core firms not only to redistribute existing ownership titles through stock rigging, but also to create and sell new ones through massive dilution. When the crash finally came, dominant capital was bailed out by the government, whereas most of the less fortunate investors, including some moderately big players, realised they were left out with a bunch of 'excessive expectations'.

From Capital Accumulation to Inflation

So far we considered the effect on accumulation of inflation, but causality also runs in reverse, with accumulation fuelling inflation. As noted earlier in the chapter, conventional economic thinking explains inflation as a monetary phenomenon of liquidity, the famous 'too much money chasing too few commodities'. And, indeed, the two often move together, although in Israel liquidity seems to follow rather than lead inflation. Either way, the correlation is descriptive more than explanatory. If the overall price level is defined as the ratio between the total quantity of money and the total volume of commodities, then rising inflation, *by definition*, is the same thing as rising liquidity. The question, therefore, is not whether or not there is too much liquidity in the system, but *why*. Free marketeers such as Milton Friedman love to blame it all on the state. It is all the policy makers' fault. They are the ones controlling the money supply; they are the ones who allow it to grow excessively; so they are responsible (Friedman and Friedman 1979: Ch. 9). But this explanation is neither persuasive nor sufficient.

The first problem, common to all statist explanations, is the assumed omnipotence of 'policy makers'. According to this logic, the decline of inflation in the Western countries since the mid-1980s was largely the result of governments and central bankers 'getting their act together'. But then, why did they not come to their senses earlier? And when they finally did see the light, why did it happen collectively? More generally, if inflation results from the whim of policy makers, why does this whim seem to move in long cycles? Unless we can answer these questions, policy making – and therefore inflation – remain 'indeterminate'.

The second problem is the complete neglect of profit. As we noted earlier, standard definitions of the 'quantity of money' such as M1, M2 and so on, depend not only on how much of it is 'supplied' by the authorities, but also on how much is 'demanded' by economic units. This latter magnitude, which is usually left out of the picture, is predicated on the *expectation of return*. Indeed, with the exception of cash, every financial asset – from bank deposits, to bank loans, to bonds to stocks – is valued proportionately to its anticipated future earnings. Over the long run, the expansion of such assets, or capital, *can be sustained only with a parallel growth of expected capital income*. This, then, is the missing prelude to the monetarist explanation. Instead of:

money growth → inflation

we should have:

growth of expected capital income → money growth → inflation

Moreover, limiting the definition of money to financial sector liabilities only is far too narrow for a 'money-based' explanation of inflation. If bank deposits are a source of excess demand, why not bonds or equities? Surely, the latter are similarly liquid and could be used in much the same way to bid up the prices of goods and services, so why not count them in?

Figure 4.15 illustrates the significance of financial assets for Israeli inflation. In it, we chart the annual rate of GDP deflator inflation, against the ratio of stock market capitalisation to GDP prevailing two years earlier. Given that the overall value of shares is a major component of the so-called 'financial assets held by the public', the tight positive correlation between the two series, existing until the late 1980s, is rather telling. Because we are using a lagged series, this correlation suggests that, during that period, the rising stock market was not only a consequence of inflation, but also one of its major fuels. In other words, if we insist on attributing inflation to bad policy, the blame should be levelled against the 'policy' of rigging the stock market and letting dominant capital print its own money, so to speak. With net investment needs falling, rising stock prices and the tidal wave of POs flooded the economy with fresh liquidity, propping up inflation. (The situation changed markedly since the early 1990s, when the resumption of growth helped absorb the liquidity of a soaring market, leaving little fuel for stoking inflation.)

From Conflict Inflation to Accumulation

According to mainstream economic theory, inflation is a real monster. It is 'a disease', writes Milton Friedman, 'a dangerous and sometimes fatal disease, a disease that if not checked in time can destroy a society' (Friedman and

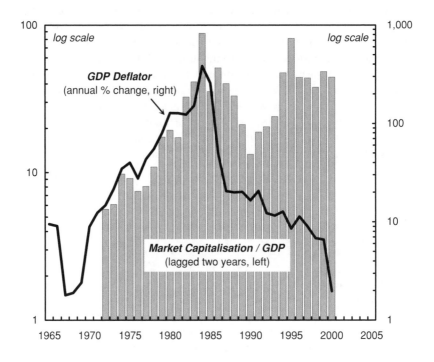

Figure 4.15   Accumulation as an Inflationary Fuel

Source: Israel's Central Bureau of Statistics; IMF through McGraw-Hill (Online).

Friedman 1979: 253). Like all diseases, explain Samuelson, Nordhaus and McCallum (1988) in their introductory textbook, inflation shows different levels of severity, ranging all the way from the 'moderate' to the 'galloping' to the 'hyper'. The first strain of the bug they associate with only the moderate cost of 'inefficiency'; the second generates 'serious economic distortions'; whereas the third, which the authors label alternatively as 'deadly virus' and 'cancer', has practically 'nothing good' about it (pp. 240–2).

Limited to the macroeconomic dimension and locked into neoclassical dogma, these characteristics fail to understand the redistributional aspect of inflation in general, and its role in differential accumulation in particular. Of course, many mainstream writers, including the ones cited above, do recognise that inflation can redistribute income. Only that in their view, this impact 'distorts' the proper distribution of income based on marginal productivity, and distortions are of course bad. But, then, since no one has ever seen marginal productivity, what exactly is the 'proper' distribution which inflation supposedly distorts? Moreover, how could the redistributional impact be universally 'bad'? After all, the loss of some is, by definition, the gain of others, so how could the two be aggregated into a single value judgement?

Distributive explanations of inflation are not new, of course. In Latin America, for instance, rapid inflation has often been associated with 'structural' and 'tug-of-war' theories. According to Hirschman (1985), however, this literature remains problematic. It shows that inflation indeed causes redistribution, but fails to explain why the same result cannot be achieved by other, more effective methods. Hirschman's criticism is relevant for our purpose, both for its insight and shortcoming.

The Latin American variety of structural inflation theories emphasise the role of production bottlenecks. Tug-of-war explanations are similar, only that instead of economic structure, they focus on the role of aggressive social attitudes. Combining the two, Hirschman offers a synthesis in which an aggressive society, when encountering structural bottlenecks, becomes prone to inflationary spirals, leading to both redistribution and restructuring.

The standard monetarist claim against this thesis, is that in the long run distribution is determined only by 'real' economic forces, not by monetary phenomena, and that inflationary redistribution, although distorting, is largely ephemeral. Hirschman agrees that the initial impact of inflation may differ from its final consequences – although that in itself, he says, does not make it neutral. The reason, he argues, is that the monetarist conception of 'real' economic forces, because of their belief in perfect competition, is far too narrow. In a non-competitive environment, the balance of political power and strategic economic positions are as 'real' as technology and physical resources. In Brazil, for instance, inflation was a principal vehicle of industrialisation. Combined with a fixed exchange rate, it undermined resource exports while encouraging machinery imports, thus contributing to an irreversible redistribution from the primary to the secondary sector.

Yet, even then, the riddle remains. Although inflation does redistribute income and alter structure, argues Hirschman, it is hardly the most 'efficient' way of doing so. In fact, most other forms of redistribution (such as universal suffrage, shorter work weeks, pension payments, public medical care, government contracts and subsidies, for instance) are far more durable, and once achieved, are more difficult to reverse. So why is it, that despite the availability of superior methods, economic agents continue to use inflation as a vehicle for redistribution?

There are two common answers, both of which are unsatisfactory according to Hirschman. One is that economic agents simply do not recognise this 'inefficiency' of inflation. Such misconceptions, though, cannot persist for long, he argues, since agents quickly learn that inflationary gains are easy to lose. The other explanation is that agents are caught in a 'prisoner dilemma', where intra-group dynamics force them to act as 'rational fools', to borrow the expression of Nobel Laureate Amartya Sen. This, however, is valid only in a competitive context. When the social arena is instead dominated by large corporations, labour unions and the state, a negotiated redistributional outcome is usually feasible without inflation. The puzzle of 'why inflation?' therefore remains.

For Hirschman, the puzzle persists because we're looking in the wrong direction. The answer, he says, lies not in the outcome of inflation, but in the *distributional struggle itself*. His explanation, somewhat reminiscent of our own power theory of accumulation, is that the real purpose of a tug-of-war inflation is not higher standards of living, but the very inflicting of damage:

> In a situation of high social tension and group antagonism, such behavior could come to be engaged in less for its normally expected material result – additional real income – than because it is enjoyed for its own sake. This means inverting the usual means–ends relationship; the gratification of intergroup hostility that is obtained by the achievement of a highly infla-tionary price or wage rise can be the real benefit, to the point where it would not matter if inflation eroded, totally and in short order, the gains achieved. (Hirschman 1985: 71)

Inflation, according to Hirschman, is in fact a relatively peaceful valve for social tensions which could otherwise culminate in an open civil war: 'with inflation', he states, 'each group is able to engage in conflictive behavior and to demonstrate its power and its antagonism to the other groups. From this point it is not far to the conclusion that such demonstration is an important function of inflation, and perhaps its real motive' (pp. 71–2).

For all its insights, Hirschman's analysis has one significant weakness: it makes inflation an *extra*-capitalist phenomenon. Although inflation cuts across different social orders, including communism, it is inherently a matter of prices and money, and is therefore essentially 'capitalistic'. To argue it is the result of vicious people playing an endless 'I'll-show-you game' against one another, and that this is a substitute for civil war, is insufficient, even if it were true. And, indeed, Hirschman does not provide evidence that the distribution of income in Latin America was largely unaltered by inflation, nor should we expect this to be the case elsewhere. As we have seen in Chapter 2, even the relatively low U.S. inflation managed to redistribute income in favour of large firms, so is it reasonable to assume that nothing of this sort happened in Latin America, where inflation was many times higher? Alternatively, could the redis-tributional impact of Germany's inflation of the 1920s be brought about by bargaining? Or can we characterise Israeli inflation of the 1970s and 1980s as a substitute for civil war? More generally, if inflation is merely a weapon in an innate conflict, why does it not persist indefinitely, but rather move in long cycles? In our view, Hirschman is right to emphasise predatory instincts, but his insight can be made much more useful as part of a broader theory of capitalism. The theory of differential accumulation could provide such framework.

Our analysis in this book argues that inflation is one of several means of differential accumulation. In the Israeli case, inflation started to rise when the conditions underwriting the earlier breadth regime were no longer sustainable. With proletarianisation and foreign aid drying up, differential accumulation by dominant capital could continue through an inflationary expansion of depth. In principle, differential accumulation could be sustained even without a major redistribution from labour to capital, provided that the core could maintain its own rate of inflation faster than the average, so as to redistribute capital income from smaller firms. In the Israeli case, though, both avenues seem to have worked in parallel.

In this context of dominant capital, politicians and central bankers operate as 'moderators' more than 'policy makers'. According to Brenner and Galai (1984), during the 1970s the Israeli government and the banks were in fact 'forced' into regulating the price of financial assets – the former in order to finance its (exogenously) growing deficit, the latter in order to raise fresh equity so as to keep their capital/loan ratio at internationally accepted levels. From a differential accumulation perspective, though, there was nothing inevitable about this process. Rising deficits and ballooning bank balance sheets happened not naturally, but as part of a broader inflationary regime. When the breadth phase was coming to a close in the late 1960s, the core groups faced two possible scenarios – a shift to depth, or collapsing differential accumulation. As it turned out, the first scenario materialised, but it could have just as well failed. In fact, the apparently 'smooth' transition from breadth to depth was predicated on a rather complex convergence of global circumstances, deliberate domestic choices, and the convenient 'folly' of Likud politicians. In this context, Israel's increasing involvement in the Middle East conflict justified higher military budgets and capital controls, which in turn helped sustain a financial explosion. And with this process in motion, the banks and the government had 'no choice' but to rig the bond and stock market, so as to prevent the process from getting out of hand.

The government's other important role was to maintain the crucial institution of indexation. As we emphasised earlier, inflation is an open-ended process, in that prices could rise without bound. But as inflation rises so does the risk of 'total loss', particularly for workers (consider the impact on the purchasing power of a fixed wage when annual inflation runs at 300 or 400 per cent). Although such losses could spell enormous gains for other social groups (as attested by the hyperinflation of Germany and Austria before the Second World War, or in Russia during the 1990s, for instance), they also create systemic risk for the social structure as whole. This is where indexation comes in.

Mainstream economists correctly point out that indexation is a major factor allowing inflation to continue. They are wrong, though, in suggesting that removing indexation will make inflation go away. Inflation exists not because of indexation, but the other way around. The main latent function of indexation is to protect *capitalists*, which it does indirectly by partly sheltering workers from the unpredictable vagaries of inflation. This point is often mis-understood and deserves further elaboration. Critiques on the left have repeatedly accused the Israeli government for fully indexing its obligations to capitalists, while keeping wages only partly indexed. Although correct, this observation is of only secondary significance. The more important service for capital is that indexation smoothes the impact on wages of inflation. The reason is that inflation could never be *fully* controlled – neither by capitalists nor by governments. Hence, if inflation is to be used as a means of differential accu-mulation, it needs indexation in order to prevent unanticipated deviations from pushing workers too close to the brink.

Of course, full indexation will make inflation useless as a means of redistri-bution. So once in place, the trick is to make indexation only *partial*, and this is where the government comes into the picture. Its role is to manipulate both the extent and timing of indexation, as it did in Israel, based on the degree to which inflation deviates from its 'desirable' path, and on the threat it posses for social stability. This also suggests that the most effective way of ending inflation is not to eliminate indexation, but rather to impose *full* indexation, as illustrated by the Brazilian *Plano Real* of 1994.

The End of Inflation

From a technical standpoint, inflation could support differential accumulation indefinitely. Politically, though, the process is unsustainable, and indeed, by the early 1980s, storm clouds began to gather. Stagnation and inflationary redistribution heightened social conflict, macroeconomic variables proved increasingly difficult to manage, and most importantly, dominant capital itself was coming under attack from new entrants lured by the immense spoils of the stock market.

Crescendo

Although the three large banks dominated the financial scene, the tidal wave created by their manipulations helped lift all boats, some with pretty lofty aspirations. One of the more important newcomers was Danot, a financial group formed by a coalition of large owners, including Moshevitch and Fromchenko from the food company Elite, Saharov from Sahar insurance, Pecker from Pecker Steel, Lautman from Delta Textile, and Proper, the country's pasta baron from Osem. In 1980, the group got itself a medium-size bank, the First International Bank of Israel (FIBI), which it purchased for $23 million from Saul Eisenberg, and which it quickly turned into an aggressive vehicle for stock rigging and POs. Within two years, FIBI was floated, fetching a market cap-italisation of $400 million. And Danot was by no means alone. The list of aspiring contenders included, among others, speculators such as Riger and Fishman, who operated the famous Ronit mutual fund; Rothschild's General Bank; United Mizrahi Bank; Saul Eisenberg and his partner Michael Albin; and, surprise surprise, the Kibbutzim, which borrowed heavily so that they too can get a share of the loot.

On the surface, the overall context looked hospitable for the newcomers. Although this was at the height of the Lebanon War, with causalities mounting and the public increasingly restless, expectations for war profits and inflationary gains seemed amply sufficient to offset the slight military inconvenience. Just to be on the safe side, though, the banks mounted mobile brokerage offices on light trucks, sending them deep into Lebanese territory, so that Israeli soldiers could continue exercising their natural right of investment, while taking periodic breaks from the fighting. And, indeed, by the end of 1982, the stock market's capitalisation reached a record $16 billion, or 88 per cent of GDP, with an estimated one-quarter of households playing the national casino.

But, then, there was also greater competition and conflict. In the beginning, this didn't seem as much of a problem, since, unlike in the goods and services market, here the struggle brought higher, not lower accumulation. The reason was simple. In order to attract clients, the contenders promised and delivered superior returns; to this, the banks responded by rigging their own yields higher, which in turn prompted the contenders into a fresh rounds of increases, and so on. Just to give the reader a feel for the magnitudes involved, in August 1982, while the Israeli army was surrounding Beirut, the banks' top six funds yielded a *monthly* dollar return of 25–30 per cent, against 60 per cent delivered by Ronit of Riger and Fishman.

And so, although everything was going up, soon enough assets started to reshuffle. Tempted by the huge differences, more and more investors preferred to have their accounts 'managed' by the new mavericks, and since the latter favoured 'speculative' stocks over the banks' own 'blue chips', the migration created selling pressures which the banks were forced to absorb at mounting costs. Moreover, smelling blood, some of the contenders became daring enough to take on the banks directly. The most intrepid were Riger and Fishman, who tried to wrestle Hasneh Insurance and Ampal Investment from Bank Hapoalim. The hostile bid for Ampal was particularly noteworthy, since, after leaving Hapoalim in 1981, Ya'acov Levinson used the company as a vehicle for siphoning the bank's assets to the United States. If Riger and Fishman had their way, the entire operation would be put at risk. The time for counterattack had come.

Collapse

The first to realise the game was over was Danot, which quickly moved to unload its investment in FIBI, hoping to pull out before things turned dicey. The timing seemed right. The prospected buyer was United Mizrahi Bank, the country's fourth largest financial institution, whose owners were willing to put $150 million for half the stocks; share prices were sky high, so the money for the deal could be easily raised through a fresh PO; and, finally, the various 'authorities', including the Finance Minister, the Governor of the Bank of Israel, and the Banks' Controller, all extended their blessing, so the deal looked set for an easy sailing.

But it was all too late. The takeover of FIBI by United Mizrahi would have created a formidable competitor to the large banks, and that, of course, was out of the question. 'We were naïve', reflected Fishman who was partner to the deal, 'failing to realise that the banks were conspiring behind our backs.... In a criminal violation of banking confidentiality, they leaked thick hints to the media that we were in financial crisis ... causing the public to gradually abandon the stocks we had interest in' (cited in Avneri 1987: 19). And then, in one swoop, the flood gates were opened. The large banks, directly and through their clients, dumped the floating shares of FIBI, along with many other stocks favoured by the speculators. Within two weeks in January of 1983, the market lost a full $4 billion, or 40 per cent of its value.

The contenders suffered a mortal blow. Danot became worthless and was dismembered two years later (with some of its owners losing control of their own companies); Ronit lost half its value, putting Riger and Fishman out of circulation for a decade; Albin fell out of favour with Eisenberg and died mysteriously during his police investigation; while Levinson, having learnt of a brewing criminal investigation into his Ampal affairs, committed suicide. Numerous smaller operators got entangled with their creditors and the law, many having to flee the country. And the Kibbutzim, which lost a fortune, fell into a debt trap from which they never fully recovered, and which marked the beginning of their end as a social institution.

And, yet, the removal of these contenders also robbed dominant capital of its main defence line. Whereas previously, bank stocks were considered a 'conservative' investment compared to the high-yielding shares promoted by the speculators, now, that the latter were beaten to pulp, the banking stocks no longer looked secure. Moreover, political folly, which until then worked wonders for dominant capital, suddenly became counter-productive. The main culprit, although blissfully ignorant of his larger role in the drama, was Finance Minister Yoram Aridor. Failing to realise the political fallout of a market crash, he stubbornly continued to 'fight' inflation by keeping the pace of currency depreciation slower than the rate of price increases. Investors, who expected an imminent exchange rate correction, naturally sold their stocks to buy dollars, and the banks, now without the speculators to defend them, had to bear the brunt. Trying to put their finger in the cracking dam, they began borrowing abroad to shore up their war chest. Their secret plan, worked out in great haste as the storm gathered momentum, was to defend a list of blue chip stocks, including their own, in the hope that, once Aridor came back to his senses and devalued the currency, investors would quickly rotate back to the resilient stock market. But Aridor, despite mounting pressures from all sides, refused to understand. And so, in October 1983, the inevitable happened. The first to pull out of the deal was Hapoalim, and once the banks' common front collapsed, the market crashed, causing another $7 billion worth of assets to evaporate into thin air.

From Price Inflation to Wage Compression

To prevent a *de*cumulation meltdown, the government stepped in with a massive bailout plan, which turned the banking stocks into government bonds for five years, redeemable at 60 per cent of their value one week before the crash. This meant further liquefaction of the monetary system, and even faster inflation. But capitalist confidence was seriously shaken, and with the middle class badly hurt and no longer willing to hold shares, the income redistribution mechanism from labour to capital was beginning to crack (see Figure 4.14). In parallel, the U.S. elite began demanding an end to the depth regime altogether. One reason was that high military spending provided Israeli armament contractors with enough of a threshold to start developing main battle systems. Their U.S. counterparts found this new development unacceptable, and so Israel was duly forced to curtail its domestic military budget (as opposed to arms imports), and abandon its grandiose plans for its own fighter aircraft. Another reason was that the U.S. Administration became increasingly concerned that inflation could destabilise its principal regional satellite. To highlight its resolve, Washington dispatched a team of U.S. economists, lead by Herbert Stein and Stanley Fischer, to draft a ten-point stabilisation programme, known as 'Herb's 10-Points'. The programme, secured by a $1.5 billion standby facility to ward off currency speculators, followed the standard IMF template of devaluation, tight monetary and fiscal policy and, of course, a significant wage erosion. Although the plan was presented as a mere 'recommendation', the sovereign Israeli government was hardly in a position to ignore it.

The result was the 1985 New Economic Plan (NEP). In the decade following the plan, Israeli economists have often congratulated the government for finally taking a bold stand, swallowing the bitter medicine they recommended all along. From the perspective of differential accumulation, however, the plan was hardly 'bold'. With both military spending and the stock market in tatters, dominant capital faced a grave risk. For decades, consensus among the elites was bolstered by an ongoing process of differential accumulation – first through breadth, and then through a concerted manipulation of depth. But with a melting stock market and the consequent collapse of differential accumulation, this consensus broke down.

It was from this point onward, when it could no longer support differential accumulation, that inflation turned into a 'public enemy'. The most pressing need was to stabilise the profit of dominant capital, and since inflation could no longer do the job, the onus fell on wages (i.e., on internal rather than external depth). In order to do so, though, it was first necessary to create the proper crisis atmosphere and a consequent need for 'sacrifice'. Paradoxically, this was not easy. The problem was that for years, workers were repeatedly told that they were the big winners from inflation (through their 'excessive' wage demand). But if so, why would they give up this perk now? Clearly, the 'cost' had to be re-articulated for them, and as it turned out there was no shortage of volunteers. Kleiman (1984), for instance, identified five heavy burdens: the wasteful activity associated with frequent re-pricing of products (such as putting new pricing stickers and making new price lists); the cost of learning new prices and the loss of human capital embedded in (ephemeral) knowledge of nominal values; the risk of capital loss from financial speculation; 'acute sense of frustration' associated with heightened uncertainty; and last but not least, the 'sorrow of lost opportunities' and the cost of mistaken decisions. According to Kleiman's own arithmetic, over the five-year period ending in 1982, the societal burden associated with these losses amounted to 3–4 per cent of GDP, which, in his opinion was what the public (that is, the workers) should be willing to forego in order to have inflation stop dead in its tracks.

And so, by the mid-1980s, the preconditions for a shift from external to internal depth were all in place: a differential accumulation crisis of unprecedented proportions, mounting pressures from the United States to change course, and an ideological front, erected with impressive academic support, on the necessity of 'sacrifice'. The clear target was labour. The breadth route was closed, and so was differential inflation. The only means of preventing further drops in differential accumulation was differential redistribution through wage erosion.

The centrepiece of the 1985 NEP was price and wage controls. The reason is that while dominant capital knew what it wanted, it could not achieve it on its own. It needed an external moderator, a 'relatively autonomous' body in the language of Poulantzas (1973: 190–3), and this is where the government again became crucial. A particular regime of differential accumulation is based on a broad consensus, common habits of thinking, and similar modes of behaviour. Since these conventions tend to acquire their own inertia, a *transition* from one regime to another often requires outside 'intervention'. The state, with its universal appearance, supplies this reliable intervention. It is reliable since state officials and institutions are locked into the logic of capital, and are therefore trusted with considerable autonomy to act within this logic, even if their policies seem counter to the immediate interests of dominant capital.

The elite does not see this in those terms, of course. Given the antagonistic appearance of differential accumulation, it rarely acknowledges, even to itself, the cooperative aspects of its endeavour. The Israeli upward price spiral was propagated by a complex set of open and tacit collusions among the big 'price makers'. This could not be openly admitted, of course, so the blame was dully assigned to 'inflationary expectations'. But then what are these expectations if not the consensus of the elite itself? To change expectations therefore is to change the outlook of the elite, and this is when an external actor like the government becomes handy.

This logic is evident in a recent assessment of the NEP written by David Brodet (1995), who, as General Manager of the Finance Ministry at the time, was responsible for wage and price controls. Orthodox macroeconomic policies, he writes, are necessary but insufficient for taming galloping inflation. The main problem is inertia, and that could be broken only with direct controls. Specifically, agents had to be 'convinced' that prices could move down as well as up, which is why he implemented the so-called 'pair policy', in which for every price the ministry raised, another was lowered.

But then changing the 'price mentality', as Brodet puts it, was largely a means to an end. In our view, the ultimate goal was to alter the 'profit mentality'. Specifically, price controls were designed, if only implicitly, to show that from now on, redistribution was to be achieved not through price inflation but through wage compression. And this was the NEP's Achilles' heel.

Unlike inflation, which leaves prices unbounded on the upside, wage compression has definite limits, particularly when combined with a highly contractionary 'stabilisation' policy. And, indeed, the economic recovery of 1985–87 was short lived, and inflation, while low by previous standards, remained at two-digit levels. The government responded by jacking up real interest rates, and growth collapsed once more. Needless to say, the official culprit was, again, labour. According to Stanley Fischer (1995: 595), things were working fine until workers started protesting their falling income, and, so, 'just as it was about to win the war, the government signed a most generous contract with the Histadrut'. From then on, it was all downhill. Workers, flooded with cash, went on a spending spree, leaving the central bank no choice but to hit the monetary brakes and kill the recovery. Obviously, life would have been so much easier if only the workers knew what was good for them.

From a differential accumulation perspective, though, macroeconomic tightening was a dead end. The substitute for depth is breadth, and indeed, it was only with the immigration boom of the 1990s that things began moving again. The growth 'miracle' which followed had little to do with bold politicians and correct policy, however. It was mostly anchored in the collapse of the Soviet Union, which unleashed an influx of a million new immigrants into Israel, and the prospects for joining the globalisation process. Together, these processes have finally convinced the Israeli elite (as well as many foreign investors) that a new breadth phase was in the making.

The new breadth regime of the 1990s, however, much like the previous depth phase of militarised stagflation, did not unfold in a vacuum. It was rather part and parcel of much broader changes affecting the nature of global accumulation. We turn to examine this broader context now, beginning with the political economy of Middle East energy conflicts.

5

The Weapondollar–Petrodollar Coalition

I warn you, that when the princes of this world start loving you, it means they're going to grind you up into battle sausage.

– Louis-Ferdinand Céline, *Journey to the End of the Night*

Although economically isolated from its neighbours in terms of trade and investment, Israel's political economy has nevertheless been deeply embedded in the larger saga of the Middle East. The twentieth century, with its endless thirst for energy, made the region crucial for its oil exports. Since the 1960s, however, oil outflows have been complemented by the newer and more precarious movement of arms imports. And as the 'petrodollar' earnings from oil and 'weapondollar' profits from arms grew increasingly intertwined, there emerged in the region a pattern of 'energy conflicts', a series of oil-related wars and revolutions which again and again rocked the Middle East, sending shock waves throughout the world.

Enigmas

Unfortunately, most of those who tried to understand this link between oil and arms have willingly put themselves into the familiar straitjacket of aggregates. The theories are numerous, but their story is almost always about 'states', 'policy makers' and the 'national interest'. Economists writing in this vein, such as Chan (1980) and Snider (1984), for instance, tend to concentrate on the issue of 'recycling'. The problem, as they see it, concerns the balance of payment. Energy crises jack up the cost of imports for oil-consuming countries, while creating trade surpluses and accumulated reserves for the oil-producing ones. A relatively efficient way to 're-balance' these imbalances, they continue, is for oil importers, mostly developed countries, to sell weapons to oil exporters. Politically, this is easy to do. Consumers in the arms-exporting countries don't care much since the shipments do not require new taxes, whereas rulers in the oil-exporting countries like the trade since it boosts their self-image and sense of security. The resulting arms race is perhaps unpleasant, but largely unavoidable; unless, of course, the producing countries agree to lower their oil prices.

The same universal language dominates the 'realist' literature of international relations. The underlying political anthropology here portrays a menacing Hobbesian environment, with each nation seeking to endure in a largely anarchic world. Survival and security in this context hinge on economic prosperity, national preponderance and military prowess, which are in turn critically dependent on the differential access to advanced technology, raw materials, and of course energy. According to the 'materialist' strand of this literature, such as Nordlinger (1981) and Waltz (1979), this dependency explains both why central decision makers insist on handling raw material and oil themselves, rather than leaving the matter to private business, and also why they seem almost trigger-happy whenever access to such resources is threatened. True, many conflicts cannot be easily explained by material interests. And yet even on such occasions, argue the realists, the national interest is usually paramount. One reason, they explain, is that the national interest could be 'ideal' as well as 'material'. And indeed, according to Krasner (1978a: Ch. 1), after the Second World War, U.S. state goals have become more 'ideological', emphasising broad aims such as 'competition' and 'communist containment' over strict access to resources (see also Lipschutz 1989). The other reason is that state officials can be wrong, misunderstand the true nature of the situation, or they can simply miscalculate the costs and benefits. But here too, even when policy seems 'nonlogical', the driving force is still – as always – the national interest (Krasner 1978a: Ch. 1).

Naturally, this type of theory can explain almost everything. The process is simple. Take any policy, and begin by looking for materialist explanations. If you find none, don't dismay. Look for ideal ones. And if that too fails, there are always errors, so you can never go wrong. Moreover, the national interest itself is a very strange concept. Since society is full of conflict, adherents of this concept argue it represents not the sum of individual interests, but rather the overall interest of the nation. In the language of Stephen Krasner, it is not the 'utility *of* the community' which matters, but rather the 'utility *for* the community', as determined by its central decision makers (1978a: 12, original emphases). However, since the decision makers themselves rarely agree on the matter, it is usually the *researcher* who ends up deciding the national interest for them (or for the reader). And the way this interest is phrased is often so loose, that it can be made consistent with virtually any line of action.

Now, to be fair, other grand narratives are also vulnerable to such ambiguities. Take the 'interest of the capitalist system', a notion often invoked by func-tionalist Marxism to rationalise developments which, on surface at least, appear contrary to the immediate interests of individual capitalists. A typical example for this is the welfare state. On the face of it, this institution undermines capitalist power. Yet, if we were to push this to the 'final analysis', the conclusion would be the opposite: by making life more bearable for the workers, the welfare state ends up keeping capitalism as a whole viable. But is this really true? Or rather, can we *prove* it is true? Another example is green-field investment. Many Marxists consider such investment as synonymous with accumulation, and therefore good for capitalism. But if so, is the century long shift from building new capacity to mergers and acquisitions, illustrated in Chapter 2, bad for capitalism? And what about a high price of oil? Or war in the Middle East? Are they good or bad for capitalism 'as a whole'? The truth is that these questions cannot be answered, and for a simple reason. The 'capitalist system', much like the 'state', is an encompassing myth. It provides the broader framework for the discussion, and therefore cannot be simultaneously used for validating or refuting a specific hypothesis within that discussion.

The problem is illustrated in Bromley's otherwise insightful analysis of world oil. His conclusion in that study is that the post-war order, and particularly the emergence of OPEC and higher prices, have in fact helped strengthened the 'general preconditions of capitalist production' under the overall auspices of U.S. hegemony (1991: 59). But what exactly are these 'general preconditions'? And if OPEC and the oil crisis have indeed boosted the system of U.S.-dominated capitalism during the 1970s and 1980s, why haven't the cartel's disintegration and lower oil prices undermined this system during the 1990s? Or have they? Surely, the world has changed in the interim. But then, it always does, so how could we ever know?

The international flows of oil and arms have been examined also from the more disaggregate perspective of the underlying industries, but here, too, there is a considerable lack of unanimity, even on substantive issues. Writing from an implicit 'instrumentalist' view, Blair (1976) and Engler (1977), for example, contend that, intentionally or not, the energy policies of parent governments (particularly the United States, Great Britain and the Netherlands) have had the effect of assisting the international oligopoly of world oil. An almost opposite view is expressed by Turner (1983) and Yergin (1991), who, in line with a more realist perspective, argue that there was a gradual but systematic erosion in the primacy of international oil companies, and that, since the 1970s, these firms were in fact acting as 'agents', or intermediaries between their host and parent governments. Studies on the international arms trade have been equally controversial. According to Sampson (1977), the absence of any international consensus on disarmament created a void, which was then filled by the persistent sales effort of the large weapon makers. And since arms exports become particularly significant in peacetime as domestic defence budgets tend to drop, the end of U.S. involvement in Vietnam during the early 1970s redirected attention to the Middle East, causing military shipments into the region to rise. Other writers, however, such as Krause (1992), reject this interpretation. The impact of private producers on arms sales policies, he claims, should not be overstated, at least not in the case of the United States, where the volume of arms exports is small relative to domestic military procurement and the contractors' civilian sales.

Whatever their insight, though, most writers tend to treat Middle East conflicts and energy crises as related though *distinct* phenomena. Wars are commonly seen as arising from a combination of local conflicts complicated by superpower interactions. Energy crises, on the other hand, are generally perceived as a consequence of changing global market conditions and institutional arrangements (such as OPEC). Some conflicts – for instance, the 1990–91 war between Iraq and the U.S.-led coalition – have been partly attributed to a struggle over the control of crude reserves, whereas others – specifically the Arab–Israeli wars of 1967 and 1973, and the Iran–Iraq conflict of 1980–88 – were seen as having aggravated ongoing energy crises. Yet, no one has so far offered a general explanation of 'energy conflicts' – that is, a framework which would *integrate* militarisation and conflict on the one hand, with global energy flows and oil prices on the other. Most significantly, existing writings on both oil and war in the region tend to deal rather inadequately, and often not at all, with the process which matters the most, namely the accumulation of capital.

As outlined in Chapter 2, during the 1970s and early 1980s the pendulum of differential accumulation swung from breadth to depth. While economic growth and corporate amalgamation receded, stagflation rose to fill the gap, contributing massively to the differential profit of dominant capital (Figures 2.6 and 2.9). A central facet of this new regime was the cycle of militarisation and energy conflicts in the Middle East, which helped both fuel inflation and aggravate stagnation the world over (Figure 2.10). Stated in this way, our argument may sound reminiscent of supply-shock theory, but the similarity is only superficial. For one, stagflation started to pick up in the early 1970s, *before* the increase in the price of oil. The oil boom certainly fuelled the process, but as a mechanism, not a cause. Second, and more importantly, to argue that oil prices were somehow a shock coming from 'outside' the system is to miss the point altogether. On the contrary, if there was indeed any 'system' here, it was one of differential accumulation. And at that particular historical junction, its engine was running in depth mode fuelled by an atmosphere of crisis emanating from the Middle East. In other words, the region was very much an integral part of the 'system'.

The purpose in this chapter is to examine the global political economy of this process. In a nutshell, our argument is that, during the 1970s, there was a growing convergence of interests between the world's leading petroleum and armament corporations. Following rising nationalism and heightened industry competition during the 1950s and 1960s, the major international oil companies lost some of their earlier autonomy in the Middle East. At the same time, the region was penetrated by large U.S. and European-based manufacturing companies which, faced with mounting global competition in civilian markets, increased their reliance on military contracts and arms exports. The attendant *politicisation* of oil, together with the parallel *commercialisation* of arms exports, helped shape an uneasy *Weapondollar–Petrodollar Coalition* between these companies, making their differential profitability increasingly dependent on Middle East energy conflicts. Interestingly, when we look at the history of the region from this particular perspective, the lines separating state from capital, foreign policy from corporate strategy, and territorial conquest from differential profit, no longer seem very solid. Many conventional wisdoms are put on their head. State policies, ostensibly aimed at advancing the national interest, often appear to undermine it; company officers and government officials, moving through a perpetually revolving door, sometimes simultaneously cater to several masters; arms races are fuelled for the sake of 'stability'; and peace is avoided for being 'too expensive'. In contrast to these anomalies, the logic of differential accumulation seems remarkably robust. It helps us make sense of corporate strategies, of foreign policies and of the link between them – and all of that within the broader context of 'energy conflicts'.

The Military Bias

The first half of the nineteenth century in Europe was marked by rising hopes for progress. The Industrial Revolution was helping humanity harness nature. The French Revolution brought new ideas of freedom. Nationalism, liberalism and socialism were breaking new ground. And absolutism was on its way out. With these changes all taking place at once, many were tempted to believe that society was on its way to a better future, one in which military conflict and war were to be rooted out. The theoretical justification for these hopes owed much to the technological determinism of French philosopher Auguste Comte. War he argued, was mainly the consequence of scarcity. Scarcity, however, was alleviated by industrialisation and technical progress, and since these were expected to continue their forward march, conflict and war were bound for extinction. And initially, he seemed vindicated. The 'bellicosity index', devised by Pitirum Sorokin and charted in Figure 5.1, shows the intensity of European military conflicts, measured by a weighted average of various indicators, as it evolved since the twelfth century (Sorokin 1962, reported in Wright 1964: 56). This intensity roughly doubled every hundred years until the seventeenth century. During the eighteenth and nineteenth centuries, however, with technical change and industrialisation picking up speed, bellicosity fell sharply, much along the lines suggested by Comte.

And yet, the drop proved a false start. By the second half of the nineteenth century, with the European powers scrambling to complete their colonial acquisitions, conflict again flared up in and outside the Continent. Sorokin's bellicosity index came back with a vengeance, soaring to record highs in the twentieth century, even without counting the Second World War and beyond. Comte was wrong. Industrialisation in general and capitalism in particular were

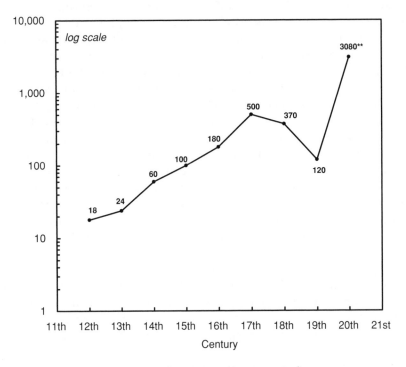

Figure 5.1   European Bellicosity Index*

* Number of wars weighted by duration, size of fighting force, number of
casualties, number of countries involved, and proportion of combatants to total
population.
** Data for the twentieth century cover the period until 1938 only.
SOURCE: Sorokin (1962) reported in Wright (1964: 56).

compatible with war after all. And indeed, by the early twentieth century, a
growing number of writers, mostly Marxist, started pondering the link between
capitalism and imperialism.

Imperialism

The seminal study on the issue, titled *Imperialism*, was written by a British left
liberal, John Hobson (1902). Many of his themes have resurfaced again and
again in subsequent works, so the argument is worth presenting, if only briefly.
During the latter part of the nineteenth century, capitalism in the leading
countries was moving from atomistic competition toward concentration and
monopoly. According to Hobson, this transition tended to redistribute income
from wages to profits, thus creating a chronic problem of 'oversavings' and

'underconsumption'. Monopoly profit, like any profit, was earmarked for green-field investment. With workers having less to spend, however, the need for such investment was much reduced. In order to avoid stagnation and crisis, the excess savings therefore had to find outlets *outside* the home country, hence the tendency toward imperialist expansion. The scramble for colonies was intense, and Africa, which in 1875 had only 10 per cent of its territory colonised, lost another 80 per cent to European powers within the next quarter of a century. And, yet, this was only ironic, since, according to Hobson, imperialism was in fact a *net loss* to society, and even to its capitalist class. A more sensible route would have been to redistribute income back from monopoly profit to wages, thereby reversing the entire causal chain from monopolisation to stagnation. So why had imperialism prevailed over redis-tribution? For Hobson, the reason was that state policy was conducted not by society at large, and not even by the capitalist class, but rather by a fairly narrow coalition for whom imperialism was indeed hugely profitable. The main profiteers were the arms producers, trading houses, the military and imperial apparatus, and above all, the financiers, whose foreign investments appreciated greatly from reduced risk premiums brought by imperial rule. The financiers, leading the pro-imperial coalition, were able to harness key politicians to their cause, enlist the possessing classes on threat of redistribution at home, and have the newspapers inflame for them the necessary atmosphere of nationalism and racism.

Marxists writers were greatly influenced by Hobson, although most tended to reject his belief that capitalism could be 'reformed'. According to Rosa Luxemburg, territorial expansion and takeover – in quest for both new markets and cheaper inputs – was in fact *inherent* in capitalism, 'the first mode of economy which is unable to exist by itself, which needs other economic systems as a medium and soil' (1913: 467). Moreover, the expansion was *necessarily violent*. 'Force is the only solution open to capital: the accumulation of capital, seen as a historical process, employs force as a permanent weapon, not only as its genesis, but further on down to the present day' (p. 371).

And indeed, according to Rudulf Hilferding (1910), imperialism projected its violence inward as much as outward, working to transform the economic, political and ideological face of the imperial countries themselves. In contrast to the classical stage, in which the various fractions of capital were politically divided, during the monopoly stage the leading elements among these fractions were fused into 'Finance Capital', an amalgamate of industry and finance controlled by the big banks. This newly welded power, argued Hilferding, drove finance capital into seeking an ever growing territory for its operations, but such expansion was meaningless unless protected by tariffs against outside competition. It was here, then, in the dual quest for territory and protection, that private capital discovered it actually needed a *strong state*:

The demand for an expansionary policy revolutionizes the whole world view of the bourgeoisie, which ceases to be peace-loving and humanitarian. The old free traders believed in free trade not only as the best economic policy but also as the beginning of an era of peace. Finance capital abandoned this belief long ago. It has no faith in the harmony of capitalist interests, and knows well that competition is becoming increasingly a political power struggle. The ideal of peace has lost its luster, and in place of the idea of humanity there emerges the glorification of the greatness of and power of the state.... The ideal now is to secure for one's own nation the domination of the world, an aspiration which is as unbounded as the capitalist lust for profit from which it springs.... Since the subjection of foreign nations takes place by force – that is, in a perfectly natural way – it appears to the ruling nation that this domination is due to some special natural qualities, in short to its racial characteristics. Thus there emerges a racist ideology, cloaked in the garb of natural science, a justification for finance capital's lust for power, which is thus shown to have the specificity and necessity of a natural phenomenon. An oligarchic ideal of domination has replaced the democratic ideal of equality. (Hilferding 1910: 335)

For Karl Kautsky, a Marxist contemporary of Hilferding, this portrayal was far too bleak. The conflict between industrial and financial capital, he argued, had not been decisively won by finance capital as Hilferding claimed. In fact, there was scope for labour opposition, in both the developed and periphery countries, to strengthen the hands of the industrial fraction. Such opposition, if successful, could redirect capitalism toward a more benign alternative, which Kautsky called 'ultra-imperialism' (1970; originally published in 1914). Exploitation would surely continue, but the exploiters, instead of locking horns in imperial destruction and inter-capitalist war, would vie for a common front. 'Hence, from a purely economic standpoint', he wrote, 'it is not impossible that capitalism may still live through another phase, the translation of cartelisation into foreign policy: a phase of *ultra-imperialism*, which of course we must struggle against as energetically as we do against imperialism, but whose perils lie in another direction, not in that of the arms race and the threat to world peace' (p. 46, original emphasis).

With hindsight, we can read here an early anticipation of the transnational corporation, of decolonisation, and of the shifting emphasis of imperialism from inter-capitalist rivalry to core–periphery struggles. But when Kautsky first articulated this view, before the First World War, he was greeted by great hostility from Lenin and Bukharin. Lenin in particular, having thrown his hopes on an imminent revolution, refused to see capitalism as culminating in anything less than Armageddon. Unequal development among the different capitalist powers, he argued, prevented any mutual cooperation among them: 'Finance capital and the trusts do not diminish but increase the differences in the rate of growth of the various parts of the world economy. Once the relation of forces is changed, what other solution of the contradictions can be found *under capitalism* than that of *force?'* (Lenin 1917: 243–4; cited from Marxist Archives, at www.marxists.org). Furthermore, if workers were sufficiently powerful to bend finance capital as Kautsky suggested, what was to prevent them from moving all the way to socialism?

Military Spending

After the Second World War, things changed drastically. In the periphery, colonialism came to an end, while in the developed core countries real wages soared and unemployment fell sharply. Was this a fundamental change, asked the Marxists? Was capitalism finally able, perhaps with the aid of government intervention, to resolve its earlier contradictions? And if so, was socialism irrelevant? According to contemporary adherents of the 'monopoly capital school', led by Baran and Sweezy, the answer to all three questions was negative. The post-war prosperity was certainly real; but it wasn't because of capitalism, but *despite* capitalism. The shift from small-scale production to big business, they argued, altered the functioning of the economy in two important respects. On the production side, large-scale undertakings, heavy R&D spending, and the incessant introduction of new technologies enabled the big oligopolies to cut cost as never before. At the same time, the strong oligopoly bias against price competition not only prevented these cost savings from being translated into lower prices, but actually introduced persistent inflation. And so, contrary to the view of classical Marxism, monopoly capitalism, by lowering cost and raising prices, created a *tendency for the surplus to rise*. For Marx, the chief menace to capitalism came from a rising organic composition of capital, leading to a tendency for the rate of profit to fall; here, on the other hand, the key issue was the rising rate of exploitation, or 'surplus' in the new terminology. But if so, what was the problem? Indeed, shouldn't a rising surplus bring *higher* profit, thus boosting capitalism even further? Not necessarily, argued Baran and Sweezy:

> According to our model, the growth of monopoly generates a strong tendency for surplus to rise without at the same time providing adequate mechanisms of surplus absorption. But surplus that is not absorbed is also surplus that is not produced: it is merely potential surplus, and it leaves its statistical trace not in the figures of profits and investment but rather in the figures of unemployment and unutilised productive capacity. (Baran and Sweezy 1966: 218)

In short, Hobson's curse was still with us. Monopoly bred redistribution, underconsumption, and therefore *falling* surplus – that is, unless absorbed by *external* offsets to savings. Contrary to the early writings on the subject, however, the most potent offsets according to Baran and Sweezy were created not by colonial expansion, but through the 'institutionalised waste' of state spending, a process first identified by Thorstein Veblen.

For external offsets to savings to be effective, the two writers argued, they needed, first, to absorb more surplus than they generated, and, second, to be available in large doses. Investment was no good here, since it usually generated more surplus than it absorbed, while exports were limited by foreign demand. Government expenditures, on the other hand, and particularly *military spending*, faced neither limitation. They were commonly 'wasteful' in the sense of absorbing but not generating surplus, and they could be extended almost at will. Technically speaking, *civilian* government spending could work in much the same way. Politically, though, it was unwelcome. The main reason was that such spending, as it pushed the economy toward full employment, undermined the social hegemony of business. According to Michal Kalecki,

> 'discipline in the factories' and 'political stability' are more appreciated by the business leaders than profits. Their class instinct tells them that lasting full employment is unsound from their point of view and that unemployment is an integral part of the normal capitalist system.... The workers would 'get out of hand,' and the 'captains of industry' would be anxious to 'teach them a lesson'.... In this situation a powerful block is likely to be formed between big business and the *rentier* interests, and they would probably find more than one economist to declare that the situation was manifestly unsound. The pressure of all these forces, and in particular of big business would most probably induce the Government to return to the orthodox policy of cutting down the budget deficit. A slump would follow in which Government spending policy would come again into its own. (Kalecki 1943b: 141, 144)

Military spending did not pose a similar threat. It did not compete directly with private interests, and while it might have lessened the disciplinary impact of unemployment, the 'shortfall' was more than compensated for by the direct use of force and violence in the name national security. And so, capitalism, according to Kalecki, tended to oscillate between two ideal types. One extreme was a democratic model in which the government, torn between supporting and legitimising accumulation, ended up creating a 'political business cycle' by its stop-go policies. The other extreme was the fascist model, in which full employment was sustained by military spending in preparation for war, and where the concentration camp substituted for unemployment as a way of pacifying workers.

Since the Second World War, argued Baran and Sweezy, the United States used armaments to write its own ticket to prosperity. According to Gold (1977), the arrangement was supported by a powerful 'Keynesian Coalition' between big business and the large unions, which, since the 1950s, consistently preferred 'military Keynesianism' and aggressive foreign policy to the more benign use of civilian spending. And the policy was not without consequences. Ten years before the publication of Baran and Sweezy's *Monopoly Capital*, Shigeto Tsuru, a Japanese political economist, wrote an article entitled 'Has Capitalism Changed' (Tsuru 1956). Having examined the sources and offsets of U.S. savings, his conclusion was that in order to maintain its prevailing growth rate, the country needed military spending equivalent to roughly 10 per cent of its GDP. However, if this proportion was to be maintained, he continued, the *absolute* level of military expenditures ten years down the road would become far too high to justify for a country in peace. And indeed, a decade later, in 1966, the United States was deeply involved in the Vietnam War, with military spending kept at close to 9 per cent of GDP.

The U.S. Arma-Core

The 'Angry Elements'

During the 1970s, other writers, such as O'Connor (1973) and Griffin, Devine and Wallace (1982), have taken the argument a step further, suggesting that government involvement, and particularly military spending, were affected not by overall macroeconomic needs or the interest of capitalists in general, but rather by the specific requirements of dominant economic groups. More significantly, however, the Korean and Vietnam conflicts of the 1950s and 1960s indicated that military spending was not only a *consequence* of economic structure, but also an important force *shaping* that structure. One of the first writers to recognise this double-sided relationship was Michal Kalecki. Much of his early writings from the 1930s and 1940s were concerned with the effect on macroeconomic performance of the 'degree of monopoly' in the underlying industries. Toward the end of his life, during the 1960s, he closed the circle, pointing to the way in which macroeconomic policy, primarily military spending, could affect the economic and social structure. In his articles 'The Fascism of Our Times' (1964) and 'Vietnam and U.S. Big Business' (1967), Kalecki claimed that continued U.S. involvement in Vietnam would increase the dichotomy between the 'old', largely civilian industries located mainly on the East Coast, and the 'new' business groups, primarily the arms producers of the West Coast. The rise in military budgets, he predicted, would effect a redistribution of income from the old to the new groups. The 'angry elements' within the U.S. ruling class would be significantly strengthened, pushing for a more aggressive foreign policy, and propagating further what Melman (1974) would later call the 'permanent war economy'.

Was Kalecki right? Had the epicentre of the U.S. 'big economy', or dominant capital in our language, indeed shifted from 'civilian' to 'military' oriented corporations? Unfortunately, the question is not easy to answer. Corporate power, we argue in this book, is a matter of differential profit. And, yet, the link between profit and production is elusive at best. If military contractors were producing only armaments and civilian firms only non-military items, the problem would have been less serious. But that is not the case in practice. Since the 1960s, most large U.S. firms have become conglomerates to a greater or lesser extent, with military contractors diversifying into civilian business and vice versa. The difficulty for our purpose is that conglomerate finance is inherently 'contaminated' by intra-firm transfer pricing, so although we may know how much a firm gets from the Pentagon in *sales revenues*, we cannot know for sure the impact this has on its *profit*.

The problem, though, is not insurmountable. In what follows, we identify the leading 'Arma-Core' of the U.S. economy, defined as the inner corporate cluster which appropriated the lion's share of defence-related contracts, and which was highly dependent on such contracts. Having identified the members of this 'Arma-Core', we then proceed to examine their combined profit relative to U.S. dominant capital as a whole. Now, although both groups derived their earnings from military as well as civilian business, and although the impact on their profit of each line of business cannot be determined with accuracy, it is safe to assume that the Arma-Core's profitability was much more sensitive to military contracts than that of dominant capital as a whole. A rise in the profit share of the Arma-Core would then indicate that Kalecki was right, and that the 'military bias' of the United States indeed enhanced the power of 'military oriented' firms. A decline in the ratio would of course suggest the opposite.

Who then was in the Arma-Core? A first approximation could be derived from data published by the U.S. Department of Defense (DoD), in its annual listing for the *100 Companies Receiving the Largest Dollar Volume of Prime Contract Awards*.[1] From this publication we can learn that military procurement was fairly concentrated, such that, over the period between 1966 and 1991, the largest 100 contractors accounted for between 62 and 72 per cent of the DoD's total prime contract awards. However, it is probably inappropriate to consider all of the leading 100 firms as members of the Arma-Core. Our tentative criterion for inclusion in this core is for the firm to be large enough to exercise political leverage, as well as significantly dependent on defence contracts, and not all of the leading 100 companies fit both characteristics. Some corporations – such as AT&T, IBM, ITT, Eastman Kodak, Ford, Chrysler, Exxon, Mobil and Texaco – were very large but depended only marginally on military contracts. Others, like Singer, Teledyne, E-Systems, Loral, FMC, Harsco and Gencorp, relied more heavily on defence sales, but were probably not big enough to exercise political leverage. Thus, concentrating only on *large, defence-dependent*

1   We ignore here parallel listings of subcontracting, foreign military sales, and contracts awarded by NASA and the Department of Energy. These contracts are significant, but their recipients tended to be the same as the DoD's prime contractors.

contractors, we end up with a more limited group of about 20 to 25 firms, which for our purpose here comprise the U.S. Arma-Core.

The precise choice of boundary between the Arma-Core and the remaining contractors is of course arbitrary to some extent, a problem which is further exacerbated by periodic changes in the ranking of firms. Given the attendant uncertainty and ambiguity, we focus on a more limited sample of only 16 corporations. These include, in alphabetical order: Boeing, General Dynamics, General Electric, Grumman, Honeywell, Litton Industries, Lockheed, McDonnell Douglas, Martin Marietta, Northrop, Raytheon, Rockwell International, Texas Instruments, Textron, United Technologies, and Westinghouse. This group is representative of the Arma-Core in that it consists of only large firms and, with only minor exceptions, it included the top ten DoD contractors in every year between 1966 and 1991.[2] During the 1966–91 period, these 16 firms received more domestic military contracts than any other comparable group of American corporations. On average, they accounted for 36 per cent of the DoD's total prime contract awards, with a floor of 30 per cent (in 1966) and a ceiling of 41 per cent (in 1985). As a group, the Arma-Core proved much more dependent on sales to the Pentagon than dominant capital as whole. For the latter, denoted here by the Fortune 500, military contracts ranged between 5 and 10 per cent of total sales. The comparable figure for the Arma-Core was 20 to 40 per cent (Nitzan and Bichler 1995: 460–1).

Turning to the crucial question of differential profitability, Figure 5.2 presents the net profit share of the Arma-Core within dominant capital. The data show that, following the Vietnam War, this share had doubled to 10 per cent by the mid-1980s, up from 5 per cent in the mid-1960s. In other words, if our interpretation here is correct, the 'permanent war economy' which existed in the United States pretty much until the end of Reagan's second presidency, seems to have indeed created an ongoing 'military bias' within the U.S. corporate sector, strengthening the relative power of military contractors. Kalecki was certainly prescient.

Corporate Restructuring and 'Military Keynesianism'

To a certain extent, this interaction between military expenditures and business realignment was also part of a broader, worldwide transformation affecting the relationships between nation states and transnational corporations. Following the Second World War, the global economic significance of the United States began to wane. The decline is evident in various indicators. For instance, whereas during the 1960s U.S. GDP measured one and half times

---

2   Excluded from the sample is Hughes Aircraft which, as a privately held firm until 1986, did not publish financial reports. Also omitted are General Motors, which entered the Arma-Core only in 1986 after acquiring Hughes Aircraft; LTV, which filed for bankruptcy protection in 1986; and Tenneco, whose annual contract awards fluctuated widely.

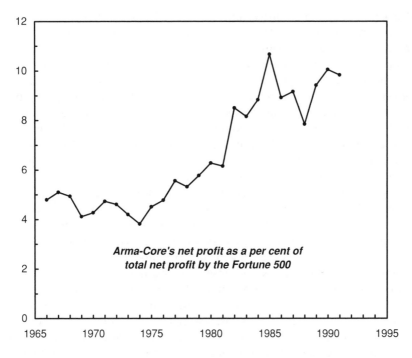

Figure 5.2   The Rise of the U.S. Arma-Core

SOURCE: Fortune; Standard & Poor's Compustat.

the combined total for the EEC's 12 countries plus Japan, by the early 1990s the ratio was only half as large. Also, as the country grew more economically open, its trade balance moved from surplus to deficit, requiring increasing doses of capital inflows to cover the shortfall. Under these circumstances, with the local market becoming relatively less important as well as increasingly contested by foreign competitors, U.S.-based firms naturally looked for further opportunities abroad. And indeed, by the early 1990s, roughly 25 per cent of their profits came from outside the country, up from less than 10 per cent in the 1960s. The foreign challenge, however, remained gruelling, and American-based firms continued their slide down the global rankings. In contrast to 1960, when the United States was home to 114 of the world's 174 largest firms, by the 1990 the number dropped to a mere 56 (figures in this paragraph are calculated from U.S. Department of Commerce through McGraw-Hill Online, and from Franko 1991).

These major transformations affected the choice of both corporate strategy and economic policy. Faced with mounting competitive pressures in civilian markets, many large U.S.-based firms found themselves increasingly drawn into the shelter of high-profit government contracts, particularly in areas such as defence, nuclear energy, space, and medical technology.[3] On the policy side, this dependency got the U.S. administration entangled in a commitment to 'military Keynesianism', which, paradoxically, grew deeper as the big corporations became more global in scope. The reason was that, with a rising share of corporate profits coming from abroad, domestic government policies affected a *diminishing* portion of corporate earnings. Or to put it somewhat differently, all other things being equal, a given increase in the companies' overall profit required a larger increment of domestic military contracts. Under these circumstances, any attempt to eliminate the 'military bias' spelled a major blow to the credibility of macroeconomic policy, and of course serious injury to some of the country's most powerful firms.

Relying on domestic military spending, however, was always a tricky business. The main problem is the mismatch existing between the requirements of *arms making* and the reality of *arms selling*. From an industrial standpoint, the technology-intensive nature of weapon making requires continuous research and development and open production lines. Furthermore, military production is highly specialised, so it cannot be easily converted into civilian use when demand for weapons slackens. These industrial considerations call for a stable growth in demand for arms – and yet, that is not what usually happens in the armament business. Perceived as a drain on the country's resources, military expenditures need to be legitimised by external threats, and these tend to fluctuate with the ups and downs of international politics and the frequency of armed conflicts. The consequence is to make domestic weapon procurement *inherently* unstable, which is of course a serious headache for the large armament producers. Clearly, if these firms are to keep their production lines open, they can never rely solely on domestic procurement, and must constantly look for 'counter-cyclical' export markets.

3   In the electronics industry, for instance, General Electric embarked on a major restructuring programme which, over the 1981–87 period, saw the company acquire some 338 business and product lines, while divesting 232 others (*Business Week*, 16 March 1987). The process, whose main goal was to move away from markets dominated by the Japanese, included the 1985 acquisition of RCA, particularly for its defence business, and the 1986 swap of GE's consumer electronic lines for Thomson's medical equipment unit (*Time*, 23 December 1985; 3 August 1987). In 1992, General Electric sold its defence electronics unit to Martin Marietta, but in turn became a major shareholder of the latter company (*Business Week*, 7 December 1992). In the aircraft industry, Lockheed left commercial aviation altogether, after its entanglement with the L-1011 airliner brought it to near bankruptcy. Similarly, McDonnell Douglas, which was initially created in 1967 when McDonnell absorbed Douglas as a means of diversifying into non-defence activity, never made any money from civilian aircraft, and, in 1991, entered into a tentative agreement to sell 40 per cent of its civilian unit to Taiwan Aerospace (*Business Week*, 14 February 1983; 23 May 1988; 2 December 1991). The deal failed to go through, and McDonnell Douglas was eventually absorbed by Boeing, which sought to bolster its position against Europe's Airbus consortium. Similar retreats plagued the automobile industry, where pressures from Japanese competition pushed U.S.-based firms back into defence-related activity. The most publicised move here was General Motors' acquisition of EDS and Hughes Aircraft, which during the 1980s turned the 'car company' into one of the country's top ten defence contractors.

Arms Exports

The perils of restricted demand are hardly new, of course. For example, during the Seven-Year War Frederick the Great found himself forced to import 32,000 rifles from abroad, and that because only a few years earlier he decided to cut down production capacity for lack of domestic demand (Frederick the Great 1979: 18). The simplest solution for this dilemma would have been to supplement the home market with foreign sales, but, initially, that was not at all obvious and for a very simple reason: weapons were usually produced by the state whose officials were hardly keen on selling them to potential enemies. Industrial advancement, however, increasingly shifted armament production into private hands, and it was this privatisation which eventually enabled the business to become truly international. The imperative of combining private ownership and foreign sales was succinctly elucidated in 1913, when, on the eve of the First World War, Krupp, the German weapon maker, got entangled in a corruption scandal. Answering his critics in the Reichstag, the Minister of War, Josias von Heeringen, defended this new system, arguing that in order to maintain sufficient capacity for wartime, military producers had to export in peacetime. This, he insisted, could be achieved only by private firms which were free from the patriotic scruples of state companies (Sampson 1977: 43). And indeed, by the end of the nineteenth century, the large armament firms – such as Krupp, Nobel, Armstrong, Vickers, Du-Pont, Electric Boat and Carnegie – were all privately owned, highly dependent on foreign markets, and most importantly, unregulated (ibid., Chs 2–4).

This structure of the military industry first came under scrutiny during the 1920s and 1930s. After the First World War, the League of Nations accused the arms companies of fermenting international conflict, causing a flurry of official investigations into the arms business. Following the Nye Committee hearings in the United States, the isolationist congress passed the 1935 Neutrality Bill, with special provision for a National Munitions Control Board to supervise American arms exports. A few years later, the 1941 Lend Lease Act brought the U.S. government further into the centre-stage of the arms trade, and by the end of the Second World War it was commonly accepted that the export of weapons was no longer a private affair, but rather a matter of foreign policy.

After the war, the 'Truman Doctrine' conceived military exports, particularly to Europe, as part of the larger effort to contain communism, a goal which would be later extended to legitimise arms shipments to South East Asia. Yet this new emphasis on broader policy goals did little to resolve the problem of unstable demand. The continued military Keynesianism of the 1950s and 1960s created the basis for an Arma-Core of large military-dependent firms, and by the late 1960s, toward the end of the United States' direct involvement in Vietnam, these corporations appeared just as vulnerable to budget cuts as the Carnegies and Du-Ponts half a century earlier. Despite several decades of change, the weapon business remained predominantly private, and with the war effort now receding, its owners were once again seeking to counteract excess capacity with foreign military sales.

Arms Exports and Corporate Profit

Interestingly, until the late 1980s most observers tended to doubt this 'economic' rationale for U.S. military exports. Such exports, they argued, were simply too small to make a difference (for instance, Krause 1992: 106). And on the surface they seemed to have a point. Domestic procurements, measured in constant 1995 prices, ranged from $61 billion in 1974, after the end of the Vietnam conflict, to $136 billion in 1987, at the peak of the Reagan build-up. The comparable figures for foreign military sales were much smaller: between $5 billion in 1963, just before the Vietnam conflict started to pick up, and $23 billion in 1987, at the height of the Iran–Iraq War (data sources in Figure 5.3). And yet the comparison is deceiving. The arms makers, like any other capitalist, are concerned not with sales but with *profits*, and these tend to be far higher in export sales. The basic reason is simple enough. The production of weapons, particularly major platforms such as tanks, aircraft and ships, involves very high research and development outlays. This fixed component is typically recovered through domestic sales, so by the time the company starts exporting, its average unit cost is far lower, and the profit per unit correspondingly higher. And indeed, an internal DoD study cited in Brzoska and Ohlson (1987: 120) estimated foreign military sales to be 2.5 times more profitable that those made to the U.S. government, while similar ratios – ranging from 2 to 2.3 – emerged from other industry sources (U.S. Congress 1991: 53).

Using these profitability indicators in conjunction with sales data, Figure 5.3 reassesses the relative importance of arms exports. The top series in the chart traces the value of domestic military shipments, measured in constant prices. The bottom series imputes the relative contribution of foreign military sales to overall military-related profit (domestic as well as foreign). The later computation is based on the conservative assumption that the export markup was twice as high as the local one, and that the ratio between the two markups remained stable over time.[4] Now, since actual markups do change over time, the ratio plotted in the chart is necessarily imprecise. Nevertheless, its overall magnitude and broad trajectory are telling. All in all, the chart suggests, first, that arms exports were probably far more important for U.S. military contractors than is commonly assumed, and, second, that this dependency has grown over

---

4 Symbolically, if (MS) is overall military sales, (MSd) is domestic sales, (MSe) is export sales, and (v) is the ratio between the export and domestic markups, then the relative contribution of military exports to military-related profit (RC) is given by the following expression:

$$RC = (v \cdot MSe) / (v \cdot MSe + MSd)$$

time. Export first became significant during the military build-down of the late 1960s and early 1970s. The United States was scaling back its direct involvement in Vietnam, and with military exports to the region continuing to rise, the ratio of export profit to total profit soared. Based on our imputation, in 1973, at the cyclical peak of the process, foreign sales accounted for up to one-third of all military-related profit. Subsequently, with President Carter reversing the spending downtrend, and with the Reagan Administration embarking on the country's largest military build-up in peacetime, arms exports became relatively less important. And yet, even in the late 1980s, when domestic spending reached record highs, exports still accounted for a sizeable one-quarter of all military-related profit. Ominously, during the 1990s, with military spending dropping and 'peace dividends' mushrooming the world over, foreign military

Figure 5.3 U.S. Military Business: Domestic and Foreign

* Manufacturing shipments of defence products. Data prior to 1968 are estimated based on pro-rated splicing with overall U.S. military expenditure.
** Based on comparison of arms export deliveries and domestic shipments of defence products, assuming the export markup is twice as high as the domestic markup. Arms exports prior to 1984 exclude military services, resulting in an estimated downward bias of 5 per cent.
SOURCE: U.S. Arms Controls and Disarmament Agency (Annual); U.S. Department of Commerce through McGraw-Hill (Online).

sales have become the profit life-line of U.S.-based contractors, accounting for an estimated 45 per cent of their total military-related earnings.

This focus on profit rather than sales helps explain why a single export deal can sometimes make or break even a large contractor. Grumman, for example, was saved from near-bankruptcy in 1974 by the sale of F-14 Tomcat fighter planes to Iran (Sampson 1977: 249–56). Similarly, during the early 1990s, the sale of 72 F-15 Eagle fighters to Saudi Arabia gave financially troubled McDonnell Douglas a temporary lease on life (*Business Week*, 16 March 1992; *Fortune*, 22 February 1993). Northrop, on the other hand, was seriously hampered by its F-20 debacle, a dedicated 'fighter for export' which the company spent $1.4 billion to develop but never managed to sell (Ferrari et al. 1987: 27).

Contrary to received wisdom, then, the evidence, however tentative, suggests that the Arma-Core was in fact very much affected by U.S. military exports. And given the growing political leverage of this core, it should be hardly surprising that foreign policy has become increasingly bound up with private profit.

Commercialising Arms Exports: From Aid to Sales

The growing interaction between trade and the flag in this area was facilitated by two related developments. The first of these developments was the *commercialisation* of arms exports. During the 1950s, when arms exports were still seen as a matter of foreign policy, up to 95 per cent of U.S. foreign military deliveries were financed by government aid. Over time, though, with the line separating state from capital becoming less and less clear, the proportions changed, and by the 1990s only 30 per cent were given as aid. The rest, up to 70 per cent, were now paid for directly by the buyer (figures computed from U.S. Defense Security Assistance Agency 1989; 1992; and U.S. Department of Commerce. Bureau of the Census Annual).

The second development, which greatly facilitated this commercialisation, was the emergence of the Middle East as the world's prime destination for exported arms. The process, illustrated in Table 5.1, shows the level of arms imports from all sources (expressed in 1987 prices), as well as their regional distribution during four distinct periods. During the first period, between 1963 and 1964, global arms imports amounted to $11.7 billion annually, with about half going to Europe (earlier data are unavailable). In the aftermath of the Second World War, the Continent was still perceived as potentially unstable, and so until the mid-1960s, the United States sent most of its military assistance to its NATO allies primarily in the form of surplus stockpile grants. Since 1965, however, the emphasis began to change. The 'hot spot' of the West–East conflict moved to South East Asia, and with it came a rapid escalation in the global armament trade. Over the 1965–73 period, world arms import rose by 65 per cent, to an annual average of $19.4 billion – with over one-third now going to East Asia. In the United States, the shift of focus from Europe to the outlying areas of the Third World brought a redefinition of arms-export policies. Weapon deliveries to Vietnam and other South East Asian countries were still financed by aid, but the European countries were now increasingly requested to pay for their U.S.-made hardware.

Table 5.1   Arms Imports by Region (annual averages)

Period	World Total ($m/year, 1987 prices)[(a)]	Of Which (per cent of world total)				
		NATO & Warsaw Pact	East Asia	Middle East	Africa	Others
1963–64	11,711	49.9	17.3	9.9	4.3	18.7
1965–73	19,356	28.9	35.2	16.8	3.8	15.3
1974–84	45,598	18.7	11.3	36.3	16.3	17.4
1985–89	51,096	18.0	12.4	32.9	9.5	27.1

(a) Constant price data are computed by dividing the original nominal figures by the U.S. implicit GDP deflator.
SOURCE: Original current-price data are from U.S. Arms Control and Disarmament Agency (Annual). (Because of repeated updates, data are from the last annual publication in which they appear.) Implicit GDP Deflator is from Economic Report of the President (Annual).

This change, which signalled a return to the pre-war commercial pattern of weapon sales, was to some extent inescapable. The post-war policy of containing communism through military aid was feasible as long as U.S. arms shipments were small and U.S. government finances solid. But as the arms race started picking up and the federal deficit ballooned, successive American administrations began to preach the merits of commercial sales. During the Eisenhower, Kennedy and Johnson governments, the trend was limited mainly to transactions with NATO, but the late-1960s entanglement in Vietnam hastened the final policy reversal. By 1969, the new 'Nixon Doctrine' stipulated that all transfers of weapons – including those going to the Third World – should, whenever possible, depend not on direct U.S. military involvement, but on the buyer's ability to pay.

Global Redistribution and the Rise of the Middle East

The single most important factor enabling this shift from aid to sales was the global income redistribution triggered by the 1973 oil crisis. The explosive growth of OPEC's revenues made the cartel's members ideal clients for weaponry, and in 1974, after the U.S. exit from Vietnam, the Middle East became the world's largest importer of armaments. As Table 5.1 shows, over the 1974–84 period, the annual arms trade rose to nearly $46 billion, up 136 per cent from the previous period, with roughly 53 per cent of the total going to the Middle East and Africa (mainly Libya and Egypt). The pivotal role here of global redistribution can hardly be overstated. Indeed, as oil revenues dropped during the latter half of the 1980s, the rapid rise in arms transfers was arrested. During 1985–89, world military imports rose only marginally, to an average annual level of $51 billion, with much of the stagnation taking place in the Middle East and Africa, whose combined share dropped to 42 per cent. (During the 1990s, the global redistribution of income has taken a new turn with the rapid growth of 'emerging markets' in Latin America, South Asia and South East Asia. Interestingly, this shift has been accompanied by a 'mini-boom' of military imports flowing into their regions, with the initial takeoff already evident in the increasing share of 'Others' recorded in Table 5.1.)

To sum up, the post-war era was marked by several important changes affecting the nature of arms production and trade. In the United States, there emerged an Arma-Core of large defence contractors, whose rising power, particularly since the Vietnam conflict, enabled it to appropriate a growing share of the profit of dominant capital. The relative growth of these companies was influenced by the continuous 'military bias' of the U.S. economy, which was itself partly the consequence of mounting global competition in civilian markets. The consolidation of this powerful group of firms strengthened their political leverage – mostly in matters affecting the domestic budget, but increasingly also in the choice of foreign policy. This latter significance stemmed primarily from the intrinsic dependence of arms production on flexible foreign demand. After the Second World War, the U.S. Administration made military exports a tool of foreign policy; but, over time, the very menu of policy options became intertwined with the development of the Arma-Core. Initially, the need for foreign markets was both limited and easily financed by U.S. military aid. However, the continuous ascent of defence-dependent corporations eventually raised arms exports up to a level which could no longer be backed solely by U.S.-government grants. The dilemma was solved by a gradual return to the pre-war pattern of commercial trade in weaponry, and what made this transition feasible was the global redistribution of income triggered by the Middle East oil crisis.

With this latter development, the U.S. Arma-Core found itself entering the centre-stage of Middle Eastern 'energy conflicts'. The consequences of this entry were far reaching. The large defence contractors which earlier depended mainly on the level of domestic military spending and foreign military aid, now found their financial fate increasingly correlated with the boom and bust of the oil business. And they were not alone. With them on the same stage were also the newly empowered OPEC governments, the governments of the imperilled Western countries, and the major petroleum companies whose dominant position in the oil world was now called into question. The emergence of the Middle East as the 'hot spot' of world conflict and the leading arms-importing region has altered the delicate relationships between these transnational corporations and both their parent and host governments. Furthermore, the seemingly circular sequence of regional wars and oil crises brought the petroleum companies into a new, and in some way unexpected alliance with the arms makers. Before we can turn to examine this alliance, however, we must look more closely at the changing circumstances affecting the petroleum industry.

Middle East Oil and the Petro-Core

The 'Demise Thesis'

The dominant view among students of the subject, is that the oil crisis of the 1970s signalled the final stage in a fundamental transformation, a trans-formation which started in the 1950s, and which eventually altered the structure of the oil industry. The first aspect of this transformation was the relative decline of the major oil companies vis-à-vis a growing number of lesser firms. After the Second World War, the 'Seven Sisters' – notably Exxon (then Standard Oil of New Jersey), Royal Dutch/Shell, British Petroleum (previously Anglo-Iranian), Texaco, Mobil, Chevron (then Socal) and Gulf – still dominated the relatively concentrated international oil arena. Gradually, however, the entrance of smaller independent companies, the growth of existing firms other than the seven largest, and the re-entry of the Soviet Union into Western energy markets, made the sector less concentrated, eroding the leading position of the oil majors. In just two decades, between 1953 and 1972, the share of the 'Seven Sisters' in the oil industry outside the United States fell from 64 per cent to 24 per cent of all concession areas; from 92 to 67 per cent of proven reserves; from 87 to 71 per cent of production; from 73 to 49 per cent of refining capacity; from 29 to 19 per cent of tanker capacity; and from 72 to 54 per cent in product marketing (Jacoby 1974: Table 9.12, p. 211).

A second and perhaps more important facet of this transformation was that the locus of control, which previously rested with the owners and officers of the large petroleum companies, had now apparently shifted into the hands of government officials, monarchs and dictators. At the 'upstream' part of the industry, the oil companies succumbed to the relentless nationalistic pressure of their host countries, and after a quarter-century of eroding autonomy eventually surrendered most of their crude oil concessions. Once begun, the transition was swift and decisive. The transnational companies, which as late as 1970 still owned about 90 per cent of all crude petroleum produced in the non-communist world, found their equity share drop sharply to only 37 per cent by 1982, most of it now concentrated in North America (figures cited in Penrose 1987: 15). A similar change occurred at the 'downstream' segment of the industry, particularly in the Western industrial countries. With the oil crisis, the cost of energy and its very availability became major policy issues with wide-ranging domestic and foreign implications; so that here, too, the firms found they had to comply with political dictates – in this case, those coming from their own parent governments. Energy in general and petroleum in particular became *political* questions, and just 'as war was too important to be left for the generals', wrote Yergin (1991: 613), 'so oil was clearly too important to be left to the oil men'.

And so emerged the 'demise thesis'. According to Turner (1983: 118–24), after the Second World War the major oil companies have come to assume various roles, acting as 'governmental agents', as 'transmission belts' between host and parent governments, as occasional 'instigators', or simply as a 'complicating factor' – but, in his opinion, all of these roles have merely added some colour to the sphere of international political economy. In the final analysis, he argues, it was the diplomats who were making the crucial decisions. The multinational petroleum companies – particularly after the oil crisis – have been pushed aside, reduced to a status of 'interested bystanders' in the high politics of world oil (pp. 147–8).

Whither the Oil Companies?

At the time, the 'demise thesis' seemed persuasive, even fashionable. It was certainly the next logical step in a long theoretical sequence, which began with the 'bureaucratic revolution' of the 1930s, continued through the 'managerial revolution' of the 1940s, and from there led to the 'technostructure' of the 1950s and 1960s, and to 'statism' in the 1970s. There was only one little problem. The evidence used to support this thesis was strangely silent on the issue which mattered most, namely the accumulation of capital. In the final analysis, capitalism emerged and expanded not because it offered a new ethos, but because that ethos helped the rising bourgeoisie alter the distribution of income from landed rent to business profit. For that reason, those who argue in favour of bureaucratic-statist determinism, or believe in the demise of big business, must go to the essence of capitalism and demonstrate that these developments have fundamentally altered the distribution of income and the mechanism of accumulation.

In this particular case, if we are to conclude that the oil majors have indeed declined, we need to be first shown not only that they lost market shares and became dependent on government policies, but also that these structural and institutional changes affected their business performance, and, specifically, their *profits*. Assuming that the large petroleum companies were squeezed between rising competition and more demanding governments, the combined pressure must have caused their net earnings to wither – either absolutely, or at least relative to some broader aggregates. And yet, this has never been demonstrated in the literature. Most studies pertaining to the 'multinational debate' in the energy sector either gloss over the issue, or simply ignore it altogether; and even where profits are referred to, the data are often incomplete and rarely analysed in a wider historical context.[5] Unfortunately, this neglect helps distort the overall picture, for while the institutional and structural indicators may imply that the major oil companies have indeed declined, the profit data seem to suggest the exact opposite!

Table 5.2 provides some long-term summary indices for the profit performance of the world's six largest petroleum companies in the early 1990s. This group – which we label here the 'Petro-Core' – consists of the original 'Seven Sisters', with the exception of Gulf which was acquired by Chevron in 1984. The comparison includes various differential accumulation indicators, relating the profit performance of the Petro-Core to corresponding figures for larger corporate groupings, including a wider international composite of petroleum firms, the Fortune 500, and the U.S. corporate sector as a whole.

The first column gives the average net rate of return for the Petro-Core (ratio of net profit to owners' equity). The overall impression from these data is that the oil crises of the 1970s and early 1980s in fact helped *boost* the profitability of the large oil companies, a notion to which we return later in the chapter. For our purpose here, though, the more interesting results are those obtained from the differential indices. In the second column, we present the rate-of-return ratio between the Petro-Core and the 'Petroleum 40–42' group of companies. This ratio is calculated by dividing the net rate of profit on equity obtained in the Petro-Core, by the matching rate attained by the Petroleum 40–42 – the latter being a broader cluster of the world's 40–42 largest non-governmental petroleum companies (including the Petro-Core firms). The results show that, during the late 1960s and 1970s, despite the competitive assaults from new entrants, the Petro-Core was able to maintain its net rate of return more or less in line with the other oil companies, and that during the 1980s it actually succeeded in surpassing them. A similar result is obtained in the third column, where we compare the net rate of return for the Petro-Core with that of U.S. dominant capital as a whole, approximated by the Fortune 500. Here, too, the large Petro-Core firms exhibit a remarkable staying power, even after the 'OPEC revolution' and the politicisation of oil in the industrialised countries. Indeed, despite the wholesale surrendering of concessions, the revoking of preferential U.S. foreign tax-credits, and a list of other adverse consequences of the new

5 Earlier pre-crisis studies are also not without fault. For example, in his work *Multinational Oil*, Jacoby (1974: 245–7) showed that the large oil companies suffered a significant decline in their foreign profitability, which he attributed to increased competition since the mid-1950s. Jacoby's methodology and implications are questionable, however. First, much of the decline of international profits in the 1950s was rooted not in more intense competition, but in higher royalties to host countries. Second, since the royalties were debited as foreign taxes against the oil companies' domestic operations, focusing only on foreign operations serves to conceal the compensating increase in domestic after-tax earnings. Indeed, as Blair (1976: 193–203, 294–320) demonstrated, the decrease in the companies' global rate of return was far smaller than the one recorded in their operations abroad. Furthermore, global profitability started to rise again in the early 1960s and, by the early 1970s, was already far higher than in the early 1950s.

oil order, the Petro-Core's rates of return in the 1970s, 1980s and early 1990s were higher than the comparable averages for U.S. dominant capital as a whole.

Table 5.2   The Petro-Core:[a] Differential Profitability Indicators (annual averages, %)

Period	Rate-of-Return Ratios			Net-Profit Ratios		
	1	2	3	4	5	6
	Rate of Return	Petro-Core ÷ Petroleum 40–42[b]	Petro-Core ÷ Fortune 500	Petro-Core ÷ Petroleum 40–42	Petro-Core ÷ Fortune 502[c]	Petro-Core ÷ All U.S. Corps
1930–39						9.1[d]
1940–49						3.3
1950–59					18.2[e]	7.2
1960–69	11.5[f]	1.01[g]	1.00[f]	61.3[g]	17.1	8.1
1970–79	14.3	0.99	1.12	61.7	18.0	9.0
1980–89	13.1	1.08	1.03	73.2	17.8	10.5
1990–91	11.5	1.03	1.20	78.1	22.3	9.1

(a) The Petro-Core consists of British Petroleum, Chevron, Exxon, Mobil, Royal/Dutch Shell, and Texaco.
(b) The Petroleum 40–42 denote the Pforzheimer & Co. group of major non-governmental petroleum corporations, representing a composite of 40–42 major worldwide oil firms aggregated on a consolidated, total company basis.
(c) The "Fortune 502" comprise the Fortune 500 corporations, as well as British Petroleum and Royal/Dutch Shell.
(d) Excluding 1931–32 in which total U.S. net corporate profits were negative.
(e) For 1954–59.
(f) For 1966–69.
(g) For 1968–69.
SOURCE: Net profit and rate of return on equity of the Petro-Core are from O'Connor (1962), *Fortune* directories and Standard & Poor's *Compustat*. Net profit of all U.S. corporations is from U.S. Department of Commerce through McGraw-Hill (Online), and from U.S. Department of Commerce, Bureau of Economic Analysis, *Statistical Abstract of the United States* (1992), Table 871, p. 542. Net profit and rate of return on equity for the Fortune 500 are from various 'The Fortune 500' listings. Net profits and rate of return on equity for the world's 40–42 leading petroleum firms are from Carl H. Pforzheimer & Co., *Comparative Oil Company Statements*, reported in the *Statistical Abstract of the United States* (Annual).

Another way to assess the differential earning power of the large oil companies is by looking at their relative share in the profit of a wider aggregate of companies. This we do in the last three columns, where we compute the share of the Petro-Core in the net profits of the Petroleum 40–42 group, the 'Fortune 502' (as defined below), and all U.S.-based corporations. Beginning with the first of these net-profit ratios (fourth column), we can see that despite the Core's relative decline in terms of economic activity (such as concessions, reserves, production, refining, transportation and marketing), its distributive share of the industry's net profit did not decrease at all. If we consider the world's largest 40–42 petroleum companies as a reasonable proxy for the international non-governmental petroleum industry, then it appears that the share of the Petro-Core in global oil profit in fact rose – from around three-fifths during the late 1960 and 1970s, to almost three-quarters by the 1980s, and then further, reaching close to four-fifths by the early 1990s. A similar picture emerges when we examine the share of the Petro-Core in the net profit of U.S. dominant capital (fifth column). Taking the Fortune 500 group again as our tentative proxy for U.S. dominant capital, and adding to its ranks the European-based British Petroleum and Royal Dutch/Shell, we can see that the profit position of the large Petro-Core firms within this modified 'Fortune 502' group has remained surprisingly unassailable. Here we have a longer time series, extending from 1954 to 1991, so the comparison is even more telling. During the late 1950s, when the oil majors were still the undisputed leaders of the international oil industry, the Petro-Core accounted for nearly one-fifth of the net profits earned by the Fortune 502 group, but that has hardly changed in the subsequent period when these firms presumably lost their pre-eminence to new entrants and politicians. The final indication for the enduring power of the Petro-Core is given by their net-profit ratio with the U.S. corporate sector as a whole – an index for which data are available since 1930 (sixth column). Following the Achnacarry and Red Line agreements of 1928, in which the large international oil companies divided the world and the Middle East between them, the Petro-Core became so powerful that, even with the Great Depression and collapsing raw material prices, it still managed to appropriate over 9 per cent of all net profits earned by U.S. corporations. The economic revival of the Second World War raised overall corporate profits, thus causing this net-profit ratio to drop significantly. However, during the 1950s, the ratio began to climb again, rising more or less continuously until, in the 1980s, it topped 10 per cent – more than the earlier record of the 1930s.

Clearly, then, as we move from means to end – that is, from economic activity to differential profitability – the historical picture seems to change, and rather significantly. What appears as the Petro-Core's relative decline from the viewpoint of exploration, production, refining and marketing, is not at all what we see when we reach the 'bottom line'. On the contrary, once we focus on the ultimate business criteria of differential accumulation, the oil crisis seems to turn from a menace to a blessing. The Petro-Core, far from losing ground, has actually held and even consolidated its leading position – relative to other international oil firms, relative to the U.S. big economy, and relative to the U.S. corporate sector as a whole.

Now, these findings are admittedly puzzling. After all, competitive pressures from new entrants and demands from governments did increase since the 1950s, so how did the Petro-Core manage to nevertheless come on top with such a feat of differential accumulation? Alternatively, given the Petro-Core's remarkable staying power, why did it give up so much control to governments? The paradox, though, is only apparent, and disappears quickly once we shift our attention from the industry's *formal* institutions to its *effective* power structure. The 1970s indeed altered the formal control of oil. But following the line of analysis first anticipated in the wake of the crisis by Blair (1976), and recently summarised by Bromley (1991), one may argue that the ultimate consequence of this transformation was to consolidate rather than undermine the relative earning power of the large petroleum companies.

Politicising Oil: From 'Free Flow' to 'Limited Flow'

Perhaps the most fundamental aspect of this transformation was the progressive *politicisation* of the oil business.[6] While this process was to a large extent continuous, it is nevertheless possible to distinguish between two qualitatively different phases. The first period, roughly until the early 1970s, could be labelled the 'free-flow' era in world oil – this in the sense that the control of oil was exercised through private ownership with state 'interference' assuming only a secondary role (Turner 1983: Chs 2–3). During the 1920s and 1930s, the inter-national petroleum arena was practically run by the large companies, particularly British Petroleum, Royal Dutch/Shell and Exxon. In 1928, the three companies, meeting in the Scottish castle of Achnacarry, divided the world between them. In that year, the same firms also signed, together with other companies, the Red Line Agreement to coordinate their activities in the Middle East.[7] Over the following three decades, explicit collusion slowly evolved into a broader system of complex arrangements and understandings, partly overt but mostly tacit, which together enabled the large oil companies to maintain their control of production, transportation, refining and marketing around the world (cf. Blair 1976: Ch. 5). However, the Second World War and the ensuing economic boom made things more complicated. First, the substitution of the United States for Britain as the leading Western power shifted the internal balance among the Seven Sisters in favour of the U.S.-based companies, undermining to some extent the group's previous cohesion. And second, the growing number of independent producers exerted downward pressure on prices, precisely at a time when rising nationalism in the Middle East and Latin America called for higher royalties. Threatened with loss of control, the large

6 Our own notion of 'politicisation' here is completely different from the realist concept of 'petro-political cycles' developed by Wilson (1987). According to the latter, during a sellers' market, producing countries are able to politicise the market in order to raise prices. During a buyers' market, on the other hand, Western countries are content letting competition reign, so as to bring prices down. Clearly, this focus on states does not allow for a *transnational* political coalition between the U.S. government, OPEC, the oil majors and the large armament contractors, along the lines developed in this chapter.

7 The extent of the companies' control during that time is well illustrated by their ability to contain the threat of oil glut throughout the Great Depression. During the 1930s, the Iraqi Petroleum Company – a joint venture between British Petroleum, Royal Dutch/Shell, CFP, Exxon, Mobil, and 'Mr 5 per cent', Calouste Gulbenkian – exercised a Veblenian policy of 'watchful waiting' throughout much of its 1928 Red Line Agreement regions. In Iraq, for example, the company actively utilised only 1 per cent of its concession; in Qatar it delayed production until 1950, some 18 years after the first exploration; and in Syria, it drilled shallow holes in order to fulfil its concession charter without producing any output (Blair 1976: 80–6).

oil companies resorted to classic predatory market practices against the independents, but that wasn't enough. And as the problem continued, the companies turned to their governments for help.

Government assistance, particularly in the United States, assumed a variety of forms, including foreign tax-credits to offset royalty payments, restrictions on the importation of cheap oil into the United States, exemptions from antitrust prosecution, and a CIA-backed coup against the Mossadeq government in Iran, to name a few. The fact that the large petroleum companies were able to secure such services is of course not entirely surprising, given their 'special relations' with successive U.S. administrations (cf. Tanzer 1969; Engler 1977). Part of this capital–state symbiosis was surely rooted in the strategic nature of oil. And yet that could by no means be the whole story. The reason, on which we shall elaborate later in the chapter, is that, on many occasions, U.S. government actions in favour of the large oil companies were patently *contradictory* to the nation's material interest.[8] Staunch realists like Stephen Krasner solved the anomaly by blaming such policies on 'nonlogical' behaviour and the 'misconceptions' of policy makers (1978a: 13–17). But there could be a much simpler explanation, namely that the oil companies, along with other dominant capital groups, were increasingly seen as synonymous with the national interest. Perhaps the best summary of this union was given by U.S. Major-General Smedley Butler:

I spent thirty-three years and four months in active service as a member of our country's most agile military force – the Marine Corps.... And during that period I spent most of my time being a high-class muscle man for Big Business, for Wall Street, and for the bankers. In short, I was a racketeer for capitalism.... Thus, I helped make Mexico and especially Tampico safe for American oil interests in 1914. I helped make Haiti and Cuba a decent place for the National City Bank boys to collect revenues in.... I helped purify Nicaragua for the international banking house of Brown Brothers in 1909–1912. I brought light to the Dominican Republic for American sugar interests in 1916. I helped make Honduras 'right' for American fruit companies in 1903. In China in 1927 I helped see to it that Standard Oil went its way unmolested. During those years, I had, as the boys in the back room would say, a swell racket. I was rewarded with honors, medals,

8 Indeed, many policy initiatives were cancelled solely due to opposition from the large companies. For example, during the Second World War, the large firms objected to the Petroleum Reserve Corporation taking control over their joint Saudi holdings, much as they opposed the Anglo-American Oil Agreement and the Saudi Arabian Pipeline. The big companies also refused to allow independent companies more than a symbolic share in the 1953 Iranian Consortium; they objected the 1970 Shultz Report which suggested to substitute tariffs for the dated system of import quotas; and they ignored the Administration's request to accommodate Libyan demands for a higher price. As a result, none of these policies and suggestions came to fruition (see Blair 1976: 220–30; Krasner 1978a: 190–205; and Turner 1983: 40–7, 152–4).

promotion. Looking back on it, I feel I might have given Al Capone a few hints. The best *he* could do was to operate his racket in three city districts. We Marines operated on three *continents*. (cited in Huberman 1936: 265–6, original emphases)

Such blunt services, however, were too crude and certainly insufficient for the post-colonial era. They were unsuited for the more subtle 'new imperialism' of transnational companies, and wholly inadequate for dealing with new problems such as business competition and the management of technical change. Since the 1960s, therefore, there emerged an urgent need for some 'external' force, a qualitatively new institutional arrangement which would bring crude production back to what the 'market can bear' – yet without implicating the oil companies as 'monopolies' and the Western governments as 'imperialists'. Historically, this institutional arrangement appeared in the form of OPEC and the upstream nationalisation of crude oil.

The broad causes for this transition have long been debated in the literature, but at least one of its consequences seems fairly clear. As Adelman (1987) rightly pointed out, the cartel achieved something which, for political reasons, the oil companies could never have pulled off on their own: a *dramatic* increase in prices. The eighteen-fold rise in the price of crude oil between 1972 and 1982 would have been inconceivable under the 'free-flow' system of private ownership. Rapid increases of such magnitude required not only a tight institutional framework, but also that oil appeared to be in short supply. The problem, though, was that oil was hardly scarce. In fact, it was abundant. The industry was plagued by chronic excess capacity (from the perspective of profit, that is), and the only way to bring this back to what the market could 'bear' was through an exogenously imposed 'crisis'. Such crisis, though, necessitates a *new political realignment*, and that is precisely what happened. With the nationalisation of crude oil, production decisions now moved to the offices of OPEC, opening the way to a new, 'limited-flow' regime.

The 'limited-flow' era worked wonders for OPEC. There can be little doubt about that. But the bonanza hardly came at the expense of the Petro-Core. On the contrary, OPEC, by working closely if tacitly with the companies, was instrumental in boosting their relative performance. The converging interests of these two groups is clearly illustrated in Figure 5.4, which shows a tight positive correlation between the value of OPEC's crude oil exports on the one hand, and the net profit of the Petro-Core on the other. A simple linear regression between the two series suggests that for every one dollar increase or decrease in export, there was a corresponding 6.7 cents change in the companies' net profit, and, moreover, that changes in the value of exports accounted for almost three-quarters of the squared variations in profits. Causality, however, was also running in the other direction, from the companies to the oil-producing countries. Although OPEC was providing the pretext for the crisis, there was still the need to coordinate output – and that it couldn't do on its own. As Blair

(1976: 289–93) and Turner (1983: 90–7) correctly indicated, managing the immense complexity of the oil arena required an overall knowledge which OPEC lacked, and which could be supplied only by the oil majors. The latter, of course, were no longer controlling output directly as producers, but they were now doing so indirectly, as the largest buyers, or 'offtakers' of crude petroleum. Interestingly, the rationale for this new alliance was delineated already in 1969 by the Saudi petroleum minister, Sheik Yamani. 'For our part', he stated, 'we do not want the majors to lose their power and be forced to abandon their role as a buffer element between the producers and the consumers. We want the present setup to continue as long as possible and at all costs to avoid any disastrous clash of interests which would shake the foundations of the whole oil industry' (cited in Barnet 1980: 61). There emerged, then, a new and more sophisticated realignment. The oil companies have indeed relinquished formal control, but that was largely in return for higher profits. Perhaps the most striking expression of this new 'trade-off' was provided by British Petroleum. The 1979 revolution in Iran deprived BP from access to 40 per cent of its global crude supplies; yet in that very year its profits soared

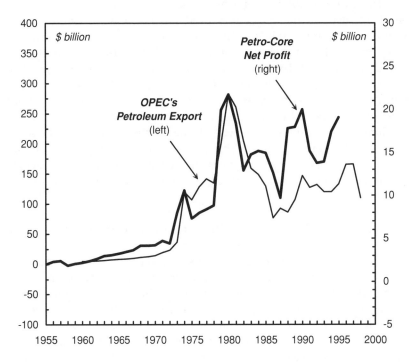

Figure 5.4   OPEC and the Petro-Core: Conflict or Convergence?

SOURCE: OPEC (Annual); Fortune.

by 296 per cent – more than those of any other major company (Turner 1983: 204; Yergin 1991: 684–7; and *Fortune*, 'The Fortune 500' 1978, 1979).

The convergence between OPEC and Western interests has long been suspected. On the eve of the first oil crisis, for example, Dan Smith suggested in *The Economist*'s survey titled 'The Phony Oil Crisis' (7 July 1973), that the U.S. Administration may have supported OPEC's drive for higher prices as a way of slowing down the Japanese economy (see also Anderson and Boyd 1984: Chs 9–11; and Terzian 1985: 188–202). Another possible reason why the U.S. government 'capitulated' and accepted separate negotiations leading to the Tehran and Tripoli Agreements of 1971, was that the large oil firms saw this as a means of checking the ominous rise of independent companies (Blair 1976: Ch. 9). In the words of Odell (1979: 216), the 1970s brought an 'unholy alliance' between the large international oil companies, the United States, and OPEC, which together sought to use higher prices as a way of boosting company profits, undermining the growth of Japan and Europe, and fortifying the American position in the Middle East. To these, Sampson (1977: 307) also added the eventual support of the British government, the Texas oil lobby, the independents, investors in alternative sources of energy, and the conservationists – all with a clear stake in more expensive oil.

In a way, then, the oil arena has evolved in a direction opposite to that of the armament industry. While the military sphere of domestic spending and arms exports has been increasingly *commercialised*, the petroleum industry has grown more *politicised*. This politicisation, however, has by no means spelled the demise of the large oil companies. On the contrary, it became a *prerequisite* for their survival. The relentless search for new reserves, along with the incessant proliferation of new technology created a constant menace of excess capacity and falling prices. At the same time, with the number of actors on the scene growing rapidly, counteracting this threat solely through corporate collusion was impractical. For the large companies, the way to overcome these challenges was to integrate their private interests into a broader political framework.

The Weapondollar–Petrodollar Coalition and Middle East 'Energy Conflicts'

And so, toward the beginning of the 1970s, several groups of large U.S.-based firms saw their interests converging in the Middle East. To recap, the first of these groups included the large weapon makers of the Arma-Core which turned to the region in search of export markets. The second cluster comprised the leading oil companies of the Petro-Core, including those based in Europe, which were now driven toward a broader alliance with OPEC. These were also joined by a second tier of interested parties, including engineering companies such as Bechtel and Fluor with big construction projects in the oil regions, as well as large financial institutions with an appetite for petrodollars. Each of these groups stood to benefit from higher oil prices; and yet none could have done so on its own. To push up the price of oil, they needed to act in concert, and this is how a 'Weapondollar–Petrodollar Coalition' between them came into being. In this section, we argue that, deliberately or not, the actions of these groups helped perpetuate an almost stylised interaction between energy crises and military conflicts. In this process of 'energy conflicts', the ongoing militarisation of the Middle East and periodical outbreaks of hostilities contributed toward an atmosphere of 'oil crisis', leading to higher prices and rising oil exports. Revenues from these exports then helped finance new weapon imports, thereby inducing a renewed cycle of tension, hostilities, and, again, rising energy prices.

From Crisis to Prices

Let's begin with prices. The common perception is that, one way or another, the price of crude oil depends on its underlying 'scarcity'. From this viewpoint, OPEC's early success is usually attributed to rapid Western growth during the 1960s and 1970s. This growth, it is argued, created 'excess demand' for oil, which in turn pushed up prices and made the cartel easy to manage. The same process, only in reverse, is said to have worked since the early 1980s. Lower industrial growth and improved energy efficiency, goes the argument, created 'excess supply', causing prices to fall and OPEC to disintegrate. Despite its popularity, however, this framework is vulnerable to both logic and fact.

From a long-term perspective, the relevant proxy for scarcity is the ratio of proven reserves to current production. Over the past three decades, due to extensive exploration, this ratio rose by a quarter – from about 30 production years in the mid-1960s, to over 40 production years during the 1990s (data from British Petroleum Annual). Now, according to the scarcity thesis, the increase should have brought crude oil prices down. And yet the exact opposite has happened. As Figure 5.5 shows, during the 1990s the real price of oil was not lower than in the 1960s, but *twice as high*. Whatever the cause for the long-term price appreciation, it was certainly *not* scarcity. And the concept is not much more useful in the short term. As we explained in Chapter 2, the argument that prices are affected by scarcity is meaningful only when such scarcity is set by natural or technical limitations. But that is by no means the case in the oil industry, which commonly operates well below its technical capacity. In this context, the impact on price of a 'shortfall' in supply is therefore a matter of sellers' collusion, not 'scarcity'.

The second problem with the scarcity thesis is that 'excess supply' and 'excess demand' reflect the difference between the *desires* of sellers and buyers; and desires, as we all know, cannot be directly observed, let alone quantified. A common way to bypass the problem, if only provisionally, is to use changes in inventories as a proxy for excess or shortage. But then the evidence from such exercise is often more embarrassing than revealing. The difficulty is illustrated

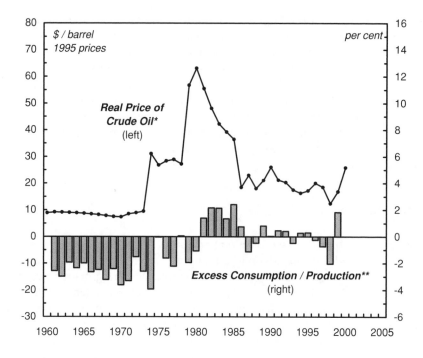

Figure 5.5 'Scarcity' and the Real Price of Oil

* Spot $ price divided by the U.S. Implicit GDP Deflator.
** World consumption less production as a per cent of their average.
SOURCE: British Petroleum (Annual); IMF and U.S. Department of Commerce
through McGraw-Hill (Online).

in Figure 5.5, where we contrast the real price of crude oil (denominated in
constant 1995 dollars), with the excess of global consumption over global
production (measured as a per cent of the average of the two). The latter variable
reflects changes in inventories, with negative values representing build-up and
positive ones denoting depletion. Now, if excess consumption indicates a
'shortage' (caused for example by unexpected rise in demand), and excess
production represents a 'glut' (triggered for instance by the unforeseen arrival
of 'distress oil'), then we should expect prices to rise in the former case and fall
in the latter. The facts, however, tell a much more confused story. During the
glut-plagued 1960s, the scarcity thesis seemed to be working, with inventories
building up and prices falling. But then things started to go wrong. Although
the inventory build-up continued through much of the early 1970s, the real
price of oil *soared*, rising by 16 per cent in 1971, 4 per cent in 1972, 6 per cent
in 1973, and 228 per cent in 1974. And indeed, according to Blair (1976: 266–8),
the 1973/74 oil crisis had nothing to do with the 'oil shortage', simply because
there wasn't any such shortage to begin with. Early in 1973, the ARAMCO

partners (Exxon, Mobil, Chevron and Texaco) were explicitly warned by the Saudis, both of the pending Egyptian attack on Israel, and of the possibility that oil would be used as a political weapon (see also Sampson 1975: 244–5). Anticipating the consequences, the companies raised production in the first three-quarters of the year, an increase which fully compensated for the eventual drop in the last quarter. All in all, OPEC production for 1973 amounted to 11.0 billion barrels, slightly higher than the 10.8 billion it should have been based on long-term growth projections (Blair 1976: 266fn). And the law of scarcity didn't seem to work much better in subsequent years. Between 1975 and 1980, inventories continued to accumulate, but the real price of oil, instead of remaining the same or falling, soared by a cumulative 135 per cent. During the first half of the 1980s, excess production gave way to excess consumption, and yet the real price of oil again refused to cooperate. Instead of rising, it fell by 71 per cent between 1980 and 1986. Even over the past 15 years, with the oil market presumably becoming more 'competitive' (notwithstanding the Gulf War of 1990–91), it is hard to see any clear relationship between excess demand and real price movements.

Last but not least, there is the issue of relative magnitudes. Indeed, even if we could ignore the direction of price movements, their amplitude seems completely out of line with the underlying mismatch between production and consumption. Over the past 40 years, world consumption was usually 2–3 per cent above or below world output. But then could such relatively insignificant discrepancies explain dramatic real-price fluctuations of tens or sometimes hundreds of per cent a year? And why are prices sometimes hyper sensitive to the mismatch, while at other times they hardly budge?

The solution for these perplexities is to broaden the notion of 'scarcity'. As a speculative commodity, the price of crude petroleum depends not only on the relationship between *current* production and consumption, but also – and often much more so – on *future* expectations. The prices buyers are willing to pay relate not only to present energy needs and the cost of alternative sources, but also to expected future prices. Similarly, sellers, both individually and as a group, are constantly weighing the trade-off between present incomes and anticipated but unknown future revenues. Moreover, these factors are not independent of each other. Indeed, buyers' willingness to pay is often affected by the apparent resolve of sellers; which is in turn influenced by the extent of consumers' anxiety. Once acknowledged, such intricacies imply that any given consumption/production ratio can be associated with a *host* of different prices, depending in a rather complex way on the nature of future expectations.

The significance of these considerations could hardly be overstated. To illustrate, consider the fact that after the emergence of OPEC, the number of primary industry players has grown appreciably – from less than a dozen in the 1960s to over 150 by the late 1970s, according to one estimate – and that still without counting governments (Odell 1979: 182). Such multiplicity should have undermined the industry's ability to coordinate output, but that is not what the facts tell us. Indeed, if we were to judge on the basis of OPEC's revenues and the companies' profits as illustrated in Table 5.2 and Figure 5.4, it would appear that collective action was indeed more effective with hundreds of participants during the 1970s and 1980s, than with only a handful before the onset of the crisis! The reason for this apparent anomaly is that, in the final analysis, the price of oil – on the open market, but also between long-term partners – depends not only on the ability to limit current output to 'what the market can bear', but also on the nature of *perceived* scarcity associated with 'external' circumstances. And in our view, since the early 1970s, the single most important factor shaping these perceptions was the vulnerability of Middle East supplies.

The global importance of Middle East oil is of course hardly new, but its significance has increased substantially since the Second World War, and particularly since the 1960s. In 1972, on the eve of the first oil crisis, the region accounted for as much as 36 per cent of the world's total production and 62 per cent of its proven reserves, up from 12 per cent and 42 per cent, respectively, in 1948 (computed from Jacoby 1974: Table 5.1, pp. 68–9; Table 5.2, pp. 74–5). But as they became more crucial, the region's oil supplies were also growing more vulnerable. The oil 'prize' acted like a magnet, turning the Middle East into an arena of superpower confrontation. And this confrontation, combined with rising nationalism, growing class inequalities, and the ancient tensions of ethnicity and religion, helped stir up instability and armed conflict. The consequences for oil were twofold. First, the region's ongoing militarisation since the late 1960s created a constant threat for future energy supplies, helping maintain high prices even in the absence of tight producer coordination. Second, the occasional outbreak of a major conflict tended to trigger an atmosphere of immediate 'energy crisis', pushing confident sellers to charge higher prices and anxious buyers to foot up the bill. And, indeed, since the early 1970s it was regional wars which perhaps more than anything affected the course of oil prices. Despite the absence of any real shortage, the onset of such hostilities – the 1973 Israeli–Arab conflict, the 1979 Islamic Revolution in Iran, the 1980 launch of the Iran–Iraq War, and the 1990/91 Gulf War – invariably generated an atmosphere of 'crisis' and 'shortage', sending prices higher. Similarly, once the crisis atmosphere dissipated – either at the end of a war, or when conflict no longer seemed threatening to the flow of oil – prices began to stagnate and then fall. The importance of these features is attested by their incorporation into common jargon. The industry's 'price consensus', for example, now customarily incorporates, in addition to its 'peacetime' base, also such items as 'embargo effects' and 'war premiums' (*Fortune*, 5 November 1990). The precise magnitude of such 'premiums' and 'effects' cannot be determined, of course, but their significance seems beyond dispute.

From Oil Revenues to Arms Imports

The weapondollar–petrodollar link was also running in the other direction, with rising oil exports helping finance military imports to fuel the regional arms race. This side of the arms–oil interaction is examined in Figure 5.6, where we contrast the annual value of foreign arms deliveries to the Middle East, with the corresponding value of the region's oil production three years earlier (both in constant dollars). The reason for the lag is that current oil revenues bear on the value of current military *contracts*, but the *delivery* of weapons, which is what we display in the chart, usually takes place later, with a lag of roughly three years.[9] We also express both the vertical and horizontal axes as logarithmic scales, in order to show the 'responsiveness' of arms imports to oil revenues. In this presentation, the slope of a trend line passing through the data indicates the per cent change of arms imports corresponding, on average, to a 1 per cent change in oil revenues three years earlier.

The first thing evident from the chart is the sharp 'structural change' affecting the relationship between the two variables. Around the early 1970s, as the oil regime shifted from 'free flow' to 'limited flow', the slope of the relationship tilted from a fairly steep position to a much flatter one. During the 1964–73 period, the trend line going through the observations had a slope of 3.3, indicating that for every 1 per cent change in oil revenues there was, three years later, a 3.3 per cent increase in arms imports. Despite this high 'responsiveness', though, the magnitudes involved were fairly small. Both superpowers were preoccupied with Europe and subsequently with East Asia, and since oil revenues increased only moderately, weapon shipments into the region, although responding eagerly, remained limited in size. By the early 1970s, however, things changed, and rather drastically. The slope of the trend line going through the 1973–97 data fell to 0.4, meaning that a 1 per cent rise in oil revenues during that period generated only 0.4 per cent increase in arms imports. And, indeed, in contrast to the 1960s, when the region's export revenues were earmarked largely for weapon purchases, now they were allocated also to a range of civilian imports, as well as being accumulated as reserves in Western banks. But, then, with the flow of oil having been 'limited' by the high politics of government and companies, and with arms exports becoming increasingly commercialised, the dollar value of both oil income and military

---

9 Conceptually, we should have contrasted arms imports with the region's *net income* from oil exports, rather than with the overall value of its oil output. The latter measure is broader, including, in addition to net export income, also production costs and the value of domestically consumed oil. Furthermore, our own measure here is imputed as the product of physical output multiplied by the average spot price, rather than measuring the actual revenues received. We use this proxy nonetheless because it is available consistently for the entire period, and since it correlates very closely with various net income series which are unfortunately available for only shorter sub-periods.

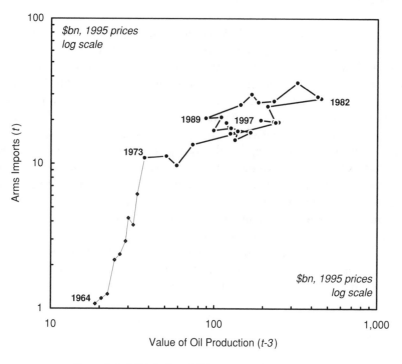

Figure 5.6   Middle East Oil Income and Arms Imports

NOTE: Value of oil production is computed as the multiple of output volume times the world spot price of crude oil. Current dollar figures for both oil production and arms imports are deflated by the U.S. implicit GDP deflator. SOURCE: British Petroleum (Annual); U.S. Arms Controls and Disarmament Agency (Annual); U.S. Department of Commerce through McGraw-Hill (Online).

imports soared to unprecedented levels toward the early 1980s – only to drop, again in tandem, when this order started to disintegrate since the mid-1980s.

The second, and perhaps more remarkable thing about Figure 5.6, is the extremely tight fit between the two series. Based on this chart, it appears that knowing the oil revenues of Middle Eastern countries was practically all that one needed in order to predict the overall value of arms deliveries three years later! Arms deliveries into the region were of course affected by numerous factors, including domestic tensions and inter-country conflicts, superpower policies to protect and enhance their sphere of influence, and the evolution of domestic arms production, to name a few. Furthermore, some arms deliveries were financed by aid or loans, so their import was not directly dependent on oil revenues. Yet, based on the chart, it would seem that these factors were either marginal, or themselves corollaries of the ebb and flow of the 'great prize' – oil.

From Differential Accumulation to 'Energy Conflicts'

We have now reached the final step of our brief statistical journey, ready to move from means to ends. Our method in this exploration was to progressively distil the interaction between oil and arms, moving from production, to sales, to profit, and, eventually, to the differential accumulation of the Weapondollar–Petrodollar Coalition. The task now is to identify the hidden links between this differential accumulation on the one hand, and Middle Eastern 'energy conflicts' on the other. Leaving the state and foreign policy for later in the chapter, and concentrating solely on the companies involved, our question is twofold. First, supposing that these firms acted in unison, how would their quest for differential accumulation relate to militarisation and conflict in the region? And, second, is this hypothetical relationship consistent with the facts?

Although the broader regime of tension and crisis was generally beneficial for the Weapondollar–Petrodollar Coalition, there were nevertheless certain differences between the interests of its armament and oil members. For the former, arms exports constituted a net addition to sales, so their gain from Middle Eastern militarisation and armed conflict was practically open ended. For the latter, however, the consequences of tension and hostilities were beneficial only up to a point, for two reasons. First, excessively high oil prices tended to encourage energy substitution, weaken profits in downstream operations, and lure entry from potential competitors. And, second, regional instability, if spun out of control, could undermine the close cooperation between the companies and oil-producing countries.

Hypothetically, then, we should expect the armament companies to have had little objection to ever-growing militarisation and conflict – this in contrast to the more qualified stance of the oil companies. Specifically, we speculate that as long as the Petro-Core companies managed to beat the 'big economy' average – that is, as long as they accumulated differentially relative to dominant capital as a whole – they judged their performance as satisfactory, and were generally content with having 'tension but not war'. However, when their rate of profit fell *below* that average, their position turned hawkish, seeking open hostilities in order to push up prices and boost their sagging performance. When that happened, the more aggressive stance of the large oil companies brought them into a temporary consensus with the leading armament firms. And it was at this point, we argue, when the Weapondollar–Petrodollar Coalition became united, that a Middle East 'energy conflict' was prone to erupt.

To see how well this hypothesis sits with the facts, consider Figures 5.7 and 5.8. The first of these charts contrasts the rate of return for the Petro-Core with the comparable rate for dominant capital as a whole, approximated here by the Fortune 500 group of companies. The second chart plots the difference between the two rates, expressed in percentage points. In both diagrams, dark areas denote a 'danger zone': a period of negative differential accumulation for the Petro-Core, and a consequent risk of a new 'energy conflict'. The eruption of each such conflict is indicated in Figure 5.8 with a little explosion sign.

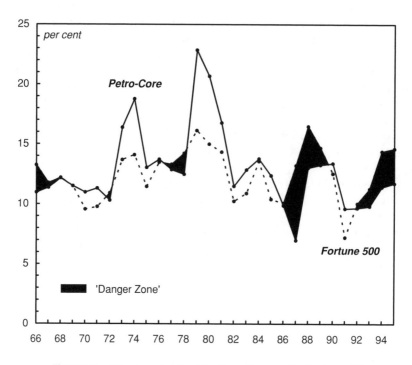

Figure 5.7   Return on Equity: The Petro-Core vs. the Fortune 500

NOTE: For 1992–93, data for Fortune 500 companies are reported
without SFAS 106 special charge.
SOURCE: Fortune; Standard & Poor's Compustat.

The evidence arising from these charts is rather remarkable. First, until the early 1990s, *every single one* of these 'danger zones' was followed by the outbreak of an 'energy conflict' – the 1967 Arab–Israeli War, the 1973 Arab–Israeli War, the 1979 Islamic Revolution in Iran and the outbreak of the 1980–88 Iran–Iraq War and, recently, the 1990/91 Gulf War. Second, the onset of *each* of these crises was followed by a reversal of fortune, with the Petro-Core's rate of return rising above the comparable big-economy average. And finally, *none* of these 'energy conflicts' erupted without the Petro-Core first falling into the 'danger zone'. (The figures also make clear that the mechanism was by no means eternal. Indeed, after the 1990/91 Gulf War, a new 'danger zone' opened up – and yet this time there was no 'energy conflict' to close it. Even the 2001 war in Afghanistan has done little to prop up prices. The reasons for this change are dealt with at the end of the chapter.)

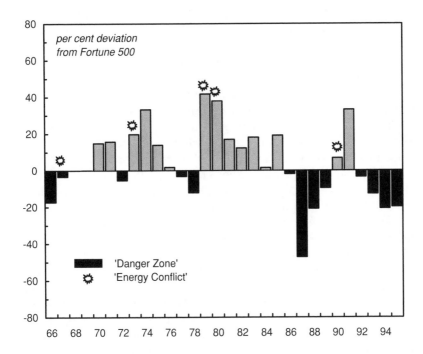

Figure 5.8   Petro-Core's Differential Accumulation and Middle East 'Energy Conflicts'

NOTE: For 1992–93, data for Fortune 500 companies are reported
without SFAS 106 special charge.
SOURCE: Fortune; Standard & Poor's Compustat.

Given the complexity of Middle Eastern affairs, these three regularities seem almost too systematic to be true. Indeed, is it possible that the differential rate of return of six oil companies was all that we needed in order to predict such major upheavals as the June 1967 War, the Iran–Iraq conflict, or the Iraqi invasion to Kuwait? And what should we make of the notion that Middle East conflicts were the main factor 'regulating' the differential accumulation of the Petro-Core? Finally, are lower-than-normal earnings for the oil majors indeed a necessary condition for Middle East energy wars? Maybe the process pictured in Figures 5.7 and 5.8 is a statistical mirage? Perhaps the real causes of energy conflicts are totally different, only that by historical fluke they happened to coincide with differential profitability?

For instance, one simple alternative, still in the realm of business explanations, is that energy conflicts were triggered by movements in profitability rather than *differential* profitability. This, however, does not seem to be the case here. The figues show that the rate of profit of the Petro-Core fell in 1969–70, 1972, 1975, 1977–78, 1980–82, 1985–87 and 1991. Energy conflicts, on the other hand, erupted only in 1967 (after the Core's profits were rising), in 1973 and 1979–80 (after they were falling) and in 1990 (after they were rising). Furthermore, despite falling profitability, no new energy conflict broke out in 1969–70, 1976, 1983 or 1988. Clearly, then, there is no straightforward connection between movements in the simple rate of profit for the Petro-Core and the occurrence of conflicts.

Another possible explanation is that energy conflicts were triggered not by setbacks for the Petro-Core, but by declining exports for the oil-producing countries. According to this argument, the destabilising impact of lower oil revenues would make governments more willing to engage in conflict in order to raise them up. The facts, however, don't seem to support this explanation either. For instance, Egyptian oil exports rose from $35 million in 1970, to $47 million in 1972, and to $93 million in 1973 (United Nations Annual). If wars were indeed contingent on falling state revenues, this should have worked *against* the Arab–Israeli conflict in 1973. Similarly with the Iran–Iraq War. The conflict erupted in 1980, after oil revenues for the two countries were *climbing rapidly*, reaching $18.4 billion for Iran and an all time high of $26.9 for Iraq; and it ended in 1988, after revenues *fell sharply* to $12.7 billion for Iran and to $15.9 for Iraq, exactly the opposite of what we would expect based on the export logic (U.S. Department of Energy Annual). Finally, the 1990 Iraqi invasion of Kuwait occurred after several years of *stable* oil revenues, with Iraqi revenues during 1987–90 hovering around $15 billion annually (ibid.). Of course, prior to his invasion to Kuwait, Saddam Hussain was under a growing financial strain accumulated during his years of fighting against Iran, so he needed much more than stable oil earnings to resolve his problems. Nevertheless, as we shall argue below, this rationale was hardly sufficient to outweigh a clear threat of forceful U.S. intervention – had there been one. Now, of course, every one of these conflicts could be explained by its own particular circumstances, many of which are related neither to oil nor arms. But recall that our purpose is to see if there was perhaps a broader logic to tie these conflicts together, and from this viewpoint, regional and local factors alone, although crucial, do not provide a picture nearly as consistent as the one offered by the Weapondollar–Petrodollar Coalition.

The corporate members of this Coalition, we argue, were not 'free riders' on the roller coaster of Middle East conflicts. Indeed, the evidence indicates not only that these companies *eventually* gained from militarisation and oil crises, but more fundamentally, that adverse drops in their differential profits have been a most effective *leading* indicator for upcoming 'energy conflicts'. This evidence cannot easily be dismissed as a chance occurrence. By the standards of empirical research, the links between differential accumulation on the one hand, and militarisation, 'energy conflicts' and oil crises on the other, are far too systematic and encompassing to be ignored. Clearly, there is need here for further exploration. How, for instance, was the weapon trade commercialised? What politicised the oil business? What role did the superpowers play in the process? How did Middle East governments, including Israel's, fit into the bigger picture? Did the large corporations shape 'foreign policy' in the region, or were they themselves instruments of such policy? Can we actually draw a line between state and capital here? Should we? Let's turn then to look more closely at the actual history of the process.

The 1967 Arab–Israeli War

Analyses of the June 1967 War are usually cast in terms of three regional processes, none of which is directly related to oil. The first process is of course the ethnic and cultural antagonism between Arabs and Jews, which began at the turn of the century, and which developed after 1948 into a nationalist clash between Israel on the one hand, and the Palestinians and the Arab states on the other (Safran 1978). The second process concerns the barriers on rapidly growing population imposed by an acute shortage of water. According to many writers this is the root cause of the conflict between Israel and its immediate neighbours, Jordan, Syria and Lebanon (Kelly 1986; Naff and Matson 1984; Rabinovitch 1983; and Sexton 1990). The third process, which received considerable attention in recent years, is the development since the 1950s of nuclear weapons by Israel (Hersh 1991). Some, such as Aronson (1992; 1994–95), see this development as crucial in determining Israel's foreign and security policies, and as a major force steering the region's recent history.

Making America 'Aware of the Issue'

Yet, the conflict was also related, even at that early stage, to the broader, *global* significance of the Middle East. The 'free-flow' era after the Second World War was marked by U.S. concerns regarding access to the region's oil fields. During the late 1940s and early 1950s, many at the State Department saw Israel as a destabilising factor. Military support to that country, argued the CIA, could provoke anti-American sentiments, weaken the U.S. position in Iran, Turkey and Greece, and possibly lead to a loss of control over the oil routes (Gazit, 1983a: 14). The Israelis, although formally non-aligned, were displeased with these negative attitudes, particularly since they had so much to offer. The sentiment of the country's elite in this matter was echoed by Gershom Schocken, editor of the daily *Ha'aretz*:

> Israel had proven its military might in the War of Independence, so making it somewhat stronger could help the West keep the political balance in the Middle East. According to this view, Israel would act as a watchdog. It wouldn't become aggressive against the explicit wishes of America and Britain. But, if, for whatever reason, the latter were to turn a blind eye, Israel could be counted on to punish those neighbours whose attitude towards the

West had become a little too disrespectful.... (*Ha'aretz*, 30 September 1951, cited in Orr and Machover 1961: 158).

Until the mid-1950s, however, Britain still seemed to be doing a good job protecting the oil routes, and with its various positions in Iraq, the oil emirates, and the Suez Canal looking secure, the Israeli overtures were politely ignored. Ben-Gurion, though, was persistent. 'It's about time to make the defence of Israel part and parcel of defending the free world', he wrote to U.S. Secretary of State John Foster-Dulles (cited in Bar Zohar 1975: 1320). To demonstrate his commitment, he offered in 1951 to secretly dispatch an Israeli battalion in order to assist the U.S. war effort in Korea, while on another occasion he proposed that Washington finance a 250,000-strong Israeli military force, dedicated to defending the region against Soviet intrusions (Gazit 1983a: 16–19). 'There was something pathetic and shameful', wrote his biographer, 'in these repeated attempts to hold on to the U.S. skirt, particularly when the latter was trying, again and again, to get rid of the embarrassing nuisance....' (Bar Zohar 1975: 1320). And yet the efforts continued. Pinchas Lavon, who replaced Ben-Gurion as Defence Minister in 1953, tried a new, bolder direction. His intention was to set up a terrorist network in the Arab countries, with the purpose of attacking U.S. embassies and cultural centres. This, he hoped, would alienate the Americans against their Arab hosts, helping them realise that their only true ally in the region was Israel (Sharet 1978: Vols. II–III). The hasty plot was uncovered, and although the affair was never thoroughly investigated, Lavon had to resign, and eventually so did Ben-Gurion. The Israeli military, though, continued the escalation, using massive 'retaliations' against Palestinian guerrillas in the hope of warming up the conflict and pulling the United States into the fold (Sharet 1978: Vol. III; Cafcafi 1994: 73).

The crowning achievement of this strategy was Israel's 1956 invasion of the Sinai peninsula, followed by Britain and France's attempt to take over the Suez Canal. *U.S. News and World Report* was quick to summarise the obvious: 'Why did Britain and France go to war against Egypt? In order to topple Nasser, to control the Suez Canal and save their oil' (9 November 1956, cited in Orr and Machover 1961: 297). The Israeli elite, on the other hand, denied any conspiracy. According to the official version, Ben-Gurion never went to France on the eve of the war to sign the Sèvres Treaty between the conspirators; there was no prior plan for France and Britain to take over the Canal in order to 'separate' the warring factions; and there was no intention to topple Nasser. The whole thing was an act of self-defence, pure and simple. Israel was threatened with annihilation, and so took a pre-emptive strike. Thirty years later, though, Shimon Peres, who participated in orchestrating the operation, presented a rather different version:

If it were not for the Suez Operation, the danger was that Britain and France would leave the Middle East before the Americans became aware of the issue, therefore allowing the Russians to penetrate and shape the region without the U.S.A. Following the Suez Operation, the Americans became committed to a regional balance. It was this commitment which shaped the U.S. stance toward the Six Day War.... (cited in Evron 1986: 164)

In other words, Ben-Gurion and his clique managed to trick their allies as well as foes. Not only was there no threat of 'annihilation', but the 'eternal Franco-Israeli friendship', which Peres always took credit for cementing, was itself merely a temporary move. The real goal was to make the Americans 'aware of the issue'.

Subcontracting

And aware they became. Following the Suez debacle, the 'free flow' of oil no longer looked secure. The emergence of Pan-Arabism and increasing Soviet intrusion into the region presented a growing threat to the feudal regimes of Saudi Arabia and surrounding sheikdoms. In 1958, Faisal, the pro-American king of Iraq was assassinated, and the 1954 Baghdad Pact erected by the British fell apart. In that same year, Syria and Egypt merged into the United Arab Republic, prompting King Hussein of Jordan to request American aid and British paratroops for his protection, and the Maronite government in Beirut to invite the U.S. marines. These developments gave rise to the new 'Eisenhower Doctrine'. According to this doctrine, the United States itself would assume military responsibility for the Persian Gulf and the Arab Peninsula (Gold 1993: 35). However, the new realignment also required to fortify the perimeter surrounding the oil region, and here Israel came in handy. Valued for its stability, pro-Western characteristics and logistical potential, it was declared a 'strategic asset' for the West (Safran 1978: Ch. 20). With persistence and a dose of good luck, the dream had finally come true.

   Initially, the State Department was careful to not openly support the Jewish state. The CIA, however, having fewer inhibitions, quickly started fashioning covert liaisons with local politicians and security officials. Many of these relations were built around a proposal by Ben-Gurion that Israel create a peripheral, pro-American alliance with non-Arab countries, such as Turkey, Iran and Ethiopia, in order to contain Arab radicalism. A central feature of this 'peripheral alliance' was a secret agreement, code-named *KK Mountain*. According to the agreement, the Israeli Mossad would become a permanent paid 'subcontractor' for the CIA, carrying out delicate operations which the U.S. legislator and judiciary would otherwise find difficult to stomach. Since the region's 'bastion of democracy' was much more lenient in these matters, the deal seemed only fair, and the Mossad quickly found itself involved in numerous proxy undertakings around the world. In the Middle East and Africa, these included military assistance to various groups and regimes, such as the royal forces in Ethiopia and Yemen, the Kurds in Iraq, the army and secret service of the Iranian Shah, the secret police in Morocco, the security forces and military of South Africa, and the rulers of Uganda, Zaire and Nigeria. Later, the Israelis would also diversify into Latin America, providing their ware and knowledge to pro-American dictatorships such as Panama, Chile, Nicaragua, Honduras, El Salvador and Guatemala (Cockburn and Cockburn 1991: Chs 5, 9, 10).

Some of these operations were allegedly part of the CIA's effort to have the new Kennedy Administration pay more attention to the Middle East. The role of the CIA is especially noteworthy, because, after the Second World War, and particularly since the early 1950s, the Agency's Middle Eastern activities were almost exclusively handled by the ARAMCO partners and Bechtel (McCartney 1989: Ch. 10). Kennedy wasn't swayed. Despite his favourable attitude toward the petroleum industry and the close oil connections of some his top officials,[10] he continued pursuing his policy of appeasement toward Nasser. However, his 'New Look' doctrine also permitted, for the first time, American military shipments to Israel. Contrary to the 'nuclear-containment' policy of his predecessors, Kennedy emphasised the use of conventional weapons and direct involvement against Soviet subversion. In 1960, he announced that he was not opposed to a 'military balance' between Israel and the Arab countries, and that in global matters the United States had 'special relations' with Israel, comparable only to its relations with Britain (Safran 1978: 581; and Gazit 1983a: 33).

Breaking Nasser's Bones Asunder

Initially, the change may have been partly motivated by Kennedy's desire to check Israel's nuclear development programme, and to prevent an out-of-control nuclear arms race between Israel and Egypt (Gazit 1983b: 49–56). Another possibility is that Kennedy was simply paying off the Jewish Lobby for financing his election campaign (Hersh 1991: Ch. 8). But toward the mid-1960s, when attempts to appease Nasser seemed to go nowhere, his successor, President Johnson, put Kennedy's 'special relations' into practice, and began sending Israel large military shipments. Despite his preoccupation with the intensifying conflict in Vietnam, Johnson was nevertheless worried about the fighting in Yemen, where Egyptian troops had on a number of occasions crossed the border into Saudi Arabia. After the end of its involvement in Libya and in the Congo, the United States ceased its economic support to Egypt altogether, and instead switched to overtly assisting the Jewish state. In 1966, at the height

10   Some of these connections involved the Texas oil associations of Vice-President Johnson, the southwestern and international oil affiliations of Secretary of the Navy Connally, the Rockefeller links of Secretary of State Dillon, and the long-term business partnership between CIA director McCone and the Bechtel family (Engler 1977: 57–8; McCartney 1989).

of its entanglement in Vietnam, Washington began giving Israel, for the first time, *heavy* assault weapons, including tanks, aircraft and missiles.

In that year, Soviet involvement in the region seemed more menacing than ever. First, Britain announced it would soon be leaving Aden, notwithstanding the ongoing Soviet-backed war in neighbouring Yemen, just south of the world's richest oil fields; then, the pro-Soviet Ba'ath party staged a coup in Syria; and finally, the Kremlin began to promote a socialist union between Egypt, Syria, Algeria and Iraq, threatening to engulf Saudi Arabia from the west and north. Given its difficulties in Vietnam, the United States was not prepared to counteract these developments directly, but Israel certainly was and did.

Toward the end of 1966, the Arab–Israeli dispute was again heating up. In November, Israel staged a massive raid into the Jordanian town of Samoa, officially in retaliation for guerrilla attacks. Then, in April 1967, an Israeli tractor, sent to cultivate a demilitarised zone just beneath the Golan Heights, sparked a border skirmish which ended with humiliating Syrian losses. Adding insult to injury, the Israelis went on to announce their intentions of forcibly dethroning the Damascus regime. Faced with mounting challenges to his Pan-Arab leadership, Nasser was more or less compelled to respond, moving two army divisions into the Sinai desert and closing the Straits of Tiran. There are, of course, other explanations. Aronson (1994–95), for instance, argues that the escalation was in fact an unintended consequence of Nasser trying to stop the development of nuclear weapons by Israel. One way or the other, it is clear that the Americans (like the French and British before them) hoped that Israel would use the opportunity to topple Nasser, and the closing of the Tiran Straits now offered the pretext for a pre-emptive strike.

Contrary to popular belief, the Israeli and American leaderships had little doubt about the outcome of the looming war. The certainty of Arab defeat was also known to Nasser – as well as to the other Arab participants – but given their internal disputes, they found it politically impossible to ignore Israeli provocations, and were thus increasingly drawn toward a point of no return.[11] Following the closure of the Straits of Tiran, Israel scheduled its attack for 25 May, but had to wait until 6 June, after Meir Amit, head of the Israeli Mossad, returned from an emergency trip to Washington with the 'green light' to 'break Nasser's bones asunder' (Haber 1987: 214–16). And so, by maintaining its loyalty to U.S. strategic interests in the region, Israel had finally succeeded in

---

11 According to former Israeli ambassador to the United States, Abba Eban, many in the State Department were convinced of Israel's military superiority and ability to win a 'crushing victory' already in the 1950s (Eban 1977: 185). After the 1967 War, IDF generals such as Ezer Weitzman, Benjamin Peled and Yitzhak Rabin, admitted quite openly that Nasser had presented no real danger. Ten days before the war, a secret CIA report delivered to Johnson accurately predicted an Israeli victory within six days. Some U.S. officials who hoped to avert a war communicated these assessments directly to Jordan and Egypt and, indeed, until the last moment, Nasser still hoped for a diplomatic resolution (Cockburn and Cockburn 1991: 140–54).

joining the U.S. orbit as an official satellite, a process which would further intensify during the 1970s and 1980s.

Preoccupied with the 'free flow' of oil, the Petro-Core may have viewed the war's outcome as highly favourable: Soviet aspirations were undermined and the cause of Pan-Arabism suffered a serious blow. However, the companies must have also noticed the positive effect the war had on their differential profitability (see Figures 5.7 and 5.8) – an ominous sign that their 'free-flow' system was itself coming to an end.[12] And as if to hasten the process, the aftermath of the war was marked by increasing arms exports. Rewarded for its victory, Israel began receiving F-4 Phantom aircraft made by McDonnell Douglas, which were previously sold only to Britain and Germany. With this, the door was now open for an arms race of sophisticated weapons, a race which would eventually help 'limit' the flow of oil and introduce the petroleum business into the new era of 'crisis'.

The 1973 Arab–Israeli War

The 1968 U.S. presidential elections brought in an administration highly attuned to the coinciding interests of oil and arms. Nixon's campaigns were supported heavily, and sometimes illegally, by contributions from both defence contractors and oil companies, while his Secretary of State Kissinger enjoyed close connections with the Rockefellers, and proposed an aggressive realpolitik which on more than one occasion entertained the feasibility of 'limited' nuclear war.[13] In the eyes of this new administration, the 1967 War did little to secure U.S. interests in the Middle East. Qaddafi's 1969 showdown with the oil companies in Libya and the attempted coup in Saudi Arabia were disconcerting reminders of pending regional hazards. Washington, so it seemed, must pay more attention, not less, to this troubled area.

The Realist View

And yet, that was easier said than done. In 1969, the United States began withdrawing its troops from Vietnam, and with warmer relations with China

12   While official crude prices had not changed, fuel prices for Western consumers rose, thus boosting the profits of the oil companies while undermining them elsewhere in the economy.
13   On Nixon's campaigns, see Sampson (1975: 205–6) and Sampson (1977: 151–2, 195). On Kissinger, see Barnet (1983: 178–9). Representatives of Rockefeller's Chase Manhattan were involved in the network of activists around Nixon's career, and some of them accepted key posts in his administration. Paul Volker, for example, was made Under Secretary of the Treasury for Monetary Affairs; John Letty became Assistant Secretary of the Treasury; and Charles Fiero became Director of the Office of Foreign Direct Investment in the Commerce Department (Barnet and Müller 1974: 251; Turner 1983: 105).

and the declaration of Détente, the new 'Nixon Doctrine' called for a lower defence budget. Instead of Kennedy's strategy to prepare for '2½ wars', Nixon and Kissinger offered resources for only '1½ wars'. In 1969, the policy kicked in, and domestic military spending started to fall. From a statist viewpoint, the result was to weaken U.S. capabilities in the Middle East, this precisely when the region emerged as one of the world's most sensitive (Gold 1993: 40). Moreover, Britain's withdrawal from its last stronghold in the Persian Gulf, together with the United States losing its last strategic air base in Libya, created a military vacuum. The solution, stipulated by Kissinger, was for the United States to concentrate only on 'core conflicts', leaving 'peripheral conflicts' to be handled by local pro-American forces. The consequences for the region were twofold. First, Washington embarked on massive arms exports, initially to Israel and the 'twin pillars', Iran and Saudi Arabia, but later also to Egypt and other countries. Second, State Department attempts at settling the Arab–Israeli conflict were now frustrated by White House support for Israel (Safran 1978: Ch. 23). With Middle Eastern affairs increasingly handled by the Nixon–Kissinger duo rather than State Secretary Rogers, Israel was now used as a threat against anti-American Arab countries (Kissinger 1979: 1285, 1289). Kissinger was particularly intimidated by what he regarded as deliberate Soviet challenges, and in 1970 worked out, together with Yitzhak Rabin, then Israel's ambassador to Washington, a joint plan for military intervention in case Syria or Iraq attacked King Hussein of Jordan.

These observations do not sit well with the realist perspective. First, given the split between the conciliatory position of the State Department and the aggressive stance of the President, it is not clear what 'national interest' American policy makers were trying to achieve. Second, the type of cannon diplomacy entertained by Kissinger did not look particularly conducive to his goal of regional stability. Indeed, according to Safran (1978: Ch. 23), the United States continued to send arms to the region, this despite its own fears that an Israeli victory against Arab aggression would cause chaos and seriously disturb the flow of oil.

The Coalition's View

From the viewpoint of the Weapondollar–Petrodollar Coalition, however, U.S. foreign policy here seems pretty consistent. Declining military spending at home hurt the large defence contractors badly (Sampson 1977: 214–21), and with pressures from these contractors coinciding with his own strategic outlook, Nixon moved to further commercialise arms exports. His new doctrine stipulated that the burden of defending U.S. allies – financially as well as in manpower – should now be borne by those allies themselves (Ferrari et al. 1987: 21). In order to do that, explained military contractor David Packard (then acting as Deputy Secretary of Defense), the United States was ready to 'give or sell [to these allies] the tools they need for this bigger load we are urging them to assume' (quoted in Sampson 1977: 243). In the Middle East, the Nixon Doctrine elevated the arms race to a new level. Commercialisation, to be sure, was not strictly enforced. Israel, for instance, was unable to pay for its rapidly rising military imports; and, yet, to its great surprise, Washington was willing to give them for free (Rabin 1979: Ch. 4).[14] Officials in Jerusalem celebrated this as a 'huge achievement' (Gazit, 1983a: 53), only that they failed to notice the even greater achievement of other states, who, unlike Israel, were both able and willing to pay.

The most 'successful' of the lot was Iran. On their visit to Tehran in 1972, Nixon and Kissinger reputedly agreed to sell Iran 'virtually any conventional arms it wanted' (cited in Sampson 1977: 252). And with this newly acquired freedom to sell, U.S. armament companies quickly started courting the country's Shah, whom Washington now appointed as 'policeman of the Gulf'. At the time, domestic sales to the Pentagon were hitting rock bottom, so military exports to Iran provided a much needed lifeline for many contractors (Figure 5.3). The extent of these exports, however, depended crucially on the petroleum revenues of the Peacock Throne, an important detail which both Nixon and Kissinger were most surely aware of.[15] And, indeed, the oil industry, too, was undergoing a profound transformation. With weakening prices and falling profitability, as illustrated in Figures 5.5 and 5.7, the large petroleum companies came to realise the potential benefit of a stronger OPEC. The cartel's apparent resolve to control output impressed the oil majors, and their London Oil Policy Group was now ready to accept a new revenue-sharing agreement (Odell 1979: 105, 215). But although the price of oil started to rise in 1971, the Petro-Core's rate of profit continued to linger and, in 1972, fell dangerously below the Fortune 500 'normal' (Figures 5.7 and 5.8).

And then came the October 1973 'energy conflict'. The war brought a sharp increase in prices, restoring the oil companies' differential profitability high above the big-economy's average. At the same time, it also generated dramatic increases in the oil revenues of Arab countries, with immediate consequences for the arms trade. In 1974, a year after the war, the Middle East surpassed South East Asia to become the world's largest market for imported weapons, with over one-third of the global trade.

14   During the 1962–66 period, Israel's annual weapon imports averaged $107 million. After the 1967 War, with the United States replacing France as the main supplier, the average almost tripled to $290 during 1967–69, and in 1970–72, with the Nixon Doctrine starting to kick in, it rose further to $550 (unpublished data from Israel Central Bureau of Statistics, courtesy of Reuven Graff).
15   Allegations that the U.S. government was promoting higher prices as a primary means of funding U.S. arms deliveries to the Shah were put forward on the CBS programme *Sixty Minutes* (3 May 1980). Kissinger, though, declined to comment (Chan 1980: 244). Kissinger was also closely associated with Rockefeller's Chase Manhattan, and it is not far fetched to assume he also contemplated the benefit for the bank from higher petrodollar deposits (*Ha'aretz*, 2 January 1981).

While there is no evidence to implicate the U.S. Administration as instigator in the conflict, there is also little to indicate it keenly tried to prevent it. To be sure, the war didn't catch the Nixon government by surprise. Warned by King Faisal of Saudi Arabia already in the beginning of 1973, the ARAMCO partners were aware of what was coming, and they passed on the information to Washington (Blair 1976: 266–8; Sampson 1975: 243–8; and Yergin 1991: 593–7). A similar message came from a CIA study (incidentally co-authored by the same analyst who anticipated that the 1967 War would last only six days), which concluded that the Egyptians were planning to attack Israel (Cockburn and Cockburn 1991: 171). Indeed, Kissinger was directly informed of the pending assault, both by Jordan's King Hussein (who between 1957 and 1977 was a paid CIA agent), and by sources close to President Sadat of Egypt (Neff 1988: 105).

The U.S. 'National Interest': What Price Stability?

These observations seem perplexing. If Nixon and Kissinger were indeed concerned with maintaining regional stability as stipulated in the realist literature, why didn't they heed Saudi requests that Washington softened its support for Israel? To suggest that this was because the Administration was by then irrevocably committed to the Israeli cause is not persuasive; for if that was the case, why did it fail to warn the Israelis of the pending calamity? Indeed, why did Kissinger caution Israel not to fire the first shot when the latter finally realised that Egypt and Syria were about to attack? One common interpretation is that Kissinger wanted the Arabs to win their self-respect and some territory, which would then be traded for peace through his own mediation (Hersh 1991: 227). However, from a statist viewpoint, Kissinger was walking on a tightrope here. The problem, according to his own admission, was how to achieve a 'balanced' outcome – one in which the war would end after Israel had recovered some of its earlier losses, but before it had the chance to destroy its opponents. For Kissinger, this must have been a real problem. He had absolute confidence in Israel's military ability and feared that an Israeli victory would be devastating for U.S. regional interests (possibly by inciting leftist coups and encouraging Soviet intervention). Yet despite the obvious danger, he stuck to his plan, moving to broker a ceasefire only at the last moment, after Israel had threatened to use nuclear weapons (Safran 1978: Ch. 23).

Clearly, then, realist calculations alone do not tell the whole story. Attuned to the plight of the oil and armament companies, Kissinger must have also pondered how an oil crisis might boost their coinciding interests. And indeed, after the war, with petrodollars and weapondollars locked in an upward spiral, peace between Israel and the Arabs was put on the backburner. The more urgent task now was to keep the 'balance of power'; and sure enough, instead of preaching reconciliation, we find the U.S. ambassador to Cairo recommending military shipments to Egypt, while his colleagues in Kuwait and Saudi Arabia explain the merit of American-made aircraft to local rulers (*New York Times*, 21 July 1975, cited in Frenkel 1991: 76). Working now for the new Ford Administration but still pursuing his original plan, Kissinger helped establish an 'interim agreement' between the warring factions. This time, though, the United States held the carrot as well as the stick; it could use Israel as a threat against pro-Soviet Arab regimes, but it could also force it to return occupied Arab land to those who promised to leave the Soviet orbit and cross the floor onto the American side (Safran 1978: Ch. 25). However, the U.S. Administration was also careful to insist that any interim agreement should not evolve into a comprehensive settlement. When in July of 1975 the Israeli government appeared willing to go to a peace conference in Geneva, President Ford threatened to withdraw American assistance (*New York Times*, 3 July 1975). The imperative of maintaining tension was spelled out clearly less than a year later. Appearing before the Jewish-American Congress in April of 1976, Henry Kissinger effectively asserted that a comprehensive Middle East peace depended not so much on the warring factions, but rather on the superpowers first agreeing on their respective spheres of influence (reported in Meyer 1976: 157).

   These pursuits on the armament front also help shed some light on the Administration's energy policy. On the surface, Washington's view on the subject seemed confused, even contradictory. Based on his analysis of over one thousand State Department cables and papers obtained under the Freedom of Information Act, Yergin (1991: 84) concluded that, between 1974 and 1981, the U.S. government in fact objected to higher oil prices. But then he simultaneously inferred that the government didn't want to see those prices lowered either (p. 643). This indecisiveness, Yergin argued, was rooted in a conflicting quest for lower energy cost at home, coupled with a richer and thus more stable Middle East. And yet, if the goal was indeed stability, why send so much armament to the region, particularly when Washington itself doubted their contribution to peace? And what about the support of Kissinger and the International Energy Agency for a 'minimum safeguard price' as a means of protecting *Western* interests? (Sampson 1975: 306; and Turner 1983: 184). Perhaps the Administration, despite its declarations to the contrary, was in fact interested in *neither lower oil prices nor regional stability*? After all, representatives of the Weapondollar–Petrodollar Coalition were now increasingly involved in 'state policy', so couldn't they have pushed things in that direction?

   The realist failure to square the circle around oil prices is only understandable. The basic reason is that, by the 1970s, while the world was already well into the 'limited flow' era, realist theories were still stuck in the 'free flow' logic. Stephen Krasner, for example, claimed that there was a negative trade-off between the level and variability of petroleum prices (1978b: 39–40). The consequence, he concluded, was that policy makers had to choose between low but variable prices, or stable but high ones. Yet, when those lines were written, this menu had already become irrelevant, and in fact misleading. From the late 1960s onward, with oil shifting to a 'limited flow' footing, the relationship between the level and variability of prices became *positive*. The choice now was not between low and variable oil prices as opposed to high and stable ones, but rather between low and stable prices against high and volatile ones. Obviously, this transition fundamentally altered the relationship between the oil companies and the so-called 'national interest'. During the early period, when the companies were concerned mainly with concessions, the Administration's willingness to have higher prices in order to secure stability and access seemed sensible. It helped the companies, as well as the broader U.S. 'national interest'. Since the late 1960s, however, harmony gave way to discord. The United States could no longer pay higher prices in order to achieve access and price stability; it couldn't, simply because access was no longer negotiable, whereas higher prices were clearly causing *greater instability*. The oil companies, on the other hand, were now interested not in access but in higher prices. Contrary to the earlier situation, therefore, there was now clear conflict between the companies and the 'national interest', and the Administration's pursuit of both instability and higher prices only indicates where its allegiances lay.

Initially, the coinciding interests of the Arma-Core and Petro-Core in regional turmoil were blurred by the imaginative use of language, which insisted on equating arms shipments with 'stabilisation'. For example, Secretary of State Rogers, who would later become a retainer for the Iranian Shah and board member of the oil company Sohio, characterised U.S. military sales as having a 'stabilising influence' – this in contrast to the 'invitation for trouble' posed by similar Soviet shipments (Engler 1977: 242). Similarly, Kissinger (1981: 182), using a more academic lingo, explained that the 'balance of power is a kind of policeman, whose responsibility is to prevent peaceful countries from feeling impotent and aggressors from becoming reckless'. Eventually, however, as the Orwellian identity of weapons and peace began to dissipate, the true forces at play came into focus.

The rising influence of the Weapondollar–Petrodollar Coalition coincided with the new policies of Jimmy Carter. Unlike Nixon's, the 'Carter Doctrine' moved from emphasising loyal proxies – chiefly Israel and the 'twin pillars', Iran and Saudi Arabia – to direct military intervention. With growing nervousness on the part of the Saudi pillar – first in response to Soviet involvement in the Horn of Africa, and later as a consequence of Soviet participation in the Yemen conflict – Carter and his national security adviser, Zbigniew Brzezinski, decided to build a 'Rapid Deployment Joint Task Force', or RDJTF (Long 1985: 62). As they saw it, the lesson from Iran was that the United States should not count on local proxies, and must use its own forces to protect its own interests (Quandt 1979: 543). This fitted well with the broader strategic rethinking in Washington. According to Brzezinski (1983: 454), events and decisions in 1979–80 had fundamentally altered the U.S. global strategic position. The Middle East – which was previously seen as semi-neutral and protected from Soviet power by a defence belt comprising Turkey, Iran, Pakistan and Afghanistan – no longer seemed invincible. As a consequence, U.S. dual commitments in Europe and the Far East were supplemented by a third strategic commitment toward what was now known as 'West Asia'. The resources needed to support this new pledge, however, were unavailable, and so in order to bypass congressional objection, part of the military deployment was financed by Saudi petrodollars (Gold 1993: 51).

Thus, notwithstanding his desire to promote world peace, President Carter was subject to considerable pressures to act otherwise. At home, his was the first administration to raise domestic military spending after almost a decade of decline (Figure 5.3). On the international arena, Carter indeed announced a policy of restraints on arms exports, which, in its first 15 months, led to the cancellation of 614 requests from 92 countries, worth over $1 billion (Ferrari et al. 1987: 25). Yet, despite these limitations, and contrary to the new statist stand on the principle of American 'self-defence', total U.S. arms exports continued to increase (albeit still slowly), particularly to the Middle East. Somewhat paradoxically, Carter, who was often perceived as a peacemaker and promoter of regional reconciliation, was also the president who contributed the most toward opening the Arab market to U.S. weaponry. In 1978, toward the Camp David Accord, he initiated the first 'combination deal', whereby U.S. armament producers *simultaneously* equipped several warring factions – a pattern which was then promptly institutionalised by other arms-exporting countries as a means of promoting peace through arms sales.[16]

The 1979 Iranian Revolution and the 1980–88 Iran–Iraq War

The Hostage Crisis

Yet the ongoing rearmament during the mid-1970s was merely sufficient to keep oil prices from falling, and in the absence of a serious upheaval, the Petro-Core's profitability in 1977 and 1978 again dropped into the 'danger zone', below the big-economy's average (Figures 5.7 and 5.8). Fortunately for the Coalition, though, help was on the way, with turmoil again starting to build up. The Islamic Revolution which began in 1978 failed to have a significant effect on the oil market, although the potential was clearly there. In this light, the involvement of the U.S. Administration in the onset of the

---

16 Israel was compensated for its withdrawal from the Sinai peninsula with two new airfields in the Negev desert worth $2.2 billion, and a 'reorganisation' package of 15 F-15 and 75 F-16 aircraft valued at $1.9 billion. The Egyptians were allowed to purchase 50 F-5 fighter aircraft worth $400 billion (with an option to buy more advanced ones later), and the Saudis bought another 60 F-15s worth $2.5 billion (*Ha'aretz*, 3 April 1983). Cyrus Vance, who participated in the negotiations as Carter's Secretary of State, was later nominated a director of General Dynamics, one of the deal's principal winners.

1979 oil crisis is noteworthy. Despite the delicate situation in Iran, President Carter quickly granted asylum to the ousted Shah, thus triggering the hostage crisis. When Iran threatened to withdraw its U.S. banking deposits, the President immediately retaliated by seizing Iranian assets.

The background leading to the seizure was outlined by journalist Anthony Sampson (1981: Ch. 17; Ha'aretz, 2 January 1981). During the period from 1976 to 1978, Iran borrowed $3.8 billion to finance arms purchases. On the eve of the Iranian Revolution, an outstanding debt of $500 million was owed to a consortium headed by Chase Manhattan, which also held $433 million in Iranian deposits. In theory, these deposits could have been withheld as a forced collateral, only that Chase had no legal right to do so – that is, unless instructed by the U.S. government for reasons of 'national security'. And as it turns out, this is precisely what happened – although not without help from David Rockefeller, the bank's chairman and one of its principal owners. Sampson reveals how Henry Kissinger, acting as a special adviser to Chase Manhattan at the time, and Jack McCloy, a former chairman of the bank, courted President Carter, who was himself closely associated with the Rockefellers through the Trilateral Commission, so that he granted asylum to the Shah despite the fragile political atmosphere. Kissinger later told Sampson that there was nothing subversive in these activities, arguing it was inconceivable that 'a few private citizens' could affect state policy. The Islamic government, in any event, was deeply offended. Turmoil ensued, and as the script unfolded, Tehran threatened to withdraw its U.S. deposits, to which Carter immediately retaliated by freezing them. The official justification was that the freeze was necessary to defend the integrity of the American banking system, although the real risk couldn't be that serious. Iran had roughly $8 billion dollars worth of deposits, but of these only $1 billion were 'call money' available on demand – less than 1 per cent of the U.S. system's outstanding cash balance. Moreover, most of these deposits were held in London, so even if drawn out, the only place for them to go was back into the Euro market. Clearly, the financial system as whole was not at threat. Certain institutions, however, particularly Chase and Citibank of the Rockefeller group, were vulnerable, and had much to gain by the freeze.

The 'Sting'

The hostage crisis in Iran sparked panic, and the price of oil finally began to rise. Adding to the turmoil, the Soviet Union invaded Afghanistan in late 1979, and in 1980 the Iraqis attacked Iran. Oil prices were now climbing beyond $35 per barrel, pulling the Petro-Core's profitability safely out of the 'danger zone'. And with Middle East oil revenues on the rise, the flow of imported weapons was also growing rapidly. To some extent, both the invasion of Afghanistan and Iraq's assault on Iran were rooted in the rising threat of Islamic funda-mentalism. Yet the U.S. government, although happy to see this threat being checked, was not entirely antagonistic to the Khomeini regime. According to several sources analysed in Cockburn and Cockburn (1991: 317–18), during the last year of his administration, Carter embarked on a 'sting operation' which, if successful, would have both helped his re-election and caused Iran to renew its demand for American weapons. The underpinnings of his strategy were relatively straightforward. With much of their sophisticated arsenal made in the United States, the Iranians were crucially dependent on U.S. spare parts and ammunition. In this context, a major conflict, preferably starting before the 1980 elections, could convince Iran to release the embassy hostages in return for American military re-supply. The unsuspecting carrier of that plan was Iraq's Saddam Hussein. With blessing from Jordan and Kuwait, promises of Saudi finances and, most importantly, a warm endorsement from Zbigniew Brzezinski, whose declared aim was to see Iran 'punished from all sides', Hussein swallowed the bait, and began advancing his forces into Iran (Cockburn and Cockburn 1991: 392). Unfortunately for Carter, the timing of the 'sting' was out of sync. Once Iraq launched its attack, his administration condemned it and began soliciting the Iranians to trade hostages for spare parts. But that was too late. Apparently, Iran already had a secret agreement with the U.S. Republican Party, according to which the hostages would be released only after the elections. And so although the weapons were ready to flow, Carter was no longer there to benefit from the deal.[17] For the Weapondollar–Petrodollar Coalition, of course, the deal was manna from heaven, regardless of who won the election – although naturally, it much preferred having Reagan on its side than Carter.

During Reagan's presidency, the Middle East was defined – in some sense paradoxically – as being increasingly important for the U.S. 'national interest'. In 1983, Reagan created a new military central command, or CENTCOM, to include the entire area of 'West Asia' from India to the Horn of Africa. CENTCOM's mandate emphasised active defence over deterrence. Its capabilities, however, were very limited. It wasn't able, for example, to counter a Soviet challenge against the oil zone in southern Iran, and certainly not to embark on a larger operation (Gold 1993: 69). Moreover, with funding being tight, the new focus on West Asia had to come at the expense of American military commitments in Europe and East Asia – this at a time when the significance to the U.S. of Middle East oil, as well as of the Soviet danger, were in fact *declining*, as we describe later in the chapter.

The Network

While the importance of oil and Soviet power were apparently waning under Reagan, the political leverage of the Weapondollar–Petrodollar Coalition was

17   The allegations about a deal between Iran and the Reagan campaign headquarters were first made by Gary Sick and others (*New York Times*, 15 April 1991; Sick 1991).

soaring to new highs. Vice-President George Bush – a former Director of the CIA and an oil millionaire in his own right – had close acquaintance with the petroleum industry, and strong ties to ultra right-wing groups. As his first Secretary of State, the President nominated Alexander Haig, previously a director of Chase Manhattan and President and Chief Executive Officer of United Technology.[18] Reagan also nominated Donald Regan, a partner and chairman of Merrill Lynch, as his Treasury Secretary. Merrill Lynch, much like Chase Manhattan and United Technology, also had special links to the Middle East. In 1978, the company acquired White Weld, an international investment firm that advised the Saudi Arabian Monetary Agency (SAMA) on how to manage its $100 billion portfolio and guided the investment of a daily inflow of about 450 million petrodollars. As his Assistant Secretary for International Affairs, Regan chose David Mulford, who until then was running White Weld's operations in Saudi Arabia (*Business Week*, 22 July 1985). Other oil-related appointments included the nomination of Paul Volker as chairman of the Federal Reserve Board, who was then succeeded by Alan Greenspan; the former was linked to the Rockefeller group, whereas the latter, besides being a groupie of Ayn Rand, was a director at both Mobil Oil and J.P. Morgan prior to his appointment.

However, the most important representatives of the Weapondollar–Petrodollar Coalition who found their way into the Reagan Administration were the veterans of Bechtel Corporation, the world's largest contractor of military installations and energy-related projects.[19] Bechtel has had a long history of building political ties at home and abroad (cf. McCartney 1989). Among other things, the company was the driving force behind the election campaigns of Presidents Edgar Hoover, Dwight Eisenhower and Ronald Reagan; it had close associates in the CIA, including Agency Directors William Casey, Richard Helms and John McCone;[20] it courted special relations with the Dulles brothers; and it has dominated decision-making at the Atomic Energy

18 Earlier, Haig served as Nixon's Deputy Assistant for National Security Affairs, as well as the White House Chief of Staff, but his leverage was now much stronger. Shiff and Yaari (1984) allege that it was he who gave Israel's Defence Minister Sharon the 'green light' to invade Lebanon in 1982. United Technology, to which Haig later returned as a special consultant, exported helicopters and aircraft engines to the Middle East. Haig was able to persuade the Israeli government to install United Technology's engines in its proposed Lavi aircraft – although the IDF preferred the alternative engines made by General Electric. Eventually General Electric came out on top. While the Lavi got cancelled, the Israeli air force, with the help of hefty bribes to IDF Brigadier General Rami Dotan, decided to equip its F-16 fighters with GE engines.

19 During the 1980s, the Bechtel family owned about two-fifths of the company's shares, with the remainder spread among the firm's senior managers. The company had to be excluded from our statistical analysis due to lack of publicly available data.

20 Supplying arms and equipment to the U.S. army during the Second World War, John McCone and his partner Steven Bechtel Sr. managed to earn in only a few years over $100 million on an investment of less than $400,000; certainly a remarkable achievement, even by the loose standards of war profiteering (McCartney 1989: 70).

Commission and the Export-Import Bank. On the international scene, Bechtel acted simultaneously as an arm of the CIA, as well as the unofficial representative of foreign governments, particularly Saudi Arabia, in the United States. These and numerous other connections, often supplemented by substantial bribes and clandestine operations, helped win Bechtel some of the world's largest construction projects.[21] But what made these projects so valuable to begin with was the unfolding 'energy crisis' since the early 1970s.

Bechtel entered the Middle East after the Second World War as a major contractor for the ARAMCO partners, but until the consolidation of OPEC its activities in the region were relatively limited. It was only with the oil price explosion of the early 1970s, that the contracts began piling up. Among others, these included the construction of natural gas projects in Algeria and Abu Dhabi, power stations in Cairo, and refineries, airports and entire petrochemical cities in Saudi Arabia. In addition, many of the company's other energy-related projects – such as Quebec's hydroelectric James Bay complex, the Alaska oil pipeline, Indonesia's liquefied natural gas facilities, and nuclear reactor plants in the United States and elsewhere – were themselves partly the consequence of rising oil prices. The company also became a major constructor of military installations – mainly for U.S. forces, but also for other sovereigns, particularly in cash-rich Arab countries.

By the early 1980s, Bechtel's international operations had risen to over one-half of its business, and the person who guided this transition since the mid-1970s was the company's president, George Shultz. Toward the 1980 election, Shultz grew worried about candidate Ronald Reagan, whose fixation on *laissez faire* and small government threatened Bechtel's lifeline. However, after a series of re-educational meetings with Bechtel executives and associates of the Rockefeller group, the presidential hopeful came back to his senses, at least enough to make Shultz an avid supporter. Once in office, Reagan began drawing on the talent of Bechtel officials. As his initial Defense Secretary he chose Casper Weinberger, who until then was a Bechtel vice-president, and in 1982, he asked Shultz to replace Haig as Secretary of State. Other Bechtel veterans with key positions in the new administration included, National Security Adviser Richard Allen; Deputy Secretary of Energy Kenneth Davis; and Philip Habib, whom Reagan sent as his Special Envoy to the Middle East while still on Bechtel's payroll.

The convergence of oil and armament interests in the Reagan Administration was paralleled to some extent in their own corporate boardrooms, mainly through interlocking directorships which provide an informal setting for exchanging ideas and coordinating collective action. For example, during the 1980s, the chairman and chief executive officer of Standard Oil of Indiana

---

21 Perhaps the largest bribe was the $200 million paid to Saudi officials in return for the $3.4 billion contract to build the new airport in Riyadh. The earliest covert operation involved the Syrian coup of 1949, after the Syrian government raised obstacles to the construction by Bechtel of a Saudi–Syrian pipeline.

(Swearingen) was a director of both Chase Manhattan and Lockheed; the board of directors of McDonnell Douglas included a director of Phillips Petroleum (Chetkovich) and a director of Shell Canada (McDonald); the chairman and president of United Technologies (Gray) was a director of both Exxon and Citibank; Boeing shared one director with Mobil and three with Chevron, including the latter's chairman (Keller); and the Chevron board included a director from Allied Signal (Hills), as well as the president and chief executive of Hewlett Packard (Yound) (based on Moody's Annual; Adams 1982).

Nourishing the Conflict

Whether the oil and armament companies indeed colluded to advance their common interests remains an open question, but the policies of the Reagan Administration certainly worked on their behalf. At home, Reagan helped consolidate the Weapondollar–Petrodollar Coalition by embarking on the largest defence build-up in peacetime, while simultaneously reducing corporate taxes. The obvious result was a rapidly rising budget deficit, which horrified the economists but delighted the arms contractors and oil companies.[22] And in the Middle East, the new Administration continued the policies of its pre-decessors, though apparently with much greater vigour. Whereas for Carter arms exports were an 'exceptional foreign policy implement', Reagan took the view that they were 'an essential element of [U.S.] global defense posture and an indispensable component of its foreign policy', moving to eliminate many of their previously imposed restrictions (U.S. Congress 1991: 20). Of course, in order to enable buyers to pay for the outgoing weapons, Middle East 'energy conflicts' had to be continuously nourished, a task to which the new Administration turned with little delay.

Building on their earlier success, Washington and Tehran were now trading regularly in exotic commodities. The United States secretly supplied weapons to the Ayatollah Khomeini, for which the latter paid with released hostages held by Iranian-backed forces in Lebanon, plus hard cash which the Americans then used to finance the Contra rebels in Nicaragua. The elaborate scheme, popularly known as the 'Iran-Contra Affair', was conceived and approved at the highest echelons, including President Reagan, Vice-President Bush, Secretary of State Shultz, Secretary of Defense Weinberger, CIA Director William Casey, and National Security Advisers Robert McFarlane and John Poindexter (*New York Times*, 19 January 1994). The purpose of the scheme, though, involved more than hostages and rebels. Its other goal, less publicised though certainly

22 The petroleum sector was a double winner under Reagan. Whereas over the 1960–80 period its effective tax rate rose from 11 to 29 per cent on an average annual profit of less than $7 billion, during the next five years earnings rose to $27 billion annually, while effective taxation dropped to 18 per cent (computed from the U.S. Department of Commerce through McGraw-Hill Online).

no less important, was to enable Iran to hold out against Iraq – but just barely, so that the war could continue for as long as possible. According to retired IDF general Avraham Tamir, Defense Secretary Haig explained to his Israeli counterpart Sharon that 'it was U.S. policy to prevent either side from winning' (Cockburn and Cockburn 1991: 328). And indeed, as journalists Waas and Unger describe in their colourful language, the Administration '"tilted" back and forth between support for Iran and support for Iraq, sometimes helping both countries simultaneously, sometimes covertly arming one side as a corrective to unanticipated consequences of having helped the other' (1992: 65). Arms shipments to sustain the Iranian war effort – ranging from $500 million to $1 billion annually, depending on the source – were handled by Israel. At the same time, the Americans also kept promoting the Iraqi cause. This was done in a variety of ways: by renewing diplomatic relations; by providing military intelligence; by granting low-interest loans; by encouraging Saudi financial assistance; by asking the Gulf states and Egypt to deliver more than $1.5 billion worth of arms and ammunition; and, finally, by allowing over $5 billion of U.S. credit – partly guaranteed by the Agriculture Department – to be covertly (and possibly fraudulently) used for Iraqi purchases of U.S. machinery and technology with military and nuclear applications (*Business Week*, 13 July 1992; Waas and Unger 1992). To facilitate payments for the war effort, it was suggested in 1984 that Bechtel construct a multibillion dollar pipeline from Kirkuk to the Jordanian port of Aqaba, so that Iraqi oil exports could bypass the hazards of the Gulf. The undertaking was endorsed by CIA Director William Casey, but apparently that wasn't enough. The main risk was Israel, whose war planes could have easily blown the project out of operation. And so Bechtel lined up an impressive battery of friends, including Swiss oil magnate Bruce Rappoport, U.S. Attorney General Edwin Meese, and National Security Adviser Robert McFarlane, whose role was to make sure such an attack wouldn't happen. Rappoport, with his reputed CIA connections and long-term friendship with Israeli Prime Minister Shimon Peres, managed to obtain a written promise, signed by Peres, that Israel wouldn't mess with the pipeline; this in return for an overall premium of about $650 million, payable in ten equal annual instalments, which would then be partly diverted to Peres' Labour Party. To further secure the arrangement, Peres was willing to freeze in a 'salvage fund' $400 million out of the U.S. military aid to Israel, and Meese and McFarlane laboured to arrange that the scheme be approved by the Overseas Private Investment Corporation (*Business Week*, 22 February 1988; Frenkel 1991: 30–4).

The Oil-Arms Bust

The project, however, never took off, perhaps because the flows of petrodollars and weapondollars were themselves beginning to recede. In 1980, the volume of Middle East oil production started to decline, and in 1982 prices followed suit.

The combined result was a steep drop in the region's oil revenues – from $197 billion in 1980 to a mere $52 billion by 1986, according to UN data. And given the intimate link from oil exports to arms imports, the consequences for the weapon makers were dire. 'We're all down now to nibbling crumbs', professed a frustrated U.S. defence executive during the 1985 Paris air show: 'The damn oil boom has gone and there is not much money around any more' (cited in Ferrari et al. 1987: 4–5). As of themselves, these developments are not entirely surprising. First, high oil prices induced greater energy efficiency, substitution to alternative sources, and further exploration and output by non-OPEC producers. Second, diversification by Saudi Arabia and Kuwait into downstream operations brought them into conflict with the companies. And finally, the Iran–Iraq War, previously a major source of 'risk' and 'scarcity', was no longer viewed as a threat for Western oil supplies.

Indeed, in this sense, the situation during the early 1980s differed from the one prevailing after the 1973 Arab–Israeli War. In the earlier conflict, the anti-Israel alliance of the Arab countries lent credibility to their 'oil weapon' and the threat of future shortages. By the 1980s, however, the OPEC front was no longer united and two important members of the cartel were themselves military foes. The disturbances occurring in the Persian Gulf, particularly the so-called 'tanker war' and attacks on oil installations, made the oil market nervous and perhaps exerted a positive influence on prices. Yet rivalry prevailed instead of cooperation, and with no end in sight to the hostilities, the likelihood of restoring OPEC's earlier cohesion seemed remote. In this respect, the overriding need of both Iran and Iraq for new weapons and ammunition only made things worse, since it forced both to stretch production to the limit, creating a gushing flow of 'distress oil'.[23] And so, from a certain point onward, the Iran–Iraq War turned from a blessing to a curse. Instead of boosting prices, it now caused them to *fall*, creating a rather taxing environment for both OPEC and the Weapondollar–Petrodollar Coalition.

Given the gravity of the situation, Saudi Arabia agreed to provide a 'cushion' for OPEC's other members, selling its oil at the cartel's official price and absorbing the demand shortfall. The cost, though, mounted quickly. The kingdom had to reduce its output from 9.8 million barrels a day in 1981, to 6.5 million in 1982 and, finally, to a mere 3.2 million in 1985, but even that failed to stabilise spot prices (OPEC Annual). Eventually, the Saudis bailed out, and as their production rose, panic ensued and the price collapsed even further.

In 1986, with the price of crude oil heading below $10 a barrel for the first time since 1973, the Petro-Core's rate of return once again dropped below the

23 Spending on the war was partly financed by foreign assistance, with Khomeini supported by both Syria and Libya, and Iraq allegedly receiving $30–60 billion in cash and replacement oil from Saudi Arabia and other Gulf states (*Business Week*, 4 June 1985; Stockholm International Peace Research Institute 1987: 303). This aid, however, was hardly sufficient for the task at hand, leaving the two countries no choice but to prime the pump.

big economy's average (Figures 5.7 and 5.8). And as the Middle East found itself entering a new 'danger zone', Vice-President Bush found himself on a mission to Riyadh, with the task of *openly* asking the Saudis to reconsider their actions and reinstate lower levels of production. Bush insisted that the government of the United States was 'fundamentally, irrevocably committed' to maintaining the free flow of oil, and that 'the interest in the United States is bound to be cheap energy prices'. However, the Vice-President also emphasised that '[there] is some point at which the national security interests of the United States say, "Hey, we must have a strong, viable domestic interest"' (*New York Times*, 7 April 1986).

The other reason for the Administration's concern for oil was the armament market. Defence procurement at home started to level off after having soared for a decade. And yet, military shipments to the Middle East, which could have partly compensated for the shortfall, were now drying up for lack of petro-dollars. Worse still, as Table 5.3 shows, competitors from other countries were now winning market share from American companies. In contrast to the period until the late 1970s, when the market was more or less under the thumb of the two superpowers, since the early 1980s suppliers from Europe and the developing world were making significant headway. By the end of the 1980s, these contenders saw their combined market share rise to more than 50 per cent, double its level a decade earlier; the share of U.S. suppliers, on the other hand, dropped to 18 per cent, down from 48 per cent.[24] A large part of this decline was due to the fact that U.S. arms shipments, despite considerable deregulation under Reagan, were still partly subjugated to 'foreign policy' considerations, whereas in other countries they were by now completely commercialised. And so, with the Iranian market having been lost to scandal, and with sales to Iraq forbidden by government decree, U.S.-based firms could only watch and see their competitors stepping in to fill the void. The lost opportunity was immense. The Iran–Iraq War, which dragged on for much of the 1980s, turned out to be the most expensive conflict since Vietnam, with the belligerent countries spending over $400 billion to fight each other. And yet, save for covert shipments, the profits from this gold mine were going not to U.S. firms, but to their rivals.[25]

24 During the 1990s, U.S. producers recovered the lost ground, although according to realist thinking they should have done far better. Indeed, with their country being the world's sole hegemon now that the Soviet Union was no more, what was to prevent them from kicking their competitors completely out of the picture? But then, the question itself is misguided. By now, U.S., European and Japanese contractors have grown increasingly intertwined through complicated supply chains and transnational cross-ownership, so that their 'state' allegiance was not always obvious. Also, and as we shall see at the end of the chapter, the U.S. 'national interest' was itself starting to shift from weaponry to other business, making competition over Middle East arms contracts seem less important.

25 Some estimates suggest that Iraq imported about $40 billion worth of arms during the period from 1980 to 1986, while Iran's foreign purchases amounted to $30 billion. The overall stake of covert U.S. shipments in these totals must have been limited. The prime suppliers for the war were based in France, the United Kingdom,

Table 5.3   Arms Exports to the Middle East

Period	Total	Supplier (per cent of total)[a]		
	($ million)	United States	Soviet Union/Russia[b]	Others
1964–73	9,447	34.4[c]	50.2	15.4
1974–78	29,000	47.6	25.9	26.6
1979–83	65,355	21.7	31.2	47.0
1984–88	89,065	18.3	29.9	51.8
1989–93	83,600	38.3	11.4	51.4
1994–97	67,300	47.1	3.9	49.0

(a) Totals may not sum up to 100 per cent because of rounding.
(b) Russia from 1992 onward.
(c) Data for the United States are for fiscal years. Total does not include the re-supply effort to Israel following the 1973 Arab–Israeli War.
SOURCE: U.S. Arms Control and Disarmament Agency (1975 Edition, p. 70; 1980 Edition, p. 160; 1985 Edition, p. 134; 1998 Edition, p. 174); U.S. Department of Commerce, Bureau of Economic Analysis, *Statistical Abstract of the United States*, 1991, Table 550, p. 340.

The 1990–91 Gulf War

With so much at stake, it was once again time for the U.S. Administration to hype the Persian Gulf as a 'vital national interest'. In a speech given in 1987, Secretary of Defense Weinberger reminded his audience that the Middle East still contained 70 per cent of the world's proven reserves. The role of the United States, he said, was to assure the region was secure, stable and, above all, free from Soviet influence and intervention. According to Weinberger's strict guidelines, the American military was practically prevented from intervening in any conflict short of a world war. The only exception was the Middle East, where direct military intrusion was deemed warranted (Gold 1993: 76). From a realist perspective, though, this new emphasis sounded a bit odd. Indeed, according to the analysis laid out in Gold (1993: 75), during Reagan's second term in office the region had become strategically *less* important to the U.S. 'national interest'. For one, the Soviet Union, locked into a losing war of attrition in Afghanistan, was no longer perceived as marching toward the Strait of Hormuz. Furthermore, although the Middle East still contained much of the world's reserves, the expansion of non-OPEC output, greater conservation, and

West Germany, Italy, South Africa, the Soviet Union, China, North and South Korea, Vietnam, Israel, Taiwan and Brazil (*Business Week*, 29 December 1986; for a full list of the 52 known participating countries, see Stockholm International Peace Research Institute 1987: Table 7.8, pp. 204–5). According to *Jane's Defence Weekly*, Iraq even supplied Iran, reselling to the latter through private dealers heavy weapons previously captured in the fighting (reported in Stockholm International Peace Research Institute 1987: 307). For detailed accounts of the arming of Iraq during and after the Iran–Iraq War, see Darwish and Alexander (1991: Chs 4–6) and Timmerman (1991).

new energy-saving technologies, have together made this oil less important than before. And, finally, the experience of the Iran–Iraq War suggested that regional conflicts could go on with oil supplies remaining cheap and plentiful. But then, these very developments, which from the viewpoint of the U.S. 'national interest' were supposedly all good, spelled serious trouble for the Weapondollar–Petrodollar Coalition. And so the escalation began.

Warming Up

Attempts to bolster U.S. military presence in the region began in 1984, when Washington tried to persuade the Persian Gulf emirates to allow the installation of American bases on their soil. The latter refused, but in 1986, when an Iraqi Mirage fighter hit an American frigate, Washington responded by sending aircraft carriers into the region. The Iranians retaliated by littering the Gulf with naval mines, to which the United States answered with mine sweepers. And, so, in 1986, when Vice-President Bush was on his mission to Saudi Arabia in an effort to raise oil prices by peaceful means, the U.S. military was already well on its way toward direct involvement in the region, a trajectory which would four years later culminate in Operation Desert Storm.

The first direct target was Libya's ruler, Muammar Qaddafi, who was increasingly blamed for fostering international terrorism. A Sixth Fleet armada of more than 45 warships, including three aircraft carriers with over 200 planes, was dispatched in March 1986 toward the renegade state. The official reason was to 'enforce the principle of freedom of the seas' against Qaddafi's unwarranted extension of Libya's territorial waters to the 32nd parallel. But as U.S. administration officials later acknowledged, the real purpose of the operation, code-named Prairie Fire, was rather different. The plan was to provoke a military response by Libya, against which U.S. forces would retaliate with escalating counter-strikes, including the destruction of the Libyan air force and bombing raids on the country's oil fields. Qaddafi, however, failed to pick up the bait and did not respond in any meaningful way (*Montreal Gazette*, 29 March 1986; *Time*, 7 April 1986). A new opportunity arose a month later, after a terrorist attack on a West Berlin discotheque ended with numerous injuries and one dead American soldier. The blame for the attack was immediately put on Libya and the fleet was sent once again toward Qaddafi's 'line of death'. But the Libyan ruler, to whom Reagan referred as the 'mad dog of the Middle East', held his fire and the military exchange was limited (*Time*, 21 April 1986). Incidentally, the Syrians, who were also blamed for being involved in the West German bombing, came out against 'U.S. aggression' in Libya, and there were increasing reports about heightening Israeli–Syrian tensions (*Time*, 26 May 1986). The attempted escalation continued, when in August, information leaked by the Administration to the *Wall Street Journal* suggested that the United States and Libya were again 'on a collision course' (*Time*, 13 October 1986).

This policy of confrontation was presented as part of a new, stronger U.S. stand against radical Middle East regimes. In 1987, however, Reagan abruptly abandoned the Libyan cause, shifting his focus back to the Persian Gulf. The official reason was again the Soviets. The 'tanker war' in the Gulf, which since 1980 had already accounted for over 300 damaged oil vessels, was suddenly made into a top priority after the Kuwaitis requested U.S. protection for their tankers. Initially, the Administration appeared reluctant, but then quickly reversed its stance once the Kuwaitis turned to the Kremlin (Gold 1993: 79–104; Darwish and Alexander 1991: 244–5). The real story, however, was more complicated. Since the beginning of 1986, the Administration was voicing open concerns that Iran was getting the upper hand in its six-year war with Iraq. But, then, in November of that year, the Iran–Contra Affair began to unravel, suggesting that part of the credit for Iran's success must go to the U.S. Administration itself. Revelations that Reagan was both condemning and supplying Tehran forced Washington to reiterate its anti-Khomeini stance, and the Kuwaiti request provided the right pretext. The Seventh Fleet assumed the role of protecting Kuwaiti tankers, and before long found itself attacking Iranian oil installations and exchanging fire with Iranian forces.

The intensified conflict and growing U.S. involvement drew the more moderate Gulf states deeper into the militarisation process. Countries such as Saudi Arabia, Kuwait, Oman and the United Arab Emirates were now looking to buy more U.S.-made weapons, which the White House was only too happy to supply.[26] The Congress, though, being far less forthcoming than the Administration, managed to block several large deals, forcing the Gulf states to look for alternative sources.[27] The biggest setback for the U.S. companies was the 1988 'deal of the century', in which the United Kingdom agreed to supply Saudi Arabia with $25 billion worth of military hardware, construction and technical support over the next two decades (*Business Week*, 12 September 1988). The end of the Iran–Iraq War in 1988 opened new business opportunities for companies which could help rebuild the war-shattered infrastructures of the two countries. The scope of the work was substantial – estimated at the time in excess of $200 billion – but then here too U.S. corporations found themselves facing stiff competition from non-U.S. rivals (*Business Week*, 29 August 1988).

26 In 1988, the Administration suggested increasing U.S. arms exports by $3.3 billion, to a level exceeding $15 billion – with proposed shipments worth $3.6 billion to Israel, $2.7 billion to Egypt, $950 million to Saudi Arabia, and $1.3 billion to other Middle Eastern countries (*New York Times*, 2 May 1988). This proposal did not prevent Secretary of State Shultz from declaring in front of the U.N. General Assembly only a few weeks later that 'developing countries must help reduce the international tension and ease the arms race' (*New York Times*, 14 May 1988).

27 In 1985, the Congress refused to approve the sale to Saudi Arabia of 40 advanced McDonnell Douglas F-15 aircraft and, in 1986, blocked the sale of 800 General Dynamics Stinger missiles. In 1988, the U.S. Senate voted to deny a Kuwaiti request for Hughes (GM) Maverick missiles and also forbade the sale of Stinger missiles to Oman (*New York Times*, 13 May 1988; *Time*, 25 July 1988).

'Danger Zone'

The Bush presidency, which began in 1989, provided continuity for the Weapondollar–Petrodollar Coalition in Washington. Some of the Coalition's representatives were by now gone, but their successors were in most cases equally aware of the oil and armament interests at stake. These included, in addition to oil millionaire George Bush, people such as Nicolas Brady, who previously ran Dillon, Read & Company when it was controlled by Bechtel, and who was now nominated Treasury Secretary; Robert Mosbacher, an oil businessman who now became Secretary of Commerce; and James Baker, a lawyer with deep ties to the oil business, who previously served under Ford and Reagan, and was now made Secretary of State (during the 1990s, Mosbacher and Baker returned to the private sector as special consultants to the energy giant Enron). Bush also wanted John Tower to become Secretary of Defense, but the former senator, who acted as retainer for five defence contractors, failed the conformation hearings. Eventually, the post went to Richard Cheney, a strong supporter of 'Star Wars' and the Contra rebels, who would later become Vice President under George Bush's son.

The Middle East situation, however, remained precarious for the Coalition. Despite the Administration's loyalty and its greater military involvement in the region, the price of oil did not recover significantly, the Petro-Core's rate of return was still in the 'danger zone', and demand for foreign weapons was stuck in the doldrums. The gravity of the situation was succinctly summarised in February 1990 by the head of CENTCOM, General Norman Schwarzkopf. Appearing in front of the Senate Armed-Forces Committee, Schwarzkopf, whose father had previously set up the dreaded Iranian SAVAK, explained the crucial and growing significance of Middle East oil. The region, he warned his audience, had 13 ongoing conflicts, and if any one of them were to develop into a full-fledged war, the consequences for the West could be dire. Despite this danger, though, he strongly recommended that the United States increase its military exports to the region in order to match disturbing advances made by foreign competitors. On the day of Schwarzkopf's speech, a 'prime Pentagon source' suggested to the *Wall Street Journal* that the Administration, now that the East–West conflict was over, should divert funds from defending Europe to protecting Saudi Arabia (cited in Frenkel 1991: 9–13). The background for these pressures was succinctly summarised two months later by an unnamed Pentagon official:

> No one knows what to do over here. The [Soviet] threat has melted down on us, and what else do we have? The navy's been going to the Hill to talk about the threat of the Indian navy in the Indian Ocean. Some people are talking about the threat of the Colombian drug cartels. But we can't keep a $300

billion budget afloat on that stuff. There is only one place that will do us as a threat: Iraq. (cited in Cockburn and Cockburn 1991: 354–5).

And, indeed, a month later Saddam Hussein finally made his move, beginning to threaten his Gulf neighbours with the dire consequences of their oil policies. After the end of the Iran–Iraq War, Hussein found himself between a rock and a hard place. His country was devastated, overburdened by $80 billion in foreign debt, and deprived of petrodollars. In order to rebuild his economy and army, he demanded that the Gulf states, which in his view benefited from Iraq fighting the fundamentalist threat for them, should now foot up the bill, forgiving their Iraqi loans and providing him with even more funds (Darwish and Alexander 1991: Chs 9–11). In parallel, he also insisted that OPEC should get its act together by reducing output and raising prices. Needless to say, neither policy sat well with his neighbours. First, they had no desire to help re-fortify Iraq only to see its claws eventually turned against them (Darwish and Alexander 1991: 256–65; Frenkel 1991: 15–18). And, second, some of the Gulf states, particularly Saudi Arabia and Kuwait, were by now sufficiently diversified into downstream operations to benefit from more moderate prices (*Business Week*, 3 July 1988, 21 January 1991). Seeing that the differences could not be settled peacefully, Hussein eventually decided to take Kuwait over. On paper at least, this would have helped him kill two birds with one stone – enlarging his own fiefdom while simultaneously limiting overproduction by 'merger'. The only problem was that there was a much bigger picture to consider, and here Hussein's calculations proved fatally wrong.

By July, with the build-up of Iraqi forces along the Kuwaiti border becoming all too evident, the United States deployed several combat ships on joint manoeuvres with the United Arab Emirates. But except for these drills its message to Iraq was ambiguous and, at times, even encouraging. To learn more on the American position, Hussein summoned the U.S. ambassador, April Glaspie. In the interview which was held on 25 July, a week before the invasion, Hussein explained his grievances against Kuwait, noting quite explicitly that Iraq intended to 'take one by one' its disregarded rights. Glaspie replied that the dispute was an internal Arab matter on which the United States had 'no position', and that she had a 'direct instruction from the President to seek better relations with Iraq'. When Hussein mentioned his demand that OPEC push the price of oil over $25 per barrel, Glaspie chose to respond that there were also many Americans who would like to see the price go above that level. On 28 July, Bush reportedly sent a message to Hussein that the use of force against Kuwait was unacceptable, but three days later his Under-Secretary of State Kelly said to reporters that the United States had 'no defence treaties with any Gulf countries'. On 1 August, despite the CIA's conclusion that an Iraqi attack was imminent, the United States still failed to voice any explicit warning (Darwish and Alexander 1991: 267–75).

Back on Top

The American stance changed drastically, however, once the Iraqis began crossing the Kuwaiti border on 2 August. Three days after the invasion, Defense Secretary Cheney and General Schwarzkopf convinced the Saudi royal family that their kingdom was Hussein's next target – a most implausible presumption by all counts as U.S. officials later admitted – persuading them to invite the deployment of 'infidel' forces on their land, something which until then the Saudis always managed to avoid (Woodward 1991: Ch. 19). During the following months, Hussein apparently attempted to seek a face-saving diplomatic solution, but to no avail. For the Americans, the opportunities offered by open confrontation were simply too great to give up.

And, indeed, the consequences of the war were highly beneficial for the Weapondollar–Petrodollar Coalition. The initial rise in the price of crude oil – from around $14 per barrel in 1990 to near $40 just before the onset of Operation Desert Storm – helped pull the Petro-Core's profitability above the big economy's average (see Figures 5.7 and 5.8). In 1991, the price per barrel declined to an average of $22 (which, incidentally, was not much below what Hussein demanded on the eve of his invasion), but that was still sufficient to keep the Petro-Core out of the 'danger zone'.[28] The price revival raised Middle East oil revenues, and although their level was still far below that of the early 1980s, the anxiety created by the war, particularly in Saudi Arabia and the adjacent sheikdoms, caused them to nervously convert more of their petro-dollars into weapondollars.

And this time, the main beneficiaries were U.S. firms, whose exports to the region in the two years following the war jumped by 45 per cent, according to the U.S. Department of Commerce. Part of the increase was in the export of civilian goods and services, mainly to Kuwait. During its short occupation, the Iraqi army engaged in systematic plunder, stealing according to some estimates $20–50 billion worth of Kuwaiti property. In addition, it also left behind war damages whose repair cost was projected at $100 billion. Perhaps not surprisingly, some of the largest reconstruction contracts went to Bechtel, beginning with a $1 billion task of extinguishing the 650 oil fires ignited by the retreating Iraqi army, and continuing with the multibillion-dollar job of restoring oil production, repairing refineries and rebuilding damaged infrastructure (*Business Week*, 18 February 1991, 6 March 1991, 11 March 1991, 17 February 1992; *Fortune*, 25 March 1991). Most of the export increase, however, was in the category of military goods and services, which rose dramatically to reinstate the United States once again as the region's prime supplier (see Table 5.3).

28   Many oil executives actually felt relieved by the more moderate prices, which were high enough for differential profitability but not for 'conspiracy theory'. Just to be on the safe side, though, some oil companies decided during the last quarter of 1990 to write off part of their higher profits against the cost of 'future environmental regulations' (*Business Week*, 11 February 1991).

On 6 March 1991, while addressing a joint session of Congress after the Iraqi surrender, George Bush exclaimed that 'it would be tragic if the nations of the Middle East and Persian Gulf were now, in the wake of the war, to embark on a new arms race' (*New York Times*, 7 March 1991). Then, on 30 May, he went further, calling the major arms-exporting countries to establish guidelines 'for restraints on destabilizing transfers of conventional arms' to the Middle East (*New York Times*, 30 March 1991). In parallel, however, the President also insisted it was 'time to put an end to micro-management of foreign and security assistance programs, micro-management that humiliates our friends and allies and hamstrings our diplomacy' (*New York Times*, 7 March 1991). To help erase some of the traces of such 'micro-management', in which both he and Ronald Reagan were explicitly implicated, Bush granted pardon in 1992 to six key figures in the Iran–Contra Affair, including a pre-emptive one to former Defense Secretary Casper Weinberger whose trial was just about to begin. Then, in line with the eternal principles of free enterprise, the Administration instructed American embassies to expand their assistance to U.S.-based military contractors, and even proposed to alter the 1968 Arms Exports Control Act, so that the Export-Import Bank could guarantee $1 billion in loan-financing for U.S. arms exports (U.S. Congress 1991: 21; *New York Times* 18 March 1991).[29] True to the time-honoured strategy of 'stabilisation through military exports', Bush proposed in January of 1991, while the Gulf War was still going, that the United States sell Saudi Arabia over $20 billion worth of armament – a deal so large that the Administration eventually had to 'slice' it into smaller pieces, for easier Congressional digestion (U.S. Congress 1991: 21).

And, so, by 1990, after a decade of losing ground to rival sellers, the United States, helped by falling exports from the former Soviet Union, was once more the largest weapon exporter to developing countries. The American comeback was especially pronounced in the Middle East – so much so that it prompted British officials to openly complain that the United States was 'monopolizing' the region's arms trade (*The Independent*, 13 December 1992). The Gulf War also helped reinstate the primacy of petroleum companies vis-à-vis their host countries. The previous political arrangement, with OPEC in the spotlight and the oil in the background, no longer seemed to work. Despite the region's militarisation, producing countries were increasingly acting at cross purposes, with Saudi Arabia, the companies' principal ally, unable to bring them back into line. And so, here too the war helped put things back in order. The region's most important suppliers – notably Saudi Arabia, Kuwait and surrounding sheikdoms – were now signatories to defence treaties with the United States and

29 Government support was not limited to defence contracts, of course. For example, both President Bush and his Secretary of State Mosbacher did not hesitate to intervene personally on behalf of AT&T, when Saudi Arabia appeared to prefer European contractors for its $8.1 billion plan to expand the kingdom's telephone network (*Business Week*, 18 February 1991). The new Clinton Administration kept up the pressure and AT&T eventually won the contract.

Britain, which effectively subordinated their oil policies to U.S. dictates. Iraq was put out of circulation by UN sanctions, and with Iran still isolated, the risk of glut was significantly limited. On the surface, then, the Weapondollar–Petrodollar Coalition looked ready to roll. But in fact, this was to be its last victory, at least for the time being. After the Gulf War, the 'danger zone' opened up once more, with oil profits falling below the average. And yet, this time around there was no new energy conflict to pull these profits back up.

The Demise of the Weapondollar–Petrodollar Coalition

The New Breadth Order

Compared with the 1970s and 1980s, the 1990s were far less hospitable to weapon dealers and oil profiteers. During the earlier period, dominant capital in the developed countries found itself well extended within its respective envelopes, its breadth potential being restricted by the post-war legacy of statism, by antitrust policies, and by capital controls. Given these barriers, differential accumulation concentrated mainly on stagflationary depth, whose main promulgators and principal beneficiaries were members of the Weapondollar–Petrodollar Coalition. But this constellation was inherently temporary. For most large firms, stagflation was a stopgap measure, to be abandoned once the pendulum swung back to breadth.

The basic conditions for renewed breadth were laid down in the late 1980s. Soviet economic liberalisation, the abandonment of import substitutions in much of the developing world, and the retreat of statism in the industrialised countries, worked to dismantle barriers on capital mobility and ease antitrust sentiments. And with controls falling apart, large firms were now more than eager to break their last, national 'envelope', moving toward integrated global ownership.[30] The differential prize was substantial. For the winners, gains from cross-border mergers and acquisitions, bolstered and replenished by green-field prospects in the developing countries, were far greater than the increasingly risky benefits from war profits and stagflationary redistribution. And as the world began shifting back to breadth, the symptoms of depth receded rapidly: world inflation fell to less than 5 per cent in 1999, down from over 30 per cent at the beginning of the decade; international hostilities were actively curtailed,

---

30 For instance, of the 599 regulatory changes recorded by the *World Investment Report* during the first half of the 1990s, 95 per cent were aimed at liberalising capital controls. Similarly, the number of bilateral investment treaties had risen to 1,330 by 1996, up from fewer than 400 in the early 1990s, with 88 per cent of the changes aimed at increased liberalisation and incentives for foreign investment (United Nations Conference on Trade and Development 1997: 18–19).

with the number of major conflicts falling to 25 in 1997, down from 36 in 1989; and military budgets the world over came under the axe, dropping by over one-third in real terms from their peak in the late 1980s.[31]

The Middle East, an epicentre for conflict and stagflation during the global depth phase, was greatly affected by this renewed breadth. The disintegration of the Soviet Union and the end of the Cold War robbed local wars of their international *raison d'être*. In parallel, the petrodollar boom, which earlier fuelled the region's military arsenals, turned into bust, making conflict difficult to sustain. The decline in oil prices and revenues also had dramatic domestic implications. Until the early 1980s, the oil bonanza helped local rulers tranquillise their domestic populations with a cocktail of large public spending and extensive internal security budgets. But with the peace blitz pulling the rug from under oil prices, the technique became expensive. According to World Bank data, GNP per capita in the Middle East and North Africa, measured in constant U.S. dollars, fell to 35 per cent of the world's average in 1998, down from 42 per cent in 1979, with the predicament being particularly severe in the Gulf countries, where per capita income, again measured in constant dollars, dropped by as much as 50–80 per cent. Starved of revenues, governments were forced to cut their budgets, and as spending declined, internal opposition, particularly from 'Islamic fundamentalism', intensified. The region's autocratic rulers were of course willing to fight such opposition nail and tooth, even with less resources. And yet, here too, global circumstances, particularly the ideological shift from statism to liberalism, put them on the defensive, weakening their self-confidence and compromising their resolve. And so, before long, many of them found themselves between a rock and a hard place. No longer awash with petrodollars, unable to pit one superpower against the other, and bogged down by domestic instability, their only way to survive was to accept U.S. protection. Those who refused, such as Libya and Iran, were doomed to isolation, whereas those opting for independent 'initiatives', such as Iraq with its invasion of Kuwait, risked severe punishment.

Israel, too, was caught largely off guard. Although its dominant capital was not directly dependent on oil, its domestic depth regime of militarised stagflation was intimately linked to the regional cycle of energy conflicts. Until the late 1980s, the local ruling class was still struggling to retain this regime, although its resolve, like that of other elites in the region, was severely weakened. The immediate reasons were the Palestinian *Intifida*, the collapse of the world market for arms exports, and increasing domestic macroeconomic instability, which, as we saw in Chapter 4, have together contributed to a massive differential accumulation crisis. The more fundamental reason, though, was the growing realisation that depth had come to an end. Global conditions

---

31   Data are calculated from International Monetary Fund (Annual), the Stockholm International Peace Research Institute (Annual), and the U.S. Arms Control and Disarmament Agency (Annual).

now required a new mechanism of accumulation, and possibly the restructuring of dominant capital itself.

The most important change in mechanism was a shift away from military conflict. On the surface, the transition seemed perplexing, even surreal. George Bush, a Weapondollar–Petrodollar loyalist, who only a few years earlier was busy promoting the Iran–Iraq conflict, and who had just completed a classic sting operation against Iraq, was now announcing in great fanfare the onset of a 'new world order' built on Middle East peace. Israeli and Arab leaders responded quickly, switching from bullets to business as if they had no animosity to overcome. And before the world could catch its breath, Prime Minister Rabin and Chairman Arafat were shaking hands on the White House lawn, celebrating the mutual recognition of their embattled nations.

The basic preconditions for this transition, though, were taking shape far from the troubled sands of the region, in the boardrooms of the world's largest corporations. Much like during the earlier transition from breadth to depth, the current swing from depth back to breadth was also accompanied by a fundamental power shift *within* dominant capital. Whereas earlier, the transition strengthened the 'angry elements' of the Weapondollar–Petrodollar Coalition, this time, it was civilian business which took the lead.

The Last Supper (Almost)

The Weapondollar–Petrodollar Coalition of course didn't give up easily. During the 1990s, it spent much time and effort trying to regroup and consolidate through corporate amalgamation, usually with full government backing. The consequence of this process was a massive centralisation in both the armament and oil sectors, culminating in the emergence of huge corporate 'clusters', illustrated in Table 5.4. In the armament sector, amalgamation was kick-started in 1993 when U.S. Defense Secretary Les Aspin invited the CEOs of the country's leading contractors to their 'Last Supper'. Military spending, he said, was poised for further declines, and with less orders to go around, the Clinton Administration wished to see its suppliers start merging. To speed up the process, the government relaxed its antitrust stance, and even reimbursed the merged firms for their amalgamation costs. It also declared that, when it came to military exports, foreign policy objectives would from now on take a back seat to profit considerations (Grant 1997). And so, over the next few years, the companies were busy buying each other out, until, in 2000, there emerged a clear pack of five leaders: Lockheed Martin (which now combined Lockheed, Martin Marietta, Loral, and much of the military lines of General Dynamics and General Electric); Boeing (which acquired McDonnell Douglas and Rockwell's aerospace defence electronics); Raytheon (which added E-Systems and the military arms of Texas Instruments and Hughes); General Dynamics (which sold many of its original military lines only to buy others from Teledyne,

Table 5.4 The World's Largest Weaponry and Oil Companies, 1999 (with major acquisitions/mergers during the 1990s)

Weaponry

1. Lockheed Martin (*defence sales $17.8bn, total sales $25.5bn, net income $382m*)
Lockheed
General Dynamics Tactical Aircraft and Space Systems (1993–94)
Martin Marietta (1994)
Loral (1996)
GE Aerospace (1997)

2. Boeing (*defence sales $16.3bn, total sales $58bn, net income $1.1bn*)
Boeing
Rockwell Aerospace and Defense Electronics (1996)
McDonnell Douglas (1997)

3. BAE Systems (*defence sales $15.2bn, total sales $19.4bn, net income $491m*)
BAE
Alenia Marconi (50% joint venture with Finmeccanica, 2000)
Saab (20% 2000)
AES (2000)
Airbus (20% joint venture with EADS, 2000)
Matra BAE Dynamics (50% joint venture with EADS, 2000)
Astrium (34% joint venture with EADS, 2000)
Eurofighter (37% joint venture with EADS and Finmeccanica, 2000)

4. Raytheon (*defence sales $14.5bn, total sales $19.8bn, net income $404m*)
Raytheon
E-Systems (1995)
Texas Instruments Defense Systems and Electronics (1997)
Hughes (1997)

5. General Dynamics (*defence sales $8.9bn, total sales $8.9bn, net income $100m*)
General Dynamics
Teledyne Vehicle Systems (1996)
Lucent's Advanced Technology Systems (1997)
GTE Government Systems (1999)
Gulfstream (1999)

6. EADS (*imputed defence sales $6.1bn, total sales $33.2bn, net income NA*)
DASA (2000)
Aerospaciale (2000)
Lagardère (2000)
Eurocopter (2000)
Dassault Aviation (45.8% joint venture with Dassault Industries, 2000)
Arianespace (22.6%, 2000)
Airbus (80% joint venture with BAE, 2000)
Matra BAE Dynamics (50% joint venture with BAE, 2000)
Astrium (66% joint venture with BAE, 2000)
Eurofighter (44% joint venture with BAE and Finmeccanica, 2000)

7. Northrop Grumman (*defence sales $6.0bn, total sales $9.0bn, net income $467m*)
Northrop
LTV Aircraft (1992)
Grumman (1994)
Westinghouse Defense and Electronics (1996)

Oil

1. Exxon-Mobil (*sales $163.9bn, net income $7.9bn*)
Exxon
Mobil (1998)

2. Royal-Dutch/Shell (*sales $105.4bn, net income $8.6bn*)
Ryal Dutch/Shell
Equilon (56% joint venture with Texaco, 1998)
Motiva (35% joint venture with Texaco and Saudi ARAMCO, 1998)

3. BP-Amoco (*sales $83.6bn, net income $5.0bn*)
BP
Amoco (1998)
Atlantic Richfield (2000)

4. Total Fina Elf (*imputed sales $82.9bn, net income $3.9bn*)
Total
Fina (1999)
Elf Aquitaine (2000)

5. Sinopec (*sales $41.9bn, net income $448m*)

6. Texaco (*sales $35.7bn, net income $1.2bn*)
Equilon (44% joint venture with Shell)
Motiva (32.5% joint venture with Shell and Saudi ARAMCO)

7. Eni (*sales $34.1bn, net income $3.1bn*)

8. Chevron (*sales $32.7bn, net income $2.1bn*)

SOURCE: *Defense News* (various issues); *Financial Times Survey of Aerospace*, 24 July 2000; *Fortune*; Moody's (Online); Charles Grant, 'A Survey of the Global Defence Industry', *The Economist*, 14 June 1997; newspaper clippings.

Lucent, GTE and Gulfstream); and Northrop Grumman (which combined Northrop and Grumman, along with the military lines of LTV and Westinghouse). Of the 16 companies which we used as a proxy for the Arma-Core, only 8 remained as independent contractors; the rest were either taken over or divested of defence holdings altogether.

And once centralisation had run its course in the U.S., the focus shifted to Europe, where in a matter of three years it gave rise to three Pan-European giants: BAE, EADS and Thomson. The European process was particularly noteworthy, since it involved cross-border amalgamation and significant privatisation in countries with strong statist traditions. The biggest amalgamate was created by UK-based British Aerospace (BAE), which took over Marconi from GEC plc., bought AES from U.S.-based Lockheed Martin, and acquired a minority stake in the Swedish-based Saab. In parallel, BAE also entered into various joint ventures with the newly formed European Aeronautic Defence and Space Company, or EADS. The latter conglomerate was created in 2000, by pooling together the various defence interests of DASA (formerly DaimlerChrysler Aerospace), France's Aerospaciale and Lagardère, and Spain's Arianespace. When EADS was formed, its largest shareholders were DaimlerChrysler, Lagardère, and the governments of France and Spain, but over 27 per cent of its stock were already publicly listed, with further privatisation to come. The third European giant, Thomson-CSF, was owned jointly by the French government, Alcatel, and Dassault Industries, with another one-third of the stocks trading freely on the market and additional privatisation in the pipeline.

The global oil sector went through similar centralisation. Unlike in defence, the process here was not openly promoted by governments, although few of the mergers faced any serious antitrust opposition. The major deals of the 1990s, listed in Table 5.4, included the acquisition of Mobil by Exxon to create Exxon-Mobil, of Amoco and Atlantic Richfield by BP, now named BP-Amoco, and of Fina and Elf Aquitaine by Total, now called Total Fina Elf.[32]

The differential financial consequences of these mergers were dramatic. The world's six largest oil firms listed in Table 5.4 had 1999 sales of $513 billion, 25 per cent more than the six companies making the Petro-Core in its peak year of 1990; and $27 billion in net profit, 24 per cent above the Petro-Core's record of 1980. In the armament sector the picture was more mixed. In 1999, the world's seven largest defence contractors listed in the table had $84.4 billion in defence revenues, compared with $61.3 billion for the 16 Arma-Core firms in their peak year of 1985. Their net profit, however, was only $2.5 billion, compared with the Arma-Core's record of $9.9 billion in 1989.

The problem for the large oil and armament companies here was that, by now, they controlled much of their universe, and that this universe was either

32 As these lines were written, Chevron and Texaco announced their intention to merge, a union which would create the world's fifth largest oil company in terms of sales.

growing slowly (as in the case of oil), or contracting (in the case of defence). Under these circumstances, internal breadth through amalgamation was inherently self-limiting, so that in this sense, government encouragement of greater centralisation merely pushed the Weapondollar–Petrodollar Coalition further toward its sectoral envelope. Beyond that point, continued differential accumulation for the Coalition depended on renewed conflict and stagflation boosting up overall profits. And yet, from the viewpoint of dominant capital *as a whole*, that route was unattractive, and in fact dangerous. By the early 1990s, civilian business offered much better ways to beat the average. Furthermore, the new civilian avenues required relative openness and stability, the very opposite of the conflict and stagflation with which the Weapondollar–Petrodollar Coalition fuelled the earlier depth regime.

The greater lure of civilian business is illustrated in Figure 5.9. The chart contrasts two series, each measuring the market capitalisation of a given corporate cluster, expressed as a share of the Standard & Poor's 500 (S&P 500), a widely used index for the largest firms listed in the United States.[33] The first series denotes the proportionate share of 26 leading aerospace and petroleum companies, a proxy for what earlier constituted the Weapondollar–Petrodollar Coalition. The second series, focusing on civilian business, measures the comparable share of 54 leading 'high-technology' companies. The focus on relative market capitalisation is indicative of how global investors view the *future* course of differential accumulation, and where profit growth is *expected* to be the fastest. From this perspective, the inverse movement of the two series points to a dramatic change occurring during the 1990s. Until the late 1980s, dominant capital was still under the fading eclipse of the Weapondollar–Petrodollar Coalition, with its representatives included in the chart accounting for close to 11 per cent of the S&P 500 total capitalisation. The 'high-technology' sector was relatively small, with less than 8 per cent of the total. Over the next decade, however, the situation has totally reversed. The armament and oil firms saw their relative share drop to about 5 per cent of the S&P 500, whereas that of the 'high-technology' companies soared to a peak of nearly 34 per cent. In 2000, 'high-technology' stocks collapsed, but even after the calamity, the sector's capitalisation was still three times larger than that of armament and oil combined. This picture is of course somewhat skewed by the much richer valuation of 'high-technology' companies, whose relative earning growth has so far lagged behind their differential capitalisation. Nonetheless, it seems evident that the Weapondollar–Petrodollar Coalition has lost its earlier primacy, and that the centre of gravity, at least for now, has shifted back to civilian business.

33 The index comprises leading companies listed on the New York Stock Exchange, American Stock Exchange and Nasdaq. Companies are usually leaders in their field and their contribution to the index are weighed by market value. In contrast to Fortune 500 companies whose 'home base' must be the United States, S&P 500 firms could be based anywhere, provided their shares are listed in the United States.

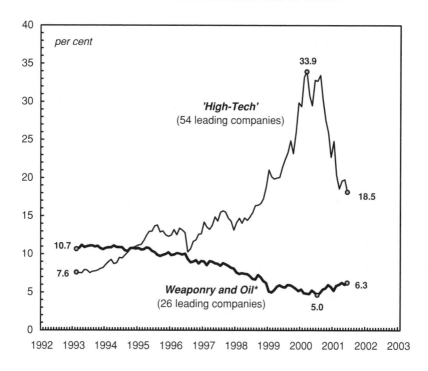

Figure 5.9   Share of Standard & Poor's 500 Market Capitalisation

* Comprises 9 aerospace/defence companies, 11 domestic integrated oil companies and
6 international integrated oil companies.
SOURCE: McGraw-Hill (Online). DRI codes: SPAEROMV, SPOILDMV, SPOILIMV for
Weaponry and Oil, SPHTECHMV for 'High-Tech'.

The fading power of the Weapondollar–Petrodollar Coalition was mirrored
in the Middle East. During the 1990s, attempts to kick-start a new 'energy
conflict' seemed to go nowhere. Every summer, tensions in the region would
rise, sometimes pulling oil prices up with them, but never enough to build up
momentum. During the early part of the decade, the main excuse were Iraqi
ceasefire violations, to which the United States and Britain eagerly retaliated
with aircraft and missile attacks. The situation again looked on the brink of
war, when in September 1994, Washington announced that Saddam Hussein
had dispatched an 80,000-strong force toward the Kuwaiti border, prompting
President Clinton to send 60,000 soldiers and 600 aircraft back to the Gulf. But
like Muammar Qaddafi before him, the Iraqi ruler preferred to ignore the 'smart'
missiles and held his fire. Since then, numerous other enemies have appeared
on the scene, from a nuclear Iran, to the Lebanese Shiites, to Islamic terrorism.
And yet, despite the hyped rhetoric and ongoing hostilities – including the
recent U.S.-led attack on Afghanistan – none of this has so far managed to significantly affect the price of oil.

The Gulf War was the Last Supper of the Weapondollar–Petrodollar Coalition, at least for the time being. During the 1990s, dominant capital as a whole was increasingly seeking cross-border expansion, a process which required tranquillity, not turmoil. Given that military conflict endangered such expansion, and that high energy prices threatened to choke the green-field potential of 'emerging markets', the Weapondollar–Petrodollar Coalition found itself increasingly isolated. And with depth giving way to breadth, it is perhaps not surprising that the 'national interest' itself was conveniently modified. As *Business Week* put it, 'The President has recognised that, in the post-cold-war era, getting global contracts for U.S. business is a matter of national security' (23 April 1994).

This neoliberal version of the national interest was eventually challenged by the 2001 attack on the Twin Towers and the Pentagon. Before turning to the present crossroad, however, we need to first travel through the transnational breadth phase of the 1990s.

6

From Foreign Investors to Transnational Ownership

The world is ours, we are its lords, and ours it shall remain.
– Jack London, *The Iron Heel*

The global order of the 1990s, argue the neoliberals, has altered the face of Israeli capitalism, and all for the better. The first and most important change was the county's increasing exposure to the vagaries of the world economy. Import duties, which averaged 13 per cent in the 1970s, dropped to 1 per cent in the 1990s, while import penetration, expressed as a share of GDP, rose from 37 per cent to more than 50 per cent over the same period.[1] Local producers, faced with these mounting pressures, were forced to shape up or give up. Israel also managed to attract foreign capital, which during the 1990s acquired large stakes in local firms. This greater openness, maintain the neoliberals, not only invigorated domestic competition, but also ushered in a fundamental transition from traditional to 'high-technology' sectors, a transition which, according to the enthusiasts, would carry the country to a fabulously prosperous future.

The second, related pillar of this transformation was the decline of the government. According to this view, the process of privatisation, hastened by the imperative of global competition, released the energy previously suffocated by public bureaucracy. In addition, international pressure forced the government to follow more responsible fiscal and monetary policies, with far less room for pork-barrel politics. True, politics, no longer the exclusive domain of dominant parties, has also become fractured and fragmented; but that only made it more democratic, argue the neoliberals.

The third and final pillar was the disintegration of organised labour, the historical arch-enemy of market efficiency in Israel. Import penetration, the arrival of hundreds of thousands of guest workers, and the effective dismantling of the Histadrut, have together reduced organised labour to a mere shadow of its past glory. For the first time in history, Israel's labour relations came to enjoy some 'flexibility'.

---

1 Figures computed from World Bank (Annual), and from Israel's Central Bureau of Statistics (Annual).

Although some of the facts portrayed here are undoubtedly true, the picture as a whole is seriously distorted. To begin with, Israel's transition toward a market economy was not at all new. It began not in the 1990s, but a century earlier, with the very first steps of Jewish colonisation in Palestine. Second, a market economy wasn't necessarily 'competitive', at least not in the way described by economics textbooks. While Israel was embracing market institutions, these institutions were based on power no less than the ones they replaced. Third, the government was far from declining. Although its direct role in production and distribution was receding, its indirect function in the institutionalisation of power was as important as ever. And fourth, the democratising impact of Israel's global integration was hardly worth bragging about. Israel's formal politics indeed appeared more open; but then it also mattered less. Effective power was increasingly capitalised in private hands, and as Israel's biggest owners integrated into a transnational capitalist class, much of what happened domestically was decided privately, and often off-shore.

The most basic fault with the neoliberal picture, however, is the notion that the 'globalisation' of Israel is, *itself*, somehow novel. As we have seen throughout the book, the country's development has been embedded in the global political economy from its pre-state beginnings. Moreover, in certain respects, the 'global imperative' was stronger earlier than now. For example, the trade deficit and the need for external financing were *five* times larger during the late 1970s and early 1980s, than presently. Similarly, the inflow of FDI has only recently surpassed its levels of the early 1960s. The purpose of pointing out these facts is not to suggest that things haven't changed. It is rather to argue that the key here is not globalisation per se, but its *specific nature*.

The essence of capitalist globalisation, we argued in Chapter 2, is the spatial integration of accumulation and ownership. Until the late 1980s, the main purpose of capital moving into Israel was to safeguard the depth regime, domestically as well as regionally. And given that this regime thrived on *inter*-national conflict, it is hardly surprising that national borders remained important. Capital crossed these borders regularly, of course. But its owners were for the most part associated with a particular state; everywhere else they were still *foreign* investors. This specific feature began to change during the 1990s, with the new regime of global breadth. Capital started breaking through its national envelopes *en masse*, and as the corporation gradually lost its national identity, its investors slowly became *transnational* owners. The purpose of this chapter is to examine how this transition affected the global political economy of Israel.

The 'Dependency'

'Mr. Begin, I have a small question for you. I got a little bulldog this morning and decided to name it after you. You wouldn't mind, would you? After all, it's a Jewish dog....' This unusual request from Californian banker Milton Petri, was addressed to Menachem Begin during a 1978 dinner party for rich Jewish donors in New York. Begin, being on his first prime ministerial visit to the United States, retained his composure. 'Mr. Petri', he replied, 'your dog is not only Jewish, he is also very rich. I would be honored if you named him after me.' Later, Petri explained: 'I donated to Begin a million greenbacks when he ran for prime minister, but then I got to know Peres; I thought he was better for Israel, so I gave him a million greenbacks, too....' (*Yediot Ahronont*, Supplement, 22 August 1986). This type of discourse wasn't new. In his memoirs, Discount chairman, Harray Recanati, recalls a similar incident from the 1950s:

> I participated in a reception for a big *Magbit* donor, who didn't hesitate attacking Eliezer Kaplan, our Finance Minister, and his General Manager David Horowitz, in their presence. He lashed at their socialist policy, which, in his view, contradicted the foundations of Judaism. I expected a sharp rebuttal, but nothing happened. The two merely calmed him down with patience and phoney reverence which disgusted me.... I felt humiliated to the bottom of my heart.... (Recanati 1984: 71)

But then what else could the Israeli politicians do? Their country was totally dependent, from the very beginning, on foreign capital, and if the donors wanted them to bow and suffer a little humiliation, so be it. They personally may have been offended, but their country survived, and *that* was the key. Or was it?

Israel's external predicament is illustrated in Figure 6.1. The chart shows two series, both expressed as a share of GDP, and smoothed as five-year moving averages. One series is Israel's trade balance, expressed against the left-hand axis, with negative readings denoting a deficit, and positive readings a surplus. The other series is the amount of foreign transfers used to finance the deficit, comprising the sum total of gifts and aid from individuals (private donations and remittances), from institutions (like the *Magbit*), and from foreign governments (Germany and the United States). This series, charted against the right-hand scale, is inverted; the lower the reading on the chart, the *greater* the transfer. In general, we can see that transfers covered the bulk of the trade deficit, but not all of it; the remainder was financed mostly by borrowing, and to a lesser extent by inward investment.

The chart makes obvious Israel's enormous dependency on foreign inflows. Since the 1950s, the country had to finance excess imports equivalent, on average, to 18 per cent of its GDP, a Herculean task by any measure. The historical development of this burden, though, remains puzzling. The trade balance, by definition, equals to the flow of capital (comprising debt, equity and transfers). What isn't always clear, though, is which of the two is the cause and which is the effect. In the United States of the 1990s, for example, the deficit was often seen, at least in part, as a *consequence* of private capital inflow. According to this view, the favourable domestic investment climate attracted

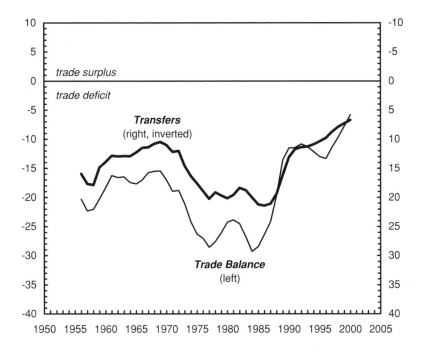

Figure 6.1   Israeli External Indicators (% of GDP)

NOTE: Series are expressed as 5-year moving averages.
SOURCE: Israel's Central Bureau of Statistics; IMF through McGraw-Hill (Annual).

capital from other countries, which in turn contributed to both faster economic growth and a stronger dollar. Since this tended to boost imports and restrict exports, the natural consequence was for the trade deficit to balloon. Obviously, this type of investment-led sequence is not what happened in Israel. In contrast to the United States, most foreign investors have generally preferred to keep their money *out* of the Holy Land, and, indeed, over the past half century, private inflows have remained negligible relative to the trade deficit (see Figure 6.5 below). Moreover, when such inflows finally started to rise during the 1990s, the trade deficit actually contracted – exactly the opposite of what we should expect from a supply-driven process. The other explanation goes in reverse, from trade to the flow of capital. The starting point here is demand. When local growth is faster than global growth, goes the argument, imports tend to rise faster than exports; the process boosts the trade deficit, and therefore calls for higher capital inflow to finance the widening gap. And yet, this logic too doesn't sit well with the Israeli fact. As the chart clearly shows, during the economic boom of the 1950s and 1960s, the trade deficit, although large by international standards, was relatively limited. In the 1970s and 1980s, on the other hand, when the economy was sinking into a deep recession, the deficit, instead of abating, rose dramatically. And when growth resumed in the 1990s, the deficit in fact shrunk. But, then, what, other than supply and demand, could explain Israel's enormous dependency on foreign inflow? Why did the economy develop such a huge trade deficit? And what accounted for the large ups and downs of these two magnitudes? The first step toward answering these questions is to disaggregate them: *Who* exactly 'depended' on the flow of capital? *Who* needed the excess imports? And how were these groups *related*? As we shall see, ordinary Israelis didn't really need most of the 'excess imports', and therefore had little reason to become 'dependent' on foreign capital. But for key groups in Israel and the United States, both the deficit and the inflow were in fact crucial. These groups – particularly the large corporations, the high political and military echelons, and the thick network of retainers, lawyers, dealers and media intermediaries supporting them – benefited greatly from the process. In the final analysis, it was they, not the country as a whole, who depended on the capital inflow. In this sense, the history of Israel's external accounts is only superficially a matter of economics. The real story is political. It concerns not so much the level of economic growth or the national saving rate, but the progressive globalisation of Israeli accumulation and its ruling class.

Zionist Donors-Investors

During the early years of the state, Israel suffered from acute foreign exchange shortages. On a number of occasions, the Finance Ministry even considered default (Horowitz 1975: 111). Agricultural exports, the country's main source of foreign earnings, were patently insufficient to cover the need for imported raw materials, weapons and industrial machinery. The shortfall was usually financed by transfers, mostly through *Magbit* donations and Israeli government bonds (whose repayment schedule made them tantamount to gifts). Since 1955, the predicament was somewhat alleviated by the arrival of German restitution payments. But with the appetite for imports growing even faster, the relief was only temporary. It was in this context that Zionist donors, mostly Jewish millionaires living abroad, rose to prominence in Israeli politics. Although their individual contributions were not always large, the country was in dire need of foreign reserves, so every dollar 'made a difference'. And that was only too convenient. For as it turned out, the contributions were equally important, if not more so, for the donors themselves, as well as for their political friends.

Most donors were connected to various Zionist organisations, often as officers and directors, and many have aligned themselves with local 'policy makers'. Take Dr Tibor Rosenbaum, who presided over the Jewish Agency and the World Zionist Organisation, while his Banque de Crédit Internationale, based in Geneva, was busy laundering money for the Mossad and the Mafia. On the request of Finance Minister Sapir, Resenbaum lent the Labour Party $300,000.

Needless to say, no one ever bothered to repay this 'loan'. Rosenbaum also 'donated' $75,000 to the party. The process was relatively straightforward. A company named Ramtam was set up, and promptly received from the Labour government a monopoly over the sale of duty free items. The owners of the company were Tibor Rosenbaum himself (48 per cent), the Labour Party (48 per cent), and Amos Manor, former head of the Shin Beit and Rosenbaum's representative in Israel (Yadlin 1980: 151). Money put into this company, as well as its monopoly profits, could then be transferred between the various participants, away from the public eye.

Such arrangements were beneficial to all sides. For the politicians, the extra-budgetary inflows were crucial. And for the donors, the sums were usually small – certainly relative to what they hoped to get in return. Indeed, although many of them felt sincere affinity to the Zionist project, they also viewed their donations as investments, a sort of down payment for future certificates, rights, grants, subsidies, tax exemptions, and even physical protection. The logic of the process was summarised, somewhat sarcastically, by Moshe Sharet. In 1953, he recorded a discussion he had with a Foreign Ministry official, regarding Samuel Bronfman, one of the heads of the *Magbit*:

A few years ago he had 100 million dollars. Now he undoubtedly has a billion. He is the richest man in the West, and possibly in the entire world. His early fortune was made smuggling booze during the Prohibition in the United States, and since then he continued to do well making whisky and other healing potions.... He showers money right and left on various institutions, in order to strengthen his position in Canada and the U.S.A., and in order to pre-empt any calamity which might befall on him. He donated a million and half to Columbia University and to McGill. He gives a lot of money to the Canadian Liberal Party, and the Catholic church also enjoys his generosity. What he fears most is legislation aimed directly at him: for instance, a law to take from every capitalist what he owns over and above five hundred million. This will have him, and only him, lose hundreds of millions in one swoop. And that is why he tries to appease, with gifts and donations, all the crucial circles. Regarding his donations to Israel, our Montreal consul, Yossef Nevo, calculated that relative to his fortune, Bronfman's donation is equivalent to Nevo giving three dollars. And with this he still lives under the illusion that people should respect him as a man, rather than as a bag of gold.... (Sharet 1978: 85)

And so emerged a network of foreign 'donor-investors', people like Bronfman, Eisenberg, Fineberg, Gaon, Hammer, Kahn, Klor, Riklis, Rotenberg, Rothschild, Warburg, Weinberg, and Wolfson, for whom Zionism and business went hand in hand. Around them, they weaved an intricate web of friends, retainers and managers, mostly drawn from the government, military and security organisations. The alliance between these two groups was the initial institution from which the internationalisation of Israeli accumulation has evolved. But it was by no means the whole story.

Corporate Cold Warriors

In fact, since the early 1970s, the relative significance of private donor-investors started to diminish. Accumulation, globally as well as locally, shifted from breadth to depth. And as the regional conflict intensified, the country's trade deficit and its financing were increasingly marked by the 'military bias' of both the United States and Israel. The core of the process was the massive rise in military imports, which soared to over 13 per cent of Israel's GDP during the late 1970s, up from less than 2 per cent in 1960 (see Figure 3.3 above). Whether or not this additional 'dependency' was necessary for most Israelis is left for the reader to decide. What *does* seem clear, however, is that for the U.S. Arma-Core, for Israel's dominant capital, and for the many intermediaries going between them, this dependency was a rich gold mine which they had no desire to abandon.

On paper, the increased trade deficit in armament – assuming 'trade' is the proper word to describe this military build-up – was accompanied by rising capital inflow; in practice, though, the money never reached Israel. Since both the equipment and its finance were provided by the U.S. government, payment would usually go from Washington directly to the relevant American supplier. The contractors of course found this 'circular finance' convenient, although that didn't keep them at home. Israel was crucial for their depth regime of 'energy conflicts', and it was therefore important to keep a close eye on the process. One way of doing so was to invest in Israel proper.

This wasn't 'ordinary' investment, though. In most cases, the contractors had little interest in building or acquiring extra capacity, and certainly not for its own sake. Their main concern was the *politics* of profit. First, being in Israel helped them safeguard their own individual share of U.S. military assistance to that country, and occasionally win additional perks through joint ventures with local firms. Second, it enabled them to closely monitor the regional conflict, and perhaps influence its course through their ties with local politicians and military officers. And last but not least, it helped them keep a lid on local competition. Domestic firms were consequently kept as second tier contractors, although that barely hurt them. In fact, the opposite was true. The presence of American 'competitors' only added to their profits. First, U.S. military imports, by fuelling the regional arms race, helped sustain healthy growth in domestic military spending. Second, the imports often made local companies entitled to reciprocal sales contracts with the U.S. government. And, third, they opened the way to joint ventures with U.S-based firms, facilitating entry to the lucrative global armament market. The process was of course complicated and often lacking in transparency. And so, around the basic equation linking U.S. and local companies, there developed an intricate network of politicians, army officers, retainers, financiers, advisers, promoters and arms dealers, whose function was to lubricate the flow of weapons and profits, in return for a share in the spoils. The protective umbrella for all of this was the good old 'national interest'.

The following examples briefly illustrate the various mechanisms at work. United Technology, for instance, bought 40 per cent of Beit Shemesh Engines. The acquisition happened after Likud Defence Minister, Moshe Arens, decided that the latter company would produce the engine for Israel's Lavi aircraft. When the Lavi was shelved under pressure from the U.S. arms lobby, United Technology promptly divested. Similarly with GTE. In 1968, when local defence spending started to rise, the company bought the government's share in Tadiran. In 1983, however, when domestic military expenditure began falling and Tadiran started selling to the U.S. military, GTE gradually pulled out. Another illustration is the partnership between Control Data and IDB in their ownership of Elbit, one of Israel's most profitable military contractors. Until its divestment in 1983, Control Data was able to share the local profit of Elbit, while simultaneously preventing it from venturing into the United States. Or the example of Siemens. In 1984, the German-based firm bought one-third of Elisra, a military contractor. Elisra was slated to 'win' a $750 million, pre-tailored contract from Bezeq, the government-owned telecom monopoly, and Siemens felt the investment was a risk worth taking. In 1984, however, things got entangled. With the Likud giving way to a government of 'national unity', other competitors suddenly appeared on the horizon. One of these was Saul Eisenberg, whose backers included Defence Minister Rabin and Prime Minister Peres. The other was ITT, represented, unofficially of course, by U.S. ambassador Samuel Lewis. Eventually Lewis prevailed, and ITT got the contract. Siemens, having been insulted, immediately liquidated its investment in Elisra (*Hadashot*, 14 October 1984).

In contrast to these investments, whose main purpose was the local market, other companies came to Israel in order to sell abroad. One of these was Loral, which entered into partnership with Elbit of IDB, as well as with Elta, a subsidiary of state-owned Israel Aircraft Industries. This entry occurred in the late 1980s, when Washington, having forced Jerusalem to abandon the Lavi fighter aircraft, agreed to offset some of its own sales (or rather, grants) to Israel with repurchases from Israeli companies. And indeed, 'shortly after signing the joint ventures', boasted Bernard Schwartz, Loral's CEO, 'we got two contracts, one from NATO, the other from the U.S.A.' (*Ha'aretz*, 18 January 1988). Another example is Northrop. During the early 1980s, the company lost more than a billion dollars on its failed F-20 'fighter for export', and was now scrambling for an alternative. One option was to jointly produce with Israel a substitute for the Lavi, which could then be sold around the world. To advance the idea, Northrop's chairman, Thomas Jones, and his Israeli retainer, former IDF air force commander Mordechai Hod, met in 1985 in New York with Israel's

Defence Minister, Yitzhak Rabin. The deal, though, never took off. Other U.S. contractors objected vehemently, and Washington demanded that Israel abandon its aspirations for a domestically produced aircraft altogether – or risk losing American assistance. From then on, it decreed, the best Israel should hope for were subcontracts from U.S. firms. And indeed, a short while later, delegations from some 20 contractors, including General Dynamics (maker of the F-16) and McDonnell Douglas (producer of the F-15 and F-18), arrived in Tel Aviv to peddle their wares and find local subcontractors to join the ride.

The Israeli newspapers described the inevitable as a 'national' humiliation and loss of autonomy; and yet, for the local armament network, this was not all bad news. Deliveries of General Dynamics' F-16, for instance, were handled by Elul Technologies, whose owners included, among others, retired air force commander, Ezer Weitzman, and former brigadier-general Aharon Yalowsky. Elul's partner to the intermediation was a Koor subsidiary named Arit, whose manager, Moshe Peled, was former head of the IDF armoured corps. Over the years, these two companies imported hundreds of aircraft, along with spare parts, worth billions of dollars, so that their own commissions must have been in the tens of millions.[2] For many domestic producers, the abandonment of local development in favour of the U.S.-made F-16 wasn't the end of the world either, since the Americans promised them plenty of subcontracts. Former air force commanders Benjamin Peled and David Ivry, for instance, who made the decision to prefer the F-16 while still in uniform during the 1970s and early 1980s, were now managers of Elbit and Israel Aircraft Industries, respectively – two companies which stood to gain handsomely from reciprocal sales to the United States.

During the mid-1980s, Israeli 'policy makers' increasingly found themselves as 'go betweens', flying back and forth across the Atlantic to mediate the various interests of American and Israel contractors. A typical illustration of the process is provided by the 1987 visit of Defence Minister Yitzhak Rabin to the United States. First, Rabin ratified a 'Memorandum of Understanding' between the two countries. Several sections of this memorandum, particularly those concerning the use of Israeli nuclear weapons to defend American interests in the region, were kept secret (perhaps in order to avoid any misunderstanding regarding Israel's delicate 'dependency' here). Second, he attended the Congressional proceedings in which the United States paid for such 'understanding' in hard cash, or rather in hardware. The package was valued at $3 billion, all in aid, with a full 60 per cent earmarked for military deliveries. The remainder of the visit was devoted to the allocation of these funds. As noted earlier, following

---

2   Exactly how much they got may never be known, since such information is conveniently secret in Israel. But the overall magnitude of commissions could be appraised, if only indirectly, from rare government audits. According to the 1986 *State Comptroller Report*, for example, between 1982 and 1984, the Ministry of Defence 'forgave' Israeli arms dealers as much as $100 million worth of commissions they were otherwise obliged to pass on to the government.

the scrapping of the Lavi, Israel was given more F-16s. As it turned out, their producer, General Dynamics, took advantage of its position to jack up prices, and Rabin was now keen on bringing them back down. For this purpose, he met with his U.S. counterpart, Defense Secretary Frank Carlucci. Israel, he told Carlucci, was an unofficial ally of the United States, and was therefore entitled to the same unit price as NATO; that is, $1.5 million less than the price quoted by General Dynamics. Carlucci promised to talk to General Dynamics. There was also another hurdle. The overall size of the rebate – $100 million – required Congressional approval, and so Rabin, saving no effort, pleaded his case with as many congressmen as he could find. Just to be on the safe side, he also travelled to General Dynamics' headquarters. Here, however, he found the going tough. The visit coincided with 'Operation Ill Wind', a massive criminal investigation into corrupt dealings between the Pentagon and its contractors. General Dynamics, faced with the prospects of large fines, was in no mood for discounts. The company also didn't like being reminded that, in lieu of the Lavi, it had to give Israeli firms subcontracts worth $150 million. Dealing with Congress proved easier. The house approved $200 million in seed money for a new Israeli project, the Arrow missile, thus breathing new life into Israel Aircraft Industries. Carlucci promised to finance 80 per cent of the project, and agreed for the remaining 20 per cent to be diverted from the economic part of the aid. Congress also approved $8 million in advanced payment, with another $17 million down the road, for developing the Popeye, a missile which state-owned RAFAEL hoped to sell to the U.S. military. And for an encore, Rabin managed to squeeze from the U.S. legislator some public relations money – $34 million for a Voice of America station in the Negev desert, and another $40 million for Israeli medical and university research. All in all, not bad for a former general who never took a course in marketing.

Between the deals, the Defence Minister also found time to negotiate the release of American-Israeli spy Jonathan Pollard; for consultations regarding the Iran–Contra scandal in which Israel was deeply involved; and of course for *Magbit* fund-raising. Other issues, such as the 'peace process', figured less prominently, and the first Palestinian *Intifada*, which erupted while the nego- tiations were going on, was naturally not even on the radar screen. But then, these issues weren't part of Israel's 'dependency'.

The Godfathers

As noted, since the 1970s U.S. aid and loans made private investors less crucial for the country's balance of payment. Indeed, although still considered 'foreign investors', by now many of them were bringing no new foreign currency into the country. Having built their power base early on, they much preferred to reap the benefits. The most prominent became 'godfathers' to one or more 'policy makers', whom they controlled and manipulated to their own ends.

Sometimes, they even bought up an entire political party. The arrangement was lucrative for both sides. The politicians would typically bestow on their godfather various 'incentives', ostensibly in order to entice him into 'investing' in the country; and if the godfather on his part chose to help these friendly public officials with some extra-budgetary financing, that too was obviously a Zionist act.[3]

One of the more colourful godfathers was Meshulam Riklis. Originally a citizen of Israel, Riklis was considered an army deserter during the 1948 War, a conflict which left 30,000 Israelis dead or wounded. In the 1960s he reappeared in his home country, this time as a foreign investor. According to his own testimony, until the early 1980s he managed to spread no less than 3 million dollars on all political parties (*Hadashot*, 29 May 1985). His biggest investment was former IDF general, Ariel Sharon. Riklis helped Sharon buy his famous ranch, and supported his ShlomZion political party. The investment soon came to fruition, and when Sharon was nominated Defence Minister in Begin's government, he turned back to repay his godfather. All Israeli arms deals must be approved by the Defence Ministry, and Sharon thought it was only appropriate that Arie Ganger, an associate of Riklis, be put in charge of such a delicate operation. The tactic, though, was a little too transparent; the arms contractors shouted foul, and the nomination was withdrawn (*Ha'aretz*, 17 January 1986). In 1982, Sharon got entangled in the Lebanon War and the massacre in Sabra and Shatila. *Time* magazine, having published its own version of events, found itself sued for libel by Sharon. The case drew considerable attention. After all, it wasn't every day that a politician from a small country took on one of the world's largest media empires. But then Sharon had his finances shored up. His expenses were offset by various friends, including arms dealers Ya'akov Nimrodi and Markus Katz, as well as godfather Riklis. The latter also dedicated Ganger, full time, to the noble cause (*Hadashot*, 14 February 1984). Following the war, Sharon was barred by the Kahan Commission from

---

3 The cost of buying up a typical Israeli politician was relatively modest. Shimon Peres, for instance, who surrounded himself with investors-donors such as Charles Bronfman, Armand Hammer, Bruce Rappoport and Saul Eisenberg, was always happy to receive little gifts. A newspaper article from the late 1980s, for example, knew to report that 'during a visit of millionaire Charles Bronfman to the official residence of his good friend, Prime Minister Shimon Peres, he was astounded to find out that the place had no wall to wall carpets. Bronfman promptly donated $25,000 for buying carpets for the house. Sonya Peres, [the Prime Minister's wife] put herself to the task, and after careful investigation called a carpet factory in Jaffa to place the order' (*Ha'aretz*, 13 February 1987). Or another illustration. When in 1987, Dr Heinrich Benedict, a West German dentist, was charged with fraud to the tune of 50 million marks, he surprised the court by pulling out an Israeli diplomatic passport and claiming immunity. As it turned out, in 1981, in preparation for the Israeli elections, Benedict fixed Shimon Peres with a new set of sparkling teeth. In return he got not only the status of a diplomat, but also Peres personally intervening on his behalf with the German authorities (*Ha'aretz*, 14 March 1988). As a side note, this last incident also serves to explain, perhaps better than any learned theory, why Israeli politicians remained indifferent to the deterioration of public health care in their country.

serving as a minister. In 1984, however, he resurfaced, this time as Industry and Trade Minister. In his new capacity, he endowed the Riklis–Ganger duo millions of dollars in tax exemptions, drawing heavy fire from the State Comptroller, and accusations of criminal conduct from members of the opposition (*Ha'aretz*, 21 May 1987; 9 July 1987; 21 March 1988; *State Comptroller Report* No. 37, 1986).

These were the heydays of the Weapondollar–Petrodollar Coalition, and so, in addition to armament, many godfathers developed a taste for oil-related assets. One of these was Bruce Rappoport, whom we already mentioned in Chapter 5 in relation to a proposed Iraqi–Jordanian pipeline, to be built by Bechtel. Rappoport was supposed to clear $2 billion worth of commissions from the deal, and then divert part of the money to Peres' Labour Party (*Ha'aretz*, 11 March 1988; *Haolam Hazhe*, 23 March 1988). Peres, of course, wasn't Rappoport's only friend in Israel. Two other retainers, Likud Finance Minister Yitzhak Modai, and Member of Knesset and future Energy Minister, Moshe Shahal, laboured relentlessly so that Paz, the country's largest oil company, be sold/given to their rich patron (at the time the government still owned a substantial stake in the company). And they almost had their way. Unfortunately for Rappoport, however, other investors also had their eyes on Paz, and some of them started leaking disturbing facts to the newspapers. One of these facts was that Rappoport's financial representative in Israel was no other than David Shoham, head of the State's Privatisation Committee in charge of the deal (*Ha'aretz*, 4 February 1988; *Ksafim*, 1 February 1988).

Another godfather with a weakness for oil was Baron Edmund de Rothschild. Over the years, Rothschild managed to accumulate numerous friends in the country. These included, among others, the late Prime Minister, Levi Eshkol, who granted the Baron sweeping tax exceptions; former head of the IDF navy, Moka Limon, whose daughter married Rothschild's son; and Arnon Gafni, former Governor of the Bank of Israel, who managed Rothschild's local finances. One of his many Israeli assets was an 18 per cent stake in the Eilat–Haifa oil pipeline. After the closure of the Suez Canal in 1967, Finance Minister Sapir wanted to build a new, $120 million pipeline from Eilat to Ashkelon, and asked Rothschild to invest. The Baron objected. The plan was not only too expensive, but would also undermine his earnings from the existing pipeline. So Sapir found another investor, the Shah of Iran, who put in half the money through IPC Holdings, a Canadian-based company. Rothschild was of course furious. He wasn't used to being 'double crossed'. But after receiving $27 million from the government in return for surrendering his exclusive 'right' to transport oil, his anger subsided somewhat (Frenkel and Bichler 1984: 161–2).

Perhaps the most noted oil magnate among the godfathers was Armand Hammer. His father was a founding member of the U.S. Communist Party and a friend of Lenin. The son was already a businessmen, although he certainly took advantage of his family background to profit from mediating between the two superpowers during the Cold War. Hammer's foray into oil was almost accidental. During the 1960s, he bought a tax shelter by the name of Occidental Petroleum. Unfortunately, or fortunately, the company, instead of losing money, struck oil in California. Then, in 1969, Hammer found himself in the midst of an international conflict. Libya's ruler, Muammar Qaddafi, kicked all Western companies out of his country, save one: Occidental Petroleum. Hammer was now really rich. It was during those boom times that he began courting the Israelis, helping their covert oil shipments bypass the Arab Boycott. Since the late 1970s, he also started rubbing shoulders with local politicians, including Peres and Begin, to whose parties he donated money. One possible reason for this generosity was that Hammer wanted them to plead his case in Washington. As it turned out, the oil magnate got entangled in illegal donations to the Nixon campaign, whom he hoped would open new business routes into the Soviet Union. Unfortunately, when William Casey became CIA Director under Reagan, these activities got Hammer branded as an 'anti-American communist'. And here, his political investments in Israel proved fruitful. Prime Minister Begin met personally with President Reagan, and the 'Hammer case' was sorted out to the satisfaction of all sides (*Haolam Hazhe*, 26 August 1987).

Sometimes, however, indirect influence proved insufficient and the godfather had to buy up an entire political party. This was illustrated in 1984, when a small ethnic party, named Tami, pulled out of the coalition, bringing down the Likud government. The man behind the deed was Swiss investor, Nessim Gaon. A native of Egypt, his business career began in Sudan, where, under the British Mandate, he made his first money from the toil of poor peasants. After Sudan won its independence, he moved to Geneva. There, together with his brother-in-law, Leon Taman, he built a multimillion dollar trading business, peddling food, commodities, real estate, and plenty of scandal around the world (*Al Hamishmar*, 30 March 1984). According to his own evidence, he was generous with all of Israel's political parties. When the Likud bloc came to power, he helped Begin's own faction, Herut, retire much of its burdensome debt. Begin was grateful, and when he travelled to Egypt after the Camp David Accord, he brought with him the two brothers-in-law, Gaon and Taman. Gaon was also standing right next to Begin when the latter received the Nobel Peace Prize in Stockholm. Of course, these dealings with the 'right' hardly came at the expense of the 'left'. Gaon was careful to also cement his relations with Peres and the Labour Party, and, as mentioned in Chapter 3, even married his daughter to the son of his local representative, Labour member of Knesset and the country's future President, Chaim Herzog. In return for these investments, Gaon hoped to win the bid for Israel's first commercial television channel. But here he was up against other heavyweights, and the bid failed. Realising that his investments were not striking the right chord, Gaon decided to pursue a more direct route. He bought himself a whole political party.

On the eve of the 1981 elections, he founded Tami, a small party headed by two colourful politicians – Aharon Ozan, a former Labour minister whom Gaon bailed out financially, and Aharon Abuhatzeira. The latter of the two had a valuable political asset. His cousin, one Baba Sali, was a local saint, whose cunning witchcraft helped him assemble a large following of obedient voters, comprised almost exclusively of poor Sephardi Jews. And so, in a curious twist of fate, Gaon the billionaire, a man whose fortune was squeezed out of the world's poorest peasants, was now speaking for Israel's 'down and out'. Naturally, the establishment didn't like this brilliant political manoeuvre, and quickly unleashed its journalists against the intruder. Gaon, on his part, retaliated with full page advertisements:

> The media has come out against me, viciously trying to smear my image. In doing so, it aggravates an already tense situation, further deepening the ethnic conflict in Israel. As President of the Sephardi Federation, I travel in the cities and development townships, talking to factory workers and school children. What I find and feel is frustration, people who live without hope, as second-class citizens.... The parties in Israel have sown hatred and rivalry between the different ethnic groups.... They split the nation by classifying Asian and North African Jews according to their origin. Is this how they treated European Jews? In my view, this is Jewish anti-Semitism.... I think the political establishment and the media are scared of losing their power.... It is well known than I support the big parties in this elections, as I did in previous ones. Other Diaspora Jews do the same to strengthen the democratic process in Israel. And yet, never before was I accused of intervening in Israel's internal affairs. Only now, when I support Tami, am I accused of such intervention.... (Ha'aretz, 26 June 1981).

Eventually, the godfather prevailed. Tami won three seats in the Knesset, and Abuhatzeira became Minister of Labour, Welfare and Immigration. Then, in 1984, Gaon's business in Nigeria took a turn for the worse. Following a coup, the new ruler, Mohammad Buhari, froze all debt services, including to Gaon and Taman, whom he accused of selling rice to Nigeria at triple the world price (Hadashot, 27 April 1984; Naylor 1987: 242). Gaon found himself stuck with no less than $100 million worth of Nigerian debt. Naturally, he turned to the Israeli government, in which he was now a major 'stakeholder', demanding collateral for the money. Prime Minister Yitzhak Shamir and opposition leader Shimon Peres agreed, and even tried to sneak the guarantees through a special Knesset subcommittee responsible for secret, 'security-related' financing. But other politicians, representing even heavier interests, leaked the proceedings, and the deal fell through. Gaon, outraged by the failure, ordered his retainer, Aharon Ozan, to pull out of the coalition and bring the government down.[4] The logic of the move was sound. The Labour Party promised Gaon to guarantee his Nigerian loans through Solel Boneh which operated in Africa. And since the

4   The other retainer, Abuhatzeira, was by now out of the loop, locked up in jail on corruption charges.

Likud was severely battered – by the Lebanon War, by the stock market crash, and by a series of resignations – an early election call seemed the quickest way to shore up Gaon's finances. Eventually, though, things worked out for all sides. Gaon settled his differences with the new Nigerian government, which proved just as corrupt as its predecessor, while Peres and Shamir cemented their own collusion through a new government of 'national unity'. The unofficial celebration was held in Gaon's Noga Hotel in Geneva, where 350 dignitaries, many of them 'foreign investors', gathered for the 1985 *Magbit* conference. The star of the conference was Henry Kissinger, who received a modest $10,000 for entertaining the distinguished guests (*Hadashot*, 4 February 1985).

For Gaon, though, this was the beginning of the end. He continued to prosper for a few years, but the scandals surrounding his operations, including his business liaisons with various dictators, such as Ferdinand and Imelda Marcos of the Philippines, and Sese Seko Mobutu of Zaire, multiplied (*Haolam Hazhe*, 8 May 1985; *Hadashot*, 23 May 1985; *Ha'aretz*, 10 October 1986; Naylor 1987: 336). In 1991, Gaon discovered a new gold mine, or so he thought, signing a barter deal to supply post-communist Russia with $1.5 billion worth of commodities in return for oil. Two years later, however, the Russian government suspended payments, alleging bribery and fraud. Gaon, who was left with huge credit obligations, sued the Russians in Stockholm's international arbitration court, as well as in Paris and in New York. His demands gradually rose from $63 million to $700 million, and, surprisingly, the court ruled in his favour. This time, though, the problem was enforcement. The world has changed, and the aging godfather, whose companies were by now being chased by creditors and the Swiss tax authorities, no longer commanded the political backwind necessary to sail the high seas of neoliberalism. Desperate, Gaon tried in 2001 to seize two Russian military jets on the grounds of the Le Bourget air show, threatening to do the same to the Russian embassy in Paris (*The Moscow Times*, 27 June 2001; *The Economist*, 5 July 2001). But that was clearly the end of the road.

The Autumn of the Patriarch

The closing of the godfathers era was best illustrated by the downfall of the 'father of all godfathers', Saul Eisenberg. Here we have the archetypal depth investor. Profit for him was a matter of politics, pure and simple. He had little respect for legal incorporation, organisational hierarchy, standard accounting practices, due diligence, and other such sublimations. The business of Eisenberg was Eisenberg: his own intimate knowledge of politics, his complicated networking, his intricate bribery schemes. His principal expertise, however, was in bridging the gap between the developed and developing economies, and that bridging, by preparing the ground for global breadth, eventually spelled his own demise.

Eisenberg was born to a religious Jewish family in Munich. When the Nazis came to power, he wandered, as a stateless refugee, across Europe. Just before the Germans invaded the Netherlands, Eisenberg, 17 years of age, managed to embark on a ship headed to Shanghai. The vessel also carried a load of frightened Chinese refugees, saved earlier from a ship sunk by the Germans. They wanted cigarettes, which gave Eisenberg his first opportunity to get something for nothing. He sold the cigarettes for a dollar a pack, having bought them at the ship's canteen for 5 cents (*Ha'aretz*, 26 December 1997). After a short stay in Shanghai, the young refugee found his way to Japan. And it was there, during the Second World War, that his business started to flourish. After the war he continued his trading, this time with the Allied Occupational Force, helping supply the raw materials needed for Japan's reconstruction.

This experience as a go-between defined his entire career. The post-war era was marked by a shift from colonialism to neo-colonialism, and it was the Eisenbergs of the world, along with the Hammers and the Khashoggis, who spearheaded the early foray of transnational firms into the developing world. Over the years, Eisenberg mediated many thousands of complicated deals, ranging from commodities, through machinery, to energy, transportation, heavy armament, and finance. His significance was evident from both his commissions and exclusivity. Those who tried to bypass him, quickly found themselves lost in a labyrinth from which only Eisenberg knew the way out. Atomic Energy of Canada, for example, learnt in 1976 that it could not sell its Candu reactor to Korea; or rather that it couldn't sell it without first paying Eisenberg his $20 million cut.[5] Similarly with Pilkington, the British glass maker, which in 1979 found out that building a $150 million factory in China would cost it another $17 million in commissions to Eisenberg.

Slowly, however, the shift from import substitution to export-led growth opened up East Asia's political economies. Eisenberg's toll booths became easier to bypass, and, as his leverage declined, he began looking for alternatives. He found these in Africa and Latin America. There, the economies were still closed, politics highly corrupt, and conflict, on which Eisenberg thrived, all pervasive.

His new business base, though, was set up in Israel. During the early 1960s, Pinchas Sapir, the country's Finance Minister, was looking for foreign investors, and Eisenberg, having heard of the various incentives, landed in Tel Aviv for a fact-finding mission. He liked what he saw, and in 1968 settled in. His reason was threefold. First, the political overhead in Israel was relatively low. Second, the policy makers' thirst for foreign capital was quenchless. In fact, it was so great, that the 'socialist' government quickly passed the so-called Eisenberg Law, which exempted him, and only him, from paying any taxes whatsoever

---

5   The affair ended in political scandal, claiming many heads in both Ottawa and Seoul, including the resignation of Korea's Prime Minister. Eisenberg himself emerged from the commotion unscathed.

for the next 30 years.[6] Finally, the country's increasing military bias provided the right milieu for Eisenberg's clandestine expertises.

And indeed, soon enough he became Israel's number one arms dealer. According to various estimates, his annual military exports during the 1980s reached $100 million. He sold everything, from aircraft and ships to ammunition and supplies – mainly to developing countries such as South Africa, Nigeria, Zaire, Colombia, Ecuador, Chile, Taiwan and China. He also became one of the country's largest military importers, representing no less than 60 foreign contractors. And like in Asia, many of his competitors and their political friends quickly found out he couldn't be ignored. In 1981, for example, Defence Minister Ariel Sharon was planning an African trip, with plenty of journalists, whose purpose was to open up new markets for Israeli armament. Eisenberg politely offered to fly Sharon, discretely and without the press, in his private jet. The minister of course refused. He had his own friends, such as arms dealers Markus Katz and Ya'akov Nimrodi, to cater to. But as the trip progressed, Sharon realised he was outmanoeuvred. On every landing he was greeted by an Eisenberg representative, already holding the exclusive right to import Israeli weapons.

Such episodes, though, were more the exception than the rule. In general, Israeli statesmen were rather happy to cooperate with their country's number one arms peddler. For example, when, in 1988, Foreign Minister Shimon Peres went to Austria to sign a trade agreement between the two countries, he was accompanied by Eisenberg's own 'foreign minister', David Kimchi. The signing ceremony was largely a formality. Kimchi, formerly a Mossad agent and Director General of Israel's Foreign Ministry, drafted the agreement three months earlier, making sure Eisenberg was given his usual exclusivity (*Haolam Hazhe*, 11 May 1988). This was not the first time Peres' flag followed Eisenberg's trade. In 1987, he went to Brazil with Eisenberg and Kimchi, who, again, arranged the visit. It wasn't entirely clear which interests Kimchi was pushing, Eisenberg's or Israel's – although that scarcely mattered, since the two were really one and the same. As one reporter put it: 'Eisenberg and Dave Kimchi work to strengthen trade and economic ties between Israel and Brazil, which is why they were invited to accompany Peres on his trip....' (*Ha'aretz*, 9 December 1987).

In the early years, Eisenberg donated mainly to the Labour Party. After 1977, however, he extended the list to include Likud and the religious parties. His political and business affairs were controlled from his Asia House, a large office building, shaped like a vessel, which he strategically inserted at the very heart of Tel Aviv, right next to America House, IBM, Koor, and the Defence Ministry. The building housed Eisenberg's own companies, as well as various related businesses, including consulates and embassies. It was also home to useful friends and politicians, such as Chaim Herzog, Yaakov Neeman, Avraham Sharir

6   Income Tax Code, Section 14A; and the Law for Encouraging Capital Investment, Chapter 7, 53.2 (1969 Amendment).

and Yigal Hurwitz. The latter, while acting as Finance Minister in Begin's government, located his own private firms in Asia House. He also arranged, entirely by coincidence of course, that the building be classified as an 'export factory', so that its owner could enjoy additional subsidies and grants (there was no need for tax exemptions, since Eisenberg already paid none).

Like Nessim Gaon, Eisenberg also bought himself a party; or rather a segment of a party, since he didn't like wasting more than necessary. His acquisition was the Liberal Party, which at the time comprised half of the Likud bloc. His most important retainers there included party leader, Simcha Erlich, who was Begin's first Finance Minister; Trade Minister Gidon Pat; and the scandal-prone Tourism Minister, Avraham Sharir, who later also became Justice Minister.[7] Sharir was given an office in Asia House, to which he promptly moved the meetings of the Knesset's crucial Finance Committee.

Eisenberg's direct manager in Israel was the skilful Michael Albin. Formerly partner to Ezer Weitzman's arms dealings, Albin was now trusted with jointly manipulating the stock market and the Liberal Party. During the early 1980s, his business activities reputedly accounted for as much as half of Eisenberg's local profits (*Hadashot*, 21 June 1984). This was the Gilded Age of the Tel Aviv market, and Albin, like Riger and Fishman, specialised in buying dormant companies, rigging their prices upwards, massively diluting the stock by selling new paper in large quantities in return for hard cash, and then dumping the corporate carcass. Occasionally, he also invested in real companies. One of these was Ata, a large but troubled textile firm which Eisenberg and Albin promised the government they would 'turn around'. They had no such intentions. After floating the company's stocks and cleaning out its coffers, they simply jumped ship. The company's hundreds of employees, many of whom worked there for more than a generation, were left free to fend for themselves.

Eventually, dominant capital grew edgy with Albin. His market manipulations put their entire system of 'regulation' at risk, and they decided to impose some checks on his wild behaviour. The task was delegated to Tel Aviv bourse chairman, Meir Het, who proposed certain amendments to the trading rules. The Knesset Finance Committee, however, rejected his proposals outright. This happened after Michael Albin, on the unprecedented invitation of Avraham Sharir, was called to testify in front of the committee. The hearings, by the way, were held at Eisenberg's Asia House (Frenkel and Bichler 1984: 150).

The cost of buying such political support was generally pretty low. Micha Reiser, for instance, a Likud member of Knesset, was acquired for various perks such as a couple of company directorships, a car and a driver, airplane tickets, and stock options; the combined value of these perks was probably less than $100,000. Securing the support of others, such as Yossef Hermelin (former head of Shin Beit), Mordechai Hod (former air force commander and representative

---

7   Sharir's scandals could fill a whole book. For a sample, see *Ha'aretz*, 9 May 1984; *Ma'ariv*, 14 May 1984; *Haolam Hazhe*, 6 March 1985; and Kotler (1988: Vol. II, pp. 12–35).

of Northrop), Eli Landau (city mayor) and various journalists, must have cost even less.[8]

Eisenberg wanted a return on these investments, and here too, much like in Asia, he focused on raw materials. One of his targets was the already mentioned oil oligopoly, Paz. In 1980, Sir Issac Wolfson, who got Paz from Sapir for practically nothing in 1957, was ready to give his share to Eisenberg for $27 million. But then, Eisenberg, whose supporters included Prime Minister Begin, Finance Minister Hurwitz, and Industry and Trade Minister Gidon Pat, found himself facing other interested parties, including the large dominant capital groups, Bruce Rappoport, and Australian millionaire Jack Liberman. After a long war of attrition, the company went to Liberman. The winning argument, hammered by his own supporter, Finance Minister Moshe Nissim, was that Liberman, being a foreign investor, would bring in much needed dollars. The Australian godfather, though, had no such intentions. As it turned out, he managed to 'discover' plenty of New Israeli Shekels, equivalent to $60 million, buried deep in the company's coffers. And since Paz was eventually sold for only $57 million, he ended up getting it for a song, and without 'investing' a single foreign dollar.

Eisenberg, in any case, didn't give up. His other target was Israel Corporation, a conglomerate with interests in over 100 subsidiaries, including Oil Refineries and Zim Shipping, which it jointly owned with the government. Initially, the takeover proceeded smoothly. Albin, as usual, manipulated the media so that the share price would fall when he was buying, only to reverse his tactics when the time came to issue new paper and realise some gain. Eventually, Eisenberg got the company, but only after sailing through some very rough water. In 1983 the stock market collapsed, and Eisenberg, perhaps for the first time in his life, found himself stuck with $40 million in losses. Needless to say, that was unacceptable, particularly since Albin seemed to have emerged unharmed, with $15 million in profit. And so, once more, Eisenberg unleashed his political power – this time against his own partner. Scandal ensued, and Albin, who found himself in police custody, eventually jumped (or was pushed) to his death from the station window.[9]

Eisenberg's last coup in Israel was the acquisition of Israel Chemicals Ltd (ICL) – a diversified producer of chemicals and fertilisers entrusted with exploiting the country's few natural resources. The company was slated for privatisation already in 1977, when the Likud first came to power, but given the

---

8 These and other names were found in Albin's papers after his death. Naturally, none of them were prosecuted.
9 Feeling betrayed, Eisenberg didn't hesitate to pull the rug from under his own family. In this particular incident, the target was his daughter Ester and her husband. The son-in-law, who earlier worked for Eisenberg together with Albin, was cut off from the business and shipped to America. Then, the daughter having been accused by her father of 'possessing stolen property', was detained by the police, her passport confiscated, so that she couldn't join her other half in America.

sensitivity of selling a 'national resource', the deed took another 20 years to complete. The sale was one of the final clashes between Israel's 'nationalist' and 'transnationalist' factions. In 1989, the nationalists, headed by Labour Finance Minister Avraham Shohat, successfully torpedoed a suggestion to sell 50 per cent of ICL to foreign investors. The benefits of privatisation, they argued, should go to the 'citizens of Israel', not foreigners (*Ha'aretz*, 23 May 1995). The particular citizen they had in mind was Saul Eisenberg. ICL, which at the time had $2 billion worth of government investment in the pipeline, was sold to Eisenberg's Israel Corporation based on a market value of only $930 million. Initially, Eisenberg bought only 25 per cent. He also had an option to buy another 17 per cent, which he hoped to muscle out for even less, once the stock price fell. But lo and behold, the price, instead of falling, rose by 33 per cent. And to make a bad situation worse, the new neoliberal officials at the Government Corporations Authority insisted Eisenberg had to take it or leave it. Grudgingly, Eisenberg bit the bullet, paying the full price for the remaining shares; but for a man who always managed to 'get something for nothing', this was a real blow. Clearly, the world was no longer what it used to be, and three weeks later, in March 1997, Eisenberg, 'one of Israel's dearest citizens', as Prime Minister Netanyahu called him, died of a heart attack (*Ha'aretz*, 28 March 1997).

Once Eisenberg was gone, his family business crumbled. With secrecy being his main asset, he was always suspicious of friends and foes alike. He did as much as he could on his own, keeping most of his records in his head. Even his wife and children were kept on a short leash, having to ask him for money when they needed it, and justify their request in writing (*Ha'aretz*, 5 August 1997). The scope of what he owned, how much it was worth, and who it should go to – all remained unclear. And the bitter family feud after his death only demonstrated that there was really no one to carry the business forward. Eisenberg's 53 per cent of Israel Corporation was therefore put on the bloc, and in January 1999 was sold to the Ofer brothers for a mere $330 million.

In contrast to the dysfunctional Eisenberg family, who lived in the world of yesterday, the Ofer clan was operating like clockwork. The two founding brothers, Yuli and Sammy, were getting older, but the younger generation was smoothly taking over. Much of the Ofers' fortune, estimated by *Forbes* at $1.9 billion in 1998, came from the seaways – primarily through their 20 per cent stake in the cruise company Royal Caribbean, and through their two commercial undertakings, Zodiac and Tanker Pacific Shipmanagement. When Israel Corporation was put up for sale, they jumped at the opportunity. One obvious reason was their desire to have Zim, the world's twelfth largest container shipping company with 2.3 per cent of the global market, added to their maritime assets (*Ha'aretz*, 28 April 2000). The other reason, less publicised but equally important, was that the 30-year Eisenberg Law was about to expire, and both seller and buyer were eager to finish the reshuffle without the taxman's intervention (*Ha'aretz*, 4 January 2000). And indeed, within two years, Israel Corporation, now owned by Ofers, unloaded $230 million worth of assets, leaving its new masters with a more focused set of holdings in chemicals (mainly through ICL), shipping (through Zim), refining (through Oil Refineries), and communication and 'high-tech' (through Tower Semiconductors). The era of the godfather came to a close.

Toward Transnationalism

The Technodollar–Mergerdollar Coalition

The decline of the Israeli godfather came as the world moved from depth to breadth. Since the late 1980s, world military spending has dropped sharply. A 'new economy', based on civilian 'high technology' was said to have emerged. Brick-and-mortar industries grew out of fashion. 'Knowledge' was the new buzz word, and information and telecommunication were the 'hot' growth sectors.[10] But, then, these changes in technology and the composition of output were themselves part of an even bigger transformation affecting the nature of *accumulation*. From the viewpoint of capital, the real issue was not production as such, but the politics of production: who controlled it, by what means, and to what ends. Until the late 1980s, such control was exercised largely through the various mechanisms of depth, including statist protectionism in a world crisscrossed with barriers and conflict. Since the early 1990s, however, as the world moved to breadth, the mechanisms, too, have changed. One of these changes was the growing state enforcement of intellectual property rights; the other was the increasing 'absorption' of technical innovators through corporate amalgamation.

And indeed, in a certain sense, contemporary technology made mergers and acquisitions perhaps more crucial than ever. The basic reason is simple enough. The emphasis of this technology on 'information' and 'communication' is inherently *integrative*; it binds together different spaces and regions. Such integration, however, also introduces new players, new forces and new rules. And these, if left unattended, tend to destabilise established power and undermine profit. The most common way of containing these centrifugal con-

10   We use inverted commas here for a purpose. The concepts of the 'new economy', 'high technology' and 'information' have become so common, that few people stop to question their meaning. First, 'information' and 'knowledge' are not some distinct, well-defined output such as furniture, houses, automobiles and computers, or production inputs such as lumber, iron ore, and microchips. Instead, they are part of that all pervasive, mysterious substance, called consciousness, which makes society possible in the first place. Second, it isn't clear how we can gauge the 'level' of technology. In what sense, for example, can we argue that the internet and the cell phone are more 'high-tech' than the internal combustion engine, the telephone, the printing press and the wheel – or for that matter, than mathematics, written language, or music? Finally, although contemporary 'high technology' does affect our world, perhaps in a big way, could we argue that this impact, taken in its totality, is greater than the impact of earlier innovations? In what units should we measure such impact?

sequences is through the centripetal, counter-force of corporate amalgamation. And so far, the method has been effective. Although liberalisation during the 1990s exposed the economies of many countries to outside 'competition', in most of them capital's share of income nevertheless rose.

The engine behind this rise was the emergence of a new, 'Technodollar–Mergerdollar Coalition'. Whereas the earlier, depth-oriented Weapondollar–Petrodollar Coalition thrived on military conflict and inflation, the interest of the new alliance lay in civilian 'high-tech' and the 'natural right to buy' anything vendible. The differential prosperity of this new coalition rested on three breadth-related poles. The first of these was *capital decontrols*, a key pre-requisite for cross-border mergers. As we argued in Chapter 2, free investment presupposed free trade; and, indeed, the 1990s saw the creation of larger 'free trade zones', most notably NAFTA and the EU, as well as lesser amalgamations such as Mercosur and EFTA. The second pole was *privatisation*. Part of this involved the sale of government-owned enterprises, but there was a much bigger prize here, namely the privatisation of government itself. According to World Bank data, average government spending on goods and services rose from less than 13 per cent in 1960, to nearly 16 per cent in the early 1990s. Much of this activity could be turned over to private hands; and since these usually ended up being the largest firms, the effect was tantamount to boosting differential accumulation through external breadth. The third, and possibly most important pole was expansion into the virgin territory of *'emerging markets'*.

The potential for differential accumulation in these markets was vast. One reason was that the entry of large Western-based companies into developing countries has been restricted for over half a century. Their presence there was therefore still limited, implying enormous room for expansion by takeover. The other reason was that, during the 1990s, the growth rates of both population and GDP per capita in these countries, although receding from their peak rates of the 1970s, were still more than twice those of the industrialised countries. True, green-field expansion created strong competitive pressures which were not necessarily favourable to differential accumulation; but it also served to replenish the pool of takeover target, thus helping extend the amal-gamation process. To put the significance of this latter potential in context, consider that during the late 1990s, 'Information Technology', the hottest growth sector of the U.S. economy, accounted for an estimated 8 per cent of GDP, and almost 15 per cent of its growth rate. Now compare this to the developing countries of East Asia and Pacific region. During the mid-1990s, these countries accounted for only 4 per cent of the world's output in constant $U.S., but for as much as *one-third* of its overall growth! The growing significance of these new markets was particularly stark relative to the diminishing role of military spending. During the 1960s, prime contract awards by the U.S. Defense Department accounted for 5 per cent of GDP, whereas overall U.S. exports to developing Asia were ten times smaller, at only one-half of 1 per cent of GDP. By the mid-1990s, however, the former had fallen by 70 per cent, whereas the latter had more than tripled to 1.7 per cent of GDP, surpassing U.S. defence procurements for the first time in history.[11]

Israel 'Opens Up'

It is within this context of breadth, 'high-tech' and the emphasis on developing countries, that the recent transition in Israel must be understood. Although Israel could be classified as a developed country by most standard indicators, from the viewpoint of global investors in the early 1990s it was still very much an emerging market – entangled in complex international and domestic controls, burdened by security concerns and instability, and far too small to bother about. Its incorporation into the new process of globalisation, therefore, required a series of fundamental changes, typical to many developing countries at the time.

The first of these changes was endorsing neoliberalism. In many countries, converting the elites proved relatively easy, since for them the globalisation 'stick' was usually accompanied by many 'carrots'. Selling neoliberalism to the underlying population, however, was a different story altogether. For most people, the change usually meant rising income inequality and the disintegration of various social support structures typical to the earlier statist order. Making them see the 'merits' of neoliberalism, or at least confusing them enough so they remained inactionary, therefore wasn't easy. The situation was in some sense reminiscent of Arthur Koestler's cynical reflection on the nature of historical change under communism. Since, according to the elite, 'ideology' always lagged behind 'reality', and given that only the elite could properly understand this discrepancy, it followed that the only path to progress was through forceful change, imposed from above (Koestler 1941). Similarly in capitalist Israel of the 1990s. Despite strong opposition from the underlying population to liberalisation and the peace process, including the murder of Prime Minister Rabin and a renewed Palestinian *Intifada*, ruling class propaganda for its 'new world order' continued unabated.

The second, more 'technical' requirement was to make capital vendible. In many developing countries, as in Israel, family ownership, high debt-to-equity ratio, and complex cross-holdings made buying assets a nightmare for foreign investors. Breaking these 'rigidities' was therefore as essential for globalisation, as it was traumatic for domestic groups. It entailed legislative and policy changes, social friction, and heightened conflict among the leading groups as they tried to reposition themselves on the changing stage.

The third necessary process was the relaxation of foreign trade barriers, and eventually, of foreign investment barriers. Again, this process too proved

---

11   Figures in this paragraph are computed from Margherio et al. (1998: Table 7, p. A1–24); World Bank (Annual); and U.S. Department of Commerce, through McGraw-Hill (Online).

difficult and drawn out. It meant that governments had to give up considerable 'autonomy', since manipulating domestic macroeconomic aggregates became inconsistent with 'self-adjusting' trade and capital flows. In the case of Israel, it also required a far broader political transformation toward peace negotiations and regional reconciliation; without this transformation, capital decontrols would have been far too risky and destabilising.

The fourth, related requirement was a change in the nature of the state itself. Once foreign and domestic capital began fusing, the resulting entities ended up transcending the geographical boundaries of their 'home' countries. Reacting to this change, governments have recently stepped up their coordination of micro- and macro-economic policies and regulations. But the 'imbalance' remained clear: whereas capital was growing *transnational*, state cooperation was still *international*. The result of this apparent unevenness was for capital to increasingly 'privatise' various state dimensions, as well as to 'incorporate' state organs and institutions from different countries as components of a worldwide mega-machine, called transnational accumulation

And, indeed, the global breadth phase may well signal the end of *nationally* based differential accumulation. One aspect of this is the change in the profit *benchmark* firms and investors try to beat. This yardstick, which previously was mostly national, has become global, even for small companies and capitalists. The other change is that *dominant capital itself* is gradually losing its 'national' character. In this regard, and particularly for our purpose here, it is also important to note a fundamental asymmetry in the way the process affects large and small markets. The size of dominant capital firms tends to be positively correlated with the size of their original 'home market'. This means that the amalgamation of two corporations, one based in a large country like the United States and the other in a small country such as Israel, is likely to be not 'a merger of equals', but a takeover of the latter by the former. It also means that dominant capital based in a small market will tend to transnationalise much faster than one based in a large market. And, indeed, as we shall see, the transnationalisation of Israel's dominant capital was remarkably rapid – so much so, that by the end of the 1990s it was no longer possible to talk about Israeli dominant capital as such. After a decade of transnational fusion, it appeared part and parcel of *global dominant capital*.

The Brodet Report

Israel's formal initiation into transnationlism began in 1995, with the publication of the so-called Brodet Report on *Aspects of Bank Holdings in Real Corporations* (Brodet et al. 1995). After decades of showing virtually no interest in the subject, the government all of a sudden became keenly concerned with corporate structure, and particularly with the fact that Israeli banks had extensive 'non-financial' holdings. A large committee, made up of public officials, businessmen, university professors and foreign experts was set up, and after short deliberations broke the astonishing news. 'The Israeli economy', it announced, 'is characterised by high corporate concentration', so much so that several large groups dominate much of the business landscape! (p. 1). These groups, explained the committee, 'are known to have had a crucial impact on the paths, behaviour and performance of the Israeli economy', and their continued dominance posed grave risk for 'the proper functioning of the market'. Among the various listed threats were instability, lower competitiveness, reduced production, higher prices and, most importantly, the scaring away of foreign investors. This was bad, very bad. It undermined the interest of the public in general and of consumers in particular, and if allowed to continue, warned the committee, could even compromise the 'proper functioning of the democratic regime' itself (p. 1).

A truly heart-warming document. What remained unclear, though, is where these allegations came from. Not that they were incorrect; but, then, how could the committee be so confident in making them? After all, with the exception of a few, largely unknown works by outsiders, the extent of the process was rarely documented, while its broader political-economy implications hardly even touched on.[12] And if corporate concentration was in fact self-evident all along, why has it become a 'problem' all of a sudden?

The answer was hidden between the lines. Although the committee spoke of concentration in general, its focus was exclusively the banking groups. The latter were still state-owned after their 1983 bailout, and the government was eager to re-privatise them. There was however a slight problem. The banks owned large chunks of the 'real' economy, so selling them to the large domestic groups, according to the Brodet Report, would have increased concentration further, amplified conflicts of interest, and destabilised their financial operations. A much better solution was to 'loosen' them up first by unbundling their real holdings, and then invite transnational corporations and foreign investors to take them over. This, it was argued, would kill two birds with one stone: on the one hand, foreign ownership would help keep the companies strong in an era of 'global competition', while on the other, domestic concentration would look lower since the new owners would be foreign.

Specifically, the committee recommended that the banks be required to reduce their holdings in any 'real' company to 20 per cent or less; that they be barred from exercising effective control over such companies (through minority holding, loans, or board members, for instance); and, finally, that they cap their overall 'real' holdings at 15 per cent of their own equity, but be allowed additional foreign holdings of up to 5 per cent of equity. According to the committee, based on 'weighing all relevant considerations', these recommen-

---

12   Rowley, Bichler and Nitzan (1988) and Bichler (1991) were perhaps the only works on the subject at the time.

dations provided the 'right balance' between alleviating concentration, keeping the banks stable, and reducing conflicts of interest (Brodet et al. 1995: 5). Precisely what these 'relevant considerations' were and how they were 'weighed' was not made clear in the report. It was also unclear how all of this would assure 'competition'. Indeed, the committee recognised that stripping banks of their non-financial subsidiaries still left the door wide open for an alternative structure, in which both were held by a 'generic' holding group (which is exactly what happened later). Conveniently, though, dealing with this concern was not part of the committee's mandate. The committee also said nothing on how to prevent the divested companies from being re-amalgamated into different groupings. Last but not least, there was complete silence on what would prevent foreign owners from cooperating with their domestic counterparts.

On the face of it, then, the whole exercise seemed rather strange. Why would the government set up a committee to deal with concentration, and then limit its scope so that its solutions could be easily circumvented? The reason was simple. The real purpose of the report was never to lower concentration, but to *change its nature*. The basic idea was to allow global investors to move in by *integrating* rather than undermining local groups. For this to happen, though, the great octopus of domestic assets had to be first chopped down into vendible units, so that they could be more easily transacted in the rapidly changing market for global ownership.

The immediate target was Bank Hapoalim. When the report was published, the bank had a vast array of precious holdings, operating across the economy. All in all, it had stakes in more than 770 companies, mostly through its ownership in six large conglomerates. One of these conglomerates was Clal, in which Bank Hapoalim had a direct 33.9 per cent stake, as well as another 6.7 per cent through its provident funds (the other large owners were IDB with 29.6 per cent, and Bank Leumi's provident funds with 6.7 per cent). The second was Koor, where Hapoalim held 22.7 per cent directly, and another 10 per cent indirectly, through its provident funds (the other owners here were Bank Leumi, and by now also U.S.-based Shamrock). The third holding was Delek, a company dealing in energy, transportation, retail and petrochemicals, and in which Bank Hapoalim had 25.5 per cent (again, together with IDB which owned 30 per cent). A fourth asset was Poalim Investment, a diversified holding group in which Bank Hapoalim held a 45 per cent stake. The fifth group was the infamous Ampal, the company which brought Hapoalim's chairman Jacob Levinson to his end, and where the bank still held 52.8 per cent of the stocks. The sixth group was a wholly owned real estate subsidiary, Diur BP, previously purchased from Solel Boneh. Extended through these various holdings, Bank Hapoalim's tentacles reached everywhere. It had stakes in ten different monopolies; it controlled leading companies in almost every sector of the economy; and it accounted for over 15 per cent of Israel's total industrial sales

(Brodet et al. 1995: Ch. 6). Clearly, there was a lot to chew on, and the wolves were lining up.

The Principal Groups

Taxes, Death and Bank Hapoalim

One of these wolves was Ted Arison, who in the early 1950s emigrated from Israel to the land of unlimited opportunities, to make a fortune in the leisure business. Like many elderly Jews, Arison wanted to spend his last years in the Holy Land, and so in 1990 he 'made Aliya' and immigrated back into Israel. There was also another reason. Arison did not like paying taxes, and he hardly did. Between 1986 and 1998, his Panamanian-registered company, Carnival Corp., made $4.7 billion in gross profit of which it managed to pay only 1.4 per cent in corporate taxes (computed from Standard & Poor's Annual). As he grew older, though, Arison realised that U.S. tax laws could make his heirs pay as much as 55 per cent in estate taxes on his personal fortune of $5 billion, and that was too much for him to stomach. The solution was to become a foreign resident. If you lived for a decade outside the United States, the tax man could no longer get you after you died. And so Arison, a 66-year-old man, moved back to Israel, and started marking time. 'All I know', he said, 'is my lawyer, he told me.... "You better live for 10 years." That's it. So I'm trying' (*Business Week*, 25 October 1999). As it turned out, though, god played tricks on him, and he died nine years later, one year short of a permanent tax holiday.

These nine years were of course not entirely wasted. Arison was a seasoned businessmen who knew what he wanted and how to get it. He started his career in Israel, where he ran M. Disengoff & Co., a small shipping business he inherited from his father. Once in America, he spent 20 years drifting from venture to venture, until he finally hit the right track. This happened in 1972, when he bought Carnival from his partner, Meshulam Riklis, for $1. The company had a single second-hand cruiser and $5 million in debt, but conditions were changing. Ocean cruising was until then an upscale market, and this, Arison realised, was his golden opportunity: if he could bring it down to the masses, they would in turn pave his way to riches. And that is exactly what happened. While in 1979 the company had revenues of only $45 million, by 1990, when Ted finally turned it over to his son Micky, middle-class 'fun-cruisers' were already generating for the Arisons $1.4 billion in annual revenues and as much as $200 million in net income.

Part of this success was undoubtedly due to Arison's patriotic acumen. By registering his company in Panama and putting most of its ships under a Liberian flag of convenience, he was able to pay little or no taxes, as well as to bypass the inconvenience of U.S. minimum-wage requirements. According to the *Wall Street Journal*, Arison's cruise employees, many of them university graduates from developing countries, were required to work for 10 months in a row with only two days vacation, while earning as little as $1.5 per day (which they were free to supplement with tips) (*Ha'aretz*, 8 September 1997). Of course, internal depth strategies of this kind were not enough, and the Arisons also went after internal breadth, expanding their leisure operations by buying other carriers, resort hotels, the PanAm airline which they merged with their own Carnival Airlines, and the NBA Miami Heat. By the late 1990s, their fortune, held mainly by father Ted and his son Micky, was estimated by *Forbes* at more than $10 billion, making them by far the richest 'Israeli' family in the world. It was clearly time to buy a bank.

Ted Arison owned a bank before – the Ensign Bank – a small Florida outfit which got him entangled in conflict of interest allegations, after it lent money to the manager of Miami's port, Carnival's home base (*Ha'aretz*, 24 July 1997). This time, however, Arison was after a much bigger prey: Bank Hapoalim. He was of course not alone. Standing against him was another group, led by Eliezer Fishman, the Israeli financial phoenix who was beaten to pulp by the large banks during the 1980s, only to rise back from the ashes and lash on them again. His consortium included investment banks Bear Sterns and Lazard Freres, American Financial Group, U.S. insurance groups Reliance and Leucadia National, and promoter and former president of Edmond Safra's Republic Bank of New York, Jeff Kyle. Arison lined up an equally impressive array, including Charles Bronfman, Goldman Sachs and George Soros. Halfway through the race, the participants' enthusiasm cooled down a bit, after the Brodet Report required that Hapoalim divested some of its prized holding. Also, the stock market was rising and that did not help either, since it threatened to make the purchase more expensive. The process even came to a temporary halt when the Likud returned to power after Rabin's assassination. Bronfman, who was closely aligned with Shimon Peres, got cold feet and began to hesitate. Arison, on the other hand, was far less concerned. In his view, 'it does not matter who is in power – right or left; the Israeli economy is so strong that even political change cannot spoil it' (*Ha'aretz*, 8 December 1997). Just to be on the safe side, though, he donated generously to Netanyahu's campaign; he also put $5 million into a new right-wing research institute, the Ariel Centre for Policy Studies, whose explicit mandate was to warn against the 'risk of peace'.[13]

Eventually, Bronfman, Goldman Sachs and Soros pulled out, seeking other ventures. Arison, though, remained persistent. He courted new partners – the Dankner family, which had close ties with Likud, along with foreign investors

---

13 'Oslo', announced the director of the centre, 'is a disaster for Israel', adding that 'Netanyahu was generous enough to help us, along with Arison, even before being elected as Prime Minister.' The centre, which Netanyahu hoped would challenge the 'old academic elites', was headed and advised by many Likud dignitaries, including former Prime Minister Yitzhak Shamir and his son, Yair Shamir; former Defence Minister Moshe Arens; future Minister for Internal Security Uzi Landau; and of course, Arison himself (*Ha'aretz*, 12 June 1998; 19 July 2000).

Len Abramson, Michael Steinheart, Charles Shustman and Lou Reinary – and by the end of 1997, his efforts finally came to fruition. His group paid the government $1.4 billion for 43 per cent of Bank Hapoalim, with an option for another 21.5 per cent later on. At the time, this was the largest corporate acquisition in Israel's history.

'Releasing Value'

Notably, a full 63 per cent of Hapoalim's purchase was financed by other banks, primarily Bank Leumi, First International Bank, Discount, and United Mizrahi Bank (whose chairman now was none other than David Brodet, head of the Brodet Committee). And this pattern was hardly unusual. According to a study by Odded Sarig, Israeli banks, which at the time were mostly government owned, financed up to 85 per cent of the privatisation and merger activity of the 1990s (*Ha'aretz*, 28 October 1997). This heavy leverage indicates that both investors and lenders expected the acquired assets to appreciate well beyond the cost of servicing the loans. And generally they were right. In 1988, Israel's stock market capitalisation was equivalent to roughly 10 per cent of outstanding bank credit, compared with an OECD average of 50 per cent; a decade later, and despite a massive credit explosion, the ratio had soared to 55 per cent, roughly the same as the OECD's (computed from World Bank Annual).

At least some of this increase, went the conventional wisdom, was due to the 'releasing of value' buried in the underlying assets. According to this argument, conglomerates like Bank Hapoalim were simply too big, too diversified and too opaque for investors to recognise their 'true' worth; and, as a consequence, their shares traded at a 'discount'. By unbundling them, and then repackaging their individual components as separate companies, their hidden value would then be 'released'. And since Israel had no capital gains tax, selling off some of these newly improved pieces could make even a highly leveraged buyout look cheap. Arison, along with many others, obviously found this logic compelling, with the result being that, between 1990 and 1998, the number of listed companies on the Tel Aviv Stock Exchange rose threefold, from 216 to 662 – a rate of increase six times faster than the world's average, and second only to Germany, which was going through a similar transformation (computed from FIBV 2000). Some of these companies were of course brand new, but many were floated subsidiaries, waiting for investors to discover their true worth.

And, yet something in this logic wasn't quite right. If conglomerate value was indeed 'invisible', how could some investors nonetheless see it before it was unbundled? And if the value was visible then it must have been already 'in the price', so how could there be any capital gain to be made? Clearly, for 'money to make money', something must happen in the middle. In the case of privatisation, this 'something' was often having the right political friends.

Arison, of course, knew this all too well. In 1995, he bought Israel's largest real estate and construction conglomerate, Housing and Construction (Shikun Ubinui). Since the company belonged to the Histadrut, and was therefore naturally 'in difficulties', Arison got his 35 per cent stake for a mere $15 million; that is, based on a company value of only $43 million. In 1998, however, Housing and Construction was already worth $278 million. What exactly happened during these two and half years to 'release' this sixfold increase in value was unclear. Arison himself knew nothing about construction. He did understand politics, though. And indeed, after the sale there were calls for independent inquiry into why the Histadrut was so eager to get rid of its prized assets, and for so little. It also turned out that Housing and Construction's chairman, Ephraim Sadka, as well as his CEO, Uzi Vardiser, each ended up with a large bundle of shares. Haim Ramon, the Histadrut chairman, of course denied any wrongdoing. Needless to say, the matter was never investigated for lack of 'public interest' (*Ha'aretz*, 17 June 1998).

Mickey Mouse Takes Over Koor

The other big Histadrut asset to be put on the blocks was Koor. Since the mid-1980s, the company faced mounting difficulties. Military spending was falling, the economic slump dried up domestic demand, and the government's 'stabilisation policy' kept interest rates high and exports uncompetitive. As a consequence, Koor accumulated close to $700 million in losses between 1985 and 1990. In 1986, the company even faced the prospect of bankruptcy, which it managed to escape only after raising $100 million in New York. The person who arranged the deal was Mike Milken of Drexel Burnham Lambert – an avid right-winger who reputedly made half a billion dollars in a single year, before being sentenced to a decade in prison for insider trading.

Classified as foreign borrowing, the deal had to be ratified by the Knesset Finance Committee, headed by Avraham Shapira. After giving his approval, Shapira extended his congratulations to Koor: 'Your success demonstrates your strength and management style, as well as the confidence your company commands around the world' (cited in Gaon 1997: 23). What he failed to mention was that at just about the same time, a New York subsidiary of Koor began lending money to Glenoit Mills, a faltering carpet mill in North Carolina, whose owner was none other than himself (*Forbes*, 11 July 1988). The impact of such manoeuvres, however, was at best cosmetic. In 1988 Koor was $250 million in the red, and having failed to repay a $20 million loan to Bankers Trust of New York, was again flirting with bankruptcy.

It was clearly time for a 'management reshuffle'. Ysha'ayahu Gavish, the last IDF general to head Koor, stepped down. His replacement was Benny Gaon, a former supermarket executive who grew up in the Histadrut, loathing everything about it. Gaon, whose name in Hebrew means 'genius', took a job nobody wanted and did everything by the neoliberal book. He cut the company's workforce to 16,000, down from 30,000; using divestment and amalgamation he reduced the number of subsidiaries to 30, down from 130; and, of course, he bolstered 'efficiency'. The employees of Koor, understandably distressed by these 'feats', protested their anger by occupying some of the company's factories. Gaon retaliated swiftly. Although formally still working for the Histadrut, and therefore in the service of his own employees, his real allegiances were clearly to mother equity and father debt. He hesitated little, and quickly dispatched the police, along with mercenaries and attack dogs, to evict the sit-in workers. For these achievements, the *Financial Times* hailed him as 'Mr Turnaround', while he himself boasted in his memoirs that only 'the daring wins'. The reality, though, was a bit more prosaic. What really turned things around was not the intrepid chairman, but the Jewish immigration from the former Soviet Union. Koor had its tentacles everywhere, and since the early 1990s, with the government again spending heavily and the economy growing rapidly, it was really difficult *not* to make money.

And then foreign investors started knocking on the door. Their entry was greatly facilitated by the 1992 election of Haim Ramon as the Histadrut's new chairman. Until then, the organisation's executives were still trying to cling onto their many corporate holdings. But the rising tide of neoliberalism and the growing deficit in their own coffers weakened their resolve, and when Ramon became chairman 'final sale' signs started appearing everywhere. Ramon himself was a corporate lawyer and a 'Third Way' neoliberal.[14] Although a Labour member of Knesset, he never had any interest in workers. The Histadrut, he announced, could not be both a labour union and an employer; it had to get rid of its business assets, and it was his job make it happen. Unlike in Poland and other former communist countries, however, the workers, who in fact owned these business assets, weren't offered the chance to receive or even buy what was really theirs. Needless to say, they never saw a cent of the proceeds. Instead, Ramon decided, on their behalf, that it was better to sell Koor to a 'stable body' – in his words, in order to 'avoid shocks' and save the company's remaining employees 'unnecessary agony' (*Ha'aretz*, 7 March 1995).

And he didn't need to look far. Gaon was already waiting around the corner with a very 'stable body' named Shamrock, an investment company jointly owned by Walt Disney's nephew Roy Disney and the General Electric pension fund. In March 1995, the deal went through, and Shamrock, headed by Stanley Gold, bought the Histadrut's 22.5 per cent stake in Koor for $252 million. The sale, Gaon declared ceremonially, 'marked an end of a chapter in the economic history of Israel' (*Ha'aretz*, 7 March 1995). And he was right. It wasn't every day that a labour union sold a company to Mickey Mouse.

14   The 'Third Way' concept was launched in 1990 by Tony Blair, who announced with much fanfare that he had finally discovered the alternative to both capitalism and state socialism. Whether he did or not is best left to experts in such matters. But it was clearly a brilliant 'alternative' for winning elections.

The Recanatis Face the Raiders

The Recanatis have had their squabbles with the law, but they never considered them as more than 'technical problems'. After the stock market crash of 1983, the Bejski Committee investigating the scandal demanded that the conspiring bankers resign, and that they be barred from ever returning to the banking business. All of them promptly complied and stepped down; with the sole exception of Raphael Recanati, who refused. His suspension came only after the government reluctantly intervened. Then came criminal charges, but they too hardly dented Recanati's confidence. In 1994, after a lengthy and much delayed trial, he and the other bankers were found guilty on various criminal counts, including banking manager felony, fraud under aggravating circumstances, securities fraud, misleading of customers, and false registration of corporate documents. All of them received fines, and most, including Raphael Recanati, were sentenced to prison. The bankers of course appealed, but the Supreme Court upheld all of their convictions, except the first (although it graciously lifted their jail sentences). As far as Raphael Recanati was concerned, this meant the case was closed. 'We were acquitted from the main charges', he claimed, 'and what remains are merely "technical" points which were left in order not to insult the [lower court] judge' (*Ha'aretz*, Annual Supplement, 15 December 1996).

And indeed, the Recanati empire remained pretty much intact. True, the Discount Bank, in which they still held a 13 per cent stake, was no longer under their control; but by now that was only one of many assets. The most important of these assets was IDB, the conglomerate which they founded in 1969 to organise their sprawling business. The family's special voting shares in this company were temporarily taken over by the government after the 1983 stock market crash, but were eventually sold back to them at bargain prices. Members of the family, including convicted felons Raphael and his son Udi, were still sitting at the helm, holding all the important levers of power. Their extensive kingdom was still safely under their command. Or so it seemed.

In Israel, the Recanatis were always leaders in business innovations. They were the first to discover the benefit of broader partnerships and alliances; the tax savings and global access provided by foreign investors; the beauty of statism and big government when budgets are rising, and of liberalism and small government in times of privatisation; the access to new saving provided by mass banking; and the promise of 'high technology'. Most importantly though, they understood, perhaps more than anyone, the power of leverage. And indeed, the Recanatis' was an 'empire by proxy'. Many if not most of their companies were held through minority ownership, bolstered on the one hand by strategic partners with whom they acted in unison, and on the other by widespread stock ownership which prevented serious outside challenges. Over the years, they created a complicated web of cross-ownership – much like the ones existing in South Africa, Korea or Japan – with many layers of ownership, and often with subsidiaries owning parts of their parent and grandparent corporations. For instance, in 1999, El-Yam Shipping, a holding company controlled by the Recanati and Carasso families, was a parent of Financial Holdings El-Yam, which was in turn a parent of IDB, which controlled IDB Development, which controlled Discount Investment Corporation, which controlled PEC, which was in turn a parent of ... El-Yam Shipping, its own grand-grand-grand-grandparent! (Ha'aretz, 31 May 1999).

This model enabled the Recanati family to control Israel's largest business complex with as little as 16 per cent of the ownership. The other strategic blocs were held by the Carasso family (16.4 per cent), and the recently added owners Goldman Sachs (9.5 per cent) and Bill Davidson (4.8 per cent) (Ha'aretz, 31 May 1999). And for a long time, that was more than enough. The key insiders cooperated in matters of internal governance, while relations with the other large groups were fortified through interlocking holdings and an intricate web of institutional arrangements. The 1990s, though, brought new winds.

First, there were growing internal squabbles. Although the various families of the Carasso clan have together held slightly more than the Recanatis, their agreement, dating back to the 1930s, was that the Carassos would always remain passive partners. In 1999, however, Raphael Recanati died, and when the throne was passed on to his son Udi and nephew Leon, some of the younger Carassos began demanding more say in management.

The more serious problems, though, came from the outside. In 1996, IDB found itself under attack from an unknown U.S.-Israeli investor, Davidi Gilo, who launched a hostile takeover bid for one of its prime assets, Scitex Corporation. The company, a maker of imaging printing equipment listed in New York, was considered one of Israel's early 'high-tech' miracles. Between 1987 and 1992, its value soared from $23 million to $1.8 billion, but then mounting global competition turned profit into losses and Scitex's market value dropped to $400 million. Gilo offered a 44 per cent premium, and IDB, which together with International Paper held only 38 per cent of Scitex, was forced to buy back its own stocks in order to ward off the invader. Eventually the defence succeeded, but Gilo was merely the beginning.

At about the same time, the Wertheimer family tried to buy out the Recanatis' share in Iscar, one of Israel's most profitable companies of which they were joint owners. Again, here too the Recanatis were vulnerable with a stake of only 25 per cent. In order to force them to sell, the Wertheimers started buying IDB stocks, raising their share to 13 per cent, up from 7. Adding insult to injury, the main sellers of IDB shares turned out to be no other than the Recanatis' long-time partners, the mutual and provident funds of Bank Leumi and Bank Hapoalim. This was indeed a totally new ballgame, a complete break with past practices of mutual understanding and common defence lines. Hapoalim's new owners viewed their assets as vendible capital; the battle drove share prices up, making for a good selling opportunity; and so they sold. In the end, the

Racanatis capitulated, swapping their minority share in Iscar for the Wertheimers' accumulated stake in IDB.

The most serious challenge, though, came from Yitzhak Tshuva, a rags-to-riches contractor who made his small fortune riding the immigration wave, and was now trying to play in the major league. His target was no other than Delek, a small conglomerate in its own right, which IDB controlled jointly with Bank Hapoalim for more than four decades. It took Tshuva only a few days to wrestle the company out of IDB, but these were clearly 'a few days which shook the world', or at least the Israeli business world. It wasn't so much that David could now take on Goliath, but rather that the Goliaths themselves were no longer buddies. Unlike in the battle for Iscar, this time the banks and their fund managers were not only willing to sell their holdings in Delek, but also to lend Tshuva the money with which to buy them in the first place. IDB held only 38 per cent of Delek, and when the other main owners stopped cooperating, the 'empire-by-proxy' was again exposed.

Clearly, the existing model was no longer working. Essentially, IDB, like the other large groups, had two basic options. It could either turn itself into a pure portfolio manager, letting others build up and sustain earning power, and then buy and sell claims on such power. Alternatively, it could 're-focus' its operations on several majority-held companies, and then work to shape and reshape its earning power on its own. Note, however, that while IDB could in principle choose one or the other, such an option is not really open for dominant capital *as a whole*. Differential earnings are based on power which must be constantly protected and increased, and that could not be done if everyone is merely a portfolio investor. This prerequisite is well recognised by the large players, so underneath the veneer of 'hostile takeovers', 'competitiveness' and 'impersonal market relations' there is always a deep layer of cooperation and understanding.

In the end, IDB chose the middle road, retaining a portfolio structure in some areas, but concentrating its power in others. Its most urgent goal was to protect its holdings in Clal, where it was already the largest owner, but still with less than half of the shares. Securing Clal, however, required a major reshuffling of assets with the other leading groups, and that is what happened next.

The Big Asset Swap

By 1997, Stanley Gold, chairman of Shamrock, was getting nervous. His two-year investment in Koor was not working well. First, his initial attempts to buy the company in the early 1990s, when the market was still cheap, lingered, and when he finally made the investment Koor was no longer a bargain. Then the market picked up, gaining as much as 70 per cent in two years. Koor's share, on the other hand, edged up by a mere 10 per cent, not even enough to service Shamrock's 63 per cent leverage. Gold, it turned out, was no wizard. Two earlier investments he made for Shamrock – one in LA Gear and the other in Grand Union – plummeted by 70 and 80 per cent, respectively (*Ha'aretz*, 7 July 1997; 23 July 1977). He was in no mood to have Koor as yet another one of his failures. The time had come to 'release value'. So far, most companies which de-conglomerated made a bundle: Bank Leumi by selling its insurance arm Migdal to the Italian company Generali; IDB by splitting its defence contractor Elbit into three separate companies; and Israel Chemicals by spinning off some of its non-core business. Now it was Koor's turn. Wasting no time, Gold started a smear campaign against Benny Gaon's managerial abilities, and even lashed at the new Likud government. 'Israel', he complained, 'is not a pretty place to invest in and support. It is no longer democratic ... and its economy may deteriorate to a situation similar to Iran, where religion determines life' (*Ha'aretz*, 21 July 1997).

Splitting up was hard to do, though. Shamrock had a mere 22 per cent of the company, with the rest held jointly by the Israeli government, Bank Hapoalim, and several large institutional investors. Not that they objected to the idea, only that the time wasn't yet ripe. It was much better to do things by consensus, with all the other big players safely on board, and preferably without Gold who was moving like an elephant in a china store. And indeed, soon enough the dust over the ownership arena settled. Bank Hapoalim was sold to the Arison/Dankner group; and then, Charles Bronfman, one of Seagram's largest owners, decided he wanted to buy Roy Disney's share in Koor. The negotiations were brief, and Shamrock, which only two years earlier was hailed by Histadrut chairman Haim Ramon as a 'stable body', received $404 million to move out.

The price was 60 per cent higher than what Gold had paid for it two years earlier. And yet Bronfman, Canada's richest man and one of Israel's shrewdest foreign investors, was hardly worried. His interests in Israel were organised through Claridge Israel, and run by Jonathan Kolber, who also owned 15 per cent of the stocks. By the mid-1990s, these assets yielded a combined return (realised and paper) of over $500 million – more than any of Claridge's other investments in the world (*Ha'aretz*, 24 July 1997). Unlike Stanley Gold, Bronfman never pretended to be a 'stable body'. His personal fortune of $3.6 billion wasn't made by 'sitting tight'. Moreover, as an investment company, Claridge's very essence was precisely to 'buy cheap to sell dear'. Nonetheless, Bronfman was very attuned to the broader implications of whom he bought from and to whom he sold.

The three conglomerates – Bank Hapoalim of the Arison/Dankner group, IDB of the Recanatis and Carassos, and Koor, which was now held jointly by the Bronfman/Kolber group and Arison/Dankner (through Bank Hapoalim) – were tightly interlocked through numerous cross-holdings. It was clearly time for a swap, and David Tadmor, the new Antitrust Commissioner, couldn't agree more. In his opinion, companies with joint ventures in certain areas tended to also not compete in other areas, even in the absence of any formal ties; such joint ventures, he said, were better dissolved. Strangely, though, instead of insisting that the joint holdings be sold to a third party altogether, or better still to several parties, Tadmor was perfectly content if one of the partners simply sold his share to the other. 'The purchase of Koor by Claridge', he claimed, 'created an exceptional opportunity to bring about a deep structural change in the market' (*Ha'aretz*, 19 July 1997; 24 July 1997). Why did he have to wait for such 'exceptional opportunity' was unclear. If there was indeed a problem, couldn't the Antitrust Commission simply step in and impose a solution? Apparently not, or perhaps it was just more convenient to 'demand' action precisely when the three conglomerates were ready to move.

At the beginning of the reshuffling process, Bank Hapoalim had a large stake in both Koor and Clal, and according to the Brodet Report, had to sell one of them – but *not* to any of the other large players. Clal, for its part, had many joint ventures with Koor and Claridge of the Bronfman/Kolber group, ventures which the Antitrust Commission wanted disbanded. The most important of these included the infrastructure conglomerate Mash'av and the 'high-technology' company ECI, as well as string of smaller firms, such as the retail chain Supersol, the telecom company Clalcom, the fuel company Sonol, and the real-estate company Shikun Ubinui (owned also by Bank Hapoalim).

And so the reshuffle began. At the end of the process, a couple of years later, the business landscape was certainly different, although hardly more 'competitive'. Bank Hapoalim, with the Antitrust Commission looking the other way, did exactly what the Brodet Report said it couldn't, selling its stake in Clal to ... IDB. The latter wasted no time, and promptly embarked on the largest merger in Israeli history, consolidating its subsidiaries IDB Development and Clal into one company. Antitrust or no antitrust, nobody would wrestle this one from them any more. Next, Koor swapped its share in Mash'av for most of IDB's stocks in ECI. Mash'av infrastructure holdings, including the cement monopoly Nesher, were now safely in the hands of the Recanatis and Carassos. Claridge on its side, exchanged its own share in ECI for additional shares in Koor, raising its control of the latter to over 35 per cent. ECI was merged with Tadiran to create the country's largest 'high-tech' company, with more than $1 billion in sales and an estimated market value in excess of $3 billion. When the changes were over, Koor had become Bronfman's second largest asset, after Seagram (*Business Week*, 21 August 1997).

'High Technology' and Domestic Power

For ideologues of the 'new economy', corporate centralisation is merely a temporary mirage, constantly threatened and continuously rolled back by innovation and technical change. The idea dates back to Alfred Marshall's notion that large firms are like trees in a forest: no matter how big they grow, eventually they die, to be replaced by new, more vigorous startups. Later on,

Joseph Schumpeter explained these dynamics by emphasising the process of 'creative destruction'. Old business structures, he argued, were constantly destroyed by the development and application of new technologies in quest for new (albeit temporary) monopoly gains. For much of the twentieth century, though, the thesis seemed hard to substantiate. Technology was of course changing, but aggregate corporate centralisation nevertheless continued to rise. The thesis supporters, however, remained adamant; and indeed, by the 1990s, they finally saw light at the end of the tunnel. For the first time in recent memory, rapid technological advances in computing, electronics and telecommunication, seemed to revolutionise business structures the world over. New 'high-tech' firms rose to challenge 'old economy' giants, competition undermined existing collusion, and governments were rapidly giving up their 'commanding heights', bowing to technical progress and the omnipotent consumer. Capitalism, argued its proponents, was finally coming into its own.

The festivities, though, proved premature. Technical change was indeed rapid, but instead of undermining business power it seemed to fortify it. Indeed, within a few years, most of the large 'high-technology' companies gravitated under the control of the same corporations, institutions and families who dominated the 'old economy'. 'Big is beautiful again', grumbled *The Economist* (21 July 2001). Of course, old money could not keep the bonanza all to itself, having to share large chunks of it with upstart techno-capitalists, such as Microsoft's Bill Gates, Paul Allen and Anthony Ballmer, Dell's founder Michael Dell, Oracle's Lawrence Ellison, and Apple's Steven Jobs. Yet, as the proceedings of the 1999 antitrust case against Microsoft suggested, in the so-called 'new economy' – perhaps more than in the 'old' one – it was not technology, but *power over technology* which counted. And indeed, in 1998, the combined net profit of the world's 445 largest software companies amounted to $11.5 billion, of which Microsoft, despite its inferior software, managed to pocket close to $8 billion, or 70 per cent of the total (*The Economist*, 13 November 1999).

The development of Israel's 'high-tech' business was hardly different. The introduction of new technologies opened various windows for change, but only for a brief historical moment, which was promptly closed after a short and brutal power struggle. The battle lured many new faces, most of whom failed and were quickly forgotten. Some, however, managed to carve a significant niche, incorporating themselves into the new emerging ownership structure. And indeed, the important change was not the incorporation of newcomers as such, but rather the very transformation of ownership toward greater vendibility, complexity and globalisation. To make our story easier to tell, we focus in this part on inward-looking, global developments, in which new technology was harnessed for the purpose of domestic power, leaving outward-looking developments for the next section.

From a domestic standpoint, the key technical changes in the 1990s were the introduction of cable and satellite delivery systems, cellular telephony, and the integration of both with traditional newsprint and television on the one hand, and with the internet on the other. Figure 6.2 outlines the ownership structure of these sectors at the end of the decade, focusing specifically of newspapers, telephone, and cable/satellite companies. The chart is incomplete in several ways: it does not cover all firms in these sectors; in omits television channels and internet companies altogether; and it does not describe all ownership ties among companies. The general picture, though, is clear enough. It reveals a massive Octopus-Hydra, whose tentacles are almost impossible to disentangle, whose heads are made up of both family firms and large publicly traded companies, and whose reach is increasingly transnational.

'New Economy' or Leveraged Hype?

One of the new 'heads' in this structure was the Dankner clan. Until the 1990s, the family's business, which consisted mainly of citrus orchards, real estate and salt production, was relatively insignificant. The dawn of the new breadth phase, though, opened up new opportunities, of which the Dankners were quick to take advantage. Soon enough, they started entering into new ventures, including energy, chemicals, banking, aviation, tourism, and of course, 'high technology'. Although they had no technical expertise or prior experience in any of these areas, the deficiency was more than compensated for by their healthy feel for investors' hype, fortuitous timing, and most of all, fondness of financial leverage. Their first major expansion took place during the deregulation wave of the early 1990s. The energy sector, which was until then controlled by an oligopoly of three companies, was opened up, and the number of competitors quickly soared to 13. The Dankners, smelling the build-up of investors' enthusiasm, bought control over Dor Energy, a small outfit which earned almost half its profit from its monopoly in the Palestinian market of the West Bank. The company was of course no match for the Israeli 'majors', but it was nonetheless a nuisance for them, and they were willing to pay a premium for its elimination. And indeed, by the late 1990s, the energy sector had re-consolidated. The number of firms dropped back to four, and Dor was bought out by Yitzhak Tshuva, who earlier wrestled the oil company Delek from IDB, and was now eager to begin swallowing his competitors.

The family's second move was to capitalise on the process of bank privatisation. They managed to join the Arison consortium in its quest for Bank Hapoalim, and when their group won the bid, the Dankners found themselves owning 12 per cent of the country's largest bank. Notably, their entire stake, worth $339 million at the time, was financed by a loan from the state-owned Leumi group. These were the happy days of Netanyahu, and the government, through Leumi, was apparently contended with the Dankners' miniscule collateral, which consisted of their newly acquired shares, plus assets whose book value was a mere $25 million. For some members of the Dankner family, though, the huge leverage was too much to stomach, and they wanted out.

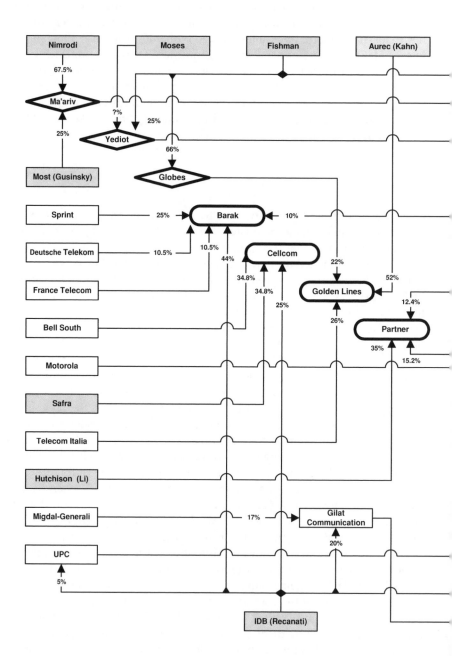

Figure 6.2 Ownership Structure of Israel's 'New Economy', 1999

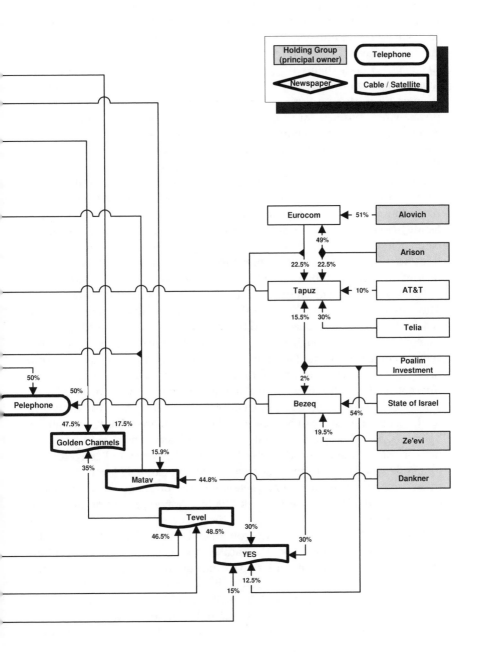

Yet this wasn't simple. With six households comprising 23 active family members, managing the Dankners' privately held assets was becoming somewhat of a nightmare. Other families – such as the Carasso clan of IDB, the Proppers of the food company Osem, and the Moseses of the daily *Yediot Aharonot* – found themselves in a similar predicament. For all of them, multiplying numbers meant intensifying family feuds and managerial paralysis. In most cases, the solution was to commodify power, by transforming the privately held business into a publicly listed corporation. The Dankners were no exception, and soon enough they too went public. The advantages were clear. First, it enabled family members to exercise 'exit' as well as 'voice', to use Hirschman's terminology (Hirschman 1970); if influencing the company from within proved difficult, they could now simply sell their stake and opt out. Second, it injected a new measure of flexibility into ownership realignments. For instance, 47 per cent of Osem was sold to the world's largest food company Nestlé, while over a quarter of *Yediot Aharonot* was sold to Israel's new media baron, Eliezer Fishman (to whom we return later). Finally and most importantly, it allowed existing owners to profit immensely from stock dilution. It was mainly this latter possibility which captured the Dankners' imagination.

The most appropriate arena for such adventures was the 'high-tech' sector. The Dankners' main asset here was their 44.8 per cent stake in Matav, one of Israel's three cable oligopolies, which they jointly owned with Ofer Nimrodi and Vladimir Gusinsky through *Ma'ariv*. Matav itself owned 15.2 per cent of the cellular company Partner (along with Hong Kong-based Hutchison, Arison, Alovich, AT&T, Telia and Poalim Investment), as well as 10 per cent of the international telephone operator Barak (along with IDB, Sprint, Deutsche Telekom and France Telecom) (see Figure 6.2). Until the late 1990s, Matav also held a 9.4 per cent share in Netia, one of Poland's largest cable and telephone operators, as well as similar investments in Hungary. The dense ownership network surrounding the Dankners' holdings here was indicative of the immense hype in which this sector was immersed, particularly since many of these companies generated huge operating losses for their owners. But, then, in the bubbled 'high-tech' sector of the 1990s, it was losses, not profits, which often made you rich.

Recall that capitalisation is based on *expected* rather than actual earnings. Under 'normal' circumstances of the so-called 'old economy', such expectations were commonly built on the basis of past and current profit trajectories. In the 'high-tech' sector of the 'new economy', however, there was no past to speak of, and often no current profit either. While this made it difficult to form any 'rational expectations', it offered fertile ground for irrational ones. And indeed, for want of a better yardstick, many investors seemed to believe that in the 'new economy', the rules of the game were somehow different. So much so, that the best future prospects were in fact offered by money-losing companies. The argument sounded simple enough: 'high-tech' ventures required massive sunk costs, leading to large current losses, which were therefore the surest omen for massive future returns. Promoters such as the Dankners of course couldn't agree more. Their company Matav, which faced a saturated market and competition from the satellite company YES, had during the late 1990s gone from profit to losses; its market capitalisation, however, soared to nearly $700 million in 1999. A large chunk of Matav's operating losses came from its stake in Partner; yet in 1999, the latter was floated in New York, quickly reaching a market value of $4.3 billion. This made Matav's share in Partner worth $645 million and the Dankners' own stake as much as $275 million (*Ha'aretz*, 29 December 1999; 3 April 2000). Such valuations offered lucrative opportunities for large POs, whose proceeds were quickly paid as dividends to the Dankners and the other key owners (*Ha'aretz*, 26 July 2001).

With so much going for it, even the Dankners began to believe in this 'high-technology' version of the Emperor's New Clothes. Yet, in their manoeuvres they were walking on a tightrope. By the end of the 1990s, they carried a debt-to-equity ratio of 10 to 1. Since their assets yielded little or no operating earnings, the only way for them to service their obligations was by realising capital gains and using POs as a source of dividends. Needless to say, this Ponzi-like strategy (named after legendary U.S. speculator, Charles Ponzi) could succeed only in a rising market; and over that the Dankners obviously had no control. In other words, the Dankners' success was built mainly on taking advantage of fortuitous circumstances, while doing little to *alter* those circumstances. Other rising capitalists, though, were trying to be more proactive.

Newspapers and Criminals

In early 1992, Ya'acov Nimrodi, one of Israel's prominent arms dealers, came under attack from the daily *Hadashot*. The paper alleged that, while acting as a middleman in the 1985 'Irangate' deals, Nimrodi embezzled money the Iranians paid Israel for its weapon deliveries. The veteran dealer was flabbergasted. Having risked his life, not to mention his money for the noble cause, he had no intention of seeing his reputation tarnished. His knee-jerk reaction was to sue the Israeli government, asking the court to clear him from any wrongdoing. But then he realised there was a better way to resolve such media-related problems: buying your own newspaper. And lo and behold, three months later the opportunity came knocking. Robert Maxwell, the master crook who owned *Ma'ariv*, Israel's second largest daily, had just died, and his receivers put the newspaper on the block. Nimrodi jumped on the opportunity, buying 50 per cent of the stocks.

Ma'ariv has had an illustrious history of very 'active', if questionable owners. Founded in 1948 by Revisionist journalists who left *Yediot Aharonot*, it was first owned by Oved Ben-Ami of the Dankner clan. Ben-Ami never served in any army. This didn't prevent him, though, from being an avid right-winger, a financial backer of the Likud, and one of the founders of Eretz Yisrael Hashlema, the right-wing umbrella organisation of Jewish settlers in the Occupied Territories. He was also one of Israel's biggest crooks, whose business deals made him the subject of numerous investigations by the State Comptroller, the tax authorities, and the police (Frenkel and Bichler 1984: 88–99). Despite his right-wing political views, *Ma'ariv* had on a number of occasions offered its services to the ruling MAPAI Party, in return for the latter closing down its own paper, *Hador* (Sharet 1978: 52, 217, 345, 384). In 1989, after Ben-Ami died, the paper was taken over by Robert Maxwell, the British press baron and undercover KGB agent, who later disappeared (or drowned) under mysterious circumstances, though not before embezzling the pension funds of his workers.

Ya'acov Nimrodi, who bought the paper from Maxwell's receivers, began his career as an Israeli intelligence attaché associated with the Iranian SAVAK, the Shah's notorious secret police. Using this experience as a launching pad, he later rode the global arms-export bonanza as one of Israel's leading weapon peddlers. By the end of the 1980s, when the depth phase of war profits was coming to a close, Nimrodi started looking for peace dividends. In 1987, a Jersey Island corporation registered under his name bought from the Leumi group 42.9 per cent of Israel Land Development (Hachsharat Hayishuv). The company was originally founded in 1909 by the Jewish Agency to redeem land for Jewish settlement, and Nimrodi's front man in the deal, Jerusalem's would-be mayor Ehud Ulmart, aptly hailed it as a 'Zionist transaction' (*Ha'aretz*, 22 October 1999). A year later, the takeover was sealed when Nimrodi acquired from the Jewish Agency the company's special 'founding shares' which gave whoever owned them absolute control. After establishing this new Zionist base for his family, Ya'acov Nimrodi stepped aside, passing the throne to his son Ofer. By the time Israel Land Development bought *Ma'ariv* in 1992, the family business was already run by this young lawyer and graduate of Harvard's business school, who, next to his father's somewhat tarnished image, looked like Mr Clean. Yet, soon enough, Ofer too found himself in trouble.

Much like the Dankners, the Nimrodis ventured into diverse areas. These included real estate, hotels, insurance, medical services, and most importantly, media and communication, where they owned *Ma'ariv*, as well as parts of Matav, Partner and Barak (see Figure 6.2). Most of their companies, however, were marginally profitable at best. Their main 'value' – if that is the proper term to use – was to help the Nimrodis milk other investors, an enterprise in which they proved second to none. In retrospect, their tactic seemed straightforward: when the market was high, they issued as much new paper as they could; when it fell, they bought on weakness, waiting for the next upswing in order to begin the cycle anew. Remarkably, the Nimrodis not only executed this strategy with great precision, but also used this to profit from their own misfortunes, so to speak.

Between 1992 and 1994, when the Israeli market was carried up on the euphoria of peace and 'emerging markets', the Nimrodis were busy diluting their shares through massive public offering of equity and debt. Secured by their special 'founding shares', they used most of the money to pay themselves huge salaries and dividends. In 1996, however, the market crashed; worse still, Ofer Nimrodi was implicated in a criminal investigation, which caused the shares of Israel Land Development to plunge even further. Yet the Nimrodis couldn't help but see the brighter side of things. Their company's stock was down to less than 30 per cent of book value; so cheap, it was worth buying again, *en masse*. And the strategy proved hugely successful. Three years later, with Ofer out of jail, the price had risen more than fivefold, and the Nimrodis were once more busy issuing fresh paper to amnesic investors and large dividends to themselves. The scheme, though, wasn't entirely foolproof: in contrast to the stock market which moved in cycles, Ofer Nimrodi's legal problems looked desperately secular. The chief executive officer of *Ma'ariv* and chairman of Israel Land Development was once again in custody, charged with eight criminal counts, including conspiracy to commit murder.

To better understand these developments, it is useful to briefly consider the background. The Nimrodis, it should be noted, did not completely plunder their companies. A good part of what they raised in the market was ploughed back into *Ma'ariv*, which they view, not without reason, as their most strategic investment. This was the era of 'communication', and newspapers were quickly becoming part of a much broader network of cables, satellites, television, telophony and the internet. *Ma'ariv* was the Nimrodis' stepping stone into this new world of opportunity, but making inroads here wasn't easy. The main problem was *Yediot Aharonot*, which in 1992 accounted for nearly 52 per cent of the daily newspaper market – compared with 15 per cent for *Ma'ariv*, the next in line. Most significantly, *Yediot Aharonot*, largely due to its far higher advertisement revenues, enjoyed gross profit margins in excess of 45 per cent, whereas *Ma'ariv* was consistently losing money (figures from *Ha'aretz*, 6 May 1998). Nimrodi managed to boost profitability somewhat, but this was clearly an uphill battle.

Competition between the two papers was heating up, and soon enough they were both wiretapping one another, as well as many other figures of greater and lesser importance. When the affair exploded in the mid-1990s, Ofer Nimrodi immediately denied any wrongdoing. Just to be on the safe side, though, he also issued a veil threat to his pursuers: 'They may be laughing now, but believe me, it is only temporary. I'll wipe away their smile pretty quickly. I'm determined, and I also have, much to their chagrin, the economic means to back my resolve' (*Ha'aretz*, Weekly Supplement, 10 July 1998). And yet, in 1998, after four years of relentlessly trying to stall and obstruct the investigation, he opted for a bargain plea, admitting all charges in return for eight months in prison. One possible reason for this sudden change of heart, was that Nimrodi realised he could not win, and that the evidence, if revealed in court, would be far more damaging than a few months in jail. But the compromise left him vulnerable, and as we noted, a year later he was charged again in the same affair – this time for conspiring to murder one of his accomplices who 'knew too much'.[15]

And the plot thickens. To the press, Ofer Nimrodi announced that 'only a sick, hallucinating mind could invent such [murder] accusations'. Yet, behind the scenes he moved swiftly, allegedly bribing top police officials so that they stalled the inquiry, and even implicating the Minister for Internal Security, Avigdor Kahalani, who ended up himself on the defendant seat (*Ha'aretz*, 22 October 1999; 18 June 2000). During the inquiry, it was also revealed that Ya'acov Nimrody asked his old friend and former arms dealer, Israeli President Ezer Weitzman, to absolve his son Ofer and roll back his earlier conviction. When Weitzman refused, a freelance journalist of *Ma'ariv* 'uncovered' evidence of the President's dubious connections with French millionaire Edward Sarusi, including secret gifts of half a million dollars. Six months later, Weitzman was forced to resign. When Shimon Peres announced his intention to replace Weitzman as President, a business associate of Ya'akov Nimrodi put the writing back on the wall, alleging that his partner paid Peres $150,000 out of his 'Irangate' sales (*Ha'aretz*, 27 June 2000).

Interestingly, the Nimrodis' legal woes didn't seem to dent their financial portfolio. On the contrary, by mid-2000, the market value of their Israel Land Development had risen threefold relative to early 1999, when their troubles began to intensify. And perhaps this shouldn't surprise us. As Rosa Luxemburg (1913) argued, brute force was by no means limited to the early 'primitive accumulation' stage of capitalism. And since the key issue here was expected earning capacity, the Nimrodis' tough tactics, as long as they boosted profit, didn't deter investors. But not entirely. Open violence made it difficult for the Nimrodis to create and capitalise 'goodwill'. In this sense, they stood out not for the use of force per se, but for the *unsophisticated* use of force, still at the level of 'badwill'. In this regard, they had much to learn from their partner, Russian investor Vladimir Gusinsky, who in a relatively short period of time managed to cover himself in a thick veneer of quasi-respectability and 'business as usual'.

The Russian Connection

Ronald Lauder was well connected in Israel. During the 1990s, the former U.S. ambassador to Austria and one-time candidate for mayor of New York, was president of the Jewish National Fund, as well as head of the Conference of Presidents of Major American Jewish Organisations. He was principal financial backer to both Benjamin Netanyahu and Nathan Sharansky, a Soviet

---

15   Initially, the prosecution alleged that Nimrodi also conspired to murder both Arnon Moses, owner of *Yediot Aharonot*, and Amos Schocken, owner of *Ha'aretz*. These additional charges were later dropped, since according to police evidence, Nimrodi changed his mind, preferring to 'squeeze' the two rather than 'crash' them (*Ha'aretz*, 7 January 2000).

'refusenick'-cum-Israeli politician, as well as founder and board chairman of Shalem Centre, a right-wing think-tank which in 1994 he spent $5 million to establish. He is also reputed to have secretly negotiated, on behalf of Prime Minister Netanyahu, a settlement over the Golan Heights with Syria's President Assad. Last but not least, his 1999 net worth of $3.9 billion made him one of the richest men in the United States, having inherited, along with his brother Leonard, the fortune of their mother, cosmetics empress Estée Lauder.

In the early 1990s, the Lauder brothers started moving into the hot communication sector. Eager to tap future advertising revenues in the new 'transition' economies, they began in 1991 by establishing Central European Media, a holding company for eleven Eastern European TV stations. Then, in 1994, they founded, together with Yitzhak Fisher, a former financial controller of the Likud, a company by the name of RSL Communication, to provide international dialling services.

In 1998, Ronald Lauder was preparing his third communication investment – a 25 per cent stake in *Ma'ariv*, for which he was willing to pay up to $33 million. The investment was supposed to boost Netanyahu's poor image in the press, whose owners didn't like watching the Prime Minister put their peace dividends at risk. With a stake in *Ma'ariv*, Lauder could have countered Netanyahu's detractors, perhaps in return for a nice slice of the telecom monopoly Bezeq, or other such prized assets. But the elections were won by Netanyahu's pale double, Ehud Barak; and Lauder's share in *Ma'ariv* was snapped from under his nose by one of Barak's own financial backers, Russian investor Vladimir Gusinsky.

Who was this Gusinsky? What was he doing in Israel? And why was he willing to pay for his stake as much as $85 million, a sum equivalent to 45 times *Ma'ariv*'s annual profit? Gusinski's appearance in Israel was part of a broader process of capitalisation and transnationalisation. The centre of this process was capital flight out of Russia and into safer havens. Although the exact figures may never be known, it is estimated that $150–300 billion, and possibly more, have left Russia during the 1990s. A large chunk of this – again, how much is unclear – moved through, or ended up in Israel, a country which had no money-laundering legislation, and whose governments always welcomed foreign funds to offset their import 'dependency'. The process attracted much attention, primarily for its alleged criminality. With reported violence in Israel rising sharply, there were increasing warnings of Russian organised crime weaving into the country's social fabric. For instance, between 1980 and 1998, the number of police investigations into attacks on human lives rose twelvefold, and into moral offences more than fourfold (Israel. Central Bureau of Statistics 1999: Table 21.11, p. 21.13). The Russian presence was particularly noted in the sex trade; so much so, that Israeli prostitutes were nicknamed 'Natasha'. During the 1990s, over 10,000 women were trafficked, often as slaves, from the former Soviet Union into Israel. These women comprised roughly 70 per cent of the local prostitution business, whose annual turnover was conservatively estimated in excess of half a billion dollars (Amnesty International 2000; Hughes 2000).

Seeking legitimacy, illicit money has also penetrated Israeli politics. According to police and media reports, former Prime Minister Netanyahu and his Chief of Staff Lieberman have had contacts with suspected Russian-based criminals, while Nathan Sharansky, a government minister whose party was supported largely by Russian immigrants, admitted to having accepted donations from Gregory Lerner, a money launderer who got himself entangled with the Russian mafia and ended up in an Israeli jail. Many of Russia's new businessmen – including notorious mobsters Eduard Ivankov and Sergei Mikhailov, as well as bigger sharks, such as Boris Berezovsky, Roman Abramovitch, Lev Leviev and Vladimir Gusinsky – have actually become Israeli citizens, at least according to their passports.

So far, however, little attention has been paid to the underlying causes of the process, namely the 'capitalisation' of Russia. As it turns out, this transition can shed light not only on the growing integration of Israeli and Russian capital, but also on the similar forces affecting their development. Perhaps the most remarkable thing about Russia's capitalisation is that it happened so quickly. The emergence of the corporation, the formation of a capitalist ruling class through differential accumulation, the pendulum of depth and breadth, and the broader transition from statism to transnationalism, have all unfolded in less than a decade. By the end of the 1990s, business enterprise in Russia was already so centralised that its head figures, now commonly referred to as 'The Oligarchs', were seeking expansion outside their country.

Russia's dominant capital, of which Vladimir Gusinsky was a noted representative, first emerged in the late 1980s, when Gorbachev, as part of his *perestroika*, opened up the banking sector for private ownership. It was then that Gusinsky, a small theatre producer and one-time taxi driver, established his Most-Bank. The number of banks quickly skyrocketed to over 1,360 in 1991, and initially competition was stiff (Schroder 1999). Soon enough, though, the nuclei of dominant capital started to emerge. During this period, the main vehicle for its differential growth was a depth regime of intense stagflation. The Russian government, faced with a collapsing tax base, turned to the printing press, causing prices to rise by 77,000 per cent between 1992 and 1996, according to IMF data. The principal winners of this policy were banks doing business with the government. Initially, their main advantage was being able to borrow from the central bank at interest rates far lower than the rate of depreciation of the rouble, and then use such loans to buy foreign currency. Eventually, when in 1994 the government switched to policy tightening, they shifted gear into buying high-yield government bonds, as well as into 'managing' government budget transfers, on which they paid little interest, and which they often embezzled (Wolosky 2000). At both stages of this lucrative business, political ties proved paramount; and indeed, only a minority of well-connected institutions – perhaps no more than 5 per cent – managed to survive the process (Schroder 1999). Within this group, a smaller cluster of banks – including Oneximbank controlled by Vladimir Potanin; Menatep of Mikhail Khodorkovsky; SBS-Agro of Alexander Smolensky; Inkombank of Vladimir Vinogradov; Alfa Bank of Mikhail Fridman; and Most-Bank of Vladimir Gusinsky – emerged as clear leaders.

The differential position of these leading financiers was further boosted by the devastation of industrial enterprise, whose output according to IMF data dropped by as much as 70 per cent between 1992 and 1996. And the depression was hardly surprising: why engage in production when the institutional structure is mired in a chaotic transition from communism, and when returns on foreign exchange and government debt are far higher and seemingly less risky? And so, Russian capitalism and its dominant capital groups were born not through economic growth, but rather out of a severe bout of stagflationary redistribution, a depth regime in which primitive accumulation was accomplished through massive *de*-industrialisation.

Of course, the highly destructive societal impact of this process meant it could last for only a brief historical moment; and if the differential gains were to be retained, depth had to quickly give way to breadth. The first steps in this transition began in 1992–93, with the incorporation of up to 80 per cent of the country's mid-size industrial cooperatives (Schroder 1999). This new vendibility made possible the beginning of conglomeration via mergers and acquisitions, whose first incarnation were the FIGs, or 'financial-industrial groups'. Some of the FIGs grew from the large banks, while others started from raw materials, or the industrial sector. Regardless of their origin, though, all were now faced with the need to break their existing sectoral envelope, and expand into other fields. Initially, however, this type of breadth movement was barred both by the stagflationary depth regime and by lack of large takeover targets, since Russia's main assets were still state-owned.

In March 1995, the leading bankers, headed by Vladimir Potanin, concocted a brilliant solution. The government, they proposed, would abandon the printing press in favour of debt financing, thus bringing Russia's inflation under control and enabling growth to resume. The finance for the operation would come from Potanin and the other large Russian bankers, so as to avoid 'dependency' on foreign loan-sharks. To secure the deal, the government would temporarily transfer to the bankers' 'custody' the shares of its large state-owned enterprises. The bankers would receive interest payments and management fees, and once the principal was repaid, would revert the shares back to the government. Of course, if the government was for some reason unable to meet its obligations, the bankers would be free to do with these shares as they saw fit. The government jumped on the proposal, dressed it up a bit to make it look more open and respectable, and then hurriedly, in less than a year, transferred Russia's most prized assets into the custody of the country's dominant capital (Lieberman and Veimetra 1996).

Needless to say, the deal was mired in controversy. There were allegations of massive corruption which priced government assets at ridiculously low prices; of bid rigging which excluded all but select insiders; and of lack of transparency which kept everyone else in the dark. There was a growing feeling that Russia's capitalism was criminal, and that the bankers were running the country like a mafia. Worse still, unlike the 'traditional' mafia which usually provided some protection to its subjects, the Russian bankers seemed to have abandoned the underlying population altogether. And indeed, since the collapse of communism, unemployment skyrocketed, wages, when they were not in arrears, were severely eroded, and public services practically disintegrated. According to the World Bank, average life expectancy, which in 1987 stood at 70 years, dropped to 64 by 1994. An anti-capitalist backlash was brewing up, and, in 1996, opinion polls suggested that the communists may well win the coming elections, putting Russia's flirt with private ownership into question.

This was a defining moment for dominant capital. Clearly, brute force, cunning and criminality were no longer enough, and if differential accumulation were to continue, capitalist power had to penetrate and alter the nature of the state itself. In short, the time had come for collective political action. In March 1996, the six 'bankers' mentioned earlier, along with a seventh capitalist, Boris Berezovsky, gathered for a strategic meeting at the World Economic Forum in Davos. Although Berezovsky himself did not own a bank, he had something far more precious: a very close relationship with President Yeltsin and his family. And so began the *semibankirshchina*, or 'the reign of the seven bank barons', named after the infamous *semiboyarschina*, the brutal regime of aristocratic officials and land owners who ruled Russia in the seventeenth century. As Berezovsky later told the *Financial Times*, the seven bank barons decided to put their combined weight behind Yeltsin, making sure he won the elections.

The bankers' principal weapon was their nearly complete control of the media. According to opinion polls, Russians trusted the media more than the President, more than the government, and even more than the Orthodox Church; and as Berezovsky boasted later on, the bankers understood this all too well. 'Information', he explained, 'is about politics; and politics is a huge part of today's Russian reality' (*Newsweek*, 19 July 1999). The consequence was the end of Russia's free press. Gorbachev's *perestroika* gave the media several years of relative autonomy; but as inflation started to spiral in the early 1990s, independent newspapers and TV stations rapidly fell prey to takeovers, and soon ended in the hands of the bankers, primarily Berezovsky and Gusinsky (Gessen 1998; Mickiewicz 1999). Having spent a few years perfecting their media skill by attacking each other, the new owners were now ready for the more complicated cooperative task of revitalising Yeltsin. And propping him up wasn't easy. The aging incumbent even suffered two heart attacks (reported as 'colds' by the media), which almost killed him. But in the end, Russians trusted the media, and the operation succeeded. Yeltsin remained 'in power'.

The use of inverted commas here is deliberate, for the lines between business and state were getting increasingly blurred. Yeltsin literally owed his victory to the bankers, and quickly gave them key positions in his administration. Perhaps the most important of these was the nomination of Vladimir Potanin, owner of Oneximbank and custodian of numerous state assets, as Vice Premier in charge of economic policy and privatisation. With these changes, Russia's dominant capital was now ready to enter the second stage of the 'loans-for-shares' programme, the one in which custody was to be converted into hard cash. And so began the twentieth century's biggest robbery.

As everyone expected, the government was unable to, and by now uninterested in, redeeming its shares; it was left to their custodians, the 'Oligarchs', to do with them as they saw fit. The privatisation advanced swiftly, although often without a clear trail to who got what, and for how much. And the opaqueness was hardly accidental. Initially, many Western observers watched the process with reserved approval. The new Russian Oligarch was often ridiculed for being unsophisticated, and criticised for his 'robber baron' tactics. But much like his U.S. counterpart a century earlier, his primitive accumulation was deemed necessary. 'He steals, but he gets things done', was the winning campaign slogan of Adhemar de Barros, a São Paulo politician (Page 1995: 151); and to many in the West, the Oligarchs seemed to be fulfilling much the same role in Russia. Indeed, the prevailing expectation was for this kind of 'wild east' to quickly set the stage for 'proper' capitalist law and order. History, however, worked out a little differently.

The Oligarchs, it turns out, were highly sophisticated, certainly more than many of their Western 'observers' and foreign partners. Unlike most outsiders, they knew Russia was still far from 'law and order', and would remain so for the foreseeable future. Under such circumstances, hard cash was far more attractive than symbolic profit, and better still, when accumulated outside the country. As a consequence, companies were bled dry by first using transfer pricing to redefine as 'cost' what Western companies would normally consider 'profit', and then channelling the proceeds to other holdings and foreign accounts. The oil company Yukos, for instance, has allegedly siphoned in this way more than $800 million in less than one year to its owner Khodorkovsky, while Aeroflot insiders are believed to have cross-subsidised foreign companies controlled by Berezovsky (Wolosky 2000; *Financial Times*, 28 July 2000).

Equally sophisticated was the way the Oligarchs structured their holdings. In contrast to the interlocking and often recursive organisation of the Japanese *Keiretsu*, Korean *chaebol*, South African conglomerates and Israeli holding groups, where firms sometimes owned each other, the FIGs were typically made 'flat', with one holding company controlling all subsidiaries, which were otherwise unconnected. Although that made the structure more vulnerable to outside takeover, given that the Oligarchs' goal was often to eviscerate rather than build up their holdings, the benefit far outweighed the risk. Using this structure, FIG owners managed to elevate bankruptcy to a level of high art, transferring good assets to other firms in their organisation, and then leaving the bankrupt company's empty shell for their creditors and minority shareholders to squabble over (Mellow 1999; *Financial Times*, 25 July 2000). The most publicised victims of this strategy were foreign investors, who, lured by a booming Russian stock market, were crowding in to plant their money in the new promised land. British Petroleum, for instance, paid $571 million for 10 per cent of Potanin's Sidanko, one of Russia's largest oil companies. The deal, signed with much fanfare in 10 Downing Street under the auspices of Tony Blair, valued the company at 10 times what Potanin paid for it a couple of years earlier. Even George Soros, the wizard of global finance, was tempted to pay $980 million for 25 per cent of Potanin's Svyazinvest Telecommunication, along with Deutsche Morgan Grenfell, which lent the company several hundred million dollars more (*Business Week*, 1 March 1999). In 1998, however, the market crashed, making these investments practically worthless. And when the minority partners and creditors came looking for remainders, they discovered that most of the leftovers were either taken over by other Oligarchs, or siphoned away, in order 'to protect the company from predators', as a Yukos official carefully explained (Lyons 1999).

At this conjunction, the tone of Western commentators began to change. If Soros could be tricked into losing 1 billion dollars in what he himself professed to be the 'worst investment of my professional career' (Soros 1998: 167), something in Russia must have gone awfully wrong. The Oligarchs were expected to open up Russia for business. Instead, they used one hand to milk foreign investors, while the other sent the money abroad, often with the help of respectable foreign institutions.[16] This charade was supposed to end after the financial crisis of 1997–98, which forced many other developing countries to welcome foreign owners as white knights of corporate salvation. Not in Russia. The Oligarchs, whose net worth was presumably wiped out by the crisis, rose from the ashes, staging what *Euromoney* called the 'waltz of the living dead', and once more taking foreign investors to the cleaners. Clearly, something had to be done, and sure enough, a *Foreign Affairs* article now argued that the real threat for U.S. 'national security' came not from the communists, but from the Russian Oligarchs (Wolosky 2000). According to the author, the Oligarchs should be targeted individually, and there was even room for temporary re-nationalisation, so that the assets could be 'properly' re-privatised.

And, indeed, by the early 2000s, Russia's capitalisation seemed to be entering a third stage. Having first moved from depth through stagflation in 1990–96,

16	The most publicised case involved the Bank of New York, whose officials were found guilty in connection with illegal transfers of billions of dollars, involving Oligarchs such as Berezovsky, Luzhkov and Khodorkovsky, Kremlin figures like Chernomyrdin and Chubais, and last but not least, Semyon Mogilevich, Russia's 'Brainy Don' of money laundering. Recently, the inquiry was extended into the possible embezzlement of $4.5 billion in IMF loans (*Newsweek*, 6 September 1999; *United Press International*, 11 July 2000; *Financial Times*, 25 July 2000).

to breadth via privatisation and merger in 1996–99, dominant capital, still in breadth mode, appeared to be taking its first transnational steps. And like previously, this transition also involved political realignment. On the surface, the drama appeared largely as a struggle between 'politicians' and 'capitalists'. Vladimir Putin, the new President, launched a well-publicised campaign against the Oligarchs, whom he accused of stealing state assets. Russia, he declared, would from now on be run not by the mafia, but by the 'dictatorship of the law'. The Oligarchs, some of whom supported Putin, rejected any wrongdoing, arguing that at the time, there was complete chaos, and, indeed, very few laws to break. Under the surface, however, the 'struggle' wasn't so much a fight between the government and the Oligarchs, as an attempt to alter the very nature of accumulation.

Ironically, one of the principal targets of these attacks was Vladimir Gusinsky, the Oligarch who has done the most to push Russian accumulation toward its next, transnational phase. In contrast to the other Oligarchs for whom the media was largely a political weapon, Gusinsky was quick to realise it could also be extremely lucrative in its own right. Initially, though, this realisation put him at odds with his fellow Oligarchs. Unlike in their more 'traditional' cash cows of energy, utilities and consumer goods, profit in the media business depended crucially on transnational integration on the ownership side, and on political liberalism on the consumption side.

The need for transnational integration meant that Gusinsky's foreign dealings were designed more to build ties than to set traps. He courted the friendship of Rupert Murdoch; brought in Newsweek as joint owner of his own newspaper Itogi; sold part of his NTV and TNT networks to the American Funds Group; acquired nearly a quarter of the Lauders' Central European Media; and of course, expanded his business in Israel. Here, in addition to his joint ownership of Ma'ariv, he also had stakes in Matav, Barak, Bezeq Internet and Dor Energy, as well as other holdings in partnership with Bank Hapoalim and United Mizrahi Bank (Broadcasting & Cable's TV International, 24 January 2000; Ha'aretz, 18 July 2000).

The other half of his media success depended on viewers' 'trust', or 'ratings' in the business lingo. This type of goodwill could be sustained only within the context of 'political liberalism' and 'freedom of the press', and, sure enough, Gusinsky became champion of both. Notwithstanding his earlier participation in the staged reinstatement of Yeltsin, Gusinsky's strong opposition to the war in Chechnya and its chief architect Putin, established him, at least in the West, as maverick and forebear of the 'New Russia'.

Needless to say, the bureaucracy and several of the Oligarchs didn't like this excessive 'openness'. And, so, once Putin became President in 2000, he immediately began harassing Gusinsky, who found himself detained on charges of forgery and fraud. The government also tried to wrestle away his Media Most, although this proved more difficult, since Gusinsky apparently eviscerated much of its assets. He himself settled, at least for the time being, in Spain, from where he continued to operate his increasingly transnational network.

The reach and complexity of this network is worth illustrating, if only briefly. In 1997, Israel was exploring the possibility of a gas project with Russia. One of the principal candidates on the Israeli side was Tahal, a water and infrastructure company, formerly owned by the government and recently acquired by a private consortium owned by Arison, Kardan and the Leumi Group. The director of the company was retired IDF general Yanush Ben-Gal, who at the time also chaired the state-owned Israel Aircraft Industry. Ben-Gal was closely associated with Dankners, whose Dor Energy was also interested in participating. The Dankners on their part had the right connections with the Likud government. They were also building up their relationship with Gusinsky, inviting him into partnership in Dor and Matav. Gusinsky was closely associated with Gazprom, which financed part of his media operations, and which was likely to take over the project on the Russian side. These connections were forging a year after Gusinsky and his friends reinstalled Yeltsin as President. It was therefore only natural that Viktor Chernomyrdin, former Prime Minister under Yeltsin and founder of state-owned Gazprom, was willing to assist Gusinsky in his various undertakings.

Gusinsky was also participating in Russian politics in yet another way, through his involvement with Russia's orthodox Jewish community. The relative cohesion of this community made it a natural interest group, and hence a prized asset to control. Israel on its part created for this purpose a semi-clandestine organisation, named Nativ, whose head, Ya'akov Kadmi, later joined Gusinsky as a business associate. Nativ, on its part, was saddling a struggle between two rival religious factions, both based in Israel, who fought for the hearts, minds and votes of the Russian Jews. One of these factions, the Russian Jewish Congress, was founded and presided by Gusinsky. The other faction, the Federation of Jewish Communities in the former Soviet Union (FJC), was founded and presided by an equally determined businessmen, Lev Leviev, whose religious support was drawn from the Lubavitch clan of Chabad Hassidim.

Leviev, a Russian-born Israeli, began his business career during the 1990s. When the Brodet Committee required that the banks unbundle their 'real' assets, he bought from the Leumi Group a controlling interest in a company named Africa-Israel. Then, using his connections with politicians and former KGB operatives in Angola, he managed to make Africa-Israel a partner, together with the Angolan government and Belgian investors, in the Angola Selling Corporation, or Ascorp. The deal gave him exclusive rights over the country's war-torn and crime-ridden diamond trade. It also increased his political leverage within Russia, where De Beers' diamond concession was about to expire. And for the time being at least, he seemed to have backed the right horse, teaming up with Berezovsky to support Putin's presidency. Berezovsky on his part, used his ORT TV channel to prop up Leviev's FJC in its successful bid to nominate Russia's Chief Rabbi (*Financial Times*, 11 July 2000).

The 'Fishman State'?

Whereas in Russia, the most demonised businessmen were the Oligarchs, in Israel it was Eliezer Fishman, the new 'Mephistopheles of finance'. As described in Chapter 4, Fishman rose to fame in the late 1970s as a highly sophisticated financier who briefly managed to outmanoeuvre the banks in their own stock market game, only to be buried under $300 million worth of unpaid obligations in the wake of the 1983 stock market crash. Ten years later, though, he was back, big time. Like a Phoenix rising from the ashes, Fishman managed not only to shake off his debts, but also to accumulate a massive portfolio of over a hundred companies – in real estate, commerce, finance and the media, among others. Many found the scope of his ownership, particularly in the 'information' sector, alarming. One journalist claimed that Fishman's power in this area made him 'the strongest man in Israel', while another went further to classify him as a 'new phenomenon' in Israeli reality, one which embodies centralised ownership and active control in the same person (*Ha'aretz*, 1 February 2000; 2 February 2000). Sooner or later, warned the Fishman bashers, this unstoppable machine would own everything, turning Israel into the 'Fishman State'.

Such fears, although not without basis, need to be qualified. To the extent that the state was being 'taken over', it was not by Fishman, but by transnational dominant capital. Power was indeed becoming increasingly centralised, but not in the hands of any one owner, or even several owners, but rather as an attribute of their *collective coordination*. The earning capacity of Fishman – and for that matter, of Bronfman, Arison and the Recanatis who owned even more – relied crucially on their direct relationship with all other owners; in addition, and perhaps more importantly, these earnings depended on the broader ideological hegemony of 'market capitalism', which dominated the state on its various organs, and which kept the underlying population, if not by conviction at least by confusion, sufficiently inactionary. Moreover, domestic owners, regardless of their relative power within Israel, could hardly exercise it in isolation from global developments. This was partly because they shared their ownership with foreign investors, but mostly since the process of global accumulation itself was crucial in determining what could and couldn't be done domestically. Indeed, over the past decade, the direction and patterns of Israeli and global accumulation have become increasingly correlated and often indistinguishable, a point to which we return toward the end of the chapter.

What made power appear somewhat new and different was the increasing centrality of financial markets, and that was also why Fishman stood out. His exceptional ability to both recognise imminent developments and effectively commodify them into capital made him a true 'captain of solvency'; in this sense, he was much like the legendary nineteenth century U.S. capitalist, Jay Gould, who let nothing detract him from his 'steadfast pursuit of strategic power and liquid assets' (Josephson 1934: 193). Fishman was the archetype 'wave watcher'. He thought, anticipated and acted via the equity and bond markets, constantly seeking to predict the 'next wave' of earning power. And given the 'forward-looking' nature of capitalisation, his success depended crucially on being able to buy such power *before* it became headline news. This ability enabled Fishman to outperform some of the more established groups, making him look omnipotent. Yet, as we shall see, his differential success remained dependent on these other groups' cooperation, consent and, ultimately, mutual fusion.

Fishman's extraordinary foresight was evident already in his early foray into real estate and commerce. After being burnt by the stock market crash in 1983, he preferred, as he put it, to talk to 'bricks and walls rather than people', and for a decade was busy buying only real estate (*Ha'aretz*, 18 February 2000). Most of his assets were acquired at bargain prices. These were obtained from the Kibbutzim (many of which were starving for cash, after having allowed Fishman and his partner Riger to 'manage' their portfolios in the 1980s); from the nearly bankrupt Histadrut, which unloaded the assets of its insurance company Hasneh; and from the Labour government, which was eager to sell him Jerusalem Economic Corporation and Industrial Buildings. His success in this area was spectacular. The reason, though, had less to do with his sudden love for bricks, and more with the changing political economy of Russia and the 'New Middle East', which pushed-pulled one million new immigrants to Israel, causing land prices to skyrocket. And indeed, between 1985 and 1995, real estate stock rose by 178 per cent in real terms, compared with 130 per cent for the market as whole, and Fishman, who bought many of his properties for pennies, made even more (Israel. Central Bureau of Statistics 1999: Table 9.12, p. 9.11). The same demographic change also contributed to his commercial success, particularly in the area of discount megastores, where he teamed up with Canadian supermarket giant Loblaw to challenge the oligopoly of Hamashbir, Blue Square and Supersol. By the mid-1990s, though, the real estate/commercial wave was clearly receding. 'The Israeli consumer', observed the sarcastic Fishman, 'is no longer content with low prices, and is now demanding a "shopping experience"' (*Ha'aretz*, 10 April 1998). It was clearly high time to look for a new wave.

And so Fishman started buying media and communication companies. His first major move was to try and get a cellular phone licence, in which he actually failed. By the mid-1990s, Israel already had two such companies – Pelephone, a joint venture of Bezeq and Motorola, and Cellcom, jointly owned by IDB, Bell South and the Safra group. Both of these got their licence for free, and, so, in 1996, the government decided it was time to issue a third licence, this time auctioned for real money. Fishman teamed up for the bid with several big players, including Morris Kahn and Koor, as well as Southwestern Bell (SBC), Mannesman, and Compagnie Générale des Eaux (CGE). Eventually, the licence went to the Partner consortium, led by Hutchison Wampoa of the Li family (see Figure 6.2). The consortium paid $400 million for this 'goodwill', which it immediately floated in New York, where its value quickly soared to over $4 billion.

Having lost a cellular battle had hardly dented Fishman's enthusiasm. To the contrary, he was determined to ride the wave by building his own communication empire (see Figure 6.2). And, indeed, soon enough he could boast that 'there is no one in Israel who is more involved in communication than me; no doubt I'm the biggest' (*Ha'aretz*, 18 February 2000). Although he didn't yet have his cellphone company, his telecom holdings already included phone operator Golden Lines, which he owned together with Kahn and Telecom Italia (after SBC left the partnership), along with an aspiration to devour part of the state monopoly Bezeq once the government finally put it on the blocks. His major coup, though, was gaining control over Israel's largest daily, *Yediot Aharonot*. In 1997, he took advantage of a family feud among the Moses clan, which had previously controlled the newspaper, to become the outfit's largest shareholder. *Yediot Aharonot* was a cash cow which gave Fishman over half of Israel's newspaper market. It was also a strategic asset which opened for him a gateway into electronic communication. The paper's large stake in the cable operator Golden Channels made Fishman a majority owner of that company; it also linked him to both IDB and UPC, which owned part of Golden Channels through their own cable company, Tevel; finally, *Yediot Aharonot*'s stake in the TV licence Reshet gave him access to television revenues.

Fishman's enthusiasm for communication was, as usual, prescient. Between 1996 and 1999, global telecommunication stock prices rose by over 350 per cent, and so did the shares of many Israeli communication companies. Significantly, though, this spectacular rise had little to do with profits; in fact, earnings per share, largely due to massive dilution, trended *downward* over the period. Yet, global investors lost none of their appetite. To the contrary. In 1996, they were still willing to pay no more than 20 dollars for every one dollar of current communication earnings (based on price-earning multiples). But as the euphoria spread, this number started rising and rising, reaching 40 dollars in 1997, 70 dollars in 1999, and a record 120 dollars in 2000 – before dropping back to less than 60 dollars by mid-2001, after the market 'corrected'.[17] The hype was so intense, that, in early 2000, the British government managed to sell five licences of 'third generation' cellular operators for as much as $34 billion, or $586 for every one of the island's inhabitants, while in August of that year, the German government auctioned its own licences for $45 billion (*The Economist*, 8 July 2000; *Financial Times*, 20 August 2000). Around the same time, Vodafone, a telecom company, purchased Airtouch for a price equivalent to $11,393 per existing subscriber, and Deutsche Telekom offered to buy VoiceStream based on $18,126 per subscriber (*Financial Times*, 21 July 2000). Excessive enthusiasm is of course not new, being part and parcel of equity

17   Computed based on the FTSE UK 350 Telecommunication Services Index, reported in McGraw-Hill (Online).

markets since their inception (Kindelberger 1978; Galbraith 1990). But the communication-led boom of the late 1990s certainly stood out in its magnitude: in the United States, it pushed the average price-earning multiple to over 30, its most 'expensive' level since 1870.

What drove this optimism? Or rather, how was this optimism *rationalised* during the euphoria, before the bitter correction deflated both prices and theory? The common explanation of the enthusiasts was technology. Improving communication, they maintained, would lower cost and increase competition, causing inflation to drop, interest rates to decline and risk premiums to contract. Whether true or not, though, such changes should affect all stocks, so the attraction of communication in particular must have come from expectations for *differential* profit growth. Where was such growth supposed to come from? Part of it, we were told, would come from market penetration. New technology, went the argument, substituted for old ways of doing things, and in the process enriched whoever happened to control it. Although this argument sounded reasonable for less developed countries, where the 'penetration potential' has for long kept investors excited, it was less persuasive for countries such as Israel. The number of Israeli cellular phone subscribers, for instance, rose from 130,000 in 1994, to 1 million in 1996, to 2 million in 1998, to 3 million in 2000, and given that Israel had only 6 million inhabitants, the market was clearly approaching saturation. The situation was similar in the cable business, where, in 1997, after seven years in operation, over 90 per cent of all households were already hooked up, compared with 66 per cent in the United States and only 7 per cent in Japan (*Ha'aretz*, 6 April 1997). True, admitted the enthusiasts, but such calculations were hopelessly backward-looking. For example, whereas yesterday's mobile phones were restricted to voice communication, today they already enabled us to hook onto the internet and e-mail, communicate through instant messaging, and access services such as travel management and Yellow Pages. Tomorrow, mobile phones would let us into the wonderful world of e-commerce, and after tomorrow, who knows (*The Economist*, 8 July 2000). In other words, although a simple headcount might suggest that markets such as Israel were close to saturation, the constant provision of *new* services was effectively making the process start over and over again.

The Politics of Communication Profits

Unfortunately, such argument confused 'industry' with 'business'. The real question here was not whether communication technology would expand and change everyday life, but would such change translate into *differential profit?* The 2001 crash of 'high-technology' stocks put a dent in such hopes. Communication technology was not easy to defend, and unless you managed to fend off competitors, your distributive share – as well as the whole profit pie

– could have easily shrank instead of growing. Even Amazon, the world's largest online retailer, couldn't show a single cent in profit, and after the initial euphoria, saw its market value collapse by 90 per cent. Moreover, as technical change blurred the traditional divides among different industries, there was little to prevent cross-business poaching from further eroding profit margins.

In other words, 'techno-profit', perhaps more than other types of profit, depended crucially on the extent to which technology could be 'protected'; as always, it wasn't technology per se, but the control over technology which mattered. And indeed, at least some of the hype surrounding the communication business was directly correlated with the changing nature of power.

The most important component of such power was undoubtedly the state. The Israeli government, of course, played a totally different tune, singing the praise of 'privatisation' and 'liberalisation'. In the late 1990s, a special committee (Wax–Brodet–Leon) warmly recommended that communication be deregulated into a 'completely competitive' sector; and before long, Likud Communication Minister, Limor Livnat, pompously announced that 'when I'm finished here, nobody will want this portfolio, since there will be little left to do.... The Israeli communication market will soon look like that of every advanced Western country, a completely competitive market' (*Ha'aretz*, 18 June 1998). Needless to say, such statements were misleading, to put it mildly. The state was in no way getting out of the communication business. On the contrary, its involvement was becoming deeper than ever. What changed was the form. Whereas earlier the state was itself an owner, now its policies – or rather, the impact of such policies on expected earnings – was gradually commodified as private capital in the hands of absentee owners. Such change in form should hardly surprise us, of course. The impact on profit of state action (or inaction) has long been commodified as capital, with investors routinely discounting into present value the expected effect of military spending, of protectionism, of lower taxes, and so on. State 'regulation' of communication profit was simply another step in the same direction.

Why was the state so crucial for 'techno-capitalisation'? In some areas, the answer was obvious. The wave spectrum, for instance, was a gift of nature belonging to no one in particular, and until recently indeed hardly a news item. Statist ideology and technological limitations restricted the business potential of broadcasting, leaving much of the spectrum in the hands of governments for purposes such as propaganda and military applications. But with technology advancing and liberalism making a comeback, wireless applications such as telephone, satellite broadcasting and the internet became lucrative business. Access to the wave spectrum has suddenly become a scarce 'resource', complete with its own expected profit and vendible capitalisation. Note, however, that profit and capitalisation here depended not on *accessing* the spectrum, which remained a gift of nature open to anyone, but on *excluding others* from such access. And this is where 'state regulation' became crucial, determining who got in and who stayed out, under what conditions, and with what consequences.

In other areas, such as cables, the role of state regulation was slightly different. Here, there were no natural limitations. Technically, anyone could lay down cables, and there was no practical limit on the number of competing wires which could be plugged into the same rational consumer. The consequence of such free-for-all chaos, of course, would be falling profit margins and business ruin, and that is precisely why state regulation was necessary. By restricting the number of cable operators and determining the conditions under which they operated, profits could be calibrated, almost at will. Again, the key question was who was doing the calibrating, how, and in whose interests.

Finally, the state had the broader role of 'defining' the proper boundaries between the different markets. The business problem here was that technical change tended to lower and sometimes eliminate entry barriers between different sectors, enabling cross-sector poaching of 'customer loyalty'. For instance, was cable TV part of the same market as satellite TV? Was television broadcasting a market of its own, or should it be treated together with telephone and the internet as part of a broader communication market? These were all crucial regulatory issues, since they determined the extent to which owners could trespass each other's territory, and hence the overall level and distribution of profit.

And so the battle for communication profit, in Israel as elsewhere, quickly became the 'battle for the state'. In 1990, the Israeli government divided the country between six cable companies, corresponding to mutually exclusive geographical regions. This helped, but only as a start. The large owners then took matters into their own hands, and began acquiring their smaller competitors until the number of companies was down to three: Matav owned by Dankner, Nimrodi and Gusinsky; Tevel held by IDB and UPC; and Golden Channels controlled by Fishman, Moses, and IDB/UPC through Tevel (see Figure 6.2). Although officially distinct, the three companies operated pretty much as a monopoly. On the production side, they used their jointly owned monopsony, ICP, to cut the cost of acquired programmes, while on the sales side, they charged almost identical prices, usually twice as high as those paid by Western European subscribers; the result was operating profit margins as wide as 65 per cent (*Ha'aretz*, 17 December 1999; 2 February 2000).

Most importantly, the three companies began coordinating their public policy stance. Initially, such coordination was unnecessary. Antitrust Commissioner David Tadmor, who previously represented Golden Channels as a private lawyer, was conveniently forthcoming; he did nothing to prevent their centralisation, and then woke up in 1999 to declare the obvious, namely that they were a monopoly. This belated regulatory insult hardly worried the cable companies; they lashed back at Tadmor, arguing that their relevant market was not cables, but television broadcasting in general, which they did not (yet) dominate. What worried them more was that some of their fellow capitalists, enticed by fat profit margins, wanted a share of the pie. The most important challenge came from a new satellite company, chaired by competition prophet David Brodet. The outfit, incorporated under the imaginative name of YES, promoted itself as a white knight fighting the evil cable barons. The facts, though, showed it was owned by similar heavyweights with much the same aspirations, including Arison, Alovich, AT&T, Telia, Poalim Investment, Bezeq, Migdal-Generali, and even one of the cable owners, IDB (see Figure 6.2).

And as the battle for profit heated up, the political arena was quickly divided into two opposing camps, both swearing allegiance to the good of the nation and the almighty consumer. On the one hand stood the supporters of YES, led by Finance Minister Avraham Shohat; on the other, the cable advocates led by Communication Minister Ben Eliezer. (Needless to say, none of these 'policy makers' dared voice a third option, let alone propose it as an actual 'policy'.) Wasting little time, the two camps began pounding each other. The cable companies tried to stall the YES licence for as long as possible, levelling veiled threats to sue state officials for damages, and keeping the supreme court busy with their petitions. Their 'foreign' partners, UPC and Southwestern Bell (SBC), pressured Prime Minister Netanyahu to annul the YES permit, and even had the American embassy accuse the government of undermining U.S. business interests.

The attack on YES, however, was merely a tactical bargaining chip. Satellite communication was of course too late to prevent, but by putting up a 'fight' and then 'conceding', the cable companies hoped to win a much bigger war. Their goal was threefold: first, to renew their exclusive free licence to deliver cable services for another 15 years; second, to extend this licence into internet and telephone services; and, third, to formally merge their three companies into one, jointly owned by Dankner, Nimrodi and Gusinsky (25 per cent), IDB and UPC (37 per cent), and Fishman and Moses (38 per cent) (Ha'aretz, 17 December 1999; 1 February 2000).

The main force behind this transformation was Eliezer Fishman. Although he vehemently denied having any interest in mergers and 'lazy money', exceptions to this rule were numerous and the cable union was surely one of them. Expected profits, he realised, depended not on politically segregating different technologies such as cable, satellite, television, phone and the internet, but rather on integrating them. Merger and conglomeration were therefore essential; and since expected earnings could be sold as current hype, Fishman was eager to move quickly, before the stock market bubble burst away with his premium. Based on comparable 'synergies', he hoped to float the merged company on Wall Street for as much as $10 billion, or five times its current value. And since time was pressing, he notified Communication Minister Ben Eliezer, that 'if the government didn't immediately accept his demands, he would close shop and move his businesses abroad' (Ha'aretz, 18 February 2000).

The YES consortium of course realised the pending danger. If Fishman and his partners had their way, their own exclusivity in satellite delivery would be at risk. Wasting no time, they demanded that the cable companies be barred from simultaneously handling delivery and contents, and that they be prevented from merging. They also had their representative, Finance Minister Shoat, strongly object the renewal of the cable licence, and demanding that it be instead re-auctioned for real money. The cable companies retaliated by unleashing their own watchdogs in the Communication Ministry. Their chief spokesman, Communication Minister Ben Eliezer, claimed that YES' stalling tactics not only harmed consumers, but also undermined Israel's technological competitiveness. Moreover, as he saw it, a cable monopoly was exactly what Israel needed, since its combined force would enable it to effectively 'compete' against the state monopoly Bezeq in telephone and internet. And last but not least, he proposed that, in light of their already massive infrastructure investments, the cable companies be spared the licence fees (*Ha'aretz*, 7 January 2000).

As the bickering went on, however, competition grew increasingly 'unregulated', turning profits into losses. Furthermore, in 2000, the 'high-tech' market finally crashed, making public offerings difficult and debt services burdensome. It was clearly time for a truce. In 2001, the cable companies therefore agreed to forgo any claim regarding satellite delivery, in return for full ownership of their physical infrastructure, including indefinite operating rights. And since the two parties came to an understanding, the government was no longer fussy about money. Whereas initially the Finance Ministry demanded $1.5 billion for the cable concession, in the end it settled for a mere $150 million (*Ha'aretz*, 7 December 2001).

High-technology communication, with its centralised ownership and deep government involvement, was obviously neither 'liberal' nor 'competitive', but rather *political* in the wider sense of the term. The key question was *who* wielded power. Was it the 'regulator', who at least in principle could carve the communication sector as he saw fit? Or was the regulator himself becoming part of the capitalisation process? Was Prime Minister Barak, who in 1999 was called to act as a modern Salomon in the cable–satellite dispute, omnipotent? Or was he merely a puppet, an eleventh player in what one journalist called 'a ten billion dollar story that only ten people understand'? (*Ha'aretz*, 19 November 1999). Was Israel's Antitrust Commission, which in 2000 was ranked by *Global Competition Review* as the world's second best after Germany's, indeed almighty? Or did it simply follow the path of least resistance?

These questions were by no means limited to Israel. In 2000, for instance, the U.S. government forced Japan, with much fanfare, to have NTT, its state-owned telephone monopoly, cut its connection charges to U.S. telecom companies. Was President Clinton advancing here the vague interest of the 'global economy', as he put it, or was his government part of a much more concrete struggle of differential accumulation? (*Financial Times*, 20 July 2000). On the face of it, with communication prices being decided at the highest level of international politics, it would seem that ultimate power lay in the hands of prime ministers and presidents; and indeed, in a recent gathering of the world's largest media moguls, one of the chief concerns was the 'threat of industry regulation' (*Financial Times*, 20 July 2000). But then, if that was the case, why all the fuss about private ownership? If governments could regulate prices, as well as contents, services, the number of operators, and so on, who needed the Fishmans of the world? The common answer was that private enterprise was more efficient than public ownership, and that its fierce competition ensured that consumers enjoyed the benefits. Yet, supposing this were true, why were governments the world over engaged in 'benign neglect', allowing ownership to become increasingly centralised and therefore less 'competitive'? Was it merely the consequence 'regulatory mistakes' as one Israeli journalist called them, or was it rather a deliberate policy of 'non-intervention', so that the large owners can work out their own arrangements? (*Ha'aretz*, 18 August 2000).

And, indeed, a quick look at Figure 6.2 above should make clear how difficult it was to even begin talking about competition and 'free enterprise' in this context. Although there were now many more 'operators' than ever before (and certainly more than during the statist stage of government monopoly), these operators were hardly independent. Instead, they were part of a single 'ownership alloy', linking the various segments of dominant capital into a structure which could no longer be disentangled. And this was only one sector. If we were to expand our picture to cover the *entire* business arena, ownership connections would quickly grow so dense that they could not be even deciphered. This also explained why new entrants, even ones as cunning and aggressive as Fishman, could not really 'take over' a business sector. As newcomers, their only way to survive was by building ties with the other dominant groups. And that was precisely what Fishman was busy doing since his comeback. Although he had several opportunities to make large gains by striking the big players, he always preferred to show his power rather than use it. For instance, the ownership battle in which Yitzhak Tshuva wrestled Delek away from IDB, was anticipated by Fishman, who for several months accumulated Delek's shares. Although he could have taken over the company himself, Fishman preferred to let someone else humiliate the Recanatis. Forgoing Delek was peanuts compared to the benefit of future cooperation with IDB.

The first implication is that, far from creating greater competition, rivalry and friction, every successful entrant – from Danker, through Nimrodi, to Gusinsky, to Fishman – helped to further consolidate the *combined* power of dominant capital. Unless such entrants became part of the structure, they would be crushed; and becoming part of the structure required that they weave themselves into it, adding more ties and in the process making the whole structure appear stronger. The second implication is that when coming to analyse the political economy of modern capital, there is no point in looking at different 'industries', or even 'sectors' defined along *production* lines. Not that these were unimportant, only that they could be misleading unless first situated within the broader structure of *ownership* and its political-economic underpinnings. And when dealing with ownership, the proper framework was quickly becoming global. As we have seen, Israel's capitalist development has been, from its inception, part of a broader global process. Until recently, domestic and international accumulation were mostly *linked* in various ways; but during the 1990s, the two processes have grown increasingly *integrated* through the transnationalisation of ownership itself. We turn to examine this later process more closely now.

Transnationalism and Israeli Technology

During the 1990s, the discovery of Israel by foreign investors had local politicians elated. Global capitalists were not only hailing the country's liberalisation and 'high-tech' credentials, but also putting their money where their mouth was, sending capital inflow soaring from zero at the beginning of the decade, to 5 per cent of GDP by its end. For former Prime Minister Netanyahu, this was clear evidence that the country was on its way to becoming a 'high-technology "tiger"'. Israel, in his view, was 'the Silicon Valley of the Eastern Hemisphere' and 'one of the great technological and entrepreneurial successes in the world'. Although the panacea didn't prevent him from losing the elections, his Labour successor, Barak, was equally enthusiastic. Israel, he declared, was evidently 'different from any other place in the world', a country of 'enormous vitality stemming from the richest possible genetic pool', which helped it become 'the most powerful of all states lying in a 1,500 km radius from Jerusalem'.[18]

But then was Jerusalem really becoming the centre of the 'high-tech' world? Was this language not a bit megalomaniacal for a country whose entire population was smaller than Chicago's? Was Israel indeed so important for foreign investors, and if so, why? What were the underlying forces integrating it into the global political economy? Did these forces justify the hyper-optimism of Israeli politicians? Did 'everybody' benefit from these developments, or was it only a minority, with the rest of the population paying the price? So far in this chapter, we have emphasised developments within Israel, keeping such questions in the background. Now, however, as we approach the end of our book, it is time to refocus the analysis, putting global developments back at the centre, and Israel, where it belongs, on the periphery.

Why Invest in Israel?

During the 1990s, investors' interest in Israel stemmed from three basic reasons. The first of these is a simple breadth rationale, reminiscent of the 'Coca Cola

18   Netanyahu is cited from the *Financial Times*, 30 January 1996, 5 July 1996, and from *Business Week*, 17 February 1997. Barak is cited from *Ha'aretz*, 19 May 2000.

Kid Syndrome'. We name this syndrome after *The Coca-Cola Kid*, an ironic film by Dusan Makavejev about a troubleshooting Coca-Cola executive, sent to Australia to fix a 'problem' in the local subsidiary. The nature of the problem: a 'blank spot' in the Australian desert, where Coca-Cola apparently had no sales. During the early 1990s, the situation in Israel was similar. For years, many transnational companies stayed away from the country, scared off by regional instability and the Arab Boycott. When the circumstances changed after the 1993 Oslo Accord, they discovered Israel was an empty spot on their maps, and rushed in with their troubleshooters to quickly fill the void. Entrants in this category included consumer-good giants Kimberly Clark, Nestlé, Unilever, and Procter & Gamble; food chains such as McDonald's and Grand Metropolitan (Burger King); raw material investors like British Gas and Volkswagen; financial groups such as Generali, Lehman Brothers, Citigroup, Republic Bank, HSBC, Chase Manhattan and Bank of America; as well as many of the world's communication giants charted in Figure 6.2. In addition to these 'direct' investments, many large companies and institutional investors began building up an Israeli 'portfolio', acquiring stocks and bonds on the open Tel Aviv and New York markets.

The second reason for investing in Israel was the government's remarkable hospitality. As we have seen earlier in this chapter, many assets taken over by foreign investors, particularly those privatised by the government and the Histadrut, were bought at bargain prices. The fullest royal treatment, however, was given to green-field investors, of which the most publicised case was Intel's. Although the company set up an Israeli subsidiary already in 1974, until recently its activities were mainly in R&D, an area where Israel was reputed to have a comparative advantage. In 1996, however, Intel made an apparently strange decision, announcing its intention to build a $1.6 billion production facility, nicknamed 'Fab 18', to manufacture microchips and flash memory. The decision was unusual since production of this sort was considered 'low-tech', and was normally carried out in developing countries, where the cost of unskilled labour was far lower. But then this specific decision had little to do with labour. According to the Israeli law of the time, green-field investors putting up factories in special 'development zones' were entitled to a grant worth up to 38 per cent of their investment, or $600 million in the case of Intel. The government also agreed to supply various facilities worth an additional $300 million, so all in all, Intel got a state subsidy equivalent to $900 million, or 56 per cent of its original investment. The public justification for the deal was that the plant created new jobs – 1,500 working for Intel and another 1,500 working for its subcontractors. The jobs were pretty expensive, however, each costing the government $300,000; for comparison, the average state subsidy per job in investor-friendly Ireland was only $15,000 (*Davar*, Weekly Supplement, 19 April 1996). But then the purpose of course was never to give this money to the plant's workers, whose annual salaries of $10,000 were deemed more than adequate. The real goal was more profit.

Exactly how much more was hard to tell since Intel kept this information to itself; the general order of magnitude, however, was easy enough to approximate. Operating at full capacity, the plant was expected to generate $1 billion or more in annual sales. Assuming pre-tax margins equal to Intel's average of one-third, this meant $333 million in annual gross profit. Now, in contrast to the United States, where Intel paid over 30 per cent of its income in taxes, in Israel it had until then managed to pay close to none. Assuming this tradition persisted, net profit would be the same as gross earnings; or $333 million. In relation to Intel's declared investment of $1 billion, this represented a 33 per cent rate of return on equity – 50 per cent higher than the firm's worldwide average of 22 per cent (computed from Moody's Online). And that too was probably a gross understatement, since Intel had the habit of using transfer pricing to inflate the value of its investment way beyond what it actually put in.[19]

This 'grant bonanza' was of course hard to ignore, and before long numerous transnational companies, from Volkswagen, through Motorola, to Toshiba, to Tower Semiconductor, were asking the government to support massive subsidy-maximising 'investments'. Even Intel could not resist and tabled expansion plans worth $2–3.5 billion. The government, although still enthusiastic, was overwhelmed; and being unable to come up with so much cash, reluctantly cut the subsidy down to 20–24 per cent.

Yet, the tidal wave of foreign money, instead of receding, continued, with much of the inflow directed into buying local 'high-technology' companies. This type of inflow was the third, and increasingly most important reason for investing in Israel. And strangely enough, there was nothing Israeli capitalists loved more than this invasion. Indeed, the ultimate dream of most startups and oligarchs alike was having their companies cannibalised by a large trans-national firm. From the perspective of the 'victim', the rationale was obvious: buyers often paid hundreds of millions and eventually billions of dollars, making the original owners fabulously rich. The motive of the buyers, however, was less clear. Why did they spend so much, particularly when the companies they bought often had only a few dozen employees, negligible sales, and little or no profit?

Competition, Power and Waste

As noted earlier, one of the basic tenets of the 'new economy' was that technical change bolstered competition. 'High-tech', argued the enthusiasts, enabled

19 In 1984, for instance, Israel's State Controller reported that of the $123 million Intel declared as investment, $109 million were financed by the government, with the remaining $14.5 million actually costing the company a mere $1.5 million. In other words, Intel's effective investment amounted to slightly more than 1 per cent of what it declared (*Ksafim*, 21 May 1984).

nimble innovators to challenge corporate dinosaurs; even the Marxists, when examining contemporary conditions, began drawing parallels with the unregulated markets of the nineteenth century; for many people competition was once more a synonym for capitalism. But was this all true? Was technical change in general, and 'high-tech' in particular, indeed making the world more competitive? Like all self-evident truths, this one too merits a re-examination.

One basic indicator for the 'intensity' of competition is the markup: when firms compete more vigorously, their markup gets squeezed; when they collude, the markup widens. Figure 6.3 provides some relevant evidence on the evolution of the markup in the United States, which is measured here by the share in value added of non-labour income (comprising pre-tax profit, rent and

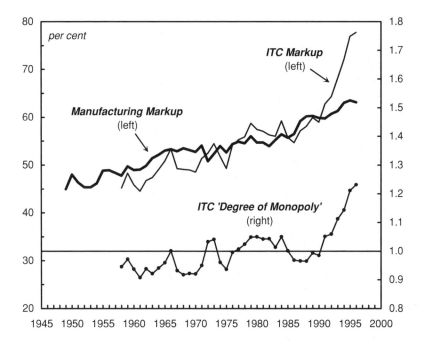

Figure 6.3   The 'New U.S. Economy': Knowledge or Power?

NOTE: *ITC* stands for Information Technology and Communication. The index here comprises hardware and equipment firms in the following 10 sectors (with SIC codes in parentheses): calculating and accounting equipment (3578), office machines nec (3579), radio & TV receiving sets (3651), semiconductors & related devices (3674), electronic capacitators (3675), electronic resistors (3676), electronic coils & transformers (3677), electronic connectors (3678), process control instruments (3823), instruments to measure electricity (3825) (definition based on Lynn Margherio et al. *The Emerging Digital Economy*, US Department of Commerce, Washington, DC, 1998, p. A1-19). The *Markup* is defined as the per cent share of non-labour income in value added. The '*Degree of Monopoly*' is given as a ratio between the ITC and Manufacturing markups.
SOURCE: U.S. Department of Commerce through McGraw-Hill (Online).

interest). The upper part of the chart displays two markup series – one for the manufacturing sector as a whole, the other for a selected subset of ten information technology and communication industries (ITC).[20]

The data indicate that during the second half of this century, the intensity of competition in manufacturing actually *declined*, with the markup rising to 63 per cent in the mid-1990s, up from 45 per cent in the late 1940s. A similar process is evident in the ITC sector, with the markup rising pretty much in tandem with the manufacturing average. Since the early 1990s, however, the two series diverged: while the manufacturing markup continued along its long-term uptrend, in the ITC sector it broke off, zooming from 59 per cent in 1990, to 78 per cent in 1996, the last year for which data are available. The bottom of the chart plots a measure of the 'degree of monopoly' of the ITC sector, computed as the ratio of the two markup series (ITC relative to manufacturing, of which it was a subset).[21] Based on this latter index, ITC was generally more competitive than manufacturing until the late 1980s (the degree of monopoly being below one), and less and less competitive than manufacturing since the early 1990s (degree of monopoly greater than one, and rising).

Now, if there was indeed a 'one-to-one' link here, leading from technology to competition, according to the chart this link must have been *negative*. As technology advanced over the past 50 years, profit margins rose; and when technical change accelerated since the early 1990s, profit margins – particularly in those sectors where the acceleration was most pronounced – soared. Technical change, so it seemed, actually *undermined* competition.

At first sight, this conclusion seems perplexing. Doesn't the spread of technical 'know-how' work to loosen market power? The answer is yes, it does. But then, technology itself is only one side of the process; the other side is the protection of technology, and it is the *balance* between them which determines power and markups. Of course, neither technology nor its protection can be quantified, so this 'balance' cannot be measured. What can be observed, though, is the 'imprint' it leaves on the markup. A falling markup suggests technical progress out-stepping protection and exclusion, a rising markup implies the opposite. Clearly, neither outcome depends on the pace of technical change per se. Thus, slow technical progress, provided that its protection builds up even more slowly, would end up leading to lower markups, making the

20 The U.S. Department of Commerce defines the Information Technology Sector as an aggregate of 40 different industries, covering hardware, software and services, communication equipment, and communication services (Margherio et al. 1998). For many of these industries, relevant data are available only since 1987. In our computations here we therefore concentrated on a sample of 10 hardware and equipment industries, for whom the data go back to 1958. These figures are of course not entirely accurate inasmuch as the *industrial* classifications on which they are based do not exactly overlap with the underlying *business* structure of firms.

21 The 'degree of monopoly' concept, mentioned already in Chapter 2, was proposed by Michael Kalecki (1943a) as a way of using income distribution indicators to link microeconomic structures with macroeconomic dynamics.

world look more 'competitive'. On the other hand, and this is probably what lies behind Figure 6.3, if technology advances in leaps and bounds, but its protection consolidates even faster, the result would be *fatter* margins.

One way of defending new technology is by enforcing 'intellectual property rights'. And, indeed, such enforcement seems to have expanded in recent decades. U.S. annual patent registration, for instance, increased by 150 per cent since 1980, to 275,000. Moreover, a growing proportion of such patents focus not on production, but directly on the business process, appropriating activities such as 'selling professional advice over the internet', or 'one-click buying'. Recently, some companies even moved into so-called 'strategic patenting', whose declared purpose was to protect *anticipated* technology (*The Economist*, 8 April 2000).

The second, and perhaps more effective counter-force to technical change is corporate amalgamation. The vendibility of capital means that even if dominant firms are unable to develop new technology in house, they can always buy it through corporate takeover. And, indeed, during the 1990s, this latter strategy was adopted by many large ITC firms, such as AOL, Microsoft, Lucent, 3Com, Nortel, and most notably, Cisco. The latter company started in the early 1980s as a local project to connect computer equipment at Stanford University. By the late 1990s, it was already a network equipment giant, with 40 per cent of the big corporate market, 18 per cent of the small and medium firm market, and 33 per cent of the internet service provider market. In 2000, this leading position pushed Cisco's sales revenues to $19 billion, its net profits to $2.7 billion, and its market capitalisation to half a trillion dollars, making it the world's most valuable company (Moody's Online; *Business Week*, 13 September 1999). Much of this growth, though, came not from developing new technology, but from buying it: between 1993 and 2000, Cisco took over 55 companies, worth more than $24 billion, for which it paid mostly with its own shares (Moody's Online; *The Economist*, 8 April 2000). According to its CEO, John Chambers, during the market boom of the late 1990s the company was willing to pay between $500,000 and $3 million per 'acquired' employee, and the reason was simple. With the exception of its early invention of routers, almost all of Cisco's subsequent technology came from the companies it bought. And Cisco was hardly alone in this; most 'high-technology' giants adopted the same model, spending on such 'intangibles' as much as $100 billion in 1998, up from $15 billion in 1990 (*The Economist*, 4 December 1999).

At the time, the popular explanation for these 'techno-mergers' was that the large companies really had no choice. Since innovation was effective only when done in small firms, or so went the argument, the giants had to wait patiently for the innovators to do their job, and then buy them out. There was another possibility, however, and that was that the large firms could certainly innovate, but simply found it cheaper to have others do the work for them. This latter rationale was eloquently described by *Fortune*:

To a certain extent, industry leaders such as America Online, Cisco Systems and Microsoft are just outsourcing part of their research and development to Silicon Valley, letting the free market apportion R&D budget to different products and independent teams. The market also provides a mechanism (called customers) to validate the results. Then the AOLs and the Ciscos use their stock as currency to buy the startup whose products are most in demand; those products then contribute (theoretically, at least) to future revenues and profit growth, giving the behemoths more currency to buy more startups. Many of the companies that aren't bought simply shrivel and die. (Schonfeld 1999)

The latter process had two important implications. First, it meant a significant income transfer from society to large ITC firms, with massive waste on the way. If Cisco or Lucent were to develop the technology themselves, they would have to bear the cost of both failure and success. But since they let others do it for them and then bought only the best outcome, they ended up paying mostly for success. From their own perspective, whether the price they paid was 'expensive' or 'cheap' could be judged only in retrospect, relative to future profits. From the viewpoint of society, though, the process was bound to generate enormous waste. The main reason was the absence of any effective mechanism to 'regulate' the number of aspiring innovators, who, as a matter of business principle, did not share their knowledge; inevitably, they ended up duplicating each other, only to see most of their inventions – some of which were very good, but not good enough – dumped on the garbage heap.

Second, the process serves to explain how profit margins in the ITC sector could soar, despite the springing into life of millions of startups. In reality, most startup companies did not compete with the large ITC firms, but rather catered to their needs. The main reason for this bifurcation was the *integrative* nature of the ITC technology. Since ITC was inherently about 'connectivity', profit in this business depended crucially on controlling the various links. Now, given the availability of many connection paths, only those with so-called 'complete solutions' stood a chance; this in turn meant that ITC companies must be *very large*, and that they must *cooperate*, openly or tacitly, on matters ranging from common technical standards to the transnational politics of intellectual property rights. Under these circumstances, most small companies had neither hope nor desire to challenge the inner circle of ITC giants. Their main promise to riches was to serve rather than fight, which they did by developing *specific* technologies to augment the giants' *overall* differential power. The result was a two-tier competition, with small firms fighting each other in a life and death trench war, only to bolster the differential accumulation of big ones. And, indeed, according to a recent study by Multex, a consulting company, during 1995–99, the top three firms – Intel, Microsoft and Oracle – managed to pocket half the profit of Nasdaq's leading 4,200 companies (*Ha'aretz*, 16

August 2001). This combination of competition, waste and power is crucial for understanding the development of 'high-technology' in Israel.

Israel's Silicon Wady: The Big 'Sale'

During the bull market of the 1990s, global ITC executives loved to praise Israel as the 'core of the internet industry', the place to be for any 'meaningful internet player'. And why wouldn't they? Israeli engineers and programmers developed for them new ITC technologies on the cheap, and praising the 'employee of the month' was always a good way to encourage harder work and further government support. But describing Israel as a 'core' was a bit excessive. The business core was still the United States and Europe. Israel was of course connected to this core, but largely as a 'putting out' system. Its companies were setting neither the pace of events, nor their trajectory. Indeed, for the most part they were simply trying to guess where the global bandwagon was going, and what technology to develop so that the giants would take them along for the ride.

This 'putting out' relationship began to emerge in the mid-1990s, with the acquisition of firms such as Nicecom by 3COM (for $53 million), of Uvic by AOL ($14.5 million), of Scorpio by U.S. Robotics ($80 million), and of Orbotech by Applied Materials ($285 million) (*Ha'aretz*, 28 November 1997). But it was only in 1998, with the publicised acquisition by AOL of Mirabilis for $407 million, that the true nature of the process came into focus. When it was sold, Mirabilis was a small outfit with no sales, no profits, and no idea how to generate them. In fact, even its software – an instant messaging system named ICQ (and pronounced 'I-seek-U') – was hardly sophisticated, having cost a mere $3 million to develop. But the buyer was after a totally different prize: ICQ's 14 million users. Mirabilis could do little with these users; for AOL they were a gold mine. Internet service providers such as AOL lived and died by the number of subscribers, and ICQ, distributed freely on the internet, gave them exclusive access to millions, with hopefully many more to come. And indeed, by 2000, with ICQ already part of AOL, the number of registered users soared to 70 million, of which 20 million were hooked on regularly for three hours a day. Notably, in this struggle for 'consumer loyalty', timing was everything. Mirabilis and AOL succeeded because they were the first to understand it and quick to act. Had they waited a while longer before signing their deal, newcomers with better products could have easily depreciated their underlying 'goodwill' to nil. And indeed, Microsoft, having entered instant messaging only a year later, found itself fighting an uphill battle, trying to wrestle AOL 'loyalists' away from their ICQ addiction.

After the Mirabilis deal, the pattern was set, with more and more takeovers of Israeli startups by ITC giants, some of which – such as the $1.6 billion sale of DSPC to Intel, the $4.5 acquisition of Chromatis by Lucent, and the $4.5

takeover of MMC by AMCC – ranging in the billions. In most cases, the target was not a production facility, but rather an R&D outfit with some type of 'goodwill'. These 'immaterial assets', however, be they special technology or customer loyalty, were valuable only insofar as they could be protected; in other words, the acquisition was not of technology, but of power over technology. Most importantly, such power was typically ineffective unless embedded within the bigger mega-machine of the acquirer.

Indeed, size was so important here that even Israel's largest ITC company, ECI Telecom, found it was too small for the brave new world of 'high-tech'. Controlled by Koor, with IDB as a minority shareholder, ECI employed 5,000 workers, who in 1999 generated $1.1 billion in sales and $102 million in net income. Its market value, however, was a mere $3 billion – less than what Lucent paid in 2000 for Chromatis's few dozen workers and their cyber-optic technology. The comparison is particularly ironic not only since many of Chromatis's workers came from ECI, but also because, at the time, ECI already possessed better technology in this very field. ECI, however, was caught off guard, and in this business late often meant never. After the Chromatis deal, both Lucent and Cisco had the required technology in their armoury, so ECI could not sell it to them again. And so Koor threw in the towel, announcing it would break ECI into five separate companies, list them in New York, and pray for 'release' of value.

But then here lay the problem. Since what the large buyers acquired was specialised knowledge, they tended to need only 'one of each'; and given that there were only so many AOLs, Intels or Lucents around, there could be only so many happy Mirabilises, DSPCs and Chromatics. For all the rest, the prospects were dim. And indeed, even at the height of the 'high-tech' euphoria, Israel had already begun to accumulate 'living dead' startups, companies whose technology was deemed inferior, and to whom venture capital was no longer available. In 2000, the value added of all startup companies, mostly in R&D, accounted for as much as 2 per cent of Israel's GDP. Yet, to the extent that this R&D aimed at making the companies attractive for takeover, it was much like treasure hunting. Sometimes, a lucky hunter would hit the jackpot and be promptly bought out by an ITC giants; but for the most part, the R&D effort would be entirely wasteful.

Of course, not all Israeli 'high-technology' companies sought a buyer. Many have in fact tried to make it alone, and some even managed to gain global prominence. In all cases, though, their fate was decided by power, not technology. During the early 1990s, Israeli 'high-tech' startups were a hot commodity on Wall Street. Technical innovations from the likes of Scitex, Indigo, Netmanage, Madge, IIS and Sapience, were seen as revolutionary, and the companies owning them were valued in the billions. The most promising was Geotek, which used military-turned-civilian telecom technology to attract half a billion dollars in venture capital from George Soros, Claridge, Vanguard, and General Motors. Within a few years, however, these companies managed to accumulate well over $1 billion in combined losses, and in most cases saw their share prices beaten to pulp. The reason was simple. They all had 'cutting edge' technology, but none of the global power to protect it.

In contrast, the few Israeli ITC companies which did grow into 'independent' stars all had this order reversed, with technology *subordinated* to power. The most noted of these were Comverse, Amdocs, and Check Point. By the end of the 1990s, the three companies, all listed in New York, had a combined workforce of more than 13,000, sales of $1.7 billion, net profit of $400 million, and market capitalisation of $50 billion – equivalent to 77 per cent of the entire Tel Aviv Stock Exchange. Their growth was both rapid and consistent: from 1996 to 1999, Check Point's net profits rose by 85 per cent annually; Comverse's by 83; and Amdocs' by 60 (Moody's Online).

And yet, although successful, all three companies were in fact far less 'independent' then they looked. Take Amdocs. The company, founded in 1982 by would-be Israeli billionaire Morris Kahn, was the world's leading provider of billing services to large telephone operators. It had only several dozen clients, with the top six accounting for over half the sales. Most importantly, its biggest customer, U.S.-based SBC, was also its largest owner, having bought half the company from Kahn in 1984, and as of 1998 still owning the largest stake of 26.5 per cent (*Ha'aretz*, 1 June 1998). Comverse, like Amdocs, was also a world leader in its field of voice messaging systems, having its voice cells embedded in 45 per cent of all mobile phones sold around the world. The company, founded in 1984, grew rapidly, and in 1998 was included in the Nasdaq 100 and S&P 500 indices, the first Israeli firm to have had the honour. However, since the mid-1990s, its field began to attract giants such as Lucent and Unisys which acquired Comverse-like companies, forcing the latter into similar amalgamation tactics. Its founder and CEO, Kobi Alexander, began talking about turning his company into an 'Israeli Cisco'. And, indeed, during the 1990s, Comverse took over eleven companies, including an $860 million merger with its main competitor, U.S.-based Boston Technologies, and a $550 million acquisition of eXalink, an Israeli startup (Moody's Online). Until recently, Check Point remained the most 'independent' of the three. Founded in 1993, the company became famous for its 'Firewall' software which protected internet systems from outside invaders. Defending profit growth, however, was a bit trickier, and here Check Point had to rely on ITC giants such as Sun, Hewlett Packard, IBM, MCI, Nokia and Deutsche Telekom to sell its software. The arrangement worked well, since, by giving these firms a 'cut' of its sales, Check Point effectively turned them from potential foes into allies (*Ha'aretz*, 25 January 1998).

Perhaps most importantly, none of these three firms could be easily labelled as 'Israeli'. They were registered and traded in New York, their head offices were in the United States, and most of their shares were owned by global investors. In Check Point, for instance, only 28 per cent of the stocks was held by the Israeli founders and managers; in Comverse 10 per cent; and in Amdocs a mere 5 per cent (in 1999 Morris Kahn sold much of his stake for $1.1 billion to U.S. investors). Last but not least, by the end of the 1990s well over half their workforce was already outside the country.

End of the Road?

The 'de-Israelisation' of Israeli firms has been going on for some time. By 2000, there were already 110 'Israeli' companies listed in New York, with a market value twice that of the 665 companies listed in Tel Aviv. An estimated 60 to 90 per cent of all new Israeli startups filed for a U.S. charter, and the state of Delaware even opened an office in Jerusalem to facilitate the process (*Ha'aretz*, 2 August 2000). Much of the haemorrhage has been blamed on the convenience of American tax laws and regulations, which made mergers and acquisitions – the *raison d'être* of most Israeli starups – easier and cheaper for U.S.-based companies. Trying to 'correct' the problem, Israel has unilaterally recognised corporate registration in the United States (naturally without asking for the same in return). It also moved to facilitate outward transfers of state-financed technology, as well as to lower capital gains tax on foreign takeovers of Israeli companies. And yet, legal reform alone could hardly reverse the trend.

In a world of free capital mobility, corporate location is primarily a question of differential profitability. Now, from the viewpoint of 'high-tech' companies, conditions in Israel could hardly get any better. This is illustrated in Table 6.1, which puts selected Israeli R&D indicators in a broader context. Consider first civilian research and development. In 1996, the last year for which data are available, Israel devoted 2.3 per cent of its GDP to this end, roughly the same as the OECD average. Focusing on civilian R&D alone, however, is highly misleading. Most of Israel's successful ITC companies were intimately linked to the military. The more established of these, such as Tadiran, ECI, Elbit and Elron, owed their initial success to IDF procurement, whereas younger ones, such as Check Point, Comverse, DSPC and Libit, were founded by veterans of IDF communication, intelligence, and computer units. (One of these military units was aptly labelled by its members as 'The Secret Unit for Producing Millionaires'.) Since the IDF did not protect its research and development by patents, its veterans took the liberty to do so instead, creating, according to one count, over 40 companies, with profits in the hundreds of millions and market capitalisation in the billions (*Ha'aretz*, Annual Supplement, 15 December 1999). The Israeli government keeps secret the amount it spends on military R&D; this, though, could be roughly estimated in the order of 2 per cent of GDP, putting Israel's overall R&D at 4.3 per cent of GDP – 85 per cent above the OECD average, and 30 per cent more than Sweden, the next country in line.[22]

22 In the U.S., UK and France, the three OECD countries with major defence budgets, roughly 15 per cent of the R&D is military (Israel. Central Bureau of Statistics 2000). Now, assuming military R&D is proportionate to overall military spending, and given that the share of military spending in GDP is three times larger in Israel than in these three countries, the implication is that the military accounts for 45 per cent of Israel's total R&D. With civilian R&D being 2.3 per cent of GDP, overall R&D – civilian and military – should then be in the order of 4.3 per cent of GDP.

Table 6.1   Comparative R&D Indicators

	Israel	OECD
R&D as a share of GDP	4.3%	2.3%
Government finance of private R&D	25.8%	6.9%
Engineers per 10,000 people	135	85 (U.S.A.) 75 (Japan)
Education spending as a share of GDP	9.4%	6.1%

SOURCE: Israel. Central Bureau of Statistics (2000); Bank Hapoalim (2000).

Looking more closely at civilian R&D, in 1996 the Israeli government accounted for 41.9 per cent of the total, somewhat higher than the OECD average of 35.5 per cent. But then that too is misleading. For a business firm, the key issue is how much of its own R&D is shouldered by the government, and here the Israeli state was exceptionally generous. Whereas in the OECD, governments financed on average 6.9 per cent of private R&D, in Israel the comparable figure was 25.8 per cent. According to the Institute for Advanced Strategic and Political Studies in Jerusalem, a right-wing think-tank advocating 'lean government', between 1968 and 1998 the Office of the Chief Scientist passed on to private firms a cumulative subsidy of $3.8 billion, measured in 1999 prices; less than 15 per cent of this money was repaid in royalties (Raskin 1999). Officials at the Industrialists' Association readily admitted that 'the grant money of the Chief Scientist was the "life line" of Israeli high technology' (*Ha'aretz*, 17 August 1999); and indeed, based on Raskin's study, in 1997 the subsidy accounted for almost 20 per cent of the pre-tax profit of ten leading 'high-technology' firms. Last but not least, the Israeli tax authorities were especially lenient with 'high-tech' companies, which typically enjoy tax holidays of two to ten years, extendable indefinitely for rapidly growing firms. The result: an effective tax rate of around 15 per cent, compared to 30–45 per cent in the United States and Europe (*Ha'aretz*, 22 June 1999).[23]

During the 1990s, Israeli 'high-tech' firms also benefited from exceptional labour market circumstances. The rapid drop in domestic military spending and the cancellation of major military projects since the late 1980s provided civilian companies with a pool of highly skilled workers. This pool was further augmented during the 1990s by the massive inflow of highly educated immigrants from the former Soviet Union. As a result, Israel recorded the highest proportion of engineers in the world (135 per 10,000 people, compared with 85 in the US and 75 in Japan); the largest proportion of science PhDs in the world (15 per 10,000 people); and the third highest proportion of graduates in Mathematics, Natural Sciences and Engineering, after Germany and England (Bank Hapoalim 2000).

23   The average tax rate for Israeli firms here pertains to 1996–98, and is based on a sample of ten leading 'high-technology' companies: ECI, Comverse, Check Point, Gilat Communication, Orbotech, DSPC, Mercury, Nice, Teva and Elbit Systems.

Yet, despite these favourable conditions – or perhaps because of them – ITC firms have begun leaving Israel. Even before the 'high-tech' meltdown of 2000–01, it was already hard to see how these greenhouse conditions could get *any better*. But, then, that was precisely what firms needed in order to stay. During the late 1990s, with the transition from military to civilian production and the economic integration of Russian immigrants more or less complete, Israel started to experience 'shortages' of skilled workers. Unlike legal and policy matters, however, these limitations were not easy to 'fix'. Israeli spending on education already accounted for 9.4 per cent of GDP, compared with an OECD average of 6.1 per cent, and was difficult to increase. Furthermore, discrimination against Israeli Arabs (20 per cent of the population) and the non-technical bias of religious education (roughly 40 per cent of secondary school students) effectively kept over half the labour force out of ITC jobs.

To complicate things further, the emergence of less developed countries, particularly India, as ITC sites, was beginning to draw attention away from Israel. India has only recently begun shedding off its statist protectionism, so its corporate grants, subsidies and tax holidays to 'new economy' firms have much more room to expand. Similarly with educational infrastructure and labour skills. Although these were inferior to Israel's in relative terms, in absolute terms they were not only far bigger, but could also expand faster. During the late 1990s, India accounted for a mere 2 per cent of world software exports. These exports, however, were growing at more than 50 per cent annually, roughly twice the world average, and if that differential were to continue, by the late 2000s India's global share could reach 20 per cent. Most importantly, these developments were already evident in the bottom line. Whereas in Israel, consistent profit growth of 70 per cent was recorded only by a select number of ITC companies, in India this was the *average* (Khozem Merchant et al. 2000).

The impact of these domestic and global forces was to further transnationalise Israel's political economy. Even without counting the arrival of over a million immigrants from the former Soviet Union, Israel's labour force was already one of the world's most transnational, with foreigners, mostly unskilled workers from poor countries, accounting for over 10 per cent of the total. During the boom years of the late 1990s, business groups also began demanding the 'importation' of skilled workers. This hasn't happened yet; but whether more foreign workers came to Israel, or Israeli companies continued to go global, the impact on 'de-nationalising' accumulation was the same.

Global Accumulation, Domestic Depletion

Since the early 1990s, Israel's ruling class incorporated itself into the new breadth order of transnational accumulation. The transition was presented, ostentatiously, as a victory for the country's enlightened leadership. 'Liberalism', 'peace', and 'high-tech', they said, finally put Israel on the road to prosperity, and, initially, many were caught by the slogans. But soon enough reality set in. Neoliberalism, people discovered, was really a new power structure; peace, a cover-up for corporate peace dividends; and 'high-tech', a way to redistribute income and wealth.

For most people, prosperity remained elusive, and the reason was simple: during much the post-war era, material standards of living had to do not with 'liberalism', 'peace', or 'high technology', but with *demographics*. In fact, in both developing and developed countries – regardless of whether they were liberal or autocratic, peaceful or militaristic, industrial or agricultural – per capita GDP growth could be almost entirely 'explained' by population growth. The two are tightly correlated, and as we showed in Figure 3.1 earlier in the book, a similar correlation exists in Israel. Of course, population growth itself does not 'create' higher standards or living, nor is it the only 'factor' at play. Whatever the explanation, however, it must lie with the broader, societal nature of production. As we argued in Chapter 2, material standards of living are a matter of *social* productivity; that is, of the *interaction and integration which link people together*. And insofar as Israeli population growth created greater social 'fusion', it also acted as a catalyst for rising societal productivity.

From this perspective, Israeli prospects in the 1980s looked dismal. As Figure 3.1 showed, annual population growth fell to 1.5 per cent, down from 5 per cent in the 1950s–1970s, and GDP per capita growth sunk. During the 1990s, the picture seemed to finally brighten. Immigration from the former Soviet Union raised population growth rates dramatically, if only temporarily, rekindling hopes for rising productivity growth. And, yet, this failed to happen. Academics and journalists insisted it was just a matter of time; demography, they observed, was on Israel's side, and with the fresh backwinds of 'free markets', 'high-tech' and 'peace', prosperity was surely around the corner. Or was it?

For dominant capital, the neoliberal order of high-tech peace was of course a bonanza. Population growth provided the needed breadth; 'peace' and 'high-tech' attracted transnational investors; liberalisation opened up the world to capital flight; and the hype generated by these developments created immense capital gains. But the differential nature of the process was inherently *redistributional*, working to both re-divide the pie and restrict its growth. For the majority of the population, therefore, the new order was the problem, not the solution.

And, indeed, in this sense the new prosperity scheme was more of a scam, built on foundations of sand. The reason is perhaps best explained through negation. Consider first the following hypothetical scenario. Suppose for the moment that the neoliberal prophets had their way, and that the entire Israeli business sector was busy developing new ITC technology. Clearly, only the best innovations emerging from this effort would be potentially usable; of these select few, only a fraction could be 'protected' by intellectual property rights; and of that fraction of a fraction, only some would end up being successfully capitalised, either as 'independent' companies, or as takeover targets. In other words, most of the effort would be wasteful. And, yet, from a global viewpoint the expense was relatively modest, and if transnational capitalists were willing to indefinitely subsidise it with their venture capital, most Israelis would have enjoyed very high standards of living, some becoming fabulously rich and the rest earning high salaries.

The global 'high-tech' crash of 2000–01 put a big dent in this blueprint. But even if growth in this sector were to resume, the idea that this could engender lasting domestic prosperity was still far fetched, to put it mildly. First, as we have seen, Israel was rapidly approaching the labour limits on further 'high-tech' expansion. In other words, even if venture capital continued to flow in, for the unlucky 80–90 per cent of the population, who just happened to be permanently stuck in 'low-tech' jobs, the benefits would be limited at best. The most they could hope for were 'trickled down' crumbs from the upper world of 'high-tech'. And even that was probably too much to expect. As it turned out, and here we come to the second fallacy of the 'high-tech' dream, Uncle Global was far less generous to Israel than he looked. In fact, it wasn't at all clear who was subsidising whom. During the 1990s, most capital inflow was earmarked for takeover, not green-field expansion. Moreover, in return for the limited green-field investment which they did make, the 'investors' demanded, on the threat of going elsewhere, that the government foot up much of the bill through grants, subsidies and tax holidays. They also insisted on broader liberalisation and tight macroeconomic policies. And the government seemed hardly in need of persuasion, with both Labour 'left' and Likud 'right' competing over who would better squeeze the underlying population in order to cater to these 'needs'.

In short, the only miracle in this 'high-tech' drama, was the ability of dominant capital to suck in resources from the rest of society, while making everyone believe this was somehow in their best interest. And, indeed, for most of the population the consequences, illustrated in Figure 6.4, were dire. Unemployment, which reached a record 11 per cent in 1992, declined somewhat during the early years of the immigration boom, but has since resumed its uptrend. In parallel, there has been a massive increase in income inequality, indicated in the chart by the soaring Gini Coefficient.[24]

The reasons for these developments are not difficult to see. On the one hand, capital gains, profits and salaries in the 'high-tech' sector have risen rapidly. On the other hand, the decline of traditional industries, the disintegration of organised labour, competition from cheap foreign workers and imports, and regressive government income policies to subsidise the few by the many, have together caused unemployment to soar and income to stagnate. During the early 1950s, 'socialist' Israel was still one of the more egalitarian countries, with

---

24   The Gini Coefficient measures inequality on a range from 0 (full equality) to 1 (full inequality with one person pocketing all the income).

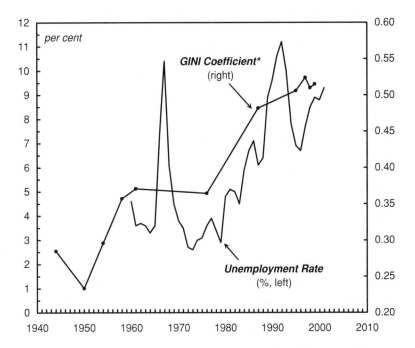

Figure 6.4   Unemployment and Income Inequality

* GINI Coefficient pertains to the distribution of pre-tax income of all earners from
all sources. Missing data are interpolated linearly.
SOURCE: Israel's Central Bureau of Statistics; Israel Finance Ministry, State Revenue
Administration.

the top 20 per cent of the population earning only 3.3 times the income of the
bottom 20 per cent. This was certainly impressive, particularly relative to 'free
market' countries such as the United States, where the comparable ratio was as
high as 9.5. By 1995, however, after two generations of 'Americanisation', the
situation was reversed. Israel was now the most unequal of all industrialised
countries, with the ratio of the top to the bottom 20 per cent reaching 21.3,
compared with 'only' 10.6 in the United States.[25]

The broader consequences of this 'high-tech dilemma' were of course hardly
unique to Israel. Inequality, unemployment and insecurity have increased in
most countries. And as disenchantment with neoliberalism spreads, even the
more vocal warriors of global breadth, such as Intel's chairman, Andi Grove,
have begun to worry:

25 Data in this paragraph are computed from the U.S. Census Bureau and from Israel's
    State Revenue Administration. Israel does not publish statistics on the distribution
    of assets, but here, too, we may well expect the extent of inequality to exceed that
    of the United States.

Suppose everything in the middle gets eliminated and society becomes [comprised of] high-paid information workers and low-paid service workers. You get into situations where the living standards and costs of the former are imposed on the latter.... I don't quite know where it will end up going, but it has become really problematical. Yet, everybody wants to emulate Silicon Valley. As they do so, they will turn the world into more islands with the same problems. (*Business Week*, 28 August 2000)

The nature of the 'problem', though, was not technology as such, but the modern power structure to which it was subjugated. Indeed, current technical know-how could not only greatly improve the material and social welfare of most people, but also eliminate some of the greater evils of poverty and insecurity around the world. And, yet, under the rule of vendible capital, it tended to create 'winner-takes-all' situations, whose impact was to heightened inequality and suffering instead of alleviating them.

The common political response to this was to reiterate the 'trickle-down' liberal argument, augmented by government initiatives to boost 'knowledge', And here, too, Israel was hardly different. The most outspoken on the issue was Benjamin Netanyahu, who often spelled out aloud what his Labour and Likud competitors were careful to hide. There was indeed a 'scary gap between rich and poor in Israel', he admitted, but the way to resolve it was certainly not by handouts. 'I don't want to create jobs,' he declared, 'I want the entrepreneur to want.' The government, of course, was not planning to pull out completely, but rather to concentrate on education. Recognising that handing out state assets to private capitalists was bound to increase social disparity, Netanyahu concocted a brilliant solution. The state, he proposed, would plow some of the privatisation proceeds, along with donations from the lucky tycoons, back into a 'special fund designed to close social gaps', and into creating 'thinking schools' to help 'balance the intellectual makeup of Israeli society' (*Ha'aretz*, 28 January 1996; 26 November 1996; 27 May 1997).

This so-called 'strategy' was highly suited for the 'new world order' of free capital mobility. Income inequality could sometimes boost growth in the initial stages of capitalist development, or at least this is what many came to believe following the empirical works of Simon Kuznets (1965; 1973). Once the economy matured and urbanised, however, the impact often became negative, since it increased savings by the affluent, while limiting consumption by the masses. In the relatively closed economies of the Cold War era, investors were forced to accept 'government intervention' and 'demand management' in order to prevent this 'imbalance' from politically undermining the capitalist order. But as the economies opened up, domestic demand was no longer a problem. If there was not enough of it at home, there was always the world. Of course, global competition was often tougher than domestic; but, then, for those able to 'merge' into transnational capital, the differential benefit usually outweighed the cost.

This process of transnationalisation, and its consequences for Israeli accumulation, are illustrated in Figures 6.5 and 6.6, respectively. The first of these figures charts the inflow and outflow of foreign direct investment (FDI), expressed as a per cent of GDP.[26] During the 1990s, inflows, which indicate the extent to which foreign owners increased their holdings of Israeli assets, have soared to an average of nearly 2 per cent of GDP, surpassing their previous record of the 1960s. At the same time, Israeli capital also began moving out. The large local firms, which earlier formed the core domestic dominant capital, have for long been 'too big' for the domestic market. But it was only during the 1990s, with the relaxation of capital controls and the realignment of tax laws along U.S. standards, that their outward movement began in earnest. Their recent 'exit' rate was roughly 1 per cent of GDP, but if local conditions continue to stagnate, the pace could accelerate.

And as the process unfolded, with foreigners buying local assets and Israelis acquiring them outside the country, the 'nationality' of capital got more and more blurred. The impact of this transnational fusion is illustrated in Figure 6.6. The chart shows the five-year moving correlation between the annual rate of change of the Tel Aviv Stock Exchange index (TASE), and the corresponding rate for the Nasdaq index, both computed from monthly data expressed in U.S. dollars. Each point on the series, therefore, represents the correlation prevailing during the previous 60 months.

The gradual increase in this correlation, illustrated by the straight regression line going through the data, shows the growing convergence between the rates of return in the two countries.[27] Until the mid-1980s, the correlation was very low, and at some point even negative. Israel was still locked in its depth regime of militarised stagflation, 'high-tech' was not yet a buzz word, capital flows were restricted, and the exchange rate regulated. But as depth gave way to breadth, and Israel moved toward ITC, liberalised its capital account, and brought inflation and currency depreciation 'under control', the correlation between the two markets rose significantly, approaching a value of 0.7 in the five years ending in 2001. Correlation does not imply causation, but in this case it is pretty clear which market is driving which.

At a Crossroads

By the end of the twentieth century, then, it seemed as if Israel's dominant capital finally realised its American dream of a 'New Middle East': local by

26 Recall that FDI figures could significantly underestimate the extent of transnational ownership changes, since these changes could also be financed through portfolio flows and local credit.
27 The correlation coefficient ranges from –1 to 1, with a value of 1 indicating the two series moving exactly together; –1 meaning they move inversely as a mirror image of one another; and 0 denoting no systematic connection.

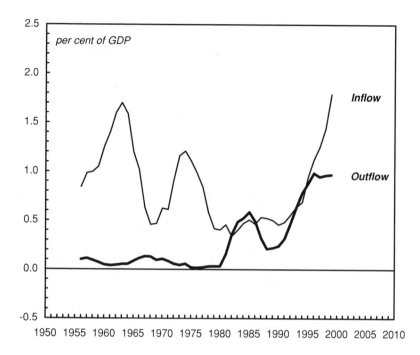

Figure 6.5   Israeli FDI Flows

NOTE: Series are smoothed as 5-year moving averages.
SOURCE: IMF through McGraw-Hill (Online).

denomination, global by accumulation. But there was a fly in the ointment. Although the transnationalisation of ownership has generally strengthened the power of dominant capital, it also made its differential accumulation vulnerable to grassroots challenges. And when the local elite sought to respond to these challenges, it found itself hampered by both inner conflict and the uncompromising dictates of global capital.

Consider first the domestic scene. The 1990s boosted the differential performance of the core groups. The underlying population, on the other hand, both Israeli and Palestinian, was rendered defenceless against the vagaries of global breadth. During the early part of the decade, this divergence was camouflaged by the growth euphoria of neoliberalism, 'high-tech' and 'emerging markets'. Toward the end of the decade, however, with the euphoria subsiding and the breadth regime running out of steam, the conflict between transnational accumulation and local well-being came back with a vengeance.

This conflict may well mark the beginning of the end of Zionism. Until recently, Israeli capitalism went well with the Zionist project. The country's ruling class, from its colonial beginnings, through its statist institutions, to its emergence as dominant capital, managed to interweave Jewish colonial ideas

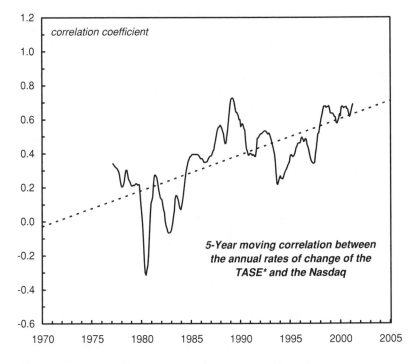

Figure 6.6   Converging Accumulation

* The TASE (Tel Aviv Stock Exchange) index is based on splicing of IMF data (until December 1976), the General Index (January 1977 to March 1993) and the Mishtanim Index (April 1993 onward). Both the TASE and Nasdaq are expressed in US$.
NOTE: Series display monthly observations. The straight line going through the observation is a linear regression.
SOURCE: IMF and Nasdaq through McGraw-Hill (Online); Tel Aviv Stock Exchange.

with capitalist praxis. During its 'militaristic' stage, it skillfully harnessed the 'national' interest to its differential accumulation. The social cohesion needed to sustain the war economy was cemented by religious and racial rhetoric, authoritarian welfare institutions, and frequent armed conflict against external enemies. The cheap labour force in the equation was provided by the Palestinians.

The shift toward transnationalism upset this delicate 'equilibrium'. With the elite increasingly focused on the Nasdaq, the 'high-tech' business, and markets in the rest of the world, the prospect of peace dividends began to look much more attractive than dwindling war profits. Dominant capital was less and less receptive to the 'garrison state', and calls for an end to the Arab–Israeli conflict mounted. Once the 'peace process' started and the globalisation wagon began rolling, however, the Zionist package began to unravel. The domestic population, no longer needed for 'national' projects, was left exposed to the harsh reality of neoliberalism. And the Palestinians, whose cheap labour was now outbid by even cheaper 'guest workers', were given their 'Palustan' – a semi-autonomous entity, with half its original territory, no army, no economic sovereignty, limited water, complete dependency on Israeli infrastructure, and hundreds of Jewish settlements and roads crisscrossing their land.

The consequences of this unravelling were quick to emerge. In 2000, the Palestinians revolted. And, yet, the Israeli elite, perhaps for the first time in its history, was caught in limbo. Torn between its Zionist past and transnational aspirations, it tried to ride both horses. Alarmed by the Palestinians' loss of fear, anxious that its army may be unable to win a guerrilla war, and aware that conflict would shatter the hard-won business confidence, it hesitated, tending to respond rather than initiate. At the same time, its fear for loss of 'Jewish cohesion' prevented it from accepting a democratic, non-racial solution to the conflict. Indeed, since the Oslo 'peace' agreement of 1993, the various Israeli governments have removed *not a single* Jewish settlement in the Occupied Territories. On the contrary, they added more.

Paradoxically, though, the demographic cohesion they were so keen on preserving was by now more a myth than reality. Massive immigration from the former Soviet Union, the importation of foreign workers, and the rapid natural growth of the local Arab population, made Israel less and less of a 'Jewish state'. Furthermore, many of the country's poor, ravaged by neoliberalism and disillusioned with the doublespeak of both Labour and Likud, shifted their allegiances to religious and ethnic political parties, such as SHAS and Yisrael Ba-aliyah. The emphasis of such parties on ethnicity, racism and religion has been welcomed by the elites as a cheap way of diverting attention from class divisions. And yet, if the underlying causes of pauperisation remain unchecked, 'containment' of this sort could easily unravel into a backlash.

To complicate things further, the Israeli elite, by endorsing transnational-isation, made itself subservient to broader processes over which it had no control. Presently, the most important of these processes is the cresting of the global breadth wave. During the 1990s, merger activity has reached all time highs. The ensuing corporate centralisation, along with informal networking and state-managed 'deregulation', helped boost cooperation and collusion among the world's largest business alliances. But globalisation also unleashed the demon of green-field growth, particularly in the developing countries, where rapid proletarianisation contributed to the gradual build-up of excess capacity. Initially, the centripetal mechanism of internal breadth was stronger than the centrifugal forces of external depth. But toward the end of the decade the tables turned. Disintegration and cut-throat competition substituted for coordination and collusion, pricing power was eroded, and the profit margins of dominant capital started to feel the pinch.

The disturbances first hit the periphery of global accumulation, where corporate coordination was the weakest. A series of cascading crises, beginning with the Mexican peso crisis of 1994, and continuing through the Asian crisis of 1997, the Russian meltdown of 1998, and the Brazilian crisis of 1999, were a clear indication that corporate amalgamation was losing the war on green-field investment. In 2000, the crisis finally reached the core Western countries, beginning with the 'high-tech' sector and quickly spreading throughout the economy. Global stock markets, anticipating the ensuing drop in earnings, went into a tailspin, and merger activity, having risen for two decades, collapsed. And then, as if to push the breadth order off the cliff, came the attacks of 11 September 2001. The breadth order of the 1990s came down crashing.

The impact on Israel was immediate and brutal. Escalating guerrilla warfare with the Palestinians, attacks in the United States, and the global 'war on terrorism' beginning with Afghanistan, delivered the rude awakening. Clearly, expectations for a 'New Middle East' and vast 'peace dividends' were a bit premature. Tourism into Israel has fallen sharply, green-field investment has come to a halt, and capital inflow has turned into a trickle. Most seriously, the global 'high-tech' meltdown buried many Israeli companies under mountains of losses. Some of the largest players, such as Koor, IDB, Fishman and the Dankers, were forced to write-off expensive acquisitions. And given that many of their acquisitions, along with green-field R&D investments, were heavily leveraged, the large banking groups were also feeling the pressure.

Israeli capitalism is clearly at a crossroads, and its future, perhaps more than ever, is bound up with global developments. Until recently, transnationalisation lent strong support to reconciliation with Arab neighbours, and to 'peace', if only paternal, with the Palestinians. The recent stalling of global breadth, however, has thrown a monkey wrench into the process. If the reprieve proves temporary, there may still be a remote chance of resolving the regional conflict. Breadth requires political stability, and dominant capital, both in Israel and globally, would seek a settlement to calm things down. But with religion winning the hearts and minds of the underlying population, time is running out. And if instead of renewed breadth, global capital settles in for an extended period of depth, the conflict and violence associated with such a regime could prove devastating for Israel and for the region.

References

Abramov, Kobby, and Yuval Zuk. 1999. Groups Controlling Listed Companies. Hebrew. *This Month in the Bourse* (August): 3–9.

Adams, Gordon. 1982. *The Politics of Defense Contracting: The Iron Triangle*. Transaction edn. New Brunswick, N.J.: Transaction Books.

Adelman, Morris Albert. 1987. The Economics of the International Oil Industry. In *The International Oil Industry: An Interdisciplinary Perspective*, edited by J. Rees and P. Odell. New York: St Martin's Press, pp. 27–56.

Aglietta, Michel. 1979. [1987]. *A Theory of Capitalist Regulation: The U.S. Experience*. London: Verso.

Aharoni, Yair. 1969. Institutional Rigidity and Resource Utilisation. Hebrew. *Economic Quarterly* 16 (62, July): 157–68.

Aharoni, Yair. 1976. *Structure and Performance in the Israeli Economy*. Hebrew. Tel Aviv: Cherikover.

Aharoni, Yair. 1991. *The Political Economy of Israel*. Hebrew. Tel Aviv: Am Oved and the Levi Eshkol Institute.

Alexander, Esther. 1975. National Income, Private Consumption, Disposable Wage and Inflation in the Israeli Market, 1968–1974: Reflections on the Impact of Inflation on Income Redistribution During Inflation. Jerusalem: n.p.

Alexander, Esther. 1990. *The Power of Equality in the Economy: Israeli Economy in the 80s*. Hebrew. Tel Aviv: United Kibbutz.

Almogi, Yossef. 1980. *Splenium Corporis*. Hebrew. Tel Aviv: Idanim.

Amit, Meir. 1999. *Head On...*. Hebrew. Or Yehuda: Hed Arzi Publishing House.

Amnesty International. 2000. *Israel: Human Rights Abuses of Women Trafficked From the Commonwealth of Independent States*: Amnesty International.

Anderson, Jack, and James Boyd. 1984. *Oil: The Real Story Behind the World Energy Crisis*. London: Sidgwick & Jackson.

Arian, Asher. 1977. The Passing of Dominance. *The Jerusalem Quarterly* 5 (Fall): 13–32.

Arian, Asher. 1985. *Politics and Government in Israel*. Hebrew. Tel Aviv: Zmora-Bitan.

Arian, Asher. 1989. *Politics in Israel: The Second Generation*. Second edn. Chatham, N.J.: Chatham House.

Arlosoroff, Haim. 1934. *The Writings of Haim Arlosoroff*. Hebrew. 6 vols. Tel Aviv: A. I. Steible.

Aronson, Shlomo. 1992. *The Politics and Strategy of Nuclear Weapons in the Middle East: Opacity, Theory and Reality*. Albany: Random House.

Aronson, Shlomo. 1994–95. *Nuclear Weapons in the Middle East. Opacity: Theory and Reality 1948–1993*. Written with the assistance of A. Brosh. Hebrew. 2 vols. Jerusalem: Academon.

Aronson, Shlomo, and Dan Horowitz. 1971. The Strategy of Controlled Retaliation. The Israel Case. Hebrew. *State and Government* 1 (1).

Arrighi, Giovanni, Kenneth Barr, and Shuji Hisaeda. 1999. The Transformation of Business Enterprise. In *Chaos and Governance in the Modern World System*, edited by G. Arrighi and B.J. Silver. Minneapolis and London: University of Minnesota Press, pp. 97–150.

Averitt, Robert T. 1968. *The Dual economy: The Dynamics of American Industry Structure*. 1st edn. New York: W.W. Norton.

Avneri, Ari. 1987. *The Gamblers: The Rise and Fall of the Captains of Finance*. Hebrew. Tel Aviv: Steimatsky.

Bank Hapoalim. 2000. High-Tech In Israel – A Status Report. *Economic Report* July: 11–20.

Bank of Israel. Monetary Department. 1998. The Money and Capital Markets, Annual Report. Jerusalem: Bank of Israel.

Bar Zohar, M. 1975. *Ben Gurion*. Hebrew. Tel Aviv: Am Oved.

Baran, Paul. A., and Paul M. Sweezy. 1966. *Monopoly Capital: An Essay on the American Economic and Social Order*. New York: Modern Reader Paperbacks.

Barkai, Haim. 1964. *The Public Sector, the Histadrut Sector and the Private Sector in the Israeli Economy*. Sixth Report, 1961–64. Hebrew. Jerusalem: Falk Centre.

Barnet, Richard J. 1972. *Roots of War*. New York: Atheneum.

Barnet, Richard J. 1980. *The Lean Years: Politics in the Age of Scarcity*. New York: Simon and Schuster.

Barnet, Richard J. 1983. *The Alliance. America, Europe, Japan: Makers of the Postwar World*. New York: Simon and Schuster.

Barnet, Richard J., and Ronald E. Müller. 1974. *Global Reach: The Power of the Multinational Corporations*. New York: Simon and Schuster.

Barnett, Michael N. 1992. *Confronting the Costs of War: Military Power, State, and Society in Egypt and Israel*. Princeton, N.J.: Princeton University Press.

Baumol, W.J., A.S. Blinder, and W.M. Scarth. 1986. *Economics: Principles and Policies – Macroeconomics*. Canadian edn. Toronto: Academic Press Canada.

Bejsky, M., V. Ziller, Z. Hirsh, Z. Sarnat, and D. Friedman. 1986. *Report of the Commission of Inquiry into the Manipulation of the Banking Shares*. Hebrew. Jerusalem: Government Printer.

Ben Dor, G. 1977. Politics and Military in Israel in the Seventies. In *The Israeli Political System*. Hebrew, edited by M. Lissak and E. Gutmann. Tel Aviv: Am Oved.

Ben-Gurion, David. 1933. *From Class to Nation: Chapters in Clarifying the Path and Purpose of the Workers Movements*. Tel Aviv: Davar.

Ben-Porath, Yoram. 1986. *The Israeli Economy: Maturing Through Crises*. Cambridge, Mass.: Harvard University Press.

Ben-Porath, Yoram. 1989. *The Israeli Economy: Maturing Through Crises*. Hebrew. Tel Aviv: Am Oved and Falk Institute.

Berglas, Eitan. 1970. Defense, Standard of Living and Foreign Debt. Hebrew. *Economic Quarterly* 17 (67, September): 191–202.

Berglas, Eitan. 1983. Defense and the Economy: The Israeli Experience. Discussion Paper 83.01, The Maurice Falk Institute of Economic Research, Jerusalem.

Bhagat, Sanjai, Andrei Shleifer, and Robert W. Vishny. 1990. Hostile Takeovers in the 1980s: The Return to Corporate Specialization. *Brookings Papers on Economic Activity: Microeconomics*: 1–85.

Bichler, Shimshon. 1991. The Political Economy of Military Spending in Israel. Hebrew. Unpublished Doctoral Dissertation, Political Science, Hebrew University, Jerusalem.

Bichler, Shimshon. 1994–95. Political Power Shifts in Israel, 1977 and 1992: Unsuccessful Electoral Economics or Long Range Realignment? *Science & Society* 58 (4): 415–39.

Bichler, Shimshon, and Jonathan Nitzan. 1996. Military Spending and Differential Accumulation: A New Approach to the Political Economy of Armament – The Case of Israel. *Review of Radical Political Economics* 28 (1): 52–97.

Bichler, Shimshon, and Jonathan Nitzan. 2001. *From War Profit to Peace Dividends: The Global Political Economy of Israel*. Hebrew. Jerusalem: Carmel.

Blair, John M. 1972. *Economic Concentration: Structure, Behavior and Public Policy*. New York: Harcourt, Brace Jovanovich.

Blair, John M. 1976. *The Control of Oil*. New York: Vintage Books.

Böhm-Bawerk, Eugen von. 1891. [1971]. *The Positive Theory of Capital*. Translated with a Preface and Analysis by W. Smart. Freeport, New York: Books for Libraries Press.

Bowring, Joseph. 1986. *Competition in a Dual Economy*. Princeton, N.J.: Princeton University Press.

Braudel, Fernand. 1985. *Civilization & Capitalism, 15th–18th Century*. Trans. from the French and Revised by Sian Reynolds. 3 vols. New York: Harper & Row, Publishers.

Brenner, Menachem, and Dan Galai. 1984. The Banking Share Crisis in Macroeconomic Perspective. Hebrew. *Economic Quarterly* (119, January): 909–13.

British Petroleum. Annual. *BP Statistical Review of World Energy*. London: The British Petroleum Company.

Brodet, David. 1995. Price Controls – Economic Solution Under Unusual Conditions. Hebrew. *Economic Quarterly* 95 (4): 607–12.

Brodet, David, Avi Ben Bassat, Raphi Barel, Ya'acov Gadish, Zvi Zussman, and Dov Lautman. 1995. *The Committee for Examining Aspects of Bank Holdings in Real Corporations*. Jerusalem: State of Israel.

Bromley, Simon. 1991. *American Hegemony and World Oil: The Industry, the State and the World Economy*. Cambridge: Polity Press.

Brown, D. 1924. Pricing Policy in Relation to Financial Control. *Management and Administration*: February, pp. 195–8; March, pp. 283–6; April, pp. 417–22.

Bruno, Michael. 1984. The Necessary Economic Policy in the Present Crisis. Hebrew. *Economic Quarterly* 30 (119): 843–7.

Bruno, Michael. 1989. External Shocks and Internal Responses: The Macroeconomic Performance of Israel, 1965–1982. In *The Israeli Economy: Maturing Through Crisis*. Hebrew, edited by Y. Ben-Porath. Tel Aviv: Am Oved, pp. 365–92.

Bruno, Michael. 1995. The Stabilisation Program – A Decade's Perspective. Hebrew. *The Economic Quarterly* 42 (4, December): 580–8.

Bruno, Michael, and Stanley Fischer. 1989. The Inflationary Process in Israel: Shocks and Adaptation. In *The Israeli Economy: Maturing Through Crisis*. Hebrew, edited by Y. Ben-Porath. Tel Aviv: Am Oved, pp. 393–417.

Brzezinski, Zbigniew K. 1983. *Power and Principle: Memoirs of the National Security Advisor, 1977–1981*. New York: Farrar Straus Giroux.

Brzoska, Michael, and Thomas Ohlson. 1987. *Arms Transfers to the Third World, 1971–85*. Oxford and New York: Oxford University Press.

Cafcafi, A. 1994. *A War of Choice. The Road to Sinai and Back 1950–1957. The Struggle of Political Doctrines in Israel of the 1950s*. Hebrew. Ramat Ef'al: Yad Tabenkin and NGO for the Heritage of Moshe Sharet.

Caporaso, James A., and David P. Levine. 1992. *Theories of Political Economy*. Cambridge: Cambridge University Press.

Caves, Richard. 1989. Mergers, Takeovers, and Economic Efficiency: Foresight vs. Hindsight. *International Journal of Industrial Organization* 7: 151–74.

Chan, Steve. 1980. The Consequences of Expensive Oil on Arms Transfers. *Journal of Peace Research* 17 (3): 235–46.

Clark, John Bates. 1899. [1965]. *The Distribution of Wealth*. New York: Augustus M. Kelley.

Coase, Ronald H. 1937. [1996]. The Nature of the Firm. In *The Economic Nature of the Firm. A Reader*, edited by L. Putterman and R.S. Kroszner. Cambridge: Cambridge University Press, pp. 89–104.

Cockburn, Andrew, and Leslie Cockburn. 1991. *Dangerous Liaison: The Inside Story of the U.S.–Israeli Covert Relationship*. 1st edn. New York: HarperCollins Publishers.

Cohen, Benjamin J. 1993. The Triad and the Unholy Trinity: Lessons for the Pacific Region. In *Pacific Economic Relations in the 1990s: Cooperation or Conflict*, edited by R. Higgott, R. Leaver and J. Ravenhill. Boulder, Colo.: Lynne Rienner Publishers, pp. 133–58.

Cournot, Augustin. 1838. [1929]. *Researches Into the Mathematical Principles of the Theory of Wealth*. Translated by N.T. Bacon. New York: Macmillan Co.

Dan & Bradstreet. 1984. *Dun's 100 Israel 1994: Israel's Leading Enterprises*. Tel Aviv: Dan & Bradstreet.

Dan, Hillel. 1963. *In the Unpaved Road: The Tale of Solel Boneh*. Hebrew. Jerusalem and Tel Aviv: Schocken.

Darwish, Adel, and Gregory Alexander. 1991. *Unholy Babylon: The Secret History of Saddam's War*. London: Victor Gollancz.

Djilas, Milovan. 1957. *The New Class: An Analysis of the Communist System*. New York: Praeger.

Doremus, Paul N., William W. Keller, Louis W. Pauly, and Simon Reich. 1998. *The Myth of the Global Corporation*. Princeton, N.J.: Princeton University Press.

Dovrat, Ephraim. 1970. Restraint Policy: An Imperative. Hebrew. *Economic Quarterly* (65–66, June): 15–17.

Eban, Abba Solomon. 1977. *Abba Eban: An Autobiography*. 1st edn. New York: Random House.

Edwards, Richard. 1979. *Contested Terrain: The Transformation of the Workplace in the Twentieth Century*. New York: Basic Books.

Eis, Carl. 1969. The 1919–1930 Merger Movement in American Industry. *The Journal of Law and Economics* 12 (2): 267–96.

Emmanuel, Arghiri. 1972. *Unequal Exchange: A Study of the Imperialism of Trade*. New York: Monthly Review Press.

Engler, Robert. 1977. *The Brotherhood of Oil: Energy Policy and the Public Interest*. Chicago and London: University of Chicago Press.

Evron, I. 1986. *Suez 1956: A New Perspective*. Hebrew. Tel Aviv: Modan.

Farjoun, Emanuel. 1978. The Palestinian Workers – An Economic Reserve Army. Hebrew. *Red Papers* (5).

Farjoun, Emanuel. 1980. The Palestinian Workers in Israel – A Reserve Army of Labour. *Khamsin* (7): 107–43.

Farjoun, Emanuel. 1983. Class Division in Israeli Society. *Khamsin* (10): 29–39.

Ferrari, Paul L., Jeffrey W. Knopf, and Raúl L. Madrid. 1987. *U.S. Arms Exports: Policies and Contractors*. Washington, D.C.: Investor Responsibility Research Center.

FIBV, International Federation of Stock Exchanges. 2000. Number of Companies With Shares Listed (Table 195), http://www.fibv.com/statistics.asp

Fischer, Stanley. 1993. Israel and its Neighbours – Growth, Stablisation and Reform in Israel. Hebrew. *Banking Quarterly* 31 (123, March): 6–27.

Fischer, Stanley. 1995. The U.S. Role in the Israeli Stabilisation Plan. Hebrew. *Economic Quarterly* 95 (4): 589–97.

Fischer, Stanley, and Ya'akov Frenkel. 1982. Stabilisation Policy for Israel. Hebrew. *Economic Quarterly* 29 (114): 246–55.

Fisher, Irving. 1906. *The Nature of Capital and Income*. New York: Macmillan.

Fisher, Irving. 1911. *The Purchasing Power of Money: Its Determination and Relation to Credit, Interest and Crises*. Assisted by Harry Gunnison Brown. New York: Macmillan.

Fleming, Marcus J. 1962. Domestic Financial Policies Under Fixed and Under Floating Exchange Rates. *IMF Staff Papers* 9 (November): 369–80.

Folkerts-Landau, David, Donald Mathieson, and Garry J. Schinasi. 1997. *International Capital Markets: Developments, Prospects, and Key Policy Issues*. Washington D.C.: International Monetary Fund.

Franko, Lawrence G. 1991. Global Corporate Competition II: Is the Large American Firm an Endangered Species? *Business Horizons* 34 (6, November/December): 14–22.

Frederick the Great. 1979. *Instructions to Commanders*. Hebrew. Translated by J. Wallach. Tel Aviv: Ma'arachot.

Frenkel, Shlomo. 1991. *Storm in the Desert: The Real Story*. Hebrew. Tel Aviv: Citrin.

Frenkel, Shlomo, and Shimshon Bichler. 1984. *The Rich Families: Israel's Aristocracy of Finance*. Hebrew. Tel Aviv: Cadim Publishing House.

Frieden, Jeffry A. 1988. [1995]. Capital Politics: Creditors and the International Political Economy. In *International Political Economy: Perspectives on Global Power and Wealth*, edited by J.A. Frieden and D.A. Lake. New York: St Martin's Press, pp. 282–98.

Friedman, Milton. 1953. *Essays in Positive Economics*. Chicago: University of Chicago Press.

Friedman, Milton. 1970. [1974]. A Theoretical Framework for Monetary Analysis. In *Milton Friedman's Monetary Framework: A Debate with his Critics*, edited by R.J. Gordon. Chicago and London: The University of Chicago Press, pp. 1–62.

Friedman, Milton, and Rose Friedman. 1979. *Free to Choose: A Personal Statement*. New York and London: Harcourt Brace Jovanovich.

Friedman, Milton, and L.J. Savage. 1948. The Utility Analysis of Choices Involving Risk. *Journal of Political Economy* 56 (4, August): 279–304.

Fukuyama, Francis. 1999. Death of the Hierarchy. *Financial Times*, 13 June, I.

Galbraith, John Kenneth. 1990. *A Short History of Financial Euphoria*. New York: Penguin.

Galin, Amira, and Yanai Tab. 1971. The Package Deal – A Turning Point in Israeli Labour Relations. Hebrew. *Economic Quarterly* 18 (69–70, July): 106–13.

Gaon, Benjamin. 1997. *The Daring Wins*. Tel Aviv: Yediot Aharonont.

Gazit, Mordechai. 1983a. Israeli Arms Purchases from the U.S. Hebrew. Policy Oriented Papers 8. The Leonard Davis Institute for International Relations.

Gazit, Mordechai. 1983b. *President Kennedy's Policy Toward the Arab States and Israel*. Hebrew. Tel Aviv: The Shiloach Centre for Middle East and African Studies.

Georgescu-Roegen, Nicholas. 1979. Methods in Economic Science. *Journal of Economic Issues* XIII (2, June): 317–28.

Gessen, Masha. 1998. De-pressed. *The New Republic*, 28 September, 16–17.

Giladi, Dan. 1973. *The Yeshuv During the Fourth Migration 1924–1929: An Economic and Political Examination*. Hebrew. Tel Aviv: Am Oved.

Gold, Dore. 1993. *U.S. Military Strategy in the Middle East*. Hebrew. Tel Aviv: Joffe Center for Strategic Studies and Ministry of Defense.

Gold, David A. 1977. The Rise and Fall of the Keynesian Coalition. *Kapitalistate* 6 (1): 129–61.

Goldberg, G. 1992. *Political Parties in Israel – From Mass Parties to Electoral Parties*. Hebrew. Tel Aviv: Tel Aviv University.

Goodman, John B., and Louis W. Pauly. 1995. The Obsolescence of Capital Controls? Economic Management in an Age of Global Markets. In *International Political Economy: Perspectives on Global Power and Wealth*, edited by J.A. Frieden and D.A. Lake. New York: St Martin's Press, pp. 299–317.

Gorani, Yossef. 1973. *Ahdut Ha'avoda 1919–1930: The Ideological Basis and Political Method*. Hebrew. Tel Aviv: United Kibbutz.

Gozansky, Tamar. 1986. *Capitalist Development in Palestine*. Hebrew. Haifa: Mifalim Universitaim.

Grant, Charles. 1997. A Survey of the Global Defence Industry. *The Economist*, 14 June, 1–18.

Greenberg, Yitzhak. 1988. *Equal Wage in the Histadrut: Family Incomes in 1924–1954*. Hebrew. n.p.: Yad Tabenkin. Institute for the Study of the Kibbutz and the Labour Movement.

Griffin, Larry J., Joel A. Devine, and Michael Wallace. 1982. Monopoly Capital, Organised Labour and Military Expenditures in the United States, 1949–1976. (In Theme Supplement: 'Marxist Inquiries: Studies of Labour, Class and State', Edited by M. Buawoy and T. Skocpol.) *American Journal of Sociology* 88: S113–S153.

Gross, Nachum T., and Yitzhak Greenberg. 1994. *Bank Ha'Poalim: The First 50 Years, 1921–1971*. Tel Aviv: Bank Ha'Poalim and Am Oved.

Haber, Eitan. 1987. *Today War Will Break Out: The Memoirs of Brigadier General Israel Lior.* Hebrew. Jerusalem: Adanim/Yediot Aharonot.

Hacohen, David. 1981. *Time to Tell.* Hebrew. Tel Aviv: Am Oved.

Halevi, Nadav, and Ruth Klinov-Malul. 1968. *The Economic Development of Israel.* New York and Jerusalem: Praeger.

Hall, R.L., and C.J. Hitch. 1939. Price Theory and Business Behaviour. *Oxford Economic Papers* (2): 12–45.

Harcourt, Geoffrey C. 1969. Some Cambridge Controversies in the Theory of Capital. *Journal of Economic Literature* 7 (2): 369–405.

Hasid, N., and O. Lesser. 1981. Economic Resources for Israel's Security. Hebrew. *Economic Quarterly* 28 (109): 243–52.

Helleiner, Eric. 1994. *States and the Reemergence of Global Finance: From Bretton Woods to the 1990s.* Ithaca, N.Y.: Cornell University Press.

Hersh, Simon M. 1991. *The Samson Option: Israel's Nuclear Arsenal and American Foreign Policy.* New York: Random House.

Hewlett, Sylvia Ann. 1980. *The Cruel Dilemmas of Development: Twentieth Century Brazil.* New York: Basic Books, Inc. Publishers.

Hilferding, Rudolf. 1910. [1981]. *Finance Capital: A Study of the Latest Phase of Capitalist Development.* Edited with an Introduction by Tom Bottomore, from a translation by Morris Watnick and Sam Gordon. London: Routledge & Kegan Paul.

Hirschman, Albert O. 1970. *Exit, Voice, and Loyalty: Responses to Decline in Firms, Organizations, and States.* Cambridge, Mass.: Harvard University Press.

Hirschman, Albert O. 1985. Reflection on the Latin American Experience. In *The Politics of Inflation and Economic Stagnation,* edited by L.N. Lindberg and C.S. Maier. Washington D.C.: Brookings Institution, pp. 53–77.

Hobsbawm, Eric J. 1975. *The Age of Capital, 1848–1875.* New York: Charles Scribner's Sons.

Hobson, John. A. 1902. [1965]. *Imperialism: A Study.* Ann Arbor: University of Michigan Press.

Hollander, Herman. 1979. *My Life and What I Did With It.* Jerusalem: Koren.

Horowitz, Dan. 1944. *The Economic Development of Israel.* Hebrew. Tel Aviv: Bialik.

Horowitz, Dan. 1975. *Life at the Centre.* Hebrew. Ramat Gan: Masada.

Horowitz, Dan. 1982. The Israeli Defense Forces: A Civilianized Military in a Partially Militarized Society. In *Soldiers, Peasants and Bureaucrats,* edited by R. Kolkowitz and A. Korbonski. London: George Allen and Unwin, pp. 77–106.

Horowitz, David, and Moshe Lissak. 1977. *From Settlement to State: Israel's Jews as a Political Community During the British Mandate.* Hebrew. Tel Aviv: Am Oved.

Horowitz, David, and Moshe Lissak. 1988. Democracy and National Security in a Continuous Conflict. Hebrew. *Yahadoot Zemanenu* 4: 27–65.

Horowitz, Dan, and Moshe Lissak. 1989. *Trouble in Utopia: The Overburdened Polity of Israel.* SUNY series in Israeli studies. Albany: State University of New York Press.

Howard, Michael Charles, and J.E. King. 1992. *A History of Marxian Economics. Volume II, 1929–1990.* Princeton, N.J.: Princeton University Press.

Huberman, Leo. 1936. [1961]. *Man's Worldly Goods: The Story of the Wealth of Nations.* New York: Monthly Review Press.

Hughes, Donna M. 2000. The 'Natasha' Trade: The Transnational Shadow Market of Trafficking in Women. *Journal of International Affairs* 53 (2, Spring): 625–51.

Huntington, Samuel P. 1975. The Crisis of Democracy: The United States. In *The Crisis of Democracy,* edited by M. Crozier, S.P. Huntington and J. Watanuki. New York: New York University Press.

Hymer, Stephen H. 1960. [1976]. *The International Operations of National Firms: A Study of Direct Foreign Investment.* Cambridge, Mass. and London, England: The MIT Press.

Ileen, Ephraim. 1985. *Hereby Signed.* Hebrew. Tel Aviv: Ma'ariv.

International Monetary Fund. Annual. *International Financial Statistics.*

Israel. Central Bureau of Statistics. 2000. *National Expenditure on Civilian Research & Development, 1989–1998.* (S.P. 1121). Jerusalem: Central Bureau of Statistics.

Israel. Central Bureau of Statistics. Annual. *Statistical Abstract of Israel.* Jerusalem: Hemed Press.

Jacoby, Neil H. 1974. *Multinational Oil: A Study in Industrial Dynamics.* New York: Macmillan.

Jensen, Michael C. 1987. The Free Cash Flow Theory of Takeovers: A Financial Perspective on Mergers and Acquisitions and the Economy. In *The Merger Boom.* Proceedings of a Conference held at Melvin Village, New Hampshire, edited by L.E. Browne and E.S. Rosengren. Boston: Federal Reserve Bank of Boston, pp. 102–43.

Jensen, Michael C., and Richard S. Ruback. 1983. The Market for Corporate Control. *Journal of Financial Economics* 11: 5–50.

Josephson, Matthew. 1934. *The Robber Barons: The Great American Capitalists. 1861–1901.* New York: Harcourt, Brace and Company.

Kalecki, Michal. 1943a. [1971]. Costs and Prices. In *Selected Essays on the Dynamics of the Capitalist Economy, 1933–1970.* Cambridge: Cambridge University Press, pp. 43–61.

Kalecki, Michal. 1943b. [1971]. Political Aspects of Full Employment. In *Selected Essays on the Dynamics of the Capitalist Economy, 1933–1970.* Cambridge: Cambridge University Press, pp. 138–45.

Kalecki, Michal. 1964. [1972]. The Fascism of Our Times. In *The Last Phase in the Transformation of Capitalism.* New York and London: Modern Reader, pp. 99–104.

Kalecki, Michal. 1967. [1972]. Vietnam and U.S. Big Business. In *The Last Phase in the Transformation of Capitalism.* New York and London: Modern Reader, pp. 99–104.

Kalecki, Michal. 1971. *Selected Essays on the Dynamics of the Capitalist Economy, 1933–1970.* Cambridge: Cambridge University Press.

Kaplan, A.D.H., J.B. Dirlam, and R.F. Lanzillotti. 1958. *Pricing In Big Business: A Case Approach.* Washington, D.C.: The Brookings Institution.

Kautsky, Karl. 1970. Ultra-Imperialism. *New Left Review* 59 (Jan/Feb): 41–6. (Original German version published in 1914).

Kelly, A. 1986. *Water and Peace.* Hebrew. Tel Aviv: United Kibbutz Publisher.

Kennedy, Paul M. 1987. *The Rise and Fall of the Great Powers.* New York, NY: Random House.

Keynes, John Maynard. 1939. Professor Tinbergen's Method. *Economic Journal* XLIX (September): 558–68.

Khozem Merchant et al. 2000. Survey of Indian Information Technology. *Financial Times,* 4 July.

Kindelberger, Charles P. 1978. *Manias, Panics, and Crashes: A History of Financial Crises.* New York: Basic Books, Inc. Publishers.

Kissinger, Henry. 1979. *White House Years.* Boston: Little Brown.

Kissinger, Henry. 1981. *For the Record: Selected Statements 1977–1980.* Boston and Toronto: Little Brown & Company.

Kleiman, A. 1992. *Double-Edge Sword: Israel Defense Exports as an Instrument of Foreign Policy.* Hebrew. Tel Aviv: Am Oved.

Kleiman, Ephraim. 1973. Money and Inflation in Israel. Hebrew. *Economic Quarterly* 20 (78–79, September): 237–46.

Kleiman, Ephraim. 1974. Inflation and the Redistribution of Public Capital. Hebrew. *Economic Quarterly* 21 (83, December): 238–56.

Kleiman, Ephraim. 1984. The Cost of Inflation. Hebrew. *Economic Quarterly* 30 (January): 859–64.

Kleiman, Ephraim. 1996. The Political Economy of Israel: Statism at a Crossroads. In *Israel Toward the 2000s: Society, Politics and Culture.* Hebrew, edited by M. Lissak and

B. Kne-Paz. Jerusalem: Magnes and the Eshkol Institute at the Hebrew University, pp. 196–216.

Knight, Frank H. 1933. [1951]. *The Economic Organization*. New York: Harper Torchbooks.

Koestler, Arthur. 1941. *Darkness at Noon*. Translated by Daphne Hardy. New York: The Macmillan company.

Kotler, Yair. 1984. *Not For Disclosure*. Hebrew. Nazarath: Shor (Modan).

Kotler, Yair. 1988. *The National Team*. Hebrew. Tel Aviv: Yarden.

Kotz, David M., Terrence McDonough, and Michael Reich, eds. 1994. *Social Structures of Accumulation: The Political Economy of Growth and Crisis*. Cambridge: Cambridge University Press.

Krasner, Stephen D. 1978a. *Defending the National Interest: Raw Materials Investments and U.S. Foreign Policy*. Princeton, N.J.: Princeton University Press.

Krasner, Stephen D. 1978b. A Statist Interpretation of American Oil Policy Toward the Middle East. *Political Science Quarterly* 94 (1, Spring): 77–96.

Krause, Keith. 1992. *Arms and the State: Patterns of Military Production and Trade*. Cambridge and New York: Cambridge University Press.

Krugman, Paul. 1994. The Myth of Asia's Miracle. *Foreign Affairs* 73 (6, November/December): 62–78.

Kuznets, Simon Smith. 1965. *Toward a Theory of Economic Growth*. With 'Reflections on the Economic Growth of Modern Nations'. New York: W.W. Norton & Company Inc.

Kuznets, Simon Smith. 1973. *Population, Capital, and Growth: Selected Essays*. New York: Norton.

Laqueur, Walter. 1972. *A History of Zionism*. New York: Schocken Books.

Lenin, Vladimir I. 1917. [1987]. Imperialism, The Highest State of Capitalism. In *Essential Works of Lenin: 'What Is to Be Done?' and Other Writings*. New York: Dover Publications, Inc., pp. 177–270.

Levhari, David. 1984. Capital Market and Monetary Policy. Hebrew. *Economic Quarterly* 30 (119): 839–40.

Leviatan, Nissan, and Sylvia Piterman. 1989. Inflationary Acceleration and the Balance of Payment Crises. In *The Israeli Economy: Maturing Through Crisis*. Hebrew, edited by Y. Ben-Porath. Tel Aviv: Am Oved, pp. 436–72.

Lieberman, Ira W., and Rogi Veimetra. 1996. The Rush for State Shares in the 'Klondyke' of Wild East Capitalism: Loans-for-Shares Transactions in Russia. *The George Washington Journal of International Law and Economics* 29 (3): 737–68.

Lipschutz, Ronnie D. 1989. *When Nations Clash: Raw Materials, Ideology and Foreign Policy*. New York: Balinger Publishing Company.

Lochery, Neill. 2000. 'New Wine Into Old Bottles': Literature on Israel in 2000. *Middle Eastern Studies* 36 (3): 209–30.

Long, David E. 1985. *The United States and Saudi Arabia: Ambivalent Allies*. Boulder, Colo.: Westview Press.

Lubell, Harold, H. Weisbrod, and R. Kahana. 1958. *Israel's National Expenditure: 1950--1954*. Jerusalem: The Falk Project for Economic Research in Israel and Central Bureau of Statistics.

Lustick, Ian. 1980. *Arabs in the Jewish State: Israel's Control of a National Minority*. Austin, Tex.: University of Texas Press.

Luxemburg, Rosa. 1913. [1951]. *The Accumulation of Capital*. With an Introduction by Joan Robinson. Translated by Agnes Schwarzschild. New Haven: Yale University Press.

Lyons, Ronan. 1999. The Waltz of the Living Dead. *Euromoney*, September, 295–304.

McCartney, Laton. 1989. *Friends in High Places. The Bechtel Story: The Most Secret Corporation and How it Engineered the World*. New York: Simon and Schuster.

McGraw-Hill. Online. *DRI Database*.

Machlup, Fritz. 1946. Marginal Analysis and Empirical Research. *American Economic Review* 36 (4, September): 519–54.

Maddison, Angus. 1991. *Dynamic Forces in Capitalist Development. A Long-Run Comparative View.* Oxford and New York: Oxford University Press.

Magdoff, Harry. 1969. *The Age of Imperialism: The Economics of U.S. Foreign Policy.* 1st Modern Reader edn. New York: Monthly Review Press.

Malone, Thomas W., and Robert J. Laubacher. 1998. The Dawn of the E-Lance Economy: Technology Allows Individuals and Companies to Operate in New Ways. *Harvard Business Review* 76 (5, September–October): 144–52.

Manne, Henry G. 1965. Mergers and the Market for Corporate Control. *The Journal of Political Economy* 73 (2): 110–20.

Margherio, Lynn, Dave Henry, Sandra Cooke, Sabrina Montes, and Kent Hughes. 1998. *The Emerging Digital Economy.* Washington D.C.: U.S. Department of Commerce.

Markham, J.W. 1955. Survey of the Evidence and Findings on Mergers. In *Business Concentration and Price Policy: A Conference of the Universities-National Committee for Economic Research.* Princeton N.J.: Princeton University Press, pp. 141–90.

Marshall, Alfred. 1920. *Principles of Economics: An Introductory Volume.* 8th edn. London: Macmillan.

Marx, Karl. 1909. *Capital: A Critique of Political Economy.* 3 vols. Chicago: Charles H. Kerr & Company.

Means, Gardiner C. 1935. *Industrial Prices and Their Relative Inflexibility.* Senate Document 13, 74th Congress, 1st Session. Washington D.C.: GPO.

Mellow, Craig. 1999. Working It Out. *Institutional Investor*, July, 121–4.

Melman, Seymour. 1974. *The Permanent War Economy: American Capitalism in Decline.* New York: Simon and Schuster.

Meyer, H.D. 1976. *The Alternative: The Turnaround in U.S. Policy and the Future of Israel.* Hebrew. Translated by Menachem Lamdan. Ramat Gan: Massada.

Michaeli, Micha. 1981. Inflation and Money in Israel After the 1977 Liberalisation. Hebrew. *Economic Quarterly* 25 (109, July): 115–36.

Mickiewicz, Ellen. 1999. Russian Television News: Owners and the Public. *Nieman Report*, Fall, 27–30.

Migdal, Joel S. 1989. The Crystallization of the State and the Struggles Over Rulemaking: Israel in Comparative Perspective. In *The Israeli State and Society. Boundaries and Frontiers*, edited by B. Kimmerling. New York: SUNY Press, pp. 1–27.

Mills, C. Wright. 1959. *The Sociological Imagination.* New York: Oxford University Press.

Mintz, Alex. 1984. The Military-Industrial Complex: The Israeli Case. In *Israeli Society and its Defense Establishment: The Social and Political Impact of a Protracted Violent Conflict*, edited by M. Lissak. London: F. Cass, pp. 103–27.

Moody's. Annual. *Industrial Manuals.* New York: Moody's Investor Service.

Moody's. Online. *FISonline.*

Mumford, Lewis. 1967. *The Myth of the Machine: Technics and Human Development.* New York: Harcourt, Brace & World, Inc.

Mumford, Lewis. 1970. *The Myth of the Machine: The Pentagon of Power.* New York: Harcourt, Brace Jovanovich, Inc.

Mundell, Robert A. 1963. Capital Mobility and Stabilization Policy Under Fixed and Flexible Exchange Rates. *Canadian Journal of Economics and Political Science* 29 (4, November): 475–85.

Naff, Thomas, and Ruth C. Matson, eds. 1984. *Water in the Middle East: Conflict or Cooperation.* Boulder, Colo.: Westview Press.

Naylor, Tom R. 1987. *Hot Money and the Politics of Debt.* Toronto: McClelland and Stewart.

Neff, Donald. 1988. *Warriors Against Israel: America Comes to the Rescue in 1973.* Brattleboro, Vt.: Amana Books.

Nelson, Ralph L. 1959. *Merger Movements in American Industry, 1895–1956.* Princeton N.J.: Princeton University Press.

Nitzan, Jonathan. 1992. Inflation as Restructuring: A Theoretical and Empirical Account of the US Experience. Unpublished PhD Dissertation, Department of Economics, McGill University, Montreal.

Nitzan, Jonathan. 1995. The EMA 'Phoenix': Soaring on Market Hype. *The BCA Emerging Markets Analyst* 4 (6, October): 10–17.

Nitzan, Jonathan. 1996. The EMA Phoenix: Shorting on Market 'Hype'. *The BCA Emerging Markets Analyst* 5 (6, October): 14–25.

Nitzan, Jonathan. 1998. Differential Accumulation: Toward a New Political Economy of Capital. *Review of International Political Economy* 5 (2): 169–217.

Nitzan, Jonathan. 2001. Regimes of Differential Accumulation: Mergers, Stagflation and the Logic of Globalization. *Review of International Political Economy* 8 (2): 226–74.

Nitzan, Jonathan, and Shimshon Bichler. 1995. Bringing Capital Accumulation Back In: The Weapondollar–Petrodollar Coalition – Military Contractors, Oil Companies and Middle-East 'Energy Conflicts'. *Review of International Political Economy* 2 (3): 446–515.

Nitzan, Jonathan, and Shimshon Bichler. 2000. Capital Accumulation: Breaking the Dualism of 'Economics' and 'Politics'. In *Global Political Economy: Contemporary Theories*, edited by R. Palan. New York and London: Routledge, pp. 67–88.

Nordlinger, Eric A. 1981. *On the Autonomy of the Democratic State*. Cambridge, Mass.: Harvard University Press.

O'Connor, Harvey. 1962. *World Crisis in Oil*. New York: Monthly Review Press.

O'Connor, James. 1973. *The Fiscal Crisis of the State*. New York: St Martin's Press.

Odell, Peter R. 1979. *Oil and World Power*. 5th edn. Harmondsworth: Penguin.

Olson, Mancur. 1965. *The Logic of Collective Action: Public Goods and the Theory of Groups*. Cambridge, Mass.: Harvard University Press.

Olson, Mancur. 1982. *The Rise and Decline of Nations: Economic Growth, Stagflation, and Social Rigidities*. New Haven: Yale University Press.

OPEC. Annual. *Annual Statistical Bulletin*. Vienna: OPEC.

Orr, Akiva, and Moshe Machover. 1961. [1999]. *Peace, Peace and No Peace*. Hebrew. Jerusalem: n.p.

Orwell, George. 1948. *Nineteen Eighty-Four*. London and Toronto: Secker & Warburg and S.J. Reginald Saunders & Co. Ltd.

Page, Joseph A. 1995. *The Brazilians*. Reading, Mass.: Addison-Wesley Publishing Company, Inc.

Parkin, M., and R. Bade. 1986. *Modern Macroeconomics*. 2nd edn. Scarborough, Ontario: Prentice-Hall Canada.

Patinikin, Don. 1965. *The Israeli Economy in the First Decade*. Hebrew. Jerusalem: Falk Centre.

Penrose, Edith Tilton. 1959. *The Theory of the Growth of the Firm*. Oxford: Blackwell.

Penrose, Edith Tilton. 1987. The Structure of the International Oil Industry: Multinationals, Governments and OPEC. In *The International Oil Industry: An Interdisciplinary Perspective*, edited by J. Rees and P. Odell. New York: St Martin's Press, pp. 9–18.

Peres, Shimon. 1995. Judging the Plan by its Implementation. Hebrew. *Economic Quarterly* 95 (4, December): 573–6.

Peri, Yoram. 1983. *Between Battles and Ballots: Israeli Military in Politics*. Cambridge and New York: Cambridge University Press.

Pigou, Arthur C. 1935. Net Income and Capital Depletion. *Economic Journal* 45: 235–41.

Poulantzas, Nicos Ar. 1973. *Political Power and Social Classes*. Translated by Timothy O'Hagan. London: New Left Books and Sheed and Ward.

Pribram, Karl H. 1971. *Languages of the Brain: Experimental Paradoxes and Principles in Neuropsychology*. Englewood Cliffs, N.J.: Prentice-Hall.

Quandt, William B. 1979. The Middle East Crisis. *Foreign Affairs* 58 (3): 540–62.

Rabin, Yitzhak. 1979. *Service Record*. Written by D. Goldstein. 2 vols. Tel Aviv: Ma'ariv.

Rabinovitch, I. 1983. The Struggle Over the Jordan Water as a Component in the Arab–Israeli Conflict. In *The Galilee Lands*. Hebrew, edited by A. Shmueli, A. Sofer and N. Kliot. Haifa: Gestlit.

Raskin, Adam. 1999. Israeli Government Research and Development Subsidies to High Technology Companies. *IASPS Policy Studies* 42: 1–25.

Ravenscraft, David J. 1987. The 1980s Merger Wave: An Industrial Organization Perspective. In *The Merger Boom*. Proceedings of a Conference held at Melvin Village, New Hampshire, edited by L.E. Browne and E.S. Rosengren. Boston: Federal Reserve Bank of Boston, pp. 17–37.

Ravenscraft, David J., and F.M. Scherer. 1987. *Mergers, Sell-Offs, and Economic Efficiency*. Washington, D.C.: The Brookings Institution.

Ravenscraft, David J., and F.M. Scherer. 1989. The Profitability of Mergers. *International Journal of Industrial Organization* 7 (1): 101–16.

Razin, Assaf. 1984. The Israeli Market 1983. Hebrew. *Economic Quarterly* 30 (119, January): 834–7.

Razin, Assaf, and Efraim Sadka. 1993. *The Economy of Modern Israel: Malaise and Promise*. Chicago: University of Chicago Press.

Recanati, Harry. 1984. *Recanati: Father and Son*. Hebrew. Jerusalem: Caneh.

Robinson, Joan. 1962. *Economic Philosophy*. Harmondsworth: Penguin.

Robinson, Joan. 1966. *An Essay on Marxian Economics*. 2nd edn. London: Macmillan.

Rosenfeld, Henry, and Shulamit Carmi. 1979. The Apropriation of Public Means and a State-Made Middle Class. Hebrew. *Journals for Research and Critisim* 2: 43–84.

Rowley, J.C.R., Shimshon Bichler, and Jonathan Nitzan. 1988. Some Aspects of Aggregate Concentration in the Israeli Economy, 1964–1986. Department of Economics Working Papers 7 (88), McGill University, Montreal.

Sadan, Ezra. 1985. National Security and National Economy. In *Israeli Security Planning in the 1980s: Its Politics and Economics*. Hebrew, edited by Zvi Lanir. Tell Aviv: Ministry of Defence, pp. 119–29.

Sadka, Ephraim, and Assaf Razin. 1995. Fiscal Balance During Inflation, The Disinflation and the Immigration: Policy Lessons. Hebrew. *Economic Quarterly* 4 (95, December): 617–42.

Safran, Nadav. 1978. *Israel, The Embattled Ally*. Cambridge, Mass.: Belknap Press.

Sampson, Anthony. 1975. *The Seven Sisters: The Great Oil Companies and the World They Shaped*. New York: Viking Press.

Sampson, Anthony. 1977. *The Arms Bazaar. The Companies, the Dealers, the Bribes: From Vickers to Lockheed*. London: Hodder and Stoughton.

Sampson, Anthony. 1981. *The Money Lenders: Bankers in a Dangerous World*. London: Hodder and Stoughton.

Samuelson, Paul A. 1974. [1977]. World Wide Stagflation. In *Collected Scientific Papers of Paul A. Samuelson*, edited by H. Nagatani and K. Crowley. Cambridge, Mass.: The MIT Press, pp. 801–7.

Samuelson, Paul A., William D. Nordhaus, and John McCallum. 1988. *Economics*. 6th Canadian edn. Toronto: McGraw-Hill Ryerson.

Sanbar, Moshe, and Shaul Bronfeld. 1973a. Thinking, Policy and Development in the Monetary Sphere, 1948–1972. Hebrew. *Economic Quarterly* 20 (77): 3–16.

Sanbar, Moshe, and Shaul Bronfeld. 1973b. Thinking, Policy and Development in the Monetary Sphere, 1948–1972 (Second Chapter). Hebrew. *Economic Quarterly* 20 (78–79): 217–36.

Scherer, F.M., and David Ross. 1990. *Industrial Market Structure and Economic Performance*. 3rd edn. Boston: Houghton Mifflin.

Schonfeld, Erick. 1999. Choice Morsels: Born to Be Bought. *Fortune*, 166–74.

Schroder, Hans-Henning. 1999. El'tsin and the Oligarchs: The Role of Financial Groups in Russian Politics Between 1993 and July 1998. *Europe-Asia Studies* 51 (6): 957–88.

Schumpeter, Joseph A. 1954. *History of Economic Analysis*. Edited from manuscript by E.B. Schumpeter. New York: Oxford University Press.

Segev, Tom. 1984. *1949: The First Israelis*. Hebrew. Jerusalem: Domino.

Sexton, R. 1990. *Perspectives on the Middle East Water Crisis: Analysing Water Scarcity Problems in Jordan and Israel*. Hebrew. London: Overseas Development Institute.

Shamir, Michal, and Asher Arian. 1982. Ethnic Voting in the 1981 Elections. *State, Government and International Relations* 19–20: 88–104.

Shapiro, Yonathan. 1975. *The Organisation of Power*. Hebrew. Tel Aviv: Am Oved.

Shapiro, Yonathan. 1977. *The Democracy In Israel*. Hebrew. Tel Aviv: Am Oved.

Shapiro, Yonathan. 1980. The End of a Dominant Party System in Israel. In *The Elections in Israel, 1977*, edited by A. Arian. Jerusalem: Academic Press, pp. 23–38.

Shapiro, Yoram. 1984. *An Elite Without Successors: Generations of Political Leaders in Israel*. Hebrew. Tel Aviv: Sifriat Poalim.

Sharet, Moshe. 1978. *Personal Diary*. Hebrew. 8 vols. Tel Aviv: Ma'ariv.

Sharkansky, Ira. 1987. *The Political Economy of Israel*. New Brunswick, N.J.: Transaction Books.

Shiff, Ze'ev, and Ehud Yaari. 1984. *War of Deception*. Tel Aviv: Schocken Publishing House.

Sick, Gary. 1991. *October Surprise: America's Hostages in Iran and the Election of Ronald Reagan*. New York: Times Books/Random House.

Skocpol, Theda. 1985. Bringing the State Back In. In *Bringing the State Back In*. Papers from a conference held at Mount Kisco, N.Y., February 1982, sponsored by the Committee on States and Social Structures, the Joint Committee on Latin American Studies, and the Joint Committee on Western European Studies of the Social Science Research Council., edited by P.B. Evans, D. Rueschemeyer and T. Skocpol. Cambridge and New York: Cambridge University Press.

Snider, Lewis. W. 1984. Arms Exports for Oil Imports? The Test of a Non-Linear Model. *Journal of Conflict Resolution* 28 (4, December): 665–700.

Sorokin, Pitirum Aleksandrovich. 1962. *Social and Cultural Dynamics*. 4 vols. New York: Bedminster Press.

Soros, George. 1998. *The Crisis of Global Capitalism. [Open Society Endangered]*. New York: PublicAffairs.

Standard & Poor's. Annual. *Compustat Research Insight CD ROM*.

Steindl, Josef. 1945. *Small and Big Business: Economic Problems of the Size of Firms*. Institute of Statistics, Monograph No. 1. Oxford: Basil Blackwell.

Stockholm International Peace Research Institute. Annual. *SIPRI Year Book: Armament, Disarmament and International Security*. Oxford: Oxford University Press.

Tanzer, Michael. 1969. *The Energy Crisis: World Struggle for Power and Wealth*. New York: Monthly Review Press.

Taylor, Alan M. 1996. International Capital Mobility in History: The Saving–Investment Relationship, NBER Working Paper No. 5943, National Bureau of Economic Research, Cambridge Mass.

Terzian, Pierre. 1985. *OPEC: The Inside Story*. Translated by M. Pallis. London: Zed Press.

Tevet, Shabtai. 1980. *David's Jealousy. The Life of David Ben-Gurion*. Vol. 2. Hebrew. Jerusalem and Tel Aviv: Schocken.

Tevet, Shabtai. 1987. *David's Jealousy. The Life of David Ben-Gurion*. Vol. 3. Hebrew. Jerusalem and Tel Aviv: Schocken.

Tilly, Charles, and Gabriel Ardant. 1975. *The Formation of National States in Western Europe*. Studies in Political Development 8. Sponsored by the Committee on Comparative Politics, Social Science Research Council. Princeton, N.J.: Princeton University Press.

Timmerman, Kenneth R. 1991. *The Death Lobby: How the West Armed Iraq*. Boston: Houghton Mifflin.

Tinbergen, Jan. 1940. On a Method of Statistical Business-Cycle Research: Reply. *Economic Journal* L (March): 141–54.

Tobin, James, and William C. Brainard. 1968. Pitfalls in Financial Model Building. *American Economic Review: Papers and Proceedings* 58 (2, May): 99–122.

Tobin, James, and William C. Brainard. 1977. Asset Markets and the Cost of Capital. In *Economic Progress, Private Values, and Public Policy: Essays in the Honor of William Fellner*, edited by B. Balassa and R. Nelson. Amsterdam and New York: North-Holland Publishing Co., pp. 235–62.

Tsuru, Shigeto. 1956. Has Capitalism Changed? In *Has Capitalism Changed? An International Symposium on the Nature of Contemporary Capitalism*, edited by S. Tsuru. Tokyo: Iwanami Shoten, pp. 1–66.

Tsuru, Shigeto. 1968. Keynes versus Marx: The Methodology of Aggregates. In *Marx and Modern Economics*, edited by D. Horowitz. New York and London: Modern Reader Paperbacks, pp. 176–202.

Tuchman, Barbara Wertheim. 1984. *The March of Folly. From Troy to Vietnam*. 1st edn. New York: Knopf: Distributed by Random House.

Tuma, Elias H. 1989. The Economies of Israel and the Occupied Territories: War and Peace – A Panel Discussion. Hebrew. *Economic Quarterly* (139): 593–606.

Turner, Louis. 1983. *Oil Companies in the International System*. 3rd edn. London and Winchester, Mass.: Royal Institute of International Affairs and Allen & Unwin.

U.S. Arms Control and Disarmament Agency. Annual. *World Military Expenditures and Arms Transfers*. Washington, D.C.: U.S. Government Printing Office (GPO).

U.S. Congress, Office of Technology Assessment. 1991. *Global Arms Trade*. OTA-ISC-460, June. Washington D.C.: GPO.

U.S. Defense Security Assistance Agency. 1989. *Foreign Military Sales, Foreign Construction Sales and Military Assistance Facts as of September 30, 1989*. Washington, D.C.: FMS Control & Reports Division Comptroller, DSAA.

U.S. Defense Security Assistance Agency. 1992. *Foreign Military Sales, Foreign Construction Sales and Military Assistance Facts as of September 30, 1992*. Washington, D.C.: FMS Control & Reports Division Comptroller, DSAA.

U.S. Department of Commerce. Bureau of the Census. 1975. *Historical Statistics of the United States. Colonial Times to 1970*. 2 vols. Washington D.C.: GPO.

U.S. Department of Commerce. Bureau of the Census. Annual. *Statistical Abstract of the United States*. Washington D.C.: GPO.

U.S. Department of Energy, Energy Information Administration. Annual. *International Energy Annual*. Washington D.C.: GPO.

United Nations Conference on Trade and Development. 2000. *World Investment Report. Cross-Border Mergers and Acquisitions and Development*. New York and Geneva: United Nations.

United Nations, Department of International and Social Affairs, Statistical Office. Annual. *Statistical Yearbook*. New York: United Nations.

Veblen, Thorstein. 1904. [1975]. *The Theory of Business Enterprise*. Clifton, N.J.: Augustus M. Kelley, Reprints of Economics Classics.

Veblen, Thorstein. 1908a. [1961]. On the Nature of Capital. I: The Productivity of Capital Goods. In *The Place of Science in Modern Civilisation and Other Essays*. New York: Russell & Russell, pp. 324–51.

Veblen, Thorstein. 1908b. [1961]. On the Nature of Capital. II. Investment, Intangible Assets, and the Pecuniary Magnate. In *The Place of Science in Modern Civilisation and Other Essays*. New York: Russell & Russell, pp. 352–86.

Veblen, Thorstein. 1923. [1967]. *Absentee Ownership and Business Enterprise in Recent Times: The Case of America*. With an introduction by Robert Leckachman. Boston, Mass.: Beacon Press.

Waas, Murray, and Craig Unger. 1992. In the Loop: Bush's Secret Mission. *New Yorker*, 2 November, 64–83.

Wallich, Henry C. 1984. Why is Net International Investment So Small? In *International Capital Movements, Debt and Monetary System*, edited by W. Engles, A. Gutowski and H.C. Wallich. Mainz: V. Hase & Koehler, pp. 417–37.

Waltz, Kenneth Neal. 1979. *Theory of International Politics*. Reading, Mass.: Addison-Wesley.

Weston, J. Fred. 1987. The Payoff in Mergers and Acquisitions. In *The Mergers and Acquisition Handbook*, edited by M.L. Rock. New York: McGraw-Hill, pp. 31–47.

Wilson, Ernest J. 1987. World Politics and International Energy Markets. *International Organization* 41 (1, Winter): 125–49.

Wolosky, Lee S. 2000. Putin's Plutocrat Problem. *Foreign Affairs* 79 (2): 18–31.

Woodward, Bob. 1991. *The Commanders*. New York: Simon & Schuster.

World Bank. Annual. *World Development Indicators CD-ROM*. Washington D.C.: World Bank.

Wright, Quincy. 1964. *A Study of War*. Abridged by Louise Leonard Wright. Chicago and London: The University of Chicago Press.

Yadlin, Asher. 1980. *Testimony*. Hebrew. Jerusalem: Idanim.

Yatziv, Gadi. 1979. The Class Basis for Party Association – The Example of Israel. Hebrew. *Research in Sociology*, Department of Sociology, Hebrew University, Jerusalem.

Yergin, Daniel. 1991. *The Prize: The Epic Quest for Oil, Money, and Power*. New York: Simon and Schuster.

Zamiatin, Eugene. 1924. [1952]. *We*. Translated and with a Forward by Gregory Zilboog. Introduction by Peter Rudy. Preface by Marc Slonim. New York: E.P. Dutton.

Zusman, Zvi. 1969. From a National Wage Policy to a Sectoral Wage Policy. Hebrew. *Economic Quarterly* 16 (64, December): 340–31.

Zusman, Zvi. 1974. The National Policy for Restraining Wages. Hebrew. *Economic Quarterly* 21 (80–81, May): 39–52.

Index